Fodor's

PERU

3rd Edition

Fodor's Travel Publications   New York, Toronto, London, Sydney, Auckland
www.fodors.com

Be a Fodor's Correspondent

Your opinion matters. It matters to us. It matters to your fellow Fodor's travelers, too. And we'd like to hear it. In fact, we need to hear it.

When you share your experiences and opinions, you become an active member of the Fodor's community. That means we'll not only use your feedback to make our books better, but we'll publish your names and comments whenever possible. Throughout our guides, look for "Word of Mouth," excerpts of your unvarnished feedback.

Here's how you can help improve Fodor's for all of us.

Tell us when we're right. We rely on local writers to give you an insider's perspective. But our writers and staff editors—who are the best in the business—depend on you. Your positive feedback is a vote to renew our recommendations for the next edition.

Tell us when we're wrong. We're proud that we update most of our guides every year. But we're not perfect. Things change. Hotels cut services. Museums change hours. Charming cafés lose charm. If our writer didn't quite capture the essence of a place, tell us how you'd do it differently. If any of our descriptions are inaccurate or inadequate, we'll incorporate your changes in the next edition and will correct factual errors at fodors.com immediately.

Tell us what to include. You probably have had fantastic travel experiences that aren't yet in Fodor's. Why not share them with a community of like-minded travelers? Maybe you chanced upon a beach or bistro or B&B that you don't want to keep to yourself. Tell us why we should include it. And share your discoveries and experiences with everyone directly at fodors.com. Your input may lead us to add a new listing or highlight a place we cover with a "Highly Recommended" star or with our highest rating, "Fodor's Choice."

Give us your opinion instantly at our feedback center at www.fodors.com/feedback. You may also e-mail editors@fodors.com with the subject line "Peru Editor." Or send your nominations, comments, and complaints by mail to Peru Editor, Fodor's, 1745 Broadway, New York, NY 10019.

You and travelers like you are the heart of the Fodor's community. Make our community richer by sharing your experiences. Be a Fodor's correspondent.

¡Feliz viaje! (Bon voyage!)

Tim Jarrell, Publisher

FODOR'S PERU
Editor: Josh McIlvain

Editorial Production: Astrid deRidder
Editorial Contributors: Aviva Baff, Nicholas Gill, Michelle Hopey, Zoe Ponce Massey, Katy Morrison, Diana P. Olano, Ruth Anne Phillips, Paul Steele, Mark Sullivan, Jeffrey Van Fleet, Doug Wechsler, Oliver Wigmore.
Maps & Illustrations: David Lindroth and Mark Stroud, *cartographers*; William Wu, *information graphics*; Bob Blake and Rebecca Baer, *map editors*
Design: Fabrizio LaRocca, *creative director*; Guido Caroti, Siobhan O'Hare, *art directors*; Tina Malaney, Chie Ushio, Ann McBride, Jessica Walsh, *designers*; Melanie Marin, *senior picture editor;* Moon Sun Kim, *cover designer*
Cover Photo: Machu Picchu: Caroline Webber/age fotostock
Production/Manufacturing: Steve Slawsky

3rd Edition

ISBN 978–1–4000–1969–4

ISSN 1542–3433

SPECIAL SALES
This book is available at special discounts for bulk purchases for sales promotions or premiums. Special editions, including personalized covers, excerpts of existing books, and corporate imprints, can be created in large quantities for special needs. For more information, write to Special Markets/Premium Sales, 1745 Broadway, MD 6-2, New York, New York 10019, or e-mail specialmarkets@randomhouse.com.

AN IMPORTANT TIP & AN INVITATION
Although all prices, opening times, and other details in this book are based on information supplied to us at press time, changes occur all the time in the travel world, and Fodor's cannot accept responsibility for facts that become outdated or for inadvertent errors or omissions. So **always confirm information when it matters,** especially if you're making a detour to visit a specific place. Your experiences—positive and negative—matter to us. If we have missed or misstated something, **please write to us.** We follow up on all suggestions. Contact the Peru editor at editors@fodors.com or c/o Fodor's at 1745 Broadway, New York, NY 10019.

PRINTED IN SINGAPORE
10 9 8 7 6 5 4 3 2 1

CONTENTS

PERU IN FOCUS

CONTENTS

ABOUT
THIS BOOK

Our Ratings

Sometimes you find terrific travel experiences and sometimes they just find you. But usually the burden is on you to select the right combination of experiences. That's where our ratings come in.

As travelers we've all discovered a place so wonderful that its worthiness is obvious. And sometimes that place is so unique that superlatives don't do it justice: you just have to be there to know. These sights, properties, and experiences get our highest rating, **Fodor's Choice**, indicated by orange stars throughout this book.

Black stars highlight sights and properties we deem **Highly Recommended**, places that our writers, editors, and readers praise again and again for consistency and excellence.

By default, there's another category: any place we include in this book is by definition worth your time, unless we say otherwise. And we will.

Disagree with any of our choices? Care to nominate a place or suggest that we rate one more highly? Visit our feedback center at www.fodors.com/feedback.

Budget Well

Hotel and restaurant price categories from ¢ to $$$$ are defined in the opening pages of each chapter. For attractions, we always give standard adult admission fees; reductions are usually available for children, students, and senior citizens. Want to pay with plastic? **AE, DC, MC, V** following restaurant and hotel listings indicate whether American Express, Diner's Club, MasterCard, and Visa are accepted. The Discover card is accepted almost nowhere in South America.

Restaurants

Unless we state otherwise, restaurants are open for lunch and dinner daily. We mention dress only when there's a specific requirement and reservations only when they're essential or not accepted—it's always best to book ahead.

Hotels

Hotels have private bath, phone, and TV and operate on the European Plan (aka EP, meaning without meals), unless we specify that they use the Continental Plan (CP, with a continental breakfast), Breakfast Plan (BP, with a full breakfast), or Modified American Plan (MAP, with breakfast and dinner) or are all-inclusive (including all meals and most activities). We always list facilities but not whether you'll be charged an extra fee to use them, so when pricing accommodations, find out what's included.

Many Listings

★	Fodor's Choice
★	Highly recommended
⊠	Physical address
⊹	Directions
⏧	Mailing address
☎	Telephone
🖷	Fax
⊕	On the Web
✍	E-mail
☑	Admission fee
☉	Open/closed times
Ⓜ	Metro stations
▭	Credit cards

Hotels & Restaurants

🏨	Hotel
⤹	Number of rooms
△	Facilities
¶◎¶	Meal plans
✕	Restaurant
⚓	Reservations
↘	Smoking
ꙮ	BYOB
✕🏨	Hotel with restaurant that warrants a visit

Outdoors

🏌	Golf
⚑	Camping

Other

☺	Family-friendly
⇨	See also
⊠	Branch address
☞	Take note

Experience Peru

WHAT'S NEW IN PERU

Better Days Ahead?

Peru is a nation on the threshold of change. Emerging from decades of corrupt governments, the Andean country is now seen as an economic power in Latin America. Despite half of its population living under poverty, Peru's economy surpasses the global average. Exports of asparagus, fish, coffee, gold, and more to China, Japan, Chile, and the U.S., are growing at a rate of 25% and are expected to reach $50 billion by the end of 2010. Private investments, including in mining and energy, have helped the investment rate of the country increase at an annual rate of 20% since 2006. Analysts expect the tourism, agriculture, and mining industries to continue to attract national and international investments for years to come.

New Old Wonder

The "Lost City of the Incas," the famed Machu Picchu, was given a breath of life—not that it needed it—when it was named one of the New Seven Wonders of the World in 2007, alongside the Great Wall of China and Taj Mahal. Too much exposure might turn out to be a bad thing; the archaeological site was put on the World Monuments Fund's 2008 Watch List of the 100 Most Endangered Sites in the world.

Food News

Declared the "Gastronomical Capital of Latin America" by the Fourth International Summit of Gastronomy Madrid Fusión in 2006, Lima is representing Peru's gastronomy, which has influences from the different cultures—African, Japanese, and Chinese, to name a few—that comprise Peru. Famous chef and businessman Gastón Acurio is making sure the world knows how delicious Peruvian specialties are by establishing Peruvian restaurants, with traditional Peruvian dishes being served in modern and innovative ways, in cities such as Bogota, Santiago, Panama, and Madrid. His restaurants in Lima include an upscale-take on cevicherias, restaurants specializing in the seafood dish ceviche, which are usually found at hole-in-the locales; and another franchise making use of sanguches, Peru's special take on sandwiches.

Peru's Jukebox

Music staples in Peru such as salsa and meringue have had new competition in recent years now that reggaeton and cumbia have joined the party. While reggaeton, a genre that combines dancehall and Latin rhythms in an urban style, is not only immensely popular in Peru but around Latin America, cumbia is the style taking over the country. The music, a variant of the African Guinean "cumbe," was at first only popular with the poorer classes in Peru. Now, elite night clubs and most radio stations play hits from bands specialized in cumbia, such as Grupo 5, Agua Marina, and Armonia 10. Some say its popularity hit an all-time high when members of the group Néctar all tragically died in a bus accident in 2007.

Soccer Dreams

While the national Peruvian soccer team has seen better days to put it nicely, its U-17 league—a youth team of players 17 years old and younger—showed what the future of soccer in Peru can be when it had a stellar run during the 2007 FIFA U-17 World Cup. The youngsters managed to beat out powerhouses Brazil in

their first game, along with Ecuador and Argentina. They were eventually eliminated by South Korea, but their effective counterattacks and impressive game plans showed the world what Peruvian soccer could be, lifting the spirits of a country that hasn't seen its players display such skill since the '70s.

Picking Up After the Earthquake

On August 15, 2007, an earthquake measuring 8.0 on the magnitude scale devastated three coastal cities in Peru: Pisco, Ica, and Chincha Alta. In terms of damages and loss of life, this earthquake was one of the worst in Peruvian history, leaving more than 500 dead, 1,300 injured, and destroying 80% of Pisco. Though it was felt in cities such as Lima and Trujillo, Pisco and its neighbors were worse hit, with sizeable aftershocks. President Garcia and his cabinet were criticized for aid that supposedly came too slowly, while organizations such as OXFAM and the Red Cross made their way to the affected regions to provide assistance. Two all-star fund-raising concerts featuring national and international singers and musicians were held a few months following the deadly quake.

Poverty

The increase in economic stability that Peru has enjoyed in recent years hasn't lowered the poverty rate much. Any visitor to Lima, Peru's capital, who looks beyond the seaside luxury buildings in Miraflores and travels outside of the city will see the "pueblos jóvenes," shantytowns where residents live without running water or electricity.

Protests

Political protests, labor strikes for improved wages, and protests against laws that adversely affect the poor are common. In February 2008 Cusco residents staged a huge three-day protest against a law passed by congress that would allow private business easier access to develop near archaeological sites, including Machu Picchu. While political protests aren't rare for Peru, this particular one cost the city the opportunity to host various meetings during a summit gathering countries from the Asia-Pacific region. For international delegates to visit Peru and not visit famed Cusco and its Inca ruins would be as if they visited Egypt and didn't go to the Pyramids.

FAQS

How difficult Is Peru to Get Around?

Thanks to more domestic flights, Peru is much easier to move about these days. Almost every worthwhile destination is within a two-hour flight from Lima. Train travel is limited, but easy to use. Traveling by car is trickier—roads are better than before, but signs aren't well-posted. Buses go everywhere, and come in all classes and sizes. In cities, cabs are available and cheap. But check for an official license.

Is Machu Picchu Hard to Get To?

Travel to Machu Picchu is so efficient that it's almost too easy. The most common method is to hop on the PeruRail from Cusco to Aguas Calientes or you can do as the Incas did and walk the path, which is a two- to four-day jaunt and highlight for those who do it. Both options are likely to be the most expensive things you'll pay for in Peru, but Machu Picchu is also one of the most amazing things you're likely to ever see.

Will I Have Trouble if I No Habla Español?

No problemo. Although it's helpful to know some Spanish, it's not a necessity, especially on an organized tour or in tourist areas. There's a strong push for tourist professionals to learn English, but cab drivers or store clerks aren't likely to know a lick. So, we suggest studying a few simple phrases. "Cuánto Cuesta?" *How much?* is a good one to start with.

What Languages Do People Speak?

The official language is Spanish and nearly everyone speaks it. But in the highlands the language the Incas spoke, Quechua, is still widely used. Older populations in indigenous communities often don't know Spanish, but younger generations do. Aymara, a pre-Inca language, is spoken among some indigenous populations around Lake Titicaca.

Are the Effects of the 2007 Earthquake Apparent?

The worst is over, thanks to relief agencies and volunteers who are still cleaning up rubble, building new homes, and redeveloping communities. The coastal towns around Ica and Pisco were hardest hit by the 8.0 quake and luckily for the tourism industry, most major hotels in Ica, along with the Ballestas Islands and Nazca Lines escaped major damage. Pisco suffered more, and several tour operators lost their businesses, but have been operating from their make-shift offices (tents) with the help of cell phones. Tourism is alive and the business is needed and wanted here.

Is the Water Safe to Drink?

Nope. But bottled water is cheap and sold nearly everywhere. So drink up the good stuff, it'll help you beat altitude sickness.

What Are the Safety Concerns?

Petty crime is the primary concern. If you're "gringo," you probably have a camera, iPod, watch, jewelry, credit cards, cash—everything a thief wants. Pickpocketing and bag slashing are the most common methods. Thieves are fast and sneaky so be alert, especially in crowded markets and bus stations, and never walk on deserted streets. In the last couple years there have been "strangle muggings," when several robbers strangle the traveler until they're unconscious, making for an easy steal, but the number has been limited.

Should I Worry About Altitude Sickness?

Yes and no. If you have health issues, you should check with your doctor before heading to high altitudes. But for everyone else, don't worry too much because nearly everyone experiences altitude sickness. The lucky ones may have a headache for the first 24 hours, while others may endure several days of intense fatigue and headaches. When up high, lay off the booze, skip the physical activity, hydrate, eat some sugar, chew coca leaves, take an ibuprofen, hydrate some more, and sleep it off. Many hotels have oxygen so don't hesitate to ask for it.

Do I Have to Pay Any Fees to Get into the Country?

No. But you pay to get out. The departure tax system (which nearly every South American country embraces) is alive and well in Peru. Be prepared to fork over S/91.96 or US$30.25 when you leave Lima for any international destination. Every time you fly domestically, you also get hit with a departure tax, but it's only S/18.39 or US$6.05. Warning: you can only pay with CASH—soles or dollars.

What's in a Pisco Sour?

A smooth sipper, pisco sours are made with 2 ounces of pisco, (a white grape brandy made from grapes grown in the Andes), ¾ ounces of freshly squeezed lime juice, a half-ounce of simple sugar syrup, 1 whipped egg white, and a few Angostura bitters. They're so tasty it's no wonder Peruvians are proud of their mildly tangy, national cocktail (and so are Chileans, who also claim the pisco sour as their national drink). Beware, they're quick to sneak up on you.

Are There Cultural Sensitivities I Should Be Aware Of?

Peruvians are very polite, so, it's customary to be the same. You'll notice that men and women kiss each other on the cheek when saying hello, and the same goes for women to women. It's nonsexual and a sign of friendliness. There's no six inches of personal space in Peru, it's more like two: people talk, walk, and sit close in general, so don't be alarmed. Peruvians, like many South American countries, are also on "Latin Time," meaning, arriving an hour late for a social engagement is considered customary. Finally, there's actually bathroom etiquette in Peru. It's polite not to throw toilet paper down the toilet and instead place it in the bin provided. Plumbing is not super-sophisticated and pipes clog frequently.

WHAT'S WHERE

The following numbers refer to chapters in the book.

2 Lima. In Peru's cultural and political center experience some of the best dining in the Americas, vibrant nightlife, and great museums and churches. See the Catedral and the catacombs at the Iglesia de San Francisco, and stroll about Miraflores for shops and eats.

Fishing boats.

3 The South. Head south for wines and piscos around Ica, duneboarding in Huacachina, the mysterious Nazca Lines, the marine life of Paracas National Perserve, and tranquil fishing villages at Pucusana and Cerro Azul. The inland area, particularly Pisco, was devastated by the 2007 earthquake.

4 Southern Coast To Lake Titicaca. Colca and Cotahuasi canyons are the world's two deepest. Peru's "second city," Arequipa, may also be its most attractive. Lake Titicaca is the world's highest navigable lake and home to the floating Uros Islands.

Pisac.

5 Cusco & the Sacred Valley. Cusco (11,500 feet above sea level) is a necessary stop on your journey to Machu Picchu. The former Inca capital has fine restaurants, hotels, churches, and museums. Take day trips to the Pisac market, and to Inca ruins at Sacsayhuamán and Ollyantaytambo.

6 Machu Picchu. The great Machu Picchu, crowded or not crowded, misty rains or clear skies, never ceases to enthrall, and the Inca Trail is still the great hiking pilgrimage. Stay in Aguas Caliente for the best access.

7 Amazon Basin. Peru's vast tract of the Amazon may contain the world's greatest biodiversity. Fly into Iquitos or Puerto Maldonado for the wildlife preserves, the lodges upriver, rainforest hikes, and boat excursions on the Amazon.

8 The Central Highlands. Festivals, craft villages, and markets dominate Huancayo and the Mantaro Valley, while the passionate Semana Santa celebrations are the rage in Ayacucho. From Lima to Huancayo, the world's highest railroad is running again—it tops out at 15,685 feet.

9 The North Coast and the Northern Highlands. Go up the coast for some of South America's best beach life and inland to the Cordillera Blanca for some of the world's highest mountains. Many of Peru's greatest archaeological discoveries were made in the north. Sites are still being uncovered in Chiclayo, Trujillo, and Chachapoyas.

Camp near Laguna Satuna, Cordillera Blanca.

QUITO ★

Portoviejo

ECUADOR

COLOMBIA

Guayaquil

Machala

Tumbes

Iquitos

7

Piura

**Pacaya-Samiria
National Reserve**

Mayobamba

Chachapoyas

Amazon River

BRAZIL

Túcume
**Pampa
Grande**

Chiclayo

Sipán

Cajamarca

9

**Gran
Pajatén**

Chán Chán

**Huacas
del Sol**

Trujillo

Pucallpa

Chimbote

Huaraz

CORDILLERA BLANCA

Pan-American Highway

Huanuco

Cerro De Pasco

Mantaro Valley

**Manu
National Park**

7

LIMA ★

2

Huancayo

Puerto
Maldonado

Pucusana

A
N
D
E
S

Huancavelica

8

**Machu
Picchu**

6

Aguas Calientes

**Tambopato-
Candamo
Reserve**

Cerro Azul

Ayacucho

Ollantaytambo

Pisac

Pisco

Abancay

Cusco

5

Paracas

Ica

Sacsayhuamán

**Paracas
National Preserve**

Huacachina

3

**Cotahuasi
Canyon**

Lake
Titicaca

BOLIVIA

Nazca

Nazca Lines

Colca Canyon

Sillustani

Juliaca

4

Arequipa

Puno

PACIFIC OCEAN

Moquegua

Tacna

CHILE

0   150 mi

0   150 km

EXPERIENCE PERU PLANNER

Time

Peru shares the Eastern Standard Time zone with New York and Miami when the U.S. East Coast is not on Daylight Savings Time. So when it's noon in Lima it will be 11 AM in Dallas and 9 AM in Los Angeles.

When to Go

Seasons flip in the southern hemisphere, but this close to the equator, "summer" and "winter" mean little. Think instead of "dry" and "rainy" seasons. Also the climates of the Costa (coast), the Sierra (mountains) and the Selva (jungle) are different.

Peru's tourist season runs from May through September, the dry season in the Sierra and Selva. The best time to visit is May through July, when the cool, misty weather is on the Costa, and the highlands are dressed in bright green under blue skies. When it's dry in the Sierra and the Selva, it's wet on the Costa, and vice versa. (But the coast doesn't get much rain any time of year.)

It never rains in the coastal desert, but a dank, heavy fog called the garúa coats Lima from June through December. Outside Lima, coastal weather is clearer and warm.

Health & Safety

Peru is safer than it has been in years, but standard travel precautions apply. Remember: you represent enormous wealth to the typical person here; the budget for your trip might exceed what many Peruvians earn in a year. Conceal your valuables, watch your things, avoid deserted locales, walk purposefully, take taxis at night, and be vigilant around scenes of commotion that may be engineered to distract you.

In terms of health and sanitation, few visitors experience anything worse than a bout of traveler's diarrhea. If you stick to upscale eateries in well-trodden destinations, you may minimize even those problems. Be wary of raw foods (peel your fruit!), and avoid drinking tap water entirely (and ice cubes). Check with your local public health department about any pre-travel immunizations or precautions (hepatitis, typhoid, malaria) recommended for Peru, and give yourself several weeks, since some procedures may require multiple injections.

High Altitude

Peru's lofty heights present you with both majesty and menace. The Andes, the country's signature geographic feature, provide a glorious backdrop. The 6,768-meter (22,204-feet) Huascarán tops Peru's peaks, and much of the center north–south band of the country sits at 3,000–4,000 meters (9,800–13,000 feet) altitude.

Treat that altitude with respect. Its consequences, locally known as soroche, affect visitors. For most, it's little more than a shortness of breath, which can be minimized by taking it easy the first couple of days and a good intake of nonalcoholic liquids. It occasionally requires immediate descent to lower altitudes. Peruvians swear by tea brewed from coca leaves, a completely legal way (legal here, at least) to prevent symptoms. We recommend a pre-trip check with your doctor to see if any underlying conditions (hypertension, heart problems, pregnancy) might preclude travel here.

Festivals & Celebrations

Fireworks and processions honor the **Virgen de la Candelaria** (February 2) in Puno and the Highlands, with the faithful following images of the Virgin Mary through the streets. Dancers depict the struggle between good and evil. (The demons always lose.)

Semana Santa (March or April) brings elaborate Holy Week processions countrywide. Ayacucho portrays the week's agony and triumph with ornate porter-borne floats emerging from palls of incense to the accompaniment of clanging bells.

Cusco's spectacular **Inti Raymi** (June 24) marks the winter solstice and reenacts age-old Inca pageantry that beseeches the sun to return. The fortress ruins of Sacsayhuaman form the stage for that proverbial cast of thousands.

Pre-dawn firecrackers rouse you out of bed. Not to worry: the revolution has not started. It's the kick-off to Peru's two-day **Independence Day** (July 28–29) parades. Independence was won in 1821.

Lima and the Central Highlands revere the **Señor de los Milagros** (October 18–28), a colonial-era image of a dark-skinned Christ that survived a 1655 earthquake that destroyed much of the capital. The devout, clad in purple robes and white sashes, carry heavy statues of Christ through the streets.

Tipping

A 10% tip suffices in most restaurants unless the service is exceptional. Porters in hotels and airports expect S/2–S/3 per bag. There's no need to tip taxi drivers, although many people round up the fare. At bars, tip about 50 céntimos for a beer, more for a mixed drink. Bathroom attendants get 20 céntimos; gas-station attendants get 50 céntimos for extra services such as adding air to your tires. Tour guides and tour bus drivers should get S/5–S/10 each per day.

First-Timer?

Build downtime into your itinerary. Don't let the churches, temples, convents, palaces, and ruins blur together.

Consider an overnight flight to Lima that arrives in the pre-dawn hours and lets you catch the first domestic flight to your final destination.

Postpone that diet. "Amazing" is the only way to describe what we think is the hemisphere's best cuisine.

Learn a few words of Spanish. Outside the tourist industry, few people speak much English. (And Spanish is a second language for many Peruvians, too.)

Pack reserves of patience. Peru offers a polished tourism product, but schedules occasionally go awry.

PERU TODAY

Government

Peruvian citizens have been on a political roller coaster for the past two decades. Current President Alan Garcia was first elected Chief of State in the 1980s. That presidency was marked by hyperinflation and the Shining Path, the terrorist group that would paralyze the country. After being accused of embezzling millions, Garcia went into exile, leaving Alberto Fujimori (elected 1990) to clean up the mess, and eventually get the upper hand against the Shining Path. Though the economy got back on track with Fujimori's austere reform program, his authoritarian policies—shutting down Congress, suspending the constitution—brought about a new set of problems.

After basically reelecting himself in 2000 through a flawed electoral process, Fujimori was eventually declared unfit by the Peruvian government. His challenger, Alejandro Toledo, won 2001's new election, beating out Garcia who had the audacity to come back and run for president again. Toledo, Peru's first indigenous president, made promises to deliver more jobs but couldn't produce them due to inexperience. By the time of the 2006 election, people were fed up with the scandals of Toledo's presidency. Garcia gave it one last shot, going up against leftist, nationalist Ollanta Humala. Peruvians gave Garcia another chance, going by the idea that voting for him was voting for "the lesser of two evils," or at least, for the devil you know.

Economy

Driven mainly by international investment, the Peruvian economy flourished in the late 1990s. This was accomplished through Fujimori's presidency, which saw the privatization of some mining, electricity, and telecommunications industries. Due to the weather effects from El Niño, worsening terms of trade, and political instability, the years ending Fujimori's term saw the economy slump. Once Toledo took over, he implemented a recovery program that had ill-effects, with the GDP growth barely making it past 0.2%. Things are now stabilizing, as the economy has grown steadily in recent years, largely due to increased exports.

Media

Fujimori's authoritative policies during the 1990s made it difficult for Peru's journalists to do their jobs. His administration was known for keeping an eye out for reporters in opposition to him. He often attempted to bribe networks so that they'd show him in a favorable light. To this day the left-leaning *La Republica* daily, who opposed Fujimori's administration, refers to him as the "ex-dictator." The situation is nowhere near what it used to be, but the topics of corruption, drug-trafficking, and the Shining Path are still dangerous subjects for reporters.

Religion

As a result of Spanish conquest, Peru remains predominantly Roman Catholic, with more than 80% of the population identifying themselves this way. Catholicism has a heavy influence on the daily life of your average Peruvian, as well as in state affairs. The newly elected president's inauguration ceremony begins with a mass in the Cathedral in Lima. Despite this overwhelming presence, some are moving toward Protestantism and Evangelicalism, which currently represent about 12% of the population. Indigenous Peruvians have also adopted Christian beliefs and fused them with their own, as

with the Pachamama (Mother Earth) representing the Virgin Mary.

Sports

Like most South Americans, fútbol (soccer) is a sport Peruvians can't live without. Today, the best teams are Universitario de Deportes, Alianza Lima, Sporting Cristal, and Cienciano. A game between Universitario and Alianza is considered a "clasico" and shouldn't be missed. Go at your own risk, however; these games have been known to get out of hand thanks to rowdy fans. Peru's national team hasn't managed to qualify for the World Cup in more than two decades. The sub-17 had a great display in the 2007 Sub-17 World Cup, showing the old-timers what a new generation of Peruvian soccer players is capable of. And although some people may not consider it a sport, bullfighting is still popular in Peru, especially in Lima. The season runs from October to December and the bloody fights—that result in the death of the bull—take place at Lima's Plaza de Acho.

Sexual Mores

Not acknowledging homosexuality and circulating machismo ideals are cultural norms in Peru. As expected in a country with almost all its citizens identifying themselves as Roman Catholics, homosexuality is still a touchy subject. Lima is one of the only cities where a small percentage of men actually feel comfortable enough to openly display their lifestyle. The chauvinistic, machismo attitude is also the cause for the stereotypical identities women and men have to endure: men being the dominant, macho ones, while women trail behind. Advancements in the workplace and in civil rights have been made, but women still face obstacles in achieving the same literacy rate as men and having reliable access to health care.

Literature

Peru's most famous writer is Mario Vargas Llosa. The novelist, who once ran for president but was defeated by Alberto Fujimori, is recognized as one of the figures responsible for the Latin American literary boom of the 1960s. His novels include comedies, murder-mysteries, and political thrillers. Several have been adapted to the big screen (*Tune in Tomorrow*) while others are frequently produced as plays around Peru (*The Feast of the Goat*). Peru's most famous poet is Cesar Vallejo. Vallejo, who only published three books of his poetry during his career, is considered one of the most innovative poets of the 20th century. Today, modern writers such as Jaime Bayly base their novels on themes such as political criticism, friendship, and sexual freedom; the latter is still a touchy subject in this very conservative country.

Music

Peruvian music can be split by regions: the sounds originating from the sierra (Andean region) and the sounds coming from the coast. "Huayno" comes from the Andes and is characterized by the use of Zampoña, a wind instrument. Its version from the region of Ayacucho is probably the most recognizable. Coastal "Musica criolla" (criollo music) has its roots in Spanish, Gypsy, and African influences. Singers such as the late Chabuca Granda popularized this genre, especially in Lima. The more modern "chicha" is a fusion of huayno, rock, and cumbia and is getting much airplay in Lima and Ollantaytambo.

TOP PERU ATTRACTIONS

Machu Picchu & the Inca Trail

(A) This "Lost City of the Incas" is the big reason why people come to Peru. The Machu Picchu ruins were built around the 1450s, only to be abandoned a hundred years later. Spanish conquistadors never found it and for centuries it stayed hidden. But in 1911, it was rediscovered by an American historian. If you're adventurous, and in good shape, the four-day Inca Trail is the classic route to Machu Picchu.

Colca Canyon

(B) Twice as deep as Arizona's Grand Canyon, Colca Canyon is typically a side-trip from Arequipa, which is a three-hour drive away. Adventure sport enthusiasts head for the Canyon's Colca River for river-rafting, while those less inclined toward danger hike the canyon for its gorgeous landscapes. The highlight is the Cruz del Condor, a mirador where visitors can spot the Andean condor in flight.

Chan Chan

(C) A UNESCO World Heritage Site since 1986, this archaeological site was home to the second largest pre-Columbian society in South America: the Chimú. The estimated 30,000 Chimú residents built the mud city between 850 and 1470. You can roam the ruins—which contain 10 walled citadels that house burial chambers, ceremonial rooms, and temples—on a day trip from the northern city of Trujillo.

Lake Titicaca

(D) At 3,812 meters, Puno's Lake Titicaca is the highest navigable lake in the world. More than 25 rivers empty into it, and according to Inca legend, it was the birthplace of the Sun God who founded the Inca dynasty. On Isla Taquile, like other islands here, Quechua-speaking people reserve the traditions of their ancestors.

Baños del Inca

(E) Six kilometers from the northern city of Cajamarca, Baños del Inca (Inca Baths) hot springs were once used by Inca Atahualpa, the last sovereign Inca Emperor. Supposedly, the emperor was relaxing in one of the mineral-rich baths when Spanish conquistadors arrived in Cajamarca. While visitors can only view the older pools that have been preserved intact, they can bathe in the newer pools built specifically for tourists.

Nazca Lines

(F) It's thought that between 900 BC and AD 600, the Nazca and Paracas cultures constructed the Nazca Lines: geometric figures drawn into the Pampa Colorado (Red Plain) in Nazca, a city south of Lima. Three hundred geoglyphs and 800 straight lines make up these mysterious figures. No one knows why these massive drawings—which include representations of a lizard, monkey, condor, and spider—were created. The only way to get a good view is to take a flightseeing tour.

Sacsayhuamán

(G) Machu Picchu isn't the only must-see Inca ruin to visit from Cusco. Used as a fortress during Pizarro's conquest, the military site of Sacsayhuamán is made of huge stone blocks; the largest is 8.5 meters high and weighs more than 300 tons. It's believed that some 20,000 men worked on the site.

Cordillera Blanco

(H) Part of the Andes range, Cordillera Blanco (White Range) has more than 50 peaks that reach 5,500 meters (18,000 feet) or higher and stretches 20 km wide and 180 km long. Mountain climbers and hikers of all skill levels can enjoy this majestic range, which is part of the Huascarán National Park.

IF YOU LIKE

Sun, surf & seafood

During the summer months (December–March), beach lovers around Peru head west to enjoy a day of surfing the Pacific Ocean waves, sunbathing on immaculate beaches, and devouring the country's freshest seafood.

Puerto Chicama. This fishing outpost north of Trujillo claims to have the world's longest left-hand point break. Surfers of all skill levels can find suitable waves year-round, but the perfect wave usually occurs between March and June.

Lima. While you can enjoy Lima's Costa Verde for a day at the beach, what truly brings visitors to this capital is the food. Lima has restaurants that specialize in everything, but "cevicherias" (restaurants dedicated to serving the seafood dish) are the staple. Check out Peruvian Chef Gaston Acurio's upscale cevicheria "La Mar."

South of Lima. Though some resorts were greatly damaged by the August 2007 earthquake, urbanites from Lima still escape to the towns of San Vicente de Cañete or Asia, a couple of hours from the capital city. Cerro Azul, a local beach town in Cañete, is a tranquil alternative to the beaches of Lima's Costa Verde. In contrast, Asia, also in Cañete, is where you'll find the young and hip surfing or dancing the night away.

Máncora. This fishing town on Peru's northern coast is the country's worst kept secret. Ask any Peruvian which is the best beach town in Peru and they will all mention this relaxed, small town. Máncora is sunny year-round and visited by beach admirers worldwide.

Ancient Archaeological Sites

The main reason travelers stop in Peru is to see the ancient ruins left by the Inca and older civilizations. Machu Picchu is the biggie, but don't stop there. Here are a few archaeological sites that are as historically interesting.

Caral. Three hours north of Lima, the archaeological ruins of Caral in the Supe Valley, shocked the world when its origins were discovered to date back to 2627 BC—1,500 years earlier than what was believed to be the age of South America's oldest civilization. Last year, 25,000 visitors came to see Peru's newest wonder.

Choquequirau. The Inca ruins of Choquequirau in Cusco is the ideal destination for those who enjoy history and trekking. Five-day trek tours are available if you wish to make the journey to this site, which has been called "Machu Picchu's sacred sister" because of the similarities in architecture.

Chan Chan. This capital of the pre-Inca Chimu empire was the largest pre-Columbian city in the Americas and the largest adobe city in the world. A 3-mile drive from Trujillo, Chan Chan is a UNESCO World Heritage Site. It's threatened by erosion because of its close proximity to the coast and its heavy rains and flooding.

Ollantaytambo. Sixty kilometers northwest of Cusco, the enormous Inca terraces of Ollantaytambo was one of the few locations where the Incas managed to defeat Spanish conquistadors. The fortress also served as a temple, with a ceremonial center greeting those who manage to get to the top.

Natural Beauty

With more than 50 natural areas or conservation units—in the forms of national parks, reserves, sanctuaries and protected rain forests—Peru is a paradise if you're seeking to be at one with nature.

Colca Canyon and Cotahuasi Canyon. The two deepest canyons in the world are in the high southern desert of Peru. Dipping down 10,600 feet and 11,000 feet respectively, there are many opportunities for hiking, intense kayaking, and bird-watching. More than just great geology, villages offer glimpses into the indigenous culture.

Huascaran National Park. In the department of Ancash, this park was established to protect the various flora and fauna, as well as the landscape of Cordillera Blanca, the "White Mountain Chain." Lucky visitors could see the speckled bear, cougar, jaguar, llama, and the Andean condor at this UNESCO World Heritage Site.

Tingo Maria National Park. While the park boasts an impressive number of 104 species of fauna and 144 species of flora, people make the trip out to tropical Tingo Maria to see the park's two main features: the chain of mountains called La Bella Durmiente because its silhouette resembles a sleeping woman; and the Cueva de las Lechuza, a cave that is home to various owls.

Rio Abiseo National Park. Try to spot the yellow-head parrot or "mono choro de cola amarilla" (yellow-tailed Woolly Monkey) in the jungles of this park in the department of San Martin. The park features the archaeological site "Gran Pajaten" of the Chachapoyas Culture, considered one of most impressive monumental complexes.

Museums

It could be argued that Peru is one big outdoor museum. However, as distinct an experience it is to visit the Chan Chan ruins, a little background information is always helpful. Museums in Peru do an excellent job of documenting the history and culture in a country overflowing with it.

Museo Santury. Home to the famed "Juanita, the Inca princess" mummy, the Museo de la Universidad Católica de Santa María, as it's formally known, is one of the main stops for anyone visiting the city of Arequipa. Juanita was discovered in southern Peru and is now kept in a cold glass box to preserve her body so that future visitors can learn about her sacrificial death.

Museo de Arte de Lima. In the Parque de la Exposicion, MALI, as it's called by Limeñans, features some of the best collections of Peruvian art. Modern and historical paintings depicting colonial Peru are alongside works by current artists such as Fernando de Szyszlo.

Museo Nacional Sicán. Twenty kilometers north of Chiclayo, this great museum focuses on the Sicán civilization, which originated in AD 750. Learn the life and death of one of their leaders, the Lord of Sicán, who was a representative of the "natural world" in their culture.

Museo Rafael Larco Herrera. This museum, one of Lima's finest, was constructed on the site of pre-Columbian pyramid houses. It's mostly known for its impressive pre-Columbian erotic pot collection. If you're not into titillating art, check out the more than 40,000 other ceramics, textiles, and gold pieces on display.

QUINTESSENTIAL PERU

Exploring the Past

Machu Picchu is great, but there's more to see of Peru's fascinating history. Stand at Cajamarca where Inca Atahualpa was captured by Spanish leader Francisco Pizzaro. Explore the ancient Moche culture by walking about its adobe pyramids. Puzzle over the mysterious Nazca Lines from the sky. Then enjoy city life in the Spanish influenced Lima, Trujillo, and Arequipa, and their colonial-era homes, churches, monasteries, and museums.

Peruvian history is best understood by visiting its people and experiencing its cultures. The islands of Lake Titicaca reveal a slice of raw ancient Andean culture. It's as if time has frozen while Quechua and Aymara families live and work off the land, eating and dressing as they did in the 16th century. It's not much different in the mountains and highlands where Quechua-speaking folks farm terraces thousands of years old.

Festival Time

Clanging bells, chanting, and wafting incense rouse you before dawn. You peer out your window: scores of people draped in bright colorful costumes walk down the street carrying a saint's figure.

Devout Catholicism, a strong indigenous tradition, and history pack the calendar with fiestas—from Lima's birthday in January, to the nationwide Semana Santa in spring, and Carnival the last two weeks of February. During Puno week, in November, citizens reenact the birth of the first Inca emperor Manco Capac who, sources say, materialized from Lake Titicaca.

Among the crosses, saints, colorful costumes, and folk songs, townspeople try their luck at bingo, and beauty queens go for the crown, while high-stepping horses compete for style points, and the Pilsen and Cusqueña beer flows freely.

High Living

Life in the Andes, the altiplano, has changed little through the centuries. In many villages Quechua is still the only language spoken. There are few cars, no computers, no ATMs, and no restaurants, though you will see locals carrying cell phones. Families live in stone and adobe huts and plumbing is a hole in the ground.

Nearly every family raises animals for food and transport. Parents harvest crops from the ancient terraces while children attend school. Cold temperatures call for hearty foods like soup, potatoes, bread, quinoa, and meats.

When it comes to fiestas, these villagers know how to let loose. No major floats needed. Parades consist of local instruments, traditional folk dances that reenact Peruvian history, hand-sewn clothing embroidered with bright colors, a crowd, and lots of alcohol.

Rituals of the Dance

Peruvian folkloric dances vary dramatically between coast and mountains.

The *marinera* is performed by a courting couple who execute elegant, complex movements while holding a handkerchief, but never touch. Trujillo is the city best known for marinera festivals and performances. A musician sits on a *cajón*, a wooden box with a sound-hole in the back, and taps out a rhythm.

The most challenging dance is the Andean *tijeras* (scissors), which involves gymnastic leaps to the strains of the harp and violin. Colonial-era priests claimed that a pact with the devil enabled dancers to swallow swords; stick pins in their faces; and eat insects, frogs, and sometimes snakes. The dance has toned down since then.

GREAT ITINERARIES

CLASSIC ANDES & THE AMAZON

Day 1: Lima

On your first full morning, take a three-hour tour to see the downtown historic center, the Museo de Oro, and (by taxi) the modern suburbs of San Isidro and Miraflores. In the afternoon visit the Museo Nacional de Antropología y Arqueología and the Museo Rafael Larco Herrera—both are in the Pueblo Libre district. Since you're in the neighborhood, finish the day by browsing through the Feria Artesanal, an artisans' market. ⇨ *Lima, Chapter 2.*

Days 2 & 3: Puno

From Lima take an early-morning flight to Juliaca, a commercial center with an airport that serves Puno and the Lake Titicaca region. Puno's 3,830-meter (12,500-feet) altitude can take your breath away. Check in your hotel and depart for a tour of the pre-Inca burial ground and stone *chullpas* at Sillustani. The next day take a boat tour of the lake, stopping at the Uros Islands and Isla Taquile. ⇨ *The Southern Coast to Lake Titicaca, Chapter 4.*

Days 4 & 5: Cusco

From Puno make arrangements with Peru Rail to take the train to Inca capital of Cusco, a 330 meter (1,083-foot) drop in altitude. Spend the day visiting Qorikancha, the MAP museum, the Museo Inka, and other architectural gems. At night indulge in new Andean cuisine at the Map Café or Inka Grill. The following day tour the Sacred Valley, stopping for the stone fort of Sacsayhuaman, the handicraft market and fantastic ruins at Pisac, a buffet Andean lunch in Urubamba, and finally at Ollantaytambo for the Inca fortress ruins. Or spend the day white-water rafting on the Urubamba or Apurímac

river. If you're hiking the four-day Inca Trail, begin here. ⇨ *Cusco & the Sacred Valley, Chapter 5.*

Days 6 & 7: Machu Picchu

Early the next morning, catch the train in Cusco to Aguas Calientes. Take the bus up the mountain to Machu Picchu, the majestic ancient citadel. For bragging rights climb Huaynu Picchu, the backdrop mountain for incredible views of the ruins below. The next morning explore the handicraft markets around town and a take a dip in the city's namesake thermal baths before returning to Cusco. ⇨ *Machu Picchu & the Inca Trail, Chapter 6.*

Days 8–11: Tambopata National Reserve

Fly out of Cusco to Puerto Maldonado where someone from your eco-lodge will meet you. You'll take a boat down the Madre de Dios river to your lodge and check in your bungalow. Your days will be filled with hikes into the National Reserve or visits to the renowned *Guacamayo clay lick,* while at night you'll take a short hike on trails near your lodge to look for monkeys or take a skiff to look for caiman and other nocturnal creatures. ⇨ *The Amazon Basin, Chapter 7.*

THE SOUTH COAST & CENTRAL HIGHLANDS

Day 1: Lima

On your first morning, tour the Plaza de Armas. In the afternoon, see the Museo Nacional de Antropología y Arqueologia and the Museo Rafael Larco Herrera and shop at the outdoor Feria Artesanal. ⇨ *Lima, Chapter 2.*

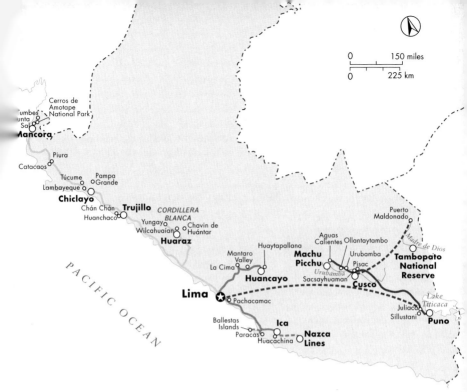

Days 2 & 3: Ica

Leave Lima early by bus or car and head south on the Pan-American highway to Ica, Peru's wine-growing area. (Allow about four hours.) Check into the Las Dunas Resort and arrange for an afternoon tour of one of the wineries and Ica's Museo Histórico Regional. The next day jump in a 4WD and drive through the desert and then test your skills at sand boarding down the dunes surrounding the *Huacachina* oasis. ⇨*The South, Chapter 3.*

Day 4: Nazca

In the morning take a five person plane to survey the lines and drawings of Nazca from the air before leaving by bus or car for Paracas. On an afternoon boat trip to the Balestas Islands you'll see sea lions, birds, and tiny Humboldt penguins, passing by the large candelabra etched on a cliff. Catch an afternoon bus

back to Ica, and overnight there. ⇨*The South, Chapter 3.*

Day 5: Lima

From Ica catch an early bus back to Lima and check back in your hotel. Take an afternoon trip to the pre-Inca pyramids at Pachacamac 30 minutes to the south or a culinary tour around the city and learn to make ceviche and the perfect pisco sour. ⇨*Lima, Chapter 2.*

Days 6–9: Huancayo

If you have timed it right you'll depart Lima's Desamparados station at 7 AM for the trip into the Central Highlands. The highest train in the world climbs to 4,818 meters (14,694 feet) at La Cima before dropping down to 3,254 meters (9,924 feet) at Huancayo. For the next two days shop for crafts and visit Andean markets in the Mantaro Valley and hike to the glacier at Huaytapallana or visit nearby Huanca ruins. If you want to volunteer in a highland village helping orphaned children or learn to weave or carve gourds from the masters, spend more time here. Otherwise, catch the train back on the fourth day. ⇨ *The Central Highlands, Chapter 8.*

THE NORTH COAST & CORDILLERA BLANCA

Day 1: Lima

On your first morning, tour the Plaza de Armas and the catacombs at San Francisco. In the afternoon, see the Museo Nacional de Antropología y Arqueologia and the Museo Rafael Larco Herrera. Have dinner in Miraflores. ⇨ *Lima, Chapter 2.*

Days 2–6: Huaraz

From Lima, drive or take an early-morning bus to Huaraz and spend the day acclimatizing while exploring the city and the nearby Wari ruins of Wilcahuaían or the sanctuary at Old Yungay, a town covered by a devastating earthquake in 1970, burying tens of thousands of people. For the next four days trek on the Santa Cruz circuit, a fantastic route in the heart of the Cordillera Blanca, or take less strenuous day trips to pristine mountain lakes and the ruins of Chavín de Huantar. ⇨ *The North Coast & Northern Highlands, Chapter 9.*

Days 7 & 8: Trujillo

From Huaraz go to Trujillo. Explore the Plaza de Armas at your leisure. The Libertador Hotel on the Plaza is a good spot for lunch or dinner. The next morning continue touring the city, visiting the beach resort of Huanchaco for lunch and spend the afternoon lounging on the beach. Local fishermen set out in their *caballitos de totora,* or reed boats. In the afternoon travel to the adobe-brick city of Chán Chán and the Huaca del Arco Iris. ⇨ *The North Coast & Northern Highlands, Chapter 9.*

Days 9 & 10: Chiclayo

Take a bus to Chiclayo (208 km/129 mi) from Trujillo. Visit the cathedral and the witches' market, where shamans and folk healers sell their herbs. The next morning tour the burial platform of Huaca Rajada to see the tomb of the Lord of Sipán and the on-site museum. Continue to Pampa Grande, site of the largest pyramid in South America. In the afternoon explore the nearby mud-brick pyramids at Tucume and the Bruning museum at Lambayeque. Overnight again in Chiclayo. ⇨ *The North Coast & Northern Highlands, Chapter 9.*

Days 11–14: Mancora

From Chiclayo take a bus or plane to Piura, where transfers to the beach paradise of Mancora can be made. In the day you'll bask in the sun or ride horses on Los Pocitas beach, learn to surf at the Municipal beach, or visit the craft town of Catacaos. For a day trip head to La Chicama to surf the worlds longest left breaking wave, to Cerros de Amotape National Park near Tumbes, or a snorkeling tour at Punta Sal. At night dine on prawns before dancing in a sandy-floored club until the sun comes up. ⇨ *The North Coast & Northern Highlands, Chapter 9.*

VISIBLE HISTORY

by Paul Steele

About 15,000 years ago, the first people to inhabit what is now Peru filtered down from Northand Central America. They were confronted by diverse and extreme environments at varying altitudes. An ocean rich in fish contrasts with sterile coastal valleys that are only habitable where rivers cut through the desert. To the east the valleys and high plateau of the Andes mountains slope down to the Amazon rainforest, home to exotic foods, animals, and medicinal plants.

Modern Peru incorporates all of these environmental zones. Long before the centralized state of the Inca empire, people recognized the need to secure access to varied resources and products. Images of animals and plants from coast and jungle are found on pottery and stone monuments in highland Chavin culture, c. 400 BC.

Around AD 500 the Nazca Lines etched out in the desert also featured exotic jungle animals.

In the 15th century the Incas achieved unprecedented control over people, food crops, plants, and domesticated animals that incorporated coast, highlands, and the semitropical valleys. Attempts to control coca leaf production in the warmer valleys may explain Machu Picchu, which guards an important trading route.

When the Spaniards arrived in the 16th century, the search for El Dorado, the fabled city of gold, extended the Viceroyalty of Peru into the Amazon lowlands. Since independence in 1821, disputes, wars, and treaties over Amazon territory have been fueled increasingly by the knowledge of mineral oil and natural gas under the forest floor.

(far left) Moche ceramic, portrait of a priest; (above) Cerro Sechin ca. 1000 BC on Peru coast; (left) Mummified corpse skull.

BIG OLD BUILDINGS
2600–1000 BC

Peru's first monumental structures were also the earliest throughout the Americas. Coastal sites like Aspero and Caral have platform mounds, circular sunken courtyards, and large plazas that allowed public civic-ceremonial participation. At Garagay and Cerro Sechin mud and adobe relief sculptures show images connected to death, human disfigurement, and human to animal transformation. A developing art style characterized by pronounced facial features like fanged teeth and pendant-iris eyes reached its height later in Chavin culture.

■ Visit:
Kotosh (⇨ Ch. 8),
Sechín (⇨ Ch. 9).

CHAVIN CULTURE
900–200BC

Chavin de Huantar, a site not far from Huaraz, was famous for its shamans or religious leaders who predicted the future. A distinctive and complex imagery on carved stone monuments like the Lanzón and Tello Obelisk featured animals and plants from the coast, highlands, and especially the jungle. The decline of Chavin de Huantar coincided with the emergence of other oracle temples such as Pachacamac, south of modern Lima. The distinctive Chavin art style, however, continued to influence later cultures throughout Peru, including Paracas on the south coast.

■ Visit:
Chavin de Huantar (⇨ Ch. 9).

ALL WRAPPED UP IN PARACAS
600–50BC

On the Paracas Peninsula the remains of an ancient burial practice are strewn across the desert. Corpses were wrapped in layers of textiles, placed in baskets, and buried in the sand. Many elaborately woven and embroidered garments that could be tens of meters long were only used to bury the dead and never worn in life. The mummy bundles of high status individuals were often accompanied by offerings of gold objects, exotic shells, and animal skins and feathers.

■ Visit:
Pachacamac (⇨ Ch. 3).

(above) Chavin de Huantar; (top right) Huaca de la Luna deity; (bottom right) Nazca ground picture of whale.

THE NASCANS

50BC – AD700

On Peru's south coast followed the Nasca, who are famous for the geoglyph desert markings known as the Nazca Lines. Thousands of long straight lines were constructed over many centuries, while around fifty animal outlines date to a more concise period of AD 400–600. An extensive system of underground aqueducts channeled water from distant mountains. In such a barren environment the Nazca Lines were probably linked closely to a cult primarily devoted to the mountain water source.

■ Visit:
Cahuachi (➪ Ch. 3),
Nazca Lines (➪ Ch. 3).

MOCHE KINGDOM

AD100 – 800

On Peru's north coast the Moche or Mochica controlled a number of coastal river valleys. Large scale irrigation projects extended cultivable land. The Temples of the Sun and Moon close to the modern city of Trujillo were constructed from millions of adobe or mud bricks and were some of the largest buildings anywhere in the ancient Americas. The high quality of Moche burial goods for individuals like the Lord of Sipan indicated a wide social gulf not previously seen in Peru. Full-time artisans produced metalwork and ceramics for Moche lords. The pottery in particular is famous for the realistic portrayal of individuals and

for the naturalistic scenes of combat, capture, and sacrifice that could have been narrative stories from Moche mythology and history. Some themes like the sacrificing of war captives in the presence of the Lord of Sipan and the Owl Priest were probably reenacted in real life. A number of severe droughts and devastating el niños rains precipitated the decline of the Moche.

■ Visit:
Pañamarca (➪ Ch. 9),
Huaca de la Luna (➪ Ch. 9),
Huaca del Sol (➪ Ch. 9).

Wari Empire begins | Chachapoyas kingdom begins

EXTENSIVE ROAD NETWORK CREATED

550   750   950

(above) Wari face neck jar; (top right) Chan Chan, (bottom right) Kuelap.

WELCOME TO THE WARI EMPIRE

550–950

A new dominant highland group, the Wari, or Huari, originated close to the modern city of Ayacucho. Wari administrative centers, storage facilities, and an extensive road network were forerunners to the organizational systems of the Inca empire. The Wari were influenced by the iconographic tradition of a rival site, Tiahuanaco, in what is now Bolivia, which exerted control over the extreme south of Peru. After Wari control collapsed, regional kingdoms and localized warfare continued until the expansion of the Inca empire.

■ Visit:
Pikillacta (⇨ Ch. 5),
Santuario Histórico Pampas de Ayacucho (⇨ Ch. 8).

CHIMU KINGDOM

900–1470

On the north coast the Chimu or Chimor succeeded the Moche controlling the coastal river valleys as far south as Lima. The capital Chan Chan was a bustling urban sprawl that surrounded at least 13 high-walled citadels of the Chimu lords. The city was built close to the ocean shore and continual coastal uplift meant that access to fresh water from deep wells was a constant problem. An extensive canal network to channel water from rivers never worked properly.

■ Visit:
Chan Chan (⇨ Ch. 9),
Huaca Esmeralda (⇨ Ch. 9).

THE FIGHTIN' CHACHAPOYAS

800–1480

In the cloud forests of the eastern Andean slopes the Chachapoyas kingdom put up fierce resistance against the Incas. The Chachapoyas are famous for their mummified dead placed in cliff-top niches and for high quality circular stone buildings at sites like Kuelap, one of the largest citadels in the world. Kuelap may have been designed as a fortification against the Wari. Later the Incas imposed harsh penalties on the Chachapoyas who subsequently sided with the Spaniards.

■ Visit:
Kuelap (Cuelap) (⇨ Ch. 9).

(left) Mama Occlo, wife and sister of Manco Capac, founder of the Inca dynasty, carrying the Moon; (above) Machu Picchu.

1

IN FOCUS VISIBLE HISTORY

C. 1400 INCA ORIGINS

The Inca empire spanned a relatively short period in Peruvian history. The mythical origins of the first Inca Manco Capac, who emerged from a cave, is typical of Peruvian ancestor tradition. Spanish chroniclers recorded at least 10 subsequent Inca rulers although in reality the earlier kings were probably not real people. The famous Inca, Pachacuti, is credited with expansion from the capital Cusco. Inca iconographic tradition that followed geometric and abstract designs left no representational images of its rulers.

■ Visit:
Isla del Sol (➪ Ch. 4).

1450 – 1527 INCA EMPIRE

Within three generations the Incas had expanded far beyond the boundaries of modern Peru to central Chile in the south and past the equator to the north. The Amazon basin was an environment they did not successfully penetrate. Although the Incas fought battles, it was a two-way process of negotiation with *curacas*, the local chiefs that brought many ethnic groups under control. The empire was divided into four *suyu* or parts, centered on Cusco. At a lower level communities were organized into decimal units ranging from 10 households up to a province of 40,000 households. Individual work for the state was known as *mit'a*. Communities forcibly resettled to foreign lands were called *mitimaes*. The Incas kept a regular population census and record of all the sacred idols and shrines. The Incas spread the language Quechua that is still spoken throughout most of Peru and in neighboring countries.

■ Visit:
Ollantaytambo (➪ Ch. 5), Machu Picchu (➪ Ch. 6), Ruins at Pisac (➪ Ch. 5).

EXTENSIVE DEPOPULATION THROUGHOUT PERU

| 1600 | 1650 | 1700 |

(above) The execution of Tupa Amaru; (left) Francisco Pizarro, Diego de Almagro, and Fernando de Luque planning the conquest of Peru.

ARRIVAL OF THE CONQUISTADORS

1527–1542

The Spanish conquistadors arrived on the coast of Ecuador and northern Peru bringing European diseases like smallpox that ravaged the indigenous population and killed the Inca king. They also introduced the name Peru. In 1532 a small band of conquistadors led by Francisco Pizarro first encountered the Inca ruler Atahualpa in Cajamarca. This famous confrontation of Old and New World cultures culminated with the capture of Atahualpa, who was later strangled. The Spaniards arrived in Cusco in 1533 and immediately took the city residences and country estates of the Inca elite for themselves. The resistance of Manco Inca could not drive the Spaniards out of Cusco, and by the end of the 1530's the Inca loyal supporters had retreated to Ollantaytambo, and then to the forested region of Vilcabamba that became the focus of Inca resistance for the next 30 years. In 1542 the Viceroyalty of Peru was created and a new capital city, Lima, became the political and economic center of Spain's possessions in South America.

■ Visit:
Cajamarca (⇨ Ch. 9),
Sacsayhuemán (⇨ Ch. 5).

END OF THE INCAS

1542 – 1572

A relatively small number of Spaniards overthrew the Incas because of support from many groups disaffected under Inca rule. Native Peruvians quickly realized, however, that these new lighter-skinned people were intent on dismantling their whole way of life. The 1560's nativist movement Taqui Onqoy, meaning dancing sickness, called on native gods to expel the Spaniards and their religion. In 1572 the Inca Tupa Amaru, mistakenly called Tupac Amaru, was captured and executed in public in Cusco.

■ Visit:
Cusco (⇨ Ch. 5).

(above) Battle of Ayacucho, Bolivar's forces establish Peruvian independence from Spain 1824; (left) Simon Bolivar, aka "The Liberator."

1

IN FOCUS VISIBLE HISTORY

SPANISH COLONIAL RULE

1572 – 1770

The Spanish crown increasingly sought more direct control over its American empire. A new viceroy, Toledo, stepped up the policy of *reducciones* in which formerly dispersed native communities were resettled into more easily controlled towns. This made it easier to baptize the native population into the Catholic church. The indigenous population was forced to work in mines such as Potosí, which became the biggest urban center in the Americas. Huge quantities of gold and silver were shipped to the Caribbean and then to Europe, and helped fund Spain's wars in Europe. Spanish hacienda estates introduced new food crops such as wheat, and new livestock like pigs and cows. The scale of native depopulation—more acute on the coast—is today reflected by the number of abandoned hillside terraces. The Inca elite and local chiefs started to adopt European dress; some found ways to prosper under new colonial regulations (like avoiding Spanish taxes if demonstrating Inca ancestry).

■ Visit:
Colonial architecture of
Arequipa (⇨ Ch. 4),
Ayacucho (⇨ Ch. 8),
Cusco (⇨ Ch. 5),
Lima (⇨ Ch. 2),
Trujillo (⇨ Ch. 9).

END OF COLONIAL RULE

1770 – 1824

The execution of the last Inca ruler in 1572 did not stop continued rebellions against Spanish colonial rule. In the eighteenth century an uprising led by the local chief José Gabriel Condorcanqui, who called himself Tupa Amaru II, foreshadowed the wars of independence that ended colonial rule in Peru and elsewhere in the Americas. Peru declared its independence in 1821 and again in 1824, when Símon Bólivar arrived from Colombia to defeat the remaining royalist forces at the battle of Ayacucho.

■ Visit:
Pampas de Quinua
(⇨ Ch. 8).

TIMELINE
| Slavery abolished
Quechua language officially recognized |
Earthquake devastates
South Peru
└ *POPULATION MIGRATION TO BIG CITIES* ┘

| 1900 | 1950 | 2000 | PRESENT |

(above) Former Peruvian President
Alberto Fujimori; (right) Lima, Peru.

REPUBLICAN ERA

1824 – 1900

Despite an initial 20 years of chaos, when every year seemed to bring a new regime, the young republic was attractive to foreign business interests. Particularly lucrative for Peru were the export of cotton and guano—nitrate-rich bird droppings used for fertilizer. Peru benefited from foreign investment such as railroad building, but an increasing national foreign debt was unsustainable without significant industrial development. Disputes with neighboring countries, especially the War of the Pacific against Chile in which Lima was sacked, land to the south ceded, and the country bankrupted, deeply affected the nation.

20TH-CENTURY PERU

1900 – 2000

For much of the nineteenth century Peru was led by presidents with military backgrounds, and military coups were interspersed with periods of civilian governments. The largest popular political movement, Alianza Popular Revolucionaria Americana, was founded by Victor Raul Haya de la Torre in the 1920s. Democratically elected presidents were rare. Old institutions like the haciendas declined and many are now abandoned ruins. In contrast, Lima's population increased rapidly with the growth of shanty towns called pueblos jóvenes.

RECENTLY . . .

1980–PRESENT

In the 1980s, the Shining Path guerrilla movement characterised a violent time in which thousands were killed. The capture of its leader, Abimael Guzmán, in 1992 has made Peru more attractive to tourism. In 1990 Peru elected as president Alberto Fujimori, who suspended the constitution to force economic reforms, and who now faces corruption and murder charges. He was succeeded by Peru's first president of largely native descent, Alejandro Toledo (2001-06). Alan Garcia, who led the country to economic disaster in the 1980s, won the election in 2006, casting himself as personally reformed and politically reformist. In 2007 an earthquake devastated southern Peru.

Lima

WORD OF MOUTH

"I love Spanish colonial architecture and Lima's historic center is beautiful. The Plaza Mayor (Plaza de Armas) is beautiful, as is Plaza San Martin. The San Francisco Monastery is very interesting."

— Bencito

WELCOME TO LIMA

TOP REASONS TO GO

★ **Neptune's Bounty:** You'll quickly encounter *cebiche*—slices of raw fish or shellfish marinated in lemon juice and covered with onions. Also try the *corvina* (sea bass) and *lenguado* (sole).

★ **Lima Baroque:** In El Centro, Iglesia de San Francisco's facade is considered the height of the "Lima Baroque" style of architecture. The crypt below stores the bones of dearly departed monks.

★ **Cool Digs:** More than 30 archaeological digs are around Lima. In Miraflores, a pre-Inca temple called Pucllana soars above the apartment buildings. In San Isidro is the temple Huaca Huallamarca.

★ **Handicrafts:** Calle Alcanflores, which runs through Miraflores, has stores selling everything from hand-woven rugs to silver-filligree jewelry.

★ **Park Life:** On weekends families and couples fill Lima's parks. Parque del Amor emphasizes its purpose with a huge statue of a couple locked in passion.

1 El Centro. The Plaza Mayor, the city's main square, is spectacular. Nearly every block has something to catch your eye, whether it's the elaborate facade of a church, the enclosed wooden balconies on centuries-old houses, or a pleasant park.

2 San Isidro. The mostly residential neighborhood grew around Parque El Olivar, a grove of olive trees. Many of the half-timbered homes are set among the gnarled trunks, evincing a fairy-tale setting. It's a fairly wealthy area but there are still budget-friendly dining and lodging options.

3 Miraflores. The heart of the modern city, Miraflores is where you'll probably spend most of your time. Its restaurants, bars, and boutiques are a big draw. Visit Parque del Amor and the string of other parks along the waterfront—the coastline view is unforgettable.

4 Barranco. The city's most bohemian neighborhood, Barranco has a fun and funky vibe. Low-key seafood eateries line the Bajada Los Baños, a cobblestone path leading down to the ocean. In the evening, it fills young people in search of a good time.

5 Pueblo Libre. This neighborhood feels like a village, which is exactly what Pueblo Libre was until the city's borders pushed outward. The city's best museum, the Museo Arqueológico Rafael Larco Herrera, is here.

GETTING ORIENTED

Most of Lima's colonial-era churches and mansions are in **El Centro**, along the streets surrounding the Plaza de Armas. From there, a speedy expressway called Paseo de la República or a traffic-clogged thoroughfare called Avenida Arequipa take you south to **San Isidro and Miraflores**, two fairly upscale neighborhoods where you'll find the bulk of the city's dining and lodging options. East of Miraflores is **Barranco**, a more bohemian suburb.

Banco de Credito, Lima.

LIMA PLANNER

The Weather

The weather in Lima doesn't vary much throughout the year. Daytime temperature rises to about 70°F, and at night it hangs around 60°F. The humidity remains low. The coastal region gets little precipitation, so you'll rarely find your plans ruined by rain.

Visitor Information

Assisting travelers is iPerú, which has English- and Spanish-language information about the city and beyond. The city runs the Oficina de Información Touristica, or Tourist Information Office, in the rear of the Municipalidad de Lima. It's a good place to pick up maps of the city, but the staff is not always that helpful.

Information iPerú (⊠ *Jorge Basadre 610, San Isidro* ☎ *01/421–1627* ⊠ *Malecón de la Reserva and Av. José Larco, Miraflores* ☎ *01/445–9400* ⊕ *www.peru.info*). **Oficina de Información Touristica** (⊠ *Paseo de los Escribianos 145, El Centro* ☎ *01/315–1505*).

Getting Here & Around

If you're flying to Peru, you'll almost certainly touch down at Aeropuerto Internacional Jorge Chávez, on the northwestern fringe of Lima. Once you're in the main terminal, hundreds of people will be waiting. Do yourself a favor and arrange for a transfer through your hotel.

Taxis are the best way to get around Lima. Use only taxis painted with a company's logo and that have the driver's license prominently displayed. It's best to negotiate the fare before you get in. A journey between two adjacent neighborhoods should cost between S/4 and S/7; longer trips should be about S/10 to S/15. If you call a taxi, the price will be roughly double. Well-regarded companies include Taxi Amigo (☎01/349–0177) and Taxi Móvil (☎01/422–6890).

Two types of buses—regular-size *micros* and the van-size *combis*—patrol the streets of Lima. Fares are cheap, usually S/1.40, or about 45¢ for a ride of any distance. First timers are intimidated by these vehicles, but they are a great way to experience the city.

Historical Walk

Almost all Lima's most interesting historical sites are within walking distance of the **Plaza de Armas**. The fountain in the center can be used as a slightly off-center compass. The bronze angel's trumpet points due north, where you'll see the **Palacio de Gobierno.** To the west is the neocolonial **Municipalidad de Lima,** and to the east are the **Catedral** and the adjoining Palacio Episcopal. The cathedral, one of the most striking in South America, should be given a look inside. Head north on Jirón Carabaya, the street running beside the Palacio de Gobierno, until you reach the butter-yellow **Estación de Desamparados,** the municipal train station. Follow the street as it curves to the east. In a block you'll reach the **Iglesia de San Francisco,** the most spectacular of the city's colonial-era churches. Explore the eerie catacombs.

2

Health & Safety

Drink only bottled water and order drinks *sin hielo* (without ice). Avoid lettuce and other raw vegetables. As for ceviche and other dishes made with raw seafood: chefs take pride in serving only what was swimming that morning, so the majority of travelers don't have a problem enjoying these delicacies.

El Centro is safe during the day, but as the locals head home in the late afternoon, so should you. The neighborhood is dicey at night. Residential neighborhoods like Miraflores, San Isidro, and Barranco have far less street crime, but you should be on your guard away from the main streets. Always be alert for pickpockets in crowded markets and on public transportation.

For robberies, contact the Tourist Police. The department is divided into the northern zone (☎01/424–2053), which includes El Centro, and the southern zone (☎01/460–4525), which includes Barranco, Miraflores, and San Isidro. English-speaking officers will help you negotiate the system. For emergencies, call the police (☎105) and fire (☎116) emergency numbers.

Tours

Lima has many top tour operators with experienced English-speaking guides for local and country-wide sightseeing. The most professional is Lima Tours, which offers tours of the city and surrounding area as well as the rest of Peru. The company is one of the few that conducts tours for gay groups. Lima Vision has some excellent city tours, including several that include lunch at a traditional restaurant or a dinner show. Other well-regarded companies include Condor Travel, Setours, and Solmartour.

Operators: Condor Travel (✉Av. Amando Blondet 249, San Isidro ☎01/442–0935 ⊕www.condortravel.com.pe). **Lima Tours** (✉Belén 1040, El Centro ☎01/619–6900 ⊕www.limatours.com.pe). **Lima Vision** (✉Jr. Chiclayo 444, Miraflores ☎01/447–7710 ⊕www.limavision.com). **Setours** (✉Av. Comandante Espinar 229, Miraflores ☎01/446–9229 ⊕www.setours.com). **Solmartour** (✉Av. Grau 300, Miraflores ☎01/444–1313 ⊕www.solmar.com.pe).

Retablos Explained

You can tell a lot about colonial-era churches by their *retablos (retables)*, the altarpieces that are almost always massive in scale and over-the-top in ornamentation. Most are made of elaborately carved wood and coated with layer after layer of gold leaf. Indigenous peoples often did the carving, so look for some atypical elements such as symbols of the sun and moon that figured prominently in many local religions. You may be surprised that Jesus is a minor player on many retablos, and on others doesn't appear at all. That's because these retablos often depict the life of the saint for which the church is named. Many churches retain their original baroque retablos, but others saw theirs replaced by the much simpler neoclassical ones with simple columns and spare design. If you wander around the church, you're likely to find the original relegated to one of the side chapels.

Updated by
Mark Sullivan

When people discuss great cities in South America, one that is often overlooked is Lima. But Peru's capital can hold its own against its neighbors. It has an oceanfront setting, colonial-era splendor, sophisticated dining, and nonstop nightlife.

It's true that the city—clogged with traffic and choked with fumes—doesn't make a good first impression. But wander around the regal edifices surrounding the Plaza de Armas, among the gnarled olive trees of San Isidro, or along the winding lanes in the coastal community of Barranco and you might find yourself charmed.

In 1535 Francisco Pizarro found the perfect place for the capital of Spain's colonial empire. On a natural port, the so-called Ciudad de los Reyes (City of Kings) allowed Spain to ship home all the gold the conquistador plundered from the Inca. Lima served as the capital of Spain's South American empire for 300 years, and it's safe to say that no other colonial city enjoyed such power and prestige during this period.

When Peru declared its independence from Spain in 1821, the declaration was read in the square that Pizarro had so carefully designed. Many of the colonial-era buildings around the Plaza de Armas are standing today. Walk a few blocks in any direction for churches and elegant houses that reveal just how wealthy this city once was.

The walls that surrounded the city were demolished in 1870, making way for unprecedented growth. A former hacienda became the graceful residential neighborhood of San Isidro. In the early 1920s, with the construction of tree-lined Avenida Arequipa, people pushed farther south to neighborhoods like bustling Miraflores and bohemian Barranco.

Almost a third of the country's population of 28 million lives here, many of them in poverty-stricken *pueblos jóvenes* in the outskirts of the city. Many residents of these "new towns" come from mountain villages, desperate for any kind of work. The lack of jobs led to a dramatic increase in crime during the 1980s and '90s.

Things have improved. Residents who used to steer clear of the historic center now stroll along its streets. And many travelers who once would have avoided the city altogether now plan to spend a day here and end up staying two or three. Not surprising, since Lima has the country's finest museums, swankiest shops, and most dazzling restaurants. It turns out that there really is a reason to fall in love with Lima.

EXPLORING LIMA

EL CENTRO

In the colonial era, Lima was the seat of power for the viceroyalty of Peru. It held sway over a swath of land that extended from Panama to Chile. With power came money, as is evident by the grand scale on which everything was built. The finely carved doorways of many private homes reach two or three stories high. At least half a dozen churches would be called cathedrals in any other city. And the Plaza de Armas, the sprawling main square, is spectacular.

But history has not always been kind to the neighborhood known as El Centro. Earthquakes struck in 1687 and 1746, leveling many of the buildings surrounding the Plaza de Armas. Landmarks, such as the Iglesia de San Agustín, were nearly destroyed by artillery fire in skirmishes that have plagued the capital. But more buildings are simply the victims of neglect. It's heartbreaking to see the wall on a colonial-era building buckling, or an intricately carved balcony beyond repair. But the city government has made an effort to restore its historic center. After years of decline, things are changing for the better.

An unhurried visit to the historic district's main attractions takes a full day, with at least an hour devoted to the Museo de Arte Nacional and the Museo de la Inquisición. ■**TIP→** Even if you're short on time, don't bypass the guided tour of the underground catacombs of the Iglesia de San Francisco. Also, you'll want to take a breather on the cathedral steps, as the locals do.

GETTING AROUND

Chances are you're staying in Miraflores or San Isidro, which are a quick taxi ride from El Centro. Since taxis take the expressway, you're downtown in 10 minutes. Much slower, but more interesting, is taking a bus. The regular-size *micros* and the van-size *combis* travel along crowded Avenida Arequipa. The journey takes a half-hour, more or less. Once you're there, the only way to get around is by foot. No problem, as the historic area is rather compact.

EL CENTRO'S CHURCHES & CATHEDRALS

❽ **Catedral.** The first church on the site was completed in 1625. The layout for this immense structure was dictated by Francisco Pizarro, and his basic vision has survived complete rebuilding after earthquakes in 1746 and 1940. Inside are impressive baroque appointments, especially the intricately carved choir stalls. Because of changing tastes, the main altar

El Centro

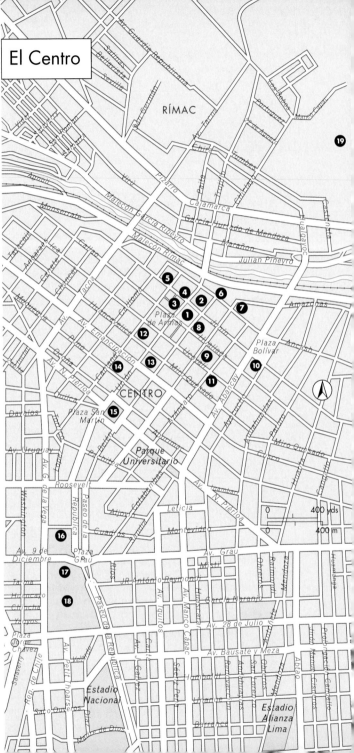

STREET SMARTS

Although El Centro is safe for daytime strolls, at night you'll want to take a taxi to your destination. If you find yourself on the street with few other people around in the late afternoon, it's probably time to hail a cab.

was replaced around 1800 with one in a neoclassical style. At about the same time the towers that flank the entrance were added. Visit the chapel where Pizarro is entombed. A small museum has religious art and artifacts. ✉ *East side of Plaza de Armas* ☎ *01/427–9647* 🎟 *S/10* ⏲ *Mon.–Sat. 10–4:30.*

5 **Convento de Santo Domingo.** The 16th-century Convent of Saint Dominic is a great place to experience life in the cloister. This sprawling structure shows the different styles popular during the colonial era in Lima. The bell tower, for instance, has a baroque base built in 1632, but the upper parts rebuilt after an earthquake in 1746 are more rococo in style. The church is popular, as it holds the tombs of the first two Peruvian saints, Santa Rosa de Lima, and San Martín de Porres. The pair of cloisters in the convent are decorated with yellow-and-blue tiles imported from Spain in the early 17th century. ✉ *Conde de Superunda and Camaná* ☎ *01/427–6793* 🎟 *S/5* ⏲ *Mon.–Sat. 9–11 and 3–6, Sun. 9–1.*

14 **Iglesia de Jesús, María y José.** The 1659 Church of Jesus, Mary and Joseph may have a plain facade, but inside is a feast for the eyes. Baroque retables representing various saints rise from the main altar. ✉ *Jr. Camaná and Jr. Moquegua* ☎ *01/427–6809* 🎟 *Free* ⏲ *Mon.–Sat. 9–noon and 3–5.*

13 ★ **Iglesia de la Merced.** Nothing about this colonial-era church could be called restrained. Take the unusual baroque facade. Instead of stately columns, the powers-that-be decided they should be wrapped with carefully carved grapevines. Inside are a series of retables that gradually change from baroque to neoclassical styles. The intricately carved choir stalls, dating from the 18th century, have images of cherubic singers. The first house of worship to be built in Lima, Our Lady of Mercy was commissioned by Hernando Pizarro, brother of the city's founder. He chose the site because it was here that services were first held in the city. ✉ *Jr. de la Unión at Jr. Miro Quesada* ☎ *01/427–8199* 🎟 *Free* ⏲ *Tues.–Sun. 8–1 and 4–8.*

7 Fodor's Choice ★ **Iglesia de San Francisco.** Bones—including thousands and thousands of human skulls—are piled in eerie geometric patterns in the crypt of this church. ■ **TIP→ This was the city's first cemetery, and the underground tunnels contain the earthly remains of some 75,000 people, which you visit on a tour (available in English).** The Church of Saint Francis is the most visited in Lima, mostly because of these catacombs. But it's also the best example of what is known as "Lima Baroque" style of architecture. The handsome carved portal would later influence those on other churches, including the Iglesia de la Merced. The central nave is known for its beautiful ceilings painted in a style called *mudejar* (a blend of Moorish and Spanish designs). On the tour you'll see the adjoining

monastery's immense collection of antique texts, some dating back to the 17th century. ⊠*Jr. Ancash 471* ☎*01/427–1381* ⊞*S/5* ⊙*Daily 9:30–5:45.*

⓫ **Iglesia de San Pedro.** The Jesuits built three churches in rapid succession on this corner, the current one dating from 1638. It remains one of the finest examples of early-colonial religious architecture in Peru. The facade is remarkably restrained, but the interior shows all the extravagance of the era, including a series of baroque retables thought to be the best in the city. ■TIP➔ **Don't miss the side aisle, where gilded arches lead to chapels decorated with beautiful hand-painted tiles.** Many have works by Italians like Bernardo Bitti, who arrived on these shores in 1575. His style influenced an entire generation of painters. In the sacristy is *The Coronation of the Virgin,* one of his most famous works. ⊠*Jr. Ucayali at Jr. Azángaro* ☎*01/428–3010* ⊞*Free* ⊙*Mon.–Sat. 7–12:30 and 5–8.*

CRAZY ABOUT FÚTBOL

Soccer—or *fútbol*—reigns supreme in Peru. When a highly contested match is televised, don't be surprised to see dozens of people in the street outside a bar or restaurant that happens to have a television. This is how most Peruvians watch matches, and it's the best way for newcomers to join in. If you want to see a match in person, they are played year-round at the 45,574-seat **Estadio Nacional** (⊠*Jr. José Díaz, El Centro* ☎*01/433–6366*), home to the national team. Tickets range from US$5 to US$25.

MUSEUMS, PLAZAS & OTHER SIGHTS

⓬ **Casa Riva-Agüero.** A pair of balconies with *celosías*—intricate wood screens through which ladies could watch passersby unobserved—grace the facade of this rambling mansion from 1760. A mildly interesting museum of folk art is on the second floor, but the real reason to come is for a glimpse into a colonial-era home. ⊠*Jr. Camaná 459* ☎*01/427–9275* ⊞*S/3* ⊙*Mon.–Sat. 10–7.*

⓳ **Cerro San Cristóbal.** Rising over the northeastern edge of the city is this massive hill, recognizable from the cross at its peak—a replica of the one once placed there by Pizarro. If the air is clear—a rarity in Lima—you can see most of the city below. The easiest way to get here is via one of the buses that circle the Plaza de Armas. An hour-long tour costs S/5. ⊠*Calle San Cristóbal.*

❾ **Casa Torre Tagle.** Considered one of the most magnificent structures in South America, this mansion sums up the graceful style of the early 18th century. ■TIP➔Flanked by a pair of elegant balconies, the stone entrance is as expertly carved as that of any of the city's churches. It currently serves as a governmental building and is not open to the public, but you can often get a peek inside. You might see the tiled ceilings, carved columns, and a 16th-century carriage. Across the street is **Casa Goyeneche,** which was built some 40 later in 1771, and was clearly influenced by the rococo movement. ⊠*Jr. Ucayali 363.*

DID YOU KNOW?

For more than 400 years, Lima's Cathedral has undergone numerous reconstructions and facelifts thanks to earthquakes.

6 **Estación de Desamparados.** Inaugurated in 1912 Desamparados Station was the centerpiece for the continent's first railway. The building, using lots of glass for natural light, was based on styles popular in Europe. The city often uses the space for temporary art exhibits, giving you a chance to check out the inside. ⊠ *Jr. Carabaya and Jr. Ancash.*

3 **Municipalidad de Lima.** Although it resembles the colonial-era buildings surrounding it, the City Hall was constructed in 1944. Step inside to see the stained-glass windows above the marble staircase. Alongside the building a lovely pedestrian walkway called the Paseo Los Escribanos, or Passage of the Scribes, is lined with inexpensive restaurants. On the south side is the tourist-information office. ⊠ *West side of Plaza de Armas* ☎ *01/315–1505 tourist office* ⊙ *Tourist office Mon.–Sat. 9–6.*

PALATIAL POST OFFICE

4 **Correo Central.** Inaugurated in 1897 this regal structure looks more like a palace than a post office. You can buy a stamp or send a package, but most people come to admire the exuberance of an era when no one thought twice about placing bronze angels atop a civic building. At one time locals deposited letters in the mouth of the bronze lion by the front doors. The Museo Postal y Filatélico, a tiny museum of stamps, is just inside the front entrance. ⊠ *Conde de Superunda, between Jr. de la Unión and Jr. Camaná* ☎ *01/427–9370* ⊠ Free ⊙ *Mon.–Sat. 8–8, Sun. 9–2.*

17 **Museo de Arte de Lima.** The facade is covered with graffiti, probably because it adjoins a busy bus stop. But the rest of the Museum of Art is lovingly cared for. Built in 1872 as the Palacio de la Expedición, this mammoth neoclassical structure was designed by Gustav Eiffel (who later built the famous tower). It contains a bit of everything, from pre-Columbian artifacts to colonial-era furniture to modern art. One of the highlights is the collection of 2,000-year-old weavings from Paracas. ■TIP→ Leave time to sip an espresso in the café near the entrance. ⊠ *Paseo Colón 125* ☎ *01/423–6332* ⊕ *museoarte.perucultural.org.pe* ⊠ *S/12* ⊙ *Thurs.–Tues. 10–5.*

16 **Museo de Arte Italiano.** Italian art in Peru? This little-known museum is one of the city's most delightful. Most of the art is about a century old, so it captures the exact moment when impressionism was melting into modernism. Don't overlook the magnificent iron door, by Alessandro Mazzucotelli. ⊠ *Paseo de la República 250* ☎ *01/423–9932* ⊠ *S/3* ⊙ *Weekdays 10–5.*

10 **Museo de la Inquisición.** Visit the original dungeons and torture chambers of the Spanish Inquisition, where stomach-churning, life-size exhibits illustrate methods of extracting "information" from prisoners. This massive mansion later served as the temporary home of Congress, which found a permanent home in the neoclassical structure across the street. The guided tour, offered several times a day in English, lets you explore the beautiful building, especially the coffered ceilings dat-

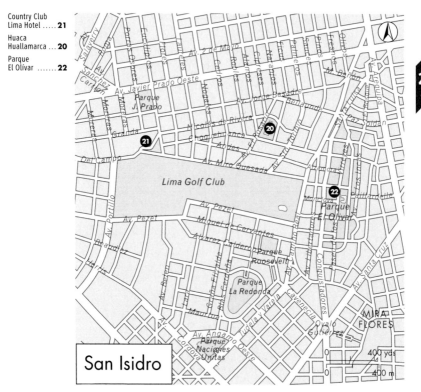

San Isidro

ing from the 18th century. ⊠*Jr. Junín 548* ☎*01/428–7980* ⊕*www. congreso.gob.pe/museo.htm* ☑*Free* ☺*Daily 9–5.*

❷ **Palacio de Gobierno.** The best time to visit the Governmental Palace is weekdays at noon, when you can watch soldiers in red-and-blue uniforms conduct an elaborate changing of the guard. (It's not Buckingham Palace, but it's impressive.) Built on the site where Francisco Pizarro was murdered in 1541, the Palacio de Gobierno was completed in 1938. The neobaroque palace is the official residence of the president. At this writing the palace had suspended tours for security reasons. Call ahead to see if tours have been resumed. ⊠*North side of Plaza de Armas* ☎*01/426–7020.*

❶ **Parque de la Exposición.** Eager to prove that it was a world-class capital, Lima hosted an international exposition in 1872. Several of the buildings constructed for the event still stand, including the neoclassical Palacio de la Expedición, which now serves as the Museo de Arte. Stroll through the grounds and you'll find the eye-popping Pabellón Morisco, or Moorish Pavilion. Painstakingly restored in 2005, this Gothic-style structure has spiral staircases leading to a stained-glass salon on the second floor. The nearby Pabellón Bizantino, or Byzantine Pavilion, needs a polish. Despite its name, it most closely resembles a turret from a Victorian-era mansion. ⊠*Av. de la Vega and Av. Grau* ☎*01/423–4732* ⊙*Daily 9–5.*

❶ **Plaza de Armas.** This massive square has been the center of the city since
★ 1535. Over the years it has served many functions, from an open-air theater for melodramas to an impromptu ring for bullfights. Huge fires once burned in the center for people sentenced to death by the Spanish Inquisition. Much has changed over the years, but one thing remaining is the bronze fountain unveiled in 1651. ■**TIP→ It was here that José de San Martín declared the country's independence from Spain in 1821.** ⊠*Jr. Junín and Jr. Carabaya.*

⓯ **Plaza San Martín.** This popular plaza is unlike any other in the city. It's surrounded on three sides by French-style buildings—most of them an oddly appealing shade of pumpkin—dating from the 1920s. Presiding over the western edge is the Gran Hotel Bolívar, a pleasant stop for afternoon tea. Several restaurants on the periphery enjoy the view of the statue of San Martín in the center. ⊠*Between Jr. de la Union and Jr. Carabaya.*

SAN ISIDRO

While strolling through the ancient olive trees of Parque El Olívar, you might be surprised that there's not a single car in sight. That's because the mostly residential neighborhood of San Isidro lacks the fast pace of the rest of the city. At its main attraction, Huaca Huallamarca, you can clamor around the ruins of this ancient temple.

Like nearby Miraflores, San Isidro is big on shopping—plenty of boutiques sell designer goods, bars serve up the latest cocktails, and restaurants dish out cuisine from around the world.

Numbers in the text correspond to numbers in the margin and on the San Isidro map.

GETTING AROUND
The best way to travel between San Isidro's widely dispersed attractions is by taxi. Walking through the neighborhood takes no more than a few hours. This is probably Lima's safest neighborhood.

WHAT TO SEE
㉑ **Country Club Lima Hotel.** Two magnificent palms stand guard at the entrance to this 1927 hotel, widely regarded as the most elegant hotel in the city. If you're here in the afternoon, you might want to stop by for the English-style tea. ⊠*Los Eucaliptos 590* ☎*01/211–9000.*

⓴ **Huaca Huallamarca.** The sight of this mud-brick pyramid catches many people off guard. The structure, painstakingly restored on the front side, seems out of place among the neighborhood's towering hotels and apartment buildings. The upper platform affords some nice views of the San Isidro. There's a small museum with displays of objects found at the site, including several mummies. This temple, thought to be a place of worship, predates the Incas. ⊠*Av. Nicolás de Rivera and Av. El Rosario* ☎*01/224–4124* ⊠*S/5.50* ⊙*Tues.–Sun 9–5.*

Even the statues find love in the Parque del Amor, Miraflores.

㉒ Parque El Olívar. This pretty park was once an olive grove, so it's no surprise that you'll find an old olive press here. The gnarled old trees, some more than a century old, still bear fruit. Yellow and red irises line the walkways. ⊠ *East of Av. Conquistadores.*

NEED A BREAK? When strolling through Parque El Olívar, stop by Pasteleria Monserrat (⊠ *Pancho Fierro 131* ☏ *01/440–0517*) for some of the neighborhood's most fanciful pastries, including little cupcakes shaped like mice.

MIRAFLORES

With flower-filled parks and wide swaths of green overlooking the ocean, no wonder travelers flock to this seaside suburb. At its center is Parque Miraflores, sitting like a slice of pie between Avenida José Larco and Avenida Diagonal. On the eastern side is the Parroquia Virgen Milagrosa, the neighborhood's largest church. The colonial-style building next door is the Municipalidad de Miraflores, where most governmental business takes place.

Where you go next depends on your areas of interest. If you're interested in ancient cultures, head to the towering temple of Pucllana. From the top you have a great view of the neighborhood. A tiny Museo Amano contains one of the city's best collections of ancient artifacts. If you have romance on your mind, go south along Avenida Diagonal— also known as Avenida Oscar Benevidas—to reach Parque del Amor.

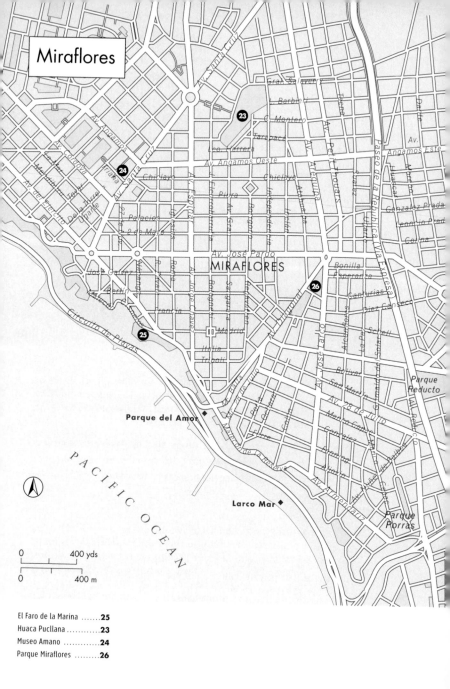

Miraflores

PACIFIC OCEAN

Parque del Amor ◆

Larco Mar ◆

0	400 yds
0	400 m

You won't be alone—this wonderful waterfront park attracts young lovers all day.

Miraflores is also the city's cultural hub. There are plenty of boutiques, galleries, and museums, as well as bars, cafés, and restaurants. Some people who find themselves in Lima for a short time never leave this little haven.

GETTING AROUND

Good times to stroll Miraflores are mid-morning, when the heat is not yet overbearing, or mid-afternoon, when you can escape the sun by ducking into a bar or café. All the stores along Avenida José Larco stay open for early-evening window shoppers. About a half hour of walking will lead you to the ocean, where you'll want to spend another hour or so strolling along the cliff. Miraflores is about 20 minutes from El Centro by taxi.

> ## LOVE PARK
>
> **Parque del Amor.** You might think you're in Barcelona when you stroll through this lovely park. Like Antonio Gaudí's Parque Güell, the park that provided the inspiration for this one, the benches are decorated with broken pieces of tile. Here, however, they spell out silly romantic sayings like *Amor es como luz* ("Love is like light"). The centerpiece is a controversial statue of two lovers locked in a lewd embrace. ⊠*Av. Diagonal.*

WHAT TO SEE

㉕ El Faro de la Marina. Constructed in 1900 this little lighthouse has steered ships away from the coast for more than a century. The classically designed tower is still in use today. ⊠*Malecón Cisneros and Madrid.*

㉓ ★ Pucllana. Rising out of a nondescript residential neighborhood is this mud-brick pyramid. You'll be amazed at the scale—this pre-Inca *huaca*, or temple, covers several city blocks. The site, which dates back to at least the 4th century, has ongoing excavations, and new discoveries are often being announced. ■**TIP→** Archaeologists working on the site are usually happy to share their discoveries about the people who lived in this area hundreds of years before the Inca. A tiny museum highlights some recent finds. Knowledgeable guides are available in Spanish and English. This site is off the beaten path, but plenty of restaurants are nearby, including the on-site Huaca Pucllana. ⊠*General Borgoño, 2 blocks north of Av. Angamos Oeste* ☎*01/445–8695* ⊕*pucllana.perucultural. org.pe* 🖃*S/7* ⊗*Wed.–Mon. 9–4:30.*

㉔ Museo Amano. Although only two rooms, this museum packs a lot into a small space. The private collection of pre-Columbian artifacts includes one of the city's best ceramics. Imaginative displays reveal how cultures in the northern part of the region focused on sculptural images, while those in the south used vivid colors. In between, around present-day Lima, the styles merged. ■**TIP→** A second room holds an impressive number of weavings, including examples from the Chancay people, who lived in the north between 1000 and 1500. Some of their work is so delicate that it resembles the finest lace. Call ahead: you need an appointment to join one of the Spanish-language tours. ⊠*Retiro 160* ☎*01/441–2909* 🖃*Free* ⊗*Weekdays 3–5 by appointment only.*

26 **Parque Miraflores.** What locals call Parque Miraflores is actually two parks. The smaller section is Parque Central, which has frequent open-air concerts. Shoeshine boys will ask whether you need a *lustre* when you stop to listen to the music. The honking noise you hear is the ice-cream vendors that patrol the park on bright yellow bicycles. A tourist-information kiosk sits on the south side. Across a pedestrian street full

> **PARAGLIDE, ANYONE?**
>
> If you walk along the ocean on a sunny day, you'll doubtless see a dozen or so brilliantly colored swaths of cloth in the sky above you. **PerúFly** (✉ *Av. Jorge Chavez 658, Miraflores* ☎ *01/444-5004* ⊕ *www.perufly.com*) offers a six-day course for about US$450.

of local artists showing off their latest works is Parque Kennedy, where the babble from a lively crafts market fills the evening air. On the eastern side is the pretty Parroquia Virgen Milagrosa (Miraculous Virgin Church). A few sidewalk cafés are behind the church. ✉ *Between Av. José Larco and Av. Diagonal.*

BARRANCO

Barranco is a magnet for young people who come to carouse in its bars and cafés. Sleepy during the day, the neighborhood comes to life around sunset when artists start hawking their wares and its central square and bars begin filling up with people ready to party. Founded toward the end of the 19th century, Barranco was where wealthy Limeños built their summer residences. The weather proved so irresistible that many eventually constructed huge mansions on the cliffs above the sea. Many of these have fallen into disrepair, but little by little they are being renovated into funky restaurants and hotels.

GETTING AROUND

To get your bearings, head to Parque Municipal, one of the nicest parks in the city. To the south, the brick-red building with the tower is the Biblioteca Municipal, or Municipal Library. Stop by the tourist office on the ground floor to pick up a map of the neighborhood. To the north is the parish church called La Santisima Cruz. To the east is Lima's own Bridge of Sighs, the Puente de los Suspiros. ■ TIP→ Directly below is the bougainvillea-shaded Bajada de Baños, lined with wonderful old houses. Head down this cobblestone street and soon you'll find yourself walking in the waves at Playa Barranquito.

Numbers in the text correspond to numbers in the margin and on the Barranco map.

WHAT TO SEE

30 **Museo de la Electricidad.** In front of this tiny museum is a cherry-red *urbanito*, or streetcar, named Breda. From Tuesday to Sunday, for about 65 cents you can climb aboard and take a three-block trip down Avenida Pedro de Osma. Inside the museum are photos of other trolleys that once rumbled along Lima's streets. The captions are only in Spanish. ✉ *Av. Pedro de Osma 105* ☎ *01/477–6577* ⊕ *museoelectri. perucultural.org.pe* ✉ *Free* ☉ *Daily 9–5.*

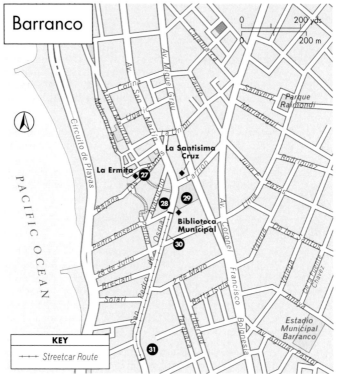

Barranco

KEY

⊷ *Streetcar Route*

❷❽ **Museo-Galería Arte Popular de Ayacucho.** An unassuming facade makes it easy to miss, but inside you'll find one of the country's best collections of folk art. ■**TIP→ One especially interesting exhibit concerns the cajones San Marcos, the boxlike portable altars that priests once carried from village to village.** Peasants began to make their own, placing scenes of local life inside. These dioramas, ranging in size from less than an inch to more than a foot wide, are still made today. ✉*Av. Pedro de Osma 116* ☎*01/247–0599* ✉*Free* ☉*Tues.–Sat. 9–6.*

❸❶ **Museo Pedro de Osma.** Even if there was no art inside this museum,
Fodor's Choice it would still be worth the trip to see the century-old mansion that
★ houses it. The mansard-roofed structure—with inlaid wood floors, delicately painted ceilings, and breathtaking stained-glass windows in every room—was the home of a wealthy collector of religious art. The best of his collection is permanently on display. The finest of the paintings, the 18th-century *Virgen de Pomato,* represents the Earth, with her mountain-shape cloak covered with garlands of corn. A more modern wing contains some fine pieces of silver, including a lamb-shape incense holder with shining ruby eyes. Make sure to explore the manicured grounds. ✉*Av. Pedro de Osma 423* ☎*01/467–0141* ✉*S/10* ☉*Tues.–Sun. 10–6.*

NEED A BREAK?
Along a walkway leading past La Ermita is the gingerbread-covered La Flor de Canela (⊠ *Ermita 102* ☎ *No phone*), a sweet little café with a porch overlooking much of Barranco. It's a great place to escape the midday heat.

㉙ Parque Municipal. Elegant swirls of colorful blooms make this park stand out from others in Lima. Here you'll find locals relaxing on the benches, their children playing nearby. ■**TIP→** Around 6 pm every evening artists who live nearby show off their latest works. ⊠ *Between Av. Pedro de Osma and Av. Grau.*

㉗ Puente de los Suspiros. The romantically named Bridge of Sighs is a lovely
★ wooden walkway shaded with flowering trees. You won't have to wait long to see couples walking hand in hand. The bridge crosses over the Bajada de Baños, a cobblestone walkway that leads to Playa Barranquito. On the far side is La Ermita, a lovely little chapel painted a dazzling shade of red. ⊠ *East of Parque Municipal.*

PUEBLO LIBRE

Instead of hurrying past, residents of Pueblo Libre often pause to chat with friends. There's a sense of calm here not found elsewhere in the capital. Plaza Bolívar, the park at the heart of Pueblo Libre, is surrounded by colonial-era buildings, many of which have shops and restaurants. On the south side, in the Municipalidad de Pueblo Libre, are governmental offices. A small gallery on the ground floor sometimes hosts painting and photography exhibitions.

Despite the pleasant surroundings, there would be little reason to venture this far if it weren't for the presence of two fine museums, the Museo Nacional de Antropología, Arqueología, e Historia del Perú, and the Museo Arqueológico Rafael Larco Herrera.

GETTING AROUND
The most convenient way to reach Puerto Libre is a quick taxi ride. There are buses, but chances are you'd have to switch once or twice to get back to your hotel.

WHAT TO SEE
Museo Nacional de Antropología, Arqueología, e Historia del Perú. The country's most extensive collection of pre-Columbian artifacts can be found at this sprawling museum. Beginning with 8,000-year-old stone tools, Peru's history is peeked at through the sleek granite obelisks of the Chavín culture, the intricate weavings of Paraca peoples, and the colorful ceramics of the Moche, Chimú, and Inca civilizations. ■**TIP→** A fascinating pair of mummies from the Nazca region are thought to be more than 2,500 years old; they are so well preserved that you can still see the grim expressions on their faces. Not all the exhibits are labeled in English, but you can hire a guide for S/15. ⊠ *Plaza Bolívar* ☎ *01/463–5070* ⊕ *mnaah.perucultural.org.pe* ⊠ *S/11* ☉ *Tues.–Sat. 9–5, Sun. 9–4.*

NEED A DRINK?
Saloon-style doors lead you into the Antigua Taberna Queirolo (⊠ *Jr. San Martín 1090* ☎ *01/463-8777*), a charming little bar about a block west of

Plaza Bolívar. Locals lean against round tables and sample the pisco bottled at the bodega next door.

Fodor's Choice ★ **Museo Arqueológico Rafael Larco Herrera.** Fuchsia bougainvillea tumbles over the white walls surrounding the home of the world's largest private collection of pre-Columbian art. The oldest pieces are crude vessels dating back several thousand years. Most intriguing are the thousands of ceramic "portrait heads" crafted more than a millennium ago. Some owners commissioned more than one, allowing you to see how they changed over the course of their lives. The *sala erótica* reveals that these ancient artists were surprisingly uninhibited. Everyday objects are adorned with images that are frankly sexual and frequently humorous. This gallery is across the garden from the rest of the museum, so you can distance the kids from it. Guides are a good idea, and are just S/25 per group. ✉ *Av. Bolívar 1515* ☎ *01/461–1835* ⊕ *www.museolarco.org* 💲 *S/25* ⊙ *Daily 9–6.*

> **SURFING**
>
> With Surf Express (✉ *568 Highway A1A, Satellite Beach* ☎ *321/779-2124* ⊕ *www.surfex. com*), surfers ride with some of the best left-breaking waves in the world, such as at Punta Rocas south of Lima. You'll want a wetsuit, because the water is chilly.

ELSEWHERE AROUND LIMA

A few of Lima's most interesting museums are in outlying neighborhoods such as Monterrico and San Borja. These neighborhoods are generally safe, but there's no reason you'd want to go out for a stroll. The most convenient way to reach them is a quick taxi ride.

WHAT TO SEE

Museo de la Nación. If you know little about the history of Peru, a visit to this fortresslike museum is likely to leave you overwhelmed. The number of cultures tracked over the centuries makes it easy to confuse the Chimú, the Chincha, and the Chachapoyas. The three floors of artifacts end up seeming repetitive. The museum is more manageable if you have a specific interest, say, if you're planning a trip north to Chiclayo and you want to learn more about the Moche people. Except for a pair of scale models of Machu Picchu, the rooms dedicated to the Inca is disappointing. ✉ *Av. Javier Prado Este 2465, San Borja* ☎ *01/476–9878* ⊕ *www.cosapi.com.pe* 💲 *S/6.50* ⊙ *Tues.–Sun. 9–6.*

Museo de Oro. When you see examples of how these societies manipulated gold—from a mantle made of postage-stamp-size pieces worn by a Lambayeque priest to an intricately designed sheet that once decorated an entire wall of the Chimú capital of Chán Chán—you begin to imagine the opulence of these ancient cities. The museum has other interesting items, including a child's poncho of yellow feathers and a skull with a full set of pink quartz teeth. Upstairs are military uniforms and weapons. None of the displays are particularly well marked, either in English or Spanish, so you might want to see the museum as part of an organized city tour; it's a pretty good deal, as you'll save the cost of a taxi. At any rate, be prepared to pay one of the steepest admissions of any of South America's museums. ⊠*Alonso de Molina 1100, Monterrico* ☏*01/345–1271* ☚*S/30* ☉*Daily 11:30–7.*

**OFF THE
BEATEN
PATH**

Pachacàmac. Dating back to the first century, this city of plazas, palaces, and pyramids, many of them painstakingly restored, was for centuries a stronghold of the Huari people. Here they worshipped Pachacámac, creator of the world. It was a pilgrimage site, and people from all over the region came to worship here. In the 15th century the city was captured by the Inca, who added structures such as the *Acllahuasi,* the Palace of the Chosen Women. When the Spanish heard of the city, they dispatched troops to plunder its riches. In 1533, two years before the founding of Lima, they marched triumphantly into the city, only to find a few remaining objects in gold. Today you can visit the temples, including several that were built before the time of the Incas. The Incas built several more structures, including the impressive Templo del Inti, or Temple of the Sun. Here you'll find a grand staircase leading up to the colonnaded walkways surrounding the temple. The site has a small but excellent museum. Although it's a quick drive from the city, the easiest way to see Pachacámac is by a half-day guided tour offered by Lima Tours and several other agencies in Lima. ⊠*31 km (19 mi) south of Lima on Carretera Panamericana Sur* ☏*01/430–0168* ⊕*pachacamac.perucultural.org.pe* ☚*S/5.50* ☉*Daily 9–5.*

WHERE TO EAT

THE SCENE

Seafood, especially *cebiche* (raw fish or shellfish in lemon juice), is a Peruvian specialty. The more mood for seafood, do as the locals do and have it for lunch.

WHAT IT COSTS IN NUEVO SOLES					
	¢	$	$$	$$$	$$$$
RESTAURANTS	under S/20	S/20–S/35	S/35–S/50	S/50–S/65	over S/65

Restaurant prices are per person for a main course.

BARRANCO

In keeping with its reputation as a bohemian neighborhood, Barranco has a slew of cozy cafés. Look for these around the Puente de los Suspiros. For more substantial fare, head to those facing Parque Municipal.

ITALIAN

$–$$ ✕**Antica Trattoria.** At this Italian-style eatery, if you want to watch the chefs prepare your meal, grab one of the rough-wood tables in the front room near the open grill. Plenty of other rooms provide more privacy. As you might expect in a restaurant that is a stone's throw from the ocean, the seafood is especially good. You can't go wrong with dishes like risotto with lobster. The more than 50 different kinds of pizza

Continued on page 64

FOOD IN PERU

by Mark Sullivan

When Peruvians talk about *comida criolla*, or typical food, they aren't talking about just one thing. This is a vast country, and dishes on the table in coastal Trujillo might be nowhere in mountainous Cusco. And all bets are off once you reach places like Iquitos, where the surrounding jungle yields exotic flavors.

REGIONAL CUISINE

THE CAPITAL

Lima cooks up the widest variety of Peruvian and international foods. One of the most influential immigrant communities is the Chinese, who serve traditional dishes in restaurants called *chifas*. One favorite, *lomo saltado*, strips of beef sautéed with onions, tomatoes, and friend potatoes, is now considered a local dish.

THE COAST

When you talk about the cuisine of the country's vast coastal region, you are talking about seafood. Peruvians are very particular about their fish, insisting that it should be pulled from the sea that morning. The most common dish is *ceviche*, raw fish "cooked" in lemon or lime juice. It comes in endless variations—all delicious.

A woman preparing *anticuchos*.

THE ALTIPLANO

Hearty fare awaits in the altiplano. Because it keeps so well over the winter, the potato is the staple of many dishes, including the ubiquitous *cau cau*, or tripe simmered with potatoes and peppers. A special treat is *pachamanca*, a Peruvian-style barbecue where meat and potatoes are cooked in a hole in the ground lined with hot rocks. In Huancayo, the local specialty is *papa a la huancai'na*, boiled potato covered in yellow chili-cheese sauce.

THE AMAZON

Fish is a staple in the Amazon, and you'll know why once you taste paiche and other species unknown outside this area. One of the best ways to try local fish is *patarashca*, or fish wrapped in banana leaves and cooked over an open fire. Restaurants here are very simple, often just a few tables around an outdoor grill.

Ceviche dish.

IT'S ALL ABOUT THE FISH

Peru's high-altitude lakes, including Lake Titicaca, and rivers spawn some very tastey *trucha* (trout).

In Peru, restaurants known as *cebicherías* serve more than the marinated fish called ceviche. The menu may intimidate those who can't tell *lenguado* (sole) from *langosta* (lobster). Don't worry—just order a series of dishes to share. Local families pass around huge platters of *pescado* until they are picked clean, then gesture to the server for the next course.

The fragrant *sopa de mariscos* is soup overflowing with *chorros* (mussels) still in their shells. *Tiradito* is similar to ceviche but leaves off the onions and adds a spicy yellow-pepper sauce. A platter of *chicharrones de calamar*, little ringlets of deep-fried squid, should be given a squeeze of lime. For a nice filet or whole fish, many restaurants suggest a dozen or more preparations. It's best grilled, or *a la plancha*.

ON THE SIDE

ELOTE
A pile of large-kernel corn.

Camote
Boiled sweet potatoes. The sweetness is a wonderful contrast to the citrus marinade.

Cancha
A basket full of fried corn that's usually roasted on the premises. Highly addictive.

Chifles
A northern coast specialty of thin slices of fried banana.

Zarandajas
A bean dish served in the northern coast.

A simple boiled potato
A dish you'll recognize.

SPUD COUNTRY

POTATO ON THE PLATE

The potato, or its cousin the yucca, is rarely absent from a Peruvian table. Any restaurant offering *comida criolla*, or traditional cuisine, will doubtless serve *cau cau* (tripe simmered with potatoes and peppers), *papa a la huancaina* (potatoes in a spicy cheese sauce), or *ocopa* (boiled potatoes in peanut sauce). Just about everywhere you can find a version of *lomo saltado*, made from strips of beef sautéed with tomatoes, onions, and fried potatoes. Some 600,000 Peruvian farmers, most with small lots in the highlands, grow more than 3,250,000 tons of potatoes a year.

GET YOUR PURPLE POTATOES HERE!
Peru's potatoes appear in all colors of the spectrum, including purple, red, pink, and blue. They also come in many strange shapes.

SCIENCE POTATO
The International Potato Center (Centro Internacional de la Papa), outside of Lima, conducts spud research to help farmers and open markets, particularly for the great variety of Andean potatoes. They recently sent 35 million potato seeds for safe-keeping to a genetic storage facility to Svaldbard, Norway, a large island of ice that is above the arctic circle—just so the Peruvian potato can outlive us all.

POTATO HISTORY

The potato comes from the Andes of Peru and Chile (not Idaho or Ireland), where it has been grown on the mountain terraces for thousands of years. There are endless varieties of this durable tuber: more than 7,000 of them, some of which are hardy enough to be cultivated at 15,000 feet. The Spanish introduced potatoes to Europe in the late 1500s.

(above) Preparing *pachamanca;* (left) Discovering the potato.

OTHER STAPLES

CORN: Almost as important as potatoes is corn. You might be surprised to find that the kernels are more than twice as large as their North American friends. Most corn dishes are very simple, such as the tamale-like *humitas*, but some are more complex, like the stew called *pepián de choclo*. A favorite in the humid lowlands is *inchi capi*, a chicken dish served with pea-nuts and toasted corn. A sweet purple corn is the basis for *chicha morada*, a thick beverage, and *mazamorra*, an even thicker jelly used in desserts. Even ancient Peruvians loved popcorn, kernels were found in tombs 1000 years old in eastern Peru. Also discovered were ceramic popcorn poppers from 3000 AD.

PEPPERS: Few Peruvian dishes don't include *ají*, the potent hot peppers grown all over the country. You'll find several everywhere—*amarillo* (yellow pepper), *rocoto* (a reddish variety), and *panca* (a lovely chocolate brown variety), but there are hundreds of regional favorites. Some, like ají *norteño*, are named for the region of origin, others, like the cherry-sized ají *cereza*, are named for what they resemble. Such is the case with the ají *pinguita de mono*, which, roughly translated, means "small monkey penis." It is one of the hottest that you'll find.

Hot pepper tip: Never rub your eyes after handling a hot pepper, and avoid contact with your skin.

FOR ADVENTUROUS EATERS

CUY: What was served at the Last Supper? According to baroque paintings hanging in the Iglesia de San Francisco in Lima and the Cathedral in Cusco, it was guinea pig. Both paintings show a platter in the middle of the table with a whole roasted guinea pig, including the head and feet.

This dish, called *cuy chactado* or simply *cuy*, has long been a staple of the antiplano. Cuy is a bit hard to swallow, mostly because it is served whole. The flavor is like pork, and can be sweet and tender if carefully cooked.

ANTOCUCHOS: When a street vendor fires up his grill, the savory scent of *anticuchos* will catch your attention. Beef hearts in the Andes are a delicacy. Marinated in herbs and spices, these strips of meat are incredibly tender. They have become popular in urban areas, and you're likely to run across restaurants called *anticucherías* in Lima and other cities.

ALPACA: Nearly every visitor to Cusco and the surrounding region will be offered a steak made of alpaca. It's not an especially tasty piece of meat, which may be why locals don't eat it very often. But go ahead—you can impress the folks back home.

(Top, right) *humita* (bottom) Peruvian eating guinea pig.

Where to Stay & Eat in Barranco

are cooked in the wood-fired oven. ⊠ *Av. San Martín and Av. Ugarte,* ☎ *01/247–3443* ☰ *MC, V.*

PERUVIAN

$–$$ ✗ **Manos Morenas.** A century-old house behind an iron gate contains one of the most atmospheric restaurants in Barranco. The tables scattered around the front porch are so inviting that you might get no farther than the front door. Past the brilliant blue facade is a warmly lighted dining room bustling with women in colorful headwraps serving tasty Peruvian fare. ■ **TIP→ The ají de gallina, a spicy stewed hen, is the best you'll find anywhere.** If you're brave, sample the *anticuchos,* skewers of beef hearts. At night Manos bursts to life with music and dancing. ⊠ *Av. Pedro de Osma 409,* ☎ *01/467–0421* ⌕ *Reservations essential* ☰ *AE, MC, V.*

¢–$ ✗ **Las Mesitas.** Filled with a dozen or so marble-topped tables, this
★   charming old-fashioned café is a block north of Parque Municipal. The constant stream of Limeños informs you that the food is first-rate. Share a few *humitas,* steamed tamales that you season with pickled onions or bright yellow hot sauce. The best are those stuffed with chicken, onions, and green corn. If the floor's pinwheel design doesn't put you off balance, then the spinning dessert display certainly will.

2

Try the *mazamorra morada*, a sweet pudding of cornmeal and candied fruit. ✉*Grau 341*, ☎*01/477–1346* ▬*MC, V.*

$ ✗**Las Terrazas de Barranco.** If you're standing in Parque Municipal, you won't miss this restaurant. Bright pink geraniums tumble down the series of terraces that give the place its name. The open-air dining room, big enough for half a dozen tables, lets you enjoy the cool breezes. The specialty is *cebiche* (chunks of raw fish marinated in lemon juice and topped with onions), and the spicy fish dish is served several ways. If you're hungrier, go for the crispy whole fish. ✉*Av. Grau 290*, ☎*01/247–1477* ▬*MC, V.*

SEAFOOD

¢–$ ✗**Javier.** Seafood restaurants are huddled together along the street leading down to the ocean—in fact, several share a single staircase. What sets Javier apart is its rooftop terrace, which overlooks the crashing waves. There's nothing fancy here, just incredibly fresh fish. Start with the *conchas a la parmasana* (clams with Parmesan cheese), then try the *lenguado a la parrilla* (fish served hot off the grill). A pisco sour—the first one is on the house—is a great way to start your meal. ✉*Bajada de Baños 403*, ☎*01/477–5339* ▬*V.*

$–$$ ✗**Vida.** Facing a cobblestone street, this butter-yellow building has an
★   unbeatable location. Wide windows in the dining room let you watch young lovers stroll across the Puente de los Suspiros. With the ocean practically at the door, it's no surprise the focus is seafood. Try the sea bass wrapped in prosciutto and sautéed in pisco, or the swordfish grilled in squid ink. If you arrive early, enjoy a pisco sour at the outdoor bar. ✉*Bajada de Baños 340*, ☎*01/252–8034* ⚑*Reservations essential* ▬*AE, DC, MC, V* ☯*Closed Mon. No dinner Sun.*

EL CENTRO

If you're looking for a fancy meal, you'll be hard-pressed to find it in El Centro. But if you want cheap, filling food, you've come to the right place. A highlight is the Barrio Chino, packed with dozens of Chinese-Peruvian restaurants called *chifas*.

CAFÉS

$ ✗**Estadio.** If you want to watch the big game—and in this country that can only mean one thing—you can't do better than this neighborhood hangout. Soccer paraphernalia covers nearly every square inch of the wood-paneled dining room. It's a sedate place during the day, and a place for a lunch of typical dishes like *ají de gallina* (chicken in a spicy sauce). ■**TIP➔** On game day things can get out of hand. If it gets too noisy inside, head outside to one of the tables facing Plaza San Martín. ✉*Av. Nicolás de Piérola 926, Lima 01* ☎*01/428–8866* ▬*AE, MC, V.*

¢   ✗**Restaurante Cardano.** This isn't the kind of old-fashioned café that has
★   been gussied up to attract tourists. It looks pretty much the same as when two Italian brothers opened for business in 1905. A huge mirror hangs over the curved wooden bar. You enter through swinging doors, and a waiter in a long white apron waves you over to an empty table. The *menú economico*, which rings up for less than two bucks, is one

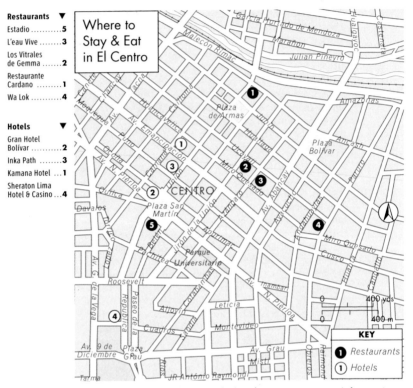

Where to Stay & Eat in El Centro

of the city's great bargains. With three courses, you certainly won't go away hungry. ⊠ *Av. Ancash 202, Lima 01* ☎ *01/427–0187* ⊟ *AE, V.*

CHINESE

$–$$$ ✕ **Wa Lok.** Of the dozens of *chifas* in Chinatown, none comes close to Wa Lok. Attention to the smallest detail makes every meal memorable; *kun pou kay tien*—chicken stir-fried with asparagus and yellow peppers—arrives garnished with an impossibly elaborate hibiscus flower carved from a carrot. Vegetarians can choose from more than 30 dishes made without meat. No matter what you order, do as the locals do and enjoy it with a glass of chartreuse-color Inca Cola. ■**TIP**➔ **If the dining room is full, don't fret; there's another branch in Miraflores.** ⊠ *Jr. Paruro 864, El Centro* ☎ *01/427–2656* ⊠ *Av. Anamos 700, Miraflores* ☎ *01/447–1329* ⊟ *AE, DC, MC, V.*

PERUVIAN

$ ✕ **Los Vitrales de Gemma.** Tucked into the courtyard of a beautiful colo-
★ nial-era building, this is one of the prettiest restaurants in the historic district. Tables covered with peach-color linens are set beneath flower-covered colonnades. The food, creative takes on old recipes, is just as appealing. Start with a spinach salad tossed with bacon, walnuts, and slices of apples, then move on to *pescado en salsa langotinos* (fish in lobster sauce) or *espagueti fruotos del mar* (pasta with seafood).

✉Jr. Ucayali 332 ☎01/426–7796 ⊟AE, DC, MC, V ⊗Closed Sun.

MIRAFLORES

Although inexpensive eateries are clustered around Parque Miraflores, the more elegant ones are scattered about, so plan on reaching them by taxi. If you want to dine with an ocean view, Miraflores has more options than any other neighborhood.

CAFÉS

¢ ✗La Buena Esquina. If you're planning a picnic, stop by this little corner bakery for tempting prepared sandwiches, such as the *tres jamones*, piled high with three kinds of ham. If you're a do-it-yourselfer, buy a baguette and some cheese and you're all set. The Good Corner is also a nice spot for afternoon coffee and pastries. ✉*José Galvez and Jorge Chavez, Lima 18* ☎*01/241–8603* ⊟*AE, DC, MC, V.*

$ ✗Café Café. The drink of choice is the cappuccino calypso, combining a jolt of joe with frangelica, Kahlua, and rum. Don't worry—you can still order your espresso straight up. Most people forgo the food, but that's a shame, as the roast-beef sandwich is a sizzling slab of meat atop a wedge of crusty bread. Even the BLT is decadent, served open face with huge chunks of avocado. This is a see-and-be-seen kind of place. Tables on the second level let you check out the crowd below, and those on the street give you an unobstructed view of Parque Central. ✉*Martir Olaya 250, Lima 18* ☎*01/445–1165* ✉*Larcomar, Malecón de la Reserva and Av. José Larco* ☎*01/445–1165* ⊟*AE, DC, MC, V.*

¢ ✗Quattro D. An emerald-green awning won't allow you to miss this oddly named café, a favorite among young couples on dates and harried parents with children in tow. ∎TIP➡ It's a good choice if you're headed to the nearby archaeological site of Pucllana. Grab a table by the window to choose from the daily specials. Most people, however, head to the counter in back to choose from the 20 or so varieties of gelato. Among the sassier tropical flavors are tamarindo and guanabana. ✉*Av. Angamos Oeste 408, Lima 18* ☎*01/447–1523* ⊟*No credit cards.*

CONTINENTAL

$$–$$$ ✗Astrid y Gaston. You can't help but watch the kitchen door—each
Fodor'sChoice dish the waiters carry out is a work of art. Take the *pato asado con*
★ *mil especies* (roast duck with 1,000 spices): the honey-brown breast is accompanied by a steamed pear and a pepper bubbling over with basil risotto. Other dishes, like the pasta with squid and artichokes, are just as astonishing. ∎TIP➡ Take advantage of the wine list—it's one of the best in town. In a colonial-style building on a quiet street, the restaurant

NUNS SINGING!

✗L'eau Vive. Calling to mind *The Sound of Music*, a group of nuns sings "Ave Maria" every night around 8:30. The holy sisters cook French food that, while not extraordinary, is satisfying. Trout baked in cognac and duck in orange sauce are two dishes that bring the locals back. In a beautifully restored mansion directly across from Palacio Torre Tagle, the restaurant is worth a visit just for a peek inside. The furnishings, especially the plastic chairs, don't do justice to the glorious architecture. ✉*Ucayali 370,* ☎*01/427–5612* ⊟*AE, MC, V* ⊗*Closed Sun.*

2

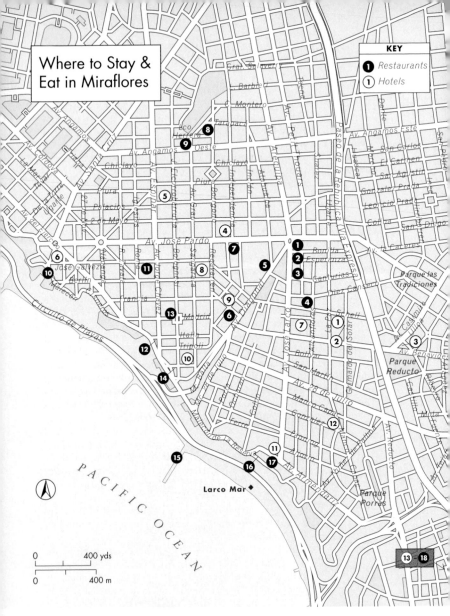

Where to Stay & Eat in Miraflores

Larco Mar ◆

P A C I F I C   O C E A N

| 0 | 400 yds |
| 0 | 400 m |

is lovely, with pumpkin-color walls and original artwork. ⊠ *Cantuarias 175, Lima 18* ☎ *01/444–1496* ⊟ *AE, MC, V* ⊘ *Closed Sun.*

$ ✗**Vivaldino.** Wrought-iron tables covered with crisp white linens and lighted with stained-glass lamps distinguish this classic eatery. Tall windows let you gaze down at the ocean. The menu tends toward Mediterranean-style fare. Try the *solomillo caprese* (bits of steak with tomatoes and mozzarella cheese) or the *pulpito parrillero* (grilled octopus with potatoes and arugula). If the dessert cart includes a mousse made with *lucuma*, a local fruit, snap one up immediately. ⊠ *Larcomar, Malecón de la Reserva and Av. José Larco, Lima 18* ☎ *01/446–3859* ⊟ *AE, MC, V.*

ITALIAN

¢–$ ✗**La Glorietta.** Locals refer to the alley west of Parque Kennedy as "La Calle de Pizza," and with good reason—it's packed with nearly identical pizza parlors. The best of the bunch is this popular place, as relaxed as the others are rowdy. There are wooden tables instead of plastic, and attentive waiters instead of disinterested teens. Best of all, the pizza isn't half bad. Enjoy it with a beer or pisco sour as one of the wandering musicians plays "Don't Worry, Be Happy" on the flute. ⊠ *Juan Figari 181, Lima 18* ☎ *01/445–0498* ⊟ *AE, MC, V.*

$–$$ ✗**Trattoria di Mambrino.** You don't even have to walk through the door
★ to know that this trattoria's pasta is fresh. Passersby pause by a window to watch cooks stuff the ravioli and drape the fettuccini on long wooden rods. But the proof is on the plate: delicious dishes like tortellini tossed with chunks of beef, mushrooms, and a touch of cream leave you satisfied but not stuffed. With room for dessert, you can be tormented by the *tormento de chocolate.* The only caveat is the service, which can be lackadaisical. ⊠ *Manuel Bonilla 106, Lima 18* ☎ *01/446–7002* ⊘ *Reservations essential* ⊟ *AE, MC, V.*

PERUVIAN

$$–$$$$ ✗**Las Brujas de Cachiche.** Although the name conjures up a haunted house, the Witches of Cachiche is a modern space with huge windows, soaring ceilings, and lots of modern art. ■**TIP**➜ **The magic is the cooking, which draws on Peru's traditional cuisines.** Don't expect dishes like baby goat roasted with herbs to be handed down from *abuela* (grandmother); the chef often adds touches from other cultures. Although there are some reasonably priced entrées, dishes like lobster will send your bill into the triple digits. The wine list has several top South American vintages. ⊠ *Bolognesi 460, Lima 18* ☎ *01/444–5310* ⊘ *Reservations essential* ⊟ *AE, DC, MC, V.*

$$–$$$$ ✗**Huaca Pucllana.** You feel like a part of history at this beautiful res-
Fodor's Choice taurant, which faces the ruins of a 1,500-year-old pyramid. ■**TIP**➜
★ **Excavations are ongoing, so you can watch archaeologists at work as you enjoy the breezes on the covered terrace.** Rough-hewn columns hold up the dining room's soaring ceiling. This is *novo andino* cuisine, which puts a new spin on old recipes. Yellow peppers stuffed with shrimp are a great way to start, and the *cabrito al horno* (roasted kid) is a work of art. Wash it all down with one of many pisco preparations. ⊠ *Av. General Borgoña* ☎ *01/445–4042* ⊘ *Reservations essential* ⊟ *AE, DC, MC, V.*

$–$$ ✕**El Señorío de Sulco.** It's no surprise that the food is so good when you learn that owner Isabel Alvarez authored several cookbooks. The antique cooking vessels hanging on the walls reveal her passion for Peruvian cuisine. Start with *chupe de camerones*, a hearty soup combining shrimp and potatoes, then move on to *arroz con pato*, duck stewed in dark beer and seasoned with coriander. For dessert there's the meringue-topped *suspiro de limeña*, which literally means "sigh of a lady of Lima." Arrive early to watch the sun set over the ocean. ✉*Malecón Cisneros 1470, Lima 18* ☎*01/441–0389* ✍*Reservations essential* ✉*AE, DC, MC, V* ☉*No dinner Sun.*

$–$$ ✕**Las Tejas.** As it's a few steps down from the street, it would be easy to pass by this family-run restaurant. That would be a shame, as it serves up some of the neighborhood's tastiest traditional cuisine. The staff will explain each dish, what part of the country it comes from, and how it's made. ■TIP→This is the best place to sample lomo saltado, slices of pork sautéed with tomatoes and onions and served over fried potatoes. You know the food is fresh, as it's prepared in the open-air kitchen inches away from the tables scattered around the covered terrace. ✉*Diez Canseco 340, Lima 18* ☎*01/444–4360* ✉*AE, DC, MC, V.*

SEAFOOD

$$–$$$ ✕**La Rosa Náutica.** One of the most recognizable landmarks in Miraflores, La Rosa Náutica is at the end of a prominent pier. The blue slate roof of the rambling Victorian-style building is visible even from miles away. In the gazebolike dining room is a view of the entire coast. Signature entrées include grilled scallops topped with a hearty cheese, but you might also consider the sea bass or the sole. Daily specials might include rock fish in salt crust. For dessert, try the *crepes suchard* filled with ice cream and topped with hot fudge. ✉*Espigón 4, Lima 18* ☎*01/447–0057* ✉*AE, DC, MC, V.*

$–$$ ✕**Segundo Muelle.** Many restaurants are along the ocean, but the crowds keep coming to this sleek eatery. The reason is the seafood, specifically the lip-smacking *cebiche*. Choose from 10 different versions, each with some type of fish, shrimp, squid, or octopus; the *mixto* lets you sample them all. Still, nothing brings a hush over the dining like when the waiter appears with *chita al plato*, a whole fish that's been grilled to perfection. ✉*Malecón Cisneros 156, Miraflores* ☎*01/241–5040* ✉*Av. Conquistadores 490, San Isidro* ☎*01/421–1206* ✉*AE, DC, MC, V* ☉*No dinner.*

STEAK

$$$–$$$$ ✕**El Rincón Gaucho.** The cowhides on the floors and the photos of prize heifers on the walls don't let you forget that this is the place for steaks. Even the menus are made of hand-tooled leather. The Argentine beef, always sliced to order, is displayed just inside the front door. The best bet for the indecisive is the *parrillada*, a mixed grill of steaks, kidneys, livers, pork chops, chicken legs, and blood pudding. The order for two will satisfy three or four people. Although the restaurant overlooks the ocean, only a handful of tables have a view. ✉*Av. Armendariz 580, Lima 18* ☎*01/447–4778* ✉*AE, DC, MC, V.*

$$–$$$ ✗La Tranquera. A butcher's front window couldn't display more cuts of meat than the glass case along the wall of this local landmark. Check out the different cuts, then inform your waiter which one you want and how it should be cooked. It will arrive at your table atop a charcoal brazier, sizzling from the grill. ■ TIP➔ Even the smallest steaks, labeled junior, are the size of a dinner plate. If you have a lighter appetite, the *costillas a la barbacoa* are basted with a tangy barbecue sauce that doesn't overwhelm the flavor of the ribs. ⊠*Av. José Pardo 285, Lima 18* ☎*01/447–5111* ▭*AE, DC, MC, V.*

SWISS

$–$$ ✗La Tiendecita Blanca. A shiny brass espresso machine is the only modern touch at this old-fashioned eatery that first flung open its doors in 1937. The fancifully painted woodwork on the doors and along the ceiling and the honey-color baby grand conjure up the Old Country. *Rösti* (grated potatoes with bacon and cheese) and five kinds of fondue, including a tasty version with ripe tomatoes, are among the traditional choices, but you may want to fast-forward to dessert, as the glass case is filled with eye-popping pies and pastries. You can also do as the locals do and buy a few crusty rolls and sit outside in Parque Miraflores. ⊠*Av. Larco Herrera 111, Lima 18* ☎*01/445–9797* ▭*AE, DC, MC, V.*

SAN ISIDRO

Most of San Isidro's restaurants are on or near Avenida Conquistadores, the neighborhood's main drag. Many of the neighborhood's restaurants are open only for lunch.

JAPANESE

$–$$ ✗Matsuei. Chefs shout out a greeting as you enter the teak-floored dining room of this San Isidro standout. Widely considered the best Japanese restaurant in town, Matsuei specializes in sushi and sashimi. If raw is not your thing, the tasty *kushiyaki*, a house specialty, is a broiled filet with a ginger-flavored sauce. There's plenty for vegetarians, including Japanese eggplant grilled to perfection and served with a sweet sesame glaze in the *goma nasu*. The building is shaded by a cluster of slender trees. ⊠*Manuel Bañón 260, Lima 27* ☎*01/422–4323* ▭*AE, DC, MC, V* ☉*Closed Sun.*

MEXICAN

$ ✗Como Agua Para Chocolate. You can't miss this cantina—the three-story structure is an eye-catching yellow trimmed with royal blue. Once you duck under the star-shape piñata hanging just inside the front door you'll realize that the dining rooms are in equally vivid shades of red and green. Happily, the food doesn't pale in comparison. Among the specials are *barbacoa de cordero,* which is lamb steamed in avocado leaves, and *albóndagas al chipotle,* a plate of spicy meatballs served with yellow rice. If you want to take home some of the magic, there's a stand selling the namesake sweets. ⊠*Pancho Fierro 108, Lima 27* ☎*01/222–0174* ▭*AE, DC, MC, V.*

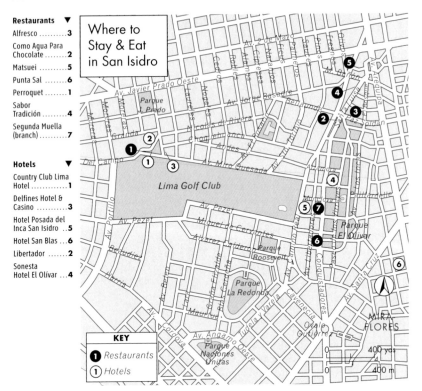

Where to Stay & Eat in San Isidro

Lima Golf Club

KEY

❶ *Restaurants*

① *Hotels*

400 yds

400 m

PERUVIAN

$$–$$$ ✗**Perroquet.** There's not a more elegant dining room than Perroquet,
tucked away in the Country Club Lima Hotel. You feel pampered in the
main room, with its upholstered chairs and tables almost overloaded
with polished crystal and china. If it's a cool evening, you might prefer the terrace and its glittering chandeliers. Yet the atmosphere never
feels stuffy, and neither does the menu. There are traditional dishes, but
they have a modern flair. Try the lamb's shin simmered for three hours
in red wine and cilantro seeds, or the salmon in a passion-fruit glaze
served over a bed of looks. After dinner, retire to the English Bar for
an aperitif. ⊠*Country Club Hotel,* ☎*511/611–9000* ⚑*Reservations
essential* ▭*AE, D, DC, MC, V.*

SEAFOOD

$–$$ ✗**Alfresco.** There's no sign at this local landmark, so look for the
colonial-style building behind a low wall. Beyond the heavy wooden
doors are an oak-paneled bar and dining rooms with potted palms and
antique furnishings. ■**TIP➔ The fish is among the best the city.** Start
with the excellent *cebiche,* available at a reasonable price. If you have
room for more, try the *pulpo a la brasa* (grilled octopus) or *fetuccini
negro con camarones* (squid-ink pasta tossed with shrimp). Accompany your meal with a selection from the long list of South American

wines. ⊠*Santa Luisa 295, Lima 27* ☎*01/422–8915* ⊟*AE, DC, MC, V* ⊗*No dinner.*

$–$$ ✕**Punta Sal.** Walls covered with stones worn smooth by the ocean add
★ an elegant touch to San Isidro's best seafood restaurant. But the real
excitement is on the platters streaming out of the kitchen. Order the
tiradito criollo, and the slices of fish arrive covered in a vivid sauce
made from yellow peppers. This place has won every award in the
book, undoubtedly because the chefs constantly look to other countries for inspiration. This is one of the few *cebicherías* serving car-
paccio. You can ask that your sole or sea bass be cooked one of 10
different ways. ⊠*Av. Conquistadores 948, San Isidro* ☎*01/441–7431*
⊠*Malecón Cisneros at Av. Tripoli,* ☎*01/242–4524* ⊟*AE, DC, MC,
V* ⊗*No dinner.*

¢–$ ✕**Sabor Tradición.** Locals can't get enough of this restaurant—maybe
because the fish dishes are so good, or maybe because the prices, including the lunch specials, are so reasonable. Deciding on an entrée can be
difficult. If you're in the mood for shrimp, you'll find it prepared at
least half a dozen ways, including *picante de camarones* (shrimp in a
spicy sauce). It's a good thing that the chef lets you sample. ⊠*Av. Santa
Luisa 156, Lima 27* ☎*01/441–8287* ⊟*AE, DC, MC, V* ⊗*Closed
weekends.* No *dinner.*

WHERE TO STAY

	Neighborhood Vibe	Pros	Cons
BARRANCO	Bohemian atmosphere appeals to younger people	Plenty of bars and restaurants, interesting architecture	Far from the sights noisy at night
EL CENTRO	Colonial-era splendor sur-rounding the Plaza Mayor	Walking distance to the city's best-known sights	Clogged with traffic dur-ing the day, deserted at night
MIRAFLORES	Bustling neighborhood filled with museums and galleries	Hundreds of dining op-tions, seaside setting, pretty parks	Traffic noise permeates even the side streets
SAN ISIDRO	Mostly residential area with a few commercial strips	Peace and quiet, espe-cially around Parque El Olivar	No major sights, a bit far from the action

THE SCENE

Lima isn't lacking for lodging—you can't go far before you see the
flurry of flags above a doorway indicating that international travelers
are welcome. If you have some money to spend, the capital has some
astonishing accommodations. For something special, pass by the towers of glass and steel and head to such charmers as the Miraflores Park
Plaza, the Country Club Lima Hotel, or the Gran Hotel Bolívar.

PLANNING

There are plenty of low-cost lodgings in Lima, many of them on quiet streets in the mostly residential neighborhoods of Miraflores and San Isidro. These areas are safe, so you don't have to worry about taking a stroll during the day, and they're quick cab rides to El Centro.

Although the historic center is much safer than it once was, it still has few decent hotels. If you decide to stay near the heart of the city, remember that you really can't go for a stroll at night. You'll also have far fewer options in terms of bars and restaurants than in other neighborhoods.

WHAT IT COSTS IN NUEVO SOLES				
	¢	$	$$	$$$	$$$$
HOTELS	under S/125	S/125–S/250	S/250–S/375	S/375–S/500	over S/500

Hotel prices are for a standard double room, excluding tax.

BARRANCO

¢   **Hospedaje Domeyer.** Barranco is the artist hangout, so it's no surprise that the hotel's common areas are furnished in what might called "thrift store chic." Bronze sculptures are scattered about and paper lanterns hang from above. It all somehow works with the old house's vividly colorful tile floors. Rooms have high ceilings and tall windows with shutters you can throw open to catch the ocean breezes. **Pros:** Near dozens of restaurants, quiet street. **Cons:** Hippy asthetic means common areas are often a jumble, bathroom walls don't extend to the ceiling. ⊠ *Jr. Domeyer 296, Lima 04* ☎ *01/247–1413* ✒ *13 rooms* ♨ *In-room: VCR. In-hotel: bar, laundry service* ⊟ *AE, DC, MC, V.*

¢   **La Quinta de Allison.** On a quiet side street in Barranco, this unassuming hotel doesn't shout to get your attention. But you should take a second look, especially because it's one of the cheapest places in the neighborhood. Rooms are on the small side, but are perfectly comfortable. A few of the more expensive rooms have whirlpool tubs. All of the neighborhood sights are within a few blocks. **Pros:** Near dozens of restaurants, quiet street, clean and confortable. **Cons:** Basic furnishings, snug common areas. ⊠ *Jr. 28 de Julio 281, Lima 04* ☎ *01/247–1515* 🖷 *01/247–6430* ✒ *20 rooms* ♨ *In-hotel: restaurant, room service, bar* ⊟ *MC, V.*

EL CENTRO

$ **Gran Hotel Bolívar.** Tastes may have changed since 1924, but this
★   grande dame retains the sumptuousness of the days when guests included Ernest Hemingway. As you enter the marble-columned rotunda, your eyes are drawn upward to the magnificent stained-glass dome. Off to one side is the wood-paneled bar, which remains as popular as ever. ■ TIP→ **The tables on the terrace are the perfect place to enjoy the best pisco sours in town.** A grand staircase sweeps you up to the

rooms, which retain lovely touches like parquet floors. Pull back the curtains for an unforgettable view of Plaza San Martín. **Pros:** Atmosphere to spare, convenient location, good value. **Cons:** Some furnishings are a bit threadbare, on a busy corner. ⊠ *Jr. de la Unión 958, Lima 01* ☎ *01/619–7171* ⊕ *www.granhotelbolivarperu.com* ⤵ *272 rooms, 5 suites* ⚘ *In-room: safe. In-hotel: 2 restaurants, room service, bar* ⊟ *AE, DC, MC, V* ☉ *BP.*

¢ 🖼 **Inka Path.** The price is the main selling point of this downtown hotel. A double room is less than $30, making this one of the city's best bargains. But you also get charm, as this second-floor lodging has rooms with double doors leading to balconies overlooking a colonial-era church. Rooms are nicer than they need to be at this price, and are scrupulously clean. **Pros:** On a quiet pedestrian street, near the major sites, welcoming staff. **Cons:** Up a very steep set of stairs. ⊠ *Jirón de la Union 654, Lima 01* ☎ *01/426–1919* ⊕ *www.inkapath.com* ⤵ *14 rooms* ⚘ *In-hotel: restaurant, bar, no elevator, laundry service* ⊟ *MC, V.*

$ 🖼 **Kamana Hotel.** Less than three blocks from the Plaza de Armas, this hotel puts you right in the middle of things. All the downtown sights are a short walk away. The best part is that you don't have to pay much for this prime spot. Rooms are quite comfortable, and the locally made textiles make each a little different. Although rooms facing the street are sunnier, ask for an inside room if traffic noise bothers you. The improbably named café, Mr. Koala, specializes in Italian fare. **Pros:** Very close to the main square, near plenty of dining options. **Cons:** A bit sterile, neighborhood is not the best at night. ⊠ *Jr. Camaná 547, Lima 01* ☎ *01/426–7204* ⊕ *www.hotelkamana.com* ⤵ *44 rooms* ⚘ *In-room: safe, Wi-Fi. In-hotel: room service, bar, laundry service, public Wi-Fi* ⊟ *AE, DC, MC, V* ☉ *CP.*

$$$$ 🖼 **Sheraton Lima Hotel & Casino.** The country's largest casino is off the marble lobby of downtown's largest hotel. You might call it a landmark, as its concrete facade is visible for miles. Perfectly serviceable rooms have subdued colors and surround an open atrium. This is a good choice for business travelers, as it has eight large meeting rooms and a convention center. Tourists appreciate that it's within walking distance of the city's historical district. The hotel is near the expressway, so it's also a short drive to San Isidro and Miraflores. **Pros:** Plenty of amenities, great casino, near several museums. **Cons:** Ugly facade, nothing Peruvian about the decor, neighborhood is dicey at night. ⊠ *Paseo de la República 170, Lima 01* ☎ *01/315–5000* ⊕ *www.sheraton.com.pe* ⤵ *438 rooms, 21 suites* ⚘ *In-room: safe, minibar, dial-up. In-hotel: 3 restaurants, bar, tennis court, pool, gym, spa, laundry service, public Internet, public Wi-Fi, airport shuttle* ⊟ *AE, DC, MC, V.*

MIRAFLORES

¢ 🖼 **El Carmelo.** A stone's throw from Parque del Amor, this little inn is on one of the neighborhood's quietest streets, yet all the excitement of Parque Miraflores is merely four blocks away. Simply furnished rooms, some with wood floors, are clean and comfortable. Some have interior windows, so ask for one facing the street. Guests mingle in a little bar in the lobby. **Pros:** A block from the oceanfront park, near many restaurants, good value. **Cons:** Basic rooms, long walk to Miraflores sights. ✉*Bolognesi 749, Lima 18* ☎*01/446–0575* 🛏*31 rooms* ♿*In-room: no a/c. In-hotel: restaurant, room service, bar, laundry service, public Internet* ⊟*AE, DC, MC, V* ⦿*CP.*

$ 🔆**La Castellana.** A favorite for years, this exuberantly neoclassical struc-
Fodor'sChoice ture resembles a small castle. The foyer, where wrought-iron lanterns
★ cast a soft glow, is a taste of what is to come. Beyond are lovely touches like stained-glass windows and a towering turret. All the wood-shuttered rooms are lovely, but especially nice are No. 10, which overlooks the sunny courtyard, and No. 15, which has a private balcony facing the front. The friendly staff goes above and beyond the call of duty, even helping with things like airplane reservations. This inn remains immensely popular, so make reservations far in advance. **Pros:** Gorgeous colonial-style building, near dozens of restaurants, great value. **Cons:** Neighborhood can be noisy on weekends, newer section not quite as charming. ✉*Grimaldo del Solar 222, Lima 18* ☎*01/444–3530* ⦿*www.hotel-lacastellana.com* 🛏*29 rooms* ♿*In-room: safe. In-hotel: restaurant, bar* ⊟*AE, DC, MC, V.*

$$$$ 🔆**DoubleTree El Pardo Hotel.** This is one hotel where you won't want to go to your room. ■**TIP→** The open-air café on the ground floor is a great place for a cocktail, while the rooftop pool and hot tub have a view that will leave you breathless. The high-tech health club, with all the latest equipment, is among the best in the city. This is primarily a business hotel, so there is a well-stocked business center and half a dozen meeting rooms. The casino addition did little for the look of the hotel, unfortunately. **Pros:** Lots of charm for a chain hotel, near lots of dining options, walking distance to all Miraflores sights. **Cons:** Bland facade, impersonal feel. ✉*Jr. Independencia 141, Lima 18* ☎*01/241–0410* ⦿*www.doubletreeelpardo.com.pe* 🛏*92 rooms, 18 suites* ♿*In-room: safe, dial-up. In-hotel: restaurant, room service, bar, pool, gym, laundry service, airport shuttle, public Internet* ⊟*AE, DC, MC, V.*

$ 🔆**Hostal Torreblanca.** With a name that refers to the gleaming white tower on its top floor, you can guess that this butterscotch-color building is distinctive. All budget hotels should have little touches like the beamed ceilings and red-tile floors found in the sunny rooms. The best of the bunch has a roaring fireplace and a balcony overlooking a circular park covered with flowers. Although the hotel is a little far from the center of Miraflores, it's just a block from the park overlooking the ocean. Many people from the neighborhood are regulars at the restaurant, which has a huge grill for sizzling steaks. **Pros:** Lots of atmosphere, near oceanfront park. **Cons:** On a busy traffic circle, long walk to restaurants. ✉*Av. José Pardo 1453, Lima 18* ☎*01/242–1876* ⦿*www.torreblancaperu.com* 🛏*30 rooms* ♿*In-room: refrigerator, Wi-Fi (some). In-hotel: restaurant, room service, bar, laundry service, public Internet, airport shuttle* ⊟*AE, DC, MC, V* ⦿*BP.*

$ 🔆**Hosteria Angiolina.** If you want to be in the middle of the action, you can hardly do better than this small hotel in Miraflores. It's on a pedestrian street, so you're spared some of the traffic noise. ■**TIP→** There are three or four restaurants just out the front door, and dozens more within

Changing of the guard, Peru-style, in front of the Palacio de Gobierno (Government Palace), in El Centro.

a few blocks. The staff is remarkable friendly, helping with everything from lugging your luggage to touring the neighborhood. The buttery yellow building has charm to spare, especially the third-floor terrace and skylight illuminated at night in a brilliant blue. **Pros:** Family-run establishment, on a quiet street. **Cons:** Basic decor, some rooms have no views, lots of stairs. ⊠ *Tarata 250, Lima 18* ☎ *01/444–3000* ⊕ *www. hosteriaangiolina.com* ⤴ *25 rooms* ⚓ *In-room: no a/c, Wi-Fi. In-hotel: laundry service, no elevator, public Internet* ⊟ *MC, V* ⧖ *EP.*

$–$$
Fodor's Choice
★

🏨 **Hotel Antigua Miraflores.** In a salmon-color mansion dating back more than a century, this elegantly appointed hotel is perhaps the city's loveliest lodging. Black-and-white marble floors and perfectly polished railings greet you as you stroll through the antiques-filled lobby. Up the wooden staircase are guest rooms with hand-carved furniture. Those in front have more character, whereas the more modern rooms in the newer section curve around a graceful fountain. Known for its impeccable service, the hotel sees repeat business year after year. The original art in the dining room is for sale. **Pros:** Gorgeous architecture, pleasant staff, residential neighborhood. **Cons:** Long walk to Miraflores sights, newer rooms have less charm. ⊠ *Grau 350, Lima 18* ☎ *01/241–6116* ⊕ *www.peru-hotels-inns.com* ⤴ *15 rooms* ⚓ *In-room: Wi-Fi. In-hotel: restaurant, bar, gym, public Internet* ⊟ *AE, DC, MC, V.*

$

🏨 **Hotel Colonial.** Elaborately carved wooden balconies accentuate the facade of this mustard-color colonial-style hotel, part of the small San Agustín chain. A huge fireplace dominates the lobby, where a graceful arch leads to the airy restaurant serving traditional fare. Religious relics such as heavy iron crosses decorate the common areas found on every floor. Rooms leading off the wrought-iron staircase have nice touches like wood wainscoting and beamed ceilings. One especially nice touch is the minuscule bar, with a vault ceiling and padded wallpaper on the walls. Here, beside the antique upright piano, chat with other guests as you enjoy a pisco sour. **Pros:** Authentic atmosphere, near plenty of dining options. **Cons:** Additions mar beauty of old house, somewhat off the beaten path. ✉ *Commandante Espinar 310, Lima 18* ☎ *01/241–7471* ⊕ *www.hotelessanagustin.com.pe* 🛏 *34 rooms* ⚷ *In-room: safe, refrigerator, Wi-Fi. In-hotel: restaurant, room service, bars, laundry service, public Internet, airport shuttle* ⊟ *AE, DC, MC, V.*

$–$$ 🏨 **Leon de Oro.** A statue of a lion stands guard at this boutique hotel in the heart of Miraflores. Don't expect the usual bright colors and colonial-style furniture. Instead you'll find muted shades and crisp lines in the generously sized rooms. The butter-soft linens on the queen-size beds and polished marble in the baths will leave you feeling pampered. For real luxury, spend a bit more on a suite and settle into your own hot tub. **Pros:** On a quiet street, professional staff, nice buffet breakfast. **Cons:** Feels more European than Peruvian, long walk to most dining options. ✉ *Av. La Paz 930, Lima 18* ☎ *01/242–6200* ⊕ *www.leondeoroperu.com* 🛏 *44 rooms, 2 suites* ⚷ *In-room: safe. In-hotel: restaurant, room service, bar, laundry service* ⊟ *AE, DC, MC, V* ⦿ *BP.*

$$$$ 🏨 **Marriott Hotel & Stellaris Casino.** This isn't a hotel—it's a small city. Just about anything you long for, whether it's a chocolate-chip cookie or diamond earrings, can be had in the shops downstairs. If not, there's the Larcomar shopping center across the street. The views are spectacular from the glass tower, which forever altered the skyline of Miraflores when it opened. On clear days the entire coastline is visible. The only disappointment is the rooms, which are luxuriously appointed but lack the slightest hint that you're in Peru. The Stellaris Casino is one of the city's most popular. **Pros:** Ocean views, near many restaurants. **Cons:** Expensive for what you get, crowded common areas, long walk to Miraflores sights. ✉ *Malecón de la Reserva 615, Lima 18* ☎ *01/217–7000* ⊕ *www.marriotthotels.com* 🛏 *288 rooms, 12 suites* ⚷ *In-room: safe, dial-up. In-hotel: 2 restaurants, bar, tennis courts, pool, gym, laundry service, public Internet, public Wi-Fi, airport shuttle* ⊟ *AE, DC, MC, V.*

$$$$ **Fodor's Choice** ★   🏨 **Miraflores Park Plaza.** Surprisingly few of the city's hotels are near the ocean, which is why this hotel is in such demand. ■ **TIP→** **If you think the views from your room are breathtaking, just head up to the rooftop pool overlooking the entire coastline.** Rooms have sitting areas that make them as big as suites, and computer connections and fax machines. Better suited for couples are the suites, which have hot tubs strategically placed beside the beds. Don't miss the Dr. Jekyll and Mr. Hyde bar, which has a hidden mezzanine for a romantic rendezvous. **Pros:** Unobstructed ocean views, lots of atmosphere, near many restaurants. **Cons:** Not walking distance to Miraflores sights. ✉ *Malecón de la Reserva 1035, Lima 18* ☎ *01/242–3000* ⊕ *www.mira-park.com* 🛏 *64 rooms, 17 suites* ⚷ *In-room: safe, refrigerator, VCR, Wi-Fi. In-hotel: 2 res-*

2

taurants, room service, bars, pool, gym, spa, laundry service, public Internet, public Wi-Fi, airport shuttle ⊟AE, MC, V.

¢ ⚏ **Las Palmas.** A block from Parque Miraflores, this apricot-color building puts you in the heart of things. The paneled lobby and wood staircase call to mind an older European pension. Upstairs, things are more modern. Many of the simply furnished rooms are on the small side, so ask to see a few before you decide. Calle Berlín, which runs along the side, is lined with several friendly little cafés serving incredibly inexpensive lunches. **Pros:** Cozy feel, near dozens of restaurants. **Cons:** Basic rooms, near some noisy bars. ⊠*Calle Bellavista 211, Lima 18* ☎*01/444–6033* ⊕*www.hotellaspalmas.com* ⤳*66 rooms, 3 suites* ⚑*In-room: no a/c. In-hotel: restaurant, room service, bar, laundry service, public Internet, public Wi-Fi* ⊟*AE, DC, MC, V.*

$ ⚏ **La Paz Apart Hotel.** For less than the cost of many shoebox-size hotel rooms you can get a generously sized one- or two-bedroom suite. Each suite at this five-story hotel has a compact kitchenette, making it perfect for anyone staying for more than a few days. The decor is clean and simple, with carefully chosen modern furnishings. The location—an easy walk from dozens of shops and restaurants—is hard to beat. **Pros:** Near dozens of restaurants, extremely friendly staff. **Cons:** Lacks a Peruvian feel, on a busy street. ⊠*Av. La Paz 679, Lima 18* ☎*01/242–9350* ⊕*www.lapazaparthotel.com* ⤳*22 suites* ⚑*In-room: safe, kitchen, Ethernet. In-hotel: restaurant, room service, bar, gym, laundry service, public Internet, public Wi-Fi* ⊟*AE, DC, MC, V* ⦿*BP.*

$ ⚏ **San Antonio Abad.** Cool breezes blow through the arches at this mansion on the eastern edge of Miraflores. Common areas have colonial-style furniture and are throughout the rambling old building. A wood staircase dominates the lobby and leads up to cozy rooms, many of which have wood floors and beamed ceilings. Some have balconies that overlook the sunny patio. The hotel is nestled in a quiet residential area. Three parks, including the lovely Parque Reducto, are within a few blocks. The shops and restaurants of Miraflores are a 10-minute walk away. **Pros:** In a quiet residential area, pretty colonial-style building, good value. **Cons:** Long walk to restaurants, some dated furnishings. ⊠*Ramón Ribeyro 301, Lima 18* ☎*01/447–6766* ⊕*www.hotelsanantonioabad.com* ⤳*24 rooms* ⚑*In-hotel: no elevator, public Internet, public Wi-Fi* ⊟*AE, MC, V* ⦿*BP.*

SAN ISIDRO

$$$$ ⚏ **Country Club Lima Hotel.** Priceless paintings from the Museo Pedro de Osma hang in each room in this luxurious lodging. The hacienda-style hotel, dating from 1927, is itself a work of art. Just step into the lobby, where hand-painted tiles reflect the yellows and greens of the stained-glass ceiling. The air of refinement continues in the rooms, all of which are draped with fine fabrics. ∎**TIP→** Many have private balconies that overlook the oval-shaped pool or the well-tended gardens. Locals frequently come by for high tea in the stained-glass atrium bar or traditional fare in the elegant Perroquet restaurant. The outdoor terrace is perfect for romantic dinners. **Pros:** Architectural gem, doting

Fodor'sChoice
★

service, one of the city's best restaurants. **Cons:** A bit removed from the action, newer sections lack the old-fashioned charm. ⊠*Los Eucaliptos 590, Lima 27* ☎*01/211–9000* ⊕*www.hotelcountry.com* ⌁*75 rooms* ⌂*In-room: safe, refrigerator, Ethernet. In-hotel: restaurant, room service, pool, gym, laundry service, public Internet, public Wi-Fi, airport shuttle* ⊟*AE, DC, MC, V.*

$$$$ 🖫**Delfines Hotel & Casino.** It's not every day that a pair of dolphins greets you near the entrance of your hotel. Yaku and Wayra do just that in the lobby of this high-rise in San Isidro. Kids love to help feed them as their parents look on from the adjacent café, where crisscrossing ribbons of steel hold aloft the glass roof. Although they're on the small side, the rooms at this business hotel are bright and comfortably furnished, and many have sweeping views of the adjacent Club Lima Golf. **Pros:** Good location for business travelers, nice views of the city. **Cons:** A long walk to dining options, expensive for what you get. ⊠*Los Eucaliptos 555, Lima 27* ☎*01/215–7000* ⊕*www.losdelfineshotel.com* ⌁*173 rooms, 24 suites* ⌂*In-room: safe, refrigerator, Wi-Fi. In-hotel: restaurant, room service, bar, pool, gym, spa, laundry service, public Internet, public Wi-Fi, airport shuttle* ⊟*AE, MC, V.*

$$–$$$ 🖫**Hotel Posada del Inca San Isidro.** With dozens of bars and restaurants within walking distance, this hotel puts you in the middle of the action. It has all the amenities—except a pool—of its neighbors, but the price tag is considerably less. Rooms are quite large, with pairs of tables to spread out your work on. Sun streams through the windows, double-paned to keep out the noise from the street. Relax with a pisco sour in Aguaymanto, the café in the corner of the lobby. Wheelchair ramps allow free movement for those who can't manage steps. **Pros:** Laid-back vibe, central location, good value. **Cons:** Chain-hotel feel, staff can seem harried. ⊠*Av. Libertadores 490, Lima 27* ☎*01/222–4373* ⊕*www.hotelposadalima.com* ⌁*45 rooms, 5 suites* ⌂*In-room: safe, refrigerator, Ethernet. In-hotel: restaurant, bar, laundry service, public Internet, public Wi-Fi, airport shuttle* ⊟*AE, DC, MC, V.*

$
★ 🖫**Hotel San Blas.** The best deal in San Isidro—maybe in the entire city—is this little gem. Its price tag is below that of many budget hotels, while its amenities are equal to those of quite a few resorts. The rooms are as big as suites and have niceties like modem connections and soundproof windows. Jacuzzis turn the baths into spas. A well-equipped meeting room on the ground floor that accommodates 30 people opens out into a sunny patio. The café in the lobby is on call if you order up a midnight snack, even if it's three in the morning. **Pros:** Spacious rooms, pretty terrace, generous breakfast buffet. **Cons:** On a busy street, long walk to restaurants. ⊠*Av. Arequipa 3940, Lima 18* ☎*01/222–2601* ⊕*www.hotelsanblas.com.pe* ⌁*30 rooms* ⌂*In-room: safe, refrigerator, Wi-Fi. In-hotel: room service, bar, laundry service, public Internet, public Wi-Fi, airport shuttle* ⊟*AE, DC, MC, V* ⦿*BP.*

$$–$$$ 🖫**Libertador San Isidro Golf.** When you want to relax, this high-rise hotel knows how to accommodate you. The staff greets you in whispered voices as you stroll through the lobby. Although the hotel is in the heart of San Isidro's business district, the rooms are surprisingly quiet. No bland furnishings—bright fabrics and original artwork make you doubt that this is a chain hotel. The restaurant, the Ostrich House, specializes in dishes made from that odd bird. **Pros:** Nice views of the city, elegant feel, good value. **Cons:** A long walk to dining options, too formal for families with kids. ✉*Los Eucaliptos 550, Lima 27* ☎*01/421–6666* ⊕*www.libertador.com.pe* 📞*53 rooms* ♿*In-room: Wi-Fi. In-hotel: 2 restaurants, room service, bar, gym, laundry service, airport shuttle, public Internet, public Wi-Fi* ▤*AE, DC, MC, V.*

$$$$ 🎨 **Sonesta Hotel El Olívar.** Stretching along an old olive grove, this lumi-
★ nous hotel has one of the most relaxed settings in San Isidro. This is especially true if you do avail yourself of the sundeck and pool on the top floor. Rooms are amply proportioned, especially those with private balconies overflowing with greenery. The clientele is mostly business travelers, so the rooms have computer connections and space to spread out. Italian cuisine is served at El Olivar, where you're treated to a view of the park. Ichi Ban serves up a vast selection of sushi and sashimi. **Pros:** Lovely location overlooking a park, top-notch dining, near shops and boutiques. **Cons:** Chain-hotel feel, far from sights. ✉*Pancho Fierro 194, Lima 27* ☎*01/221–2121* ⊕*www.sonesta.com* 📞*134 rooms, 11 suites* ♿*In-room: safe, refrigerator, Ethernet. In-hotel: 2 restaurants, room service, bar, pool, gym, laundry service, public Internet, public Wi-Fi, airport shuttle* ▤*AE, DC, MC, V.*

NIGHTLIFE & THE ARTS

Lima may not be the city that doesn't sleep, but it certainly can't be getting enough rest. Limeños love to go out, as you'll notice on any Friday or Saturday night. Early in the evening they're clustered around movie theaters and concert halls, while late at night they are piling into taxis headed to the bars and clubs of Miraflores and Barranco. Ask at your hotel for a free copy of *Peru Guide*, an English-language monthly full of information on bars and clubs as well as galleries and performances.

THE ARTS

GALLERIES

Miraflores is full of art galleries that show the works of Peruvian and occasionally foreign artists. **Corriente Alterna** (✉*Av. de la Aviación 500, Miraflores* ☎*01/242–8482*) often has works by notable new artists. In the rear of the Municipalidad de Miraflores, the **Sala Luis Miró Quesada Garland** (✉*Av. Larco Herrera and Calle Diez Canseco, Miraflores* ☎*01/444–0540*) sponsors exhibits of sculpture, painting, and photography. **Trapecio** (✉*Av. Larco Herrera 743, Miraflores* ☎*01/444–0842*) shows works by contemporary Peruvian artists.

In San Isidro **Artco** (✉*Calle Rouad and Paz Soldán, San Isidro* ☎*01/221–3579*) sponsors cutting-edge art, sometimes involving different mediums such as painting and video. **Praxis** (✉*Av. San Martín 689, at Diez Canseco, Barranco* ☎*01/477–2822*) has constantly rotating exhibits of international artists experimenting with different forms.

The courtyard of the mansion-museum, Casa Riva-Agüero, in El Centro.

MUSIC

The Orquesta Sinfónica Nacional, ranked one of the best in Latin America, performs at the Museo de la Nación's **Auditoria Sinfónica** (⊠*Av. Javier Prado Este 2465, San Borja* ☎*01/476–9878*). In the heart of Barranco, the **Centro Cultural Juan Parra del Riego** (⊠*Av. Pedro de Osma 135, Barranco* ☎*01/477–4506*) sponsors performances by Latin American musicians.

In the Municipalidad de Miraflores, the **Centro Cultural Ricardo Palma** (⊠*Av. Larco Herrera 770, Miraflores* ☎*01/446–3959*), sponsors cultural events throughout the week, including films, poetry readings, and concerts. The **Instituto Cultural Peruano Norteamericano** (⊠*Av. Angamos Oeste and Av. Arequipa, Miraflores* ☎*01/446–0381*) offers music ranging from jazz to classical to folk.

NIGHTLIFE

BARS

When you're in Barranco, a pleasant place to start off the evening is **La Posada del Mirador** (⊠*Ermita 104, Barranco* ☎*01/477–9577*). The bar has a second-story balcony that looks out to sea, making this a great place to watch the sunset. There's often a lively crowd of travelers hanging out on the covered terrace of **Mochileros** (⊠*Av. Pedro de Osma 135, Barranco* ☎*01/247–1225*). Local bands perform on the weekends at this bar, which is in a century-old house.

CLOSE UP

2

Peña Party

The most popular weekend destinations are *peñas*, bars that offer *música criolla*, a breathless combination of Peruvian, African, and other influences. The music is accompanied by flashily costumed dancers whipping themselves into a frenzy. Depending on the venue, these shows can be exhilarating or just plain exhausting. Ask locals to recommend one not geared to tourists. Most peñas start the show at 10:30 or 11 and continue until the wee hours of the morning.

The most upmarket of the peñas is found in Barranco at **Manos Morenas** (⊠ *Av. Pedro de Osma 409, Barranco* ☎ *01/467–0421*). Extravagantly costumed performers hardly seem to touch the ground as they re-create dances from around the region. The musicians, switching instruments half a dozen times during a song, are without equal. The place feels like a theme park, partly due to the long

tables of picture-taking tourists. Vying for the tourist market is **La Candelaria** (⊠ *Av. Bolognesi 292, Barranco* ☎ *01/247–1314*), which is recognizable from the fiery torches flanking the front door. In the main room, the dancers have plenty of room to show off their steps. The facade may be dull, but the attitude is anything but at **De Rompe y Raja** (⊠ *Jr. Manuel Segura 127, Barranco* ☎ *01/247–3271*). Slightly off the beaten path, this peña attracts mostly locals to its shows with *música negra*, a black variant of *música criolla*.

Junius (⊠ *Av. Independencia 125, Miraflores* ☎ *01/617–1000*) has dinner shows featuring traditional dances. It's geared mostly to tourists. An older crowd heads to **Sachún** (⊠ *Av. del Ejército 657, Miraflores* ☎ *01/441–4465*). The draw, it seems, are the sentimental favorites played by the band.

Facing Barranco's main square is **Juanito's** (⊠ *Grau 274, Barranco* ☎ *No phone*), one of the neighborhood's most venerable establishments. Built by Italian immigrants in 1905, the former pharmacy retains its glass-front cabinets. Today, however, the bottles inside are filled with wine and spirits. **Posada del Ángel** (⊠ *Av. Pedro de Osma 164, Barranco* ☎ *01/247–0341*) retains its Victorian-era warmth. It's one of the few bars in Barranco where you can actually hold a conversation.

Miraflores lets you sample beers from around the world. If you're longing for a pint of Guinness, head to **Murphy's Irish Pub** (⊠ *Schell 627, Miraflores* ☎ *01/242–1212*). The wood paneling and the well-worn dart board may convince you that you're in Ireland. If you prefer a good pilsner, try **Freiheit** (⊠ *Lima 471, Miraflores* ☎ *01/247–4630*). The second-story establishment is a favorite among college students.

DANCE CLUBS

In Barranco, the most popular dance club is the second-floor **Déjà Vu** (⊠ *Av. Grau 294, Barranco* ☎ *01/247–3742*). A triangular wood staircase leads up to a collection of odd-shape rooms where little tables are pushed together to accommodate big groups. The dance floor, off to one side, is something of an afterthought. Should the noise get to you, head out to the balcony overlooking the central square. Near Parque Miraflores is **Tequila Rocks** (⊠ *Calle Diez Canseco 146, Mira-*

flores ☏*01/444–3661*), a downtown *discoteca* that's been popular for years. Drink specials bring in the crowds.

GAY & LESBIAN CLUBS

After 10 PM you'll definitely want to stop for a drink at **La Sede** (✉*Av. 28 de Julio 441, Miraflores* ☏*01/242–2462*), one of the city's more sophisticated bars. After midnight you should head to the most popular disco, **Downtown Todo Vale** (✉*Pasaje Los Pinos 160, Miraflores* ☏*01/444–6433*). A balcony filled with comfy couches overlooks the cavernous dance floor. Psychotic drag queens dressed as hula dancers or space mutants shout epithets from the stage at the appreciative crowd of men and women. There's a more laid-back scene at **Punto 80** (✉*Manuel Bonilla, Miraflores* ☏*01/446–7567*), a neighborhood hangout.

LIVE MUSIC

Clubs with live music are scattered all over Miraflores. In Barranco **El Ekeko** (✉*Grau 266, Barranco* ☏*01/477–5823*) is the most elegant of the live music venues. Head upstairs to the main room, where tall windows crowned with yellow-and-green stained glass recall when this neighborhood was a retreat for the rich and powerful. Locals who pack the place enjoy Latin-flavored music, from calypso to cha-cha-cha. Slightly more sedate than most clubs is **La Estación** (✉*Av. Pedro de Osma 112, Barranco* ☏*01/467–8804*). In an old train station, the warmly lighted space specializes in folk music. **La Noche** (✉*Bolognesi 307, Barranco* ☏*01/477–4154*) is at the far end of a pedestrian street called Bulevar Sánchez Carrión. The rock and jazz bands booked here appeal to a youthful, noisy crowd. Escape to an outdoor patio or a second-story balcony to check out who is coming and going.

★ It's easy to miss the **Jazz Zone** (✉*Av. La Paz 656, Miraflores* ☏*01/241–8139*), as the unassuming little club is down an alley. You head up a bright red stairway to the dimly lighted second-story lounge. Expect jazz flavored with local rhythms. Flashing lights let you know you've arrived at **Satchmo's** (✉*Av. La Paz 538, Miraflores* ☏*01/444–4957*), which is as overblown as the Jazz Zone is understated. The music, from all around Latin America, attracts a slightly older crowd.

SHOPPING

Hundreds of stores around Lima offer traditional crafts of the highest quality. The same goes for silver and gold jewelry. Wander down Avenida La Paz in Miraflores and you'll be astounded at the number of shops selling one-of-a-kind pieces of jewelry; the street also yields clothing and antiques at reasonable prices. Miraflores is also full of crafts shops, many of them along Avenida Petit Thouars. For upscale merchandise, many people now turn to the boutiques of San Isidro. For original works of art, the bohemian neighborhood of Barranco has many small galleries.

MALLS

★ Limeños love to shop, as you'll discover when you walk through any of the city's massive malls. With more than 200 shops, **Jockey Plaza** (⊠*Av. Javier Prado 4200, Surco* ☎*01/435–1035*) is by far the largest in Lima. Just about every chic boutique has opened a branch here. The only trouble is that it's in Surco, a hike from most hotels. Right in the heart of things is **Larcomar** (⊠*Malecón de la Reserva and Av. José Larco, Miraflores* ☎*01/620–7583*), a surprisingly appealing shopping center in Miraflores. It's built on a bluff below Parque Salazar, so it's almost invisible from the street. Its dozens of shops, bars, and restaurants are terraced and have views of the ocean.

PISCO STOP

Founded in 1880, **Santiago Queirolo** (⊠*Av. San Martín 1062, Pueblo Libre* ☎*01/463–1008*), has had years to perfect their pisco, and even won the prize for the country's best pisco back in 2002. Besides four types of pisco, also sample seven types of wine and two champagnes. Take a peek at how they're brewed and bottled at the factory in Pueblo Libre.

MARKETS

On the northern edge of Miraflores, Avenida Petit Thouars has at least half a dozen markets crammed with vendors. They all carry pretty much the same merchandise. To get a rough idea of what an alpaca sweater or woven wallet should cost, head to **Artesanías Miraflores** (⊠*Av. Petit Thouars 5541, Miraflores* ☎*No phone*). It's small but has a little of everything. Better-quality goods can be found at **La Portada del Sol** (⊠*Av. Petit Thouars 5411, Miraflores* ☎*No phone*). In this miniature mall the vendors show off their wares in glassed cases lighted with halogen lamps. Some even accept credit cards. Ask a local about the best place for handicrafts and you'll probably be told to go to **Mercado Indios** (⊠*Av. Petit Thouars 5245, Miraflores* ☎*No phone*). Among the mass-produced souvenirs are a few one-of-a-kind pieces.

SPECIALTY SHOPS

ANTIQUES

Dozens of shops selling *antigüedades* crowd Avenida La Paz, making this street in Miraflores a favorite destination for bargain hunters. Toward the back of a little cluster of shops, **El Arcón** (⊠*Av. La Paz 646, Miraflores* ☎*01/447–6149*) packs an incredible variety into a small space. Head to the rooms in back for fearsome masks and colorful weavings dating back almost a century. **Antigüedades Siglo XVIII** (⊠*Av. La Paz 661, Miraflores* ☎*01/445–8915*) specializes in precious metals. Don't miss the case full of silver *milagros*, or miracles. These heart-shape charms were once placed at the feet of religious statues in gratitude for answered prayers. Brooding saints dominate the walls of **El Frailero** (⊠*Av. La Paz 551, Miraflores* ☎*01/447–2823*). These small statues and paintings, most of which were made for private homes, date back to the colonial period.

CLOTHING

Lots of stores stock clothing made of alpaca, but one of the few to offer
★ articles made from vicuña is **Alpaca 111** (✉ *Av. Larco 671, Miraflores*
☎ *01/447–1623* ✉ *Larcomar Malecón de la Reserva and Av. José
Larco, Miraflores* ☎ *01/241–3484*). This diminutive creature, distant
cousin of the llama, produces the world's finest wool. It's fashioned
into scarves, sweaters, and even knee-length coats. There are branches
of the store in Hotel Los Delfines, Miraflores Park Hotel, and Sonesta
Posada del Inca El Olívar.

There are several other shops specializing in alpaca in Miraflores. **All
Alpaca** (✉ *Av. Schell 375–377, Miraflores* ☎ *01/446–0565*) sells sweaters and other pieces of clothing in sophisticated styles. Bright colors
reign at **La Casa de la Alpaca** (✉ *Av. La Paz 665, Miraflores* ☎ *01/447–
6271*). The patterns are updated takes on Andean designs.

FABRIC

Inspired by Peru's proud past, the wonderful weaves at **Silvania Prints**
(✉ *Calle Diez Canseco 378, San Isidro* ☎ *01/242–2871*) are printed
by hand on the finest cotton. Buy them already fashioned into everything from scarves to tablecloths. **Lanifico** (✉ *Av. Alberto del Campo
285, San Isidro* ☎ *01/264–3186*) offers fine fabrics made from baby
alpaca—wool from animals no older than two years. Beautifully made
lace tablecloths and placemats are on display at **El Taller** (✉ *Av. Libertadores 260, San Isidro* ☎ *01/422–9613*). There's a wide selection of
thread if you feel inspired to make your own.

HANDICRAFTS

For beautiful pottery, head to **Antisuyo** (✉ *Tacna 460, Miraflores*
☎ *01/447–2557*), which sells only traditional pieces from around the
country. Tiny *retablos* (boxes filled with scenes of village life) are among
the eye-catching objects at **Raices Peru** (✉ *Av. La Paz 588, Miraflores*
☎ *01/447–7457*). For one-of-a-kind pieces, **Coral Roja** (✉ *Recavarren
269, Miraflores* ☎ *01/447–2552*) sells work made on the premises. The
little red building is the place to go for original designs.

★ **Anonima** (✉ *Av. Libertadores 256, San Isidro* ☎ *01/222–2382*) is
known for its handmade glass bowls, vases, and other objects in wonderfully wacky color combinations. On a quiet street in San Isidro,
Indigo (✉ *Av. El Bosque, San Isidro* ☎ *01/440–3099*) lets you wander through at least half a dozen different rooms filled with unique
items. There's a selection of whimsical ceramics inspired by traditional designs, as well as modern pieces. In the center of it all is an
open-air café.

JEWELRY

For one-of-a-kind gifts, try **Migue** (✉ *Av. La Paz 311, Miraflores*
☎ *01/444–0333*), where you'll find jewelers fashioning original pieces
in gold and other precious metals.

For sterling you can't beat the classic designs at **Camusso** (✉ *Av. Bena-
vides 679, El Centro* ☎ *01/425–0260* ✉ *Av. Rivera Navarrete 788, San
Isidro* ☎ *01/442–0340*), a local *platería*, or silver shop, that opened its

doors in 1933. Call ahead for a free guided tour of the factory, which is a few blocks west of El Centro. Chic designs fashioned in silver are the trademark of **Ilaria** (⊠*Av. Dos de Mayo 308, San Isidro* ☎*01/221–8575* ⊠*Los Eucaliptos 578, San Isidro* ☎*01/440–4875*). The store has two branches in San Isidro.

LIMA ESSENTIALS

TRANSPORTATION

BY AIR

Numerous airlines handle domestic flights, so getting to any of the major tourist destinations is no problem. You can often find space at the last minute, especially outside of high season. Lan, which in the past few years has become the carrier with the most national flights, departs several times each day for Arequipa, Cusco, Juliaca, Puerto Maldonado, and Trujillo. Aero Cóndor has daily flights to Arequipa Cusco, and Iquitos. Star Perú flies to Arequipa, Cusco, Juliaca, Iquitos, and Trujillo, and Taca Peru flies to Arequipa and Cusco.

Carriers Aero Cóndor (☎*01/614–6014* ⊕*www.aerocondor.com.pe*). **Lan** (☎*01/221–3764* ⊕*www.lan.com*). **Star Perú**. ☎*01/705–9000* ⊕*www.starperu. com*. **Taca Peru** (☎*01/446–0033* ⊕*grupotaca.com*).

Airport Information Aeropuerto Internacional Jorge Chávez (⊠*Av. Faucett s/n* ☎*01/517–3100* ⊕*www.lap.com.pe/ingles*).

BY BUS

Two types of buses—regular-size *micros* and the van-size *combis*—patrol the streets of Lima. You won't have to wait long for a bus; on major thoroughfares it's not uncommon to have half a dozen or more waving you aboard. You simply hop on at any intersection and pay the conductor as you leave. Fares are cheap, usually S/1.40, or about 45¢ for a ride of any distance. It's difficult to tell where buses are headed, as the signs on the windshields indicate only the end points of the route. The conductors hang out the door and announce the route with the speed of an auctioneer. A better way to discern the route is by the signs along the sides. The names of the major streets traveled will be listed. If a bus travels on a section of Avenida Arequipa, the sign will say AREQUIPA. If it travels the entire distance, it will say TODO AREQUIPA. When you want to get off, simply tell the conductor *la proxima esquina*, meaning "the next corner."

RENTING A CAR

Most rental agencies also offer the services of a driver, a good solution for those who want the freedom of a car without the hassle of driving on Lima's busy streets. In addition to offices downtown, Avis, Budget, Hertz, and National all have branches at Jorge Chávez International Airport that are open 24 hours. (The Avis desk is just outside the inter-national-arrivals terminal.)

Contacts Avis (⊠*Av. Larco 1080, Miraflores* ☎*01/446–4533*). **Budget** (⊠*Mo-*

reyra 569, San Isidro ☎ *01/442–8703*). **Hertz** (✉ *Av. Cantuarias 160, Miraflores* ☎ *01/447–2129*). **National** (✉ *Av. España 453, El Centro* ☎ *01/433–3750*).

CONTACTS & RESOURCES

BANKS & EXCHANGE SERVICES

Automatic-teller machines are ubiquitous in Lima, and several are in the arrivals hall of the airport. All accept cards on both the Plus and Cirrus networks, and most offer the choice of withdrawing either Paruvian soles or U.S. dollars.

On Avenida José Pardo, the main commercial street in Miraflores, there's a bank on nearly every block. When exchanging money, you will usually be asked to show your passport.

Banks Banco Continental (✉ *Av. Grau and Unión, Barranco* ✉ *Av. José Pardo and Jorge Chavez, Miraflores* ✉ *Av. Conquistadores and Conde de la Monclova, San Isidro*). **Banco de Credito** (✉ *Av. José Larco and Schell, Miraflores* ✉ *Av. José Pardo between Recavarren and Libertad, Miraflores*). **Banco Santander** (✉ *Carabaya and Ucayali, El Centro*). **Interbank** (✉ *Av. José Larco and Schell, Miraflores* ✉ *Jr. de la Unión and HuancavelicaEl Centro*).

INTERNET

The city's dozens of Internet cafés usually charge S/2–S/3 an hour. All have speedy connections and pleasant surroundings.

Internet Cafés Cybersandeg (✉ *De la Union 853, El Centro* ☎ *01/427–1695*). **Dragon Fans** (✉ *Calle Tarata 230, Miraflores* ☎ *01/446–6814*). **Jedi** (✉ *Av. Diagonal 218, Miraflores* ☎ *01/447–9290*).

MAIL

Send important packages from the FedEx office in Miraflores or the DHL and UPS offices in San Isidro.

Post Offices Centro (✉ *Jr. Junín, between Jr. de la Unión and Jr. Camaná* ☎ *01/427–0370*). **Miraflores** (✉ *Av. Petit Thouars 5201* ☎ *01/445–0697*). **San Isidro** (✉ *Av. Libertadores 325* ☎ *01/422–0981*).

Shipping Services DHL (✉ *Calle Los Castaños 225, San Isidro* ☎ *01/517–2500*). **FedEx** (✉ *Pasaje Mártir José Olaya 260, Miraflores* ☎ *01/242–2280*). **UPS** (✉ *Av. del Ejercito 2107, San Isidro* ☎ *01/264–0105*).

MEDICAL

Several clinics have English-speaking staff, including the Clinica Anglo-Americana and Clinica El Golf. Both are in San Isidro.

Hospitals Clinica Anglo-Americana (✉ *Av. Alfredo Salazar, San Isidro* ☎ *01/221–3656*). **Clinica El Golf** (✉ *Av. Aurelio Miro Quesada, San Isidro* ☎ *01/264–3300*).

The South

WORD OF MOUTH

Nasca Lines are amazing and well worth the trip. If you get at all air sick take something beforehand, because you don't want to spoil a pretty short flight by feeling bad…and don't try taking photos out of the window.

—Mincepie

WELCOME TO THE SOUTH

TOP REASONS TO GO

★ **Mysteries in the Desert:** Marvel over the mysterious Nazca Lines, giant figures etched into the desert floor by an enigmatic ancient civilization.

★ **Island Life:** Boats cruise around the Islas Ballestas for viewing sea lions, condors, flamingoes, and millions of guano-producing sea birds in the Paracas National Reserve.

★ **Fun with Grapes:** Go wine tasting in the grape-growing valleys of Lunahuaná and Ica and sample Peru's most famous drink, pisco, in the best *bodegas* (traditional wineries).

★ **Staying Seaside:** Tranquil beaches and fishing villages dot the coast just south of Lima. Top-notch surfing awaits at Punta Hermosa and Punta Rocas, and Pucusana is a charming, cliffside resort town.

★ **Sandboarding:** Test your nerve and skill sandboarding down the giant dunes at the oasis town of Huacachina, then nurse your injuries in the lagoon's magical healing waters.

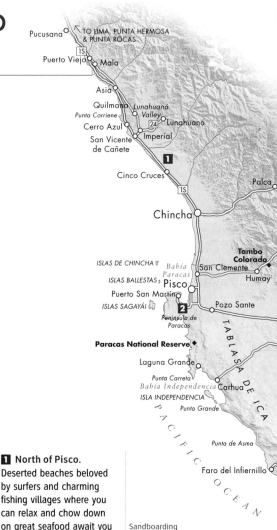

1 North of Pisco. Deserted beaches beloved by surfers and charming fishing villages where you can relax and chow down on great seafood await you in one of Peru's favorite and most accessible holiday regions. Forget the noise and chaos of Lima and head to gorgeous Pucusana or tiny Cerro Azul to enjoy the quiet life, or grab your board and hop a bus to Punta Hermosa where the surf's always up.

Sandboarding

Desert lagoon, Huacachina, Ica.

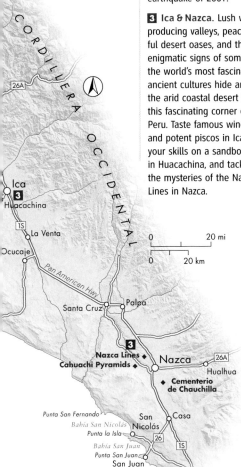

2 Pisco & the Paracas Peninsula. Rugged beaches and tiny rocky islands swarm with amazing wildlife on this part of the Peruvian coast, where Spanish-style villas perch on the shoreline waiting for their summer-holiday residents. In Pisco town, the always dusty streets are even more so as residents start the long process of rebuilding their lives after the disastrous earthquake of 2007.

3 Ica & Nazca. Lush wine-producing valleys, peaceful desert oases, and the enigmatic signs of some of the world's most fascinating ancient cultures hide among the arid coastal desert in this fascinating corner of Peru. Taste famous wines and potent piscos in Ica, test your skills on a sandboard in Huacachina, and tackle the mysteries of the Nazca Lines in Nazca.

GETTING ORIENTED

3

Southern Peru is connected to Lima by the Pan-American Highway, which runs down the coast to Pisco and the Paracas Peninsula before cutting inland to Ica and Nazca. Between Lima and Pisco are a variety of small coastal towns all located just off the Panamericana. Towns are laid out in the usual Spanish colonial fashion around a central Plaza de Armas. This is usually a good place to look for services such as banks, lodgings, and transport.

Man showing off Peruvian grapes.

THE SOUTH PLANNER

When to Go

Although the weather in southern Peru is fairly even and arid throughout the year, the best time to visit is in summer and autumn, November through April, when the rivers are ripe for rafting and kayaking and harvest festivals spice up the small towns. Around Christmas, Carnival, the grape harvest, Easter, the mid-June religious festivals, and Peru's independence day in July, hotels are often booked to capacity.

Health & Safety

The main health advice for the rest of Peru also applies to this region: Don't drink the water (or use ice), and don't eat raw or undercooked food.

Theft can be a problem in crowded tourist areas, such as beaches, or on economy-class transport. Police are helpful to most foreign travelers, but procedures can be slow, so take care with your valuables. If you lose something important, like your passport, report it to the police and to your embassy.

Emergency Services: Emergency Central ☎*105.* **Fire** ☎*116.* **Medical Alert** ☎*22540.* **Police** ☎*105.* **Red Cross** ☎*26587.*

Getting Around

With the Panamericana following the coastline all the way to Chile, Southern Peru is prime territory to explore by road. Bus travel is easy and inexpensive. Larger companies such as Soyus serve all major towns. Minivans called combis, and share taxis, shuttle between smaller towns and usually depart from the Plaza de Armas.

By Bus: Numerous companies work the route from Lima to Arequipa. Always take the best service you can afford— aside from the comfort issue, cheaper carriers have less stringent safety standards and the section of highway between Pisco and Tacna is notorious for robbery, especially on overnight services. Cruz del Sur provides the most reliable service. Ormeños has the most departures from Ica, although the quality of their vehicles and onboard service is notoriously patchy.

By Car The Pan-American Highway runs the length of southern Peru, some of it along the coast, some through desert, and some over plateaus and mountains. It's paved and in good condition, but have fully equipped first-aid and repair kits packed. Besides breakdowns, hazards include potholes, rock slides, sandstorms, and heat. You'll find many service stations along this route, most of which have clean bathrooms and convenience stores. Off the highway conditions are less predictable. Roads may be poor in the eastern highlands and around the Paracas Reserve. Four-wheel-drive vehicles are recommended for all driving except within major cities.

Your only real options to rent a car are in Lima or Arequipa.

Restaurants & Hotels

Casual dress is the order of the day. Reservations are seldom necessary. If you're on a budget, look for the excellent value set menus during lunchtime, where a three-course meal can be as little as S/3. Throughout the south seafood is king, and your chef might blend local farm goods and the catch of the day with international seasonings. In Ica, try *tejas,* candies made of *manjar blanco,* a sweet, puddinglike milk spread. A treat available only during harvest festivals is *cachina,* a partially fermented wine.

Accommodations in southern Peru range from luxury resorts to spartan *hostals* that run less than S/10 per night. Hotels rated $$$$ usually have more than standard amenities, which might include such on-site extras as a spa, sports facilities, and business and travel services, and such room amenities as minibars, safes, faxes, or data ports. Hotels rated $$$ and $$ might have only some of the extras. Accommodations rated ¢–$ are basic and may have shared baths or be outside the central tourist area. If you're arriving without a reservation, most towns have accommodations around the Plaza de Armas or transport stations.

WHAT IT COSTS IN NUEVO SOLES

RESTAURANTS				
¢	$	$$	$$$	$$$$
under S/20	S/20–S/35	S/35–S/50	S/50–S/65	over S/65

HOTELS				
¢	$	$$	$$$	$$$$
under S/125	S/125–S/250	S/250–S/375	S/375–S/500	over S/500

Restaurant prices are per person for a main course. Hotel prices are for a standard double room, excluding tax.

Pisco Know-how

Spend any amount of time in the south of Peru, and it won't be long before someone offers you a pisco, Peru's national liquor and a southern specialty. At up to 40% proof it can be too much for some palates, so if you're unused to drinking spirits straight up remember that the secret to pisco drinking is to first swirl the pisco around the glass, and then, before taking a mouthful, inhale the vapors. Exhale as you swallow for a much smoother and more pleasurable drop! Salud!

Attention: Terremoto!

After the devastating shock of the force 8 earthquake that shook Peru's southern coast in 2007, the town of Pisco and its surrounds have a long road to recovery. Be aware of this when travelling through this part of the country. In particular expect to find infrastructure such as accommodation and dining options changing rapidly as reconstruction takes place. Try to impact positively on these towns: help to boost the economy by using locally owned businesses rather than chain hotels or restaurants.

By Katy
Morrison

From vineyards to arid coastal desert, surf beaches to rolling sand dunes, the area south of Lima is wild, contradictory, and fascinating. Jump a bus on the Pan-American Highway, which cuts a black ribbon of concrete south all the way to Chile and you'll see mile after mile of nothing but sand, cactus, and wind-torn brush clinging to the stark, rocky earth.

It seems arid and inhospitable, yet keep traveling and you'll begin to discover the reasons why this region has been home to some of the world's most amazing ancient civilizations. Lush desert oases hide among the sweeping dunes, fertile river valleys tuck swatches of green into the gray folds of the mountains, and amazing wildlife lounges offshore on rocky islands.

This region was home to the Nazca, a pre-Colombian civilization that created the enigmatic Nazca Lines. ■ **TIP→Hundreds of giant diagrams depicting animals, humans, and perfectly drawn geometric shapes are etched into the desert floor over areas so vast that they can only be seen properly from the air.** The mystery of how, why, and who they were created for is unexplained, although theories range from irrigation systems to launch pads for alien spacecraft.

This is also where the Paracas culture arrived as early as 1300 BC and over the next thousand years established a line of fishing villages that exist today. The Paracas are long gone, and the Inca Empire conquered the region in the 16th century, yet the Paracas left behind some of Peru's most advanced weavings, ceramics, stone carvings, metal jewelry, and thousands of eerie cemeteries in the desert.

Yet it's not all ancient civilizations, pottery, and mysterious drawings. With a sunny climate, great wines, and charming fishing villages, this region has been a favorite holiday destination for generations of Limeñans anxious to escape the big city. It's also been a commercial hub. For years during the mid-19th century the region was the center of Peru's riches, which took the rather odorous form of guano—bird droppings (found in vast quantities on the islands off the coast of Paracas) that are a rich source of natural fertilizer. Shipped to America and Europe from the deep-water port of Pisco, the trade proved so lucrative that there was even a war over it—the Guano War of 1865–66 where Spain battled Peru for possession of the nearby Chincha Islands.

Today the region capitalizes on its natural beauty, abundant wildlife and enigmatic archaeological sites to draw tourists from all parts of the world. ■TIP➜When the earthquake struck the coast of Pisco on August 15, 2007, it was a double calamity for the region. Settled above the Nazca and South American tectonic plates, southern Peru is no stranger to earthquakes and Pisco town has been destroyed several times over the course of its history. Tsunamis, some 7 meters (23 feet) high, often accompany the quakes and can splash in as much as 1 km (½ mi) from the coast. The 2007 quake that leveled much of Pisco and left the fishing industry in tatters due to boat damage also severely affected the region's tourism. As people struggled in the aftermath to rebuild houses, churches, hospitals, and roads, reduced tourist numbers have further strained the precarious economy.

With wines and piscos to taste in Ica, dunes to board down in Huacachina, mysterious Lines to puzzle over in Nazca, and tranquil fishing villages to relax in in Pucusana and Cerro Azul, this part of Peru will seduce and charm you. Forget the whistle-stop tour and hire a car or take a bus along the Panamericana, stopping whenever and wherever you feel the urge. From Lima the road leads to Pisco, where you can choose side trips southwest to Paracas National Reserve, the Islas Ballestas, or east to Ayacucho. Continuing south, you'll pass through the desert towns of Ica and Nazca, take-off point for flights over the Nazca Lines as well as trips east to Cusco and Machu Picchu. Farther south is the lovely colonial town of Arequipa, the largest settlement in the region, as well as the gateway to some of the world's deepest canyons and Lake Titicaca. From Arequipa, it's a long, parched desert drive to Tacna at the Chilean border. The "gringo trail" it may be, but just because the path is well-beaten doesn't mean there's not always something new to discover.

NORTH OF PISCO

Tired of the noise, smog, and traffic chaos of Lima? A couple of hours drive south is all that's required to leave behind any trace of the big city. Glistening beaches, tranquil fishing villages, and great surf spots are on this easily accessible section of the Peruvian coast. This is the favored weekend getaway for wealthy Limeñans whose grand summer residences lie side-by-side with local fishermen's houses. Follow their lead and head south to enjoy the sun, sand, and the freshest seafood you'll ever eat.

GETTING AROUND
Traveling from town to town is easy in this part of Peru—distances are short and no town is more than an hour or so from the last. ■TIP➜Car rental is a convenient way to get around, although you'll have to organize

this in Lima as there are no rental services between Lima and Arequipa. If you don't have a rental car, hotels and travel agencies in Pisco offer four-hour tours of Tambo Colorado for around S/60.

Minibuses (called combis) shuttle between most towns and are the cheapest, although not the most comfortable, way of getting around. Look on the side of the combi for the painted signs displaying its route. If you choose to travel by taxi, agree on a price before setting off.

From Cerro Azul, combis depart to Cañete from the Plaza de Armas for S/1. To get to Luanahuaná, take a combi from Canete to Imperial for S/0.70, then another combi to Luanahuaná for S/3. Soyuz and Flores both offer a bus service between Cañete and Pisco for S/3.

PUCUSANA

67 km (42 mi) south of Lima on the Carretera Panamerica Sur.

Welcome to the Riviera, Peru-style. Colorful fishing boats jostle for space in the crowded harbor, fantastic cebicherias dish up the day's catch on the waterfront, and expensive holiday houses for Lima's wealthy occupy the hillsides. Pucusana is a gem well-known to locals but undiscovered by many foreign tourists. Arrive in the Peruvian summer (December to March) and you'll find this harbor town packed with vacationing Limenans who flock here for its beautiful setting, tranquil atmosphere, and the freshest seafood around. During the rest of the year you may have the town to yourself. The tiny brown-sand beaches of Las Ninfas and Pucusana Playa lie around the harbor and are good for a dip if you don't mind the boats—the more adventurous can swim (or take a boat ride) to La Isla—the island on the other side of the harbor with another small beach. For a better swimming spot take a five-minute walk around the point to get to the beach of Naplo.

If the chilly waters don't tempt you, stroll through the fishmarket to see the day's catch and stop for a *cebiche* at one of the tiny stalls on the beach. Afterward walk away from the harbor toward the cliff to watch the waves crash through the **Boquerón del Diablo.** Balancing things out in the biblical stakes is the Rostro de Cristo, a rock formation on the side of the hill containing the Boquerón said to resemble the profile of Christ. It's a little hard to make out so you may need a local to point it out.

WHERE TO STAY

¢   ⊞ **El Mirador.** Don't be put off by the steep climb up to this family-run guesthouse. Perched high on the hillside overlooking the harbor this charming spot wins the prize for the best views in town. Blue-and-white decor and glittering ocean views lend a ramshackle Mediterranean air while the warm welcome from hostess Elizabeth and her grandchildren is truly Peruvian. Rooms are basic but comfortable and let's face it, with views this good who wants to stay indoors? Grab a chair or a hammock on the wide veranda and enjoy the sunset, or, if you're here during the summer months (December—February) when the restaurant is functioning, let Elizabeth cook you up a home-style Peruvian

Surfing

CLOSE UP

South of Lima you'll find a string of sandy beaches, most of them backed by massive sand dunes. The water is cold and rough, the waves are big, and lifeguards are nonexistent.

Sound appealing? Then pick up your board and head south to see why Peru is becoming one of South America's hottest surfing destinations.

For a sure bet, head to **Punta Hermosa,** a town near Km 44 on the Pan-American Highway (about an hour's drive south of Lima), which with its numerous reefs and coves has the highest concentration of quality surf spots and breaks all year round.

Fancy yourself a pro? The largest waves in South America, some 7 meters (20 feet) high, roll into nearby **Pico Alto,** with nearly 20 good breaks around the Pico Alto Surf Camp. Paddle out from Punta Hermosa via Playa Norte to reach the reef, although be warned—these waves are for the very experienced and crazy only!

Excellent surfing is also much closer to shore at the town of **Cerro Azul,** at Km 132 of the Panamericana. Long tubular waves break right in front of the town, so be prepared for an audience. A pleasant fishing village, Cerro Azul is a popular weekend and holiday destination and the beach gets crowded during peak times. Go mid-week if you want the place to yourself.

Peru doesn't have a huge surfing tradition, but to see where a small slice of local history was made, head to **Punta Rocas,** 42 km south of Lima, where in 1965 Peruvian surfer Felipe Pomar converted himself into something of a national hero when he won the World Surfing Championships.

Costa Verde

The reef-break here provides a classic wave for beginners and advanced surfers alike.

There's even some decent surfing in the middle of Lima. Just off the coast of Miraflores, on the **Costa Verde** beach road you can find four surfable beaches, all within a 15-minute walk of each other. Right near the Rosa Nautica restaurant, Redondo, Makaha, La Pampilla, and Waikiki are breaks for beginners but with their proximity to the city the water can be more than a little polluted. Think you've just paddled past a jellyfish? It's more likely a plastic bag.

Surfing in Peru is best from March to December, with May probably being ideal. Although the climate is dry year-round, in winter the Pacific Ocean can get very chilly (although it's never particularly warm and wetsuits are advisable year-round), and coastal fog can leave you with little to look at.

–Katy Morrison

meal. If you visit during the peak periods of Christmas and New Year, book ahead. **Pros:** Spectacular views over the harbor, welcoming reception, veranda for lounging on. **Cons:** Hard climb up some steep stairs to hotel, no vehicle access, no off-season restaurant. ⊠*Prolg. Miguel Grau Mz. 54 Lote 1* ☎*01/430–9228* ⌂*6 rooms* ⌂*In room: no a/c, no phone. In-hotel: restaurant, no elevator, laundry service, parking (no fee)* ⊟*No credit cards.*

CERRO AZUL

131 km (81 mi) south of Lima; 15 km (9 mi) north of Cañete.

"Aqui esta tranquilo" say the locals, and tranquil it certainly is in this small fishing town between Cañete and Pucusana. The hustle and bustle of the old days, when the town made its living as a port for the exportation of guano and pisco, is long gone and now the only industry you'll see is the fishermen repairing their nets down by the waterfront.

Limeñans trickle in on the weekends, arriving as much for the town's charmingly off-beat character as for the peace and quiet. ■**TIP**➜**On the weekend you'll find the local brass band parading through the streets before and after the church services.** The local church, instead of ringing its bell, sets off fireworks in the Plaza de Armas as an unconventional call to prayer.

Walk along the waterfront where fish restaurants dish up deliciously fresh ceviche, then, if you're not too full, scramble over the dunes behind the pink and green former customs house to find what remains of the ancient Inca sea-fort of Huarco. In the evenings head to the Plaza, where several tiny restaurants serve up soups and chifa for a little over S/4.

WHERE TO STAY

¢   ☷ **Hostal Cerro Azul.** In a town short on accommodation this little hostel is one of the most reliable options and fills up quickly on weekends and holidays. Relaxed and low-key, what this place lacks in character it makes up for by being a step away from the beach. Single travelers and couples may find the standard rooms rather small and dark. Groups are more fortunate—spacious apartments sleeping up to eight are a good deal and come with their own private terraces for lounging on and taking in the sea views. Between December and February the small cafeteria on the premises functions as a restaurant, serving up Peruvian and fish dishes. **Pros:** Close to the beach, good lodgings for groups, pricing packages for longer stays. **Cons:** Small rooms, no restaurant during the off-season, off-season repairs leave the place looking a little chaotic. ⊠*Puerto Viejo* ☎*01/284–6052* ⊕*www.cerroazulhostal.com* ⌂*12 rooms, 4 apartments* ⌂*In room: no a/c, no phone, refrigerator (some), no TV (some). In-hotel: restaurant, no elevator, laundry service, parking (no fee)* ⊟*AE, DC, MC, V.*

¢–$ ☷ **Las Palmeras.** Although worn around the edges these days, this long-running hotel still merits a mention for its prime beach-front location. With their old-fashioned furnishings the rooms may not be very stylish, but many have excellent sea views and tiny balconies. During the summer months the pool and terrace overlooking the beach are pleasant spots to kick back with a pisco sour. Be warned—bring your own party if you want to stay here during the off-season—with only a skeleton service (no pool, no restaurant, and practically no staff) it may feel a little lonesome. **Pros:** Beachfront location, sea views from most rooms, pool during summer months. **Cons:** Worn-looking rooms, highly scaled back service during off-season. ⊠*Puerto Viejo* ☎*01/284–6005* ⮵*16 rooms* ⌂*In room: no a/c, no phone. In-hotel: restaurant, bar, pool, no elevator, laundry service, parking (no fee)* ⊟*AE, DC, MC,V.*

GRAPE HARVEST

If you happen to be in the San Vicente de Cañete region in March, drop by Cañete, which holds one of Peru's most exciting *Fiestas de la Vendimia* (grape-harvest festivals) on the first weekend of that month. The event stems from the town's proximity to the **Valle Cañete**, best known for its fertile vineyards that produce some of Peru's greatest wines. During the rest of the year there's little in Cañete to hold your interest, and most people head straight to the far nicer town of Cerro Azul, 30 minutes to the north.

LUNAHUANÁ

150 km (93 mi) south of Lima; 83 km (51 mi) from Pucusana; 85 km (54 mi) north of Pisco.

Flanked by arid mountains, the beautiful valley of the Río Cañete cuts a swathe of green inland from Cañete to reach the tiny but charming town of Lunahuaná, nestled against the river. It's the center for some of Peru's best white-water rafting. The season is from December to March when the water is at its highest, creating rapids that can reach up to class IV. Most of the year, however, the river is suitable for beginners. Rafting companies offering trips line Calle Grau in town.

If you're more interested in whetting your palate, Lunahuaná is a great spot to enjoy the products of the region—wines and piscos from the surrounding wineries and freshwater prawns straight from the river. ■**TIP→In March you can celebrate the opening of the grape pressing season at the Fiesta de la Vendimia.** The rest of the year, join the locals and while away the afternoon trying the variety of cocktails from the pisco stands dotted around the flower filled main plaza—the maracuya (passionfruit) sour is a winner. If the cocktails, sun, and lazy atmosphere don't get the better of you, just down the road from Lunahuaná lies the **Incahuasi** ruins—an Inca site said to have been the military headquarters of Túpac Yupanqui. There's not a great deal to see, although Inca enthusiasts may find it interesting.

WHERE TO STAY

$ 🏨**Río Alto Hotel.** Just ½ km from Lunahuana, this hacienda-style hotel has a family vibe and is popular with visitors from Lima. Cozy public spaces with bamboo decor, a flower-filled courtyard, and the sounds of the river create a restful atmosphere. ■**TIP→The restaurant's terrace is a great spot to enjoy pisco sours or river-prawns while keeping an eye on** the kids in the nearby pool. Rooms are small, although they have broad windows, slightly worn but comfortable furnishings, private bathrooms, and TVs. For groups, there are two fully equipped bungalows; one sleeps five (S/243), the other sleeps seven (S/340). **Pros:** Riverside location, pool, flower-filled terrace to kick back in. **Cons:** Small rooms, out of town location, no travel services. ⊠ *Cañete–Lunahuana Hwy., Km 39.5* ☎ *01/284–1125* ⊕ *www.rioaltohotel.com* ⇥ *23 rooms, 2 bungalows* ⚒ *In-room: no a/c, kitchen (some), refrigerator (some). In-hotel: restaurant, bar, pools, no elevator, parking (no fee)* ⊟ *AE, DC, MC, V.*

$ 🛏 **Villasol Hotel.** Listen to the sounds of the Rio Cañete from your room or enjoy the river views while floating lazily in the swimming pool at this large hotel that makes the most of its spectacular riverside location. The pool area, with its terraced lawns, access to the riverbank, and two saunas, is a winner, as is the cavernous on-site restaurant with its menu designed by renowned Peruvian chef Michel Vasquez Rebaza. Ignore the terrible plastic floor tiles in the otherwise comfortably furnished rooms and head straight for the windows for the spectacular views over the Rio Cañete. A few extra dollars gets you a room with a private balcony and river views. **Pros:** Riverside location, spectacular pool area, river views from some rooms. **Cons:** Some rooms only have views to the lawn, unimaginative room furnishings, parking on the front lawns. ⊠ *Cañete–Lunahuana Hwy., Km 37.5* ☎ *01/284–1127* ⊕ *www.hotelvillasolperu.com* ⇥ *55 rooms* ⚒ *In-room: no a/c, refrigerator (some). In-hotel: restaurant, room service, bar, pool, saunas, no elevator, parking (no fee)* ⊟ *AE, DC, MC, V.*

AFRO-PERUVIAN BEAT

A sprawling town midway between Cañete and Pisco, Chincha is famous for its riotous Afro-Peruvian music. If you're nearby during late February, head here to celebrate the Fiesta de Verano Negro when Chincha and neighboring El Carmen shake their booty day and night in the peñas and music clubs of El Carmen. A highlight is El Alcatraz, a dance in which a hip-swiveling male dancer tries to set his partner's cloth tail on fire with a candle. There's not a lot to see outside of festival time, especially after the 2007 earthquake leveled much of El Carmen and left its historic peñas in ruins.

TAMBO COLORADO

Fodor's Choice ★ *48 km (30 mi) southeast of Pisco.*

Tambo Colorado is one of Peru's most underrated archaeological sites. This centuries-old burial site, extremely well-preserved in this bone-dry setting, was discovered beneath the sand dunes by Peruvian archaeologist Julio Tello in 1925. Dating back to the 15th-century, Tambo Colorado or Pucahuasi in Quechua (*Huasi* means "resting place," and *puca* means "red," after the color of the stone it was built from), is thought to have been an important Inca administrative center for passing traffic on the road to Cusco. It was also where Inca runners waited to relay messages. With runners waiting at similar stations every 7 or so kilometers, messages could be passed from one end of the country to the other in just 24 hours.

The site comprises several sections laid out around a large central plaza. ■TIP→Notice that the plaza's distinctive trapezoid shape is reflected throughout the site—look for trapezoid windows and other openings—and thought to have been an earthquake-proofing measure, necessary in this extremely volatile region. The site has withstood the test of time, but that hasn't stopped generations of visitors from etching personalized graffiti into its walls. A small museum is on-site, which has some of Julio Tello's original finds, including funeral *fards* (burial cocoons), dating from 1300 BC to AD 200 and wrapped in bright cotton and wool textiles embroidered with detailed patterns. Some skulls showed evidence of trepanation, a sophisticated medical procedure involving the insertion of metal plates to replace sections of bone broken in battles where rocks were used as weapons. Samples from Tello's original dig are also on display at the Museo Julio Tello near Paracas. ⌧*Paracas Bay* ☎*No phone* ⌸*S/7.50* ☉*Daily 9–5.*

If you have time, drive up the road past Tambo Colorado to the **Puente Colgante** *(suspension bridge).* The original wooden bridge built in the early-20th-century bridge and a newer one installed in 2004 span the river side by side. If you're brave, cross the older version.

Catch your breath and drive up to **Huaytara,** a beautiful modern Catholic church built on the foundation of an Inca temple 2,800 meters (9,200 feet) above sea level.

PISCO & THE PARACAS PENINSULA

With spectacular natural surroundings and diverse wildlife, Pisco and neighboring Paracas have long been featured as a stop on Peru's well-beaten tourist trail. At just half a day's drive from the capital, for many years Pisco was a favorite holiday destination for Limeñans anxious to escape the big smoke. ■TIP→Sadly, the earthquake that struck in August 2007 left little of the colonial town standing, and both the city and country reeling with the scale of the destruction. Life continues, however, and as Pisco rebuilds itself, the rugged coastline of the Paracas Peninsula and spectacular rocky Ballestas Islands draw visitors keen to experience the area's wild scenery and to see flamingos, penguins, sea lions, and every imaginable type of guano-producing sea bird.

PISCO

30 km (19 mi) south of Chincha.

Lending its name to the clear brandy that is Peru's favorite tipple and a source of fierce national pride, the coastal town of Pisco and its surroundings hold a special place in the national psyche. It's the point where the Argentinean hero, General San Martín, landed with his troops to fight for Peru's freedom from Spanish rule. It's the city where *pisco,* the clear grape alcohol that is the country's national drink, was invented, and it's also an important sea port that had its heyday during the 1920s, when guano (bird droppings used as fertilizer) from the nearby Islas Ballestas were worth nearly as much as gold.

Modern-day Pisco shows little evidence of its celebrated past. Instead, what you'll find is a city struggling to get back on its feet after the disaster of August 2007, when a force 8 earthquake shook the town for three minutes. Disregard for planning permission, illegal building extensions, and the use of adobe (mud brick) as the main building material had left a vast number of Pisco's buildings unable to withstand the quake, and hundreds of lives were lost as homes, churches, and hospitals collapsed during the tremor.

Undoubtedly a town that's had more than its fair share of hardship and natural disaster, 2007 was not the first time Pisco has suffered from earthquake damage. The city stands where it does today because an earthquake in 1687, and pirate attacks in its aftermath, destroyed so many structures that viceroy Count de la Monclova decided to give up on the old location and start afresh where the city lies today.

Modern-day Pisco is not giving up, however, and the town is working hard to rebuild itself (we hope with more stringent building standards in place). For travelers, it's still the best jumping-off spot from which to explore the surrounding region's wildlife, scenery, and wines. National Pisco Day, the third Saturday in September, draws thousands to the drink's birthplace. ■TIP➜For travelers wishing to assist Pisco's recovery, there are numerous opportunities to volunteer. While organizations active in the area vary over time, a good place to start looking for current opportunities is www.idealist.org. Even those without the time to volunteer should know that every Nuevo Sol spent in local businesses is contributing to the region's economy.

GETTING AROUND
Transport within Pisco is generally not necessary: the central area is easily covered on foot, although those venturing out at night should take a taxi. If you arrive by bus you may find yourself dropped off at the Pisco turn-off on the Panamericana rather than in town itself—ask for a direct service. If you do end up disembarking on the highway there are taxis waiting, which make the run into town for around S/5. Drivers who work this route have a bad reputation for taking travelers only to hotels from which they receive a commission—always insist on being taken to the destination of your choice and ignore anyone who tells you that the hotel has closed, moved, or changed its name.

ESSENTIALS
BUS **Empresa José de San Martín** (✉2 de Mayo y San Martín ☎034/543–167). **Ormeños** (✉Av. San Francisco ☎056/532–764). **Paracas Express** (✉Pan-American Hwy., Km 447 ☎056/533–623). **San Martín** (✉San Martín 199 ☎056/522–743 or 051/363–631).

CURRENCY **Banco de Crédito** (✉Plaza de Armas). **Banco de la Nación** (✉Calle San Francisco, primera cuadra).

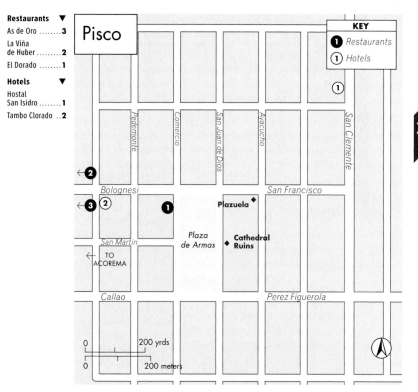

MEDICAL **San Juan de Dios (Hospital)** (✉ *Calle San Juan de Dios, tercera cuadra* ☎ *056/532-332*).

POLICE **Comisaría Sectorial** (✉ *Calle San Fransisco, primera cuadra* ☎ *056/532-884*).

WHERE TO EAT

¢–$$ ✕**As de Oro.** It may look a little like a gas station cafeteria but what this restaurant lacks in style it makes up for with terrific local cuisine, especially fresh seafood. Try the tangy ceviche or one of the seafood stews; if you like heartier fare, sample roast chicken and grilled meats. If you want to nosh between meals, there are plenty of salads, soups, coffees, and desserts. ✉ *Av. San Martín 472* ☎ *056/532-010* ▭ *AE, DC, MC, V* ☾ *Closed Mon.*

¢ ✕**El Dorado.** On the Plaza de Armas this simple eatery is a perennially popular spot with locals and tourists alike. The menu is of the standard chicken-and-rice or beef-and-rice variety but the servings are generous and the set menu, consisting of an entrée, main, and drink is good value at S/8. This is a good spot to try the famous Peruvian dish lomo saltado—a heaping pile of sliced beef, tomato, rice, and fries. ✉ *Calle Progreso 171* ☎ *056/311-740* ▭ *No credit cards.*

¢–$ ✕**LaViña de Huber.** Locals recommend this restaurant on the outskirts of town as the best around, and judging from the lunchtime crowds, they

CLOSE UP

Pisco Country

El Pisco es Peruano! and don't try to tell the locals any different. This clear brandy that takes its name from the port town of Pisco is Peru's favorite tipple and a source of fierce national pride. It would take a brave and foolish man to raise the suggestion that pisco was invented in Spain, or worse still, in neighboring Chile. Yes, when in Peru, the only thing you need to know is that el pisco es 100% Peruano.

Fiery and potent, Pisco is hands-down the most popular liquor in Peru, and is drunk on just about every social occasion. Invited to someone's house for dinner? Chances are you'll be welcomed with a Pisco Sour, a tart cocktail made from pisco, lime juice, and sugar. Heading to a party? You're sure to see at least a couple of people drinking Peru Libres—a Peruvian take on the classic cuba libre, using pisco instead of rum and mixed with Coca-Cola. Of course, the real way to drink pisco is *a lo macho*—strong and straight up. It will certainly put hairs on your chest.

Pisco is derived from grapes, like wine, but is technically an *aguardiente*, or brandy. Through a special distillation process involving a serpentine copper pipe, the fermented grapes are vaporized and then chilled to produce a clear liquor. Four kinds of grapes are used: quebranta grapes make *pisco puro*; quebranta grapes mixed with torontel and muscatel grapes produce *pisco acholado*; and quebranta, torontel, muscatel and albilla grapes combined make *pisco aromatico*.

Legend has it that pisco got its name from sailors who tired of asking for "aguardiente de Pisco" and shortened the term to pisco. (The name meant "place of many birds" in the language of the indigenous people, and it still refers to the port city as well as a nearby river.)

Today Peru produces more than 200 million liters annually, 70% of which is exported to the United States. In 1988 the liquor was designated a national patrimony, and each year Peruvians celebrate an annual Pisco Festival in March as well as the National Day of the Pisco Sour every February 8.

Bottoms up!

–Brian Kluepfel & Katy Morrison

---

can't be too far wrong. Run by three brothers who take turns in the kitchen, this friendly spot cooks up hip modern Peruvian cuisine with enticing dishes such as sole fillets rolled with bacon and served with passionfruit dipping sauce, or fish stuffed with spinach and sautéed in a pisco and pecan broth. Everything is delicious and the portions are enormous so order a few dishes to share. ✉*Prolg. Cerro Azul, next to Parque Zonal* ☎*056/533–199* ▭*No credit cards*.

WHERE TO STAY
The 2007 earthquake destroyed many accommodations in Pisco and at this writing no large hotels were in operation. The options listed below are structurally sound and well-built buildings that survived the quake. If you decide to stay elsewhere, stay away from hotels housed in precarious-looking multistory adobe constructions.

¢   🏨**Hostal San Isidro.** A relaxing oasis away from the dust of the Pisco streets, this friendly, family-run guesthouse is a top place to drop your bags and rest your weary bones. The cozy rooms have bright Peruvian motifs and there's a sunny patio and swimming pool to hang out in. Complimentary coffee in the morning and a free laundry service ensures that you'll leave feeling and looking rejuvenated and ready for the next adventure. The hostel is near the cemetery; take a taxi if arriving at night. **Pros:** Very welcoming hosts, great pool, free laundry service. **Cons:** Near the cemetery, expensive dorm rooms, high walls somewhat fortresslike. ⊠*San Clemente 103* ☎*056/536–471* ⊕*www.sanisidrohostal.com* 🛏*18 rooms* ♿*In-room: no a/c, no phone, Wi-Fi. In-hotel: pool, no elevator, laundry service, public Internet, public Wi-Fi* ▭*No credit cards.*

¢   🏨**Tambo Colorado.** Waiting with a complimentary pisco sour to welcome new arrivals, the gregarious hosts of this new hostel near the Plaza de Armas do all they can to make guests feel at home. There's a pretty central patio and bamboo-covered bar to lounge in and practice your Spanish with the chatty owners, and the spacious rooms overlooking the patio are modern and attractively furnished. ■**TIP➜**If you like the pisco sour, the hosts are more than happy to share their secrets with a class on how to prepare this famous Peruvian cocktail. **Pros:** Welcoming atmosphere, complimentary pisco sour, close to the Plaza de Armas. **Cons:** Rooms facing street can be noisy, no restaurant, no credit cards. ⊠*Bolognesi 159* ☎*056/531–379* ⊕*www.hostaltambocolorado.com* 🛏*16 rooms* ♿*In-room: no a/c, no phone, Wi-Fi. In-hotel: café, bar, no elevator, laundry service, public Internet, public Wi-Fi, parking (free)* ▭*No credit cards.*

ISLAS BALLESTAS

15 km (10 mi) south of Pisco.

Spectacular rocks pummeled by waves and wind into *ballestas* (arched bows) along the cliffs mark the Islas Ballestas, a haven of jagged outcrops and rugged beaches that shelter thousands of marine birds and sea lions. You're not allowed to walk on shore, but you wouldn't want to—the land is calf-deep in *guano* (bird droppings). Anyway, a boat provides the best views of the abundant wildlife: sea lions laze on the rocks surrounded by penguins, pelicans, seals, boobies, cormorants, and even condors, which make celebrity appearances for the appreciative crowds in February and March. On route to the islands is Punta Pejerrey, the northernmost point of the isthmus and the best spot for viewing the enormous, cactus-shape **Candelabro** carved in the cliffs. It's variously said to represent a symbol of the power of the northern Chavín culture, a Masonic symbol placed on the hillside by General Jose San Martín, leader of the liberation movement, or a pre-Inca religious figure.

GETTING AROUND

Most travelers make Pisco a base from which to visit the nearby Islas Ballestas, and the majority of hotels will assist with organizing tours including transport to and from the port. To visit Islas Ballestas, you must be on a registered tour, which usually means an hour or two cruis-

Seals observe congregation of floating humans at Isla Ballestas.

ing around the islands among sea lions and birds. Motorboat tours usually leave from the El Chaco jetty at 8 and 10 AM. For the calmest seas, take the early tour. ■ TIP→ You'll be in the open wind, sun, and waves during boat trips, so dress appropriately, and prepare your camera for the mists in July and August. Bring a hat, as tourists are moving targets for multitudes of guano-dropping seabirds. Also, be prepared for the smell—between the sea lions and the birds the odor can drop you to your knees. It takes about an hour to reach the park from the jetty; you're close when you can see the Candelabra etched in the coastal hills. A two-hour tour costs around S/50. Some tours continue on to visit the Paracas Peninsula during the afternoon for around S/25 extra. Combis and colectivos make the run between Pisco and Paracas for S/2.

Several companies in Pisco sell Paracas–Ballestas packages, most work in conjunction with hotels and guesthouses who can help making bookings. One of the most reputable is **Paracas Overland** (☎ 056/533–855 ⊕ www.paracasoverland.com.pe).

Ballestas Expeditions (☎ 056/532–373), whose owner Lucho Astorayme has been going out to the islands since he first accompanied his fisherman dad more than 30 years ago, is another reputable tour operator.

CLOSE UP

Area Tours

In Ica, Costa Linda and Pelican Travel Service offer tours of the city and can arrange trips to Paracas National Park and the Nazca Lines. One fellow you can't miss in Ica is Roberto Penny Cabrera, a direct descendent of Ica's founding family with a home right on the Plaza de Armas. After a long career in mining, Roberto started his company, Ica Desert Trip Peru, and began offering tours of the nearby desert in his fully equipped four-wheel-drive Jeep. He's fascinated with the fossils of gigantic sharks and whales he's come across and has a collection of huge incisors that would make Peter Benchley jump.

Guided tours of Paracas National Park and the Ballestas Islands are offered by Zarcillo Connections in Paracas and the often-recommended Paracas Overland in Pisco (although currently without an office due to earthquake damage). Ballestas Travel Service represents several travel agencies who sell park packages. Just about every hotel in Pisco and Paracas will assist booking tours, and most include transport to and from the dock at Paracas. Make sure your boat has life jackets.

Most hotels can arrange tours of the Nazca Lines, but several travel companies also specialize in local explorations. The going rate for a flight over the lines ranges US$40–US$60, depending on the season. Book ahead, because the flights are often sold out. The inexpensive and often recommended Alegría Tours includes stops at several archaeological sites, maps, guides, and options for hiking the area. Nasca Trails arranges flights over the Nazca Lines, trips to the Pampas Galeras vicuña reserve, and tours of the Cementerio

Chauchills in Spanish, Italian, French, German, and English.

Make sure the guide or agency is licensed and experienced. Professional guides must be approved by the Ministry of Tourism, so ask for identification before you hire.

ICA

Ica Desert Trip Peru (Roberto Penny Cabrera) (✉ *Bolivar 178, Ica* ☎ *056/231–933* ✉ *icaderttrip@ yahoo.es*).

NAZCA LINES

Alegría Tours (✉ *Calle Lima 168, Nazca* ☎ *056/522–444 or 056/506–722* ✉ *alegriatours@hotmail.com*). **Nasca Trails** (✉ *Ignacio Morsequi, Nazca* ☎ *056/522–858* ✉ *nasca@ correo.dnet.com.pe*).

PARACAS & ISLAS BALLESTAS

Ballestas Travel Service (✉ *San Francisco 249, Pisco* ☎ *034/533–095*). **Costa Linda** (✉ *Prolongación Ayabaca 509, Ica* ☎ *056/234–251*). **Paracas Overland** (✉ *Pisco* ☎ *056/533–855* ⊕ *www.paracasoverland.com.pe*). **Pelican Travel Service** (✉ *Independencia 156, Galerías Siesta, Ica* ☎ *056/225–211*). **Zarcillo Connection** (✉ *Paracas* ☎ *056/536–543* ⊕ *www.carcilloconnections.com*).

3

PARACAS NATIONAL RESERVE

15 km (10 mi) south of Pisco.

If a two-hour jaunt around the Islas Ballestas doesn't satisfy your thirst for guano, sea lions, and sea birds, then a land trip to the 280,000-hectare (700,000-plus-acre) Reserva Nacional de Paracas just might.

This stunning coastal reserve, on a peninsula south of Pisco, teems with wildlife. Pelicans, condors, and red-and-white flamingos congregate and breed here; the latter are said to have inspired the red-and-white independence flag General San Martín designed when he liberated Peru. On shore you can't miss the sound (or the smell) of the hundreds of sea lions, while in the water you might spot penguins, sea turtles, dolphins, manta rays, and even hammerhead sharks.

Named for the blustering *paracas* (sandstorms) that buffet the west coast each winter, the Reserva Nacional de Paracas is Peru's first park for marine conservation. Organized tours take you along the thin dirt tracks which crisscross the peninsula, passing by sheltered lagoons, rugged cliffs full of caves, and small fishing villages. This is prime walking territory, where you can stroll from the bay to the **Julio Tello Museum,** and on to the fishing village of **Lagunilla** 5 km (3 mi) farther across the neck of the peninsula. Adjacent to the museum are colonies of flamingos, best seen June through July (and absent January through March, when they fly to Sierra). Hike another 6 km (4 mi) to reach **Mirador de Lobos** (Sea-Lion Lookout) at Punta El Arquillo. Carved into the highest point in the cliffs above Paracas Bay, 14 km (9 mi) from the museum, is the **Candelabra.** Note that you must hire a guide to explore the land trails.

GETTING AROUND

Minibus tours of the entire park can be arranged through local hotels and travel agencies for about S/25 for five hours. A taxi from Pisco to Paracas runs about S/14, or you can take a half-hour Chaco–Paracas–Museo *combi* to El Chaco for S/2. From Paracas, you can catch a slow motorboat to the reserve and islands.

BEACHES

Most beaches at Paracas are rugged and scenic, top-notch for walking but dangerous for swimming due to rip tides and undertow. Beware in the shallows, too—there are often stingrays and giant jellyfish. Calmer stretches include La Catedral, La Mina, and Mendieta, as well as Atenas, a prime windsurfing section. Dirt roads lead farther to Playa Mendieta and Playa Carhaus. Small, open restaurant shacks line the more popular beaches.

WHERE TO STAY & EAT

Sleepy Paracas really only comes alive during the Peruvian summer (December to March), when city-dwellers arrive to set up residence in their shore-front holiday homes. If visiting out of season, be warned—many hotels close during the low season, or take the opportunity to scale back their service and concentrate on repairs.

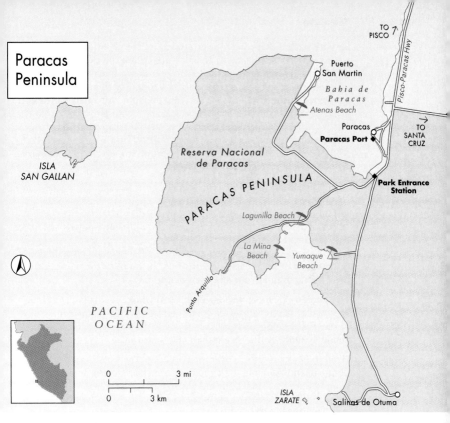

Paracas Peninsula

ISLA SAN GALLAN

TO PISCO

Puerto San Martin

Bahia de Paracas

Atenas Beach

Pisco-Paracas Hwy

Paracas

Paracas Port

TO SANTA CRUZ

Reserva Nacional de Paracas

PARACAS PENINSULA

Park Entrance Station

Lagunilla Beach

La Mina Beach

Yumaque Beach

Punta Arquillo

PACIFIC OCEAN

0   3 mi
0   3 km

ISLA ZARATE

Salinas de Otuma

$ ★ ✕ **El Chorito.** Spacious, light-filled, and with minimalistic white decor and polished wood, this eatery would not look out of place in a much larger and more cosmopolitan city. The emphasis is on seafood, dished up in delicious creations such as conchitas à la parmesana (baked mussels with Parmesan cheese). The dish to try is the *cebiche asesino,* or "killer ceviche," which packs a spicy punch. ⊠*Av. Paracas s/n, in front of Plazuela Abelarolo Quiñorez* ☎*056/545–045* ▭*AE, MC, V.*

$$ ▦ **Hotel Condor Club & Beach Resort.** A good spot if you're looking to really get away from it all, this beachfront hotel is a long, hot walk out of town. If you don't fancy being confined to eating in the hotel, then consider this option only if you have your own transport. It's a peaceful spot, however, and is one of the few out-of-town options open year-round. The spacious rooms are done in muted shades that match the landscape and some have private terraces with ocean or garden views. **Pros:** Beachfront location, sea views, tranquil setting. **Cons:** A long walk from town, no pool during the off-season, very slow in off-season. ⊠*Santo Domingo Urb.* ☎*056/545–080* ⊕*www. resortelcondor.4t.com* ⇆*10 rooms* ⌂*In-hotel: restaurant, room service, bar, pools, laundry service, parking (no fee)* ▭*AE, V* ▯◀*CP.*

¢ ▦ **Refugio del Pirata.** Friendly and terrifically located for those heading out to early-morning boat tours, this ramshackle guesthouse is popular with backpackers and tour groups alike. The slightly worn-looking rooms may be nothing to write home about, but the breakfast terrace with views over the port is the best spot in town from which to catch up on postcard writing or enjoy a pisco sour. Try to get a room with sea views; those that face the internal corridor are small and dark. **Pros:** Central location in town, terrific terrace with port views, easy to organize tours via the affiliated travel agency on the ground floor. **Cons:** No restaurant, rooms lack style. ⊠ *Av. Paracas Lote 6* ☎ *056/545–054* 🔃 *14 rooms* ⚙ *In-room: no phone. In-hotel: bar, no elevator, laundry service, public Internet, parking (no fee)* ▭ *No credit cards.*

ICA & NAZCA

South of Pisco, the thin black highway cuts through desert vast and pale as cracked parchment, and there's nothing but sand and sky as far as the eye can see. As you gaze out the bus window at mile upon endless mile of arid coastal desert, you'd be forgiven for thinking that there's little to hold your attention in this part of Peru.

You couldn't be more wrong. With good wines, year-round sunshine, spectacular desert landscapes, and giant desert drawings left by one of the world's most mysterious and enigmatic ancient cultures, there's definitely more to this region than meets the eye.

Head to Nazca to puzzle over the mystery of the world-famous Nazca Lines—giant drawings of animals, geometric shapes, and perfectly straight lines that stretch for miles across the desert floor. Who created them and why? Theories range from ancient irrigation systems to alien spaceship landing sites. Hop on a light aircraft for a dizzying overflight and try and cook up your own theory.

Or try tackling the easier problem of discerning which of Ica's numerous bodegas produces the best pisco, and if you're around in March, have a go at stamping the grapes during the pressing season.

Adrenaline seekers will find their mecca in Huacachina, where the dazzling dunes can be explored in a hair-raising dune buggy ride, and slide down on a sandboard. The oasis town just outside Ica also draws the health-conscious, who come to enjoy the lagoon's reputedly magical healing qualities.

ICA

56 km (35 mi) southeast of Paracas.

A bustling commercial city with chaotic traffic and horn-happy drivers, Ica challenges you to find its attractive side. Step outside the city center, however, and you'll see why this town was the Nazca capital between AD 300 and 800, and why the Nasca people couldn't have picked a better place to center their desert civilization. Set in a patch of verdant fields and abutted by snow-covered mountains, Ica is serene, relaxing, and cheerful, with helpful residents—likely due as much to the nearly never-ending sunshine as to the vast selection of high-quality wines and piscos produced by dozens of local bodegas. This is a town of laughter and festivals, most notably the Fiesta de Vendimia, the wine-harvest celebration that takes place each year in early March. Ica is also famous for its pecans and its high-stepping horses called *caballos de paso*.

The city's colonial look comes from its European heritage. Ica was founded by the Spanish in 1536, making it one of the oldest towns in southern Peru. The city suffered badly in the August 2007 earthquake, however, and sadly many of the colonial-era buildings, including most of the famous churches, were destroyed.

Today Peru's richest wine-growing region is a source of national pride, and its fine bodegas are a major attraction. Most are open all year, but the best time to visit is February to April, during the

grape harvest. The Tacama and Ocucaje bodegas are generally considered to have the best-quality wines and the Quebranta and Italia grape varietals are well regarded. ■TIP➔The Peruvian autumn is the season for Ica's Fiesta de la Vendimia, where you can enjoy parades, sports competitions, local music, and dancing, and even catch beauty queens stamping grapes. It's also a great time to be introduced to the vast selection of local wines and piscos, as well as an opportunity to try homemade concoctions not yet on the market.

The city's excitement also heightens for such festivals as February's Carnival, Semana Santa in March or April, and the all-night pilgrimages of El Señor de Luren in March and October. Other fun times to visit are during Ica Week, around June 17, which celebrates the city's founding, and the annual Ica Tourist Festival in late September.

GETTING AROUND

Surrounded as it is by vineyards, tourism in Ica is all about wineries. Most are close to the city and are easily accessed by road. ■TIP➔If you don't have your own car (or you don't want to be designated driver on a winery trip), pick the wineries you'd like to see and ask a taxi driver to make you a price. Or hop on one of the prearranged tours offered by most hotels. The going rate for a four-hour taxi ride taking in three wineries close to the city is around S/50; if you go on a formal tour you'll pay up to S/40 per person.

Taxis in Ica include the noisy but distinctive three-wheeled "moto-taxis." A taxi ride between Ica and Huacachina costs S/3–S/4.

The bus company Ormeños has the most departures from Ica, although the quality of their vehicles and onboard service is notoriously patchy. Buses usually depart from the park at the western end of Salaverry, including to Lima (5 hours, S/16), Pisco (1 hour, S/4), and Nazca (3 hours, S/7). Taxis *colectivos* to Lima (3 ½ hours, S/42) and Nazca (2 hours, S/7) leave from the southwest corner of Municipalidad and Lambayeque when full.

ESSENTIALS

BUS   **Ormeños** (✉ *Lambayeque 180* ☎ *056/215–600*).

CURRENCY   **Banco de Crédito** (✉*Av. Grau 105* ☎*056/235–959*).

INTERNET   **Cetelica** (✉*Huánico* ☎*056/221–534*).

MAIL   **Post Office** (✉*Lima y Moquegua* ☎*056/221–958*). **DHL** (✉*Av. San Martín 398* ☎*056/234–549*).

VISITOR INFO   **Inrena** (✉*Petirrojos 355* ☎*01/441–0425*). **Tourist Office** (✉*Cajamarca 179*).

WINERIES

If you can't imagine anything better than sampling different varieties of wine and pisco at nine in the morning, then these winery tours are most definitely for you. Most wineries in the Ica region make their living from tourism and as a way of boosting sales devote a good portion of the winery tour in the tastings room. Tours are free although the guides do appreciate tips.

■**TIP**➔**Peruvians like their wines sweet and their pisco strong.** If you're unused to drinking spirits straight up, follow this tried and true Peruvian technique for a smoother drop—after swirling the pisco around the glass, inhale the vapors. Before exhaling, take the pisco into your mouth and taste the flavor for four seconds. As you swallow, exhale!

❶ After suffering earthquake damage in 2007, this 16th-century farm hacienda has taken the opportunity to overhaul its now very modern operation. Internationally renowned, **Bodega Hacienda Tacama** produces some of Peru's best labels, particularly the Blanco de Blancos. Stroll through the rolling vineyards—still watered by the Achirana irrigation canal built by the Inca—before sampling the end result. The estate is about 11 km (7 mi) from town. ✉*Camina a la Tinguiña s/n* ☎*056/228–395* ✒*Free* ☉*Weekdays 9–2.*

❷ Look for **Bodega El Carmen,** a small winery on the right side of the road, when you're driving south into Ica; it makes a good stop for sampling fine pisco. Look for the ancient grape press, which was made from an enormous tree trunk. ✉*3 km (2 mi) north of Ica, Guadalupe* ☎*056/233–495* ✒*Free* ☉*Mon.–Sat. 10–4.*

❸ A sunny brick archway welcomes you to the large, pleasant **Bodega Vista Alegre,** which has been producing fine wines, pisco, and sangria since it was founded by the Picasso brothers in 1857. The largest winery in the valley, this former monastry is a popular tour bus stop so come early to avoid the groups. Tours in English or Spanish take you through the vast pisco and wine-making facilities at this industrial winery, before depositing you in the tasting room. Take a taxi or city buses 8 or 13 to get there. *Don't walk from downtown Ica,* as robberies have been reported along this route. ✉*Camina a la Tinguiña, Km 205* ☎*056/238–735* ✒*Free* ☉*Weekdays 9–2.*

❹ One of the more fun alcohol-making operations to visit is **Bodega Lazo,** owned by Elar Bolívar, who claims to be a direct descendent of the Libertador Simón Bolívar himself (some locals shrug their shoulders at this boast). Nonetheless, Elar's small artisanal operation includes a creepy collection of shrunken heads (Dutch tourists, he says, who didn't pay their drink tab), ancient cash registers, fencing equipment, and cop-

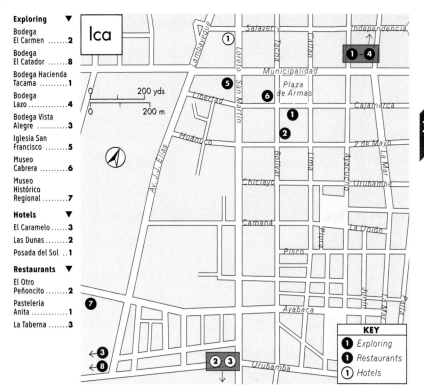

ies of some of the paintings in Ica's regional museum. The question is, who really has the originals—Elar or the museum? As part of your visit, you can taste the bodega's recently made pisco, straight from the barrel. Some organized tours include this bodega as part of a tour. It's not a safe walk from town, so take a cab if you come on your own. ⊠ *Camino de Reyes s/n, San Juan Bautista* ☎ *056/403–430* 🔘 *Free.*

8 A favorite stop on the tour circuit, the family-run **Bodega El Catador** produces wines and some of the region's finest pisco. If you're here in March, watch out for the annual Fiesta de Uva where the year's festival queen tours the vineyard and gets her feet wet in the opening of the grape-pressing season. If you miss the festival, check out the photos in the small museum near the restaurant. The excellent Taberna restaurant and bar is open for lunch after a hard morning's wine tasting. If you don't want to drive, take a taxi or wait at the second block of Moquegua for Bus 6 (S/1), which passes by about every half hour. ⊠ *Pan-American Hwy. S, Km 294, Fondo Tres Equinas 102* ☎ *056/403–295* 🔘 *Free* 🕐 *Daily 8–6.*

WHAT TO SEE

5 Soaring ceilings, ornate stained-glass windows and the fact that it's the only one of Ica's colonial era churches left standing after the 2007 earthquake makes **Iglesia San Francisco** the city's grandest religious building.

DID YOU KNOW?

That's not a wave and that's not snow either. Sandboarding down the giant dunes of Huachachina has become an extremely popular and fun sport. Sorry, no gondolas.

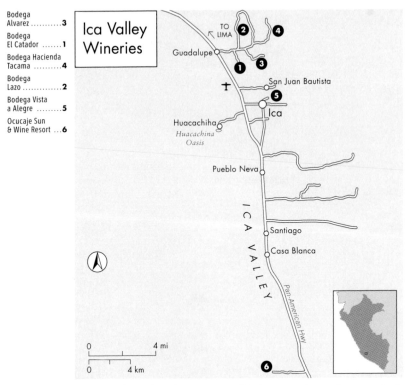

Ica Valley
Wineries

Yet even this colossal monument didn't escape the quake unscathed.
■ **TIP→If you look on the floor toward the front of the church you can see
the gouges left in the marble blocks by falling pieces of the church altar.** It's
said that the statues of the saints stood serenely throughout the quake
and didn't move an inch. ⊠ *At Avs. Municipalidad y San Martín* ☎ *No
phone* ⊠ *Free* ⊘ *Mon.–Sat. 6:30–9:30 and 4:30–7:30.*

6 Curious to know the *real* meaning of the Nazca Lines? Head to **Museo
Cabrera**—a small, unmarked building on the Plaza de Armas, which contains a collection of more than 10,000 intricately carved stones and boul-
ders depicting varied pre-Colombian themes ranging from ancient surgical
techniques to dinosaurs. The charismatic and eccentric owner, Dr. Javier
Cabrera, has studied the stones for many years and is more than happy to
explain to you how they prove the existence of an advanced pre-Colombian society who created the Nazca Lines as a magnetic landing strip for
their spacecraft (he even has the diagram to prove it!). ⊠ *Bolívar 170*
☎ *056/231–933 or 056/213–026* ⊠ *S/10 with guided tour* ⊘ *Weekdays
9:30–1 and 4:30–7, weekends by appointment only.*

7 It may be a little out of the way, but don't let that stop you from visit-
Fodor'sChoice ing the fantastic **Museo Histórico Regional** with its vast and well-preserved
★   collection on regional history—particularly from the Inca, Nazca, and
Paracas cultures. Note the quipas, mysterious knotted, colored threads

thought to have been used to count commodities and quantities of food. ■**TIP➔Fans of the macabre will love the mummy display, where you can see everything from human mummies to a mummified bird.** The squeamish can head out back to view a scale model of the Nazca Lines from an observation tower. You can also buy maps (S/0.50) and paintings of Nazca motifs (S/4). The museum is about 1½ km (1 mi) from town. It's not advisable to walk, so take the opportunity to jump into one of the distinctive three-wheeled *mototaxis* that will make the trip for around S/2. ⊠*Ayabaca s/n* ☎*056/234–383* ✒*S/11, plus S/4 camera fee* ☻ *Weekdays 8–7, Sat. 9–6, Sun. 9–1, or by appointment.*

WHERE TO EAT

¢–$$ ✕**Pasteleria Anita.** High ceilings lend an openess to this popular spot on the Plaza de Armas, which makes it perfect for people-watching. Everything from cappucino to shrimp cocktail is available, and although it's not the cheapest venue in town, the range of delicious pastries and locally made chocolate make it a top pick for sweet-tooths. ⊠*Jr. Libertad 133, Plaza de Armas* ☎*056/218–582* ▬*AE, DC, MC, V.*

¢–$ ✕**El Otro Peñoncito.** Three generations have had a hand in this family business, one of the oldest and most respected restaurants in Ica. Dishing up traditional Peruvian cuisine and the self-proclaimed best pisco sours around, this classic spot is a welcome change from the usual fried chicken and rice joints on every other corner. Local specialties include the *pollo a la Iqueña* (chicken in a rich pecan, pisco, and spinach sauce) and the traditional *papa a la huancaina* (potatoes with cheese sauce). Owner Hary Hernandez says he won't accept credit cards, although precious stones, gold, and silver are fine. Art by Iqueño artists adorns the walls. ⊠*Bolívar 255* ☎*056/233–921* ▬*No credit cards.*

$$ ✕**La Taberna.** After a hard morning's wine tasting, stop in this cheerful open-air restaurant in Bodega El Catador to top up your carbohydrates and soak up the pisco. Like an outdoor rural dining room, this pleasant spot dishes up local specialties such as *carapulcra con sopa seca* a stew of dried potatoes and dried meat, washed down with one of El Catador's excellent wines. If you want to keep up the pace, Catador's bar with its extensive range of piscos is within arm's reach. ⊠*José Carrasco González, Km 296* ☎*056/403–295* ▬*AE, MC, V.*

WHERE TO STAY

$ ☷**El Carmelo Hotel & Hacienda.** Hotel or bodega-related theme park? It's hard to tell at the oddball spot on the road between Ica and Huacachina, where rooms are built around a central courtyard complete with ancient grape-press and working pisco distillery. It's strange but it works, giving the place a unique and charming air. ■**TIP➔There's something for everyone—an adventure playground for the kids, a small zoo, and of course, the bodega.** Rooms are simple but comfortable with pastel furnishings and wood fittings. In March, you're invited to use your feet in the annual grape pressing. **Pros:** Wicker-filled open-air sitting room, chance to see the pisco-making process up close, zoo to entertain the kids. **Cons:** Out of town location, rooms are on the small side, eccentric design. ⊠*Pan-American Hwy., Km 301.2* ☎☎*056/232–191*

⊕www.elcarmelohotelhacienda.com ⊷58 rooms ⟁In-room: no a/c, Wi-Fi. In-hotel: restaurant, bar, pool, no elevator, laundry service, public Wi-Fi, parking (no fee) ▭AE, MC, V.

$$–$$$ ✕⊡ **Hotel Las Dunas.** For a taste of the good life, Peruvian style, head to
★ this top-end resort on the road between Ica and Huacachina. A cluster of whitewashed buildings at the foot of the dunes, this colonial-style holiday resort is a favorite getaway for Peruvian families. ■ **TIP→ Llamas roam freely in the grounds. The ponds and canals that run between the buildings are full of fish.** Spacious rooms have balconies overlooking lush lawns, and suites have sunny courtyards and whirlpools. You can dine poolside or in a breezy gazebo at the restaurant and enjoy such dishes as flounder with seafood sauce and spicy *lomo saltado* an enormous pile of stir-fried beef, tomatoes, chips and rice. Rent sand boards, play golf on the dunes, ride horseback, or fly over the Nazca Lines (S/350) from the hotel's airstrip. Book weekdays to save 20%. **Pros:** Beautiful grounds, activities for children, top restaurant. **Cons:** Out of town, resort aesthetic, rooms look a little frumpy for the price. ⊠*La Angostura 400* ☎*056/256–224* ✑*dunas@invertur.com.pe* ⊷*130 rooms, 3 suites* ⟁*In-room: no a/c (some), safe, refrigerator, Wi-Fi (some). In-hotel: restaurant, bars, golf course, tennis court, pools, gym, bicycles, no elevator, laundry service, public Internet, parking (no fee), no smoking rooms* ▭*AE, DC, MC, V.*

$–$$ ⊡ **Ocucaje Sun & Wine Resort.** The focus is on all the best of southern Peru: sunshine and good wines. Popular with well-heeled Limeños, it feels like a comfortable Spanish country home, but rooms have all the amenities. Well outside Ica, this remote bodega and resort is all about relaxation and restoring your spirits—which you can do by lying beside the attractive pool, getting a spa massage, or exploring the nearby historic sights. A continental breakfast is available for S/15 and during the evening the restaurant dishes up the usual criollo and Peruvian fare, just with slightly more style. Wash it all down with an excellent wine from the award-winning bodega. **Pros:** Beautiful grounds, excellent wines from the award-winning bodega, tourist services. **Cons:** Remote location, inaccessible via public transport. ⊠*Pan-American Hwy. S, Km 334, Av. Principal s/n* ☎*056/836–101* ⊕*www.hotelocucaje.com* ⊷*55 rooms* ⟁*In-room: refrigerator. In-hotel: restaurant, room service, bar, tennis court, pool, gym, spa, bicycles, no elevator, laundry service, parking (no fee)* ▭*AE, DC, MC, V.*

¢ ⊡ **Posada del Sol.** Surly staff and a noisy street frontage take the shine off this small hotel in central Ica, yet given the dearth of decent lodgings it remains one of the best options in town. The rooms are clean but characterless, and some only have internal windows. The corner suites are far nicer with lots of natural light and space but are only for heavy sleepers on account of the horn-happy drivers on the road below. **Pros:** Central location near the Plaza de Armas, secure, comfortable beds. **Cons:** Noisy street frontage, standard rooms only have internal windows, unhelpful staff. ⊠*Esquina Loreto y Salvaverry 193* ☎*056/238–446* ⊷*50 rooms* ⟁*In-room: no a/c. In-hotel: no elevator, laundry service, public Internet, parking (no fee)* ▭*No credit cards.*

SHOPPING

Ica is an excellent place to pick up Peruvian handicrafts with regional styles and motifs. Tapestries and textiles woven in naturally colored llama and alpaca wool often have images of the Nazca Lines and historical figures. In particular, look for *alfombras* (rugs), *colchas* (blankets), and *tapices* (hangings).

HUACACHINA

3

5 km (3 mi) southwest of Ica.

Drive 10 minutes through the pale, mountainous sand dunes southwest of Ica and you'll suddenly see a gathering of attractive, pastel-color buildings surrounding a patch of green. It's not an oasis on the horizon, but rather the lakeside resort of Laguna de Huacachina, a palm-fringed lagoon of jade-color waters whose sulfurous properties are reputed to have healing powers. The view is breathtaking: a collection of attractive, colonial-style hotels in front of a golden beach and with a backdrop of snow-covered peaks against the distant sky. In the 1920s Peru's elite traveled here for the ultimate holiday, and today the spacious resorts still beckon. The lake is also a pilgrimage site for those with health and skin problems, and for sand boarders who want to tackle the 100-meter (325-foot) dunes and budget travelers who pitch tents in the sand or sleep under the stars.

EN ROUTE About 40 km (27 mi) southeast of Huacachina is **Bodega Ocucaje,** a famous winery in an old Spanish mansion, whose vintages—including the famous Vino Fond de Cave—are considered among Peru's best. Also on the property is the Ocucaje Sun & Wine Resort, actually a charming inn that offers accommodation packages with dining, sports, and winery tours. ⊠*Av. Principal s/n* ☎*056/836–101* ⊕*www.ocucaje. com* ☜*S/15* ⊗*Weekdays 9–noon and 2–5, Sat. 9–noon.*

WHERE TO STAY & EAT

¢ ✕**Arturo's Restaurant Taberna.** In a town severely lacking dining options, this new restaurant holds some promise. With plastic furniture and a concrete floor, it's not winning any style prizes, but the hearty Peruvian cooking hits the spot and with most meals going for around S/7 to S/10 it's by far the best deal on food in town. Owner Arturo has grand plans to turn it into a more upmarket eatery, so expect changes. There's a good selection of wines from the local bodegas, and prices are almost as cheap as buying direct from the winery. ⊠*Av. Perotti, lote 3* ☎*No phone* ⊟*No credit cards.*

¢ ✕🏨**Carola del Sur.** This place is party central, just follow the sounds of Bob Marley drifting on the night air and you'll be sure to end up here. Rooms are basic but then again, people don't come here to hang out in their rooms. Instead, they spend their time lounging by the pool, playing with (and rescuing their belongings from) Marvin, the resident spider monkey, and chowing down on great Peruvian and international food in the central bar and restaurant. Carola del Sur is affiliated with Casa de Arena just up the road, together they run an extensive and professional dune buggy service. **Pros:** Good restaurant and bar, pool has views of the dunes, Huacachina's largest and longest running dune buggy service. **Cons:** Terrible fluorescent lighting in the rooms, small windows, loud music makes getting an early night impossible. ⊠*Av Perotti s/n, Balneario de Huacachina* ☎*056/215–439* ☞*50 rooms* ⚘*In-room: no a/c, no phone, no TV. In-hotel: restaurant, bar, pool, no elevator, laundry service, parking (no fee)* ▬*No credit cards.*

¢ 🎏 **El Hauchachinero.** Hands-down Huacachina's best budget lodging, this is a beautiful bargain in the oasis of Peru. Clean, safe, and with its own little bar featuring a mural of Ica's now-disappeared camel herd, this place is very popular, so call ahead or risk missing out. Thoughtful design touches are everywhere, from the Peruvian art and artesanía adorning the walls to the gorgeous bamboo fittings and wooden balconies and walkways. If you want to relax, the pool area with its hammocks for lounging in is super inviting. If you're feeling more adventurous, head out on a dune buggy and sand-boarding tour. The collection of raucous parrots will ensure that you're up in time for breakfast. **Pros:** Fantastic pool area with hammocks for lounging, dune-buggy service and sandboard rental, attractively furnished rooms and common areas. **Cons:** Often full, noisy parrots. ⊠*Av. Perotti, Balnearia de Huacachina* ☎*056/271–435* ⊕*www.elhuacachinero. com* ☞*21 private rooms, 3 shared rooms* ⚘*In-room: no phone, no TV. In-hotel: bar, pool, no elevator, laundry facilities, parking (no fee)* ▬*No credit cards* ❌*CP.*

Fodor's Choice
★

$ 🎏 **Hosteria Suiza.** It may not be the most jumping joint in town, but this guesthouse is a good spot for enjoying the beauty of the desert landscape and lush oasis without having to deal with the constant party that exists in some other hotels. The gorgeous manicured garden with pool and outdoor parrilla (barbecue) looks right onto the dunes, and some rooms have balconies overlooking the oasis. **Pros:** Peaceful atmosphere, lovely garden, great pool. **Cons:** No restaurant, furnishings are a little old-fashioned. ⊠*Balneario de Huacachina* ☎*056/238–762* ⊕*www. hostesuiza.com* ☞*17 rooms* ⚘*In-hotel: restaurant, bar, pool, no elevator, parking (no fee)* ▬*V* ❌*CP.*

$$–$$$ ❌🎏 **Hotel Mossone.** Imagine life as it was in Huacachina's heyday in the oasis's original hotel. With a picture-postcard location fronting onto the lagoon and gorgeous Spanish colonial–style architecture, this graceful spot is as popular now as it was in the 1920s. An internal courtyard lined with tall ficus trees is the focal point of this century-old mansion. Watch out for Jennifer, the (male) tortoise who likes to stroll here during the day. Rooms look out onto gardens overflowing with flowers and the elegant bar and restaurant have splendid lake views. The hotel provides free bicycles and sand boards for guests, but if you're staying elsewhere you can still stop in for excellent *comida criolla* (cuisine rich in peppers, onions and other spices), especially *papas a la huancaina.* a potato dish served with a creamy mustard sauce. **Pros:** Fantastic location in front of the lagoon, great pool, the elegant lounge bar is the best spot in town from which to watch the sun set over the dunes. **Cons:** Rooms look a little tired, hotel is often full with tour

Fodor's Choice
★

SAND BOARDING

Ever fancied having a go at snow-boarding but chickened out at the thought of all those painful next-day bruises? Welcome to the new adventure sport of sand boarding, a softer and warmer way to hit the slopes. Surrounded by dunes, Huacachina is the sand-boarding capital of the world: every year European sports fans arrive here in droves to practice for the international sand-surfing competitions on Cerro Blanco, the massive dune 14 km (8 mi) north of Nazca.

With no rope tows or chairlifts to get you up the dunes, the easiest way to have a go at sand boarding is to go on a dune buggy tour, offered by just about every hotel in town. In these converted vehicles you'll be driven (quickly) to the top of the dunes, upon which you can board, slide, or slither down to be picked up again at the bottom. Drivers push their vehicles hard, so be prepared for some heart-stopping moments. Carola del Sur guesthouse has the biggest fleet of dune buggies and runs two tours daily at 10 AM and 4 PM. The tours last around two hours and cost S/40.

groups. ⊠ *Balneario de Huacachina s/n* ☎ *056/213–630, 01/261–9605 in Lima* 🖷 *034/236–137* 🖅 *41 rooms* 🔊 *In-room: safe, refrigerator. In-hotel: restaurant, bar, pool, billiards room, bicycles, laundry service, public Internet, parking (no fee)* ☰ *AE, DC, MC, V.*

NAZCA

Fodor's Choice ★ *120 km (75 mi) southeast of Ica.*

What do a giant hummingbird, a monkey, and an astronaut have in common? Well, apart from the fact that they're all etched into the floor of the desert near Nazca, no one really seems to know. Welcome to one of the world's greatest mysteries—the enigmatic Nazca Lines. A mirage of green in the desert, lined with cotton fields and orchards and bordered by crisp mountain peaks, Nazca was a quiet colonial town unnoticed by the rest of the world until 1901, when Peruvian archaeologist Max Uhle excavated sites around Nazca and discovered the remains of a unique pre-Colombian culture. Set 598 meters (1,961 feet) above sea level, the town has a dry climate—scorching by day, nippy by night—that was instrumental in preserving centuries-old relics from Inca and pre-Columbian tribes. ■TIP➡The area has more than 100 cemeteries, where the humidity-free climate has helped preserve priceless jewelry, textiles, pottery, and mummies. Overlooking the parched scene is the 2,078-meter (6,815-foot) Cerro Blanco, the highest sand dune in the world

Even with the knowledge of the Nazca culture obtained from the archeological discoveries, it was not until 1929 that the **Nazca Lines** were discovered, when American scientist Paul Kosok looked out of his plane window as he flew over the (⊠ *Pampas de San José, 20 km (12 mi) north of Nazca town*). Almost invisible from ground level, the Lines were made by removing the surface stones and piling them beside the lighter soil underneath. More than 300 geometrical and biomorphic figures, some measuring up to 300 meters (1,000 feet) across, are etched into the desert floor, including a hummingbird, a monkey, a spider, a pelican, a condor, a whale, and an "astronaut," so named because of his goldfish-bowl-shape head. Theories abound as to their purpose, and some have devoted their lives to the study of the Lines. Probably the most famous person to investigate the origin of the Nazca Lines was Kosok's translator, German scientist Dr. Maria Reiche, who studied the Lines from 1940 until her death in 1998.

GETTING AROUND

Be prepared: Nazca is all about tours and it may seem like everyone in town is trying to sell you one at once. The minute you poke your nose outside the bus door you'll be swamped with offers for flights over the lines, hotels, and trips to the Chauchilla cemetery. Be wise about any offers made to you by touts at the bus station—if it's cheap, there's probably a good reason why. That said, a tour with a reputable agency is a great way to catch all of Nazca's major sites. Recommended agencies include Alegria Tours and Nasca Trails.

All buses arrive and depart from the óvalo (roundabout). To see the lines from ground level, taxis will make the 30-minute run out to the mirador for around S/40, or do it the local way and catch any north-bound bus along the Panamericana for just S/3. ■TIP➡Flights over the lines are best in early morning before the sun gets too high and winds make flying uncomfortable. Standard flights last around 30 minutes and cost between $40US and $60US, depending on the season. You'll also have to pay an airport tax of S/10 (watch out for cheeky operators who will try and tell you that the tax is $10US, it's not!). You can buy flight tickets from travel agencies and many hotels in town, or directly from the airline offices near the airport. Buying tickets in advance will save you time. Tickets are available on the spot at the airport but as planes won't take off until all seats are filled you may spend most of your morning hanging around the dusty Panamerica Sur watching while others take off and land.

FLIGHTS FOR THE LINES
Nazca Lines tours on Aero Cóndor, which depart from the small Aeropuerto Nazca, cost S/191 for a 40-minute flight plus lunch, a tour of Nazca's archaeological museum, and a trip to the *mirador*. Note that these flights are often overbooked year-round. Less expensive flights on Aero Ica and upstarts Aero Montecarlo, Aero Palpa, Aeroparacas, Alas Peruanas, TAE, Travel Air, and Taxi Aereo have similar services. As these latter lines are small operations with varying office hours, check at the airport for schedules. Most sightseeing flights depart from Nazca, although Aero Paracas also originates in Lima and Pisco. ■TIP➡Arrive early to check-in for your flight, as many are full and there's a chance you'll get bumped if you're late.

Carriers Aero Condor (⊠ *Camino Real 355, San Isidro, Lima* ☏ *01/442–5215* ⊠ *Panamericana Sur, Km 446, Nazca* ☏ *056/522–402* ⊕ *www.aerocondor. com.pe*). **Aero Ica** (⊠ *Hotel Maison Suisse, Nazca* ⊠ *Tudela and Varela 150, Lima* ☏ *01/440–1030*). **Aero Palcazu** (⊠ *Calle León Bauman 101, San Borja Sur, Lima* ☏ *061/990–0247*). **Aero Paracas** (⊠ *Teodoro Cardenas 470, Lince,*

Lima ☎*01/265–8073 or 01/265–8173* ✉*Lima 169, Nazca* ☎*056/521–027* ✉*Panamericana Sur, Km 447* ☎*056/522–688*). **Sabsa** (✉*Panamericana Sur, Km 447, Nazca* ☎*056/523–863*).

ESSENTIALS

BUS · **Cruz del Sur** (✉*Av. Los Incas* ☎*034/522–484* ⊕*www.cruzdelsur.com.pe*). **Wari Tours** (✉*Pan-American Hwy.* ☎*056/534–967*).

CURRENCY · **Banco de Crédito** (✉*Lima y Grau*).

INTERNET · **Speed Service** (✉*Bolognesi 299* ☎*056/522–176*).

MEDICAL · **Hospital de Apoyo** (✉*Calle Callao s/n* ☎*056/522–486*). **Es Salud** (✉*Juan Matta 613* ☎*056/522–446*).

MAIL · **Post Office** (✉*Jr. F. de Castillo 379* ☎*056/522–947*).

POLICE · **Comisaría Sectorial** (✉*Av. Los Incas* ☎*056/522–2084*).

WHAT TO SEE

To see where a lifelong obsession with the Nazca lines can lead you, head to the **Casa-Museo Maria Reiche**, former home of the German anthropologist who devoted her life to studying the mystery of the lines. There's little explanatory material among the pottery, textiles, mummies, and skeletons from the Paracas, Nazca, Wari, Chincha, and Inca cultures, so don't expect any of the area's mysteries to be solved here, but the museum does a great job of showing the environment in which Maria lived and worked, and her vast collection of tools, notes, and sketches is impressive. A scale model of the lines is behind the house. Take a bus from the Ormeño terminal to the Km 416 marker to reach the museum, which is 1 km (½ mi) from town. ✉*Pan-American Hwy., Km 416, San Pablo* ☎*034/255734* 💲*S/3.50* ⊙*Daily 9–4.*

Everyone comes to Nazca for the lines, but it's worth a visit to the **Tallera de Artesania de Andres Calle Flores.** Mr. Flores is a 91-year-old wonder who years ago discovered old pottery remnants and started making new pottery based on old designs and forms. Andres's son, Tobi, hosts a funny and informative talk in the kiln and workshop, and afterward you can purchase some beautiful pottery for S/30 to S/60. It's a quick walk across the bridge from downtown Nazca; at night, take a cab. ✉*Pje. Torrico 240, off Av. San Carlos* ☎*56/522–319* 💲*Free* ⊙*By appointment only.*

For an overview of the Nazca culture and the various archaeological sites in the region, the Italian-run **Museo Antonini,** is the best museum in town. The displays, made up of materials excavated from the surrounding archaeological digs, are heavy on scientific information and light on entertainment, although the display of Nazcan trophy skulls will appeal to the morbid among us and textiles fans will appreciate the display of painted fabrics from the ancient adobe city of Cahuachi. All the signage is in Spanish, so ask for the translation book at the front desk (there's only one copy, however). ■**TIP→Don't miss the still-working Nascan aqueduct in the back garden.** ✉*Av. de la Cultura 600* ☎*056/265–421* 💲*S/15, S/20 with a camera* ⊙*Daily 9 AM–7 PM.*

AROUND NAZCA

In the midst of the pale, scorched desert, the ancient **Cementerio de Chauchilla** is scattered with sun-bleached skulls and shards of pottery. *Huaqueros* (grave robbers) have ransacked the site over the years, and while up until a couple of years ago the mummies unearthed by their looting erupted from the earth in a jumble of bones and threadbare weavings, they are now housed neatly inside a dozen or so covered tombs. It's nevertheless an eerie sight, as the mummies still have hair attached, as well as mottled, brown-rose skin stretched around empty eye sockets and gaping mouths with missing teeth. Some are wrapped in tattered burial sacks, though the jewelry and ceramics with which they were laid to rest are long gone. Tours from town take about three hours and cost around S/30. Visits to the cemetery are also packaged with Nazca Lines flights. ⌂*30 km (19 mi) from Nazca, the last 12 km (7 mi) of which is unpaved* ☎*No phone* ☐*S/5* ⊙*Daily 8–6.*

Within a walled, 4,050-square-yard courtyard west of the Nazca Lines are the **Cahuachi Pyramids,** an ancient ceremonial and pilgrimage site. Six adobe pyramids, the highest of which is about 21 meters (70 feet), stand above a network of rooms and connecting corridors. Grain and water silos are also inside, and several large cemeteries lie outside the walls. Used by the early Nazca culture, the site is estimated to have existed for about two centuries before being abandoned about AD 200. Cahuachi takes its name from *qahuachi* (meddlesome). El Estaquería, with its mummification pillars, is nearby. Tours from Nazca visit both sites for around S/60 and take four hours. ⌂*34 km (21 mi) west of Nazca* ☎*No phone* ☐*Free* ⊙*Daily 8–5.*

The wooden pillars of **El Estaquería,** carved of *huarango* wood and placed on mud-brick platforms, were once thought to have been an astronomical observatory. More recent theories, however, lean toward their use in mummification rituals, perhaps to dry bodies of deceased tribal members. You can take a private tour of the site for about S/17 with a three-person minimum. ⌂*34 km (21 mi) west of Nazca* ☎*No phone* ☐*Free* ⊙*Daily 8–4.*

WHERE TO STAY & EAT

¢–$ ✕**Cevicheria "El Limón."** It may not look like much, but this small restaurant next door to Hotel Alegría serves a variety of delicious Peruvian dishes. The ceviche (sliced fish and seafood marinated in lemon juice) is the best in town and has made this restaurant a favorite with locals and travelers. Friendly and attentive service round out the experience, although the music (which at the time we visited seemed to be Greatest Hits of the '90s played on Andean pan-flute) leaves something to be desired. Top off with the best pisco sour in town for a truly Peruvian experience. ⌂*Calle Lima 168* ☎*056/523–877* ▭*V.*

¢ ✕**Chifa Nam Kug.** Enduringly popular, this landmark chifa near the Plaza de Armas continues to satisfy the crowds with cheap Chinese fare. There's not much that sets this chifa apart from any other in Peru, but the food is delicious and a two-course lunch is just S/5. Fried rice

Continued on page 130

by Ruth Anne Phillips

NAZCA LINES

On the surface of the southern Peruvian coastal desert or "Pampa" between the Nazca and Ingenio River valleys are the Nazca Lines. The Nazca Lines are enormous figures, geometric designs and straight lines etched into the desert's surface called geoglyphs. There are more than 1,000 enormous figures, geometric shapes and straight lines, some arranged as ray centers. While the most famous of the lines appear on the Pampa de San José near Nazca as well as on the hillsides of the valleys of the Río Grande de Nazca, the geoglyphs are throughout a larger area that comprises 400 square miles.

*Nazca images shown in relation to each other; not at true scale.

INGENIO VALLEY

Panamericana Hwy.

Hevon

Spiral

Spider

Rose

Lizard

Watch Tower

Tree

Hands

Hummingbird

One of the hummingbirds is five times the length of a large airplane.

Condor

Monkey

Dog

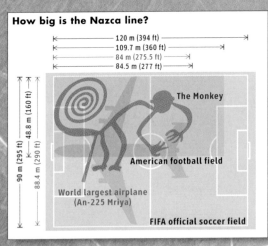

How big is the Nazca line?

120 m (394 ft)
109.7 m (360 ft)
84 m (275.5 ft)
84.5 m (277 ft)

90 m (295 ft)
48.8 m (160 ft)
88.4 m (290 ft)

The Monkey

American football field

World largest airplane
(An-225 Mriya)

FIFA official soccer field

THINGS TO LOOK FOR

Shell

Parrot

The biomorphic designs include monkeys, birds, a spider, plants, and a number of fantastical combinations and somewhat abstracted humanoid creatures. One of the monkeys is 180 feet long while a hummingbird is five times the length of a large airplane. At least 227 spirals, zigzags, triangles, quadrangles, and trapezoids make up the geometric designs, with one trapezoid measuring over 2,700 feet by 300

A trapezoid.

feet. The straight lines represent the greatest proportion of the geoglyphs: 800 single or parallel lines stretch on for miles, ranging in width from less than two feet to hundreds of feet.

Many of the lines haphazardly overlap each other, which indicates that as a group they were not pre-planned.

CONSTRUCTION

Modern archaeologists have recreated surprisingly simple construction methods for the geoglyphs using basic surveying techniques. Sight poles guided the construction of straight lines and strings tied to posts helped create circular designs. Wooden posts that may have been used as guides or end markers and an abundance of fancy potsherds, possibly used in rituals, have been found along many of the lines.

AGE

The extremely dry climatic conditions of the Pampa have helped preserve the lines; most date from c. 500 AD, during the florescence of the Nazca culture (c. 1–700 AD). A small number, however, may date to after the Nazca period to as late as 1000 AD.

Panamericana Hwy.
(18 miles from Nazca to Ingenio Valley)

Astronaut

TO
NAZCA

HISTORY AND MYSTERY

An archaeologist examines the lines.

Though the Nazca Lines are difficult to see from the ground due to their enormous size, some can be seen from nearby hillsides. It's widely believed that the lines were first properly seen from an airplane, but they were "discovered" by archaeologists working near Cahuachi in the mid-1920s. American archaeologist, Alfred L. Kroeber was the first to describe them in 1926, but it was Peruvian archaeologist Toribio Mejía Xesspe who conducted the first extensive studies of the Nazca Lines around the same time.

By the late 1920s, commercial planes began flying over the Pampa and many reported seeing the Nazca Lines from the air. It was not until American geographer and historian, Paul Kosok and his second wife Rose, flew over the Nazca drainage area in 1941, however, that the Nazca Lines became a widely known phenomenon in the United States and Europe.

THE CREATIVE PROCESS

The dry desert plain acts as a giant scratchpad as the darker oxidized surface can be swept away to reveal the lighter, pale pink subsurface. Many of the shapes are made with one continuous line that has piles of dark rocks lining the edges creating a dark border.

Stylistic comparisons between the figural Nazca Lines and images that appear on Nazca ceramics have helped establish their age.

THEORIES ABOUND

The Nazca Lines have incited various scholarly and popular theories for their construction and significance. Kroeber and Xesspe, observing the lines from the ground, believed that they served as sacred pathways. Kosok, seeing the lines from the air, observed the sun setting over the end of one line on the day of the winter solstice and thought they must have marked important astronomical events. German mathematician Maria Reiche, who studied the lines and lived near them for decades, expanded upon Kosok's astronomical theories. Modern scholars, however, have demonstrated that the lines' alignment to celestial events occurred at a frequency no greater than chance. Other theories posit that they were made for earth, mountain, or sky deities. After Cahuachi was determined in the 1980s to have been a large pilgrimage center, the idea that the lines acted as a sacred pathway has gained new momentum. Another plausible theory suggests that the Nazca Lines marked underground water sources.

IT'S THE ALIENS, OF COURSE

Popular theories have promoted the "mystery" of the Nazca Lines. One influential author, Erich von Däniken, suggested in his 1968 best-selling book *Chariots of the Gods* (reprinted several times and made into a film) that these giant geoglyphs were created as landing

Spaceman figure, San Jose Pampa

markers for extraterrestrials. Archaeologists and other scientists have dismissed these theories. The aliens deny them as well.

VISITING THE NAZCA LINES

The "Candelabra of the Andes" or the "Paracas Candelabra" on the Peninsula de Paracas.

The best way to view the Nazca Lines is by air in small, low-flying aircraft. Local companies offer flights usually in the early morning, when viewing conditions are best. You can fly over several birds, a few fish, a monkey, a spider, a flower, a condor, and/or several unidentified figures. While seeing the amazing Nazca Lines is a great experience, the sometimes questionable-looking airplanes with their strong fumes and pilots who seem to enjoy making nausea-inducing turns and twists make it an adventure for the strong in spirit (and stomach).

Nazca

KEY

1 Restaurants

① Hotels

0 _____ 200 yrds

0 _____ 200 meters

Restaurants ▼
Chifa Nam Kug **4**
Cevicheria El Limon **1**
Via la Encantada **2**
Restaurant Don Carlos **3**

Hotels ▼
Casa Andina **5**
Hotel Alegría **3**
Hotel Maison Suisse **1**
Hotel Majoro **2**
Hotel Navzca Lines **4**

dominates the menu, but the garlic beef and fried prawns entrées are excellent. ⊠*Bolognesi 448* ☎*056/522–151* ⊟*No credit cards.*

¢ ✕**Restaurant Don Carlos.** For a truly local experience, follow the crowds to this tiny restaurant, which dishes up tasty Peruvian meals in huge portions. The restaurant won't dazzle you with its design, but what it lacks in style it more than makes up for with home-style Peruvian cuisine just like your grandmother used to make it (or your grandmother's Peruvian cousin). The set-lunch—a soup, a main course, and a drink—is a steal at only S/4.50 and you may need to fight to get a table. The menu changes daily but specialties include *aji de gallina,* chicken in creamy hollandaise sauce served with boiled rice and a sliced egg. There's no street sign; look for "Restaurant" painted over the door. ⊠*Calle Fermín del Castillo 375* ☎*056/524–087* ⊟*No credit cards.*

¢–$$ ✕**Via La Encantada.** This stylish eatery on restaurant row adds some
Fodor'sChoice class to the Nazca dining scene. ■**TIP➜With food that is as modern as**
★ **the decor, this is the best spot in town to try Peruvian-fusion cuisine.** The *pollo a lo Oporto,* chicken in a port wine sauce, is a stand-out, as is the cocktail list, including tri-color Macchu Pichu pisco. Head upstairs for a spot on the balcony overlooking the street, and while there, sneak a peek through the back window and you can see the parrilla chef working over the restaurant's giant barbecue. ⊠*Calle Bolognesi 282* ☎*056/524–216 or 056/964–3426* ⊟*V.*

WHERE TO STAY

$ ✕🖭**Casa Andina.** A relative newcomer, this hotel, part of a national
Fodor'sChoice chain, offers the best value for the money of any of Nazca's top-end
★ lodgings. Catering to business travelers and tourists, the smartly furnished rooms come fully equipped with safes and Wi-Fi Internet access, and a small business center has computer access and endless coffee and tea. Those interested strictly in pleasure can instead spend their time relaxing by the hotel's small pool. **Pros:** Wi-Fi Internet access in rooms, welcoming service. **Cons:** Small pool. ⊠*Bolognesi 367* ☎*056/523–563* ⊕*www.casa-andina.com* ☌*60 rooms* ♿*In-room: safe, Wi-Fi. In-hotel: restaurant, bar, pool, no elevator, laundry service, public Internet, public Wi-Fi, parking (no fee), no-smoking rooms* ⊟*AE, DC, MC, V* ◉*CP.*

$ 🖭**Hotel Alegría.** Long a favorite with travelers, this classic Nazca hotel has recently had a facelift and is now better than ever. Clean, comfortable rooms are set around a sunny courtyard with swimming pool—a perfect spot to relax after a dusty morning flight over the lines. The reception is extremely welcoming, and knowledgeable staff can help book flights and tours. Across from the bus station, the hotel is often full. Call ahead or risk missing out. **Pros:** Friendly staff, good pool, book exchange. **Cons:** Smallish rooms, no Internet access, often full. ⊠*Calle Lima 166* ☎🖶*056/522–702* ☌*42 rooms, 3 bungalows* ♿*In-room: no a/c (some). In-hotel: restaurant, pool, no elevator, laundry service, parking (no fee)* ⊟*No credit cards* ◉*BP.*

$$ 🖭**Hotel Maison Suisse.** Although a bit worn-looking these days, this long-running hotel across from the airport provides a peaceful green

refuge from the Nazca dust. Kids splashing in the small pool and the school-canteen–like decor in the dining area give the hotel an atmosphere of a summer holiday camp, with bungalow-style accommodation dotted among the palm trees and green lawns. The underground bar is definitely the coolest room in the hotel. The hotel also runs Aero Ica, so arranging flights over the lines is a breeze. **Pros:** Peaceful, convenient for the airport, lovely garden. **Cons:** Out of town, small pool, characterless rooms. ⊠*Km 445, Pan-American Hwy. S* 🕾🕾*056/522–434* 🛏*39 rooms, 6 suites* △*In-hotel: restaurant, bar, pool, no elevator, laundry service, parking (no fee)* ☰*AE, V.*

$ 🕍**Hotel Majoro.** In fragrant gardens surrounded by cotton fields, this quiet, 80-year-old hacienda and former Augustine convent 1½ km (1 mi) from the airport offers a taste of life on a coastal farm. ■**TIP➜Set in 15 acres of gorgeous gardens, the hotel offers simple but charming rooms set around courtyards and overlooking colorful blossoms.** Having been given a facelift in the last couple of years, the hotel feels reinvigorated, and you'll appreciate the Nazca-theme decorative touches. The excellent restaurant serves local specialties, and the English-speaking staff can organize horseback rides, mountain-bike trips, or four-wheel-drive excursions. **Pros:** Peaceful atmosphere, charming gardens, good travel services. **Cons:** Out of town, popular with tour groups, some airplane noise. ⊠*Pan-American Hwy. S, Km 452* 🕾*056/522–750, 01/451–3897 in Lima* 🖥*01/562–3451* ⊕*www.hotelmajoro.com* 🛏*62 rooms* △*In-room: no a/c, Wi-Fi. In-hotel: restaurant, room service, bar, pools, bicycles, no elevator, laundry service, parking (no fee)* ☰*DC, MC, V* ⦿*BP.*

$$ 🕍**Hotel Nazca Lines.** Mixing colonial elegance with all the mod-cons, **Fodor's**Choice this top-end hotel is a Nazca landmark. Formerly the home of Maria
★   Reiche, this historic hacienda has long drawn international tourists and adventurers seeking to solve the mysteries of the lines. Stylish colonial rooms with private terraces and piped-in music deliver a touch of the good life, and the enormous central courtyard with its inviting pool make it hard to drag yourself away to explore the lines. With nightly planetarium shows and lectures about the lines, you can attempt to solve the mystery without leaving poolside. Delicious meals served on a tiled walkway beside the courtyard are worth the expense, and non-guests can have lunch and use the pool for S/16. The hotel is extremely charming—the staff, perhaps overwhelmed by the tour groups that march nightly through the doors, not so much. **Pros:** Magnificent pool, nightly lectures, colonial charm. **Cons:** Busy staff, tour groups, expensive. ⊠*Jr. Bolognesi* 🕾*056/522–293, 01/261–9605 in Lima* 🖥*056/522–112* 🛏*78 rooms* △*In-room:safe, refrigerator. In-hotel: restaurant, bar, pool, no elevator, laundry service, public Internet, public Wi-Fi, parking (no fee), no-smoking rooms* ☰*AE, DC, MC, V.*

The Southern Coast to Lake Titicaca

WORD OF MOUTH

"We took the tours to the floating islands and to Taquille. This was excellent as well. Taquille is absolutely beautiful and we had the opportunity to eat "locally" which was one of the best meals of the whole trip."

—aszatkowski

WELCOME TO THE SOUTHERN COAST TO LAKE TITICACA

TOP REASONS TO GO

★ **Wild Rivers:** Fantastic rapids and gorges make Colca Canyon and Cotahuasi Canyon the region's best-known kayaking and rafting spots.

★ **Folk Fiestas:** Whether it's Carnivál in Puno, Arequipa's annual Anniversary or Semana Santa in Chivay, Peru's culture is celebrated with more than 300 festive folkloric dances and brightly colored costumes.

★ **Wildlife:** Llamas, vicuñas, and alpaca roam the Reserva Nacional Salinas y Aguada Blanca, giant Andean condor soar above Colca Canyon, and rare bird species nest at Lake Titicaca and in the coastal lagoons of Meija.

★ **Shopping:** Along with Arequipa's alpaca stores, this region is also a mine of yarn, leather products, guitars, and antiques.

★ **Floating Islands:** On Lake Titicaca, made from the lake's tótora reeds, the series of Uros islands float, providing residence to more than 3,000 Aymara and Quechua inhabitants.

1 The Southern Coast. Small fishing villages dot the vast desert coastline from Chala to the Chilean border. With fresh seafood and plenty of sun, coastal towns like Chala, Camaná, and Mollendo buzz with people from December to March. Outside this time, the flat beaches, dramatic cliffs, and icy waters seem almost alone.

2 Colca & Cotahuasi Canyons. Canyon country is dusty and dry, a place of striking geology, wildlife, and history. It's also a playground for adventure sports lovers. Five hours northeast of Arequipa is Colca Canyon, the second deepest gorge in the world. It's home to the intense Río Colca, 14 tiny villages, the giant Andean Condor, and great hiking. Nine hours away is Colca's sister gorge, the world's deepest canyon, Cotahuasi Canyon.

The Cathedral, Arequipa.

3 Arequipa. Arequipa is known as La Cuidad Blanca or the white city for its dazzling white volcanic rock, which nearly all the Spanish-colonial buildings are constructed from. The most Spanish city in all of Peru, it's also the most romantic one. Its home to Juanita the ice mummy, the Santa Catalina Monastery, and scores of museums.

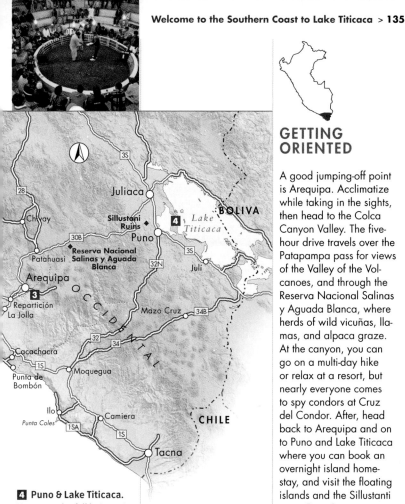

GETTING ORIENTED

A good jumping-off point is Arequipa. Acclimatize while taking in the sights, then head to the Colca Canyon Valley. The five-hour drive travels over the Patapampa pass for views of the Valley of the Volcanoes, and through the Reserva Nacional Salinas y Aguada Blanca, where herds of wild vicuñas, llamas, and alpaca graze. At the canyon, you can go on a multi-day hike or relax at a resort, but nearly everyone comes to spy condors at Cruz del Condor. After, head back to Arequipa and on to Puno and Lake Titicaca where you can book an overnight island home-stay, and visit the floating islands and the Sillustani ruins. From Puno, some head to Bolivia while others go to Cusco by train, bus, or plane. Similarly, you can travel to Puno from Cusco and begin your exploration in the opposite direction.

4 **Puno & Lake Titicaca.**
Known as the folkloric capital of Peru, Puno's annual festivals shine with elaborate costumes, music, and dancing in the streets. Puno has quality hotels and good restaurants, and it's the jumping-off point to Lake Titicaca, the world's highest navigable lake and the reason travelers come here. Outdoor adventures and unique island cultures can be found throughout the lake's more than 50 islands.

Children in traditional costume

THE SOUTHERN COAST TO LAKE TITICACA PLANNER

Weather Wise

Southern coastal Peru is always warm and arid. In the mountains and high plains, from May through early November the blistering sun keeps you warm, but nights get cold. Rainy season is from mid-November until April, when it's cooler and cloudy, but rain isn't a guarantee. Use sunscreen, even if it's cloudy.

Health & Safety

Health Mountain towns and Lake Titicaca are home to *soroche* (altitude sickness). Temporary cures include *mate de coca* (coca tea) or *chancaca* (crystallized pure cane sugar). Drink lots of bottled water and forgo alcohol.

Safety Colca Canyon is safe as are Arequipa and Puno. However, don't walk alone at night, know where your money is, and educate yourself on the good and bad parts of town. Police presence has increased in Arequipa. Use only recommended taxi companies or have someone call you one. But walking around the Plaza, even at night, is safe in Arequipa. Hiking El Misti alone is not recommended. Puno is generally safe in the tourist areas, but at night the port and the area in the hills are not safe.

Getting Around

By Air: Flights take between 30 minutes and an hour to fly anywhere in southern Peru, and a one-way ticket costs $50 to $100. LanPeru has daily flights between Lima and Rodríguez Ballón Airport, 7 km (4½ mi) from Arequipa. Aerocondor (⊕ www.aerocondor.com.pe) and Star Peru (⊕ www.starperu.com) also have daily flights. All three airlines operate daily flights to Aeropuerto Manco Cápac in Juliaca, the closest airport to Puno and Lake Titicaca. It takes 45 minutes to drive from Juliaca to downtown Puno.

By Bus: The road between Arequipa and Puno has been paved, so instead of 20 hours, now it only takes 5–6. Service is also good between Puno and Cusco, and so is the road between Puno and Copacabana in Bolivia. Cruz del Sur (⊕ www.cruzdelsur.com.pe), CIVA, Imexso, Inka Express, Flores and Ormeños (⊕ www.grupo-ormeno.com.pe) have offices in Puno and Arequipa. For your comfort and safety, take the best service you can afford. There have been holdups on night buses from Arequipa to Nazca and Puno to Cusco. Several bus companies sell tickets that go direct, so buy one of those. Bus stations in Peru are known for crime, mostly theft of your belongings, so always hold on to your bags.

By Car: Car rental services are in Arequipa center and at the airport. Keep your car travel to daylight hours: night driving poses a number of risks—blockades, crime on tourists, and steep roads. A 4x4 is needed for the canyons. While the road from Arequipa to Chivay has improved, the last hour of the journey is rough and has steep cliffs. Use even more caution if traveling into Cotahuasi Canyon: only a quarter of the 12-hour ride is paved.

By Train: Train travel on Peru Rail (⊕ www.perurail.com) is slow, but scenic and more relaxing than a bus playing reggaeton. A Pullman train ticket means more comfort, not to mention a meal and increased security. The train only goes from Cusco to Puno. It's a popular way to take in the dramatic change of scenery as you ride over La Raya pass at 4,315 meters (14,156 feet). The trip takes about nine hours. For a full listing of PeruRail trips, check out ⊕ www.orient-express.com. It's now possible to book online.

Restaurants & Hotels

If you can't wait to try cuy (guinea pig) or if you prefer wood-fired pizza, Arequipa and Puno have some excellent restaurants, ranging from gourmet novo-Andino cuisine to traditional fare and international grub. Food in Arequipa is known for strong, fresh flavors, from herbs and spices to vegetables served with native Andean foods like grilled alpaca and ostrich steaks. If you're headed to the coast, hold out for the freshest fish around, as cheap, delicious seafood and shellfish are the specialty. In the mountains, the cool, thin Andean air calls for hearty, savory soups and heaps and heaps of carbs in the form of the potato. Whether they're fried, boiled, baked, with cheese, in soup, alone, potatoes you will be eating. In Puno fresh fish from the lake is served in almost every restaurant. Puno also has a special affliction for adobe oven, wood-fired pizza.

Arequipa and Puno are overloaded with hotels. This is good for you, the traveler, considering you reap the benefit of great service for a low price. Puno lives and breathes for tourists. While a few chain hotels are in the lake-side city, most are small boutique hotels with local owners pinning to get in on the tourist boom in this otherwise agricultural town. As a commercial business center, Arequipa has more high-end hotels that cater to the business traveler, and given its fame for being the romance city, it also has lots of small inns.

WHAT IT COSTS IN NUEVO SOLES

RESTAURANTS				
¢	$	$$	$$$	$$$$
under S/20	S/20–S/35	S/35–S/50	S/50–S/65	over S/65

HOTELS				
¢	$	$$	$$$	$$$$
under S/125	S/125–S/250	S/250–S/375	S/375–S/500	over S/500

Restaurant prices are per person for a main course. Hotel prices are for a standard double room, excluding tax.

Taxi Thoughts

Ask any Arequipeños and they'll tell you Arequipa has three major concerns: earthquakes, the looming threat of volcanoes, and taxis.

Arequipa has the most taxis per capita of any city in Peru. Pint-size yellow cars, namely miniature Daewoo Ticos, clog the streets. Pollution is high, accidents aplenty, and rush-hour traffic rivals that of Los Angeles.

About 40 years ago, driving taxis became the hot job to have, especially for young people looking to make a quick sole. As the industry grew, immigrants from Bolivia, Chile, and elsewhere came swarming in, creating stiff competition. Soon paying off government agents for valid taxi licenses became commonplace. Officially, this practice no longer occurs, but there remains an overload of little yellow hotwheels. In fact, in 2006 a United Nations study on air pollution in Arequipa, said on average 50 cars per minute cross the Plaza de Armas. The study also said that since 1992 the number of taxis in Arequipa has increased by more than 250%!

In no other part of Peru does the scenery change so rapidly and dramatically. Peru's southern desert coast is a vast plain against the Pacific Ocean. Unpopulated and underdeveloped, life is about fishing. Little villages are full of hole-in-the-wall cevicherias and miles of beach.

Arequipa, Peru's second largest city, is a Spanish-colonial maze, with volcanic white sillar buildings, well-groomed plazas, and wonderful food, museums, and designer alpaca products. Arequipa is close to Colca Canyon, where many head to see the famed gorge for its stunning beauty, depth, and Andean condors. Several hours farther out is the very remote Cotahuasi Canyon, the world's deepest gorge.

Second in tourism to Machu Picchu, Lake Titicaca is home to the floating islands. The Los Uros islands are nearly 40 man-made islands—constructed from the lake's tortora reeds—and are literally floating. The natives are the Quechua and Aymara peoples, who still speak their respective languages.

Puno, an agricultural city on the shores of Titicaca is the jumping-off point for exploring the lake, and is Peru's folkloric capital. A dusty-brown city most of the time, Puno is a colorful whirlwind during festivals. The region's many fiestas feature elaborate costumes, story-telling dances, music, and lots of merrymaking. Each November and February, Puno puts on two spectacular shows for local holidays.

THE SOUTHERN COAST

The southern coast is a vast rugged desert, with jutting cliffs and a handful of green valleys. Not nearly as populated as the north coast, the southern shore is slower paced. It's perfect for light hiking, bird-watching, fishing, sampling fresh seafood, and sunbathing. Unfortunately, swimming is not advised, thanks to the strong Humboldt Current, which makes this section of the Pacific icy-cold and creates a strong undertow. There isn't much happening here, but the fresh ocean breeze and nearly 600 km (372 mi) of beachfront make it a good place to get off the gringo trail and relax. The Mejia Lagoons with its large bird sanctuary, the beaches of Mollendo, and the pre-Inca ruins of Puerto Inca are the most interesting places to visit. Summer season is from December to March when towns along the coast swoon with southern Peruvians on vacation. Outside this time, they're like ghost towns.

The economy along the coast revolves around catching fish, and cooking it. From Chala to Chile, endless cevicherias dish-up ceviche and serve lobster-size shrimp *camarones*, another local specialty.

GETTING AROUND

The southern coast begins about an hour southwest of Nazca, along the Pan-American Highway where the road starts to parallel an ancient 240-km (149-mi) Inca footpath to Cusco. This path was once used for transporting goods and for communication between the Sacred Valley and Puerto Inca. Discovered in the 1950s, the small bay of Puerto Inca was the shipping port for the Incas. Today it's the most important archaeological and historic ruin along the southern coast.

About 10 km (6 mi) to the south of Puerto Inca is Chala, a coastal community with a good beach, some great seafood and not much else. More excitement can be found 222 km (138 mi) south of Chala, along the Pan-American to the larger, more populated beach town, Camaná.

From December to March you won't see many international travelers in Camaná but you will see herds of vacationing Arequipeños and Puneños (people from Puno) who flock to Camaná for its long stretches of beach, vibrant nightlife, and volleyball tournaments. Camaná resembles a clean Daytona Beach and attracts a mainly youthful crowd, but because it's only 2.5 hours from Arequipa, it yields all ages.

Farther down the coast, about 126 km (78 mi) from Camaná, you'll hit the charming Spanish-colonial village of Mollendo which has the nicest beaches in the south. Five kilometers (3 mi) down the coast from Mollendo is also the Mejia Lagoons, a protected sanctuary with an abundance birds.

CHALA

173 km (107 mi) southwest of Nazca.

If you're driving along the coast, Chala, with nearby Puerto Inca, is a good place for an afternoon stretch. The coastal village is surrounded by quiet beaches. The shore is lined with hole-in-the-wall restaurants, which lack names but serve enormous plates of fresh-cooked fish. There isn't much here, but after grabbing a bite you can walk along the beach, Playa Grande, or visit the ruins of Puerto Inca.

Informally, the village is now split into two, Chala Sur and Chala Norte. The town isn't large enough to warrant such separation, but the north (Chala Norte) is an older, dodgy part of town, and the south (Chala Sur) is the newer section of town.

WHAT TO SEE

Playa Grande is a gorgeous stretch of soft sand cradled by dark rocky coves that jut out into the Pacific. If you enjoy fishing, watching the fishermen bring home loads of fresh jumbo shellfish and fish is a sight not to miss. The action can be seen from the main pier (more like a small dock) and it's also perfect for casting a line (bring your own).

Puerto Inca is 10 km (6 mi) north of Chala and is the old Inca port at the base of an ancient 240-km (149-mi) Inca footpath to Cusco. This path was once used for transporting goods and messages between the Sacred Valley and the coast. ■ TIP➡Nearly every 7 km (4 mi) along the path you'll see a post where Inca runners relayed notes and changed messengers so that news could be passed from the coast to the mountains within 24 hours. Still in excellent condition, the road exemplifies how important the ocean resources were to the Inca Empire and how resourceful the Incas were. You can hike in for a few miles on the trail or walk around the ruins in Puerto Inca where you'll find a cemetery temple and many tools used by the coastal Incas. Watch your step: large holes in the ground mark where drying and storage buildings once stood. To get to Puerto Inca, you can walk from Chala in two hours, or get dropped off at Km 603 and hike 3 km (2 mi). If you take a colectivo, you will be packed in like a sardine, but it only costs about S/3. A taxi from Chala runs about S/17.

WHERE TO STAY

¢–$ ☷ **Hotel Puerto Inka.** This economical resort is in a small, quiet bay. Depending on the day you might encounter archaeologists or ecologists, honeymooners, tour groups, and backpackers. The rooms are large and hot water is always available. Camping on the beach is also an option for S/13. The on-site restaurant cooks great breakfasts and good fish plates for dinner but their day long à la carte menu is hits or miss. The bilingual staff is helpful and since Chala has little to offer, the hotel provides lots to keep you entertained: two private beaches, kayak and wave-running rentals, hiking trails, evening bonfires, endless games of volleyball, a good outdoor bar, and proximity to the ruins. If you rent a room, you also have use of the swimming pool, but campers don't. **Pros:** Lots of activities, large, clean rooms, near the ruins. **Cons:** Restaurant is inconsistent, hotel is sometimes too crowded. ⊠*Pan-American Km 610* ☎*054/778–458* ☎☐*054/272–663* ⊕*www. puertoinka.com.pe* ⇨*24 rooms* ⟳*In- room: no a/c, safe (some). In-hotel: restaurant, bar, pool, beachfront, water sports, no elevator, laundry services, public Internet, parking (no fee), no-smoking rooms* ▭*AE, MC, V* ⦿*CP.*

CAMANÁ

222 km (138 mi) south of Chala.

Known for its beaches, Camaná is a magnet for Arequipeños in the summer months (December–March). Outside this time, this small fishing village, like all the other coastal villages, is nearly empty.

Camaná, the capital of the province with the same name, played an important role during colonial times when supplies were unloaded here before being transferred to Arequipa and to the silver mines in Posotí, Bolivia. It was also once home to the Waris, Collaguas, and Incas. But perhaps the most significant history was more recent—and devastating. In 2001 Camaná was on the brink of becoming the coast's next big tourist destination, but a tsunami, resulting from a 8.4 earthquake, leveled hotels, homes, and restaurants. Eight-meter high (26 feet) waves wiped-out most beach resorts along the popular beach La Punta. Camaná is slowly becoming a beachgoers' haven again.

RESERVA NACÍONAL PAMPAS GALERAS

Take the paved road (Hwy. 26) east from Nazca for two hours and you'll reach this nature reserve with herds of the rare, slender brown vicuña. Established in 1967 the 6,500-hectare park is composed of flat, windy grasslands where Andean condors and guanaco can also be spotted. A military base is on the site, and a park guard records all entrances and exits. Admission is S/7; the park is open daily 8–6.

4

La Punta is Camaná's most popular beach, a stretch of brown granular sand, 5 km (3 mi) from town. While the waves are small and not much swimming goes on here, there's lots of sunbathing, beer-sipping, and volleyball. Discos and bars stand edge to edge, among little hotels and cafés, which provide an alternative to bronzing and bikini-watching. ■TIP➜At the very south of La Punta is an area called the caves, a small rocky inlet that's good for wading. Just outside of town **La Miel** is a rocky inlet with calm waters. It's a popular place for camping and watching sunsets. No matter which beach you hit, bring an umbrella and strong sunscreen—there's no shade.

ESSENTIALS

CURRENCY **Banco de Crédito BCP** (✉ *Av. 9 de Noviembre 139*). **Banco Continental BBVA** (✉ *28 de Julio 405*).

WHERE TO STAY & EAT

¢ ✗**Cevicheria Rosa Nautica.** Not to be confused with the famous Lima institution, this Rosa Nautica isn't nearly as fancy, pricy or as good, but it makes an effort. A hole-in-the-wall, family-style restaurant serves heaping plates of mostly ceviche. If you want to share it's possible to order it *para compartir.* Try the mixto. ✉*La Punta, Camaná* 📞*No phone* ▭*No credit cards.*

¢ 🏨**Hotel de Turistas.** Beautiful colonial architecture makes this hacienda
☾ an attractive inn that has lured travelers since the 1960s. Spacious accommodations have high ceilings, arched doorways, and long windows overlooking lush gardens. The newer additions of the indoor sauna and hot tub are nice, and children can play in the outdoor pool, which has water slides. The restaurant serves a good breakfast and dishes out local delicacies and desserts all day. **Pros:** Hot water, sauna, friendly atmosphere. **Cons:** Furniture doesn't match, sells out quickly in summer. ✉*Av. Lima 138* 📞*054/571–113* ⤶*21 rooms* ☾*In-room: safe(some). In-hotel: restaurant, room service, bar, pool, no elevator,*

laundry service, parking (no fee) ⊟*AE, DC, MC, V* ⦿|*BP.*

¢ ⚹ **Sun Valley.** Go to this resort near
☾ the beach for water sports and sand boarding. After a day of play you can relax in a modern, if blandly decorated, clean room with a hot bath. The restaurant serves Peruvian comfort food. **Pros:** Clean, modern, near the beach. **Cons:** Small rooms. ⊠*Cerrillos 2, Km 843* ☎*054/283–056 or 054/969–4235* ✉*eridv@hotmail.com* ⇥*42 rooms* ⟨⟩*In-room: no a/c, safe (some). In-hotel: restaurant, bar, pool, gym, water sports, no elevator, laundry service, parking (no fee)* ⊟*AE, DC, MC, V* ⦿|*BP.*

PETROGLYPHS

Toro Muerto is the world's largest petroglyph field, where hundreds of volcanic rocks are thought to have been painted more than 1,000 years ago by the Huari (or Wari) culture. There are sketches of pumas, llamas, guanacos, and condors, as well as warriors and dancers. Head higher for expansive views of the desert. It's hot and windy, so bring water, a hat, and sunglasses. Toro Muerto is 40 km (25 mi) northeast of Canaña.

MOLLENDO

113 km (70 mi) southwest of Arequipa.

Mollendo is a cheerful, Spanish-influenced town with colorful, colonial architecture and 35 km (21 mi) of clean, sandy beach. The brightly painted colonial homes and groomed plazas appear as if they were plucked from the Costa del Sol in Spain. A great place to view these homes is around Plaza Bolognesi and Plaza Grau. Castle Forga, a bright yellow colonial-style castle, perches over a cliff above the sea. While Castle Forga is vacant and not technically a museum, visitors are allowed to look around, though the hours are inconsistent. Mollendo is the most attractive beach community in the Southern coast. The water is still not desirable for a swim but the waves are fairly subdued. A strong recycling program keeps the beaches clean. You'll also find many of the freshest cevicherias in the south.

BEACHES

Five primary beaches are along the coast of Mollendo, which start in the northern part of town and progressively get nicer as they continue south. The first beach, **Primera Playa**, is a small stretch of sand complete with a beach club ambience including lifeguards, a bathhouse (with toilets and showers), a parking area, snack shop, a swimming pool, and tennis courts. There's a S/7 fee for use of the pool and facilities.

The second beach, **Segunda Playa**, is your standard beach with sun, sand, and waves, but the hard-to-miss yellow Castle Forga, which sits atop a large cliff, separates the second and third beach, **Playa Tercera**, at which point the beaches get more exclusive. On Playa Tercera tents and umbrellas are for rent and it's a sea of red and blue awnings. Along the beach are lifeguards and a few outdoor seafood restaurants. The fourth beach, **Albatros**, is larger than Tercera and also includes rental umbrellas. Finally, the fifth beach, **Las Rocas**, or the Rocks, is wider and cleaner, with permanent tents and umbrellas set up, and a sea of wealthy Peruvian sunbathers.

Although it's not technically one of Mollendo's beaches, **Catarindo** is 2 km (1.2 mi) north of Mollendo on the Pan-American. A small inlet, it has almost no waves and is the place to swim, or to put in a kayak.

WHERE TO STAY & EAT

¢ ✕**Restaurant Marco Antonio.** This charming hole-in-the-wall is a family operation—your fish is cooked upstairs and brought down a winding stairway to the Spartan but comfortable dining area. The catch of the day varies with the season, but it's always fresh and delicious. Ask for the criolla style mixto. ⊠*Comercio 254–258, Parque Bolognesi* ☎*No phone* ☐*V.*

¢ ▦**Hostal Cabaña.** We wouldn't recommend this place for your honeymoon, there are no frills and the old lodge feels camp-like, but it's clean, and has what you'll need to get a good night rest after a day at the beach. **Pros:** Large rooms, private bath, and hot water. **Cons:** A little loud on the weekends. ⊠*Comercio 240* ☎*054/534–57* ⚒*In-room: no a/c. In-hotel: restaurant (breakfast only), no elevator, laundry service, parking (no fee)* ☐*No credit cards* ��*CP.*

SANTUARIO NACIONAL LAGUNAS DE MEJÍA

5km (3 mi) south of Mollendo

Down the coast from Mollendo are the **Mejía Lagoons.** The reserve protects wetlands, including swamps, salt marshes, and totora reeds. More than 200 bird species have been sighted here, including the rare red-fronted coot and the Chilean flamingo. ■**TIP➔While the most pleasant season is October to May, the best sightings are from January to April at the crack of dawn.** The reserve is open from sunrise to sunset and the cost of admissions is S/5 or a three-day pass for S/10. From Mollendo it takes about 15 minutes to reach the lagoons. Colectivos run frequently between the two and cost S/1, 20 centivos. ⊠*Km 32, Carretera Mollendo, Valle Tambo, Arequipa* ☎*054/800–004.*

CROSSING INTO CHILE

The border with Chile, about 40 km (25 mi) from Tacna, is open daily and very easy to cross. From Tacna there are scores of colectivos that will give you a ride to the other side for S/20, or you can take a bus from Tacna, which is headed to Arica and departs hourly. Yet another option is to take a train.

Typically drivers will help with border formalities, even the colectivos. The road journey takes about an hour. Any train aficionado will enjoy the slow, somewhat bumpy, but beautiful train ride from Tacna to Arica, which takes more than an hour and costs S/6.

CLOSE UP

On The Menu

With the altitude and cool weather, southern Peru is famous for its hearty and savory soups. Quinoa and potatoes typically provide the base, and with the emergence of novo-Andina cuisine, the addition of meats, vegetables, and spices make these soups a meal unto itself. Cheese, potatos, cuy, and quinoa make up the diets in traditional villages around Lake Titicaca and the canyons.

SEAFOOD

In coastal towns you'll dine in *cebecherías* and more upscale *marisquerías* (seafood restaurants). The best are along the coast and in Puno.

Ceviche: Fish or shellfish marinated in lime juice, cilantro, onions, tomatoes, and chilies) is always on the menu, served raw as a salad or cocktail and usually accompanied by *canchas,* toasted corn kernels sprinkled with salt. *Ceviche mixto* is a mix of shellfish and fish and is best along the coast.

Escabeche: Raw fish and prawns with chilies, cheese chunks, sliced eggs, olives, and onions, and found in Arequipa.

MEATS

lomo saltado: sautéed beef strips with garlic, tomatoes, onions, chilies, and fried potatoes.

lomo a la huancaina: beef strips with egg and cheese sauce.

Filet de cuy: A novo-Andino style of cuy cut in filets instead of whole found in Arequipa at select restaurants.

cuy chactado: roasted guinea pig.

SOUPS AND STEWS

Créma de Quinoa: creamed soup made of quinoa. Found in mountainous areas like Lake Titicaca and the Canyonlands.

chupe verde: potatoes, cheese, eggs, and herbs; found in Arequipa and Canyonlands.

hualpa chupe: chicken, chilies, and spices; found in Arequipa.

chupe de camarones: spicy shrimp stew; found on the coast.

sopa a la criolla: onions, peppers, and potatoes; found in Arequipa.

Mollejitas: chicken innards are the specialty in Arequipa.

BAKED GOODS & DESSERTS

Panaderías (bakeries) and *pastelerías* (pastry shops) are places to find fresh-baked rolls and *pan integral* (grain bread).

alfajores: (shortbread).

cocadas al horno: (macaroons).

ganja blanco: (boiled evaporated milk and sugar mixed with pineapple or peanuts.

Queso Helado: The signature ice cream of Arequipa. Creamy coconut ice cream with cinnamon.

churros: fried dough sprinkled with sugar.

mazamorra morada: purple maize, cinnamon, milk, and sugar—a specialty from small street stands in Arequipa.

REFRESHMENTS

The Mountain Dew–like Inka Cola is the local soda brand. Regional beers includes Cusqueña and Arequipeña. *Chicha* or *chicherias* (a fermented corn drink) is the national beverage for fiestas and celebrations, not to be confused with *chicha morada* (a nonalcoholic drink from purple corn). *Vino Calliente* is hot-mulled red wine served across the country but especially in the highlands and in Puno.

COLCA CANYON & COTAHUASI CANYON

COTAHUASI CANYON

★ *50 km (31 mi) north of Colca Canyon.*

Colca Canyon may be the region's most famous natural attraction, but at 3,354 meters (11,001 feet), Cotahuasi is the world's deepest gorge, beating Colca Canyon by 163 meters (534 feet). It's nearly twice as deep as the Grand Canyon. The canyon has been carved by the Río Cotahuasi, which changes into Río Ocuña before connecting to the Pacific. Its deepest point is at Ninochaco, below the quaint administrative capital of Quechualla, and accessible only by kayak; kayak explorations first documented the area in the mid-1990s and measured its depth. Since then, paddling Cotahuasi river's Class V rapids is to kayakers what scaling Mount Everest is to mountaineers.

> **ADVANCE PREP**
>
> Cotahuasi is not traveler-savvy yet so it's not possible to show up in a town, buy a map, hire a guide, and get on your way. You'll want to buy a map of the canyon at the Instituto Geográfico Militar in Lima or at the South American Explorers in Lima or Cusco.

The ride from Arequipa to the Cotahuasi Canyon ranks with the great scenic roads of the world. As you pass Corire and Toro Muerto, the road rides the western side of snow-capped Nevado Coropuno (21,079 feet), Peru's third-highest volcano, for spectacular views as you descend into the valley of Cotahuasi. ■TIP→Logistically speaking, it's a bumpy 11- to 13-hour bus ride or 10 hours by four-wheel drive from Arequipa. The pavement ends in Chuquibamba. Some of the road from Chuquibamba to Cotahuasi, the longest stretch of the ride, is in the process of being graded. There's no fee to enter the canyon.

GETTING THERE

Cotahuasi Canyon is a travel destination in the making, but outside of expert extreme sports enthusiasts, few people venture here. Unless you're taking a bus, driving anything but a 4x4 is asking for trouble. The jagged, rocky dirt roads are full of cliffs and narrow corners. Dry for most of the year, the roads get muddy from December to April (rainy season), a time when you're also likely to encounter random streams flowing across the road.

Hire a guide, regardless of season and not just for safety. Since this region is so remote, you're likely to see a lot more with a guide. All buses travel through the night; three bus companies go from Arequipa to Cotahuasi daily, each leaves around 5 PM, arriving in Cotahuasi village in time for sunrise: Transportes Cromotex (☎054/421–555), Transportes Reyna (☎054/430–612), and Alex Bus (☎054/424–605).

■TIP→If you're driving, know that gas stations are few between the long stretch from Corire (near Toro Muerto) to the village of Cotahuasi.

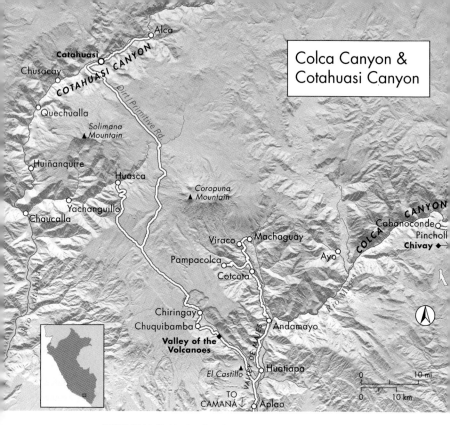

Colca Canyon &
Cotahuasi Canyon

COTAHUASI VILLAGE & VICINITY

Cotahuasi is the largest town in the region and the first you'll stumble upon. In the hills at 2,680 meters (8,620 feet), whitewashed colonial-style homes line slim, straight lanes before a backdrop of Cerro Hiunao. Most visitors kick-off their stay in this Quechua-speaking community of 3,500 residents, where there are a few hostels, restaurants, a small tienda (grocery store), a bell tower, and Plaza de Armas. It's also where most hiking trails begin or end. Many families rent burros (mules) to tourists to help carry their load, especially kayakers who walk eight hours down to the gorge with their boats.

Below the village of Cotahuasi is the valley of Piro, the gateway to the canyon, which is close to Cataratas de Sipia, a 150-meter (462-foot), 10-meter-wide waterfall. ■TIP➔Sipia Falls is the most visited attraction in the entire canyon. Three hours farther south along a thin track against the canyon wall—which climbs to 400 meters (1,312 feet) above the river—you'll reach Chaupo, a settlement surrounded by groves of fruit trees. You can camp here and hike through Velinga to ruins at Huña before reaching Quechualla where you can see the ancient farming terraces of Maucullachta, an old Wari-city across the gorge.

In Cotahuasi Village, the route forks, leading the northeast along the Rio Cotahuasi or due north. Either way is possible by 4x4, colectivo, or on foot. Heading northeast, about 10 km out of town, you'll discover the village of Tomepampa. After that is the small town of Alca, near the hot springs of

Luicho and farther along the road. Even further east is Puica at 3,700 meters (8,440 feet). Traveling northwest from Cotahuasi village will lead you to Pampamarca, a town known for weaving exquisite rugs. Two hours by car, Pampamarca is three hours from the hot springs of Josla and the Uskuni of Uskuni.

OUTDOOR ACTIVITIES

Many operators in Arequipa and Cusco offer multiday excursions. Most tours are at least four days, five nights and some last up to 17 nights. A few local hikers provide custom tours for visitors as well.

HIKING Cotahuasi Canyon is an awesome place to explore by foot. The backdrop of snow-capped Volcano Coropuna and Solimana is fantastic, the high desert plains offer a rest from the steep upward rocky canyon terrain, and the untouched villages provide a cultural aspect. Hikes can go between 6,000 feet and 21,000 feet in height so prepare for the altitude. Temperatures remain about 65–70°F during the day, dipping below 45° on any given night. Ancient Inca paths wind throughout the canyon and its terraces. ■TIP➡Beware, many of these ancient trails are narrow, rocky, and hang over the side of the canyon. Newer trails parallel some of the ancient ones, and are generally safer.

Sipia Falls is a solid three- to four-hour trek from Cotahuasi Village and it's a hard-on-your knees hike down that includes two bridge crossings, but the first taste of being in the canyon is a surreal experience. It's also possible to reach the falls by hailing a colectivo or in your own 4x4 from the Cotahuasi road to the Sipia Bridge where the road ends. From here it's a 45-minute hike to the falls.

If you're going on a multiday excursion, continue on the trail from Cotahuasi to Sipia to the Chaupo Valley and the citrus tree village of Velinga, a good place to camp. From Velinga it's on to Quechualla where you'll pass through the 1,000-year-old old Wari ruins, rock forests, and cactus forests. One of the last major points along this route is Huachuy where you can again camp. Beyond this point things get trickier as you'll have to cross the Rió Cotahuasi. Many guides use a cable system to reach Yachau Oasis, Chaucalla Valley, and eventually Iquipi Valley.

WHITE-WATER Kayakers and white-water rafters can challenge the rapids anywhere
RAFTING from the upper Cotahuasi, near the village, almost to the Pacific. The river is divided into four sections: the Headwaters, beginning upstream from Cotahuasi village, Aimaña gorge, Flatwater Canyon, and the Lower Canyon.

The Lower Canyon is a mix of Class III and V rapids, without much portage. Most rafting tour operators put-in at the village of Velinga and use this part of the river for tours. These tours are done fairly frequently by operators from Arequipa. Depending upon skill level and adventure craving kayakers tend to put-in up river and have to portage on several occasions.

Kayakers put-in at Headwaters in the village of Chuela. Here the rapids ring in at a Class III, but by the time the Aimaña gorge starts in the waters tug at Class V. White-water season is June through November when the rapids are Class III to V. But the best time to go is mid-May to mid-June. The water is snowmelt so wetsuits are necessary.

VALLEY OF THE VOLCANOES

This spectacular, 65-km (40-mi) crevasse north of Colca Canyon includes a line of 80 extinct craters and cinder cones. Looming over the scene is active Volcán Coropuna, the third highest peak in Peru. Andagua, at the head of the valley, has the best tourist facilities in the area. The valley is about five hours by a rocky, half-paved, half-dirt road from Colca Canyon. There are several multiday hikes from Colca Canyon that must be arranged in Arequipa. If you're going to Cotahuasi or Colca Canyon, you're bound to pass through this high-altitude valley.

COLCA CANYON

30 km (19 mi) north of Toro Muerto.

Flying overhead, you can't miss the green, fertile trough as it cuts through the barren terrain, but it's all an illusion; only scrub brush and cactus cling to the canyon's sheer basalt sides and miles of ancient terraces. ■TIP➔The canyon is named for the stone warehouses (colcas) used to store grain by an ancient society living along the walls of the gorge.

Carved into the foothills of the snow-covered Andes and sliced by the silvery Río Colca, Colca Canyon drops 3,182 meters (10,607 feet) down. The more adventurous can embark on a multiday hike into the canyon—typically a two-, three-, or five-day excursion. Bird lovers (and anyone with an eye for amazement) can visit the Cruz del Condor. Culture seekers can spend a night with a native family. Light hikers and archaeology aficionados can observe points along the rim, or those seeking pure relaxation can hit one of the all-inclusive lodges with horseback riding and thermal baths.

Cruz del Condor is a haunt for the giant birds, particularly at dawn, when they soar on the winds rising from the deep valley. At 1,200 meters (4,000 feet), the "condor cross" precipice between the villages Pinchollo and Cabanaconder is the best place to spot them. ■TIP➔From June to August, you're likely to spot close to 20 or more condors during a morning visit. By October and November many of the female birds are nesting, so your chances of eyeing flocks are slim, but you'll likely spot a few birds.

Llamas take the high road in Colca Canyon.

GETTING AROUND

By hiring a private guide, renting a four-wheel-drive vehicle, joining a tour from Arequipa, or going by bus you can explore the area. Arequipa is the jumping-off point for nearly everyone headed to Colca Canyon. Chivay is the first town you'll come to. The ride takes about five hours from Arequipa. The road takes you through the Reserva Nacional Aguada Blanca y Salinas and over the Patapampa Pass where at 4,825 meters you can view nearly the entire Valley of Volcanoes. The road is only paved about half of the way; going toward the Patapampa Pass is dirt, but has been graded and smoothed out. The last quarter of the ride is rocky. Most everyone going to Colca Canyon will experience altitude problems along the way, so bring plenty of water. Some of the nicer hotels will have oxygen tanks.

Taxis are a good way to go from town to town if long hikes or mountain biking isn't your thing. Taxis line up around the Plaza de Armas in Chivay. Most rides will cost S/15–S/20.

CHIMAY

The largest town in the Colca Canyon region is Chivay, a small, battered-looking village with a population of 3,000. Most tourist facilities are here, which are not many, but include restaurants,

SCARY BRIDGES

A hallmark of Cotahausi Canyon is its bridges, which are all hanging (and swinging) across the Río Cotahuasi. They're cool to look at, nerve-racking to consider, but there's only one way over.

CLOSE UP

Canyon Life

Quechua farmers once irrigated narrow, stacked terraces of volcanic earth along the canyon rim to make this a productive farming area. These ancient fields are still used for *quinoa* and *kiwicha* grains, and barley grown here is used to brew Arequipeña beer.

Most of those who live along the rim today are Collagua Indians, whose settlements date back more than 2,000 years. Their traditions were persevered through the centuries. In these unspoiled Andean villages you'll still see Collaguas and Cabana people wearing traditional clothing and embroidered hats. Spanish influence is evident in Achoma, Maca, Pinchollo, and Yanque, with their gleaming white *sillar* (volcanic-stone) churches.

Seeped in colorful folklore tradition, locals like a good fiesta. Some of the larger festivals include La Virgen del Candelaria, a two-day fiesta in Chivay on February 2 and 3; later in the month Carnivál is celebrated throughout the valley. Semana Santa (holy week) in April is heavily observed, but for more a more colorful party don't miss Chivay's annual anniversary fiesta on June 21. From July 14 to 17 the Virgen del Carmen, one of the larger celebrations kicks off with parades on both ends of the canyon: Cabanaconde and Chivay. All Saints Day is well-honored on November 1 and 2 as is La Virgen Imaculada on December 8.

hotels, a medical clinic, and a tourist information center. As you approach Chivay, you'll pass through a stone archway signifying the town entrance, where AUTOCOLCA, the government authority over Colca Canyon, stops cars to ask if they are headed to see the condors. If you're headed to Cruz del Condor or any of the churches in the 14 villages you must purchase a S/35 entry ticket, which will be asked for again at the entrance of the Mirador. Nearly all agency tours do not include this entry fee in their all price.

Chivay marks the eastern end of the canyon's rim, the other end is Cabonconde, a developing village where most multiday hikes into the canyon begin and end. As you come into Chivay the road splits off into two: one, less traveled because of its rocky rutted surface, goes along the canyon's northern edge to the villages of Coporaque, Ichupampa, and Lari; the other follows the southern rim and although it's a bumpy dirt road, it's better for travel and leads to Cruz del Condor, and the small towns of Yanque, Maca, and Cabanaconde.

OUTDOOR ACTIVITIES

Most organized adventure sport activities should be arranged from Arequipa, especially kayaking, rafting, and multiday treks into the canyon. Many upper-tier hotels and resorts offer packages, have their own tour guides, and have activities like horseback riding and mountain bike rentals. So check with your hotel before booking anything else. There's only one official tour operator in Chivay and it specializes in mountain bike rentals. However, local guides for hiking can be hired by asking around; the most experienced guides are in Cabanaconde and Chivay. The average price is S/59 or US$20 a day for a local guide.

HIKING Bring lots of water (the valley has water, but it's grossly expensive, as it's "imported" from Arequipa), sunscreen, a hat, good hiking shoes, high-energy snacks, sugar or colca leaves to alleviate the altitude sickness, and layer your clothes. One minute the wind may be fierce and the next you may be sweltering in the strong sun.

> **HIGH SUN**
>
> Don't forget sunblock! At high altitudes the rays can be fierce, even with clouds. Often the brisk mountain temperatures fake you into thinking it's too cool for a burn.

4

Along the Canyon: Along the south side of the canyon it's possible to do an easy hike from the observation points between Cruz del Condor and Pinchollo. Paths are along the canyon rim most of the way; however, in some places, you have to walk along the road. The closer to Cruz del Condor you are the better the paths and lookouts get.

Another short hike, but more uphill, is on the north rim starting in Coporaque. At the Plaza de Armas, to the left of the church in the corner of the Plaza you'll see an archway. Go through the archway and take a right uphill and you'll be on the trail, which goes from wide to narrow, but is defined. ■TIP➜Following it up about an hour, you'll come to ancient burial tombs (look down) with actual skeletons. The trail climbs up a cliff, which overlooks the valley. It's about a two-hour hike to the top and in some spots is very steep and rocks are crumbly. After the tombs the path becomes confusing and splits in many directions.

Into the canyon: Trails into the canyon are many as well as rough and unmarked, so venture down is with a guide. Several adventure tour operators provide governmental certified hiking guides; local guides are also easily found. Packages range from two- to eight-day treks. The Cabanaconde area is the entry point for most of these.

The most popular multiday hike is the three-day/two-night trek. Starting about 20 minutes (by foot) east of Cabanaconde at Pampa San Miguel, the trail to San Juan Chuccho (one of the larger villages along the river) begins. The steep slope has loose gravel and takes about four hours. In San Juan Chuccho sleeping options are family-run hostels or a campsite. Day two consists of hiking on fairly even terrain through the small villages of Tapay, Cosnirhua, and Malata before crossing the river and into the lush green village of Sangalle, or as locals call it, Oasis, a mini-paradise along the Río Colca, with hot springs and waterfalls. On day three, you'll hike four to five hours uphill to the rim and arrive in Cabanaconde by lunch.

We do not recommend hiking alone here. So many paths are in this area that it can be overwhelming to even the most experienced trekkers.

WHITE-WATER RAFTING The Río Colca is a finicky river. Highly skilled paddlers long to run this Class IV–V river. Depending upon the season, the water level and the seismic activity of the local volcanoes, the rapids change frequently. In some areas it's more than a Class V and in other areas it's slow enough that it could be considered a Class II–III. Below Colca Canyon

Llamas, Vicunas & Alpacas

Alpaca

Llamas, vicuñas, guanacos, and alpacas roam the highlands of Peru, but unfortunately not in the great herds of pre-Inca times. However, there are always a few around, especially the domesticated llama and alpaca. The sly vicuña, like the guanaco, refuses domestication. Here's a primer on how to tell them apart.

The Alpaca is the cute and cuddly one, especially while still a baby. It grows a luxurious, long wool coat that comes in as many as 20 colors and its wool is used in knitting sweaters and weaving rugs and wall hangings. Its finest wool is from the first shearing and is called "baby alpaca." When full-grown it's close to 1½ meters (4.9 feet) tall and weighs about 7 kg (15 pounds). Its size and the shortness of its neck distinguish it from the llama. There are two types of alpaca. The common huancayo with short thick legs and the suri, least predominant and a bit taller and also nicknamed the Bob Marley for its shaggy curly dreadlocks that grows around its face and chest.

The Guanaco, a cousin of the delicate vicuña, is a thin-legged wild endangered camelid, with a coarse reddish brown coat and a soft white underbelly. Its hair is challenging to weave on its own, so often it's mixed with other fibers, like alpaca. The guanaco weighs about 200 pounds and can be up to 5 feet long and 3–4 feet high. Eighty percent of Guanacos live in Patagonia, but the other 20% are scattered through the altiplano of southern Peru, Chile, and Bolivia. It's the only camelid that can live at sea level and in the high-altitude Andes.

The Llama is the pack animal with a course coat in as many as 50 colors, though one that's unsuitable for weavings or fine wearing apparel. It can reach almost 2 meters (6 feet) from its hoofs to the top of its elongated neck and long, curved ears. It can carry 40–60 kg (88–132 pounds), depending on the length of the trip. It can also have some nasty habits, like spitting in your eye or kicking you if you get too close to its hind legs.

The Vicuña has a more delicate appearance. It will hold still (with help) for shearing, and its wool is the most desirable. It's protected by the Peruvian government, as it was almost killed off by unrestricted hunting. It's the smallest of the Andean camelids, at 1.3 meters (4 feet) and weighs about 40 kg (88 pounds) at maturity. It's found mostly at altitudes over 3,600 meters (12,000 feet).

—By Joan Gonzalez

conditions on the Río Majes (the large downstream section of the Río Colca) are reliable with superb white-water rafting. Skilled rafters start in Huambo by renting mules for S/20 and for the next eight hours descend to the river. The waters at this point rank in at Class III, but when the Río Mamacocha dumps in it's Class IV and V rapids.

> **BRING CASH!**
>
> There are no ATMs in the Colca Canyon or valley area, nor is it possible for credit cards to be processed. Soles and U.S. dollars (no bills larger than $10) are accepted.

Paddlers who have tried to run the entire river through the canyon have had more casualties than successes. There are a few well-known operators to consider, which is important given the river's intensity.

CANYON TOUR OPERATORS IN AREQUIPA:

For about S/140 per day you can hire **Carlos Zárate Aventuras** (⊠*Santa Catalina 204* ☎*054/263–107* ⊕*www.zarateadventures.com*) and his hiking and mountain guides, who conduct tours in Spanish, English, and French. Other travelers interested in multiday trekking trips of Colca Canyon, Misti, and Chachani use **Land Adventures** (⊠*Santa Catalina 118-B* ☎*054/204–872* ⊕*www.landadventures.net*)

For the standard tour of Colca Canyon turn to **Colonial Tours** (⊠*Santa Catalina 106* ☎*054/286–868*) a specialist in the one- and two-day tour. Most agencies selling the one- and two-day tours pool their customers and send them with Colonial, so check here first. Upscale travelers go with **Condor Travel** (⊠*Santa Catalina 210 in la Casona de Santa Catalina shopping center, another office at 117 Santa Catalina* ☎*054/237–821* ⊕*www.condortravel.com*).Slightly less expensive, but still good is **Giardino** (⊠*Jerusalén 604-A* ☎*054/221–345* ⊕*www.giardinotours.com*)

The king of all kayaking and rafting operators in Peru, **Cusipata Viajes y Turismo** (⊠*Jerusalen 408-A, Arequipa* ☎*054/203–966* ⊕*www.cusipata.com* ✉*cusipata@gmail.com*) puts on multiday runs down the Colca, Cotahuasi, and the Chili rivers. All guides are trained in first aid and Swiftwater Rescue. Class IV, V, and VI rafting adventures through the Colca Canyon are operated May through September by **Apumayo Expediciones** (⊠*Garcilaso 316-A, Cusco* ☎☎*084/246–018* ⊕*www.apumayo.com*).

WHERE TO STAY & EAT

Chivay is tiny, but has plenty of small budget hotels and a few restaurants. You'll come into town on 22 de Agosto, which leads to the Plaza de Armas, where you'll find **Lobo's Pizzeria, McElroy's Pub** (a gringo magnet owned by a true Irishman), and **El Balcón de Don Zacarias,** which serves very good traditional food. An organic novo-Andino restaurant, **Kantua,** on Calle Garcilazo 510, is worthy of a visit.

If you're planning on staying one night in Colca Canyon it makes sense to stay in Chivay. If you'll be in the area for longer, we recommend one of the lodges in the valley, which are more inclusive and offer activities like hiking, biking, horseback riding, and have a restaurant on-site.

CHIVAY

$ **Casa Andina.** This hotel seems like a Swiss ski lodge, with bungalow
☾ cabins made of locally quarried rock. Medium-size rooms with rustic furnishings have private baths with hot water. The restaurant serves excellent Peruvian fare. **Pros:** Planetarium and observatory, good breakfast, cozy lounge and fireplace. **Cons:** No easy access to the outdoors, small bathrooms. ⊠ *Calle Huayna Capac s/n, Chivay* ☎ *054/53–1020* ☎ *054/53 1098* ⊕ *www.casa-andina.com* ⇨ *52 rooms* ⚹ *In-room: safe, refrigerator (some), Wi-Fi (some). In-hotel: restaurant, bar, no elevator, laundry service, public Internet, public Wi-Fi, parking (no fee), no-smoking rooms* ⊟ *AE, DC, MC, V* ⊙ *BP.*

$ **✕ Pozo del Cielo.** Across the river on top of a hill on the outskirts of
★ Chivay sits one of the most quaint lodges in the valley. A series of chalets are made of adobe, wood, and stone. Simple rooms have beds piled with warm blankets and include a modern bathroom. The dark-wood window shades and low wooden doorways seem out of a fairy tale. All rooms lead to the main lodge by narrow, outdoor cobbled stone pathways. In the lodge the restaurant is composed of endless windows and an adobe fireplace. ■**TIP→The views over Chivay, the valley, and volcanoes are stunning.** Good novo-Andino food is served and there's always hot tea. **Pros:** Hot-water bottles at bedtime for extra warmth, on the outskirts of Chivay, good views. **Cons:** Must walk outside to get to breakfast, no bureaus or closets. ⊠ *In Chivay: Calle Huáscar B-3 Sacsayhuaman. In Arequipa: Pasaje Apurímac 113* ☎ *054/531–041 Chivay, 054/205–838 Arequipa* ☎ *054/202–606* ⊕ *www.pozodelcielo. com.pe* ⇨ *20 rooms* ⚹ *In-room: no a/c, no phone, safe (some), no TV (some). In-hotel: restaurant, room service, bar, no elevator, laundry service, parking (no/fee), no-smoking rooms* ⊟ *AE, MC, V* ⊙ *BP.*

AROUND THE VALLEY

$$$$ **✕ Las Casitas del Colca.** It doesn't get better than this, at least not in
Fodor's Choice Colca. The region's newest hotel is also the most luxurious, and by far
★ the most expensive. It's an all-inclusive resort with cooking and painting classes, fly-fishing, horseback riding, hiking tours, and a full-service spa. Thatch-roof bungalows with terraces have spectacular views over the silvery Río Colca. ■**TIP→All outdoor terraces also have small private hot springs tubs, an open-fire pit, and couches.** Rooms are bright with comfortable furnishings, including wrought-iron beds piled with heaps of elegant bedding and leather armchairs. The smooth stone floors are heated and the deep bathtubs have glass ceilings so at night you can also soak in the amazing stars above. An on-site novo-Andino restaurant serves creative fare made using vegetables from the garden. All meals are offered à la carte. **Pros:** All-inclusive, heated floors, private hot springs. **Cons:** Pricey. ⊠ *Parque Curiña Yanque* ☎ *051/610–8300* ☎ *051/242–3365* ⊕ *www.lascasitasdelcolca.com* ⇨ *19 rooms, 1 suite* ⚹ *In-room: no a/c, safe, refrigerator, no TV, Wi-Fi. In-hotel: restaurant, room service, bar, pools, spa, bicycles, no elevator, laundry service, con-*

cierge, executive floor, public Internet, public Wi-Fi, parking (no fee), no-smoking rooms ⊟*AE, MC,V* ⦿*|AI.*

$ ╳⊡ **La Casa de Mama Yacchi.** Perhaps the best food around, and the best pillows, too. Owned by the same folks of Casa de Mi Abuela in Arequipa, this rustic thatched-roof hotel is a great economical choice. Its main lodge is cozy and the restaurant specializes in local fare, such as the alpaca barbeque, and there's a good bar. The rooms are simple bungalows with standard beds and excellent bedding. On the north rim, in Coporaque, it's very peaceful. Horseback riding and hikes can be arranged daily. **Pros:** Delicious food, good water pressure, and pillows. **Cons:** Gets cold, far from Cruz del Condor. ⊠*Calle Jerusalén 606, Coporaque* ☎*054/241–206* 🖷*054/242–761* ⊕*www.lacasade-mamayacchi.com* ⮏*50 rooms* ♿*In-room: no a/c, no phone, safe. In-hotel: restaurant, bar, no elevator, laundry service, parking (no fee), no-smoking rooms* ⊟*No Credit Cards* ⦿*|BP.*

$$ ⊡ **Colca Lodge.** The hotel's understated look, with adobe and clay walls
🕭 and thatched roof, compliment the terrain. The location between Yanque
★ and Ichupampa offers plenty to do, including canyon hikes, horseback rides, biking, and trout fishing. It's family-friendly and kids will love the nonstop activities. Rooms are simple, perhaps too much so, but the heat works thanks to the solar panel system. Above all, this hotel has the best hot springs around. Next to the river, they're made of stone, and have a spectacular view. **Pros:** Lots of activities, hot springs, solar heating. **Cons:** Hot springs are closed in February and March, rooms are plain. ⊠*Fundo Puye s/n, Caylloma, Yanque* ☎*054/202–587* 🖷*054/220–407* ⊕*www.colca-lodge.com* ⮏*25 rooms* ♿*In-room: safe (some). In-hotel: restaurant, room service, bar, pool, bicycles, no elevator, laundry service, parking (no fee), no-smoking rooms* ⊟*AE, MC, V* ⦿*|BP.*

HOMESTAYS In the small settlements of Cabanaconde, Coporaque, Ichupampa, Madrigal, and Yanque you can experience local life by staying with families. In addition to exploring ruins and historic sites with family guides, you'll help out with daily chores and participate in seasonal festivities. This option is difficult to arrange in advance and from afar, but possible. Colonial Tours in Arequipa can make advance arrangements but details will be limited. These types of trips should only cost about US$20, including private transportation to the canyon from Arequipa.

If you don't mind uncertainty, it's quite simple to come to Chivay or Cabanaconde and ask around about staying with a family. Locals are friendly and know families in the canyon who want visitors. Arriving as early as possible is essential. It takes a few hours to network, find a family, and travel to their village.

AREQUIPA

150 km (93 mi) south of Colca Canyon; 200 km (124 mi) south of Cotahuasi Canyon.

Cradled by three steep, gargantuan, snow-covered volcanoes, the charming white-stoned Arequipa shines under the striking sun at 2,350 meters (7,709 feet). This settlement of 1 million residents grew from a collection of Spanish-colonial churches and homes constructed from white *sillar* (petrified volcanic ash) gathered from the surrounding terrain. The result is unique—short gleaming white buildings contrast with the charcoal-color mountain backdrop of El Misti, a perfectly shaped cone volcano.

The town was a gathering of Aymara Indians and Inca when Garci Manuel de Carbajal and nearly 100 more Spaniards founded the city on August 15, 1540. A mix of Spanish and Creole cultures, traditions have carried on through the centuries, giving the settlement a European flavor.

After the Spanish arrived, the town grew into the region's most profitable center for farming and cattle-raising—businesses that continue to be important in Arequipa's economy. The settlement was also on the silver route linking the coast to the Bolivian mines. By the 1800s Arequipa had more Spanish settlers than any town in the south.

Arequipeños call their home *Cuidad Blanca*, "White City," and the "Independent Republic of Arequipa"—they have made several attempts to secede from Peru and even designed the city's own passport and flag. ■TIP➜On August 15, parades, fireworks, bullfights, and dancing celebrate the city's founding.

Arequipa enjoys fresh, crisp air, and warm days averaging 23°C (73°F) and comfortable nights at 14°C (57°F). To make up for the lack of rain, the Río Chili waters the surrounding foothills, which were once farmed by the Inca and now stretch into rows of alfalfa and onions.

GETTING AROUND

Walking is the best option around the city center. Most sights, shops, and restaurants are near the Plaza de Armas. For a quick, cheap tour, spend S/3 and catch a Vallecito bus for a 1.5-hour circuit around Calles Jerusalén and San Juan de Díos. Most sites are open morning and afternoon, but close for a couple of hours midday. Churches usually open 7 to 9 AM and 6 to 8 PM, before and after services. Taxis are everywhere and cost about S/3 to get around the center or to Vallecito.

Arequipa has two bus terminals side by side on Avenida Ibañez and Avenida Andrés Avelino Cáceres. Most people leave out of the older Terminal Terreste, where most bus companies have offices, while the newer terminal Terrapuerto sees less traffic.

In Arequipa the airport is large and it's easy to hail a taxi to your hotel. Many hotels also offer pick-up and drop-off. The cost is about S/15.

PRECAUTIONS Wear comfortable walking shoes, and bring a hat, sunscreen, a Spanish dictionary, some small change, and a good map of town. Be streetsmart in the Arequipa market area—access your cash discreetly and keep your valuables close. At 2,300 meters (7,500 feet) Arequipa is quite high. If you're coming directly from Lima or from the coast, carve out a day or two for acclimatization.

ESSENTIALS

CURRENCY **Banco Continental BBVA** (⊠ *San Francisco 108*). **Banco de Trabajo** (⊠ *Calle Moral 201*). **Banco de Crédito BCP** (⊠ *San Juan de Dios 123* ☎ *054/283–741*). **Caja Municipal Arequipa** (⊠ *La Merced 106*). **Scotiabank** (⊠ *Mercaderes 410*).

INTERNET **C@tedral Internet** (⊠ *Pasaje Catedral 101* ☎ *054/282–074*). **Cybermarket** (⊠ *Santa Catalina 115* ☎ *054/284–306*).

MAIL **Serpost Arequipa** (⊠ *Calle Moral 118* ☎ *054/215–247* ⊕ *www.serpost.com.pe* ☾ *Mon.–Sat. 8–8, Sun. 9–2*). **DHL** (⊠ *Santa Catalina 115* ☎ *054/234–288*).

MEDICAL **Clínica Arequipa SA** (⊠ *Puente Grau y Av. Bolognesi* ☎ *054/253–416 or 054/253–424*). **Hospital Goyeneche** (⊠ *Av. Goyeneche s/n, Cerado* ☎ *054/231–313*). **Honorio Delgado Espinoza Regional Hospital** (⊠ *Av. A. Carrión s/n* ☎ *054/231–818, 054/219–702, or 054/233–812*).

POLICE **Police** (⊠ *Av. Emmel 106, Yanahuara* ☎ *054/254–020*). **Policía de Tourismo** (⊠ *Jerusalén 315* ☎ *054/201–258*).

RENTAL CAR **Akal Rent A Car** (⊠ *Av. Bolognesi 903 Cayma* ⊕ *www.akalrentacar.com*). **Avis Arequipa** (⊠ *Ugarte 216* ⊕ *www.avisperu.com*). **Exodo** (⊠ *Manuél Belgrado F-1, Urb. Alvarez Thomas* ☎ *054/423–756*). **Hertz** (⊠ *Palacio Viejo 214*, ☎ *054/282–519* ⊕ *www.hertz.com* ⊠ *Rodriguez Ballón Airport* ☎ *054/443–576*).

TAXI **Taxi Turismo Arequipa** (☎ *054/458–888 or 054/459–090* ⊕ *www.taxiturismo. com.pe*). **454545** (☎ *054/454–545*).

VISITOR INFO **Iperu Oficina de Información Turística** (⊠ *Portal de la Municipalidad 110, Plaza de Armas*, ✑ *iperuarequipa@promperu.gob.pe* ⊠ *Santa Catalina 210, Casona Santa Catalina* ☎ *054/221–227* ⊠ *Rodríguez Ballón Airport,, 1st fl., Main Hall* ☎ *054/444–564*). **Touring and Automobile Club of Peru** (⊠ *Goyeneche 313* ☎ *054/603–131 or 054/603–333* ✑ *arequipa@touringperu.com.pe*).

WHAT TO SEE

❸ **Casa del Moral.** One of the oldest architectural landmarks from the Arequipa Baroque period was named for the ancient mora tree (mulberry tree) grows in the center of the main patio. One of the town's most unusual buildings, it now houses the Banco Sur, but it's open to the public. Over the front door, carved into a white sillar portal, is the Spanish coat of arms and includes a baroque-mestizo design that combines puma heads with darting snakes from their mouths—motifs found on Nazca textiles and pottery. Inside the house is like a small museum with alpaca rugs and soaring ceilings, polished period furniture, and a gallery of colonial period Cusco School paintings. Originally a lovely old colonial home, it was bought in the 1940s by the British consul and renovated to its former elegance in the early 1990s. ⊠ *Moral 318*

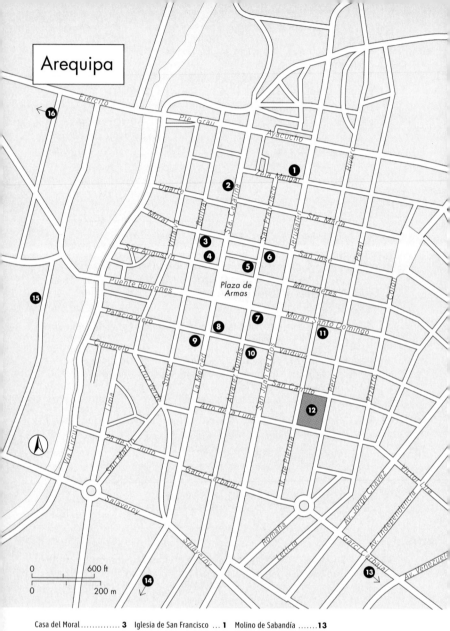

Arequipa

Plaza de Armas

0 ____ 600 ft
0 ____ 200 m

and Bolívar ☎054/214-907 ☒S/6
🕑 *Mon.–Sat. 9–5, holidays 9–1.*

➒ Casa Goyeneche. An attractive 1888 Spanish-colonial home, ask the guard for a tour, and you'll enter through a pretty courtyard and an ornate set of wooden doors to view rooms decorated in period-style antiques and Cusco School paintings. ☒ *La Merced 201 y Palacio Viejo* ☎054/352–674 ☒*Free, but if you get a tour a small donation is expected* 🕑 *Weekdays 9:15–3:15.*

4

➏ Casa Tristan del Pozo. This small museum and art gallery was built in 1738 and is now the Banco Continental. Look for the elaborate puma heads spouting water. Inside you'll find colonial paintings, ornate Peruvian costumes, and furniture. ☒*San Francisco 108* ☎054/21–2209 ☒*Free* 🕑 *Weekdays 9:15–12:45 and 4–6:30.*

➍ Casona Iriberry. Unlike the other mansions, Casona Iriberry has religious overtones. Small scriptures are etched into its structure, exemplifying Arequipa's catholic roots. The back of the house is now the Centro Cultural Cháves la Rosa, which houses some of the city's most important contemporary arts venues, including photography exhibits, concerts, and films. The front of the compound is filled with colonial-period furniture, paintings, and decor. ☒*Plaza de Armas, San Augustin y Santa Catalina* ☎054/20–4482 ☒*Free to look around, admission price for certain events* 🕑 *Mon.–Sat. 9–1 and 4–8.*

➎ ★ Catedral. You can't miss the imposing twin bell towers of this 1612 cathedral, whose facade guards the entire eastern flank of the Plaza de Armas. ■ TIP➔As the sun sets the imperial reflection gives the Cathedral an amber hue. The inside has high-vaulted ceilings above a beautiful Belgian organ. The ornate wooden pulpit, carved by French artist Rigot in 1879, was transported here in the early 1900s. In the back, look for the Virgin of the Sighs statue in her white wedding dress, and the figure of Beata Ana de Los Angeles, a nun from Santa Catalina monastery who was beatified by Pope John Paul II when he stayed in Arequipa in 1990. A fire in 1844 destroyed much of the cathedral, as did an 1868 earthquake, so parts have a neoclassical look. In 2001 another earthquake damaged one of the bell towers, which was repaired to match its sister tower. ☒*Plaza de Armas, between Santa Catalina and San Francisco* ☎054/23–2635 ☒*S/7* 🕑 *Daily 7:30–11:30 and 4:30–7:30.*

⓯ Convento de la Recoleta. One of Peru's most extensive and valuable libraries is in this 1648 Franciscan monastery. With several cloisters and museums on-site, it's a wonderful place to research regional history and culture. Start in the massive, wood-paneled, wood-floored library, where monks in brown robes quietly browse among 20,000 ancient books and maps, the most valuable were printed before 1500 and are kept in glass cases. Pre-Columbian artifacts and objects collected by missionaries to the Amazon are on display, as is a selection of elegant colonial and religious artwork. Guides are available, just remember to tip. To reach the monastery, cross the Río Chili by Puente Grau. It's a 10- to 15-minute walk from the Plaza de Armas. ⊠ *Recoleta 117* ☎ *054/27–0966* 💲 *S/2* 🕑 *Mon.–Sat. 9–noon and 3–5.*

❼ Iglesia de la Compañía. Representative of 17th-century religious archi-tecture, the complex was built by the Jesuits in 1573. ■ **TIP→** A series of bone-white buildings incorporate many decorative styles and touches. The detail carved into the sillar arcades is spectacular. The side portal, built in 1654, and main facade, built in 1698, show examples of Andean mestizo style with carved flowers, spirals, birds—and angels with Indian faces—along gently curving archways and spiral pillars. Inside, **Capilla St. Ignatius** (St. Ignatius Chapel) has a polychrome cupola and 66 canvases from the Cusco School, including original 17th-century oil paintings by Bernardo Bitti. Hike up to the steeple at sunset for sweeping views of Arequipa. The former monastery houses some of the most upscale stores in the city and contains two cloisters, which can be entered from General Morán or Palacio Viejo. The main building is on the southeast corner of the Plaza de Armas. ⊠ *General Morán at Álvarez Tomás* ☎ *054/21–2141* 💲 *Chapel S/6* 🕑 *Church weekdays 9–12:30 and 3–6, Sat. 11:30–12:30 and 3–6, Sun. 9–12:30 and 5–6.*

❶ Iglesia de San Francisco. This 16th-century church has survived numer-ous natural disasters, including several earthquakes that cracked its cupola. Inside, near the polished silver altar, is the little chapel of the Sorrowful Virgin, where the all-important Virgin Mary statue is stored. ■ **TIP→** On December 8, during Arequipa's Feast of the Immaculate Con-ception, the Virgin is paraded around the city all night atop an ornate car-riage and surrounded by images of saints and angels. A throng of pilgrims carry flowers and candles. Visit the adjoining convent S/5 to see Arequi-pa's largest painting and a museum of 17th-century religious furniture and paintings. ⊠ *Zela 103* ☎ *054/223–048* 💲 *Free* 🕑 *Church: Mon.–Sat. 7 AM–9 AM and 5–8, Sun. 7–noon and 5–8. Convent: Mon.–Sat. 9–12:30 and 3:30–6. Closed Sun.*

⓫ Iglesia y Convento de Santo Domingo. With hints of Islam in its elegant brick arches and stone domes, this cathedral carries an aura of ele-gance. Step inside to view simple furnishings and sunlight streaming through stained-glass windows as small silver candles flicker along the back wall near the altar. A working Dominican monastery is in back. ⊠ *Santo Domingo y Piérola* ☎ *054/213–511* 💲 *Free* 🕑 *Weekdays 6:45–noon and 3–7:45, Sat. 6:45–9 AM and 3–7:45, Sun. 5:30 AM–1.*

⓮ La Mansión del Fundador. First owned by the founder of Arequipa Don Garcí Manuel de Carbajal, La Mansión del Fundador is a restored colo-nial home and church. Alongside the Río Sabandía, the sillar-made home perches over a cliff and is about 20 minutes from the center. Said to have been built for Carbajal's son, it became a Jesuit retreat in the 16th cen-tury and in the 1800s was remodeled by Juan Crisostomo de Goyeneche y Aguerreverre. While intimate, the chapel is small and simple, but the home is noted for its vaulted arch ceilings and spacious patio. There's also a cafeteria with a bar on-site. To reach the home, go past Tingo

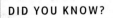

DID YOU KNOW?

You can look for the marriage of classic church styles with Andean details carved into the archways of the 16th century-built Igelsia de la Compañía.

Courtyard in Monasterio de Santa Catalina, Arequipa.

along Avenida Huasacanche. ⊠*Av. Paisajesta s/n, about 6.5 km outside of Arequipa, Socobaya* ☎*054/442–460* ✉*S/9* ⊘*Daily 9–5.*

⑫ Mercado San Camilo. This jam-packed collection of shops sells everything from snacks and local produce to clothing and household goods. You can find it around Perú, San Camilo, Piérola, and Alto de la Luna. ⊠*San Camilo 352* ☎*No phone* ✉*Free* ⊘*Daily 7–5.*

⑬ Molino de Sabandía. There's a colorful story behind the area's first stone *molina* (mill), 7 km (4 mi) southeast of Arequipa. Built in 1621 in the gorgeous Paucarpata countryside, the mill fell into ruin over the next century. Famous architect Luis Felipe Calle was restoring the Arequipa mansion that now houses the Central Reserve Bank in 1966 when he was asked to work on the mill project. By 1973 the restoration of the volcanic-stone structure was complete—and Calle liked the new version so much that he bought it, got it working again, and opened it for visitors to tour. Bring your swimsuit and walking shoes in good weather; there's a pool and trails around the lovely countryside. Adjoining the site is Yumina, which has numerous Inca agricultural terraces. If you're not driving, flag a taxi for S/16 or take a colectivo from Socabaya in Arequipa to about 2 km (1 mi) past Paucarpata. ⊠*8 km (5 mi) south of Arequipa, Sabandia,* ☎*No phone* ✉*S/7* ⊘*Daily 9–6.*

② **Monasterio de Santa Catalina.** A city unto itself, this 5-acre complex of
Ⓒ mud-brick, Iberian-style buildings surrounded by vibrant fortress like
Fodor'sChoice walls and separated by neat, open plazas and colorful gardens, is a
★ working convent and one of Peru's most famed cultural treasures.
■TIP➜Founded in 1579 and closed to the public for the first 400 years, Santa
Catalina was an exclusive retreat for the daughters of Arequipa's wealthiest
colonial patrons. Visitors can catch a peek at life in this historic monastery. Narrow streets run past the Courtyard of Silence, where teenage
nuns lived during their first year, and the Cloister of Oranges, where
nuns decorated their rooms with lace sheets, silk curtains, and antique
furnishings. Though about 400 nuns once lived here, fewer than 30 do
today. Admission includes a one-hour guided tour (tip S/10–S/20) in
English. Afterward, head to the cafeteria for the nuns' famous *torta de
naranja* (orange cake), pastries, and tea. There are night tours on Tuesday and Thursday, but check the times before you go, as they sometimes
change. ⊠ *Santa Catalina 301* ☎ *054/229-798* 🎟 *S/30* ⊗ *Daily 9–5;
last entry at 4; night tours Tues. and Thurs., 7–9.*

⑩ **Museo Arqueológico.** With a solid collection of native pottery and textiles, human-sacrificed bones, along with gold and silver offerings
from Inca times, this archaeology museum at the Universidad de San
Augustín provides a background on local archaeology and ruins. Apply
to the director for an appointment to visit; once you're approved, you'll
have an expert guide to tell all the stories behind the displays. ⊠ *Av.
Independencia, between La Salle y Santa Rosa* ☎ *054/288–881* 🎟 *S/3*
⊗ *Weekdays 8:15–4:15.*

⑧ **Museo Santuarios Andinos.** Referred to as the Juanita Museum, this fasci-
Fodor'sChoice nating little museum at the Universidad Católica Santa Maria holds the
★ frozen bodies of four young girls who were apparently sacrificed more
than 500 years ago by the Inca to appease the gods. The "Juanita"
mummy, said to be frozen around the age of 13 was the first mummy
found in 1995 near the summit of Mt. Ampato by local climber Miguel
Zarate and anthropologist Johan Reinhard. ■TIP➜When neighboring Volcán Sabancaya erupted, the ice that held Juanita in her sacrificial
tomb melted and she rolled partway down the mountain and into a cra-
ter. English-speaking guides will show you around the museum, and
you can watch a video detailing the expedition. ⊠ *La Merced 110*
☎🕾 *054/215–013* 🎟 *S/11* ⊗ *Mon.–Sat. 9–6, Sun. 9–3.*

⑯ **Yanahuara.** The eclectic little suburb of Yanahuara, northwest of the
★ city, is perfect for lunch or a late afternoon stroll. The neighborhood
is above Arequipa and has amazing views over the city at the lookout
constructed of sillar stone arches. On a clear day views of volcanos El
Misti, Chachani, and Picchu can be had. Stop in at the 1783, mestizo-
style Iglesia Yanahuara. The interior has wrought-iron chandeliers and
gilt sanctuaries surrounding the nave. Ask to see the glass coffin that
holds a statue of Christ used in parades on holy days. To reach Yanahuara, head across the Avenida Grau bridge, then continue on Avenida
Ejército to Avenida Lima, and from here, it's five blocks to the Plaza.
It's a 15-minute walk or an 8-minute cab ride from the city center.

WHERE TO EAT

Comida Arequipa (Arequipan cuisine) is a special version of *comida criolla*. Perhaps the most famous dish is *rocoto relleno*, a large, spicy red pepper stuffed with meat, onions, and raisins. Other specialties to try are *cuy chactado* (roasted guinea pig), and *adobo* (pork stew), a local cure for hangovers. Picanterías are where locals head for good, basic Peruvian meals and cold Arequipeña beer served with *cancha* (fried, salted corn).

The west side of the Plaza de Armas has dozens of restaurants along the balcony above the Portal San Augustín. The first blocks of Calle San Francisco and Calle Santa Catalina north of the Plaza de Armas, are lined with cafés, restaurants, and bars.

¢ ✕ **Café Peña Anuschka.** European expats and travelers craving the sour flavorings of German cuisine frequent this busy, dinner-only restaurant. You can also drop in after supper for a fruity cocktail or coffee and a freshly baked German pastry. The café, open 7–9 PM, transforms into a peña with live music Friday and Saturday nights. ⊠*Santa Catalina 204* ☎*054/213–221* ⊟*No credit cards* ☉*Closed Sun. No lunch.*

¢ ✕ **La Canasta.** Follow the scent of fresh baguettes to this bright little bakery where crusty French loaves are baked twice a day. Settle into the courtyard with a friend to trade tastes of grainy, buttered slices, and small sweets. You'll also find such Peruvian starches as *pan de yema* (regional brioche) and *pan de tres cachets* (a croissant filled with dulce de leche). ⊠*Jerusalén 115* ☎*054/204–025* ⊟*No credit cards* ☉*Closed Sun.*

¢ ✕ **Cusco Coffee Company.** If you're missing home, this Starbucks-esque coffee shop, owned by a Peruvian and American couple, will fix any caffeine craving. You can order-up fresh ground coffee drinks, or if tea is your thing, go for a mate (try the eucalyptus), and there's a small selection of desserts. Comfortable leather couches make this a great place to plan your day or read the International Herald. ⊠*La Merced 135* ☎*054/281–152* ⊟*AE, D, MC, V.*

¢–$ ✕ **Fory Fay Cevicheria.** Ask any Arequipeño to name their favorite fish **Fodor'sChoice** joint and Fory Fay tops the list. For more than 22 years they've served ★ some of the freshest ceviche (raw fish marinated in lime juice) around. Its owner, the personable Alex Aller, grew up in the coastal port of Mollendo and travels there daily to check on the catch. Fishing bric-a-brac and photos of New York, where Aller once lived, line the walls. ⊠*Alvarez Thomas 221* ☎*054/242–400* ⊟*AE, MC, V.*

¢ ✕ **Helados Artika.** The small, retro-style *helados* (ice-cream) café next ★ to La Compañía is the perfect stop after shopping around town. We recommend the famous Arequipeño *queso* cheese ice cream—it's sweet milk with cinnamon and a dash of coconut. If you're in for a fruitier treat go for a scoop of the guanabana. Open from 8 AM until 10 PM. ⊠*Morán 120* ☎*054/284–915* ⊟*No credit cards.*

¢ ✕ **Lakshmivan.** A herbivore's paradise, this tasty vegetarian restaurant will delight any traveler in search of leafy greens. Inexpensive and mostly organic, it's been an Arequipa staple for more than 25 years. Specializing in soups and salads (16 different kinds), all meals fuse

Short Trips from Arequipa

Reserva Nacional Salinas y Aguada Blanca. Herds of beige-and-white vicuñas, llamas, and alpacas graze together on the sparse plant life in the midst of the open fields that encompass this vast nature reserve of dessert, grass, and lakes. Wear good walking shoes for the uneven terrain and bring binoculars. Also bring a hat, sunscreen, and a warm jacket, as the park sits at a crisp 3,900 meters (12,800 feet). The reserve is 35 km (22 mi) north of Arequipa, just beyond El Misti. If you're headed to Colca Canyon from Arequipa, you have to pass through the reserve to get there.

Yura. About a half-hour drive from Arequipa, this serene little town is settled in the western foothills of the Volcán Chachani. Take the road 27 km (17 mi) farther to reach the famous thermal baths where you can take a dip in naturally heated water that ranges from 70 to 82°F. You can soak in any weather and enjoy a picnic along the river in summertime. If you don't bring your own food, you can lunch at the Hotel Libertador. Admission to the hot springs is S/10, and they're open daily from 6 AM sunrise until 3 PM. From San Juan de Dios, you can catch buses to Yura for S/3.

healthy ingredients with Peruvian flavors. You can sit outside in the courtyard among the colorful blossoms and birds, or inside, amid dazzling watercolor portraits by local artists. ⊠*Jerusalén 408* ☎*054/228–768* ▭*No credit cards.*

$ ✕**Ka Hing.** Fondly referred to as "El Chifa" by locals, this was the first real Chinese restaurant in town. Aside from traditional Chinese food, dishes fuse Chinese with indigenous Peruvian delights, like *arroz chaufa,* rice with native Peruvian vegetables and sautéed meats. It's a favorite of families, so make reservations for weekends and holidays. ⊠*Dolores 144* ☎*054/247–500* ▭*AE, MC, V.*

¢ ✕**Mandala.** Tasty vegetarian comfort foods at this innovative eatery will have vegans rejoicing. Whether it's soy pizza, soy curry, or soy burgers, there's almost an endless menu of soy delights, and gluten is popular, too. Open for breakfast, lunch, and dinner, this Peruvian-style restaurant serves creative vegetarian fare from Arequipan criolla to pastas to Chinese dishes and desserts. The healthy, natural ingredients result in a low-calorie menu that can offset a night of empañadas and pisco. ⊠*Jerusalén 207* ☎*054/229–974* ▭*No credit cards.*

$–$$$ ✕**El Mesón del Virrey.** This spacious upscale restaurant is donned in
★ antiqued Spanish-colonial motif. The meat-heavy menu is infused with Italian and coastal influences. ■**TIP➜Quinoa con Camarones (quinoa with shrimp) is one of the best dishes in Arequipa.** Much like a risotto, the quinoa is cooked in a creamy tomato sauce with vegetables and a large fresh jumbo-size shrimp that looks more like a lobster. Lamb, beef, alpaca, and ostrich can also be enjoyed. The pisco sour is one of the best around. Hear live music nightly from 8 to 10. ⊠*San Francisco 305* ☎*054/202–080* ▭*AE, D, MC, V.*

¢ ✕**Mixto's Cebichería.** Above the Catedral, this ultraromantic spot serves up some great seafood dishes. Ceviche is the focus, but you'll also find shellfish empañadas and mixed stews. They also serve pastas, salads, and grilled meats. It's not the culinary gem it once was, but the food remains good and it's a beautiful spot. On the terrace above the Cathedral entrance, the views of the city and El Misti are stunning. ⊠ *Pasaje Catedral 115* ☎ *054/205–343* ⊟ *AE, MC, V.*

$ ✕ **Nina Yaku.** This exclusive novo-Andino restaurant creates innovative Peruvian-style pastas, meats, and vegetarian dishes, all presented artfully. Drizzled in flavorful sauces, from sweet and tangy to savory and rich, the alpaca and beef are especially appetizing. It's a relaxing spot for after-dinner cocktails; ask for the *vino caliente*, mulled hot red wine. Reservations accepted. ⊠ *San Francisco 211* ☎ *054/281–432* ⊟ *AE, D, MC, V* ⊘ *Closed Sun.*

¢–$$$ ✕ **Las Quenas.** This rustic restaurant, filled with antiques and musical instruments, offers complete immersion into Arequipan life and traditions. Lunch and tea are served daily, but set dinners are the specialty, served nightly except Sunday to the accompaniment of a live folkloric performance. Dinners start at 8, and there's an extra S/5 charge if you stay for the music, which lasts until after midnight. ⊠ *Santa Catalina 302* ☎ *054/281–115* ⊟ *AE, DC, MC, V* ⊘ *closed Sun.*

¢–$ ✕ **Sambambaia's.** Specializing in classic Andean meat and fish dishes, try the chef's favorite, a tender, juicy lomo al vino tinto, but if you're craving more familiar fare, order a wood-oven pizza or the grilled chicken. ■ **TIP➔Live Latin jazz plays on Friday nights**. If you're not eating dinner, you can pay S/5 for the performance, which begins at 8. In the quiet residential neighborhood of Vallecito, it's a 10-minute walk from the Plaza de Armas. Reservations accepted. ⊠ *Luna Pizarro 304, Vallecito* ☎ *054/223–657* ⊟ *AE, DC, MC, V.*

$–$$$ ✕ **Sol de Mayo.** This charming garden restaurant in the colonial Yana-
★ huara neighborhood is worth the expense to taste true Arequipan cooking. Specialties include *ocopa arequipeña* (boiled potato slices in spicy sauce and melted cheese), and *rocoto relleno* (spicy peppers stuffed with cheese, meat and raisins). Only open for lunch. ⊠ *Jerusalén 207, Yanahuara* ☎ *054/254–148* ⊟ *AE, D, MC, V.*

¢ ✕ **Sulz.** Come hungry to this spacious, elegant restaurant that serves Arequipan food at its best. Enormous rooms packed with tables accommodate the flood of local families and tourists. If you can't decide what to order from the extensive menu, choose the Triple, which includes *rocoto* (a large red chili pepper), *chicharran* (pork rind), and *patitas de carnero* (mutton in sauce). There's a S/25 fee for patrons on weekend and holiday nights, when the live orchestra plays to those on the dance floor. ⊠ *Progreso 202A* ☎ *054/449–787* ⊟ *No credit cards.*

$ ✕ **Tradición Arequipeña.** It may be a S/8 taxi ride to this restaurant in
Fodor's Choice the Paucarpata district, but locals come in droves for the fantastic
★ Arequipan food. The decor is Peruvian country, but the flavors lean toward Creole. Get ready for *cuy chactado* (deep-fried guina pig) and *ocopa arequipeña* (potato-based dish with garlic, olives, onion, and fresh cheese). If you crave seafood, try the *Chupe de Camarones* (a creamy shrimp chowder). Open from noon to 7, it's primarily a lunch-only venue Sunday through Thursday, but on Friday and Saturday it doesn't close until 10 (sometimes later) when live music can be heard,

Where to Stay & Eat in Arequipa

KEY

❶ Restaurants

① Hotels

Plaza de Armas

| 0 | 600 ft |
| 0 | 200 m |

Restaurants ▼

Café Peña Anuschka **7**
La Canasta **5**
Cusco Coffee Company **3**
Fory Fay **2**
Helados Artika **4**
Ka Hing **20**
Lakshmivan **16**
Mandala **10**

El Mesón del Virrey **11**
Mixto's Cebichería **6**
Nina Yaku **9**
Las Quenas **14**
Sambambaia's **1**
Sol de Mayo **17**
Sulz **18**
Tradición Arequipeña **19**

La Trattoria del
Monasterio **15**
El Turko II **12**
Zig Zag **8**
Zig Zag Creperie **13**

Hotels ▼

Casa Andina Private
Collection Arequipa **4**
Casa Arequipa **5**
La Case de Melgar **3**
La Casa de Mi Abuela **1**
Hostal Santa Catalina **2**

including an orchestra on Saturday nights. Reservations recommended. ⊠*Dolores 111, Paucarpata* ☎*054/426–467* ☐*AE, D, MC, V.*

Fodor'sChoice ✕**La Trattoria del Monasterio.** Designed by Gaston Acurio, of Lima's elite
★ Astrid y Gaston restaurant, the Italian food is some of the best in Peru. Its location in the Monasterio de Santa Catalina (the entrance is outside the compound) is enough to make this place special. Homemade pastas, raviolis, gnocchi, risottos, paired with seafood, meats and creative, savory sauces are offered. There's an extensive wine list. ⊠*Santa Catalina 309* ☎*054/204–062* ☐*AE, V.*

¢–$$ ✕**El Turko II.** Artsy and hip, this café serves up a flavorful fusion of Mediterranean and Turkish fare with a distinct Peruvian twist. Known for their kebab plates, we also suggest trying the tangy red pepper and eggplant sauce with grape leaves and rice. The chain of restaurants include El Turko, El Turko III, Istanbul, and Fez, which all adorn Calle San Francisco, accept for El Turko III, which can be found at the airport. There isn't too much variation among the restaurants, but El Turko II has the most variety, and is the only one to take credit cards. ⊠*San Francisco 315* ☎*054/215–729* ☐*AE, D, MC, V.*

¢ ✕**Zig Zag Creperie.** This artistic, Euro-styled restaurant offers more than 100 crêpes, filled with a veriety of sauces, as entrées and desserts. Little sister to the Zig Zag restaurant on Calle Zela, look for such crêpe specialties as the Cubana, filled with banana slices, sugar, and rum. Exotic fruit juices like the *boa–boa* (tropical fruit punch) can be had, as can a glass of vino (wine) or high-grade espresso drinks. Check out the terrace for great views of the Monastery de Santa Catalina and volcanos. Look for the restaurant in the Alianza Francesa compound. Open until 11:30. ⊠*Santa Catalina 208* ☎*054/206–620* ⊕*www.zigzagrestaurant.com* ☐*AE, D, MC, V.*

$–$$$ ✕**Zig Zag Restaurant.** Everything at Zig Zag—from its grand iron spiral staircase to its novo-Andino cuisine, extensive wine list and decadent desserts—is done with exquisite detail and attention. Using a fusion of gourmet techniques from the Alps and Andes, the menu is a harmonious mix of fresh local foods. Try the quinoa potato gnocchi, the meat fondue or the notable Trios, a prime cut of three meats: alpaca, ostrich, and beef, slow-cooked and served on a hot stone with three dipping sauces. Call ahead and reserve one of the romantic balcony nooks. Top it all off with a chocolate mousse. ⊠*Zela 210* ☎*054/206–020* ⊕*www.zigzagrestaurant.com* ☐*AE, D, MC, V.*

WHERE TO STAY

$$$$ ⌂**Casa Andina Private Collection Arequipa.** Over-priced, but as upscale
★ as it gets, this is the place to go for top-of-line amenities. Housed in the city's former coin mint and national historical monument, this mid-size hotel opened in February 2008. Draped in Andean weaves and adorned with newfangled furniture, the rooms are large, yet cozy with plush modern bedding and elegant fixtures. Many rooms have romantic views of the city. Two colonial courtyards beg for a night walk. The gourmet restaurant serves creative novo-cuisine in its hip dining area and there's even a coin museum in honor of the building's

SOUNDS OF NIGHT

Peñas start the party early, around 8 or 9 PM, and many of the traditional restaurants sponsor a show on Friday and Saturday nights. A quiet restaurant can quickly turn into a Broadway-like show and you could very well become the star.

Most of the after-dark entertainment revolves around a number of cafés and bars near the city center along Calle San Francisco. Close by on Calle Zela, near the Catedral de San Francisco, bars seem to change daily,

and on Calle Santa Catalina you'll find small cafés that suit the more artsy, avant-garde folk. In a seedier section across town, teenagers and twentysomething Arequipeños head to discos and Salsatecas on Avenida Dolores.

4

history. **Pros:** New, comfortable bedding, large bathrooms, top-of-the-line. **Cons:** Expensive. ⊠ *Ugarte 403* ☎ *054/226–907* 🖷 *054/226–908* ⊕ *www.casa-andina.com* ⇙ *41 rooms, 1 presidential suite, 6 regular suites* ⚭ *In-room: no a/c, safe, refrigerator (some), DVD (some), Wi-Fi. In-hotel: restaurant, bar, laundry service, concierge, executive floor, public Internet, public Wi-Fi, airport shuttle, parking (fee), no-smoking rooms* ⦿*BP.*

$–$$

Fodor'sChoice

★

🏨 **Casa Arequipa.** With seven individually designed rooms, all donned in luxuriously high-quality motif and bedding, every last detail has been thought of—and applied. It's so personalized it's like you're visiting your best friends. This neocolonial boutique hotel books up fast and has won several awards. Filled with antique furnishings typical of the region, the hand-carved beds are piled high with alpaca blankets and 400 count sheets to counter the cool Andean air, and there are room heaters as well. The extra charm comes from those who run it, the hospitable staff (they'll retrieve your luggage from the airport if it's delayed, iron your clothes, and throw you a party for your birthday). A lavish breakfast buffet includes an assortment of coffee, tea, breads, fruits, and eggs, served in the dining room. In an upscale, residential neighborhood, it's a 10- to 15-minute walk from the center of town. **Pros:** Impeccable service, new and comfortable bedding, quiet neighborhood, large rooms, will arrange trips to Colca Canyon. **Cons:** Not near any stores, need a taxi at night. ⊠ *Av. Lima 409, Vallecito* ☎ *054/284–219, 202/518–9672 from U.S.* ⊕ *www.arequipacasa.com* ⇙ *7 rooms* ⚭ *In-room: no a/c, safe, DVD (some), Wi-Fi. In-hotel: restaurant, room service, bar, no elevator, laundry service, concierge, public Internet, public Wi-Fi, airport shuttle, parking (no fee), no-smoking rooms* ⊟ *AE, DC, MC, V* ⦿*BP.*

¢

★

🏨 **La Casa de Melgar.** In a beautiful tiled courtyard surrounded by fragrant blossoms and dotted with trees is this 18th-century home, believed to have been the one-time temporary residence of Mariano Melgar, Peru's most romantic 19th-century poet. This brightly blue and adobe-color Spanish-colonial has double rooms that have towering, vaulted

DID YOU KNOW?

El Misti is still an active volcano, though its last major eruption is believed to have been in the late 15th century.

brick ceilings, as well as private baths with hot water. The single suite has an original cookstove from its early days. A small on-site café, Flor de Café serves breakfast. **Pros:** High on the charm-scale, garden is great for relaxing, quiet, close to shops and restaurants. **Cons:** Rooms can get cold in rainy season, some have thin walls, front desk staff can be curt. ⊠*Melgar 108* ☏☐*054/222–459* ⊕*www.lacasademelgar. com* ⤴*30 rooms, 1 suite* ⅋*In-room: no a/c, safe. In-hotel: café, no elevator, laundry service, parking (no fee)* ❄CP ⊟V.

$ 🏨**La Casa de Mi Abuela.** An old stone wall circles this famous budget-
☺ traveler haunt. Extensive gardens, with 2,000 square meters of green
★ space grace this compound-like resort, but the English-speaking owners show their sense of humor in its centerpiece: a rusted Fiat van. The basic, wood-paneled standard rooms with well-worn furniture and tiny bathrooms do the job, but for only $10 more, the new junior garden suites—with contemporary furnishings and amenities—are much nicer. Regardless of the room, the elaborate breakfast buffet in the garden terrace is hard to top. ■**TIP➜At night you can clean up, read a book in a hammock, listen to the live piano music at the bar or take a dip in the pool.** It's a five- to seven-minute walk to the Plaza de Armas. **Pros:** Best breakfast buffet in town, free airport pick-up, large grounds, security gate. **Cons:** Standard room bathrooms are old and small, lots of tour groups. ⊠*Calle Jerusalén 606* ☏*054/241–206* ☐*054/242–761* ⊕*www.lacasademiabuela.com* ⤴*57 rooms* ⅋*In-room: no a/c, safe (some), kitchenette (some), refrigerator (some), Wi-Fi. In-hotel: restaurant, bar, pool, no elevator, laundry service, concierge, public Internet, public Wi-Fi, airport shuttle, parking (fee)* ⊟*AE, DC, MC, V* ❄BP.

¢ 🏨**Hostal Santa Catalina.** This bright-yellow hostel (and it's very much like a youth hostel, minus the youth part) offers shared and private quarters. The clean rooms, friendly owners, dependable hot water, and laundry facilities attract repeat customers—mostly European—year-round, so call ahead for reservations. Check out the stunning views on the roof terrace, or kick back in the central courtyard and read your guidebook while your clothes hang to dry in the sunshine. **Pros:** Great place to meet other travelers, central location, friendly staff. **Cons:** Old furniture and bedding, a bit noisy, communal bathrooms (not all). ⊠*Santa Catalina 500* ☏*054/243–705 or 054/221–766* ⤴*8 rooms, 3 dorms* ⅋*In-room: no a/c, no phone, safe (some). In-hotel: restaurant, no elevator, laundry facilities, concierge, public Internet, parking (no fee)* ⊟*No credit cards* ❄EP.

NIGHTLIFE

Ad Libitum (⊠*San Francisco 233* ☏*054/993–1034*) is a relaxed artistic heaven for thirsty locals in need of cheap cocktails and music. **Déja Vu** (⊠*San Francisco 319B* ☏*054/221–904*), open 9 AM to 4 AM, is a popular place to have a light meal. The two-floor venue has live Latin pop music and/or a DJ spinning every night with a dance club downstairs. **Café Bar Istanbul** (⊠*San Francisco 231-A* ☏*54/203–862, shares with El Turko, its owners*) is a tiny eclectic bar, great for martinis and small bites to eat. The **Instituto Cultural Peruano Norteamericano** (⊠*Melgar 109* ☏*054/243–201* ⊕*www.cultural.edu.pe*) hosts evening concerts of traditional and classical music. Down the street you'll find **Jenízaro**

(✉*Melgar 119* ☎*054/391–020*), a popular local bar with rock music and a small dance floor. **Kibosh** (✉*Zela 205* ☎*054/203–837*) has a lively night scene, good pizza and beer, and is a popular dance bar. For a more laid-back atmosphere, try the Canadian-owned **La Café Art Montréal** (✉*Calle Ugarte 210* ☎*054/931–2796*) for some live Latin jazz music Wednesday through Saturday. **La Troica** (✉*Calle Jerusalén 522-A* ☎*054/225–690*), open Monday through Saturday from 7 PM, specializes in Afro-Peruvian music, but also has groups from all over South America and sometimes a folkloric show on Saturday. For other good peña shows we recommend Las Quenas and Tradicion Arequipeña (see restaurants).

Although not as gay-friendly as Lima, there's a small progressive gay and lesbian scene. **SKP** (✉*Calle Villalba 205* ☎*054/934–7169 or 054/934–2108*), a gay and lesbian disco, opens at 8 PM, no cover charge before 11 PM. Closed Monday and Tuesday. **Open Night** (✉*Corner of Salaverry and Jorge Chavez* ☎*054/960–0981*) is a gay and lesbian bar/disco with live concerts on weekends.

SHOPPING

Arequipa has the widest selection of Peruvian crafts in the south. Alpaca and llama wool is woven into brightly patterned sweaters, ponchos, hats, scarves, and gloves, as well as wall hangings, blankets, and carpets. Look for *chullos* (woolen knitted caps with ear flaps and ties), transported from the Lake Titicaca region. Ceramic *toros* (bulls) are a local favorite to hold flowers or money, and you can even see them sitting in the rafters of homes to bring good luck.

At the Plaza San Francisco, the cathedral steps are the site of a daily flea market that has delicate handmade jewelry. Across the street at the Fundo el Fierro, crafts vendors tout bargains on clothing, ceramics, jewelry, and knickknacks in a cobblestone courtyard; deals can be had until about 8 PM. Arequipa is also an excellent place to purchase inexpensive, but well-constructed handmade guitars. Avenida Bolognesi has lines of such workshops. Behind the cathedral on the narrow Pasaje Catedral, boutiques sell jewelry and knickknacks made of Arequipa agate and along Santa Catalina there are many clothing stores.

Alpaca 21 (✉*Claustros de la Compañia, General Morán 118* ☎*054/239–624*) sells high-quality baby alpaca clothing and accessories, especially children's and men's. If you're looking for baby alpaca yarn **Alpa Wool** (✉*Santa Catalina 120-B* ☎*054/220–992*) carries a small selection of high-quality and cheap baby alpaca yarn. **Camping Equipment** (✉*Jerusalén 307* ☎*054/331–248*) carries everything for a last-minute outdoor adventure. **Curiosidades** (✉*Zela 207* ☎*054/232–703*) is a five-and-dime type of curiosity shop carrying everything from furniture and weapons to postcards and silver. For high-quality, reasonably priced jewelry, stop at **L. Paulet** (✉*Claustros de la Compañia, General Morán 118* ☎*054/287–786*). **Ranticuy Baby Alpaca** (✉*Claustros de la Compañia, General Morán 118* ☎*054/232–801*) intricately designed sweaters and accessories made with lots of bright colors.

PUNO & LAKE TITICACA

PUNO

975 km (609 mi) southeast of Lima.

Puno doesn't win any beauty pageants—brown unfinished cement homes, old paved roads, and a dusty desert has been the landscape for years. It's a sharp contrast to Puno's immediate neighbor, Lake Titicaca. Some people arrive in town, and scram to find a trip on the lake. Don't let the dreary look of Puno stop you from exploring its shores; it's considered Peru's folklore capital.

Puno retains traits of the Aymará, Quechua, and Spanish cultures that settled on the northwestern shores of the lake. ■ TIP→**Their influence is in the art, music, dance, and dress of today's inhabitants, who call themselves "Children of the Sacred Lake."** Much of the city's character comes from the continuation of ancient traditions—at least once a month a parade or a festival celebrates some recent or historic event.

SAFETY
Walking around the port after dark is not smart. When the sun goes down, the port gets desolate and unsuspecting tourists become targets for crime. So if you're at the handicraft market or are getting back from an outing on the lake, and suddenly it's dusk, catch a cab.

GETTING AROUND
Restaurants, shops, Internet services, banks, and drug stores line the four-block pedestrian-only street Jirón Lima, between Pino Park (sometimes called Parque San Juan after the San Juan Bautista Church nearby) and the Plaza de Armas.

Puno has tricycle taxis, which resemble Asian tuk-tuks, and are driven by bicycle peddlers with a supped-up carriage and costs only S/1 to go nearly anywhere in the city. However, if you're heading to a mirador high up on the hill, and you don't want the peddler to keel over, take an auto taxi, which costs S/3.

The bus Terminal Terreste is at 1 de Mayo 703 and Bolivar and many companies also have offices here.

ESSENTIALS
BUS **Cruz del Sur** (✉ Terminal Terrestre C-10 ☎ 051/368–524 ⊕ www.cruzdelsur. pe). **CIVA** (✉ Terminal Terrestre C-35 ☎ 051/365–882). **Imexso** (✉ Terminal terrestre C-14 ☎ 051/369–514). **Inka Express** (✉ Jr. Melgar N 226, ☎ 051/365–654). **Panamericano** (✉ Terminal Terrestre C-12 ☎ 051/354–001).

CURRENCY **Banco de Crédito BCP** (✉ Jr. Lima 510 ☎ 051/352–119). **Banco Continental BBVA** (✉ 400 Jr. Lima). **Scotiabank** (✉ Plaza de Armas, corner of Duestra and Jr. Lima).

INTERNET **Choz@Net** (✉ Jr. Lima 339, 2nd Floor ☎ 051/367–195). **La Casa del Corregidor** (✉ Deustua 576 ☎ 051/351–921 ☉ Tues.–Sat. 10–10). **Top Net** (✉ 208 Duestra).

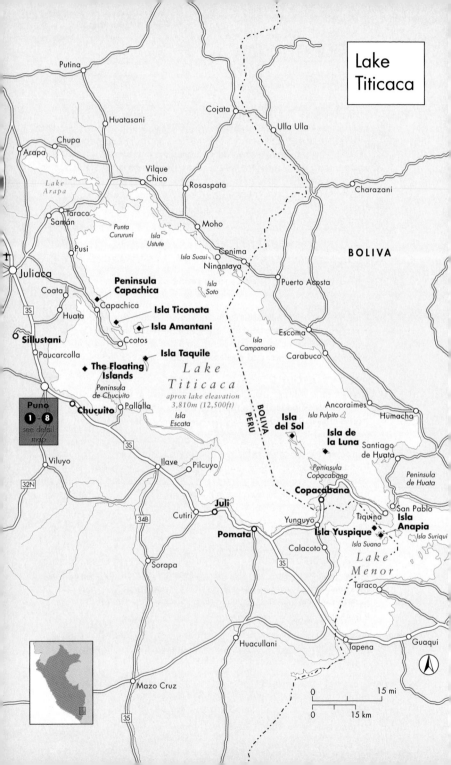

Lake
Titicaca

Putina

Huatasani

Cojata

Ulla Ulla

Chupa

Arapa

Vilque
Chico

Rosaspata

Charazani

*Lake
Arapa*

Taraco
Samán

Moho

BOLIVA

*Punta
Cururuni*

*Isla
Ustute*

Conima

Pusi

Ninantaya

Isla Suasi

Juliaca

**PENINSULA
CAPACHICA**

*Isla
Soto*

Puerto Acosta

Coata

Capachica

Isla Ticonata

Huata

3S

Isla Amantani

Escoma

Ccotos

*Isla
Campanario*

Sillustani

Carabuco

Paucarcolla

Isla Taquile

*Lake
Titicaca*
*aprox lake eleavation
3,810m (12,500ft)*

**The Floating
Islands**

*Peninsula
de Chucuito*

Ancoraimes

Isla Pulpito

Humacha

Puno
1 – **8**
see detail
map

Pallalla

Chucuito

*Isla
Escata*

**Isla
del Sol**

**Isla de
la Luna**

Santiago
de Huata

3S

Viluyo

Ilave

Pilcuyo

*Peninsula
Copacabana*

*Peninsula
de Huata*

32N

Copacabana

Juli

Cutiri

Yunguyo

Tiquina

San Pablo

**Isla
Anapia**

34B

Pomata

Calacoto

Isla Yuspique

Isla Suriqui

Isla Suana

*Lake
Menor*

Sorapa

Taraco

Huacullani

Tapena

Guaqui

Mazo Cruz

35

0   15 mi

0   15 km

BOLIVA
PERU

CLOSE UP

Festival Time!

While anytime of year is suitable for traveling to Puno and Lake Titicaca, visiting during a festival of dance, song, and parades is ideal. The streets are flooded with people; the folklore experience is passionate and very fun. Preserving the choreography of more than 140 typical dances, Puno's most memorable celebration is the *Festival of the Virgin de la Candelaria* (candle), held on February 2 and during carnival. A cast of several hundred elaborately costumed Andean singers, dancers, and bands from neighbor-

ing communities parades through the streets carrying the rosy-white complexioned statue of the Virgin. During the rest of the year, the statue rests on the altar of the San Juan Bautista Church. Puno week, as it's informally known occurs the first week of November and is equally fun. When Puno isn't having a celebration, it reverts to its true character, that of a small, poor Andean agriculture town. On the lake, Isla Taquile celebrates a vivid festival the last week of July.

MAIL **Serpost Puno** (✉ *Av. Moquegua 269* ☎ *051/351–141* 🕙 *Mon.–Sat. 8–8*).

MEDICAL **Carlos Monge Medrano Hospital** (✉ *Kil. 2 of Huancane Hwy., sector San Ramon, Juliaca* 🕙 *Daily 24 hours* ☎ *051/321—901, 051/321-750, 051/321-131, 051/321-370*). **Manuel Nuñez Butron National Hospital** (✉ *Av. El Sol 1022* 🕙 *Daily 24 hours* ☎ *051/351-021 or 051/369-286, 051/369-696*).

POLICE **Police** (✉ *Jr. Deustua 530* ☎ *051/366-271 or 051/353-988*). **Policía de Tourismo** (✉ *Jr. Deustua 538* ☎ *051/354-764, 051/354-774, or 051/353-3988*).

TAXI **Radio Taxi Milenium** (☎ *051/353-134*). **Servitaxi Turistico** (☎ *051/369-000*). **Tonocar Titikaka** (☎ *051/368-000*).

TRAIN **PeruRail** (✉ *Estacion Puno, La Torre 224* ☎ *084/238-722* ⊕ *www.perurail.com* 🕙 *Weekdays 7-5, weekends 7-noon*).

VISITOR INFO **Iperu Oficina Información Turística** (✉ *Corner of Jr. Deustua and Jr. Lima, Plaza de Armas,* ☎ *051/365-088* ✉ *iperupuno@promperu.gob.pe*).

WHAT TO SEE

❷ **Catedral.** Etchings of flowers, fruits, and mermaids playing an Andean guitar called the *charango* grace the entrance of the Spanish baroque-style church. Sculpted by Peruvian architect Simon de Asto, the 17th-century stone cathedral has one of the more eclectically carved facades of any church in the area. Plain on the inside, its main decorations are a silver-plated altar and paintings from the Cusco School. ✉ *Plaza de Armas* 🎟 *Free* 🕙 *Daily 7–noon and 3–6, Sat. 7–noon and 3–7.*

❶ **Conde de Lemos Balcony.** An intricately carved wooden balcony marks the home where viceroy Conde de Lemos stayed when he arrived in Puno to counter rebellion around 1668. Behind the Catedral it is today home of the National Culture Institute of Puno. ✉ *Corner of Calles Deustua and Conde de Lemos* 🎟 *Free* 🕙 *Weekdays 8:30-4.*

❸ **La Casa del Corregidor.** Reconstructed more than five times, this 17th-century colonial, once a chaplaincy is now a brightly colored cultural

Fodor's Choice ★

center. It was originally home to Silvestre de Valdés, a Catholic priest who served as a *corregidor* (a Spanish official who acts as governor, judge, and tax collector) and oversaw construction of the nearby Catedral. The house had a long history of changing owners until its present owner, Sra. Ana Maria Piño Jordán, bought it at public auction. ■ TIP➡ **Now a vibrant cultural locale, with an arts cooperative, it houses a fair-trade café and a few upscale handicraft stores.** The exhibition hall displays works by local artists, and hosts music events. ⊠ *Deustua 576* ☎ *051/351–921 or 051/365–603* ⊕ *www.casadelcorregidor.com. pe* ⊗ *Mon.–Sat. 9–10, Sun. 2–8.*

★ **Museo Carlos Dreyer.** An exhibit of 501 gold pieces, called the "Great
❹ Treasure of Sillustani" has classified the intimate museum as one of the most important regional archaeological museums in southern Peru. The museum is named for famed Puno painter and antiques collector, Carlos Dreyer Spohr. You can view the oil canvasses by Dreyer and explore exhibits of pre-Hispanic and colonial art, weavings, silver, copper works, delicate Aymará pottery, pre-Inca stone sculptures, and historical Spanish documents on the founding of Puno. ⊠ *Conde de Lemos 289* 📱 *S/15* ⊗ *Mon.–Sat. 9:30–7:30, Sun, 2–7:30.*

❼ **Cerrito de Huajsapata.** A statue honoring Manco Cápac, the first Inca and founder of the Inca empire, sits on this hill overlooking Puno. Legend has it that there are caves and subterranean paths in the monument, which connect Puno with the Koricancha Temple in Cusco. It's technically a 10-minute walk from town, but it's all uphill and a bit off the beaten path where a few robberies have been reported, so stick with a group or take a taxi. ⊠ *4 blocks southwest of Plaza de Armas.*

❺ **Iglesia San Juan Bautista.** This 18th-century church has been entrusted with the care of the *Virgin of the Candlemas,* the focus of Puno's most important yearly celebration in February, the Festival de la Virgen de la Candelaria. The statue rests on the main altar. ⊠ *Jr. Lima and Parque Pino.*

❽ **El Yavari.** The restored Victorian iron ship was built in Birmingham,
★ England, in 1861. It was subcontracted by the Peruvian Navy to patrol the waters of Titicaca, so it was dismantled and its 2,766 pieces and two crankshafts were loaded onto a freighter and shipped to the Peruvian Port of Arica on the Pacific coast, which today belongs to Chile. Mules and porters carried the pieces 290 mi through the Andes mountains to Puno. The journey took six years and it was Christmas Day 1870 before it was reassembled and launched on Lake Titicaca. Now a museum, it's docked at the end of a pier by the Sonesta Posada del Inca Hotel. After remaining idle for 40 years, the vessel took a trial run in 1999 after volunteers rebuilt its engine. ⊠ *Avenida Sesquicentenario 610, Sector Huaje, pier behind Posada del Inca Hotel* ☎ *051/369–329* ⊕ *www.yavari.org* 📱 *Donation* ⊗ *Daily 8–5.*

❻ **Museo de la Coca & Costumbres.** A hidden gem, this museum pays tribute
★ to the infamous coca leaf and Peruvian folklore. The quaint museum, tucked away on a second-floor building is sliced into rooms, one that houses the folklore exhibit and the other displays everything you'd

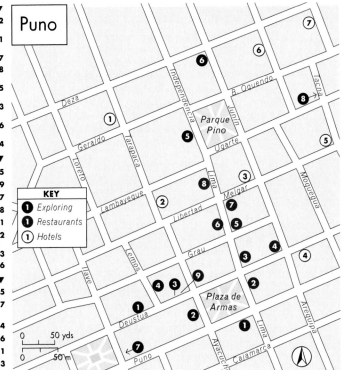

ever want to know about the coca leaf. Presented in English and Spanish, displays are well-constructed with educational videos and photographs. The mission is not to promote coca, but merely to share the plants' history and culture. You can enlist the help of a bilingual guide if you wish or mosey on your own. The folklore exhibit displays elaborately constructed costumes worn during festivals and shares the history behind the dances. ✉*Jr. Deza 301* ☎*051/977–0360* ⊕*www. museodelacoca.com* ✉*S/5* ☉*Daily 9–1 and 3–8.*

WHERE TO EAT

Many small, restaurants line Jirón Lima, and include a mix of novo-Andino and classic regional foods. On the menu you'll find fresh fish from the lake, an abundance of quinoa dishes, along with typical Peruvian fare like *lechón al horno o cancacho* (highly spiced baked suckling pig); *pesque o queso de quinua* (resembling ground-up barley), prepared with cheese and served with fish fillet in tomato sauce; *chairo* (lamb and tripe broth cooked with vegetables, and frozen-dried potato known as *chuño*). Particularly good are *trucha* (trout) and *pejerrey* (Kingfish mackerel) from the lake.

¢–$$
Fodor'sChoice
★

✗**Coco K'intu.** It's probably the best restaurant to hit town since Apu Salkantay opened its doors 13 years ago. Not surprising, both are owned by members of the Martinez family. ■TIP➔It's novo-Andino cuisine at its finest, taking traditional food and making creative, sophisticated, down-right delicious entrées. The food bursts with flavor, especially the *sopa incasica*, a thick, creamy quinoa soup with peppers and onions, and a kick of spice. Slow-cooked alpaca entrées include the *alpaca con salsa de maracuya*, a tender alpaca steak cooked in a passionfruit sauce. The creative concoctions go on and on. Open for breakfast, lunch, and dinner. ⊠ *Jr. Lima 401* ☎ *051/365–566* ▭ *V.*

¢–$$ ✕ **Restaurant Museo La Casona.** Museum-like, this quaint 17-year-old institution is filled with wrought-iron antiques and artwork including a display of antique irons and sewing machines. Divided into four intimate rooms, the polished hardwood floors, lace tablecloths, and burning candles is like having dinner at great-grandma's. Luckily there are no old home odors here, only savory aromas of hearty soups and grilled meats and fish. Try local fare, such as *lomo de alpaca* (alpaca steak) or one of their thick soups (the cream of quinoa is amazing) made with vegetables and meat or fish. Ask for the Menu Turistico and have a great set meal for S/25, and a pisco sour for less than S/6. ⊠ *Av. Lima 517* ☎ *051/351–108, or 051/967–9207* ▭ *AE, V.*

¢–$ ✕ **Apu Salkantay.** Dark rustic wooden fixtures and an adobe wood stove, along with a cozy ambience and modern novo-Andino cuisine, keep this candle-lighted restaurant a favorite with tourists and locals. While we think the best-tasting pizza is made here, there's a whole delectable menu to choose from. For lunch or dinner try the *Trucha ahumadas* (smoked trout), or the blackberry beef, an alpaca steak, fresh soup, or one of the flavorful vegetarian dishes, all prepared with natural ingredients. Service can be a little slow, but perhaps they're perfecting their product, so order-up a hot mulled wine and relax by the fire. ⊠ *Lima 425* ☎ *051/363–955* ▭ *V.*

¢–$ ✕ **Don Piero.** Colorful paintings of Quecha people partaking in various rituals hang above you as you enjoy such typical dishes as barbecued chicken, fresh fish (pejerrey and *trucha*—trout) fried in oil and garnished with potatoes and toasted chili peppers. Local musicians entertain on most nights. It's open for breakfast, lunch, and dinner. ⊠ *Lima 364* ☎ *051/365–943* ▭ *No credit cards.*

¢–$ ✕ **Mojsa.** The window seats overlooking the Plaza de Armas are for a romantic dinner or a cup of fresh local coffee. Mojsa, which mean delicious in Armaya language, serves reasonably priced novo-Andino cuisine, fused with fresh traditional and crilloa flavors. Tender, juicy cuts of grilled beef and alpaca for less than S/20 are favorties, but creative pastas and crispy brick-oven pizza are also good. Open for breakfast, lunch, and dinner. ⊠ *Lima 635, Plaza de Armas* ☎ *051/363–182.*

¢–$ ✕ **La Plaza.** A grand colonial dining room with hand-carved fixtures
★   gives this restaurant a sense of old-world Europe. Prices are inversely proportional to the large portions, so try a hearty regional dish like *chairo puneño* (soup with dehydrated potatoes and beef), *cuy* (guinea pig), or *trucha* (trout). A separate location named La Hosteria, two blocks away on Avenida Lima, has a similar menu. ⊠ *Jr. Puno 425, Plaza de Armas* ☎ *051/366–871* ▭ *AE, DC, MC, V.*

¢ ✕ **CECOVASA.** In La Casa del Corregidor, this charming and poetic café is run by a union of eight cooperatives and coffee producers who grow and sell organic fair-trade coffee. Grown locally, eight java varieties are available to taste, along with a collection of teas, cocktails, smoothies, and healthy café foods including salads, soups, sandwiches, along with more sweet treats like cakes and pies. A book exchange and sun-filled patio make this a great relaxation station. ⊠*Deustua 576, La Casa del Corregidor* 🕾*051/351–921* 🗖*No credit cards.*

WHERE TO STAY

Puno can be cold so bring warm clothes. Not even the fanciest hotels have internal heating systems, but most have portable electric heaters. Always ask about heat when you book and ask for extra blankets. Most hotels in the small towns outside Puno are run-down and not recommended.

$$$$
🕒
FodorsChoice
★
🔾**Casa Andina Private Collection Suasi.** An ecological paradise for those who can afford it, at this exclusive hotel on Isla Suasi on Lake Titicaca you can hike among wild llamas, canoe, study astronomy, learn Andean spirituality, marvel at flower-filled terraces, discuss ecosystems, or just relax with a massage. Rooms are comfortable and most have balconies. All meals are provided in the gourmet restaurant (or BBQ pit) and for an extra special treat, a private cottage comes with your own butler. It's three hours from Puno. **Pros:** Cultural activities, child-friendly. **Cons:** Charges extra for transportation. ⊠*Isla Suasi Lago Titicaca* 🕾*051/950–4235* 🖷*051/365–333* 🌐*www.casa-andina. com* 🛏*24 rooms, 2 suites* 🔾*In-room: no a/c, no phone, safe (some), kitchenette (some), Wi-Fi. In-hotel: restaurant, room service, bar, spa, beachfront, water sports, no elevator, laundry service, public Internet, public Wi-Fi, airport shuttle, no-smoking rooms* 🗖*AE, DC, MC, V* 🍴*FAP and AI.*

$$$$
★
🔾**Titilaka.** Peru's Inkaterra, an elite ecotourism hotel group, now has a property in Lake Titicaca. While the facade won't woo you, the sleek and luxurious inside matches the classic euro-contemporary motif Inkaterra is known for. All rooms have nice furnishings, high-quality linens, plasma TVs, and heated floors. The new resort is all-inclusive and offers an off-the-beaten-path location, overlooking the lake next to the Chucuito Peninsula, on Peninsula Titilaka, about a 30-minute boat ride from Puno. Titilaka offers excursions to the islands, gourmet cuisine, massage services, and a heated outdoor pool. **Pros:** All inclusive, heated floors. **Cons:** Secluded, far from Puno. ⊠*Huenccalla, Centro Poblado Menor de Titilaca, District of Plateria, Peninsula Titilaka* 🕾*800/422–5042 from USA, 511/610–0400 in Peru* 🌐*www.inkaterra. com* 🛏*18 suites* 🔾*In-room: refrigerator, Wi-Fi. In-hotel: restaurant, room service, bar, pool, spa, beachfront, water sports, no elevator, laundry service, concierge, executive floor, public Wi-Fi, airport shuttle, parking (no fee), no-smoking rooms* 🗖*AE, MC, V* 🍴*AI.*

$$$
★
🔾**Libertador Hotel Isla Esteves.** The Libertador, a gleaming white, futuristic-looking, low-rise hotel, which functions more like a resort, is 5 km (3 mi) from Puno. One of the area's most luxurious lodgings, it's on Isla Esteves, an island in Lake Titicaca, but which is connected to the mainland by a causeway. Rooms and bathrooms are all comfortable, large, clean, and modern, without any distinct ambience. While taxis are the only way to get into town, after a long day if you're too beat to head

into town, you're in luck because there's an upscale international restaurant, Los Uros, a coffee shop, and cozy bar that has beautiful night views, good pisco sours, and a fireplace. **Pros:** Knowledgeable staff, on the lake, heating, Jacuzzi and sauna. **Cons:** Five minutes from town, rooms lack charm. ⊠*Isla Esteves* ☎*051/367–780* ⊕*www.libertador. com.pe* ↻*111 rooms, 12 suites* ♿*In-room: safe, refrigerator (some), DVD (some), Wi-Fi. In-hotel: 2 restaurants, room service, bar, gym, beachfront, laundry service, concierge, executive floor, public Internet, public Wi-Fi, airport shuttle, parking (no fee), no-smoking rooms* ▭*AE, DC, MC, V* ⍂*BP.*

$$ ⊡**Casa Andina Private Collection** Out of the three Casa Andina properties in Puno, this lakeside hotel is the best. Just outside of town, the two-floor building has large stone and slate walls, and a fireplace in the lobby. Clean rooms and baths share a similar style and are basic, full of natural light, and have all modern amenities, even cribs for babies if needed. A restaurant serves up good novo-Andino food and the bar is probably too well-stocked. The only real downside: even with space heaters, it tends to get cold. **Pros:** Good atmosphere, oxygen tank, great terrace. **Cons:** Gets cold, rooms are small. ⊠*Av. Sesquicentenario 1970-1972, Sector Huaje* ☎*051/363–992* ☎*051/364–082* ↻*45 rooms, 1 suite* ♿*In-room: no a/c, safe, refrigerator (some), DVD (some), Wi-Fi. In-hotel: restaurant, room service, bar, laundry service, concierge, executive floor, public Internet, public Wi-Fi, airport shuttle, parking (no fee), no-smoking rooms* ▭*AE, DC, MC, V* ⍂*BP.*

$$ ⊡**Sonesta Posadas del Inca.** Weavings, polished wood, and native art give character to this thoroughly modern Sonesta hotel on the shores of Lake Titicaca. It's 5 km (3 mi) from the center of town and has its own dock that extends out into the lake with the *El Yavari*, the world's oldest motorized iron ship anchored at the end. Rooms are clean and plain. Eating in the hotel's restaurant, Inkafé is a pleasure, as large picture windows offer a panoramic view of the lake. It's one of few hotels in town that has accessible rooms for people with disabilities. **Pros:** On the lake, good heating, comfortable beds, near El Yavari. **Cons:** Five minutes from town, smallish rooms. ⊠*Sesquicentenario 610, Sector Huaje* ☎*051/364–111* ☎*051/363–672* ⊕*www.sonesta. com* ↻*62 rooms* ♿*In-room: safe, refrigerator (some), DVD (some), Wi-Fi (some). In-hotel: restaurant, room service, laundry service, concierge, executive floor, public Internet, public Wi-Fi, airport shuttle, parking (no fee), no-smoking rooms* ▭*AE, DC, MC, V* ⍂*BP.*

$ ⊡**Colon Inn.** With an air of old Europe, this Belgian-owned 19th-century republican-era inn is draped in dark mahogany wood and colonial furnishings. But at the center of this three-story hotel is a sky-lighted atrium with overflowing greenery and several tables. Rooms are clean and comfortable with outdated flowery comforters. All room sizes vary, from tiny to extra large, so ask to see your options. On the top floor a bar carries an impressive selection of European wines. The small restaurant prepares a quality breakfast buffet. Both eateries prepare meals throughout the day. **Pros:** A hospitable staff speaks English, free coca tea is always on hand, great water pressure. **Cons:** Dark ambience, small bathrooms. ⊠*Calle Tacna 290* ☎*051/351–432* ⊕*www.*

coloninn.com ⤶*22 rooms, 1 suite* ♿*In room: no/ac, safe, Wi-Fi. In-hotel: restaurant, bar, no elevator, laundry service, concierge, executive floor, public Internet, public Wi-Fi, airport shuttle, no-smoking rooms* ⊟*DC, MC, V* ⦿❘*BP.*

$ 🖃**Hotel Ferrocarril.** The original building dates from 1899, but continuous remodeling has kept it up-to-date in a kitschy sort of way. Large black-and-white tile floors decorate the lobby, and the overall feel is of a 1970s high school with extra wide hallways, tiered windows, and pink trim. Exquisitely clean, it's basic. All rooms have private baths with 24-hour hot water, and something most other hotels don't: central heating. It's a good budget choice. **Pros:** Near train station, friendly staff. **Cons:** Old beds and small rooms. ✉ *Av. La Torre 185* ☎*051/351–752* ⊕*www.hotelferrocarril.com* ⤶*30 rooms* ♿*In-room: no a/c, safe. In-hotel: restaurant, no elevator, laundry service, no-smoking rooms* ⊟*AE, MC, V* ⦿❘*CP.*

$ 🖃**Hotel Italia.** A lovely, flower-filled courtyard, rooftop terrace, and scrumptious restaurant are all pluses at this hotel a block from Parque Pino. Rooms are simple but comfortable, with parquet floors and wood furniture; those on the fourth floor have lake views. As the former "it" hotel no major renovations have occurred in several years to keep up with the more modern hotels. **Pros:** Friendly Peruvian–Italian owner is always around to help, excellent soups, active communal lounge. **Cons:** Furniture is old and bathrooms are small. ✉ *Theodoro Valcarcel 122* ☎*051/367–706* ⊕*www.hotelitaliaperu.com* ⤶*33 rooms* ♿*In-room: no a/c, safe (some). In-hotel: restaurant, bar, no elevator, laundry service, public Internet, airport shuttle, parking (no fee), no-smoking rooms* ⊟*MC, V* ⦿❘*CP.*

$ 🖃**Hotel La Hacienda.** Panoramic views of Lake Titicaca and its surroundings can be viewed from the endless window-filled restaurant atop of this Spanish-colonial hotel, two blocks from Plaza de Armas. All rooms are spacious, bright, and clean. The bedding, especially the pillows, is plush. Most rooms have big bay windows for a view of the city or lake. A grand spiral staircase extends through all six floors. **Pros:** Free Internet, large bathrooms, complimentary pisco sour upon arrival. **Cons:** Can be noisy along Avenida Deustra. ✉ *Deustua 297* ☎*051/365–134* ⊕*www.lahaciendapuno.com* ⤶*58 rooms* ♿*In-room: no a/c, safe, Wi-Fi. In-hotel: restaurant, room service, bar, laundry service, concierge, public Internet, public Wi-Fi, airport shuttle, no-smoking rooms* ⊟*DC, MC, V* ⦿❘*BP.*

$ 🖃**Qelqatani.** This small hotel on a quiet street about a five-minute walk from Jirón Lima is an affordable and cozy place to lay your head after a day on the lake. Rooms and private baths are large; beds are new; and all rooms have individual space heaters. In the morning a large breakfast spread is served and at night a lengthy cocktail menu can double your fun. **Pros:** Excellent staff, quiet good place to meet other travelers. **Cons:** Dark interior, carpets are getting old, Internet is slow. ✉ *Tarapacá 355* ☎*051/366–172* ⊕*www.qelqatani.com* ⤶*39 rooms, 3 suites* ♿*In-room: no a/c, safe, Wi-Fi. In-hotel: restaurant, bar, laundry service, public Internet, public Wi-Fi, airport shuttle, parking (no fee), no-smoking rooms* ⊟*AE, MC, V* ⦿❘*BP.*

¢–$ 📺**Intiqa Hotel.** Looking as if it were lifted out of Soho, all the rooms
★   are spacious, sleek, and modern, and have lots of natural light, flat-
screen TVs with Direct TV, plush brown bedding, and polished hardwood floors. Indigenous art hangs on the walls. Stained-glass windows,
which permeate light from the hotel's large atrium, line the hallways.
A service-oriented staff is helpful and can help plan local trips. **Pros:**
Big bathrooms, spacious rooms, new. **Cons:** Breakfast café doesn't have
enough seating. ⊠*Tarapacá 272* ☎*051/366–900* ⊕*www.intiqahotel.
com* ⇨*17 rooms* ⚒*In-room: no a/c, safe, Wi-Fi. In-hotel: restaurant,
laundry service, public Wi-Fi, airport shuttle, parking (no fee), no-
smoking rooms* ⊟*AE, MC, V* ⦿*CP.*

NIGHTLIFE

Classic Bar (⊠*Tarapaca 330* ☎*051/363–596*) has no frills, but it's a
favorite local hangout. For a more posh experience the **Colors Lounge**
(⊠*Lima 342* ☎*051/369–254*) is the most Manhattan-styled bar in
Puno and attracts an older crowd. Head to **Domino** (⊠*Libertad 437*)
for a Latin salsa dancing experience. After dinner the restaurant **IncaBar**
(⊠*Jr. Lima 348* ☎*051/368–031*) turns into a low-key lounge where
you'll find a thirties-and-over crowd. For live rock and pizza check
out **Kamizaraky Rock Pub** (⊠*Pasaje Grau 148*). One of the best pubs
in town, **Positive** (⊠*Jr. Lima 378, 1st fl.* ⊕*www.positive-bar.com*) is
a cozy watering hole that plays reggae and rock while serving up an
eclectic cocktail menu, which includes drinks like the "Amanti Island"
for a pricey S/12. **Pub Ekeko's** (⊠*Lima 365* ☎*051/365–986*) is a town
staple for soccer. When there are no games on, there's music and dancing. The quiet downstairs venue serves wood-fired pizza.

SHOPPING

For fine alpaca clothing head to the Peruvian retail chain **Alpaca 111**
(⊠*Jr. Lima 343* ☎*051/366–050*). Unique suede products with a Bolivian flair are sold at **Arte Inca Artesanias** (⊠*Jr. Lima 423* ☎*No phone*)
Casa del Artesano (⊠*Lima 549* ☎*No phone*) sells a modest selection
of locally made alpaca items, including sweaters, scarves, and ponchos.
Also look for Puno's signature pottery, the Torito de Pucara (Little Bull
from Pucará). The pot is a receptacle used to hold a mixture of the
bull's blood with chicha (a drink) in a cattle-branding ceremony. If you
don't find what you want here, just walk on down Calle Lima, as there
are more artisans' shops along the way.

■**TIP**➔**Never walk to the docks after the sun has set, robberies are frequent at night.** Model reed boats, small stone carvings, and alpaca-wool
articles are among the local crafts sold near the Port at Puno's **Mercado
Artesanal** (⊠*Av. Simon Bolivar and Jr. El Puerto* ☎*No phone*). If you
find you aren't dressed for Puno's chilly evenings, it's the place to buy
a good woolen poncho for less than US$10. Open 8–6. Make sure you
know where your wallet or purse is while you're snapping a photo of
the colorful market.

Punto Fino sells high-end silver jewelry, hats, and alpaca products
such as the premier Alpaka Studio clothing line. (⊠*Jr. Lima 423-B*

☎051/366-579). **Q'ori Ch'aska** (✉*Jr. Lima 435* ☎051/364–148) is a small store where you'll find ceramics and jewelry.

LAKE TITICACA

Forms Puno's eastern shoreline.

Stunning, unpredictable, and enormous, Lake Titicaca is a world of unique flora, fauna, cultures, and geology. Lago Titicaca, which means lake of the grey (titi) puma (caca) in Quechua, borders Peru and Bolivia, with Peru's largest portion to the northwest. While Peru boasts the largest port in Puno, Bolivia's side has Isla del Sol and Isla de la Luna, two beautiful islands with great views and Inca ruins.

The Bahía de Puno, separated from the lake proper by the two jutting peninsulas of Capaschica and Chucuito, is home to the descendents of the Uro people, who are now mixed with the Aymará and Quechua. The lakeshores are lush with totora reeds—valuable as building material, cattle fodder, and, in times of famine, food for humans.

Although it's generally cold, the beaming sun keeps you warm and if you don't watch it, burned.

GETTING AROUND
A boat is necessary for traveling the lake. Most people go to the islands with a tour, but colectivo boats in Puno Bay will transport you for S/10–S/25. Most boats are super slow, super old, and they won't leave port unless at least 10 people are smushed aboard. A four-hour trip will take only an hour in one of the newer speedboats that the higher-end tour companies now use.

TICONATA ISLAND
A hidden island in a corner of Lake Titicaca, Ticonata is one of the greener islands on the lake. It has a warm microclimate that allows lush green grass to grow, crops to bloom, and many birds to be spied. In 2004 the Quechua-speaking natives of this island were nearly gone—only two families remained on the island. But a community-based project began to teach locals how to use their resources for travel tourism. Today more than a dozen families have returned and ancient island practices are being taught to younger generations. Only a small number of visitors are allowed at a time and the focus of a trip is to help families farm and fish while learning the ancient traditions of the Ticonatas.

It's typically a two-day trip that starts by visiting the floating islands, then the Capachica Peninsula and Llachon, where you can hike through an original pre-Inca path or kayak in the lake. Following a picnic lunch, you head to Ticonata. ■TIP➜After helping families farm, or fish, you help prepare dinner, followed by a bonfire and native dances. In the morning you'll head to Amantani Island by rustic sailboats and then back to Puno. Most visits need to be arranged by Edgar Adventures. A group tour is easier to book, but a private tour is an option as is volunteering on the island for several days.

LLACHON PENINSULA

One of the peninsulas that form the bay of Puno, Llachon juts out on the lake near Amantani and Taquile. ■ TIP➜The land is dry and barren with rows of pre-Inca terraces, and original ancient paths and trails, which are great for exploring. You can venture out yourself from the port in Puno via water colectivo and then arrange a homestay once in Llachon, or for slightly more money, you can have a tour operator arrange the accommodations for you. By land back from Puno it's about 2–3 hours. Llachon is also a great place to kayak. Kayaking operator Titikayak has lots of trips around here.

ANAPIA & YUSPIQUE ISLAND

In the Winaymarka section of Lake Titicaca, near the Bolivian border are the Aymara-speaking islands of Anapia and Yuspique. This off-the-beaten-path two-day trip can be done with a tour operator or on your own. With 280 families living on the islands, very few people speak English or even Spanish, but rather traditional Aymara.

The trip usually begins in Puno where you board a bus for two hours to the village of Yunguyo near Punta Hermosa where you catch a 1.5-hour sailboat ride to the flat, but fertile Anapia. On arrival hosts will meet visitors and guide them back to their family's home for an overnight stay. The day is then spent farming, tending to the animals, or playing with the children, and also includes a hiking trip to nearby Yuspique Island, where lunch is cooked by the women on the beach. Typically, *huatia,* potatoes cooked in a natural clay oven and buried in hot soil with lots of herbs, is served along with fresh fish. Yuspique is not very populated, but is home to more than 100 wild vincuñas.

After returning to Anapia you'll follow an evening's activities of traditional family life, such as music or dance. All Ways Travel and Edgar Adventure run tours. Proceeds go to the families. You can do this trip on your own by following the itinerary and taking a water colectivo from Punta Hermosa to Anapia.

TOURS OF LAKE TITICACA

Excursions to the floating islands of the Uros as well as to any of the islands on Lake Titicaca can be arranged through tour agencies in Puno. Most tours depart between 7:30 and 9 AM, as the lake can become choppy in the afternoon. You also can take the local boat at the Puno dock for about the same price as a tour, although boats don't usually depart without at least 10 passengers.

OPERATORS **All Ways Travel** (✉ *Jr. Tacna 285* ☎ *051/355–552* ⊕ *www.allwaystravelperu. com*). **Condor Travel** (✉ *Tarapacá* ☎ *051/364–763* ⊕ *www.condortravel.com.pe*). **Edgar Adventures** (✉ *Jr. Lima 328* ☎ *051/353–444* ⊕ *www.edgaradventures. com*). **Kingdom Travel** (✉ *Jr. Lima 369* ☎🖷 *051/364–318* ✍ *kingdomperu@ hotmail.com*). **Kontiki Tours** (✉ *Jr. Melgar 188* ☎ *051/353–473* ⊕ *www.kontikip-eru.com*). **Solmartour** (✉ *Jr. Libertad 229–231* ☎ *051/352–901* ⊕ *www.solmar. com.pe*). **Titikayak Kayak Tours** (✉ *Jr. Bolognesi 334* ☎ *051/367–747* ⊕ *www. titikayak.com*). **Turpuno** (✉ *Jr. Lima 208 Ofic. 5 Segundo Piso,* ☎🖷 *051/352–001* ⊕ *www.turpuno.com*).

Continued on page 191

THE ISLANDS
of Lake Titicaca

According to legend, under orders from their father, the Sun God, the first Inca—Manco Cápac—and his sister—Mama Ocllo rose from the deep blue waters of Lake Titicaca and founded the Inca empire. Watching the mysterious play of light on the water and the shadows on the mountains, you may become a believer of the Inca myth.

Reed Boat Head, Uros

This is the altiplano—the high plains of Peru, where the earth has been raised so close to the sky that the area takes on a luminous quality. Lake Titicaca's sharp, sparkling blue waters may make you think of some place far from the altiplano, perhaps someplace warm. Then its chill will slap you back to reality and you realize that you're at the world's highest navigable lake, 12,500 feet above sea level. The lake's surface covers 8,600 sq km (3320 sq mi) and drops down 287 meters (942 ft) at its deepest.

Most of Lake Titicaca is a National Reserve dedicated to conserving the region's plant and animal life while promoting sustainable use of its resources. The reserve extends from the Bay of Puno to the peninsula of Capachica. It's divided into two sectors: one surrounds the Bay of Puno and protects the resources of the Uros-Chuluni communities; the other, in the Huancané area, preserves the totora-reed water fields and protects the nesting area of more than 60 bird species, including the Titicaca flightless grebe.

DID YOU KNOW?

The floating islands likely date from before the Inca empire. But since the reeds are constantly replenished, they've found a way to remain forever young.

THE FLOATING ISLANDS

Uru indian woman and totora reeds boat.

ISLAS LOS UROS

Islas Los Uros, known as the Floating Islands, are man-made islands woven together with mud and tótora reeds that grow in the lake shallows. Replenished often with layers because the underbelly reeds rot, these tiny islands resemble floating bails of hay. Walking on them feels like walking on a big waterlogged sponge, but they are sturdy.

VISITING

Trips to the Los Uros typically take three hours and can be arranged from the port in the Puno Bay or with a guide through one of the many agencies in town. While some travelers marvel at these 40-plus islands, some call them floating souvenir stands. Yes, locals sell trinkets, but visiting the floating islands is a glimpse into one of the region's oldest cultures, the Uros. Now mixed with Aymara culture it's a form of human habitation that evolved over centuries. The closest group of "floating museums" is 10 km (6 mi) from Puno.

ISLAND LIFE

The islanders make their living by fishing, trapping birds, and selling visitors well-made miniature reed boats, weavings, and collages depicting island life. You can hire an islander to take you for a ride in a reed boat. Although there's no running water, progress has come to some of the islands in the form of solar-powered energy and microwave telephone stations. Seventh Day Adventists converted the inhabitants of one island and built a church and school, the only structures not made of mud and reeds.

HOMESTAY TIP

It's tradition for most families not to have visitors help in the kitchen, and on several islands families will not eat with visitors. It's also customary to bring a gift—usually essentials like fruit, dried grains, matches, and candles.

TAQUILE & AMANTANI ISLANDS

Folk dances on Taquile island.

TAQUILE ISLAND

35 km (22 mi) west of Puno in the high altitude sunshine, Taquile's brown dusty landscape contrasts with green terraces, bright flowers, and the surrounding blue waters. Snow-capped Bolivian mountains loom in the distance.

Taquile folk are known for weaving some of Peru's loveliest textiles, and men create textiles as much as the women. Islanders still wear traditional dress and have successfully maintained the cooperative lifestyle of their ancestors. The annual Taquile festival the third week of July is a great time to visit.

Taquile is on a steep hill with curvy long trails, which lead to the main square. There are two ways to reach the top of Taquile where there are Inca and Tiahuanaco ruins—you can climb up the 528 stone steps, or take a longer path.

AMANTANI ISLAND

The island of Amantani is 45 km (28 mi) from Puno and almost two hours away by boat from Taquile. Amantani has pre-Columbian ruins, and a larger, mainly agrarian society, whose traditional way of life has been less exposed to the outside world until recently. Not as pretty as Taquile, Amantani is dusty and brown.

Locals were losing population to the mainland before a community-based project helped them dive into the tourist industry and organize homestays. Although the project has been a success, make sure you will be your host's only guests for a more intimate experience.

Most of the younger generations speak Spanish and even a smidgen of English, but the older generation speaks only Quechua. Amantani has a population of 3,500 Quechua. Sacred rituals are held in its two pre-Inca temples, dedicated to the earth's fertility.

Amantani woman spinning yarn from wool.

ISLA DEL SOL, BOLIVIA

Adventurous travelers, with a couple days to spare, will want to journey on to Bolivia. After crossing the border, and getting to the pleasant lakeside town of Copacabana (visit the striking Moorish-style cathedral), go on by boat to the Isla del Sol, Lake Titicaca's largest island, where there are tremendous views, Inca ruins, and hotels.

Isla del Sol is the best place to visit and to stay on the lake and is the mythological birthplace of the Incas. The views of the Cordillera Real mountains are amazing, especially at dawn and dusk, and the island has beautiful white sandy beaches and an extraordinary terraced landscape. Ruins include the Inca palace of Pilkokaina and a strange rock formation said to be the birthplace of the sun and moon, and an excellent Inca trail across the island. Alternatively, you can just laze around and soak up the cosmic energy.

En route to Isla del Sol, boats sometimes stop at **Isla de la Luna**, where the ruins of Iñacuy date back to the Inca conquest. You'll find an ancient con-

vent called Ajlla Wasi (House of the Chosen Women). Stone steps lead up to the unrestored ruins of the convent.

The legends that rise out of Lake Titicaca are no more mysterious than discoveries made in its depths. In 2000 an international diving expedition bumped into what is believed to be a 1,000-year-old pre-Inca temple. The stone structure is 660 feet long and 160 feet wide, with a wall 2,699 feet long. The discovery was made between Copacabana and the Sun and Moon islands.

(pictured top and bottom) Isla del Sol, the Island of the Sun, on Lake Titicaca, Bolivia.

SILLUSTANI

30 km (19 mi) northwest of Puno.

High on a hauntingly beautiful peninsula in Lake Umayo is the necropolis of Sillustani. Twenty-eight stone burial towers represent a city of the dead that both predated and coincided with the Inca empire. ■TIP→The proper name for a tower is ayawasi (home of the dead), but they're generally referred to as chullpas, which are actually the shrouds used to cover the mummies inside. This was the land of the Aymará-speaking Colla people, and the precision of their masonry rivals that of the Inca. Sillustani's mystique is heightened by the view it provides over Lake Umayo and its mesa-shape island, El Sombrero, as well as by the utter silence that prevails, broken only by the wind over the water and the cries of lake birds.

Most of the chullpas date from the 14th and 15th centuries, but some were erected as early as AD 900. The tallest, known as the Lizard because of a carving on one of its massive stones, has a circumference of 28 feet. An unusual architectural aspect of the chullpas is that the circumference is smaller at the bottom than the top. To fully appreciate Sillustani, it's necessary to make the long climb to the top; fortunately, the steps are wide and it's an easy climb. Some school children will put on dances; if you take photos of mothers, children, and pet alpacas, a donation of a couple of soles will be appreciated.

CHUCUITO

20 km (12 mi) southeast of Puno.

Chucuito (in Aymará *Choque-Huito*, Mountain of Gold) is the first of several small towns that dot the lake as you travel from Puno into Bolivia. If you aren't interested in architecture, colonial churches, or don't care to see another undeveloped Peruvian town, then chances are you won't enjoy these little towns. Having said that, Chucuito, surrounded by hillsides crisscrossed with agricultural terraces, has one novelty you won't find elsewhere—its Temple of Fertility, or Templo de Inca Uyu.

The temple is the most interesting thing to see in Chucuito. Almost a ghost town, the main plaza has a large stone Inca sundial as its centerpiece. There are two Renaissance-style 16th-century churches, **La Ascunción** alongside the plaza and the **Santo Domingo** on the east side of town. Neither one has been maintained, but both are open for services.

Templo de Inca Uyu. This "temple" doesn't quite meet the dictionary's description of a temple as a stately edifice, but that's what it's called. ■TIP→It's an outdoor area surrounded by a pre-Inca and Inca-made stone walls that block the view of a "garden" of anatomically correct phallic stone sculptures. Each 3-foot-tall penis statue points toward the sky at the Inca sun god, or toward the ground to the Pachamana, the mother earth. It's better known as the Temple of the Phallus. In ancient times it was—and is still today—visited by females who sit for hours on the little statues believing it will increase their fertility. *S/5.*

JULI

On Lake Titicaca, 84 km (52 mi) southeast of Puno.

At one time this village may have been an important Aymará religious center, and it has served as a Jesuit training center for missionaries from Paraguay and Bolivia. Juli has been called "Little Roma" because of its disproportionate number of churches. Four interesting churches in various stages of restoration are **San Pedro Mártir, Santa Cruz de Jerusalén, Asunción,** and **San Juan de Letrán.** The latter has 80 paintings from the Cusco School and huge windows worked in stone. Juli has a Saturday morning bartering market in the main square. It's not a handicraft market, but a produce and animal market where the barter system is in full effect and the trade of animals is interesting to watch. It starts at 9 AM and is done by noon.

POMATA

108 km (67 mi) southeast of Puno.

The main attraction in the small lakeside town of Pomata is the church of **Santiago Apóstol de Nuestra Señora del Rosario.** It was built of pink granite in the 18th century and has paintings from the Cusco School and the Flemish School. Its mestizo baroque carvings and translucent alabaster windows are spectacular. Its altars are covered in gold leaf. Pomata is also famous for its fine pottery, especially for its Toritos de Pucará (bull figures).

BOLIVIA SOJOURN

You'll hear lots of talk about crossing Lake Titicaca from Peru to Bolivia via hydrofoil or catamaran. At this time you can not go completely across without stopping at the border and walking from Peru into Bolivia or vice versa.■ TIP➔You can still use hydrofoils and catamarans in your journey to Bolivia's side of the lake from Copacabana on the Bolivian side, then on to the Sun and Moon islands for an overnight or two on Sun Island.

Copacabana is a pleasant, if touristy, town which provides easy access to the lake and the surrounding countryside. It's also a major pilgrimage destination for devout Bolivians at Easter and lost South American hippies all year. The breathtaking Moorish-style **Cathedral,** built between 1610 and 1619, is where you'll find the striking sculpture of the Virgin of Copacabana. If you see decorated cars lined up in front of the cathedral, the owners are waiting to have them blessed. You can combine your visit with the semi-scramble up past the stations of the cross on the hill above the town. If the climb doesn't knock you out the view will.

At the Inca Utama Resort & Spa at the Huatahata harbor you can spend a couple of days relaxing and visiting the Andean Roots Cultural Complex. The observatory with a rollback roof gives you a view of southern-hemisphere stars through powerful telescopes donated by NASA.

Bolivia's unit of currency is the boliviano—though Bolivians often refer to their currency as *pesos*. The exchange rate is about S/1 to (B)2.6.

CROSSING THE BORDER

Bolivia now requires U.S. citizens to obtain a visa to travel in the country. For a price tag of $100, the visa is good for up to 90 days in a calendar year. The application can be done by mail or in person at any Bolivian Consulate, not by the Internet. Additionally a yellow fever vaccination certificate is also necessary to show upon entry. At this writing, you were allowed to pay a US$100 fine for not having a visa and get into the country. How long this will last is anyone's guess, but you could always give it a try.

If you're taking a bus from Puno, three hours into the ride the bus will stop just after Yunguyo for border-crossing procedures. Most higher-end bus services hand you immigration forms on the bus. As you leave Peru you'll get off to get an exit stamp from the Peruvian immigration, and then walk through to the small Bolivian immigration building, where you get an entrance stamp and will have to show your visa. From there you catch up with your bus, which will be waiting for you. Keep all immigration documents, your passport and visa safe; you may need these when leaving Bolivia.

GETTING AROUND

The border-crossing tours have packages from US$150 to US$400. Reputable agencies include Crillón Tours and Transturin Ltd; based in Bolivia, tours go from Puno to La Paz and vice versa. Both include a pick-up from your hotel in Puno, transfer by first-class bus to the border in Yunguyo (a three-hour drive). After crossing the border you take a bus to Copacabana, a funky beach town (30 minutes). The most expensive—and comfortable way—to get to the Isla del Sol and Isla de la Luna is by hydrofoil from the **Inca Utama Hotel** but cheaper boats leave from Copacabana all day. The journey takes about three hours and costs (Bs)30. Once you are on the island, it's walking all the way.

TOUR COMPANIES **Crillón Tours** (⊠ Av. Camacho 1223, La Paz ☎ 591/02/233-7533 ⊕ www.titicaca. com ✉ Titicaca@entelnet.bo). **Crillón Tours** (⊠ 1450 S. Bayshore Dr., Suite 815, Miami, ☎ 305/358-5853 ✉ darius@titicaca.com). **Transturin** (⊠ Av. Arce 2678, La Paz, Bolivia ☎ 591-2/242-2222 ⊕ www.transturin.com).

WHERE TO STAY

$$–$$$ **Inca Utama Hotel & Spa.** The best lodging on Lake Titicaca's Bolivian side is the Inca Utama Hotel & Spa at Huatajata, home harbor for Crillón Tours' hydrofoils on Lake Titicaca. At the Kallawaya natural spa, relax through hydrotherapy with mud or salt baths, and massages. There are two restaurants, Sumaj Untavi, with nightly folkloric shows, and La Choza Nautica, where you can watch the sunset over

Lake Titicaca. A second-floor bar–lounge is also a nice place to relax. On premises are the Altiplano and Eco museums, with exhibits on Andean cultures. In the Andean Roots Cultural Complex, learn about Andean customs and medicines and meet a natural-medicine doctor who can tell your fortune by casting sacred coca leaves. The complex also has its own herds of llamas, alpacas, and vicuñas. Run through Crillón Tours. **Pros:** Educational, fireplace, bar, spa. **Cons:** Difficult location, rooms can get cold. ⊠ *86 Carretera Asfaltada, Huatajata, Bolivia* ☎ *02/733–7533* ⊕ *www.titicaca.com* ➥ *70 rooms* ♿ *In-room: safe (some), Wi-Fi. In-hotel: 2 restaurants, room service, bar, gym, spa, beachfront, laundry service, public Internet, no-smoking rooms* ⊟ *AE, MC, V* ⦿*CP.*

$$ 📷 **La Posada del Inca Eco-Lodge.** This restored colonial-style hacienda on Isla del Sol sits high on a bluff surrounded by pine and eucalyptus trees and overlooking Lake Titicaca. If you're not up to the climb, you can ride up on a mule, but if that seems too drastic, go up in a comfortable (by comparison) golf cart, over a narrow road. You can also walk up a winding stone path in 30–40 minutes with llamas carrying your luggage. Said to be the cradle of Inca civilization, myth has it that Manco Capac and Mama Ocllo, the first Incas rose from lake near Isla del Sol. The Posada, part of the Crillon Tours complex uses solar energy and has electric blankets and heaters in all rooms to keep you toasty. Meals are family-style around a long dining-room table, and their soups and stews are hearty and healthful. You can also have lunch or dinner in the famed Uma Kollo restaurant below the posada. All rooms are cozy and decked out with antiques for an old hacienda style. In a small town with minimal shopping just above the hacienda, you can watch the islanders planting crops on old Inca terraces. Reservations are made though Crillon Tours. **Pros:** Eco-friendly clean, excellent food. **Cons:** Hard to get to. ⊠ *Isla del Sol, Lake Titicaca, Bolivia* ☎ *591-2 233–7533 or 591-1/233–9047 Bolivia:, 305/358–5353 U.S.* 🖨 *591/211–6481* ➥ *20 rooms* ♿ *In-room: safe (some). In-hotel: restaurant, room service, bar, beachfront, no elevator, laundry service, public Internt, no-smoking rooms* ⊟ *AE, MC, V* ⦿*CP.*

Cusco & The Sacred Valley

WORD OF MOUTH

Cusco is an amazing city! The Incan walls are so impressive and the architecture is beautiful. We also enjoyed seeing the ruins at Sacsayhuaman.

—luv2globetrot

WELCOME TO CUSCO & THE SACRED VALLEY

Santo Domingo Church in Cuzco

TOP REASONS TO GO

★ **Alpaca Clothing:** Nothing says "Cusco" quite like a sweater, shawl, poncho, or scarf woven from the hair of the cute and cuddly alpaca.

★ **Andean Cuisine:** Where else in the world will you find roasted *cuy* (guinea pig) and alpaca steaks rubbing shoulders on fine-dining menus?

★ **Inca Architecture:** How did the Inca construct stone walls so precisely using 15th-century technology? How could they position a temple so it would be illuminated best at the exact moment of the solstice? Ponder history's secrets.

★ **Layered Religion:** Like that church's architecture? Take a closer look at the walls—every Catholic church was built on the site, and often on the foundation of, an Inca *huaca*, or sacred place.

★ **Hotels with History:** Cusco's hostelries brim with history. Many are former convents, monasteries, dwellings of sacred women, or palaces of Spanish conquerors.

1 Plaza de Armas.
Flanked by the city's most impressive colonial churches and lying on hallowed Inca ceremonial ground, Cusco's Plaza de Armas is the city's heart. You'll find ancient Inca walls holding up baroque colonial buildings, inside of which lie some of the city's most contemporary restaurants and shops.

2 North of the Plaza de Armas. Step back in time as you puff your way uphill from the Plaza de Armas to the charming cobbled streets of San Blas. The traditional stomping ground of Cusco's artists and artisans, this area is becoming the hippest part of Cusco, with funky modern restaurants and bars side by side with traditional galleries of Cusqueñan art.

CORDILLERA URUBAMBA

Ollantaytambo

Urubamba
Salineras
Yucay
Maras
Huayllabamba **Huayllabamba**
Moray
Racchi
Chinchero

Huarocondo   Lake Huaypo   Lake Piuray
Chuso

Zurite
Iscuchaca

Anta   **Tambomachay**
2

1 Cusco
3

3 **South of the Plaza de Armas.** Head away from the colonial center to the city's more modern section, through which runs the traffic-heavy Avenida El Sol. There's noise, pollution, and roast chicken shops everywhere, yet even in the midst of this colonial and Inca gems are found—here lies Cusco's star attraction, Qorikancha the Sun Temple.

5 **Sacred Valley of the Inca.** The Urubamba River meanders through a tranquil valley between the towns of Pisac and Ollantaytambo north of Cusco, which offers a good selection of hotels and restaurants, stunning views and a slower pace of life than the big city. The lower elevation and warmer temperatures are added bonuses.

GETTING ORIENTED

At the center of Cusco is the colonial Plaza de Armas, slightly sloped, with streets heading downhill, most prominently the Avenida El Sol, leading to the more modern sections of the city. Heading uphill takes you to the city's older neighborhoods, notably the artisan quarter of San Blas and its web of pedestrian-only walkways. If you look up, you'll see that towering over the lot is the archaeological site of Sacsayhuamán, which sits just to the left of the Christo Blanco. This white Christ statue is most clearly seen at night when it's lighted by floodlights. The Urubamba mountain range on the north side and Cusco and environs on the south side watch over the river basin known as the Sacred Valley. Transportation to the Sacred Valley is straightforward, with roads fanning out from the Urubamba, the valley's small hub city and back to Cusco.

4 **Side Trips—The Southeastern Urubamba Valley.** What really made the Inca civilization so successful? Their appreciation of a good view! Gorgeous Andean landscapes characterize almost every important Inca site in the area surrounding Cusco.

5

CUSCO & THE SACRED VALLEY PLANNER

Health & Safety

Altitude Sickness: Known as *soroche*, you'll likely encounter altitude sickness at Cusco's 3,500-meter (11,500-foot) elevation. Drink lots of fluids but eliminate or minimize alcohol and caffeine consumption. Most large hotels have an oxygen supply for their guests' use. The prescription drug acetazolamide can help. Check with your physician about this, and about traveling here if you have a heart condition or high blood pressure, or are pregnant.

Warning: Sorojchi pills are a Bolivian-made altitude-sickness remedy whose advertising pictures a tourist vomiting at Machu Picchu. Its safety has not been documented, and we don't recommend trying it.

Water: Tap water is not safe to drink here. Stick with the bottled variety, *con gas* (carbonated) or *sin gas* (plain).

Safety: Security has improved dramatically in Cusco. A huge police presence is on the streets, especially around tourist centers such as the Plaza de Armas. Nonetheless, petty crime, such as pickpocketing, is not uncommon: use extra vigilance in crowded markets or when getting on and off buses and trains. Robbers have also targeted late-night, early-morning revelers stumbling back to their hotels.

Getting Around

By Air: Aero Condor (⊕ *www.aerocondor.com.pe*) flies daily from Cusco to Lima. LanPeru (⊕ *www.lan.com*) connects Cusco with Lima, Arequipa, Juilaca, and Puerto Maldonado. Star Perú (⊕ *www.starperu.com.pe*) and TACA Peru (⊕ *www.taca.com*) fly from Cusco to Lima.

By Bus: Cusco's bus terminal is at the Terminal Terrestre on Pachacútec, not far from the airport. The best company running from Cusco is Cruz del Sur. Bus travel between the Cusco and the Sacred Valley is cheap, frequent . . . and sometimes accident-prone.

By Car: For exploring the Sacred Valley, a car is the best option. The vehicular tourist route ends at Ollantaytambo. Cusco is the only place to rent a vehicle. However, you won't need or want to drive inside the city; heavy traffic, lack of parking, and narrow streets, many of them pedestrian only, make a car a burden.

By Taxi: Cusco's licensed taxis bear a black-and-gold checkered rectangle on each side, and a light-color official taxi sticker on the windshield. Fares are S/2 within the central city and S/3 after 10 PM. Have your hotel or restaurant call a taxi for you at night.

Honda Motokar taxis—semi-open, three-wheeled motorized vehicles with room for two passengers—ply the streets of Sacred Valley towns. Touring the Sacred Valley from Cusco with one of the city's taxis costs about US$50.

By Train: PeruRail's *Andean Explorer* departs from Cusco (at Wanchaq Station on Pachacutec) Monday, Wednesday, and Saturday at 8 AM for Puno, with a stop in Juliaca. The scenic journey takes 10 hours. There is no rail service between Lima and Cusco.

Two classes of daily service to Machu Picchu depart from Cusco's San Pedro station. Purchase tickets in advance from the PeruRail sales office at Cusco's Wanchaq Station or from a travel agency. Trains depart super early in the morning. The luxury Hiram Bingham service departs from the station in Poroy at 9 AM. *See The Train To Machu Picchu in chapter 6.*

Buying a Boleto Turístico

Offering access to 16 of Cusco's best-known tourist attractions, the *boleto turístico* is the all-in-one answer to your tourism needs. Or is it? The scheme, in which you pay S/70 (S/35 for ISIC student card holders), certainly has its critics. Most agree that the ticket represents good value only if you visit nearly all the sites included. Under the scheme, however, no site can charge its own entry fee—so if you want to visit one site, you pay for them all! Certain big name attractions (such as the Cathedral) have withdrawn from the boleto turisico in order to levy their own fees. Regardless, if you want to see sites like Sacsayhuamán and Pisac, you have to buy the ticket, which can be purchased at either location of the **Oficina Ejecutiva del Comité Boleto Turístico** (OFEC ⊠ Av. El Sol 103 ☎ 084/227–037 ⊠ Garcilaso and Heladeros ☎ 084/226–919 ⊕ www.boletoturisticodelcusco.com), open Monday through Saturday 8 to 5 and Sunday 8 to 2.

For S/40 you can buy a *boleto parcial* (partial ticket) good for admission for one day only at Sacsayhuamán, Qenko, Puka Pukara, and Tambomachay, the four Inca ruins nearest Cusco. Another partial ticket, also S/40, is valid for two days at farther-flung ruins of Pisac, Chinchero, and Ollantaytambo in the Sacred Valley and Tipón and Pikillacta in the Southeastern Urubamba Valley.

If you're interested in only Cusco's cathedral and Qorikancha, as are many short-term visitors, then the boleto turístico is of no use. The cathedral, the Church of La Compañía, the church of San Blas, and the religious art museum are now united under their own *boleto intergral* (integral ticket), which you can purchase at the cathedral for S/15 (S/7.50 with an international student ID). The ticket is valid for 10 days, and the price includes a headset audioguide at each location. If you're not interested in visiting all four, it's possible to pay individual admission prices, but the four-in-one price is a bargain, and the sights are close together.

The Qorikancha, arguably Cusco's most fabulous tourist sight, levies its own admission price; it's not a member of the boleto turístico partnership. The equally wonderful Museo Inka and Museo de Arte Precolombino also charge admission independently.

Weather Wise

Cusco's high season is June through early September (winter) and the days around the Christmas and Easter holidays. Winter means drier weather and easier traveling, but higher lodging prices and larger crowds. Prices and visitor numbers drop dramatically during the November through March summer rainy season, except around the holidays.

South America Explorers

The **South American Explorers** is a membership organization. Its US$50 annual dues get you a wealth of information at its clubhouse in Cusco, as well as in Lima and other South American cities. (⊠ Choquechaca 188, Bell 4 ☎ 084/245–484 ⊕ www. saexplorers.org ⊙ May–Sept., weekdays 9:30–5, Sat. 9:30–1; Oct.–Apr., weekdays 9:30–5).

by Katy Morrison & Jeffrey Van Fleet

"Bienvenidos a la ciudad imperial del Cusco," announces the flight attendant when your plane touches down. "Welcome to the imperial city of Cusco." This royal greeting hints at what you're in for in Cusco, one of the world's great travel destinations.

The city has stood for nine centuries in this fertile Andean valley, 3,500 meters (11,500 feet) above sea level. Once the capital of the Inca empire, Cusco fell to Spanish conquistadors in 1533, when the empire was weakened from civil war. Peruvian independence was declared in 1821, and now Cusco is home to the indigenous mestizo culture of today.

According to tradition, the Inca Manco Capac and his sister-consort Mama Occlo founded the city. They envisioned Qosqo (Cusco) in the shape of a puma, the animal representation of the Earth in the indigenous cosmos, which is evident today if someone traces the animal outline for you on a city map. But not all was Inca in southern Peru, a point that gets lost in the tourist trek from one Inca ruin to the next. The presence not far from Cusco of Pikillacta, a pre-Inca city constructed by the Wari culture that thrived between AD 600 and 1000, is an indication that this territory, like most of Peru, was the site of sophisticated civilizations long before the Inca appeared.

By the time Francisco Pizarro and the Spanish conquistadors arrived in 1532, the Inca empire had spread from modern-day Ecuador in the north down through Peru and Bolivia to Chile. How did such a vast empire fall to a few hundred Spaniards? At the time, the empire, though large, was divided and severely weakened by a civil war. The Spanish brought guns and horses, which the Inca had never seen, and new diseases, against which they had no immunity. The Spanish seized Atahualpa, the recently instated Inca ruler who was in Cajamarca to subdue rebellious forces, and the rest of the population was quickly overwhelmed.

After the 1532 conquest of the Inca empire, the new colonists overlaid a new political system and new religion onto the old. They also superimposed their architecture, looting the gold, silver, and stone, and grafting their own churches, monasteries, convents, and palaces onto the foundations of the Inca sites. The juxtaposition can be jarring. The Santo Domingo church was built on top of the Qorikancha, the Temple of the Sun. And it's downright ironic to think of the cloistered convent of Santa Catalina occupying the same site as the equally cloistered Acll-awasi, the home of the Inca chosen women, who were selected to serve the sun in the Qorikancha temple. The cultural combination appears in countless other ways: witness the pumas carved into the cathedral doors. The city also gave its name to the Cusqueña school of art, in which New World artists combined Andean motifs with European-style painting, usually on religious themes. You'll chance on paintings that could be by Van Dyck but for the Inca robes on New Testament figures, and last supper diners digging into an Andean feast of guinea pig and fermented corn beer.

Throughout the Cusco region, you'll witness this odd juxtaposition of imperial and colonial, indigenous and Spanish. Traditionally clad Quechua-speaking women sell their wares in front of a part-Inca, part-colonial structure as a business executive of European heritage walks by carrying on a cell-phone conversation. The two cultures coexist, but have not entirely embraced each other even five centuries after the conquest.

The Río Urubamba passes, at its closest, about 30 km (18 mi) north of Cusco and flows through a valley about 300 meters (980 feet) lower in elevation than Cusco. The northwestern part of this river basin, romantically labeled the Sacred Valley of the Inca, contains some of the region's most appealing towns and fascinating pre-Columbian ruins. A growing number of visitors are heading here directly upon arrival in Cusco to acclimatize. The valley's altitude is slightly lower and its temperatures slightly higher, and make for a physically easier introduction to this part of Peru.

CUSCO

If you arrive in Cusco with the intention of hopping on the train to Machu Picchu the next morning, you'll probably only have time to take a stroll though the Plaza de Armas and visit Qorikancha (Temple of the Sun) and the Catedral. However, we recommend spending at least two days in Cusco before venturing off to Machu Picchu, giving yourself time to acclimate to the altitude and get to know this city of terra-cotta roofs and cobblestone streets. The churches close for a few hours in the middle of the day. Most of the city's museums close on Sunday.

Cusco takes its newest role as tourist favorite in stride, and absorbs thousands of travelers with an ample supply of lodgings, restaurants, and services. That a polished infrastructure exists in such a remote, high-elevation locale is a pleasant surprise.

ACCLIMATIZING THE COCA WAY

Take it easy! Cusco is a breathless 3,300 meters (10,825 feet) above sea level—a fact you'll very soon appreciate as you huff and puff your way up its steep cobbled streets. With 30% less oxygen in the atmosphere, the best way to avoid altitude sickness is to take it easy on your first few days. There's no point in dashing off on that Inca hike if you're not acclimatized—altitude sickness is uncomfortable at best and can be very dangerous.

Locals swear by *mate de coca,* an herbal tea brewed from coca leaves that helps with altitude acclimatization. Indigenous peoples have chewed the leaves of the coca plant for centuries to cope with Andean elevations. But the brewing of the leaves in an herbal tea is considered a more refined and completely legal way to ingest the substance, in Andean nations at least. Most restaurants and many hotels have a pot steeping constantly.

GETTING AROUND

Cusco's Aeropuerto Internacional Teniente Alejandro Velasco Astete (CUZ) is about 15 minutes from the center of town. An army of taxis waits at the exit from baggage claim, and charge S/5 to take you to the city center.

Cusco's center city is most enjoyably explored on foot. Many of the streets open to vehicular traffic are so narrow that it's simply faster to walk. ■TIP➡Cusco streets have a habit of changing names every few blocks, or even every block. Many streets bear a common Spanish name that everyone uses, but have newly designated street signs with an old Quechua name in order to highlight the city's Inca heritage: the Plaza de Armas is Haukaypata, the Plaza Regocijo is Kusipata, Triunfo is Sunturwasi, Loreto is Intikijlli, Arequipa is Q'aphchijk'ijllu, and intermittent blocks of Avenida El Sol are labeled Mut'uchaka. And so on.

ESSENTIALS

AIRPORT **Aeropuerto Internacional Teniente Alejandro Velasco Astete** (⊠ *Av. Velasco Astete s/n* ☎ *084/222–611*).

BUS **Cruz del Sur** (⊠ *Pachacutec 510* ☎ *084/221–909*). **Ormeño** (⊠ *San Juan de Dios 657* ☎ *084/227–501*).

CURRENCY **Banco de Crédito** (⊠ *Av. El Sol 189* ☎ *084/263–560*). **Banco Wiese Sudameris** (⊠ *Maruri 315* ☎ *084/264–297*). **Diners Club** (⊠ *Av. El Sol 615* ☎ *084/234–051*). **Western Union** (⊠ *Av. El Sol 627A* ☎ *084/248–028*).

INTERNET **Intinet** (⊠ *Choquechaca 115* ☎ *084/258-390*). **Mundo** (⊠ *Santa Teresa 172* ☎ *084/260–285*). **Telser** (⊠ *Calle del Medio 117* ☎ *084/242–424*).

MAIL **SERPOST** (⊠ *Av. El Sol 800* ☎ *084/224–212*). **DHL** (⊠ *Av. El Sol 627* ☎ *084/244–167*). **Scharff International/FedEx** (⊠ *Pardo 978* ☎ *084/223–140*).

MEDICAL **Clínica Pardo** (⊠ *Av. de la Cultura 710, Plaza Tupac Amaru* ☎ *084/240-387* ⊕ *www.clinicapardo.com*). **Hospital Regional** (⊠ *Av. de la Cultura s/n* ☎ *084/223–691*).

POLICE **Policía Nacional** (☎ 084/249–659). **Tourist Police** (✉ Monumento a Pachacutec, Av. Saphi s/n ☎ 084/249–654).

RENTAL CAR **Avis** (✉ Garcilaso 210 ☎ 084/241–824). **Herz** (✉ Av. El Sol 808 ☎ 084/248–800). **Explores Transportes** (✉ Plateros 356 ☎ 084/261–640). **OSDI Rent-a-Car** (✉ Urb. Mateo Pumacahua B-10 ☎ 084/251–616).

TAXI **Alo Cusco** (☎ 084/222–222). **Llama Taxi** (☎ 084/222–000). **Taxi Turismo Cusco** (☎ 084/245–000).

TRAIN **Peru Rail** (✉ San Pedro station, Cascapara near Santa Clara ☎ 084/233–551 ⊕ www.perurail.com ✉ Wanchaq station, Pachacutec near Tullumayo ☎ 084/238–722 ⊕ www.perurail.com).

VISITOR INFO **Dirección Regional de Industria y Turismo** (Dircetur) (✉ Mantas 117 ☎ 084/222–032 ☼ Weekdays 8–7, Sat. 8–2). **iPerú** (✉ Av. El Sol 103 ☎ 084/252–974 ☼ Daily 8:30–7:30)

5

AROUND THE PLAZA DE ARMAS

For thousands of years the heart of Cusco, formerly called Haukaypata and now known as the **Plaza de Armas**, continues to catch the pulse of the city. Yet where you once would have found Inca ceremonies and parades in front of the many palaces that stood here, today you'll find a more modern procession of postcard sellers, shoe-shiners, and photographers angling for your attention. It's no surprise that they congregate here—with the stupendous **Catedral** dominating the northeastern side of the Plaza, the ornate **Iglesia de La Compañía** sitting to the southeast, and gorgeous Spanish-colonial arcades forming the other two sides, the Plaza is one of the most spectacular areas of Cusco.

WHAT TO SEE

❽ **Catedral.** Dominating the Plaza de Armas, the monumental Cathedral **Fodor'sChoice** is one of Cusco's grandest buildings. Built in 1550 on the site of the **★** palace of the Inca Wirachocha and using stones looted from the nearby Inca fortress of Sacsayhuaman, the Cathedral is a perfect example of the imposition of the Catholic faith on the indigenous population. The grander the building, went the theory, the more impressive (and seductive) the faith. With soaring ceilings, baroque carvings, enormous oil paintings, and glittering gold-and-silver altars, the Cathedral certainly seemed to achieve its aim.

Today Cusco's Cathedral is one of the town's star attractions, noted mainly for its amazing collection of colonial art that mixes Christian and non-Christian imagery. Entering the Cathedral from the Sagrada

UNA FOTO AMIGO?

Cusco is one of the most colorful cities in the world, and you can't be here for more than five minutes without noticing all the women and young girls walking the streets in full traditional costume, most towing a llama or endearingly cuddling a lamb or puppy. They are more than happy to pose for photos. In fact, that's how they make their money, so make sure you pay up when asked. The going rate for a photo is S/1.

Familia chapel, head to your right to the first nave where you'll find the famous oil painting (reputed to be the oldest in Cusco) depicting the earthquake that rocked the town in 1650. Among the depictions of burning houses and people fleeing, you'll see a procession in the Plaza. Legend has it that during the earthquake, the citizens took out from the Cathedral a statue of Jesus on the cross and paraded it around the Plaza—halting the quake in its tracks. This statue, now known as the Señor de los Temblores, or Lord of the Earthquakes, is Cusco's patron, and you'll find him depicted in many Cusqueñan paintings—you'll recognise him by his frilly white skirt.

To see the famous statue, head across the Cathedral to the other side, where in the nave and to the right of the passage connecting the Cathedral to the adjoining Iglesia del Triumfo, you'll find el Señor himself. The dark color of his skin is often claimed to be a representation of the indigenous people of Cusco; the scientific explanation is that it's natural discoloration due to the statue's age.

Those interested in the crossover between indigenous and Catholic iconography will find lots to look at. Figures of pumas, the Inca representation of the earth, are carved on the enormous main doors, and in the adjoining Iglesia del Triumfo you'll see an Andean Christ in one of the altars flanking the exit. ■**TIP➜No one should miss the spectacular Last Supper, painted by the indigenous artist Marcos Zapata, where you'll see the diners tucking into a delicious feast of cuy (guinea pig) and chicha (corn beverage)!**

The cathedral's centerpieces are its massive, solid-silver altar, and the enormous 1659 María Angola bell, the largest in South America, which hangs in one of the towers and can be heard from miles away. Behind the main altar is the original wooden *altar primitivo* dedicated to St. Paul. The 64-seat cedar choir has rows of carved saints, popes, and bishops, all in stunning detail down to their delicately articulated hands.

Labels in Spanish and English are slowly being added to the more famous attractions in the Cathedral. ■**TIP➜If you're interested in a more in-depth look, enlist the services of a guide—they're easy to spot by their tracksuit-jacket uniforms.** Agree on a price before you start. An audio-guide system is currently in the works; these should be included in your ticket price when they are up and running. ⊠*Haukaypata (Plaza de Armas)* ☎*084/254–285* 🎫*S/16 or Boleto Integral* ⊙*Daily 10–6.*

❼ Convento de Santa Catalina de Siena. An extensive collection of Cusqueñan religious art is the draw at this still-working Dominican convent, which incorporates a 1610 church with high and low choirs and baroque friezes. Although there's not much to show of it these days, the convent represents another example of the pasting of Catholic religion over indigenous faiths—it was built on the site of the Acllawasi, the house of some 3,000 Inca chosen women dedicated to teaching, weaving Inca ceremonial robes, and worship of Inti, the Inca sun god. ⊠*Santa Catalina Angosta s/n* ☎*084/223–245* 🎫*Boleto Turístico* ⊙*Mon.–Thurs. and Sat. 9–5, Fri. 9–3:30.*

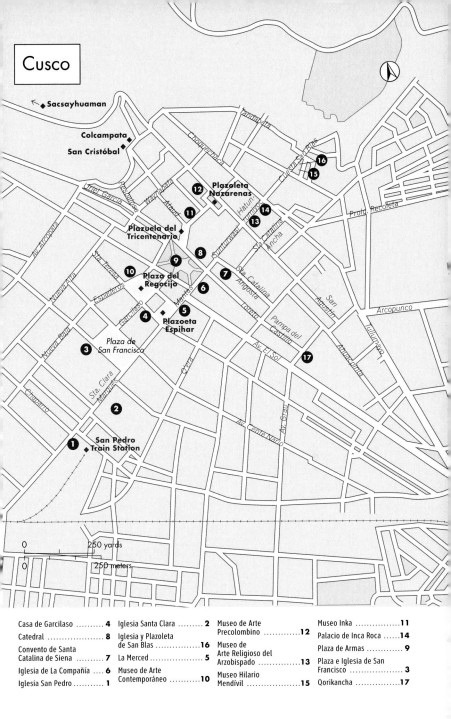

Cusco

← Sacsayhuaman

Colcampata
San Cristóbal

Plazoleta Nazarenas **12**

Plazuela del Tricentenario

Plaza del Regocijo **10**

Plazoeta Espihar

Plaza de San Francisco

San Pedro Train Station

0   250 yards

0   250 meters

DID YOU KNOW?

On Cusco's Plaza de Armas, the Cathedral was constructed atop the foundations of an Inca palace.

6 Iglesia de La Compañía. With its ornately carved facade, this Jesuit church on the Plaza gives the Cathedral a run for its money in the beauty stakes. The Compañía, constructed by the Jesuits in the 17th century, was intended to be the most splendid church in Cusco, which didn't sit too well with the archbishop. The beauty contest between the churches grew so heated that the pope was forced to intervene. He ruled in favor of the Cathedral, but by that time the Iglesia was nearly finished, complete with baroque facade to rival the Cathedral's grandeur. The interior is not nearly so splendid, however, although it's worth seeing the paintings on either side of the entrance depicting the intercultural marriage between a Spanish conquistador and an Inca princess. If you don't have a boleto integral, the church is open several times a day for mass and tourists are admitted under the condition that they participate in the mass—start wandering around and taking photos and you'll be shown the door. ⊠*Haukaypata (Plaza de Armas)* ☎*No phone* ☜*S/10 or Boleto Integral* ⊗*Mon.–Sat. 9–11:45 and 1–5:30, Sun. 9–10:45 and 1–5:30; Masses: Mon.–Sat. 7 AM, noon, 6, and 6:30 PM, Sun. 7:30, 11:30 AM, and 6 and 7 PM.*

11 Museo Inka. Everyone comes to "ooh" and "eeww" over this archaeological museum's collection of eight Inca mummies but the entire facility serves as a comprehensive introduction to pre-Columbian Andean culture. Jam-packed with textiles, ceramics, and dioramas, there's a lot to see but the displays look dated and there's not much in the way of English-language labeling. So brush up on your Spanish or hire a guide. One room is dedicated to the story of Mamakuka ("Mother Coca") and documents indigenous people's use of the coca leaf for religious and medicinal purposes—coca tea is used to relieve altitude sickness. The building was once the palace of Admiral Francisco Aldrete Maldonado, the reason for its common designation as the Palacio del Almirante (Admiral's Palace). ⊠*Ataúd at Córdoba del Tucumán* ☎*084/237–380* ☜*S/10* ⊗*Weekdays 8–6, Sat. 9–4.*

9 Plaza de Armas. With park benches, green lawns, and splendid views of the Cathedral, Cusco's gorgeous colonial Plaza de Armas invites you to stay awhile. Pull up one of those park benches and the world will come to you—without moving an inch you'll be able to purchase postcards, paintings, and snacks, organize a trip to Machu Pichu, get your photograph taken, and get those dirty boots polished. ■**TIP➜What you see today is a direct descendant of imperial Cusco's central square, which the Inca called the Haukaypata (the only name indicated on today's street signs) and it extended as far as the Plaza del Regocijo.** According to belief, this was the exact center of the Inca empire, Tawantinsuyo, the Four Corners of the Earth. Today, continuing the tradition, it's the tourism epicenter. From the Plaza you'll see the Cathedral and Iglesia de la Compañía on two sides, and the graceful archways of the colonial *portales,* or covered arcades, lining the other sides. Soft lighting bathes the plaza each evening and creates one of Cusco's iconic views. On Sunday mornings a military parade marches on the cathedral side of the plaza, drawing hundreds of spectators and a few protesters. Enjoy the views of colonial Cusco but remember that any attempt to sit on one of those inviting green lawns will prompt furious whistle-blowing from the guards!

NEED A BREAK?
Half café, half cultural center, the second-floor La Tertulia sits just off the Plaza de Armas. It's a place to curl up with a cup of coffee in front of a cozy fireplace on a chilly day. Donate the book you've just finished to the book exchange and grab another or browse the selection of foreign newspapers and magazines. Good breakfast options are on offer for early risers; lunch and dinner are the usual alpaca and chicken fare. ⊠ *Procuradores 44* ☎ *No phone* ⊗ *Daily 8–10* ▭ *No credit cards.*

HEY TOURIST!

The ubiquitous TOURIST INFORMATION signs are storefront travel agencies anxious to sell you tours rather than provide unbiased, official sources of information.

NORTH OF THE PLAZA DE ARMAS

Huff and puff your way up the narrow cobbled streets north of the Plaza de Armas to the trendy artisan district of San Blas. This is *the* spot in Cusco to pick up treasures such as ornate *Escuela Cusqueña*–style paintings and carved traditional masks. The streets are steep but you'll have plenty of opportunity to catch your breath admiring the spectacular views along the way.

WHAT TO SEE

⑯ **Iglesia y Plazoleta de San Blas.** The little square in San Blas has a simple adobe church with one of the jewels of colonial art in the Americas—the pulpit of San Blas, an intricately carved 17th-century cedar pulpit, arguably Latin America's most ornate. Tradition holds that the work was hewn from a single tree trunk, but experts now believe it was assembled from 1,200 individually carved pieces. Figures of Martin Luther, John Calvin, and Henry VII—all opponents of Catholicism—as well as those representing the seven deadly sins are condemned for eternity to hold up the pulpit's base. The work is dominated by the triumphant figure of Christ. At his feet rests a human skull, not carved, but the real thing. It's thought to belong to Juan Tomás Tuyrutupac, the creator of the pulpit. ☎ *084/254–285* ▭ *S/10 or Boleto Integral* ⊗ *Church Mon.–Sat. 8–6, Sun. 10–6.*

⑫ **Museo de Arte Precolombino.** For a different perspective on pre-Colombian ceramics head to this spectacular new museum, known as MAP, where art and pre-Colombian culture merge seamlessly. Twelve rooms in the 1580 Casa Cabrera, which was used as the convent of Santa Clara until the 17th century, showcase an astounding collection of pre-Columbian art from the 13th to 16th centuries, mostly in the form of carvings, ceramics, and jewelry. The art and artifacts were made by the Huari and Nasca, as well as the Inca, cultures. The stylish displays have excellent labels in Spanish and English that place the artifacts in their artistic and historical context. On the walls is commentary from European artists on South American art. Swiss artist Paul Klee wrote: "I wish I was newly born, and totally ignorant of Europe, innocent

Fodor's Choice
★

of facts and fashions, to be almost primitive." Most Cusco museums close at dark but MAP remains open every evening. ✉ *Plazoleta Nazarenas 231* ☎ *084/233–210* 💰 *S/20* ⏱ *Daily 9 AM–10 PM.*

13 Museo de Arte Religioso del Arzobispado. The building may be on the dark and musty side, but this San Blas museum has a remarkable collection of religious art. Originally the site of the Inca Roca's Hatun Rumiyoq palace, then the juxtaposed Moorish-style palace of the Marqués de Buenavista, the building reverted to the archdiocese of Cusco and served as the archbishop's residence. The primary repository of religious art in the city, many of the paintings in the collection are anonymous but you'll notice some by the renowned indigenous artist Marcos Zapata. A highlight is a series of 17th-century paintings that depict the city's Corpus Christi procession. Many of the works in the museum's 12 rooms are not labeled so you may want the services of a guide. ✉ *Hatun Rumiyoq and Herejes* ☎ *084/222–781* 💰 *S/10 or Boleto Integral* ⏱ *Mon.–Sat. 8–6, Sun. 10–6.*

15 Museo Hilario Mendívil. As San Blas's most famous son, the former home of 20th-century Peruvian religious artist Hilario Mendívil (1929–77), makes a good stop if you have an interest in Cusqeñan art and iconography. Legend has it that Mendívil saw llamas parading in the Corpus Christi procession as a child and later infused this image into his religious art, depicting all his figures with long, llamalike necks. ■ **TIP→** In the small gallery are the maguey-wood and rice-plaster sculptures of the Virgin with the elongated necks that were the artist's trademark. There's also a shop selling Mendívil style work. ✉ *Plazoleta San Blas 634* ☎ *084/232–231* 💰 *Free* ⏱ *Mon.—Sat. 9–1 and 2–6.*

FodorsChoice ★

14 Palacio de Inca Roca. Inca Roca lived in the 13th or 14th century. Halfway along the palace's side wall, nestled amid other stones, is the famous 12-angled stone, an example of masterly Inca masonry. There's nothing sacred about the 12 angles: Inca masons were famous for incorporating stones with many more sides than 12 into their buildings. If you can't spot the famous stone from the crowds taking photos, ask one of the shopkeepers or one of the elaborately dressed Inca figures hanging out along the street to point it out. Around the corner is a series of stones on the wall that form the shapes of a puma and a serpent. Kids hang out there and trace the forms for a small tip. ✉ *Hatunrumiyoq and Palacio and Herrajes.*

San Blas. For spectacular views over Cusco's terra-cotta rooftops head to San Blas, the traditional old Bohemian quarter of artists and artisans and one of the city's most picturesque districts. Recently restored, its whitewashed adobe homes with bright-blue doors shine anew.

■ TIP→The area is fast becoming the trendiest part of Cusco, with many of the city's choicest restaurants and bars opening their doors here. The Cuesta de San Blas (San Blas Hill), one of the main entrances into the area, is sprinkled with galleries that sell paintings in the Cusqueña-school style of the 16th through 18th centuries. Many of the stone streets are built as stairs or slopes (not for cars) and have religious motifs carved into them.

OFF THE BEATEN PATH

Colcampata. The 15-minute walk to Colcampata offers a tour through colonial neighborhoods in the heights above the city. Following Procuradores from the Plaza de Armas to Waynapata and then Resbalosa, you'll come to a steep cobblestone staircase with a wonderful view of La Compañía. Continuing to climb, you'll find the church of San Cristóbal, which is of little intrinsic interest but affords another magnificent panorama of the city. The church stands atop Colcampata, believed to have been the palace of the first Inca ruler, Manco Capac. The Inca wall to the right of the church has 11 niches in which soldiers may once have stood guard. Farther up the road, the lane on the left leads to a post-conquest Inca gateway beside a magnificent Spanish mansion.

SOUTH OF THE PLAZA DE ARMAS

After the colonial charm of central Cusco and San Blas, head south of the Plaza for a timely reminder that you're still in Peru. Traffic, smog, and horn-happy drivers welcome you to the noisy and unattractive Avenida El Sol, where the colonial charm of the city is hidden but for one glaring exception: Cusco's if-you-have-time-for-only-one-thing tourist attraction, the Qorikancha, or temple of the sun. Don't miss it.

WHAT TO SEE

Casa de Garcilaso. You'll find a bit of everything in this spot, which may leave you feeling like you've seen it all before. Colonial building? Check. Cusqueña-school paintings? Check. Ancient pottery? Check. Inca mummy? Check. This is the colonial childhood home of Inca Garcilaso de la Vega, the famous chronicler of the Spanish conquest and illegitimate son of one of Pizarro's captains and an Inca princess. Inside the mansion, with its cobblestone courtyard, is the Museo de Historia Regional, with Cusqueña-school paintings and pre-Inca mummies— one from Nazca has a 1½-meter (5-foot) braid—and ceramics, metal objects, and other artifacts. ⊠ *Heladeros at Garcilaso* ☎ *084/223–245* ▭ *Boleto Turístico* ☾ *Mon.–Sat. 8:30–5.*

Iglesia San Pedro. Stones from Inca ruins were used to construct this church. Though spartan inside, San Pedro is known for its ornately carved pulpit. The vendors you see on the front steps are a spillover from the nearby central market. Though colorful, this neighborhood shopping area is not the safest for tourists—leave important belongings in your hotel room. ⊠ *Santa Clara at Chaparro* ☎ *No phone* ▭ *Free* ☾ *Mon.–Sat. 7–11:30 and 6–7:30.*

Iglesia Santa Clara. Austere from the outside, this incredible 1588 church takes the prize for most eccentric interior decoration. ■ TIP→Thousands

Tours of Cusco, the Sacred Valley & Machu Picchu

The typical tour of the Cusco region combines the city with the Sacred Valley and Machu Picchu in three whirlwind days, including the full boleto turístico. We recommend devoting five days to get the most out of your visit—including one day to get acclimated to the high altitude.

Many excellent tour operators and travel agents are in Cusco, and some have offices in Lima. Several companies specialize in adventure tours, others in rafting excursions, still others in llama-assisted treks.

Several outfitters offer rafting trips on the Río Urubamba, close enough to Cusco to be done as a day excursion from the city. The river is navigable year-round, with rains turning it into a Class V from November–May, but a more manageable Class III the rest of the year. All also do multiday trips to the Río Apurimac, outside the Sacred Valley south of Cusco, during its May–December rafting season.

SELECTING A TRAVEL AGENCY

"Holaaaa—trip to Machu Picchu?" With so many touts in Cusco's streets hawking tours to Peru's most famous sight, it's tempting to just buy one in order to make them stop asking. Anyone who offers an Inca Trail trek departing tomorrow should be taken with more than a grain of salt—Inca Trail walks need to be booked months in advance. Don't make arrangements or give money to someone claiming to be a travel agent if they approach you on the street or at the airport in Cusco or Lima. Instead choose an agency that has a physical address. Better yet, select one that is listed in this book or on www.peru.info. Below are several reputable travel agencies.

Action Valley operates an adventure park near Poroy with double-cord bungee jumping, catapult swing, paragliding, and environmentally friendly paintball. Guides speak German and Hebrew in addition to English and Spanish. ⊠ *Santa Teresa 325, Cusco* ☎ *084/240–835* ⊕ *www. actionvalley.com.*

Amazing Peru organizes group and individual guided tours, including two types of trips to Cusco and Machu Picchu. Transportation services and accommodations are top-notch, and the guides are flexible and extremely helpful. ☎ *01/243–7704 in Lima, 800/704–2915 in North America* ⊕ *www.amazingperu.com.*

Andina Travel specializes in trekking, especially alternatives to the Inca Trail, as well as offering all the standard Sacred Valley and Machu Picchu tours. ⊠ *Plazoleta Santa Catalina 219, Cusco* ☎ *084/251–892* ⊕ *www. andinatravel.com.*

Tame rafting trips on the Urubamba River are operated year-round by **Apumayo Expediciones** ⊠ *Garcilaso 265, Cusco* ☎🖷 *084/246–018* ⊕ *www.apumayo.com.*

Enigma specializes in small, customized adventure trips throughout the region. Enjoy trekking, rafting, mountain climbing, mountain biking, or horseback riding led by professional guides. ⊠ *Jr. Clorinda Mato de Turner 100, Cusco* ☎ *084/222–155* ⊕ *www. enigmaperu.com.*

Explorandes is large and long-running company that organizes customized guided trips and expeditions through the Andes in Peru and Ecuador, including rafting and trekking trips around Cusco. ⊠ *Av. Garcilazo 316, Cusco* ☎ *084/238–380, 01/445–*

0532 in Lima ⊕ www.explorandes.com.

Globos de los Andes floats you above the Sacred Valley on hot-air balloon tours. ⊠ Av. de la Cultura 220, Cusco ☎ 084/232–352 ⊕ www.globosperu.com.

Inkaterra is a top-end agency specializing in nature-orientated trips to Machu Picchu, but can customize tours that include Cusco and the Sacred Valley with however much guide accompaniment as you need. ⊠ Andalucía 174, Miraflores, Lima ☎ 01/610–0400 in Lima, 084/245–314 in Cusco, 800/442–5042 toll-free in North America ⊕ www.inkaterra.com.

Instinct leads Cusco city tours, Inca Trail hikes, walking and rafting trips along the Tambopata River, and more. ⊠ Av. de la Cultura 1318, Cusco ⊠ Calle 25 No. 129, San Isidro, Lima ☎ 084/233–451 ⊕ www.instinct-travel.com.

Marle's Travel Adventure offers trekking excursions and rents or sells camping equipment, in addition to doing all the standard Sacred Valley tours. ⊠ Plateros 328, Cusco ☎ 084/233–680 ✎ marlestraveladventure@yahoo.com.

Mayuc is known for its rafting excursions but also offers good city and Sacred Valley tours. ⊠ Portal de Confiturías 211, Haukaypata, Plaza de Armas, Cusco ☎ 084/242–824 ⊕ www.mayuc.com.

Overseas Adventure Travel offers fully escorted 11-day tours of Cusco and the surrounding region with groups no larger than 16 people. A popular OAT add-on is a trip to Ecuador's Galápagos Islands.

☎ 800/493–6824 in North America ⊕ www.oattravel.com.

River Explorers takes you on one- to six-day rafting and kayaking excursions on the Urubamba and Apurimac rivers, and offers the standard trekking tours. ⊠ Plateros 328, Cusco ☎ 084/233–680 ⊕ www.riverexplorers.com.

Urubamba-based **Sacred Valley Mountain Bike Tours** rents mountain bikes for $25 per day and $15 per half-day, and leads cycling excursions throughout the valley. ⊠ Jr. Convención s/n, Urubamba ☎ 084/201–331 ⊕ www.machawasi.com.

Cusco-based **SAS Travel** has made a name for itself in trekking circles, but can also customize tours and accommodations in the region. ⊠ Garcilaso 270 ⊠ Portal de Panes 167, Haukaypata, Plaza de Armas, Cusco ☎ 084/249–194 or 084/255–205 ⊕ www.sastravelperu.com.

Swissraft-Peru runs multiday trips on class II, II, IV, and V rapids. ⊠ Heladeros 129, Cusco ☎ 084/264–124 ⊕ www.swissraft-peru.com.

For a tame adventurer, **Wilderness Travel** has a Peru Llama Trek that follows an off-Inca trail route to Machu Picchu where llamas carry your gear and you have the trail to yourself until near the end. ⊠ 1102 9th St., Berkeley, ☎ 510/558–2488, 800/368–2794 in U.S. ⊕ www.wildernesstravel.com.

Mainly for experienced adventurers, **X-treme Tourbulencia** leads mountain climbing and biking, trekking, and multisport trips. ⊠ Plateros 358, Cusco ☎ 084/224–362 ⊕ www.x-tremetourbulencia.com.

5

of mirrors cover the interior, competing with the gold-laminated altar for glittery prominence. Legend has it that the mirrors were placed inside in order to tempt locals into church. Built in old Inca style, using stone looted from Inca ruins, this is a great example of the lengths that the Spanish went to in order to attract indigenous converts to the Catholic faith. ⊠*Santa Clara* ☎*No phone* ✆*Free* ⊙*Daily 7–11:30 and 6–7:30.*

5 La Merced. The church may be overshadowed by the more famous Cathedral and Iglesia de la Compañía, but La Merced contains one of the city's most priceless treasures—the Custodia, a solid gold container for communion wafers more than a meter high and encrusted with thousands of precious stones. ■**TIP➔Two of the city's most famous conquistadors are buried here—Diego de Almagro and Gonzalo Pizarro.** Rebuilt in the 17th century, this monastery, with two stories of portals and a colonial fountain, gardens, and benches, has a spectacular series of murals that depict the life of the founder of the Mercedarian order, St. Peter of Nolasco. ⊠*Mantas 121* ☎*084/231–831* ✆*S/3* ⊙*Church: Mon.–Sat. 7–7:30 AM and 5–8 PM, Sun. 7–noon and 6:30–7:30 PM; museum: Mon.–Sat. 8–12:30 and 2–5:30.*

10 Museo de Arte Contemporáneo. Take a refreshing turn back toward the present in this city of history. Yet even the modern-art museum, in the Cusco municipal hall, focuses on the past. Twentieth-century artists have put a modern-art spin on imperial and colonial themes. ⊠*Kusipata s/n (Plaza Regocijo)* ☎*084/240–006* ✆*Boleto Turístico* ⊙*Weekdays 9–5.*

3 Plaza e Iglesia de San Francisco. Close to the Plaza de Armas, this plaza is a more local hangout. There's not a lot to see, apart from an intriguing garden of native plants. More interesting, if you've wandered this way, is the church with its macabre sepulchers with arrangements of bones and skulls, some pinned to the wall to spell out morbid sayings. A small museum of religious art with paintings by Cusqueña-school artists Marcos Zapata and Diego Quispe Tito is in the church sacristy. ⊠*3 blocks south of Plaza de Armas* ☎*084/221–361* ✆*S/1* ⊙*Weekdays 9–noon and 3–5.*

17 Qorikancha. If the Spanish came to the new world looking for El

Fodor'sChoice Dorado, the lost city of gold, they must have thought they'd found it
★ when they laid eyes on Qorikancha. Built during the reign of the Inca Pachacutec to honor the Sun, Tawantinsuyos' most important divinity, Qorikancha translates as "Court of Gold." Conquistadors' jaws must have dropped when they saw the gold-plated walls of the temple glinting in the sunlight. Then their fingers must have started working because all that remains today is the masterful stonework.

If Cusco was constructed to represent a puma, then Qorikancha was positioned as the animal's loins, the center from which all creation emanated; 4,000 priests and attendants are thought to have lived within its confines. Walls and altars were plated with gold, and in the center of the complex sat a giant gold disc, positioned to reflect the sun and bathe the temple in light. At the summer solstice, sunlight reflected into a niche in the wall where only the Inca were permitted to sit. Terraces that face it were once filled with life-size gold-and-silver statues of plants and animals. ■**TIP→Much of the wealth was removed to pay ransom for the captive Inca ruler Atahualpa during the Spanish conquest, blood money paid in vain since Atahualpa was later murdered.** Eventually, Francisco Pizarro awarded the site to his brother Juan. Upon Juan's death, the structure passed to the Dominicans, who began to construct the church of Santo Domingo, using stones from the temple and creating perhaps Cusco's most jarring imperial–colonial architectural juxtaposition.

An ingenious restoration to recover both buildings after the 1953 earthquake lets you see how the church was built on and around the walls and chambers of the temple. In the Inca parts of the structure left exposed, estimated to be about 40% of the original temple, you can admire the mortarless masonry, earthquake-proof trapezoidal doorways, curved retaining wall, and exquisite carvings that exemplify the artistic and engineering skills of the Inca. Bilingual guides lead tours every day except Sunday; the service is included in your admission price. A small museum down the hill with an entrance on Avenida El Sol contains a few artifacts from the site but doesn't warrant a huge amount of your time. ⊠*Pampa del Castillo at Plazoleta Santo Domingo* ☎*No phone* ☜*Ruins and church, S/10; museum, Boleto Turístico* ☉*Ruins and church, Mon.–Sat. 8:30–5:30, Sun. 2–5; museum, Mon.–Sat. 9–5:30, Sun. 9–1.*

WHERE TO EAT

THE SCENE

Cusco's dining scene is surprisingly vast. You'll encounter everything from Andean grills to Middle Eastern kebab shops. Restaurant employees on Cusco's Plaza de Armas and Plateros and Procuradores streets—any of these could be renamed "Restaurant Row"—stand in their doorways, touting their establishments, menus in hand, to entice you in. For better hygiene and more sophisticated cuisine, head into the trendy San Blas district, where you'll find some of the city's top restaurants tucked away down the ancient cobbled streets. Browsing any menu you're sure to come across the Andean specialties of *cuy* and *alpaca*. The former, you'll know as guinea pig and is usually served roasted (sometimes with peppers stuffed charmingly in its mouth!). The latter is the cute furry llamalike creature you'll see wandering the Cusco streets with its indigenous owner for photo ops.

PLANNING

Lunch is served between 1 and 3. Dinner begins around 7, and most restaurants start winding down service at about 9. Most places do stay open continually throughout the afternoon.

WHAT IT COSTS IN NUEVO SOLES					
RESTAURANTS	¢	$	$$	$$$	$$$$
under S/20	S/20–S/35	S/35–S/50	S/50–S/65	over S/65	under S/20

Prices are per person for a main course.

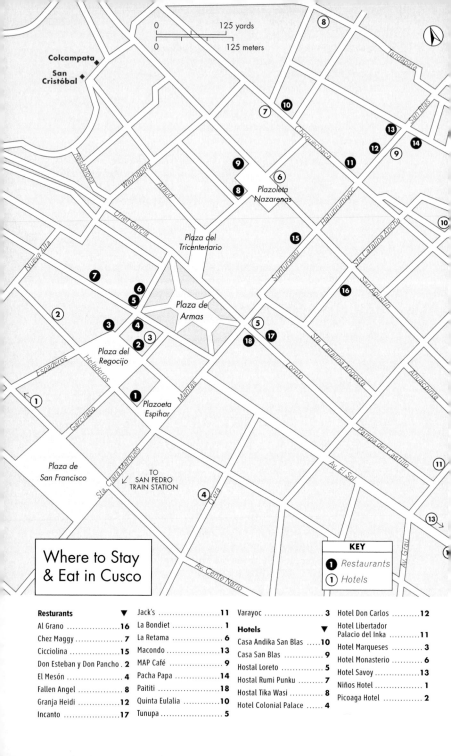

Where to Stay & Eat in Cusco

KEY

❶ Restaurants

① Hotels

CAFÉS

¢ ✗**La Bondiet.** You could be in Europe in this stylish café close to the Plaza, and although we all know that you come to Peru to experience Peru, we all need a break sometimes. ■**TIP→**This is a great spot to regroup and recaffeinate after a hard morning's sightseeing. The coffee is great, there's a huge range of mouthwatering cakes and slices to dig into, and the unusual "Inca Punch" (a milk punch with a shot of pisco) awaits those who need something a little stronger. ⊠*Heladeros 118* ☎*084/246–823* ☐*V.*

┌─────────────────────────────────┐
│ **CORN A 100 WAYS**   │
│   │
│ Corn is the other staple of the │
│ Peruvian diet—wander the streets │
│ of Cusco long enough and   │
│ you'll soon see it being popped, │
│ steamed, and roasted into a   │
│ healthy carbo-snack. *Chicha,* a │
│ corn beer drunk at room tempera- │
│ ture and sold from rural homes   │
│ that display a red flag (and in │
│ many restaurants) is a surprisingly │
│ tasty take on the old corn cob. │
└─────────────────────────────────┘

¢ ✗**Jack's.** Scrummy all-day breakfasts await at this bright and busy Aus-
★ sie-owned café in San Blas. Dishing up granola and yogurt, toasties, or a gordo brekkie with bacon and eggs, sausages, cheese, and salad, Jack's is a stand-out hit. Come during peak season and you may have to line up to get a table. Everything is prepared in-house, including the delicious breads, and the coffee is to die for. Don't think that breakfast is just a day-time food either, this jumping spot stays open well into the night. ⊠*Choquechaca 509* ☎*084/254–606* ☐*No credit cards.*

CONTINENTAL

¢–$$ ✗**Fallen Angel.** Suppress your gasps as you walk in: images of heaven,
Fodor'sChoice hell, earth, limbo, and purgatory, and everything in between greet you.
★ ■**TIP→**This was one of Francisco Pizarro's houses, and it's doubtful that he envisioned anything so avant-garde. You'll dine off bathtubs that double as fish tanks, watched over all the while by baroque angels (not the waiters!). The steak-driven menu, just like the decoration, is absolutely fabulous darling. ⊠*Plazoleta Nazarenas 221* ☎*084/258–184* ☐*AE, DC, MC, V* ⊘*No lunch Sun.*

GERMAN

¢–$ ✗**Granja Heidi.** You won't offend the owner if you ask, "Are you Heidi?" but that's actually the name of the mule who resides on the nearby farm where the owners get much of the produce for this San Blas restaurant. Yep, it's all about the farm here and while the farm-fresh yogurt is good, the farmer attitude may be a little harder to stomach. The menu is lactose-driven; look for yogurts and curds accompanying crepes and fruits. Dinner means meat and vegeterian dishes, soups, and stir-fries. ⊠*Cuesta San Blas 525* ☎*084/238–383* ☐*No credit cards* ⊘*Closed Sun.*

LATIN

¢–$$ ✗**Macondo.** Part art gallery, part café, and entirely hip, the Macondo takes its name from the land of magical realism in Gabriel García Márquez's *One Hundred Years of Solitude.* Like the novel's invented land, this eatery dishes up what they like to call "invented food" with mouthwatering Neuevo-Peruvian dishes such as "euphoria chicken" served in a mango and orange sauce or alpaca mignon with white wine and mushrooms. Bring your old books to swap at the book exchange. ⊠ *Cuesta San Blas 571* ☎ *084/229–415* ⊟ *V* ⊗ *No lunch Sun.*

MEDITERRANEAN

$–$$ ✗ **Cicciolina.** Everyone seems to know everyone and greet each other
Fodor's Choice   with a peck on the cheek at this second-floor eatery, part lively tapas
★   bar, part sit-down, candle-light restaurant. The bar wraps around the kitchen area where a small army of cooks prepare your food. You'll strain to see as they set out each new platter of tapas—perhaps some bruschetta or prawns and sweet potato in wasabi sauce—and be tempted to say, "I want one of those." The restaurant half of Cicciolina is much more subdued, with a complete selection of homemade pastas with Mediterranean sauces on the menu. You can order off the restaurant menu in the tapas bar, but not the other way around. ⊠ *Sunturwasi 393, Triunfo* ☎ *084/239–510* ⊟ *AE, DC, MC, V.*

$–$$ ✗ **Incanto.** Stylish contemporary design in an Andean setting has made this large upmarket restaurant near the Plaza a hit with those looking for a classy night out. Dishing up Mediterranean-Andean fusion cuisine as well as more traditional dishes such as delicious thin-crust pizza, this has got to be the only place in the world where you'll find ravioli of *aji de gallina*, a traditional creamy chicken sauce usually served with rice, on the menu. Wander down the back to the open kitchen, and don't forget to have a look at the original Inca wall on the way. ⊠ *Catalina Angosta 135* ☎ *084/254-753* ⊕ *www.cuscorestaurants.com* ⊟ *AE, DC, MC, V.*

PAN-ASIAN

¢   ✗ **Al Grano.** Don't let the Andean tapestries and replica Inca stone wall fool you: this small restaurant off the Plaza de Armas specializes in Asian rice plates. It offers a fantastic selection of affordable dishes from India, Thailand, Malaysia, Sri Lanka, Vietnam, Myanmar, and Indonesia. You have a choice of eight prix-fixe dinners every evening, each including one of a rotating selection of entrées. The rich dessert cakes and brownies *are* Peruvian rather than Asian, however. ⊠ *Santa Catalina Ancha 398* ☎ *084/228–032* ⊟ *No credit cards* ⊗ *Closed Sun.*

PERUVIAN

$ ✗ **Don Esteban y Don Pancho.** Contemporary Andean cuisine is the flavor of this new addition to Cusco's dining scene. Starched white tablecloths and impeccable service lend a polished air, although design touches such as a cobbled floor and natural fibers are reminders that you're in the Andes. The menu is as well-crafted as the service, with traditional Peruvian Criolle dishes. The carapulcra, dried potato with pork ribs, and the traditional bean dish tacu tacu are stand outs. Even if you don't eat, drop in for cocktails—the Chicha Tu May, which puts a twist on the pisco sour by adding a dash of ruby-red chicha, is a happiness inducer. ⊠ *Portal Espinar 144, Plaza Regocigo* ☎ *084/244–664* ⊕ *www.donestebanydonpancho.com* ⊟ *AE, DC, MC, V.*

DID YOU KNOW?

Since the late 1500s a procession carries statues of saints from area churches to the Cathedral for Cusco's Corpus Christi celebration (60 days after Easter).

$$$$ ✕**MAP Café.** Museum eateries rarely warrant guidebook listings, but this small, elegant café inside the glass-enclosed courtyard of the Museo de Arte Precolombino is actually one of the city's top restaurants. Dishing up novel and exciting twists on traditional Peruvian cuisine, try tuna with an Andean chili chutney or baked cuy, served with an accompaniment of pureed Andean potatoes. The menu is prix-fixe after 6 PM. ⊠*Plazoleta Nazarenas 231* ☎*084/242–476* ⚖*Reservations essential* ⊟*AE, DC, MC, V.*

$–$$$$ ✕**El Mesón de Espaderos.** You'll drink in the city's history as you dine on a rustic second-floor terrace with stucco walls and high-beamed ceilings above the Plaza de Armas. ■**TIP➔The parrilladas (barbecued meats) are the best in Cusco.** The platter for one person is more than enough for two, and the *Parrilla Inca,* with its mix of Andean meats, provides a good opportunity to try that cuy (guinea pig) that you've been putting off. Vegetarians may want to pass, or resign themselves to dining from the salad bar. ⊠*Espaderos 105* ☎*084/235–307* ⊟*AE, DC, MC, V.*

$–$$$ ✕**Pacha Papa.** If you've been putting off trying the famous Andean
Fodor's Choice   dishes of guinea pig or alpaca, then wait no longer. This fabulous res-
★   taurant is hands-down the best place in town for Peruvian food. Based on a typical open-air quinta, wooden tables are scattered around a large patio, warmed on those chilly Andean nights by the huge bread oven, which takes pride of place at the front, and an underground oven where one of the star dishes, pachamanca, is cooked then disinterred before your eyes. The menu takes influences from all over Peru and the waiters are happy to explain what makes each dish special. Try the delicious anticuchas de alpaca, skewers of tender alpaca meat with local spices, and don't miss the sensational adobo de chancho, a tangy pork stew with meat that melts in your mouth. The star dishes of cuy al horno, baked guinea-pig, or the underground-oven baked *pachamanca* stew where different types of meats are slow roasted together with potatoes and aromatic herbs (pacha is Quechua for ground, manca means pot) have to be ordered 24 hours in advance, so plan ahead. ⊠*Plazoleta San Blas 120* ☎*084/241–318* ⊟*AE, DC, MC, V.*

$–$$$ ✕**Paititi.** On the Plaza de Armas, this quiet, tourist-oriented restaurant that encompasses part of the original Inca wall has good fish, especially the grilled or fried trout. It's also a fine place to initiate yourself to alpaca: Paititi's specialty is this peculiarly Andean delicacy basted in a sauco (cranberry-like Peruvian fruit) sauce. Additional lures are live folk-music shows nightly and a free pisco sour for all diners. ⊠*Portal de Carrizos 270, Plaza de Armas* ☎*084/252–686* ⊟*AE, DC, MC, V.*

¢–$ ✕**Quinta Eulalia.** A quinta is a típico semi-open air Peruvian restaurant, and Eulalia's is the oldest such place in the city, cooking up hearty, filling portions of down-home food since 1941. Chicharrones (fried pork and cabbage), trucha al horno (oven-baked trout), and cuy chactado (guinea pig with potatoes) are specialties. ⊠*Choquechaca 384* ☎*084/234–495* ⊟*No credit cards* ☻*No dinner.*

¢–$$$ ✕**La Retama.** One of the better offerings on the Plaza, this tourist-oriented second-floor eatery wins points for its view over the Cathedral and Iglesia de la Compañía. Pull up a stool on the balcony to drink in the vista while you tuck into an Andean river trout in garlic sauce or trout ceviche. A cozy fireplace, Andean tapestries, and a nightly folk-music show complete the experience. ⊠*Portal de Panes 123, Plaza de Armas* ☎*084/226–372* ▤*MC, V.*

$–$$$$ ✕**Tunupa.** With subdued lighting and thoughtful design touches that include Andean textiles on the walls, this Tunupa effectively plays down its barnlike size. An endless buffet combines traditional Andean delicacies, such as alpaca and cuy, with more familiar Thai and Japanese offerings, and there's platter after platter of desserts, and free pisco sours. A nightly show to boot makes this upstairs venue on the Plaza de Armas hugely popular with tour groups. More intimate seating is on the balcony (glassed-in for those chilly Andean nights), but bookings are advisable regardless of your group size. Try the carpaccio *de lomo* (beef marinated in herbs, olive oil, and Parmesan cheese) and finish with a rich *suspiro a la limeña*, a sweet Peruvian mousse. ⊠*Portal de Confiturías 233, Plaza de Armas* ☎*084/252–936* ▤*AE, DC, MC, V.*

PIZZA

¢ ✕**Chez Maggy.** If the mountain air is a little chilly, warm up in front of the open brick ovens that produce the café's great pizzas and calzones. (Peruvian food is on the menu, but everyone comes for the pizza.) Four branches in Cusco are within a block of each other. The tables are smaller and more intimate at the main location on Plateros, but you're sure to trade tales with other travelers around the corner at Procuradores 344, as seating is at very long wooden tables. You'll also find Maggy and her pizza at Procuradores 365 and 374. ⊠*Plateros 348* ☎*084/234–861* ▤*AE, DC, MC, V.*

SWISS

¢–$$ ✕**Varayoc.** A step away from the Plaza madness, this tranquil spot is a perfect place to catch your breath and plan the day's next activity. Soft colors, exposed wood beams, and whitewashed walls create a soothing atmosphere, enhanced by the sounds of an Andean harp played live during the evenings. For a midday snack, try their good coffee, tasty pastries, and swiss food with crepes and fondues being the house specialties. ⊠*Espaderos 142* ☎*084/232–404* ▤*AE, MC.*

WHERE TO STAY

THE SCENE

No matter what your travel budget, you won't be priced out of the market staying in Cusco: luxury hotels, backpackers' digs, and everything in between await. Most lodgings discount rates during the unofficial off-season of September through May. With a few exceptions, absent are the international hotel chains. In their place are smaller, top-end, independently run lodgings offering impeccable service, even if they lack swimming pools and concierges. Lodgings in all price ranges, whether housed in a former 17th-century convent or newly built, mimic the old Spanish-colonial style of construction arranged around a central courtyard or patio.

5

You may have to adjust your internal thermostat in moderate or budget lodgings at this altitude, but all provide extra blankets. And the hot water might not be on all day, or could be lukewarm at best, even though hotels in this price range say they have *agua caliente*. Larger accommodations keep an oxygen supply on hand for those having trouble adjusting to the thin air.

THE PLANNING

Lodgings in Cusco keep shockingly early checkout times. (Flights to Cusco arrive early in the morning.) ■TIP➔Expect to have to vacate your **room by 8 or 9 am, though this is less strictly enforced in the off-season.** Most lodgings will hold your luggage if you're not leaving town until later in the day. Breakfast, at least a continental one (and usually something more ample), is included in most lodging rates.

WHAT IT COSTS IN NUEVO SOLES				
HOTELS	¢	$	$$	$$$	$$$$
	under S/125	S/125–S/250	S/250–S/375	S/375–S/500	over S/500

Prices are for a standard double room, excluding tax.

$$$ ⊡ **Casa Andina San Blas.** Taking its lead from the Spaniards, Casa Andina
★ is slowly colonizing Cusco all over again with five branches now existing in various locales throughout the city. Part of a national chain, all of the Casa Andina hotels exude professionalism and are great value for money. Fortunately for them, this is where the resemblance ends, as each hotel differs in style. The San Blas branch, in a colonial house perched up on the hillside offers great views over the city's terra-cotta rooftops. The modern and comfortable rooms are tastefully furnished with Andean touches. **Pros:** Good value for top-end lodgings, excellent location with spectacular views over Cusco, professional atmosphere and pleasant service. **Cons:** Can be a hard walk uphill to get here, some rooms have sub-par views over the neighboring houses. ⊠*Chihuampata 278* ☎*084/263–694* ⊕*www.casa-andina.com* ➾*38 rooms* ⌂*In-room: safe. In-hotel: restaurant, bar, laundry service, no elevator, public Internet, public Wi-Fi, airport shuttle, no-smoking rooms* ⊟*AE, DC, MC, V.*

$$ ⊡ **Casa San Blas.** This small hotel with a large staff—there's a 2-to-
★ 1 staff-to-guest ratio—prides itself on exceptional service. Regular rooms are quite comfortable, with colonial-style furniture and hardwood floors, but with more modern amenities than this restored 250-year-old house would imply. The top-floor suites and one apartment are similar in style, but larger, with wood-beamed ceilings and great views over the city. The spacious apartment is a great option for those considering a longer stay, and has a fully equipped kitchen. All rooms are decorated with handmade textiles (each with a design reflecting the room's name), which can be purchased if you want a keepsake. ■TIP➔The hotel sits a block off the Cuesta San Blas, the "staircase" street **leading up from the Plaza de Armas, and could not be more central for sightseeing. Pros:** Exceptionally warm welcome from the staff, the mas-

sage service is a great way to soothe away those sightseeing aches, fantastic location. **Cons:** Regular rooms are relatively pricey, it's a steep uphill walk to get here, the adjoining restaurant is extremely small (but cozy!). ☒*Tocuyeros 566, San Blas* ☎*084/237–900, 888/569–1769 toll-free in North America* 🖷*084/251–563* ⊕*www.casasanblas.com* ⌨*12 rooms, 4 suites, 1 apartment* ⌂*In-room: safe, Wi-Fi. In-hotel: restaurant, bar, no elevator, laundry service, public Internet, public Wi-Fi, airport shuttle, no smoking rooms* ▤*AE, DC, MC, V* ◉❘*BP.*

$ ❑**Hostal Rumi Punku.** A massive stone door—that's what Rumi Punku means in Quechua—opens onto a rambling complex of balconies, patios, gardens, courtyards, terraces, fireplace, and bits of Inca wall scattered here and there. It all links a series of pleasantly furnished rooms with hardwood floors and comfy beds covered with plush blankets. The top-level sauna and gym has stupendous views of the city. Expansions were being planned at this writing, so watch out for changes. **Pros:** Great views from the upstairs sauna, good hot water 24 hours a day, charming rambling layout. **Cons:** Lots of stairs, no restaurant, located a huff and puff up the hill. ☒*Choquechaca 339* ☎*084/221–102* 🖷*084/242–741* ⊕*www.rumipunku.com* ⌨*20 rooms* ⌂*In-room:Wi-Fi. In-hotel: bar sauna, no elevator, laundry service, public Internet, public Wi-Fi* ▤*AE, DC, MC, V* ◉❘*CP.*

$ ❑**Hostal Tika Wasi.** On a lovely, winding street in the San Blas neighborhood, the hugely popular Tika Wasi has a flower-filled garden, around which cluster modern carpeted rooms with huge windows and stupendous views. **Pros:** Gorgeous garden with hanging chairs to lounge in, spectacular views over Cusco, tranquil atmosphere. **Cons:** No vehicle access, lots of stairs, often full. ☒*Tanda Pata 491* ☎🖷*084/231–609* ✐*tikawasi@hotmail.com* ⌨*22 rooms* ⌂*In-room: no phone (some). In-hotel: bar, no elevator, laundry service* ▤*No credit cards* ◉❘*BP.*

¢ ❑**Hotel Colonial Palace.** Built inside the 17th-century Convent of Santa Teresa, this hotel has simply furnished rooms on two floors laid out around two lovely courtyards. The former convent forms the older wing. Its rooms have character, if occasional leaky faucets. You'll find more modern furnishings in the newer wing in front of the old convent, though it's still constructed in the colonial style. The staff is exceptionally friendly and eager to please. **Pros:** Central location, colonial charm, how often do you get to sleep in a convent? **Cons:** Not much is "palatial" about the simple rooms, breakfasts on the patio can make for a chilly early morning. ☒*Quera 270* ☎*084/232–151* ⊕*www.colonialpalace.net* ⌨*48 rooms* ⌂*In-hotel: no elevator, laundry service, no-smoking rooms* ▤*AE, MC, V* ◉❘*CP.*

$$$ ❑**Hotel Don Carlos.** Part of a Peruvian minichain of hotels, the high-rise Don Carlos caters to business travelers. The hotel is not the most stylish, but rooms are comfortable and those facing the street have double-glazed windows, a rare concession in this land of noisy buses and horn-happy drivers. **Pros:** Away from the tourist hub, double-glazed windows keep out the chill and the noise, cozy downstairs bar. **Cons:** Unattractive location right on the Avenida El Sol, rooms are

5

small for the price, only one computer for guests to use. ⊠*Av. El Sol 602* ☎*084/226–207* ⊕*www.hotelesdoncarlos.com* ↩*50 rooms* ♿*In-room: safe, refrigerator. In-hotel: restaurant, room service, bar, laundry service, public Internet, airport shuttle, no-smoking rooms* ▤*AE, DC, MC, V.*

$$$$ 🏨**Hotel Libertador Palacio del Inka.** Close enough, but still removed from the hubbub of the Plaza de Armas, this hotel on the tiny Plazoleta Santo Domingo was the last home of Francisco Pizarro, the first governor of Peru. The glass-covered lobby may look like an airport, but it gives you a good idea of the sleek contemporary design that is the signature of this hotel chain. The modern rooms have colonial touches, some with original furniture, and all have central heating to keep out the chill. The plush bar makes a mean pisco sour. **Pros:** Contemporary rooms with all the conveniences, some rooms have views to the Sun Temple, close to the action, but not in the thick of it. **Cons:** A bit too near the unattractive Avenida El Sol, modern rooms lack the character of other lodgings, customer service has been reported to be uneven. ⊠*Plazoleta Santo Domingo 259* ☎*084/231–961, 01/442–1995 in Lima* ⊕*www.libertador.com.pe* ↩*254 rooms, 14 suites* ♿*In-room: safe, refrigerator, Wi-Fi. In-hotel: restaurant, bar, room service, gym, concierge, laundry service, public Internet, public Wi-Fi* ▤*AE, DC, MC, V* ⦿*BP.*

$ 🏨**Hostal Loreto.** You can't get much closer to the Plaza de Armas than this hostel in a colonial building around a small attractive sunlit courtyard. The tiny establishment has four rooms built against the original Inca wall, as well as other simple, less-interesting rooms. The friendly, eager-to-please owners live on the premises. **Pros:** Right on the Plaza, sleeping next to original Inca walls in some rooms makes for an authentically Cusqueñan experience, close to everything. **Cons:** Being right in the thick of things makes escaping the hustle and bustle a challenge, rooms are rather dark and uninspired, paying for location rather than charm. ⊠*Intik'ijllu (Loreto) 115* ☎*084/226–352* ✉*loretohostal@yahoo.com* ↩ *13 rooms* ▤*MC* ♿*In-room: no TV (some). In-hotel: no elevator, laundry service, airport shuttle, public Internet* ⦿*CP.*

$–$$ 🏨**Hotel Marqueses.** Spectacularly carved wooden doors, an intricately paved courtyard and Cathedral views will immediately impress you in this impeccably restored 16th-century building near the Plaza. Rooms congregate around an arcaded courtyard with grand old staircases and are furnished in full colonial style with tapestry bed covers and period details. Shell out a few extra soles to get a two-level suite, with balconies from which you can see the Cathedral, colonial paintings on the walls and wonderful carved wood throughout. **Pros:** Wonderful period details, views of the Cathedral from some rooms, good value suites. **Cons:** In the heart of the tourist action, standard rooms are a decided cut below the quality of the suites. ⊠*Garcilaso 256* ☎*084/264–249* ⊕*www.hotelmarqueses.com* ↩*30 rooms* ♿*In room: safe, refrigerator (some). In-hotel: bar, no elevator, laundry service, public Internet, airport shuttle, no-smoking rooms* ▤*AE, DC, MC, V* ⦿*BP.*

$$$$ 　⊡**Hotel Monasterio.** Indisputably Cusco's top hotel is this beautifully
Fodor'sChoice　restored 1592 monastery of San Antonio Abad, a national historic
★　monument. Planners managed to retain the austere beauty of the complex—the lodging even counts the original chapel with its ornate gold
altar and collection of Cusqueño art—yet updated the compact rooms
with stylish colonial furnishings and all the mod-cons such as remote
operated window blinds and TVs that pop out of cabinet tops. The
public spaces such as the elegant lounge bar and serene cloisters will
take your breath away. ■**TIP➜For those having trouble getting it back,
the hotel even offers an in-room oxygen enrichment service, the only such
hotel system in the world.** For S/100 per night you can elect to have
your room pressurized with a flow of enriched oxygen, much like in
an airplane cabin, duplicating conditions of those 1,000 meters (3,300
feet) lower than Cusco. **Pros:** Stylish rooms with all the conveniences,
stunning public spaces, attentive service. **Cons:** Rooms are small for
the price-tag, *everything* (including Internet access) is charged, the
piped choral music can get annoying. ⊠*Palacio 136, Plazoleta Nazarenas* ☎*084/240–696, 01/242–3427 in Lima* ⊕*www.monasterio.
orient-express.com* ➳*120 rooms, 6 suites* ⟁*In-room: safe, refrigerator. In-hotel: 2 restaurants, bar, spa, concierge, laundry service, public
Internet, public Wi-Fi* ▤*AE, DC, MC, V* ⦿*BP.*

$$ 　⊡**Hotel Savoy.** Although looking dated these days, the Savoy remains
popular with the local business set for being well away from the tour-
ist hubbub of the Plaza de Armas. The mirrored colonial-style lobby
introduces you to this hotel's conservative, yet friendly, style. Dark
carved wood is everywhere: the front desk, the mailboxes, the eleva-
tors, the room doors, and the dressers and headboards inside the car-
peted rooms. The rooftop Sky Room provides a panoramic view of the
city, although it's usually occupied by conference groups. **Pros:** Away
from the bustle, comfortable lobby, friendly staff. **Cons:** The inconve-
nient location means a hike to get into town, a casino adjoins the lobby,
the design is dated and could do with a make-over. ⊠*Av. El Sol 954*
☎*084/222–122* ⊕*www.savoycusco.com* ➳*115 rooms, 6 suites* ⟁*In-
room: safe (some), refrigerator (some), Wi-Fi (some). In-hotel: room
service, bar, laundry service, public Wi-Fi* ▤*AE, DC, MC, V* ⦿*BP.*

¢ 　⊡**Niños Hotel.** If you prefer lodging with a social conscience—and even
★　if you don't—this is a great budget find; proceeds from your stay at the
"Children's Hotel" provide medical and dental care, food, and recre-
ation for 250 disadvantaged Cusqueño children who attend day care
on the premises and cheerfully greet you as you pass through the court-
yard. Rooms tend toward the spartan side, with painted hardwood
floors but firm, comfy mattresses and an endless supply of hot water.
A few other rooms as well as four apartments with shared bath, for
longer stays, are down the street on Calle Fiero. The catch? The place
is immensely popular. Make reservations weeks in advance. **Pros:** Won-
derfully welcoming staff, charming colonial building, you can sleep
soundly with the knowledge that your money is going to a good cause!
Cons: Slightly out of the way, some rooms are small. ⊠*Meloq 442*
☎⌂*084/231–424* ⊕*www.ninoshotel.com* ➳*20 rooms, 13 with bath*

5

⌂*In-room: no phone, no TV. In-hotel: no elevator, laundry service, no-smoking rooms* ▭*No credit cards.*

$$$ ▦**Picoaga Hotel.** An upscale option at a fraction of the price of some Cusco lodgings, this hotel mixes the best of the new and old Cusco. The front half drips with colonial charm—rooms are set around an attractive arcaded courtyard in the 17th-century former home of the Marquis of Picoaga. Behind is a modern wing with a restaurant that overlooks the Plaza de Armas. Rooms in the front colonial section are charming, although for style and comfort, the minimalist modern rooms with their truly enormous beds can't be beaten. The bar, with its open wood fire, huge leather couches and cozy atmosphere, is the best spot in Cusco on a cold Andean night. **Pros:** Good value for top-end lodgings, mix of modern and colonial room options, great view from the restaurant. **Cons:** Can be either overrun with tour groups or eerily empty, among the favorite stomping ground of Cusco's street sellers. ✉*Calle Santa Teresa 344* ☎*084/252–330* ⊕*www.picoagahotel. com* ⥅*72 rooms* ⌂*In-room: safe, Wi-Fi. In-hotel: restaurant, room service, bar, concierge, laundry service, public Internet, public Wi-Fi* ▭*AE, DC, MC, V* ⏏|*BP.*

NIGHTLIFE & THE ARTS

Cusco is full of bars and discos with live music and DJs playing everything from U.S. rock to Andean folk. Though dance places levy a cover charge, there's usually someone out front handing out free passes to tourists—highly discriminatory, but in your favor. (Most of the dance locales cater to an under-thirty crowd.) Bars frequently position someone in front to entice you in with a coupon for a free drink, but that drink is sometimes made with the cheapest, gut-rottingest alcohol the bar has available.

BARS & PUBS

For a cold beer and English soccer broadcast via satellite, try **Cross Keys** (✉*Portal Confiturías 233, Plaza de Armas* ☎*084/229–227*), a pub that will make London expats homesick. Challenge the regulars to a game of darts at your own risk. **El Muki** (✉*Santa Catalina Angosta 114* ☎*084/227–797*), resembling a little cave, is popular with the younger crowd, and has the younger music to match. The second-floor, dark-wood **Paddy Flaherty's** (✉*Sunturwasi [Triunfo] 124* ☎*084/247–719*) mixes pints of Guinness and old-fashioned Irish pub grub with Philly steaks, pita sandwiches, and chicken baguettes. The second-floor **Norton Rat's** (✉*Intik'ijllu [Loreto] 115* ☎*084/246–204*) is Cusco's answer to a U.S.-style sports bar, with billiards, burgers, darts, and a big-screen satellite TV showing U.S. sports. In San Blas, the intimate **7 Angelitos** (✉*Siete Angelitos 638* ☎*084/806–070*) often highlights live or recorded Creole music from Peru's coast.

DANCE CLUBS

Step into the Plaza at night and you'll be fighting off offers of free entry passes and free drinks from touts eager to get you into their sticky-carpeted venue. The drinks may be rotten and the music may be reggaeton, but they're good fun if you want to boogie. Reputed to be Cusco's first disco, dating all the way back to 1985, **Kamikase** (⊠*Kusipata 274, Plaza Regocijo* ☎*084/233–865*) is a favorite gringo bar, though plenty of locals visit, too, and has a mix of salsa, rock, and folk music. **Mama Africa** (⊠*Portal de Panes 109, Plaza de Armas* ☎*084/245–550*), Cusco's hottest reggae and hip-hop dance venue, is also part travel agency and cyber café. Dance the night away at **Ukukus** (⊠*Plateros 316* ☎*084/233–445*), a hugely popular pub and disco that hops with a young crowd most mornings until 5 AM.

FOLKLORE

A fun addition to the boleto turístico scheme is the **Centro Qosqo de Arte Nativo** (⊠*Av. El Sol 604* ☎*084/227–901*). The cultural center holds hour-long folkloric dance performances in its auditorium each night at 7, with introductions in Spanish and English. You may be one of the lucky audience members called up to participate in the final number. But you do need to buy the boleto turístico to be admitted.

If you don't fancy the show at the Centro de Arte Nativo or don't have the full boleto turistico, many of the restaurants around the Plaza de Armas offer you a similar package. Starting at around 8 PM you'll be treated to an Andean folkloric show while you're dining, the cost of which is usually included in the meal price. **Tunupa** (⊠*Portal de Confiturías 233, Plaza de Armas* ☎*084/252–936*) has a nightly folklore show along with fine dining. At **La Retama** (⊠*Portal de Panes 123, Plaza de Armas* ☎*084/226–372*) you'll enjoy Andean music during dinner each evening. **Paititi** (⊠*Portal de Carrizos 270, Plaza de Armas* ☎*084/252–686*) presents a folklore show during dinner most nights. **Bagdad Café** (⊠*Portal de Carnes 216, Plaza de Armas* ☎*084/239–949*) has live music during dinner many nights of the week, but with no fixed schedule.

GAY & LESBIAN

Rainbow flags fly everywhere in Cusco and you might think the city is just really gay-friendly. But you're actually seeing the flag of Cusco, based on the banner of Tawantinsuyo, the Inca empire. The gay scene is actually pretty limited. **Fallen Angel** (⊠*Plazoleta Nazarenas 221* ☎*084/258–184* ⊕*www.fallenangelincusco.com*) sponsors occasional gay and lesbian events, such as cabaret nights, holiday celebrations, and parties. Check out the Web site for dates and more information.

LECTURES & MUSEUMS

Most museums close their doors before dark, but the **Museo de Arte Precolombino** (⊠*Plazoleta Nazarenas 221* ☎*084/233–210*) stays open until 10 each evening year-round, if your nightlife tends toward the artsy pre-Columbian kind. Top off an evening of intellect with a late-night bite at the museum's snazzy, glassed-in **MAP Café** (☎*084/242–476*).

If you're up for an intellectual, but fun, evening, **South American Explorers** (⊠*Choquechara 188* ☎*084/245–484* ✎*cuscoclub@saexplorers.org*) holds talks on themes of tourist or cultural interest every Thursday

DID YOU KNOW?

The Inca rebuilt Cusco in the shape of a puma. Do you know what part of the body *you're* standing in?

evening at 6. The subject might be a mini-Quechua lesson, the difference between real and fake alpaca clothing, or the screening of a Latin American film. The cost is a nominal S/3 for nonmembers, and the gatherings are a great way to meet other travelers. Drop the friendly folks an e-mail and ask to be put on their mailing list.

THEATER

Fodor's Choice Cusco's newest entertainment addition, **Kusikay** (⊠ *Teatro Garcilaso,*
★ *Calle Unión 117* ☎ *01/618–3838 in Lima* ⊕ *www.kusikay.com*), should not be missed. Devoted to presenting Andean history and mythology, Kusikay is a theater-dance-acrobatics spectacular, with some of the best costumes this side of Cirque du Soleil. It's a surprisingly modern setup, with moving sets and a huge cast of more than 30 actors. Each show runs for around a year; all take local history and mythology as their subject. ■TIP→This is a great opportunity to hear Quechua spoken, as the performances mix Spanish and Quechua dialogue. Brochures in English explain the plot, and kids will be entranced by the colorful spectacle and acrobatics.

SHOPPING

Cusco is full of traditional crafts, artwork, and clothing made of alpaca, llama, or sheep wool. Beware of acrylic fakes. For the best quality products, shop in the higher end stores. The export of artifacts would require a government permit, so banish any thoughts of waltzing off with the Inca ruler Pachacutec's cape for a song.

Vendors, usually children, will approach you relentlessly on the Plaza de Armas. They sell postcards, finger puppets, drawings, and CDs of Andean music. A simple "no, gracias" is usually enough to indicate you're not interested. Several enclosed crafts markets are good bets for bargains. Even the upscale shops are sometimes amenable to offering a discount if these three conditions are met: 1) it's the September–May off-season; 2) you came into the store on your own, without a guide who will expect a commission from the shop; and 3) you pay in cash.

ART REPLICAS

Apacheta (⊠ *Santa Catalina Ancha 313* ☎ *084/238–210*) deals in replicas of pre-Columbian art, mostly ceramics, and contemporary designs. The shop works directly with its artisan suppliers, giving fair prices to them and to you, and a high degree of attentive service. **Ilaria** (⊠ *Portal de Carrizos 258, Plaza de Armas* ☎ *084/246–253*) is Cusco's finest jewelry, with an ample selection of replicas of colonial-era pieces.

CERAMICS

In San Blas, the **Galería Mérida** (⊠ *Carmen Alto 133* ☎ *084/221–714*) sells the much-imitated ceramics of Edilberto Mérida. **Seminario** (⊠ *Portal de Carnes, Haukaypata, Plaza de Armas* ☎ *084/246–093*) is the outlet in Cusco of famed ceramics maker Pablo Seminario. Prices are lower at the source in the Sacred Valley town of Urubamba.

CRAFTS & GIFTS

Galería Latina (⊠ *San Agustín 427* ☎ *084/246–588*) is a reasonably priced crafts shop with many original pieces, tapestries, ceramics, and alpaca clothing among them. Religious art, including elaborately costumed statues of the Virgin Mary, is sold at the shop at the **Galería Mendívil** (⊠ *Plazoleta San Blas* ☎ *084/226–506*).

Triunfo is lined with crafts shops as far as San Blas. One of the best, **Muñecas Maxi** (⊠ *Sunturwasi [Triunfo] 393* ☎ *084/225–492*), sells dolls in historical and local costumes. You can even have one custom-made. Also on display are *retablos* (wooden boxes) that show Cusco's most popular sites and alpaca jackets decorated with local weavings. In San Blas, **Hecho en Cusco** (⊠ *Carmen Alto 105* ☎ *084/221–948*) has high-quality cotton T-shirts with simple, stylized designs of pumas, serpents, and birds, definitely a cut above the ubiquitous Cusqueña beer shirts.

TEXTILES

Long-established **Kuna** (⊠ *Kusipata 202, Plaza Regocijo* ☎ *084/243–233*) has alpaca garments, and is the only authorized distributor of high-quality vicuña scarves and sweaters. Outlets are at the Libertador and Monasterio hotels as well as at the airport. **Perú Étnico** (⊠ *Portal Mantas 114* ☎ *084/232–775* ⊠ *Portal de Carnes 232, Haukaypata, Plaza de Armas* ☎ *084/238–620* ⊠ *Heladeros 172* ☎ *084/229–184*) has three downtown locations with fine alpaca coats, sweaters, scarves, and shawls. **Alpaca's Best** (⊠ *Portal Confiturias 221, Haukaypata, Plaza de Armas* ☎ *084/249–406*) also has a good selection of jewelry. **Royal Knitwear** (⊠ *Plaza Regocijo 203* ☎ *084/261–452*) sells alpaca and pima cotton garments at stores in Cusco and Lima, and it also exports its products to shops in the United States, Europe, Japan, and Australia. **Maqui Arte** (⊠ *Sunturwasi [Triunfo] 118* ☎ *084/246–493*) has high-quality alpaca products, including sweaters, jackets, and even colorful alpaca shoes.

Alpaca gets the camelid's share of attention for use in making fine garments, but **La Casa de la Llama** (⊠ *Palacio 121* ☎ *084/240–813*) sells a fine selection of expensive clothing made from the softer hairs sheared from its namesake animal's chest and neck. It's difficult to tell the difference in texture between llama and adult alpaca, at least in this shop.

Several artisan markets and cooperatives populate the city. The **Center for Traditional Textiles of Cusco** (⊠ *Av. El Sol 603* ☎ *084/228–117*) is a nonprofit organization dedicated to the survival of traditional textile weaving. Weavers from local villages work in the shop, and the on-site museum has informative exhibits about weaving techniques and the customs behind traditional costume. Sweaters, ponchos, scarves, and wall hangings are sold at fair-trade prices. The municipal government operates the **Centro Artesanal Cusco** (⊠ *Tullumayo and El Sol* ☎ *No phone*), containing 340 stands of artisan vendors. The **Feria**

CLOSE UP

Alpaca Or Acrylic?

Vendors and hole-in-the-wall shop-keepers will beckon you in to look at their wares: "One of a kind," they proudly proclaim. "Baby alpaca, hand woven by my grandmother on her deathbed. It's yours for S/70."

Price should be the first giveaway. A real baby-alpaca sweater would sell for more than S/200. So maintain your skepticism even if the label boldly states 100% BABY ALPACA. False labels are common on acrylic-blend clothing throughout the Cusco area. Which brings us to our next clue. A good-quality label should show the maker's or seller's name and address. You're more likely to find quality goods at an upscale shop, of which there are several around town. Such a business is just not going to gamble its reputation on inferior products.

Texture is the classic piece of evidence. Baby-alpaca products use hairs, 16–18 microns in diameter, taken from the animal's first clipping. Subsequent shearings from a more mature alpaca yield hairs with a 20-micron diameter, still quite soft, but never matching the legendary tenderness of baby alpaca. (For that reason, women tend toward baby-alpaca products; men navigate toward regular alpaca.) A blend with llama or sheep's wool is slightly rougher to the touch and, for some people, itchier to the skin. And if the garment is too silky, it's likely a synthetic blend. (The occasional 100% polyester product is passed off as alpaca to unsuspecting buyers.)

While "one of a kind" denotes uniqueness—and, again, be aware that much of what is claimed to be handmade here really comes from a factory—the experts say there is nothing wrong with factory-made alpaca products. A garment really woven by someone's grandmother lacks a certain degree of quality control, and you may find later that the dyes run or the seams come undone.

—by Jeffrey Van Fleet

Inca (⊠ *At San Andrés and Quera*) is small and informal, but bargains can be found.

SIDE TRIPS FROM CUSCO

Cusco may be endearingly beautiful, but with the constant hassle to *buy buy buy*, it's not the most relaxing place on earth. Yet just outside the city lies one of Peru's most spectacular and serene regions, filled with Andean mountains, tiny hamlets, and ancient Inca ruins. In a half-day trip you can visit some of Peru's greatest historical areas and monuments, such as Sacsayhuamán, perched high on a hill that overlooks the city, or the slightly less famous, but nonetheless spectacular, sights of Qenko, Puka Pukara, and Tambomachay.

The romantically named Sacred Valley of the Inca attracts the puma's share of visitors going to Machu Picchu. But along the highway that runs southeast of Cusco to Sicuani are lesser-known Inca and pre-Inca sites in a region locals call the Valle del Sur. ■TIP→You may have these magnificent ruins all to yourself, as they are off the traditional tourist circuit.

SACSAYHUAMÁN

2 km (1 mi) north of Cusco.

Fodor's Choice
★   Towering high above Cusco, the ruins of Sacsayhuamán are a constant reminder of the city's Inca roots. You may have to stretch your imagination to visualize how it was during Inca times—much of the site was used as a convenient source of building material by the conquering Spanish, but plenty remains to be marveled at. Huge stone blocks beg the question of how they were carved and maneuvered into position, and the masterful masonry is awe-inspiring. If you're not moved by stonework, the spectacular views over the city are just as eye-catching.

If the Incas designed Cusco in the shape of a puma, then Sacsayhuamán represents its ferocious head. ■TIP→Perhaps the most important Inca monument after Machu Picchu, Sacsayhuamán is thought to have been a military complex during Inca times. From its strategic position high above Cusco, it was excellently placed to defend the city, and its zigzag walls and cross-fire parapets allowed defenders to rain destruction on attackers from two sides.

Construction of the site began in the 1440s, during the reign of the Inca Pachacutec. It's thought that 20,000 workers were needed for Sacsay-huamán's construction, cutting the astonishingly massive limestone, diorite, and andesite blocks—the largest is 361 tons—rolling them to the site, and assembling them in traditional Inca style to achieve a perfect fit without mortar. The probable translation of Sacsayhuamán, "city of stone," seems apt. The Inca Manco Capac II, installed as puppet ruler after the conquest, retook the fortress and led a mutiny against Juan Pizarro and the Spanish in 1536. Fighting raged for 10 months in a valiant but unsuccessful bid by the Inca to reclaim their empire. History records that thousands of corpses from both sides littered the grounds and were devoured by condors at the end of the battle.

Today only the outer walls remain of the original fortress city, which the Spanish tore down after the rebellion and then ransacked for years as a source of construction materials for their new city down the hill, a practice that continued until the mid-20th century. One-fifth of the original complex is left; nonetheless, the site is impressive. Sacsayhuamán's three original towers, used for provisions, no longer stand, though the foundations of two are still visible. The so-called Inca's Throne, the Suchuna, remains, presumed used by the emperor for reviewing troops. Today those parade grounds, the Explanada, are the ending point for

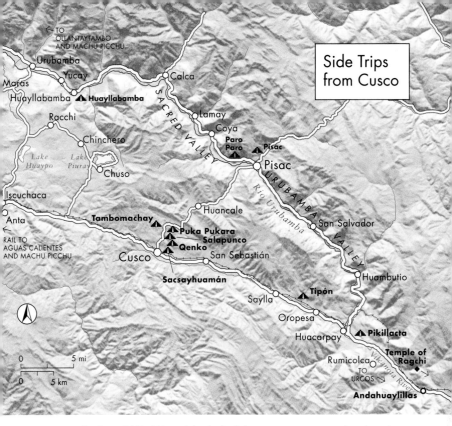

Side Trips
from Cusco

TO
OLLANTAYTAMBO
AND MACHU PICCHU

Urubamba
Yucay
Calca
Maras
Huayllabamba ⏶ Huayllabamba
Lamay
Racchi
Coya
Paro
Chinchero
Paro ⏶
Pisac
Lake
Huaypo
Lake
Piuray
Chuso
Pisac

Iscuchaca
Huancale
San Salvador
Anta
Tambomachay ⏶
Puka Pukara
Salapunco
RAIL TO
AGUAS CALIENTES
AND MACHU PICCHU
Qenko
Cusco
San Sebastián
Huambutio

Sacsayhuamán
Tipón ⏶

Saylla
Oropesa

Huacarpay
Pikillacta ⏶

5 mi
Rumicolca
TO
URCOS
Temple of
Ragchi

5 km
Andahuaylillas

the June 24 Inti Raymi festival of the sun, commemorating the winter
solstice and Cusco's most famous celebration.

These closest Inca ruins to Cusco make a straightforward half-day trip
from the city, and provide a great view over Cusco's orange rooftops.
If you don't have a car, take a taxi, or if you want to test yourself, the
ruins are a steep 25-minute walk up from the Plaza de Armas. ■TIP➔A
large map at both entrances shows the layout of Sacsayhuamán, but once
you enter, signage and explanations are minimal. Self-appointed guides
populate the entrances and can give you a two-hour tour for S/30. Most
are competent and knowledgable, but depending on their perspective
you'll get a strictly historic, strictly mystical, strictly architectural, or
all-of-the-above type tour. (But all work the standard joke into their
spiel that the name of the site is pronounced "sexy woman.")

It's theoretically possible to sneak into Sacsayhuamán after hours, but
lighting is poor, surfaces are uneven, and robberies have occurred
at night. ⊠ *Km 2, Hwy. to Pisac* ☏ *No phone* ✉ *Boleto Turístico*
☉ *Daily 7–6.*

QENKO

4 km (2½ mi) north of Cusco.

It may be a fairly serene location these days, but Qenko, which means "zigzag" was once the site of one of the Incas' most intruging and potentially macabre rituals. Named after the zig-zagging channels carved into the surface, Qenko is a large rock thought to have been the site of an annual preplanting ritual in which priests standing on the top poured chicha, or llama blood, into a ceremonial pipe, allowing it to make its way down the channel. If the blood flowed left, it boded poor fertility for the coming season. If the liquid continued the full length of the pipe, it spelled a bountiful harvest. ■TIP➜**Today you won't see any blood, but the carved channels still exist and you can climb to the top to see how they zigzag their way down.** Other symbolic carvings mix it up on the rockface too—the eagle-eyed might spot a puma, condor, and a llama. ⊠*Km 4, Hwy. to Pisac* ☎*No phone* 🎫*Boleto Turístico* ⊙*Daily 7–6.*

PUKA PUKARA

10 km (6 mi) north of Cusco.

Little is known of the archaeological ruins of Puka Pukara, a pink-stone site guarding the road to the Sacred Valley. Some archaeologists believe the complex was a fort—its name means "red fort"—but others claim it served as a hunting lodge and storage place used by the Inca nobility. Current theory holds that this center, likely built during the reign of the Inca Pachacutec, served all those functions. Whatever it was, it was put in the right place. Near Tambomachay, this enigmatic spot provides spectacular views over the Sacred Valley. Pull up a rock and ponder the mystery yourself. ⊠*Km 10, Hwy. to Pisac* ☎*No phone* 🎫*Boleto Turístico* ⊙*Daily 7–6.*

TAMBOMACHAY

11 km (6½ mi) north of Cusco.

Ancient fountains are at this tranquil and secluded spot, which is commonly known as "El Baño del Inca," or, Inca's Bath. The name actually means "cavern lodge" and the site is a three-tiered *huaca* built of elaborate stonework over a natural spring, which is thought to have been used for ritual showers. Interpretations differ, but the site was likely a place where water, considered a source of life, was worshipped (or perhaps just a nice place to take a bath). The huaca is almost certain to have been the scene of sacred ablutions and purifying ceremonies for Inca rulers and royal women. ⊠*Km 11, Hwy. to Pisac* ☎*No phone* 🎫*Boleto Turístico* ⊙*Daily 7–6.*

SALAPUNCO

5 km (3 mi) northeast of Cusco.

In a culture that worshipped the sun, dark and cavernous Salapunco denotes an intriguing change. A collection of small caves that once held Inca mummies, Salapunco is thought to have been devoted to the worship of the moon. Inside each of the caves were altars and walls decorated with puma and snake motifs, the Inca symbols for earth and the underworld, respectively. The largest cavern saw elaborate full-moon ceremonies in Inca times. The position of the entrance allows the interior to be bathed once a month by the light of the moon. Unfortunately all the mummies are long gone. ⊠*Km 5, Hwy. to Pisac* ☏*No phone* 🖃*Free* ☉*Daily 7–5:30.*

SOUTHEASTERN URUBAMBA VALLEY

5

The Río Urubamba runs northwest and southeast from Cusco. The northwest sector of the river basin is the romantically named "Sacred Valley of the Inca" and attracts the puma's share of visitors. But along the highway that runs southeast of Cusco to Sicuani are a number of lesser-known Inca and pre-Inca sites in a region locals call the Valle del Sur. You may find that you have these magnificent ruins all to yourself.

Admission to Tipón and Pikillacta is included in the Boleto Turístico, as well as in a lower-price boleto parcial that includes admission to the ruins of Pisac, Chinchero, and Ollantaytambo in the Sacred Valley. These sights are easy to visit by car during a day trip from Cusco; you'll find only very rugged lodging if you choose to stay.

TIPÓN

26 km (15½ mi) southeast of Cusco.

Everyone has heard that the Incas were good engineers, but for a real look at just how good they were at land and water management, head to Tipón. Twenty kilometers or so south of Cusco, Tipón is a series of terraces, hidden from the valley below, crisscrossed by stone aqueducts and carved irrigation channels that edge up a narrow pass in the mountains. A spring fed the site and continually replenished a 900-cubic-meter reservoir that supplied water to crops growing on the terraces. ■TIP➜So superb was the technology that several of the terraces are still in use today, and still supplied by the same watering system developed centuries ago. The ruins of a stone temple of undetermined function guard the system, and higher up the mountain are terraces yet to be completely excavated. Unfortunately, the rough dirt track that leads to the complex is in wretched condition. If you visit, either walk up (about two hours each way) or go in a four-wheel-drive vehicle (about 45 minutes to the site and 30 minutes back). ⊠*4 km (2½ mi) north of Km 23, Hwy. to Urcos* ☏*No phone* 🖃*Boleto Turístico* ☉*Daily 7–6.*

PIKILLACTA

6 km (3½ mi) east of Tipón; 7 km (4 mi) south of Oropesa

For a reminder that civilizations existed in this region before the Incas, head to Pikillacta, a vast city of 700 buildings from the pre-Inca Wari culture, which flourished between AD 600 and 1000. Over a 2 km site you'll see what remains of what was once a vast walled city with enclosing walls reaching up to 7 meters (23 feet) in height and many two-story buildings, which were entered via ladders to doorways on the second floor. Little is known about the Wari culture, although the empire once stretched from near Cajamarca to the border of the Tiahuanaco empire based around Lake Titicaca. It's clear, however, that they had a genius for farming in a harsh environment and like the Incas built sophisticated urban centers such as Pikillacta (which means the "place of the flea"). At the thatch-roofed excavation sites, uncovered walls show the city's stones were once covered with plaster and whitewashed. Across the road lies a beautiful lagoon, Lago de Lucre. ⊠ *Km 32, Hwy. to Urcos* ☎ *No phone* 🎟 *Boleto Turístico* ⊙ *Daily 7–6.*

RUMICOLCA

3 km (2 mi) east of San Pedro de Cacha.

An enormous 12-meter- (39-foot-) high gate stands at Rumicolca. It served as the border checkpoint and customs post at the southern entrance to the Wari empire. The Inca enhanced the original construction of their predecessors, fortifying it with andesite stone and using the gate for the same purpose. ⊠ *Km 32, Hwy. to Urcos* ☎ *No phone* 🎟 *Free* ⊙ *Daily 24 hrs.*

ANDAHUAYLILLAS

40 km (32 mi) southeast of Cusco.

The main attraction of the small town of Andahuaylillas, 8 km (5 mi) southeast of Pikillacta, is a small 17th-century adobe-towered church built by the Jesuits on the central plaza over the remains of an Inca temple. The contrast between the simple exterior and the rich, expressive, colonial baroque art inside is notable: fine examples of the Cusqueña school of art decorate the upper interior walls. ■TIP➜Traces of gilt that once covered the church walls are still visible. The church keeps no fixed hours. Ask around town for someone to let you inside. The town's name is a corruption of *Antawaylla*, Quechua for "copper prairie." ⊠ *Km 40, Hwy. to Urcos* ☎ *No phone* 🎟 *Free.*

TEMPLE OF RAQCHI

4 km (2½ mi) east of San Pedro de Cacha.

The ruins of this large temple in the ancient town of Raqchi give little indication of their original purpose, but if size counts, then they are truly impressive. ■TIP➜Huge external walls up to 12 meters (39 feet) high still tower overhead. You'll be forgiven for thinking that the place was once an Inca version of the Colossium, or a football stadium. Legend has it that the Temple of Raqchi was built in homage to the god Viracocha, to ask his intercession in keeping the nearby Quimsa

Peruvian women lead furry animals by the Inca site of Sacsayhuamán.

Chata volcano in check. The ploy worked only some of the time. The site, with its huge adobe walls atop a limestone foundation, performed multiple duty as temple, fortress, barracks, and storage facility. ⊠ *Km 80, Urcos–Puno Hwy.* ☎ *No phone* 🎫 *S/5* ⊙ *Daily 9–5:30.*

SACRED VALLEY OF THE INCA

A pleasant climate, fertile soil, and proximity to Cusco made the Urubamba River valley a favorite with Inca nobles, many of whom are believed to have had private country homes here. Inca remains, ruins, and agricultural terraces lie throughout the length of this so-called Sacred Valley of the Inca. Cusco is hardly the proverbial urban jungle, but in comparison the Sacred Valley is positively captivating with its lower elevation, fresher air, warmer temperatures, and rural charm. You may find yourself joining the growing ranks of visitors who base themselves out here and make Cusco their day trip, rather than the other way around.

WHEN TO GO
The valley has increasingly taken on a dual personality, depending on the time of day, day of the week, and month of the year. Blame it on Pisac and its famous three-times-weekly market. Every Cusco travel agency offers a day tour of the Sacred Valley each Tuesday, Thursday, and Sunday to coincide with the town's market days, and they all seem to follow the same schedule: morning shopping in Pisac, buffet lunch

in Urubamba, afternoon browsing in Ollantaytambo. You can almost always sign up for one of these tours at the last minute—even early on the morning of the tour—especially if you're here in the September-to-May off-season. On nonmarket days and during the off-season, however, Pisac and the rest of the Sacred Valley is a relatively quiet. In any case, the valley deserves more than a rushed day tour if you have the time.

GETTING AROUND

Highways are good—the main east-west road crossing the valley is potholed between Pisac and Urubamba, but in better shape beyond Urubamba to Ollantaytambo—and traffic is relatively light in the Sacred Valley, but any trip entails a series of twisting, turning roads as you head out of the mountains near Cusco and descend into the valley. ■TIP➔Watch for the rompemuelle signs warning you of the series of speed bumps as you pass through populated areas. The road to Machu Picchu ends in Ollantaytambo; beyond that point, it's rail only.

TARAY

23 km (14 mi) north of Cusco.

The road from Cusco leads directly to the town of Taray. The Pisac market beckons a few kilometers down the road, but Taray makes a worthwhile pre-Pisac shopping stop.

Awana Kancha, whose Quechua name loosely translates as "palace of weaving," provides an opportunity to see products made from South America's four camelids (alpaca, llama, vicuña, and guanaco) from start to finish: the animal, the shearing, the textile weaving and dyeing, and the finished products, which you can purchase in the show room. ⊠*Km 23, Carretera a Pisac* ☎*084/203–287* ⊕*www.awanakancha. com* ☎*Free* ☉*Daily 8–5.*

PISAC

9 km (5 mi) north of Taray.

The colorful colonial town of Pisac, replete with Quechua-language masses in a simple stone church, a well-known market, and fortress ruins, comes into view as you wind your way down the highway from Cusco. (You're dropping about 600 meters (1,970 feet) in elevation when you come out here from the big city.) Pisac, home to about 4,000 people, anchors the eastern end of the Sacred Valley. An orderly grid of streets forms the center of town, most hemmed in by a hodgepodge

BOLETO TURÍSTICO

Three Sacred Valley sites (the ruins at Pisac, Chinchero, and Ollantaytambo) fall under Cusco's Boleto Turístico scheme (*See Buying a Boleto Turístico at the start of this chapter.*) The ticket's 10-day validity lets you take in these three attractions as well, and is the only way to gain admission. An abbreviated S/40 ticket, valid for two days, gains you admission to the three sites in the valley.

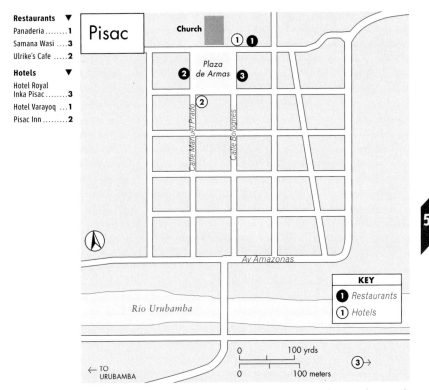

of colonial and modern stucco or adobe buildings, and just wide enough for one car at a time. (Walking is easier and far more enjoyable.) The level of congestion (and fun) increases dramatically each Tuesday, Thursday, and especially Sunday when one of Peru's most celebrated markets comes into its own, but much more spectacular are the ruins above.

WHERE TO EAT

¢ ✗**Panadería.** The unnamed bakery just off the Plaza Constitución is a Pisac institution. Vegetarian empanadas and homemade breads are delivered from the clay oven and into your hands. The lines are long on Tuesday, Thursday, and Sunday market days but it's worth the wait. ✉*Mariscal Castilla 372* ☏*No phone* ▭*No credit cards* ⊘*No dinner.*

¢ ✗**Samana Wasi.** The Quechua name of this basic restaurant on the central square translates as "house of rest," and the owner claims that this is Peruvian cuisine, fresh and made-to-order. It doesn't get any fresher than the trout caught in the nearby Urubamba River. These folks also dish up a spicy *cazuela de gallina* (chicken stew). If it's a nice day, grab one of the tables on the shady interior courtyard. ✉*Plaza Constitución 509* ☏*084/203–018* ▭*No credit cards.*

¢ ✕**Ulrike's Café.** German transplant Ulrike Simic and company dish up food all day long, the perfect refueling stop during a day of market shopping. Breakfast gets underway, before the market does, at 7 AM. ■TIP➜**Stop by for the S/15 prix-fixe lunch, with a lot of vegetarian options on the menu, a real rarity in this part of Peru.** Yummy brownies, muffins, cheesecake, and chocolate-chip cookies are the draw all day long between rounds of shopping. ⊠*Plaza Constitución 828* ☎*084/203–061* ▤*No credit cards.*

WHERE TO STAY

$$ ▦**Hotel Royal Inka Pisac.** Just outside of town is the newest branch of Peru's Royal Inka hotel chain, and the closest lodging to the Pisac ruins. Bright carpeted rooms congregate around acres of wooded and flowered grounds, and have print spreads and drapes and white walls. All third-level rooms have a fireplace. With all the activities and facilities here, a rarity in the Sacred Valley, you really never have to leave the grounds. **Pros:** Lots of activities. **Cons:** Outside of town. ⊠*Km 1½, Carretera a Pisac Ruinas* ☎*084/203–064, 800/664–1819 in North America* ▤*084/203–065* ⊕*www.royalinkahotel.com* ⇆*80 rooms* ⌂*In-room: no a/c, safe. In-hotel: 2 restaurants, room service, bar, tennis court, pool, bicycles, no elevator, no-smoking rooms* ⑂*BP.*

¢ ▦**Hostal Varayoq.** Look for the huge carved-wood doors and the international flags flying from the front. You're a half-block off the plaza on a quiet pedestrian-only street. The first floor contains a little shopping arcade, complete with empanada vendor and a collection of *cuy* (guinea pigs) scurrying around their own little toy castle. (They can end up as your dinner in the patio restaurant if you so desire.) Rooms circle the patio on the second floor, and have stucco walls, carpeted floors and brightly colored furnishings and carved armoires. **Pros:** Great value, off the main plaza. ⊠*380 Mariscal Castilla* ☎*084/223–638* ✉*luzpaz3@hotmail.com* ⇆*8 rooms* ⌂*In-room: no a/c, no phone. In-hotel: restaurant, no elevator, laundry service* ▤*No credit cards* ⑂*BP.*

¢ ▦**Pisac Inn.** Here's the best budget option in town, and it's on the main square. Common areas have murals crafted by the Peruvian-American owners; Andean tapestries hang in the rooms. The continental breakfast is S/10 extra, and the Pisaq's small café dishes up pizza on market days. **Pros:** Good pizzeria. **Cons:** Some rooms slightly run down. ⊠*Plaza Constitución 333* ☎*084/203–062* ⊕*www.pisacinn.com* ⇆*12 rooms, 7 with bath* ⌂*In-room: no a/c, no phone, no TV. In-hotel: bicycles, no elevator, laundry service* ▤*No credit cards.*

YUCAY

46 km (28 mi) northwest of Pisac.

The explosive growth of nearby Urubamba has practically engulfed the tiny village of Yucay, to the point of barely being able to tell where one ends and the other begins. Yucay proper is only a few streets wide, with a collection of attractive colonial-era adobe and stucco buildings,

Continued on page 247

Valley in the vicinity of Ollantaytambo near Cusco, Peru.

TOURING THE SACRED VALLEY
by Jeffery Van Fleet

You've come to Cusco to see Machu Picchu, but you'll spend at least one day touring the Sacred Valley. Not only is it chock-full of major archaeological and other sights, but its small towns and easy-living pace invite you to slow down. If the Inca emperors favored the warm, fertile valley as a place for cultivation and recreation, so should you.

The Sacred Valley follows the Urubamba River from the town of Pisac, about 30 km (18 mi) northeast of Cusco, and ends 60 km (36 mi) northwest of Pisac at Ollantaytambo. Beyond that point, the cliffs that flank the river grow closer together, the valley narrows, and the agriculturally rich floodplain thins to a gorge as the Urubamba begins its abrupt descent toward the Amazon basin.

What makes the valley "sacred"? The Inca named rivers by sector and called this stretch of the Urubamba Wilcamayu, "the sacred river." Spanish explorers applied the concept to the entire valley, calling it the Valle Sagrado. The tourist industry likes the appealing, evocative name, too.

The entire area, though very rural, is served by good roads and public transportation except to the Moray and Salineras sites. The best options are to rent a car or join a tour.

SACRED VALLEY

2,460m (8,072ft)
Machu Picchu

Aguas Calientes
2,082m (6,833ft)

Pacaymayu

Sayacmarco

Llactapata

Huayllabamba

CORDILLERA

Ollantaytambo
One of the region's loveliest towns, with its namesake ruins high above, marks the beginning of the Inca Trail and has a rail connection to Machu Picchu.

Ollantaytambo
2,800m (9,186ft)

Yucay & Urubamba
Two pleasant towns with some good hotels and restaurants are alternatives to staying in the "big city" of Cusco.

URUBAMBA

SACRED VALLEY

Salineras
These terraced Inca salt pans are still used today.

Salineras

Moray

Maras

Urubamba

Yucay

Huayllabamba

Huayllabamba

Racchi

Iscuchaca

Chinchero

Río Urubamba

Calca

Moray
This site is an ancestor of the modern experimental agricultural station. The Inca created varying environmental zones with their enormous circular terraces.

Chuso

Lamay

Coya

0   5 mi

0   5 km

Sacsayhuamán
Tambomachay

3,310m (10,860ft)

Huancale

Paro Paro
Pisac

Cusco

Puka Pukara
Qenko

Pisac
3,444m (11,300ft)

Pisac Market
Travelers throng Pisac's famous twice-weekly market; this is one of Peru's most touristy things to do. On Sunday, catch the colorful mass.

Pisac Ruins
A masterpiece of Inca engineering, centuries later the site is in remarkable condition, with masonry more precise than Machu Picchu's.

San Sebastián

San Salvador

Saylla

Tipón

PISAC

Pisac market vendor

PISAC MARKET

Pisac's famous market—held each Tuesday, Thursday, and Sunday—draws locals and tourists alike. Fruits, vegetables, and grains share the stage with ceramics, jewelry, and woolens on the central plaza and spill over into the side streets. Sellers set up shop about 8 AM on market days and start packing up at about 3 PM. The market is not so different from many others you'll see around Peru, only larger. Go on Sunday if your schedule permits; you'll have a chance to take in the 11 AM Quechua Mass at the Iglesia San Pedro Apóstolo and watch the elaborate costumed procession led by the mayor, who carries his *varayoc*, a ceremonial staff, out of the church afterward. Sunday afternoon sees bands and beer tents—this is small-town Peru at its best. ⏲ Sun., Tues., and Thurs. 8–3 or 4.

PISAC RUINS

From the market area, drive or take a taxi S/10–S/15 one-way up the winding road to the Inca ruins of Pisac. Visiting on market day is your best bet for finding easy transportation up; the alternative is a steep two-hour walk from town. It's most crowded on Sunday; the rest of the week there will be few other people.

Archaeologists originally thought the ruins were a fortress to defend against fierce Antis (jungle peoples), though there's little evidence that battles were fought here. Now it seems that Pisac was a bit of everything: citadel, religious site, observatory, and residence, and may have served as a refuge in times of siege. The complex also has a temple to the sun and an astronomical observatory, from which priests calculated the growing season each year. Narrow trails wind tortuously between and through solid rock. You may find yourself practically alone on the series of paths in the mountains that lead you among the ruins, through caves, and past the largest known Inca cemetery (the Inca buried their dead in tombs high on the cliffs). Just as spectacular *as* the site are the views *from* it.

Farther above are more ruins and burial grounds, still in the process of being excavated. ▨ Boleto Turístico ⏲ Daily 7–6.

Inca Pisac ruins on a high bluff.

5

IN FOCUS TOURING THE SACRED VALLEY

OLLANTAYTAMBO

Women in Ollantaytambo, Peru.

The town is pronounced "oy-yahn-tie-tahm-bo" but everyone calls it "Ollanta" for short. It was named for Ollantay, the Inca general who expanded the frontiers of Tawantinsuyo as far north as Colombia and as far south as Argentina during the reign of the Inca Pachacutec. The general asked for the hand of the emperor's daughter, a request Pachacutec refused. Accomplished though Ollantay was, he was still a commoner. The general rebelled against the ruler and was imprisoned. Ollantay's love may have met a bad end, but yours will not when you glimpse the stone streets and houses, mountain scenery, some of the most lush territory in the valley, and great ruins.

FORTRESS OF OLLANTAYTAMBO

Walk above the town to a formidable stone structure where massive terraces climb to the peak. It was the valley's main defense against the Antis from the neighboring rain forests. Construction began during the reign of Pachacutec but was never completed. The rose-color granite used was not mined in this part of the valley. The elaborate walled complex contained a temple to the sun, used for astronomical observation, as well as the Baños de la Ñusta (ceremonial princess baths), leading archaeologists to believe that Ollantaytambo existed for more than defensive purposes.

The fortress was the site of the greatest Inca victory over the Spanish during the wars of conquest. The Manco Inca fled here in 1537 with a contingent of troops after the disastrous loss at Sacsayhuamán and routed Spanish forces under Hernando Pizarro. The victory was short-lived: Pizarro regrouped and took the fortress. ⊠ Plaza Mañay Raquy ⚏ Boleto Turístico ⏱ Daily 7–6.

OLLANTAYTAMBO HERITAGE TRAIL

This self-guided trail allows you to tour the original layout of the town, following a series of blue plaques that outline important sites. Attribute the town's distinctive appearance to Inca organization. They based their communities on the unit of the cancha, a walled city block, each with one entrance leading to an interior courtyard, surrounded by a collection of houses. The system is most obvious in the center of town around the main plaza. You'll find the most welcoming of these self-contained communities at Calle del Medio.

Inca ruins, Ollantaytambo.

and a pair of good-choice lodgings on opposite sides of a grassy plaza in the center of town.

WHERE TO STAY & EAT

$$ ⌂ **La Casona de Yucay.** The 1810 home of Manuel de Orihuela hosted South American liberator Simón Bolívar, and you can stay in Room 136 where he slept during his 1825 visit. Spacious rooms contain colonial-style furnishings and are arranged in blocks around four courtyards, lush with flowered gardens. **Pros:** Historic setting. **Cons:** Some people think history is boring. ⌂*Plaza Manco II 104* ☏*084/201–116* 🖷*084/201–469* ⊕*www.hotelcasonayucay.com* ↩*53 rooms* ⌂*In-room: no a/c, safe, no TV. In-hotel: restaurant, room service, bar, spa, no elevator, laundry service, public Internet* ▭*AE, DC, MC, V.*

$$$ ✕⌂ **Sonesta Posada del Inca Valle Sagrado.** In the heart of the Sacred Val-
★ ley is this 300-year-old former convent (monastery). The cobblestone walkways are the perfect complement to the well-preserved colonial-era church on the grounds. The rooms, with tile floors, wood ceilings, and hand-carved headboards, have balconies that overlook the gardens or the terraced hillsides. A few rooms have access for people with disabilities, a rarity in this part of the country, but they must be reserved in advance. The restaurant has excellent regional fare and a popular Sunday lunch buffet. **Pros:** Good restaurant, historic setting. **Cons:** Some people prefer modern. ⌂*Plaza Manco II 123* ☏*084/201–107, 01/712–6060 in Lima, 800/766–3782 in North America* ⊕*www.sone-staperu.com* ↩*84 rooms* ⌂*In-room: no a/c, safe. In-hotel: restaurant, bar, spa, laundry service, public Wi-Fi* ▭*AE, MC, V.*

URUBAMBA

2 km (1 mi) west of Yucay; 29 km (17 mi) northwest of Chinchero.

Spanish naturalist Antonio de León Pinedo rhapsodized that Urubamba must have been the biblical Garden of Eden, but you'll be forgiven if your first glance at the place causes you to doubt that lofty claim: the highway leading into and bypassing the city, the Sacred Valley's administrative, economic, and geographic center, shows you miles of gas stations and convenience stores. But get off the highway and get lost in the town's tidy streets, awash in flowers and pisonay trees, and enjoy the spectacular views of the nearby mountains. You might agree with León Pinedo after all. Urubamba holds little of historic interest but the scenery, a decent selection of hotels and restaurants, and easy access to Machu Picchu rail service make the town an appealing place in which to base yourself.

Cusco transplants and husband-and-wife team Pablo Seminario and Marilú Bejar and their German shepherds run the **Cerámica Seminario** in the center of town. They take the valley's distinctive red clay and turn it into ceramic works using modern adaptations of ancient indigenous techniques and designs. ⌂*Berriozabal 111* ☏*084/201–002* ⊕*www.ceramicaseminario.com* ⊙*Daily 8–7.*

ESSENTIALS

CURRENCY Banco de la Nación (⊠ *Mariscal Castilla s/n* ☎ *084/201–291*).

MAIL SERPOST (⊠ *Jr. Comercio 535, Urubamba*).

WHERE TO STAY & EAT

$–$$ ✕ **Inka's House.** Urubamba has become buffet-lunch central—it's the midday stopping point for the organized Sacred Valley day tours—but this second-floor restaurant on the main road in the center of town is the best of the bunch. Whether you come in a group or on your own, the friendly staff greets you with a complimentary pisco sour before you get up from your table to get in line for a more than ample supply of food. (You can order from the à-la-carte menu, too.) It's all to the accompaniment of live Andean folk music. ⊠ *Av. Ferrocarril s/n* ☎ *084/434–616* ⊟ *AE, DC, MC, V.*

¢ ⊡ **Hospedaje Los Jardines.** An extensive remodeling and refurbishing has given a much-appreciated spruce up to a longtime budget favorite in the center of town. Five rooms populate a rambling house behind a wall on a quiet street. All have hardwood floors, tile baths, and attractive Venetian blinds. Lovely wood headboards and dressers and armoires fill each room in this entirely no-smoking property. Breakfast is an extra S/10, and served in an antique-filled dining room. **Pros:** Cozy setting, good value. **Cons:** Not for people seeking more than serviceable. ⊠ *Jr. Padre-Barre s/n* ☎ *084/201–331* ⊕ *www.machawasi.com* ⇌ *5 rooms, 3 with bath* ⌂ *In-room: no a/c, no phone, no TV (some). In-hotel: bicycles, no-smoking rooms* ⊟ *No credit cards.*

$–$$ ⊡ **Hotel San Agustín.** The San Agustín, part of a small Peruvian hotel chain, is the quintessential two-in-one lodging. On the main road is a modern hacienda-style hotel with gleaming rooms, modern services, and all the comforts you could desire. Up the hill is the converted Recoleta, a 16th-century Franciscan monastery with a cavernous dining room; guest rooms with hardwood floors, white walls, and Cusqueña paintings, and a bell tower with great views of the valley. There are fewer services at the monastery, though most guests—the Recoleta has a devoted artistic, New Age clientele—don't mind. All have access to the facilities down the hill. **Pros:** Historical setting. **Cons:** Dim lighting in monastery setting. ⊠ *Km 69, Carretera Pisac–Ollantaytambo* ☎ *084/201–444 or 084/201–666* ⊕ *www.hotelessanagustin.com.pe* ⇌ *65 rooms, 5 suites* ⌂ *In-room: no a/c, no phone, no TV (some). In-hotel: 2 restaurants, room service, bar, pool, no elevator* ⊟ *AE, DC, MC, V* ⊚ *CP.*

$$$–$$$$ ⊡ **Sol & Luna Lodge & Spa.** A lovely addition to the Sacred Valley of the Inca, this hotel has bungalows surrounded by flower gardens. Nearby are the Perol Chico stables, where you can book trips through this beautiful valley on the stable's famous Peruvian *caballos de paso*. The Viento-Sur Adventure Club at the hotel also offers paragliding, biking, and walking tours. **Pros:** Tranquil setting, many activities. **Cons:** A few miles outside of town. ⊠ *Fundo Huincho, 2 km west of Urubamba* ☎ *084/201–620* ⊟ *084/201–184* ⊕ *www.hotelsolyluna.com* ⇌ *28 bungalows* ⌂ *In-room: no a/c, safe, DVD (some), no TV (some). In-*

Trails Other Than The Inca Trail

Trekking to this Inca site of Choquequirao is a serious trek of at least four days.

The popularity of the Inca Trail and the scarcity of available spots have led to the opening of several alternative hikes of varying length and difficulty.

The three- to seven-day **Salcantay** trek is named for the 6,270-meter (20,500-foot) peak of the same name. It begins at Mollepata, four hours by road from Cusco, and is a strenuous hike that goes through a 4,800-meter (15,700-foot) pass. The Salcantay excursion joins the Inca Trail at Huayllabamba.

The **Ausangate** trek takes its name from the Nevado Ausangate, 6,372 meters (20,900 feet) in elevation, and requires a day of travel each way from Cusco in addition to the standard five–six days on the trail. Nearly the entire excursion takes you on terrain over 4,000 meters (13,100 feet).

Relatively new to the region's trekking scene are four-day hikes through the **Lares Valley**, north of Urubamba and

Ollantaytambo. The excursion offers a cultural dimension, with stops at several villages along the way. The Lares trek compares in difficulty to the Inca Trail.

Various treks bearing the name of **Choquequirao** take in ruins that some have trumpeted as "the new Machu Picchu," another long-lost Inca city. The site, still little excavated and not yet accessible to mass tourism, sits at 3,100 meters (10,180 feet). The four- to 11- day treks entail a series of steep ascents and descents.

The **Chinchero–Huayllabamba** trek has two selling points: it can be accomplished in one day—about six hours—and is downhill much of the way, although portions get steep. The hike begins in Chinchero, north of Cusco, and offers splendid views as you descend into the Sacred Valley.

DID YOU KNOW?

These salt pans at Salineras were built by the Inca and collect the mineral rich waters of a nearby spring until they evaporate, leaving the salt residue.

hotel: restaurant, room service, bar, pool, spa, laundry service ▭AE, *DC, MC, V* ⫶◯⫶*BP.*

CHINCHERO

28 km (17 mi) northwest of Cusco.

Indigenous lore says that Chinchero, one of the valley's major Inca cities, was the birthplace of the rainbow. Frequent sightings during the rainy season might convince you of the legend's truth. Chinchero is one of the few sites in the Sacred Valley that's higher (3,800 meters or 12,500 feet) than Cusco.

Tourists and locals frequent the small but colorful Sunday artisan market on the central plaza, an affair that gets rave reviews as being more authentic and less touristed than the larger market day in neighboring Pisac. A corresponding Chinchero produce market for locals takes place at the entrance to town.

Little remains of indigenous interest in Chinchero, today a collection of winding streets and adobe houses. After the disastrous defeat by the Spanish at Sacsayhuamán, the Inca Manco Capac passed through here in flight to the fortress at Ollantaytambo, scorching the earth in his wake, Chinchero included.

A 1607 colonial **church** in the central plaza was built on top of the limestone remains of an Inca palace, thought to be the country estate of the Inca Tupac Yupanqui, the son of Pachacutec. ⊠*Plaza de Armas* ☎*No phone* ⌨*Boleto Turístico* ◷*Tues.–Sun. 8–5.*

WHERE TO STAY & EAT

¢ ⫶▦⫶**La Casa de Barro.** Chinchero now has lodging in the form a cute hotel in an odd location. The "house of adobe," with its ochre walls and eucalyptus-wood roof merits consideration. Rooms have wood floors, bright spreads, drapes and throw rugs, and big windows with views of the valley. Some come with their own small balconies. **Pros:** Cozy setting, good value. **Cons:** Isolated location. ⊠*Miraflores 147* ☎*084/306–031* ⊕*www.lacasadebarro.net* ⤳*11 rooms* ⌂*In-room: no a/c, no phone, no TV. In-hotel: dining room, bar, no elevator, laundry service* ▭*No credit cards* ⫶◯⫶*BP.*

MORAY & SALINERAS

48 km (29 mi) northwest of Cusco.

Scientists still marvel at the agricultural technology the Inca used at Moray. Taking advantage of four natural depressions in the ground and angles of sunlight, indigenous engineers fashioned concentric circular irrigation terraces, 150 meters (500 feet) from top to bottom, and could create a difference of 15°C (60°F) from top to bottom. ■**TIP➜The result was a series of engineered miniclimates perfect for adapting, experimenting, mixing, matching, and cultivating foods, especially varieties of maize, the staple of the Inca empire, normally impossible to grow at this altitude.**

Though the technology is attributed to the Inca, the lower portions of the complex are thought to date from the pre–Inca Wari culture.

The famed terraced Inca salt pans of Salineras are still in use and also take advantage of a natural phenomenon: the Inca dug shallow pools into a sloped hillside. The pools filled with water, and upon evaporation salt crystallized and could be harvested.

Neither site keeps opening hours or has an admission charge. They're difficult to reach, and almost an impossibility during the rainy season. No public transportation serves Moray or Salineras. A taxi can be hired from Maras, the closest village, or from Cusco. Alternatively, it's a two-hour hike from Maras to either site.

OLLANTAYTAMBO

19 km (11 mi) west of Urubamba.

Poll visitors for their favorite Sacred Valley community and the answer will likely be Ollantaytambo, which lies at the valley's northwestern entrance. Ollantaytambo's traditional air has not been stifled by the invasion of tourists.

■TIP➜Ollantaytambo makes a superb base for exploring the Sacred Valley and has convenient rail connections to Machu Picchu.

Ollantaytambo is also the kick-off point for the Inca Trail. You'll start here at nearby Km 82 if you wish to hike to the Lost City. Walk up for to discover the **fortress of Ollantaytambo,** one of the most fantastic ruins in the Sacred Valley.

ESSENTIALS
INTERNET   Cyberpath (⊠ *Convención s/n* ☎ *084/204–149*). Museo CATCCO (⊠ *Patacalle s/n* ☎ *084/204–024*).

WHAT TO SEE
The small but informative **Museo CATCCO,** the Spanish abbreviation for "Andean Center for Technology and Culture of Ollantaytambo," has local history, culture, and ethnology exhibits with bilingual descriptions, one of the few such institutions around that make that concession to non-Spanish speakers. ■TIP➜You can buy pottery at an adjoining ceramics workshop. ⊠ *Patacalle s/n* ☎ *084/204–024* ⊕ *www.catcco.org* ⊠ *S/5* ☉ *Tues.–Sun. 10–1 and 2–4.*

WHERE TO STAY & EAT
$ ⊞ **Albergue Ollantaytambo.** Everyone in town knows the Albergue, right at the train station, owned by exuberant longtime American resident and artist Wendy Weeks. Dark-wood rooms here are spacious but rustic, with historic black-and-white photos from the region. The lodging has homey touches like a wood-fired sauna, huge breakfasts, and a cozy sitting room. Reserve in advance: the place is popular with groups about to embark on, or just returning from, the nearby Inca Trail. Pros: Convenience to rail station, relaxing sauna. Cons: It's no secret. ⊠ *Estación de Ferrocarril* ☎ *084/204–014* ⊕ *www.elalbergue.com* ⇥12

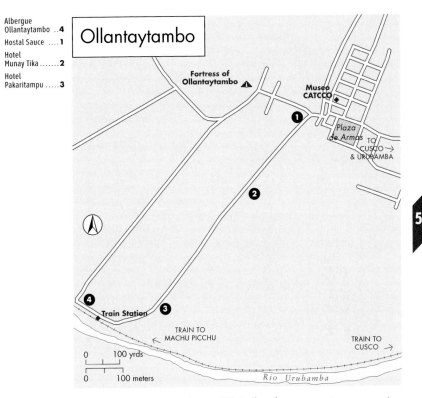

Ollantaytambo

rooms ⓢ *In-room: no a/c, no TV. In-hotel: restaurant, room service, bar, bicycles, no elevator, laundry facilities* ▭*V* ⦿*BP.*

¢ ⊡**Hotel Munay Tika.** Now that the nearby Albergue Ollantaytambo has gone upscale, this is the new best of the rock-bottom budget places in town. Rooms congregate around a flowered garden and have wood floors. Common areas have nice touches like a fireplace and sauna. **Pros:** Good value, pretty garden. **Cons:** Few amenities. ⊠*Av. Estación s/n* ☎*084/204–111* ✉*munaytika@latinmail.com* ⤶*24 rooms* ⓢ*In-room: no a/c, no phone, no TV. In-hotel: restaurant, bar, no elevator* ▭*No credit cards* ⦿*BP.*

\$\$ ✗⊡**Hotel Pakaritampu.** Ollantaytambo's best lodging has a Quechua

Fodor's Choice name that translates as "house of dawn." Fireplaces, and reading

★ rooms with Cusqueño art, invite you to settle in with a good book and a hot cup of coffee on a chilly evening. Rooms, with modern furnishings, plush blue comforters, and green-tile bathrooms, extend through two buildings. The on-grounds orchard supplies the fruit that ends up on your breakfast plate, and in the Peruvian cuisine served in the restaurant. **Pros:** Tranquil setting, good restaurant. **Cons:** Not for the party types. ⊠*Av. Ferrocarril s/n* ☎*084/204–020, 01/242–6278 in Lima* ☎*084/204–105* ⊕*www.pakaritampu.com* ⤶*32 rooms, 1 suite*

⟠ *In-room: no a/c, no TV. In-hotel: restaurant, bar, no elevator, laundry service, public Internet* ☐AE, V ♋BP.

$$ ▦ **Hotel Sauce.** The name has nothing to do with cooking sauces. Instead, it's a type of tree found in the Sacred Valley. Thanks to the hotel's hillside location, half of the vaulted-ceiling rooms have a superb view of the Ollantaytambo ruins. The cozy lobby fireplace is usually stoked with a fire on brisk evenings. **Pros:** Good value, great views. **Cons:** Not for those who like huge hotels. ✉ *Ventiderio 248* ☎084/204–044 ⎙084/204–048 ⊕*www.hostalsauce.com.pe* ⟿8 *rooms* ⟠ *In-room: no a/c, no TV (some). In-hotel: bar, no elevator, laundry service, public Internet* ☐V ♋BP.

Machu Picchu & the Inca Trail

WORD OF MOUTH

That first look was awesome. My daughter and I literally stopped in our tracks and just stared—and then looked at each other in total amazement. It lived up to every expectation imaginable! The scale was immense; the details elaborate; the stonework an almost unbelievable engineering feat. It was beautiful, and there was an air of mystery just as I'd hoped! We were mesmerized.

—althom1122

WELCOME TO
MACHU PICCHU & THE INCA TRAIL

TOP REASONS
TO GO

★ **Discover Ancient Kingdoms:** Hiram Bingham "discovered" Machu Picchu in 1911. Your first glimpse of the fabled city from the Funeral Rock will be your own discovery, and every bit as exciting.

★ **The Trail:** The four-day hike of the Inca Trail from near Ollantaytambo to Machu Picchu is Peru's best-known outdoor expedition. Spaces fill up quickly, but never fear: tour operators have opened up some alternative treks.

★ **Ye Olde Technology:** It was the 15th century, yet the Inca made the stones fit perfectly without mortar. The sun illuminates the windows perfectly at the solstice, and the crops grow in an inhospitable climate. And they did it all without bulldozers, tractors, and Google Earth.

★ **Mystery:** Mystics, shamans, spiritualists, astrologers, and UFO spotters, professionals and wannabes, flock to this serene region. Even the most no-nonsense curmudgeons find themselves contemplating history's secrets.

1 Machu Picchu. The two words that are synonymous with Peru evoke images of centuries-old Inca emperors and rituals. Yet no one knows for certain what purpose this mountaintop citadel served or why it was abandoned. Machu Picchu is an easy day trip from Cusco, but an overnight in Aguas Calientes gives you more time to explore and devise your own theories.

2 The Inca Trail. A 50 km (31-mi) sector of the original Inca supply route between Cusco and Machu Picchu has become one of the world's signature treks. No question: you need to be in good shape, and the four-day excursion can be rough going at times, but it's guaranteed to generate bragging rights and immense satisfaction upon completion.

3 **Aguas Calientes.** Far below the ruins sits the slightly ramshackle, but thoroughly pleasant town of Aguas Calientes, officially called Machupicchu. (No one uses the official name to avoid confusing the town with the ruins.) This is where the train from Cusco arrives, and you hop on the bus to Machu Picchu.

GETTING ORIENTED

The famed ruins of Machu Picchu, accessible only via rail or foot, lie farther down the Río Urubamba, among the cloud forests on the Andean slopes above the Amazon jungle.

Inca Drawbridge, Machu Picchu.

6

URUBAMBA

Río Urubamba

Ollantaytambo

SACRED VALLEY

Salineras

Rapchi   Maras

Moray

VILCABAMBA

Lake Huaypo

Huarocondo

TO CUSCO

Zurite   Iscuchaca

Machu Picchu

MACHU PICCHU & THE INCA TRAIL PLANNER

When To Go	Health & Safety
All the high-season/low-season trade-offs are here. Winter (June through August) means drier weather and easier traveling, but it's prime vacation time for those in the northern hemisphere. Don't forget that three major observances—Inti Raymi (June 24), Peru's Independence Day (July 28), and Santa Rosa de Lima (August 30)—fall during this time, and translate into exceptionally heavy crowds of Peruvian travelers. The result is higher winter lodging prices and larger crowds. Prices and visitor numbers drop dramatically during the summer rainy season (October through April). For near-ideal weather and manageable crowds, consider a spring or fall trip.	**Altitude:** Machu Picchu and the Inca Trail are a breath-catching 300–700 meters (980–2,300 feet) *lower* than Cusco. But to be on the safe side about altitude effects, locally known as *soroche*; get an ample intake of fluids, but eliminate or minimize alcohol and caffeine consumption. (Both can cause dehydration, already a problem at high altitudes.) Smoking aggravates the problem. Some large hotels have an oxygen supply for their guests' use. The prescription drug acetazolamide can help offset the alkalosis caused by low oxygen at high elevations.
	Water: Tap water is generally not safe to drink. Stick with the bottled variety, *con gas* (carbonated) or *sin gas* (plain). The San Luis brand is for sale everywhere.
	Crime: Aguas Calientes employs a cadre of tourist police, decked out in baseball caps and white or blue shirts that say TOURIST SECURITY MACHUPICCHU.
In January and February the weather could most likely wreak havoc with your travel plans. But it's also the time when you can enjoy Machu Picchu without the crowds. Mudslides are an occasional problem when visiting during the October–April rainy season. It's rare, but visitors have been stranded at Machu Picchi or between Aguas Calientes and Cusco if the slides block the way, but usually only very briefly.	## Getting Around
	It's an easy train ride from Cusco to Machu Picchu, Most visitors board the train in Cusco, however—or on foot along the famed Inca Trail to reach the remains of Machu Picchu. *For information about seeing the region with tour operator, see Ch. 5 "Tours of Cusco, the Sacred Valley & Machu Picchu." You cannot drive here.*
	By Train: Unless you're doing the long hike, a train is how you'll get to Machu Picchu. The Vistadome and Backpacker trains leave from Cusco's San Pedro station. They make stops at Poroy, Ollantaytambo, Km 88 (the start of the Inca Trail), and Km 104 (the launch point of an abbreviated two-day Inca Trail). The luxury Hiram Bingham leaves from Poroy, some 15 minutes from Cusco. *(For a full review of options see The Train To Machu Picchu in this chapter.)*

Restaurants & Hotels

The town of Aguas Calientes near Machu Picchu has numerous restaurants (although the menus don't vary much) and the employees will do everything they can to entice you to eat in their establishments. Lunch is served between 1 and 3, the busiest time for restaurants here. Dinner begins around 7, and most restaurants start winding down service at about 9. Most places do stay open in the afternoon if you wish to dine outside these hours.

A few in-town lodgings line the railroad tracks—that's not as down-at-the-heels as it first sounds: the tracks are one of two main streets in Aguas Calientes. Those hostelries have rooms facing the Vilcanota River. Aguas Calientes' budget lodgings are utilitarian places to lay your head, with a bed, a table, a bathroom, and little else. A handful of hotels offer surprising luxury for such an isolated location. Their rates can be shockingly luxurious, too.

The Big Four lodgings here (Sanctuary Lodge, Inkaterra, Sumaq, and Hatuchay Tower) meet their guests on the rail platforms—look for their signs when you get off the train—and deliver your luggage right to your hotel room. (They deliver your luggage from hotel to train for your departure, too, but reconfirm this; the train might pull out with you, minus your bags.) Smaller hotels usually meet guests with advance reservations just outside the train station.

Lodgings keep surprisingly early checkout times. (Hotels free up the rooms for mid-morning Cusco–Machu Picchu trains.) Expect to vacate by 8 or 9 AM, though this is less strictly enforced in the off-season. All hotels will hold your luggage if you're not leaving town until later in the day.

Most hotels keep the same official rates year-round but unofficially discount rates during the off-season of mid-September through May.

WHAT IT COSTS IN NUEVO SOLES

RESTAURANTS				
¢	$	$$	$$$	$$$$
under S/20	S/20–S/35	S/35–S/50	S/50–S/65	over S/65
HOTELS				
¢	$	$$	$$$	$$$$
under S/125	S/125–S/250	S/250–S/375	S/375–S/500	over S/500

Restaurant prices are per person for a main course. Hotel prices are for a standard double room, excluding tax.

Overnight

Many travelers associate the terms "day trip" with Machu Picchu, but an overnight at Machu Picchu (in Aguas Caliente, the town below the site) lets you explore long after the day-trippers have left the mountain, and head back up early the next morning, an especially tranquil time before the midday heat and next round of visitors appear.

Crowded House

It took the outside world almost four centuries to discover the existence of Machu Picchu, the fabled "Lost City of the Inca." After a visit to the ruins during the June–August high season, you'll swear the world is determined to make up for lost time.

On a high-season weekend, Machu Picchu might host in excess of 3,000 visitors a day. By September, daily totals fall to 1,500 visitors, and a typical February day, in the lowest of the low season, sees a relatively paltry 1,000 people pass through the entry turnstiles.

A current plan would cap numbers at 2,500 visitors per day. The Instituto Nacional de Cultura, which oversees Machu Picchu, is searching for ways to spread the numbers out more evenly over the year. Incentives may be offered for coming during the off-season.

AGUAS CALIENTES

But for the grace of Hiram Bingham, Aguas Calientes would be just another remote, forgotten crossroads. But 1911, and the tourist boom decades later, forever changed the community. At just 2,040 meters (6,700 feet) above sea level, Aguas Calientes will seem downright balmy if you've just arrived from Cusco. There are but two major streets—Avenida Pachacutec leads uphill from the Plaza de Armas, and Avenida Imperio de los Incas isn't a street at all, but the railroad tracks; there's no vehicular traffic on the former except the buses that ferry tourists to the ruins. You'll have little sense of Aguas Calientes if you do the standard day trip from Cusco. But the town pulses to a very lively tourist beat with hotels, restaurants, Internet cafés, hot springs, and a surprising amount of activity even after the last afternoon train has returned to Cusco.

ESSENTIALS

CURRENCY **Banco de Crédito** (⊠ *Av. Imperio de los Incas s/n* ☏ *084/211–342*).

INTERNET **Inkanet** (⊠ *Av. Imperio de los Incas s/n* ☏ *084/211–077*).

MAIL **SERPOST** (⊠ *Av. Pachacutec 20*).

WHAT TO SEE

A warren of vendors' stalls, generally referred to as the **Mercado** (market), lines the couple of blocks between the rail station and the bus stop for shuttle transport up to the ruins. Most newly arrived passengers fresh off the train are anxious to get to the bus and up to Machu Picchu, but you'll likely find yourself with more time to spend in the afternoon before your train leaves. Don't expect anything *too* out of the ordinary; it's standard, decent souvenir fare, mainly T-shirts, wood carvings, and weavings. ⊙ *Daily 8–6.*

Aguas Calientes (literally "hot waters") takes its name from the thermal springs, the **Aguas Termales,** that sit above town. Don't expect Baden Baden, but if you aren't too fussy, this can be a refreshing dip at the end of a hot day. ⊠ *Top of Av. Pachacutec* ☏ *No phone* ☝ *S/10* ⊙ *Daily 6* AM–8 PM.

The **Museo de Sitio Manuel Chávez Ballón,** the area's newest attraction, would go in the don't-miss column were it not for its odd location. The museum, dedicated to the history, culture, and rediscovery of Machu

Picchu, sits on the way up to the ruins about 2 km (1 mi) from the edge of town at the entrance to the national park. The buses that ferry visitors up to Machu Picchu normally do not stop along the way, but the museum's in-town office, next to the Insituto Nacional de Cultura just off the main plaza can arrange transportation for S/10 one-way. Hoofing it is the best way to get here. Plan on about a 30-minute walk. The museum provides valuable bilingual insight into South America's premier tourist attrac-

> ## INDIGENOUS TERMINOLOGY
>
> Stick to the term "indigenous" (*indígena*) to describe Peru's Inca-descended peoples. Avoid "Indian" (*indio*), which is considered pejorative here, that is, unless you're describing an Indian restaurant. Likewise, among people in Peru, "native" (*nativo*) and "tribe" (*tribú*) conjure up images best left to old Tarzan movies.

tion, which you don't get at the ruins themselves. ⊠*Puente de Ruinas, 2 km (1 mi) from Aguas Calientes* ☎*No phone* 🖃*S/20* ⊗*Daily 9–4.*

WHERE TO EAT

6

Pizza has taken Aguas Calientes by storm, though the town's ubiquitous pizzerias *do* offer other items on their menus. The pies are slid in and out of traditional Peruvian wood-burning clay ovens. The end product is a moist, cheesy baked pie.

¢ ✕**Chez Maggy.** A branch of the well-known Maggy's in Cusco is the best of the ubiquitous pizzerias in Aguas Calientes, and this branch even serves it fresh out of the requisite clay oven for no extra charge. ⊠*Pachacutec 156* ☎*084/211–006* 🖃*AE, MC, V.*

$–$$ ✕**Indio Feliz.** An engaging French-Peruvian couple manage the best res-
Fodor'sChoice taurant in Aguas Calientes, and this pink bistro is possibly the only
★ restaurant in town *not* to have pizza on its menu. Quiche lorraine, ginger chicken, and spicy *trucha macho* (trout in hot pepper and wine sauce) are favorites here, and are usually part of the more reasonably priced (S/40) prix-fixe menu, all to the accompaniment of homemade bread. Top it off with a fine coffee and apple pie or flan for dessert. The restaurant presents each diner with a tiny ceramic pot or bowl as its calling card. An expansion in 2008 allowed room for a bar and an upstairs outdoor terrace, but has not compromised the intimacy of one of Peru's best restaurants. ⊠*Lloque Yupanqui 4* ☎*084/211–090* 🖃*AE, MC, V* ⊗*No dinner Sun.*

¢–$ ✕**Pueblo Viejo.** Lively conversation fills this restaurant just off the Plaza de Armas. Everyone gathers around the grill where cuts of beef, lamb and trout are prepared Argentine parrillada style, with rice, vegetables, and fries. Off to the side is the requisite clay oven where pizzas are baked, yet this is one of the few places that does not trumpet the pizza on its menu. ⊠*Pachacutec s/n* ☎*084/211–193* 🖃*AE, DC, MC, V* ⊗*No lunch Sun.*

Continued on page 279

JOURNEY TO
MACHU PICCHU
MACHU PICCHU & THE INCA TRAIL

MACHU PICCHU & THE INCA TRAIL

Guardhouse

The exquisite architecture of the massive Inca stone structures, the formidable backdrop of steep sugarloaf hills, and the Urubamba River winding far below have made Machu Picchu the iconic symbol of Peru. It's a mystical city, the most famous archaeological site in South America, and one of the world's must-see destinations.

The world did not become aware of Machu Picchu's existence until 1911 when Yale University historian Hiram Bingham (1875–1956) announced that he had "discovered" the site. "Rediscovery" is a more accurate term; area residents knew of Machu Picchu's existence all along. This "Lost City of the Inca" was missed by the ravaging conquistadors and survived untouched until the beginning of the 20th century.

You'll be acutely aware that the world has since discovered Machu Picchu if you visit during the June–mid–September high season. Machu Picchu absorbs the huge numbers of visitors, though, and even in the highest of the high season, its beauty is so spectacular that it rarely disappoints.

DISCOVERY

American explorer and historian Hiram Bingham, with the aid of local guides, came across the Lost City in 1911. Though the name appeared on maps as early as 1860, previous attempts to find the site failed. Bingham erred in recognizing what he had uncovered. The historian assumed he had stumbled upon Vilcabamba, the last real stronghold of the Inca. (The actual ruins of Vilcabamba lie deep in the rain forest, and were uncovered in the 1960s.)

Bingham, who later served as governor of and senator from Connecticut, transported—some say stole—many of Machu Picchu's artifacts to Yale in 1912. They are still on display at the Peabody Museum. The museum is in no hurry to give them back, but negotiations, often contentious, are under way to return some of the treasures to Peru.

In 1915, Bingham announced his discovery of the Inca Trail. As with Machu Picchu, his "discovery" was a little disingenuous. Locals knew about the trail, and that it had served as a supply route between Cusco and Machu Picchu during Inca times. Parts of it were used during the colonial and early republican eras as well.

Though archaeological adventuring is viewed differently now, Bingham's slog to find Machu Picchu and the Inca Trail was no easy feat. Look up from Aguas Calientes, and you still won't know it's there.

HISTORY

Ever since Bingham came across Machu Picchu, its history has been debated. It was likely a small city of some 200 homes and 1,000 residents, with agricultural terraces to supply the population's needs and a strategic position that overlooked—but could not be seen from—the valley floor.

New theories suggest that the city was a transit station for products, such as coca and hearts of palm that were grown in the lowlands and sent to Cusco. Exactly when Machu Picchu was built is not known, but one theory suggests that it was a country estate of an Inca ruler named Pachacuti, which

means its golden age was in the mid-15th century.

Historians have discredited the romantic theory of Machu Picchu as a refuge of the chosen Inca women after the Spanish conquest; analysis shows a 50/50 split of male and female remains.

The site's belated discovery may indicate that the Inca deserted Machu Picchu before the Spanish conquest. The reason for the city's presumed abandonment is as mysterious as its original function. Some archaeologists suggest that the water supply simply ran out. Some guess that disease ravaged the city. Others surmise it was the death of Pachacutec, after which his estate was no longer needed.

"INDIANA" BINGHAM

Hiram Bingham at Machu Picchu, 1912.

A globe-trotting archaeological explorer, which was an especially romantic figure in early 20th century America, Hiram Bingham was a model for the Indiana Jones character in the film *Raiders of the Lost Ark*.

Guardhouse

House of the Terrace Caretaker

EXPLORING THE RUINS

Everyone must go through the main entrance to have their ticket stamped. Those arriving from the Inca Trail enter the park via a path leading past the Guardhouse, away from the main entrance but they must exit the park, then enter again through the ticket booth. From there you work your way up through the agricultural areas and to the urban sectors.

View from the Guardhouse

There are almost no signs inside to explain what you're seeing; booklets and maps are for sale at the entrance. Restrooms are outside the front gate, but not inside the ruins.

The English-language names to the structures within the city were assigned by Bingham. Call it inertia, but those labels have stuck, even though the late Yale historian's nomenclature was mostly offbase.

The Guardhouse is the first structure you encounter after coming through the main entrance. The Inca carved terraces into the hillsides to grow produce and minimize erosion. Corn was the likely crop cultivated. The semitropical climate meant ample rain for most of the year.

The House of the Terrace Caretaker and Funeral Rock are a 20-minute walk up to the left of the entrance, and provide the quintessential Machu Picchu vista. You've seen the photos, yet nothing beats the view in person, especially with a misty sunrise. Bodies of nobles likely lay in state here, where they would have been eviscerated, dried, and prepared for mummification.

The Temple of the Sun is a marvel of perfect Inca stone assembly. On June 22 (winter solstice in the southern hemisphere), sunlight shines through a small, trapezoid-shape window and onto the middle of a large, flat granite stone presumed to be an Inca calendar. Looking out the window, astronomers saw the constellation Pleiades, revered as a symbol of crop fertility. Bingham dubbed the small cave below the Royal Tomb, though no human remains were found here.

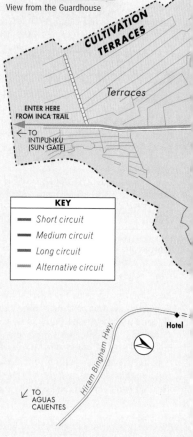

CULTIVATION TERRACES

Terraces

ENTER HERE
FROM INCA TRAIL

← TO
INTIPUNKU
(SUN GATE)

KEY
▬▬▬ *Short circuit*
▬▬▬ *Medium circuit*
▬▬▬ *Long circuit*
▬▬▬ *Alternative circuit*

Hotel

Hiram Bingham Hwy.

↙ TO
AGUAS
CALIENTES

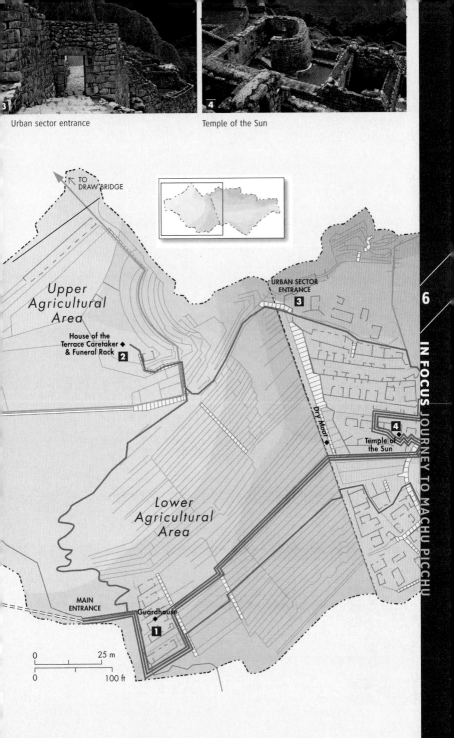

Urban sector entrance

Temple of the Sun

TO
DRAW BRIDGE

URBAN SECTOR
ENTRANCE
3

Upper
Agricultural
Area

House of the
Terrace Caretaker ◆
& Funeral Rack **2**

Dry Moat ◆

Temple of
the Sun
4

Lower
Agricultural
Area

MAIN
ENTRANCE

Guardhouse
1

0   25 m
0   100 ft

5 Principal Temple

6 Temple of the Three Windows

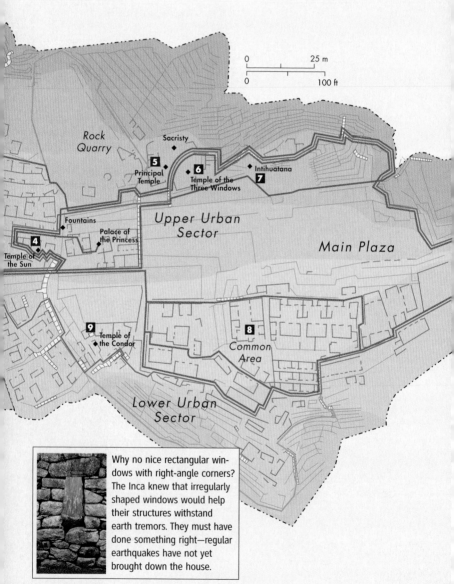

0   25 m

0   100 ft

Rock Quarry

Sacristy

5 Principal Temple

6 Temple of the Three Windows

Intihuatana **7**

Upper Urban Sector

Main Plaza

Fountains

Palace of the Princess

4 Temple of the Sun

9 Temple of the Condor

8

Common Area

Lower Urban Sector

Why no nice rectangular windows with right-angle corners? The Inca knew that irregularly shaped windows would help their structures withstand earth tremors. They must have done something right—regular earthquakes have not yet brought down the house.

Intihuatana

Common Area

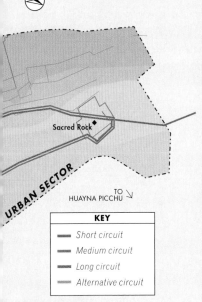

Sacred Rock◆

URBAN SECTOR

TO HUAYNA PICCHU ↘

KEY
▬▬▬ Short circuit
▬▬▬ Medium circuit
▬▬▬ Long circuit
▬▬▬ Alternative circuit

Temple of the Condor.

Fountains. A series of 16 small fountains are linked to the Inca worship of water.

Palace of the Princess, a likely misnomer, is a two-story building that adjoins the temple.

The Principal Temple is so dubbed because its masonry is among Machu Picchu's best. The three-walled structure is a masterpiece of mortarless stone construction.

Sacristy, At this secondary temple next to the primary temple, priests may have prepared themselves for ceremonies.

Temple of the Three Windows. A stone staircase leads to the three-walled structure. The entire east wall is hewn from a single rock with trapezoidal windows cut into it.

Intihuatana. A hillock leads to the "Hitching Post of the Sun." Every important Inca center had one of these vertical stone columns (called gnomons), but their function is unknown. The Spanish destroyed most of them, seeing the posts as objects of pagan worship. Machu Picchu's is one of the few to survive—partially at least. Its top was accidentally knocked off in 2001 during the filming of a Cusqueña beer commercial.

The Sacred Rock takes the shape in miniature of the mountain range visible behind it.

The Common Area covers a large grassy plaza with less elaborately constructed buildings and huts.

Temple of the Condor is so named because the positioning of the stones resembles a giant condor, the symbol of heaven in the Inca cosmos. The structure's many small chambers led Bingham to dub it a "prison," a concept that did not likely exist in Inca society.

DID YOU KNOW?

The step terraces you see here allowed residents to engineer different micro climates and cultivate a variety of corn. The structures also minimized erosion.

THE SKINNY ON MACHU PICCHU

DAY TRIPPING VS. OVERNIGHT

You can visit Machu Picchu on a day trip, but we recommend staying overnight at the hotel near the entrance or at a hotel in Aguas Calientes. A day trip allows you about four hours at Machu Picchu. If you stay overnight you can wander the ruins after most tourists have gone.

BUYING A TICKET

If you arrive without an admission ticket, you must purchase one in Aguas Calientes at the Instituto Nacional de Cultura (Avenida Pachacutec s/n, open daily 5 AM–10 PM) just off the Plaza de Armas. There is no ticket booth at the ruins' entrance. Your ticket must be used within three days. It's valid for multiple admissions on one calendar day only; a return visit the next morning means a new ticket. ☎ *084/211–067, 084/211–256 in Aguas Calientes* ✉ *S/120, S/60 with International Student Identity Card. Daily 6 AM–5:30 PM.*

CATCHING THE BUS

If you're a day-tripper, follow the crowd out of the rail station about two blocks to the Consettur Machupicchu shuttle buses, which ferry you up a series of switchbacks to the ruins, a journey of 20 minutes. Buy your S/40 round-trip ticket at a booth next to the line of buses before boarding. If you're staying overnight, check in to your lodging first, and then come back to buy a bus ticket.

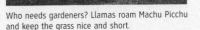

Who needs gardeners? Llamas roam Machu Picchu and keep the grass nice and short.

Buses leave Aguas Calientes for the ruins beginning at 6:30 AM and continue more or less hourly, with a big push in mid-morning as the trains arrive. The last bus up leaves about 1 PM. Buses start coming back down about 11:30 AM, with a last departure at 5:40. If you're heading back to Cusco, take the bus back down at least an hour before your train departs.

BEING PREPARED

Being high above the valley floor makes you forget that Machu Picchu sits 2,490 meters (8,170 ft) above sea level, a much lower altitude than Cusco. It gets warm, and the ruins have little shade. Sunscreen, a hat, and water are musts. Officially, no food or drinks are permitted, but you can get away with a bottle of water. Large packs must be left at the entrance.

PRACTICALITIES

A snack bar is a few feet from where the buses deposit you at the gate to the ruins, and the Machu Picchu Sanctuary Lodge, the only hotel up here, has a S/100 lunch buffet open to the public. Bathrooms cost S/1, and toilet paper is provided. There are no bathrooms inside the ruins.

THE INCA TRAIL, ABRIDGED

Some Cusco tour operators market a two-day, one-night Inca Trail excursion as the **Sacred Inca Trail** or **Royal Inca Trail.** It's easier to procure reservations for these trips, but advance reservations with a licensed operator are still essential. The excursion begins at **Km 104,** a stop on the Cusco–Machu Picchu trains. A three-hour walk along the occasionally very steep path brings you to **Huiñay Huayna** (also called Wiñaywayna) a terrace complex and the same camp site from which the longer trekking trips begin their pre-sunrise walk to the ruins. Following another couple of hours' walk, you'll arrive at Machu Picchu late in the afternoon via Intipunku, the classic Machu Picchu overlook. You spend the night at a hotel in Aguas Calientes. The second day is not a trail hike, but a visit to the ruins.

EXPLORING BEYOND THE LOST CITY

Huiñay Huayna

Several trails lead from the site to surrounding ruins.

If you come by train, you can take a 45-minute walk on a gentle arc leading uphill to the southeast of the main complex. **Intipunku**, the Sun Gate, is a small ruin in a nearby pass. This small ancient checkpoint is where you'll find that classic view that Inca Trail hikers emerge upon. The walk along the way yields some interesting and slightly different angles as well. Some minor ancient outbuildings along the path occasionally host grazing llamas. Intipunku is also the gateway to the **Inca Trail**. A two- or three-hour hike beyond the Intipunku along the Inca Trail brings you to the ruins of **Huiñay Huayna**, a terrace complex that climbs a steep mountain slope and includes a set of ritual baths.

Built rock by rock up a hair-raising stone escarpment, The **Inca Bridge** is yet another example of Inca engineering ingenuity. From the cemetery at Machu Picchu, it's a 30-minute walk along a narrow path.

The **Huayna Picchu** trail, which follows an ancient Inca path, leads up the sugarloaf hill in front of Machu Picchu for an exhilarating trek. Climbers must register at the entrance to the path behind La Roca Sagrada (the Sacred Rock). Limited to 400 visitors daily, no one is permitted entry after 1 PM—the limit is reached long before 1 PM in the high season—and all must be out by 4 PM. The walk up and back takes at least two hours and is only for the sure-footed. Bring insect repellent; the gnats can be ferocious. An alternate route back down takes you to the Temple of the Moon. The map at the entrance to the Huayna Picchu trail designates it as the Great Cave.

Looking down onto Inca ruins at base of Huayna Picchu.

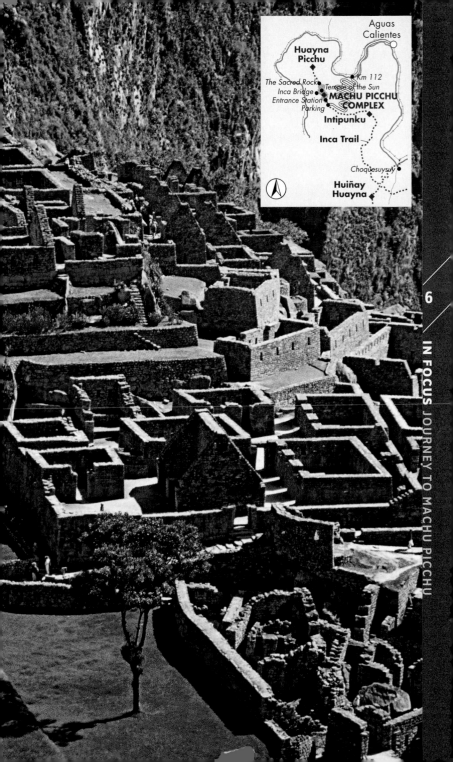

Aguas
Calientes

Huayna
Picchu

The Sacred Rock
Inca Bridge
Entrance Station
Parking

Km 112
Temple of the Sun
MACHU PICCHU
COMPLEX

Intipunku

Inca Trail

Choquesuysuy

Huiñay
Huayna

Walking the Inca trail through the Sacred Valley.

Inca Trail

Patallaqta

Train to Machu Picchu

INCA TRAIL

The Inca Trail (*Camino Inca* in Spanish), a 50-km (31-mi) sector of the stone path that once extended from Cusco to Machu Picchu, is one of the world's signature outdoor excursions. Nothing matches the sensation of walking over the ridge that leads to the Lost City of the Inca just as the sun casts its first yellow glow over the ancient stone buildings.

Though the journey by PeruRail is the easiest way to get to Machu Picchu, most travelers who arrive via the Inca Trail wouldn't have done it any other way. There are limits on the number of trail users, but you'll still see a lot of fellow trekkers along the way. The four-day trek takes you past ruins and through stunning scenery, starting in the thin air of the highlands and ending in cloud forests. The orchids, hummingbirds, Andean condors, and spectacular mountains aren't bad either.

The impressive Puyupatamarca ruins.

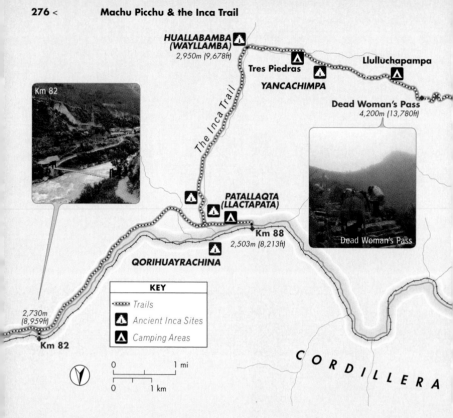

Km 82

**HUALLABAMBA
(WAYLLAMBA)** 🏕
2,950m (9,678ft)

Tres Piedras ⛺

YANCACHIMPA

Llulluchapampa ⛺

The Inca Trail

Dead Woman's Pass
4,200m (13,780ft)

**PATALLAQTA
(LLACTAPATA)** 🏕
⛺

Km 88
2,503m (8,213ft)

Dead Woman's Pass

QORIHUAYRACHINA ⛺

KEY

- ⋯⋯ *Trails*
- 🏕 *Ancient Inca Sites*
- ⛺ *Camping Areas*

*2,730m
(8,959ft)*

Km 82

0 ———— 1 mi
0 ———— 1 km

C O R D I L L E R A

INCA TRAIL DAY BY DAY

The majority of agencies begin the Inca Trail trek at **Km 82** after a two-to three-hour bus ride from Cusco.

DAY 1

Compared to what lies ahead, the first day's hike is a reasonably easy 12 km (7½ mi). You'll encounter fantastic ruins almost immediately. An easy ascent takes you to the first of those, **Patallaqta** (also called Llactapata). The name means "town on a hillside" in Quechua, and the ruins are thought to have been a village in Inca times. Bingham and company camped here on their first excursion to Machu Picchu. As at most Inca sites, you'll see three levels of architecture representing the three spiritual worlds of the Inca—the world above (a guard tower), the world we live in (the main complex), and the world below (the river and hidden aqueducts).

At the end of the day, you arrive at **Huayllabamba** (also called as Wayllamba), the only inhabited village on the trail and your first overnight

DAY 2

It's another 12-km (7½-mi) hike, but with a gain of 1,200 m (3,940 ft) in elevation. The day is most memorable for the spectacular views and muscular aches after ascending **Dead Woman's Pass** (also known as Warmiwañuscca) at 4,200 m (13,780 ft). The pass is named for the silhouette created by its mountain ridges—they resemble a woman's head, nose, chin, and chest.

A tricky descent takes you to **Pacaymayu,** the second night's campsite, and you can pat yourself on the back for completing the hardest section of the Inca Trail.

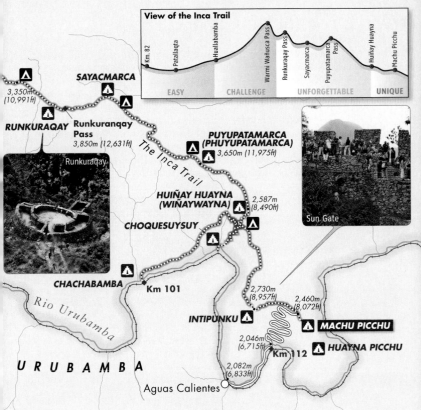

View of the Inca Trail

Km 82 · Patallaqta · Huallabamba · Warmi Wañusca Pass · Runkuraqay Pass · Sayacmarca · Puyupatamarca Pass · Huiñay Huayna · Machu Picchu

EASY   CHALLENGE   UNFORGETTABLE   UNIQUE

SAYACMARCA
3,350m (10,991ft)

RUNKURAQAY   Runkuranqay Pass
3,850m (12,631ft)

Runkuraqay

The Inca Trail

PUYUPATAMARCA (PHUYUPATAMARCA)
3,650m (11,975ft)

HUIÑAY HUAYNA (WIÑAYWAYNA)
2,587m (8,490ft)

Sun Gate

CHOQUESUYSUY

CHACHABAMBA   Km 101

2,730m (8,957ft)

2,460m (8,072ft)

Rio Urubamba

INTIPUNKU
2,046m (6,715ft)

MACHU PICCHU

Km 112   **HUAYNA PICCHU**

U R U B A M B A
2,082m (6,833ft)

Aguas Calientes

DAY 3

Downhill! You descend to the subtropical cloud forest where the Amazon basin begins. There's some of the most stunning mountain scenery you'll see during the four days. The ruins of **Runkuraqay** were a circular Inca storage depot for products transported between Machu Picchu and Cusco.

You also pass by **Sayacmarca**, possibly a way station for priests traversing the trail.

Most excursions arrive by mid-afternoon at **Huiñay Huayna** (also known as Wiñaywayna), the third-night's

stopping point, at what may now seem a low and balmy 2,712 m (8,900 ft). The first possibility of a hot shower and a cold beer are here.

There is time to see the ruins of **Puyupatamarca** (also known as Phuyupatamarca) a beautifully restored site with ceremonial baths, and perhaps the best ruins on the hike. At this point you catch your first glimpse of Machu Picchu peak, but from the back side.

DAY 4

This is it. Day 4 means the grand finale, arrival at **Machu**

Picchu, the reason for the trail in the first place. You'll be roused from your sleeping bag well before dawn to arrive at the ruins in time to catch the sunrise. You'll be amazed at the number of fellow travelers who forget about their aching muscles and sprint this last stretch.

The trail takes you past the **Intipunku,** the Sun Gate. Bask in your first sight of the ruins and your accomplishment, but you'll need to circle around and enter Machu Picchu officially through the entrance gate.

PREPPING FOR THE INCA TRAIL

YOU MUST GO WITH A GUIDE

The days of setting off on the Inca Trail on your own, along with free-for-all rowdiness and litter, ended years ago. You must use a licensed tour operator, one accredited by the Unidad de Gestión Santuario Histórico de Machu Picchu, the organization that oversees the trail and limits the number of hikers to 400 per day, including guides and porters. There are some 30 such licensed operators in Cusco.

WHEN TO GO

May through September is the best time to make the four-day trek; rain is more likely in April and October and a certainty the rest of the year. The trail fills up during the dry high season. Make reservations months in advance if you want to hike then—weeks in advance the rest of the year. The trek is doable during the rainy season, but can become slippery and muddy by December. The trail closes for maintenance each February.

GETTING READY

Tour operators in Cusco will tell you the Inca Trail is of "moderate" difficulty, but it can be rough going, especially the first couple of days. You must be in decent shape, even if your agency supplies porters to carry your pack—current regulations limit your load to 20 kg (44 lb). The trail is often narrow and hair-raising.

As the mountains sometimes rise to over 13,775 feet, be wary of altitude sickness. (Give yourself two or three days in Cusco or the Sacred Valley to acclimatize.)

Your gear should include sturdy hiking boots, a sleeping bag (some outfitters rent them); clothing for cold, rainy weather, a hat, and a towel. Also bring plenty of sunblock and mosquito repellent. Toilet paper is essential.

There are seven well-spaced, designated campsites along the trail.

WHILE YOU'RE HIKING

Coca Leaves: Although after Day 2 it is a gradual descent into Machu Picchu, you're still high enough to feel the thin air. You'll notice porters chewing coca throughout the trek. It's like drinking a cup of coffee. Coca leaves are a mild stimulant as well as an appetite, pain, and hunger suppressant. You'll only need about one bag of your own (about S/1) for the trail. To properly enjoy the leaves, take about 15 of them and pick the stems off. Stack them on top of each other and roll into a tight little bundle. Place the bundle between your gum and cheek on one side, allowing the leaves to soften up for about two minutes. Eventually start chewing to let the juice out. It's quite a bitter taste, but you'll feel better.

Bathrooms: Toilets could be a lot worse. You won't be able to sit down, but most porcelain-lined holes in the ground do flush. Bathrooms usually have working sinks, too. You must bring your own toilet paper wherever you go. Camp sites all have toilets, but the trail itself does not.

Luggage: Check with your tour operator before you go, and pack as lightly as possible. If you hire porters, they're probably going to be carrying a lot more than just your things on their backs. So an American-style backwoods backpack may not be the right piece of luggage—it weighs a lot on its own and is an awkward shape for the porters to incorporate into their massive bundles. Instead, check with your operator. They may suggest a simple duffle bag.

Walking the Inca Trail

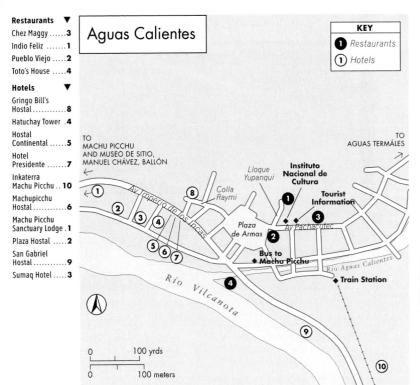

KEY

❶ Restaurants

① Hotels

Aguas Calientes

TO
MACHU PICCHU
AND MUSEO DE SITIO,
MANUEL CHÁVEZ, BALLÓN

TO
AGUAS TERMÁLES

Av. Imperio de los Incas

Lloque
Yupanqui

Instituto
Nacional de
Cultura

Colla
Raymi

Tourist
Information

Plaza
de Armas

Av. Pachacutec

Bus to
Machu Picchu

Río Aguas Calientes

Río Vilcanota

Train Station

0   100 yrds

0   100 meters

6

$-$$ ✕**Toto's House.** Long tables are set up in the center of this cavernous restaurant to accommodate the tour groups who come for the huge buffet lunch (S/50). Grab one of the smaller tables with a river view by the window or out on the front patio if you come on your own. Evenings are more sedate—that's the case with the dining scene in all the restaurants here—with such dishes as *trucha andina* (Andean trout), ceviche, and *chicharrón* (pork rinds and cabbage), all to the entertainment of a folklore music show. ✉*Av. Imperio de los Incas* ☎*084/211–020* ▤*AE, DC, MC, V.*

WHERE TO STAY

$$ ⊞**Gringo Bill's Hostal.** Bill has hosted Machu Picchu travelers for almost a quarter century, and his was one of the first lodgings in town. This rambling house has stone walls chock full of plants just off the Plaza de Armas. The corner rooms with balconies and windows get the best ventilation and have the greatest views. The small restaurant downstairs will even prepare a box lunch (S/15) for your day's excursion. This long-time budget option has added a few amenities in the past two years, but unfortunately, has raised its rates more than we think is warranted. Pros: Cozy setting, good place to meet other travelers.

Train To Machu Picchu

Venders hope you'll buy some culture before boarding the train back to Cusco.

At least two PeruRail trains depart from Cusco's San Pedro station daily for Aguas Calientes, near Machu Picchu. The Vistadome leaves at 6 AM and arrives in Aguas Calientes at 9:40. It returns from Aguas Calientes at 3:30 PM, arriving in Cusco at 7:25. A second Vistadome service departs at 6:15 AM. The round-trip fare is S/429. Snacks and beverages are included in the price, and the cars have sky domes for great views. The return trip includes a fashion show and folklore dancing.

The Backpacker train leaves Cusco at 7 AM, arriving in Aguas Calientes at 10:40. It leaves Aguas Calientes at 5 PM, getting back to Cusco at 9:25. The round-trip fare is S/290. Conditions are comparable to second-class trains in Western Europe and are quite comfortable.

A second Vistadome or Backpacker train may be added during the June–August high season, depending on demand.

All trains make an exaggerated series of five zigzag switchbacks, climbing as they leave from Cusco before descending into the lower-altitude Sacred Valley. Trains stop at Poroy, Ollantaytambo, Km 88 (the start of the Inca Trail), and Km 104 (the launch point of an abbreviated two-day Inca Trail). Arrival is in Aguas Calientes, where you catch the buses up to the ruins.

The return trip takes longer, but you can disembark in Poroy, about 15 minutes by highway from Cusco, where an Asociación de Agencias de Turismo de Cusco bus meets every Cusco-bound train. The fare is a time-saving S/5, and the bus deposits you on Cusco's Plaza de Armas.

Vistadome and Backpacker trains depart from Cusco's San Pedro station, where, in theory, same-day tickets can be purchased but waiting that late is risky. Purchase tickets in advance from the PeruRail sales office at Cusco's Wanchaq Station, weekdays from 7 to 5, and weekends and Peruvian holidays from 7–noon—note that PeruRail does not accept credit cards—or from a travel agency. (Most tour packages include rail tickets as well as bus transport to and from Aguas Calientes and Machu Picchu and admission to the ruins, and lodging if you plan to stay overnight.) Also in theory, PeruRail accepts e-mail reservations through its Web site: you send them the names, passport numbers, and travel dates of all passengers—but no credit-card numbers—then take the confirmation they send you to Wanchaq Station upon your arrival in Cusco and pay for your tickets in cash. At best, that procedure is cumbersome, and we hear frequent reports of e-mails not being answered or confirmations never received.

PeruRail's luxury Hiram Bingham train proffers a class of service unto itself (with prices to match). Trains depart from Poroy station, about 15 minutes outside Cusco, eliminating the tedious switchbacks necessary for the other trains to get out of and into the city. Departure time is a more leisurely 9 AM daily except Sunday, arriving at Aguas Calientes at 12:30 PM. Return service leaves Aguas Calientes at 6:30 PM, returning to Poroy at 10. The timetable permits you to stay at the ruins for a few hours after the day visitors have departed on the mid-afternoon trains back to Cusco. Trains consist of two dining cars, a bar car, and a kitchen car, and evoke the glamour of the old Orient Express rail service, no surprise, since Orient Express is the parent company of PeruRail. The S/1,775 round-trip price tag includes brunch on the trip to Machu Picchu, bus transport from Aguas Calientes up to the ruins and back in vehicles exclusively reserved for Hiram Bingham clients, admission to the ruins,

guide services while there, and an afternoon buffet tea at the Machu Picchu Sanctuary Lodge. The trip back entails cocktails, live entertainment, and a four-course dinner.

If you're using the Sacred Valley as your base, PeruRail operates a daily Vistadome train departing from Ollantaytambo at 7 AM, with arrival in Machu Picchu at 8:20. Other trains leave Ollantaytambo at 10:30 AM and 2:55 PM, arriving at Aguas Calientes about 75 minutes later. Return trains leave Aguas Calients at 8:35 AM and 1:20 and 4:45 PM. Round-trip fare is S/362. Shuttle buses connect Ollantaytambo to Urubamba. This service can give you more time to spend at the ruins than you'd have with a Cusco departure, or flexibility of travel at various times of day. A daily Backpacker train departs Ollantaytambo at 9:05 AM, arriving at Aguas Calientes at 11. Return from Aguas Calientes is at 4:20 PM, with arrival in Ollantaytambo at 6. Round-trip fare is S/260.

PeruRail's service is generally punctual. Schedules and rates are always subject to change, and there may be fewer trains per day to choose from during the December to March low season.

Tourists are not permitted to ride the Tren Local, the less expensive, but slower train intended for local residents only.

INFORMATION
Asociación de Agencias de Turismo de Cusco (⊠ *Nueva Baja 424, Cusco* ☎ *084/222–580*). **PeruRail** (⊠ *San Pedro station, Cascapara near Santa Clara, Cusco* ☎ *084/233–551* ⊕ *www.perurail.com* ⊠ *Wanchaq station, Pachacutec near Tullumayo, Cusco* ☎ *084/238–722* ⊕ *www.perurail.com*).

6

Cons: Price not quite justified. ⊠*Colla Raymi 104, Aguas Calientes* 🕾🖳*084/211–046* ⊕*www.gringobills.com* ⇗*20 rooms* ⚘*In-room: no a/c. In-hotel: restaurant, bar, pool, spa, no elevator, laundry service* ⊟*AE, V* ⦿❘*MAP.*

$$$–$$$$ 🖳**Hatuchay Tower.** Aguas Calientes' "high-rise" hotel towers a whole four floors above the river at the edge of town on the road heading to the ruins. Carpeted rooms are comfortable with modern furnishings and amenities, but the interior design is nothing out of the ordinary. **Pros:** Good location. **Cons:** Not exceptional. ⊠*Carretera a Machu Picchu* 🕾🖳*084/211–201 in Aguas Calientes* 🕾*01/447–5776 in Lima* 🖳*01/446–5776 in Lima* ⊕*www.hatuchaytower.com* ⇗*37 rooms, 5 suites* ⚘*In-room: no a/c, safe. In-hotel: restaurant, room service, bar, laundry service, public Wi-Fi, no-smoking rooms* ⊟*AE, DC, MC, V* ⦿❘*BP.*

¢ 🖳**Hostal Continental.** This old budget standby is the best of the rock-bottom lodgings in Aguas Calientes, and a definite cut above the standard backpacker digs. Rooms are small and basic, but so are the prices. All have white walls, two beds, a table and chair, and an abundant supply of hot water. Rates include breakfast at the Hotel Presidente, a couple of doors down. **Pros:** Hot water, good budget choice. **Cons:** Few amenities. ⊠*Av. Imperio de los Incas 165, Aguas Calientes* 🕾*084/211–078* ✉*sierraandina@gmail.com* ⇗*16 rooms* ⚘*In-room: no a/c, no phone, no TV. In-hotel: laundry service* ⊟*No credit cards* ⦿❘*BP.*

$ 🖳**Hotel Presidente.** Orange, and open, the Presidente is the best moderately priced hotel in Aguas Calientes. Carpeted rooms have modern furnishings, and about half have big windows and balconies that overlook the Río Vilcanota. These folks also manage three hostales (small hotels)—the Continental, the Machupicchu, and the Plaza—with simpler furnishings nearby. Pros: Good value, some good views. Cons: Nothing fancy. ⊠*Av. Imperio de los Incas s/n, Aguas Calientes* 🕾*084/211–034* 🖳*084/229–591* ✉*sierraandina@gmail.com* ⇗*28 rooms* ⚘*In-room: no a/c, no TV (some). In-hotel: restaurant, no elevator, laundry service* ⊟*No credit cards* ⦿❘*BP.*

$$$$ ✕🖳**Inkaterra Machu Picchu .** A five-minute walk from the center of town
Fodor's Choice takes you to this stunning ecolodge in its own minitropical cloud for-
★ est. The stone bungalows, none with the same design, have a rustic elegance, with exposed beams and cathedral ceilings. Activities include a one-day Inca Trail trek, bird-watching excursions, and orchid tours, as well as a twilight nature walk. The restaurant overlooking the surrounding hills is first-rate—try the delicious *crema de choclo* (corn chowder). The place was renamed in 2007, but everyone still refers to it as the Machu Picchu Pueblo Hotel. **Pros:** Natural setting, many activities. **Cons:** Expensive. ⊠*Av. Imperio de los Incas s/n, Aguas Calientes* 🕾*084/211–032, 01/610–0404 in Lima, 800/442–5042 in North America* 🖳*084/211–124, 01/422–4701 in Lima* ⊕*www.inkaterra. com* ⇗*83 rooms, 2 suites* ⚘*In-room: no a/c, no TV. In-hotel: 2 restaurants, room service, bar, pool, spa, laundry service, public Internet* ⊟*AE, DC, MC, V* ⦿❘*MAP.*

The pros of spending a night at the Sanctuary Lodge.

¢ 🏨 **Machupicchu Hostal.** Rooms are lined motel-style the length of a small courtyard and are simply furnished. You'll find three huge double rooms at the back facing the river. An ample breakfast is included in the rates and served at the Hotel Presidente next door. **Pros:** Best rooms face the river. **Cons:** Pretty basic. ⊠ *Av. Imperio de los Incas 135* ☎ *084/211–034* 🖷 *084/229–591* ✉ *sierraandina@gmail.com* 🛏 *12 rooms* ⛁ *In-room: no a/c, no TV* ▭ *No credit cards* ⦿*BP.*

$$$$ ✕🏨 **Machu Picchu Sanctuary Lodge.** This hotel at the entrance to Machu Picchu puts you closest to the ruins, a position for which you pay dearly. But not only will you have the thrill of watching the sun rise over the crumbling stone walls, you'll be the first ones through the ruins' gate in the morning, and have the place to yourself after most of the tourists depart each afternoon. The lodge has been completely renovated by Orient Express, which has taken over the property. The restaurant has an excellent international menu that makes it worth a special trip, and serves a popular S/100 buffet lunch open to the public. **Pros:** Prime location at ruins' entrance. **Cons:** Expensive. ⊠ *Machu Picchu* ☎ *084/211–094, 01/610–8300 in Lima, 800/237–1236 in North America* 🖷 *084/211–246* 🌐 *www.machupicchu.orient-express.com* 🛏 *29 rooms, 2 suites* ⛁ *In-room: no a/c, no phone, safe, refrigerator, VCR. In-hotel: 3 restaurants, room service, bar, no elevator, laundry service, no-smoking rooms* ▭ *AE, DC, MC, V* ⦿*FAP.*

¢ 🏨 **Plaza Hostal.** The small Plaza faces the river on the road heading out of town up to the ruins. Rooms are simply furnished. Opt for one with its own small balcony. An ample breakfast is included in the rates and served at the Hotel Presidente around the corner. **Pros:** Good location and price. **Cons:** Some rooms better than others. ⊠*Carretera a Machu Picchu* ☎*084/211–192* ⊠*084/229–591* ✎*sierraandina@gmail.com* ⌦*7 rooms* ♿*In-room: no a/c, no phone, no TV. In-hotel: no elevator, laundry service* ⊟*No credit cards* ⦿*BP.*

¢   ⬚ **San Gabriel Hostal.** A friendly couple manages this inexpensive hotel above their restaurant a few minutes' walk from the center of town. Rooms face the river and are simply furnished with a bed, a table, and a tiled bath. If you come here on a very basic budget this is a decent choice. **Pros:** Inexpensive, friendly. **Cons:** Few amenities. ⊠*Av. Imperio de los Incas 39* ☎*084/234–986* ⌦*7 rooms* ♿*In-room: no a/c, no phone, no TV. In-hotel: restaurant, no elevator* ⊟*No credit cards* ⦿*CP.*

$$$$ ✕⬚ **Sumaq Hotel.** Machu Picchu's late-2007 entry into the luxury-lodg-
Fodor's Choice   ing sweepstakes promises to give the Sanctuary Lodge and Inkaterra a
★   real run for their money. At this hotel at the edge of town on the high-way heading up toward the ruins, the list of nice touches and amenities goes on and on: grand staircases, elegant restaurant with a terrific cross selection of Peruvian cuisine, huge rooms, some with fireplace, all with wood-beam ceilings, flat-screen TVs, box spring mattresses, porcelain basin sinks, and sinfully fluffy towels. ■**TIP→ Sumaq means "beautiful" in Quechua and the name is apt.** Rates include a breakfast buffet and lunch or dinner. **Pros:** Many amenities, great restaurant. **Cons:** Luxury costs. ⊠*Carretera a Machu Picchu, Aguas Calientes* ☎*084/211–059, 01/447–0579 in Lima* ⊠*084/211–114, 01/445–7828 in Lima* ⊕*www.sumaqhotelperu.com* ⌦*60 rooms* ♿*In-room: safe, refrigerator, DVD, Wi-Fi. In-hotel: restaurant, room service, bar, spa, laundry service, public Internet* ⊟*AE, DC, MC, V* ⦿*MAP.*

The Amazon Basin

WORD OF MOUTH

"Beautiful rainforests for walks. Fragrant flowers. Villages. Fishing. Visited a school and played soccer with the kids. Herbal face and body treatments from the Amazon ladies (not in a spa, just from plants along the walks). Fresh, fresh foods. Quiet. And, ah, those wonderful hammocks for relaxing in the afternoon rains. Loved it. But about 3 days without electricity and running water was enough."

—kywood1955

WELCOME TO
THE AMAZON BASIN

TOP REASONS
TO GO

★ **The River:** The Amazon is a natural choice for adventures, but sign up with a tour operator, who will know the safest places to go boating, canoeing, swimming, and fishing. Piranhas and anacondas live in some streams.

★ **Wild Things:** Peru's Amazon basin has more than 50,000 plant, 1,700 bird, 400 mammal, and 300 reptile species. Bring binoculars.

★ **Bass Fishing:.** Anglers test out their skills versus the peacock bass, one of the world's strongest freshwater fighters.

★ **River Lodges:** Staying at a lodge up the Amazon is almost a prerequisite to visiting the Amazon basin, where the life of the river and jungle surround you.

★ **Bird World:** The incredible array of fantastical-looking birds will make an avian fanatic out of you. A boat cruise by the Allpahuayo-Mishana National Reserve, Tamshiyacu Tahuayo Reserve, and Pacaya Samiria National Reserve could add a hundred to your list.

1 Madre de Dios. The national parks, reserves, and other undeveloped areas of the southern department of Madre de Dios are among the most biologically diverse in the world. The jungle frontier city of Puerto Maldonado is mostly used by travelers as a place to fly into, board a boat, and go to the jungle lodge. The truth is that you don't come for a city experience.

2 Iquitos & Environs. Three of the most desirable ecodestinations can only be accessed by boat—Allpahuayo-Mishana Nacional Reserve, Tamshiyacu Tahuayo Reserve, and Pacaya Samiria National Reserve. The reserves are the best places for bird-watching, wildlife observation, and admiring undisturbed rain forest. The jungle-locked city of Iquitos has a party-going, city-on-the-edge attitude with more than 400,000 cooped-up residents.

Iquitos.

ECUADOR

Gueppi

Pantoja

Napo River

AMAZON BASIN

Allapahuayo Mishana
National Reserve

Tigre River

Santa Maria de Nanay

**Pacaya Samiria
National reserve**

Marañón River

Requena

Santa Isabel

Orellana

Ucayali River

Pucallpa

16 B

Puerto
Inca

Huanuco

Puerto
Bermudez

CORDILLERA CENTRAL

GETTING ORIENTED

The logistics of travel and isolation make it unlikely that you could visit both the northern and southern Amazon regions—separated by 600 km (370 mi) at their nearest point—during one trip to Peru. The city of Iquitos is the jumping-off point for the northern Amazon; Puerto Maldonado, for the south. Some 1,200 km (740 mi) and connecting flights back in Lima separate the two cities. Neither will disappoint, and both are dotted with the region's famed jungle lodges.

COLOMBIA

CONAPAC
Biological Reserve

Amazon

Iquitos   Caballococha

Tamshiyacu Tahuayo
Reserve

Nauta

BRAZIL

0   100 mi

0   100 km

Tree frog in Amazon rain forest.

Park Nacional
Alto Purus

Atalaya   Iñapari

Iberia

Manu   Puerto
Biosphere Reserve   Maldonado
        Boca Manu

        Itahuania
        Shintuya   **1**
                26 B
C O R D I L L E R A   Parque Nacional   **BOLIVIA**
                        Bahuaja-Sonene
Machu Picchu
    Urubamba   Pisac   U R U B A M B A
        Cusco   3S

Black berries.

THE AMAZON BASIN PLANNER

Weather Wise

The best time to visit the Amazon basin is during the "dry season." Although there's no true dry season in a rain forest, it rains less during July and August; it rains most in January and February, and it's hotter between February and June. For Amazon cruises out of Iquitos, high water season is best (mid-November–June). Although there's no true peak tourist season, plan well in advance anyway, as some jungle lodges often take in large groups, and cruise boats can be full.

All southern Amazon-basin reserves are best visited between May and October, the driest months; the lodges are open year-round, though rivers may overflow and mosquitoes are voracious during the worst of the rainy season. Tambopata sees a well-defined wet season/dry season; Manu's rainfall is more evenly dispersed throughout the year. During the dry season, especially July, sudden *friajes* (cold fronts) bring rain and cold weather to Madre de Dios, so be prepared for the worst. Temperatures can drop from 32°C (90°F) to 10°C (50°F) overnight. No matter when you travel, bring a rain jacket or poncho and perhaps rain pants.

Health & Safety

Traveler's Stomach. Avoiding an upset stomach and diarrhea can be difficult. Drink only bottled water, and use it even to brush your teeth. Peel fruits and vegetables before you eat them. Fasting while maintaining a strict regimen of hydration (bottled water only) is the quickest way to cure traveler's stomach.

Malaria. There is no vaccine but prescription drugs help minimize your likelihood of contracting this mosquito-borne illness. Strains of malaria are resistant to the traditional regimen of chloroquine. There are three recommended alternatives: a weekly dose of mefloquine; a daily dose of doxycycline; or a daily dose of Malarone (*atovaquone/ proguanil*). Any regimen must start before arrival and continue beyond departure. Ask your physician. Wear long sleeves and pants if you're out in the evening, and use a mosquito repellent containing DEET.

Yellow Fever. The Peruvian Embassy recommends getting a yellow-fever vaccine at least 10 days before visiting the Amazon. Though recent cases of yellow fever have occurred only near Iquitos, southern Amazon lodges in Manu and Tambopata tend to be sticklers about seeing your yellow-fever vaccination certificate. Carry it with you.

Emergencies. The Policia Nacional (P 082/803–504 or 082/573–605), Peru's national police force, handles emergencies. At jungle lodges minor emergencies are handled by the staff. For serious emergencies, the lodge must contact medical services in Puerto Maldonado or Cusco.

Restaurants & Hotels

You can dine out at restaurants only in Iquitos and Puerto Maldonado, the Amazon basin's two cities. Your sole dining option is your lodge if you stay in the jungle. Meals are served family-style at fixed times with everyone seated around a big table, and you can swap stories with your fellow lodgers about what you saw on your day's excursion. The food, usually made of local ingredients, is quite tasty.

Puerto Maldonado and Iquitos have typical, albeit small, hotels—ones where, presuming availability, you can show up on a moment's notice, sign in, and secure a room. Iquitos has a few hotels geared to business travelers. Beyond the Amazon's two cities lie the region's jungle lodges. They vary in degree of rusticity and remoteness, usually reachable only by boat. They range from camping sites a cut above the norm to full-fledged ecolodges with private baths and solar-powered lighting. Most make do without electricity, however. Showers will be refreshingly or bracingly cold, though some lodges can now heat the water.

All lodges offer some variation on a fully escorted tour, with packages from one to several nights including guided wildlife-viewing excursions. Confirm that lodge beds have mosquito nets and that all meals are included. Many lodges quote rates per person for tours that last more than one day—it's not realistic to stay for just one night. That said, the price ranges given for lodges in this chapter reflect the cost of one night's stay for two people.

Although travel agencies selling package tours via Lima or Cusco accept credit cards, most jungle lodges cannot, as they do not have electricity or phone wires. All lodges accept soles, and most accept U.S. dollars for drinks and souvenirs.

Language

Guides and staff at the jungle lodges speak English. The person on the street in this remote region probably knows only Spanish. You'll hear indigenous languages such as Ese'eja in remote areas.

Ribereños

Peruvians in the Amazon are mostly a mix of one or more native populations with some Spanish ancestry. Ribereños, as they're called, live simple lives close to the land and water, much like their native ancestors. They depend on fish and crops for their survival. A visit to a Ribereño community is unforgettable, educational, and often the highlight of a tour of the region. Also, not far from Iquitos are numerous small communities of Amazon peoples. They include the Yagua, Bora, Huitoto, Ticuna, and Cocama groups, whose people generally don't speak Spanish. If you do visit a native village, be sure to take small bills (nuevo soles or dollars) to buy artisan items.

WHAT IT COSTS IN NUEVO SOLES

RESTAURANTS				
¢	$	$$	$$$	$$$$
under S/20	S/20–S/35	S/35–S/50	S/50–S/65	over S/65
HOTELS				
¢	$	$$	$$$	$$$$
under S/125	S/125–S/250	S/250–S/375	S/375–S/500	over S/500

Restaurant prices are per person for a main course. Hotel prices are for a standard double room, excluding tax.

By Rhan Flatin
Updated by
Michael Collis

Peru's least-known region occupies some two-thirds of the country, an area the size of California. The *selva* (jungle) of the Amazon basin is watered by the world's second longest river and its tributaries. What eastern Peru lacks in human population it makes up for in sheer plant and animal numbers, more than you knew could exist, for the viewing. There are lodges, cruise boats, and guides for the growing number of people who arrive to see the spectacle.

The northern Amazon is anchored by the port city of Iquitos. Iquitos is the gateway to the world's largest and most diverse natural reserve, the Amazon rain forest. From Iquitos you can head for the jungle to explore the flora and fauna.

Though the area has been inhabited by small indigenous groups for more than 5,000 years, it wasn't "civilized" until Jesuit missionaries arrived in the 1500s. The Spanish conquistador Francisco de Orellana was the first white man to see the Amazon. He came upon the great river, which the indigenous people called Tunguragua (King of Waters), on his trip down the Río Napo in search of El Dorado. He dubbed it Amazonas after he met with extreme opposition from female warriors along the banks of the river.

The area was slow to convert to modern ways, and remained basically wild until the 1880s, when there was a great rubber boom. The boom changed the town of Iquitos overnight; rubber barons installed themselves in lavish palaces, and the city's population exploded. Local people were put to work as rubber tappers—at the time, rubber was a natural commodity that was hunted rather than farmed, and the tappers would head into the jungle and collect the sap from rubber trees. The boom went bust in the first part of the 20th century, when a British entrepreneur transported some seeds out of Brazil and began building plantations on the Malay Peninsula. You can still see remnants of the boom in the somewhat dilapidated palaces in Iquitos and along the banks of the Amazon and its tributaries, where Rivereños (the river people) eke their survival from the river and small plots of farmland.

Most of the indigenous tribes—many small tribes are in the region, the Boras, Yaguas, and Orejones being the most prevalent—have given up their traditional hunter-gatherer existence and now live in small communities along the backwaters of the great river. You will not see the remote tribes unless you travel far from Iquitos and deep into the jungle, a harrowing and dangerous undertaking. What you will see are people living along with nature, with traditions that date back thousands of years: a common sight might be a fisherman paddling calmly up the Amazon in his dugout canoe, angling to reel in something upriver.

The lesser-known southern Amazon region has to be satisfied with the big river's tributaries. Few travelers spend much time in Puerto Maldonado, the capital of Madre de Dios department, using the city instead as a jumping-off point to the Manu and Tambopata reserves. Manu is the less accessible but more pristine of the two Madre de Dios reserves, but Tambopata will not disappoint.

Be prepared to spend some extra soles to get here. Roads, when they exist, are rough-and-tumble, and often impassible during the November through April rainy season. Rivers also overflow at this time. A dry-season visit entails the least fuss. You'll most likely jet into Iquitos or Puerto Maldonado, respectively the northern and southern gateways to the Amazon. Each receives several daily flights from Lima. From each it's usually a boat ride to reach the region's famed lodges.

MADRE DE DIOS

Do the math: 20,000 plant, 1,200 butterfly, 1,000 bird, 200 mammal, and 100 reptile species (and many more yet to be identified). The southern sector of Peru's Amazon basin, most readily approached via Cusco, is famous among birders, whose eyes glaze over in amazement at the dawn spectacle of macaws and parrots visiting the region's famed *ccollpas* (clay licks). Ornithologists speculate that the birds ingest clay periodically to detoxify other elements in their diet. Madre de Dios also offers a rare chance to see large mammals, such as tapirs and, if the zoological fates smile upon you, jaguars. Animal and plant life abound, but this is the least populated of Peru's departments: a scant 76,000 people reside in an area slightly smaller than South Carolina, and almost two-thirds of them are in Puerto Maldonado.

The southern Amazon saw little incursion at the time of the Spanish conquest. The discovery in the late 19th century of the *shiringa*, known in the English-speaking world as the rubber tree, changed all of that. Madre de Dios saw outside migration for the first time with the arrival of the *caucheros* (rubber men) and their minions staking out claims. The discovery of gold in the 1970s drew new waves of fortune seekers to the region.

Tourism and conservation have triggered the newest generation of explorers in the species-rich southern Amazon. Two areas of Madre de Dios are of special interest. One is around the city of Puerto Maldonado, including the Tambopata National Reserve and the adjoining Bahuaja-Sonene National Park; easily accessible, they offer lodges amid primary rain forest and excellent birding. Tambopata also exists for sustainable agriculture purposes: some 1,500 families in the department work to extract Brazil nuts from the reserve, an economic incentive to keep the forest intact, rather than cut it down for its lumber. The Manu Biosphere Reserve, directly north of Cusco, though more difficult to reach, provides unparalleled opportunity for observing wildlife in one of the largest virgin rain forests in the New World.

PUERTO MALDONADO

500 km (310 mi) east of Cusco.

The inland port city of Puerto Maldonado lies at the meeting point of the Madre de Dios and Tambopata rivers. The capital of the department of Madre de Dios is a rough-and-tumble town with 46,000 people and nary a four-wheeled vehicle in sight, but with hundreds of motorized two- and three-wheeled motorbikes jockeying for position on its few paved streets.

The city is named for two explorers who ventured into the region 300 years apart: Spanish conquistador Juan Álvarez de Maldonado passed through in 1566; Peruvian explorer Faustino Maldonado explored the still-wild area in the 1860s, never completing his expedition, drowning in the nearby Madeira River. Rubber barons founded this youngster of Peruvian cities in 1912, and its history has been a boom-or-bust roller-coaster ride ever since. The collapse of the rubber industry in the 1930s gave way to decades of dormancy ended by the discovery of gold in the 1970s and the opening of an airport 10 years later.

Puerto Maldonado bills itself as the "Biodiversity Capital of the World," and makes the best jumping-off point for visiting the Tambopata National Reserve sector of Peru's Amazon rain forest. ■**TIP→** **Few travelers spend any time in the city, heading from the airport directly to the municipal docks, where they board boats to their respective jungle lodges.** Still, Puerto Maldonado has a handful of decent hotels. And this is the only place to use an ATM machine, cash a traveler's check, or log on to the Internet.

GETTING HERE & AROUND

It's fun to get around town in Puerto Maldonado's fleet of Honda Motokar taxis, semi-open three-wheeled motorized vehicles with room for two passengers in the back seat. Every motorbike in town also provides taxi service. You may define that as "fun" or "danger." Hold on for dear life, and don't expect a helmet.

CLOSE UP

Amazon Tours

MADRE DE DIOS

One of the most experienced guide services, **Manu Expeditions** offers 5- to 9-day camping trips. ⊠ *Urbanizació Magisterio 2nda Etapa, G-5, Cusco* ☎ *084/226–671* ⊕ *www.manuexpeditions.com.*

Manu Nature Tours operates the only full-service lodge within the Manu Biosphere reserve, and has a cloud-forest lodge. The Manu Lodge is often used by scientists who are studying the reserve's ecology. ⊠ *Av. Pardo 1046, Cusco* ☎ *084/252–721* ⊠ *Conquistadores 396, San Isidro, Lima* ☎ *01/442–8980* ⊕ *www.manuperu.com.*

InkaNatura Travel manages lodges in Manu and the Tambopata National Reserve. ⊠ *Manuel Bañon 461, Lima* ☎ *014/402–022* ⊠ *Calle Ricardo Palma 11, Cusco* ☎ *084/255–255, 877/827–8350 in U.S.* ⊕ *www.inkanatura.com.*

Inkaterra Nature Travel sets up tours to Reserva Amazonica in the Tambopata with rain-forest walks, night hikes, and a visit to Rolin Island in the Madre de Dios. ⊠ *Andalucía 174, Miraflores, Lima* ☎ *016/100–400, 800/442–5042 in U.S.* ⊕ *www.inkaterra.com* ⊠ *Procuradores 48, Cusco* ☎ *084/245–5314.*

Pantiacolla organizes ecotours in Manu and operates a series of bungalows overlooking the Alto Madre de Dios river. ⊠ *Plateros 360, Cusco* ☎ *084/238–323* ⊕ *www.pantiacolla.com.*

Peruvian Safaris offers a customized visit of Puerto Maldonado, Tambopata, and Manu, and a tour of the reserves around Iquitos. ⊠ *Alcanfores 459,* *Miraflores, Lima* ☎ *01/447–8888* ⊕ *www.peruviansafaris.com.*

Rainforest Expeditions runs three- to seven-day tours including nights at the company's two Amazon lodges: the Tambopata Research Center and Posada Amazonas. ⊠ *Av. Aramburu 166, Miraflores, Lima* ☎ *01/421–8347, 877/905–3782 in U.S.* ⊠ *Sunturwasi 350 (Triunfo), Cusco* ☎ *084/232–772* ⊠ *Arequipa 401, Puerto Maldonado* ☎ *082/571–056* ⊕ *www.perunature.com.*

IQUITOS AREA

Dawn on the Amazon Tours and Cruises has customized ecocruises from one day to two weeks. Two comfortable boats explore throughout the Amazon reserves. ⊠ *Maldonado 185, Iquitos* ☎ *065/223-730* ⊕ *www.dawnontheamazon.com.*

Explorama Tours offers three- to five-day boating and hiking trips along the Amazon River, including stays at the Explorama and ExplorNapo lodges. ⊠ *Av. de la Marina 350, Iquitos* ☎ *065/252–530, 800/707–5275 in U.S.* ⊕ *www.explorama.com.*

International Expeditions has four luxurious wooden riverboats that ply back and forth between their lodge and Iquitos with excursions into Pacaya Samiria. Cruises can be booked only from the company's offices in the United States. ⊠ *1 Environs Park, Helena,* ☎ *800/633–4734* ⊕ *www.internationalexpeditions.com.*

Paseos Amazonicos runs a variety of trips and operates lodges in both the Madre de Dios and Iquitos area reserves. ⊠ *Calle Pevas 246, Iquitos* ☎ *065/233–110* 🖷 *065/233–110* ⊕ *www.paseosamazonicos.com.*

7

Madre de Dios

BRAZIL

Iñapari

Iberia

BOLIVIA

MADRE DE DIOS

0   40 miles
0   60 km

Las Piedras R.

Manu R.

Pariamanu R.

Manu Biosphere
Reserve

Lago
Valencia

Boca
Manu

Madre de Dios R.

Puerto
Maldonado

Fitzcarrald I.

Laberinto

Alto Madre de Dios R.

Itahuania

Lago
Sandoval

Shintuya

Colorado R.

Inambari R.

Tambopata
National Reserve &
Bahuaja-Sonene
National Park

Atalaya

Urubamba

26 Paucartambo

110

Pisac

CUSCO

Cusco

3

28

PUNO

ESSENTIALS

CURRENCY   Banco de Crédito (⊠Arequipa 334 ☎082/571–001).SERPOST (⊠León
Velarde 675 ☎082/571–088). Transtours/DHL (⊠González Prada 341
☎082/572–606).

MEDICAL   Hospital de Apoyo Santa Rosa (⊠Cajamarca 171 ☎082/571–719 or
082/571–046).

VISITOR INFO   Dirección Regional de Industria y Turismo (⊠Fitzcarrald 411 ☎082/
571–164).

WHAT TO SEE

The southern Amazon has a skyscraper! The 35-meter (115-foot)
Obelisco, a strangely designed building that's shaped like a prison-
guard post but colored like it belongs on a different planet, is a few
blocks north of Puerto Maldonado's downtown. Bas-relief scenes from
the history of Madre de Dios decorate the lookout tower's base, and
the top has a vista of the nearby rain forest and the city. As Puerto
Maldonado doesn't quite glitter in the evening, the best views are during the day. ⊠Fitzcarrald and Madre de Dios ☎082/572–993 ⊠S/1
⊙Daily 8–8.

WHERE TO STAY & EAT

¢ **Hotel Cabaña Quinta.** The rambling chestnut-wood Victorian-style house, the tropical veranda, the arched doorways, the latticework, and the red-and-green *sangapilla* plants in the garden could have come right out of a Graham Greene novel. The rooms are a little less evocative but pleasantly furnished with wood paneling, print spreads, and drapes. The restaurant is one of Puerto Maldonado's best and serves a small menu of fish, meats, and soups, with plenty of yucca (cassava) chips on the side. **Pros:** Good restaurant, pleasant staff. **Cons:** Fairly basic. ⊠*Cusco 535* ☎☎*082/571–045* 🛏*51 rooms, 3 suites* ⚒*In-hotel: restaurant, airport shuttle* ⊟*V* ⍟*BP.*

¢–$ 🏨 **Hotel Don Carlos.** By Tambopata River, this Don Carlos is more rustic than the other modern business-class hotels in this small Peruvian chain. Unexciting rooms with high ceilings and tile floors enclose a pleasant garden and a much appreciated pool, one of the few around. **Pros:** Pool, quiet. **Cons:** Rooms are boring. ⊠*León Velarde 1271* ☎*082/571–029* ⊕*www.hotelesdoncarlos.com* 🛏*31 rooms* ⚒*In-hotel: restaurant, pool, laundry service, airport shuttle* ⊟*AE, DC, MC, V* ⍟*BP.*

$ 🏨 **Wasai Maldonado Lodge.** The Wasai gives you that jungle-lodge feel right in town, a block from the Plaza de Armas. Bungalows on stilts are scattered on a hill leading down from the lobby toward the pool and gazebo-style restaurant. The shady grounds overlook the Madre de Dios River, and the well-ventilated, thatched-roof, tornillo-wood bungalows make for a surprisingly cool place in the otherwise sweltering center of Puerto Maldonado. You can rent motorbikes and bicycles here. **Pros:** Convenient, activities. **Cons:** You're still in Puerto Maldonado. ⊠*Bellinghurst s/n* ☎*082/572–290* ⊕*www.wasai.com* 🛏*18 cabins* ⚒*In-room: no phone, refrigerator. In-hotel: restaurant, bar, pool, bicycles* ⊟*AE, DC, V* ⍟*BP.*

NEAR PUERTO MALDONADO

The Madre de Dios River heads from Puerto Maldonado east to the Bolivian border. The river defines the northern boundary of the Tambopata National Reserve and passes some nearby, easy-to-reach jungle lodges.

On your way down the river, tour guides will point out Madre de Dios's best-known faux site, the abandoned **ship of Carlos Fermín Fitzcarrald,** the most famous of the 19th-century *caucheros* (rubber barons). The wreckage is not Fitzcarrald's vessel, but that of a hospital ship that ran aground in the 1960s. ⊠*4 km (2½ mi) east of Puerto Maldonado.*

Changes in the course of the Río Madre de Dios have created several so-called oxbow lakes, which were formed when riverbeds shifted and the former beds filled with water. **Lago Sandoval,** east of Puerto Maldonado in the Tambopata National Reserve, is the most famous of these. It brims with parrots and macaws, but also plenty of waterfowl, most notably herons and kingfishers. The lake is a 30-minute boat ride from Puerto Maldonado; once you disembark there's an easy 2-km (1-mi) hike to the actual lake. ⊠*9 km (5½ mi) east of Puerto Maldonado.*

Lago Valencia is two hours northeast of Puerto Maldonado, just outside the boundaries of Tambopata. You can make it an all-day journey in a dugout locals call a *pequepeque.* ■TIP➔ **Regardless of your mode of transport, expect to see abundant wildlife, avian (herons, cormorants, and flamingos) and otherwise.** Turtles abound, and your best chance of glimpsing caimans (like a small alligator) is around sunset. The elusive and endangered giant otter is also known to live in the oxbow lakes. A community of the indigenous Ese'eja is nearby. This section of the river is a favorite lucky site for Madre de Dios's gold panners. Carry your passport on the trip to Valencia; you'll be a mere 5 km (3 mi) from the Bolivian border, and Peruvian authorities inspect documentation for those who float this close. ⊠*23 km (14 mi) east of Puerto Maldonado.*

WHERE TO STAY

$$$$ ⌂**Reserva Amazónica.** A 45-minute boat ride downriver from Puerto Maldonado on the Madre de Dios River, this is the most accessible of the jungle lodges. Private bungalows, set amid trees beside the river, have flush toilets, showers, and porch hammocks, but no electricity. Because the lodge is relatively close to Puerto Maldonado, large mammals are rare, but visitors often see smaller ones, such as anteaters and agoutis. For wildlife viewing, consider a day trip to Lago Sandoval. On rare occasions, the giant Amazon river otter may be seen. The lodge runs an environmental-education program for children. A typical jungle dinner—fried bananas, *pacamoto* (fish or chicken cooked inside bamboo over coals), and fresh papaya—is very good. **Pros:** Easy ride to get to, good excursions, children's programs. **Cons:** Perhaps too many guests (for the jungle) for some. ⊠*Km 15, Madre de Dios River, Madre de Dios* ☎*082/572–283* 🖷*082/572–988* ⊕*www.inkaterra.com Reservations in Lima:* ⊠*Andalucía 174, Miraflores, Lima* ☎*016/100–400* 🖷*014/224–701 Reservations in Cusco:* ⊠*Procuradores 48, Cusco* ☎*084/245–5314* ⬳*30 rooms* ⌂*In-room: no phone, no TV. In-hotel: restaurant, bar, spa* ⊟*AE, MC, V* ⦿*FAP.*

$ ⌂**Sandoval Lake Lodge.** InkaNatura Travel operates this lodge, the
Fodor'sChoice closest to Puerto Maldonado. To get here, you take a 30-minute boat
★ ride east on the Madre de Dios River and then hike through a forest trail for about 2 mi, then get in a canoe for a 30-minute paddle to the lodge. The lodge overlooks Lago Sandoval, and the scenery is spectacular. A stay includes excursions to the lake and rain forest, bilingual guides, and presentations. There is some electricity! **Pros:** Beautiful location, good excursions, hot showers, monkeys. **Cons:** The boat-hike-boat route there won't be for everyone. ⊠*30 min by boat from Puerto MaldonadoReservations:* ⊕*Calle Ricardo Palma 11, Cusco* ☎*084/255–255, 877/827–8350 in U.S.* 🖷*084/245–973* ⊕*www.inkanatura.com* ⬳*25 rooms* ⌂*In-room: no a/c, no phone, no TV. In-hotel: bar, library, store* ⦿*AI.*

Continued on page 301

THE JUNGLE LIFE

by Doug Wechsler

Green-winged Macaw (Ara chloroptera) foraging high in rain forest canopy.

An observant naturalist living in the Peruvian Amazon can expect to see something new and exciting every day in his or her life. To the casual traveler much of this life remains hidden at first but reveals itself with careful observation.

Western Amazonia may be the most biologically diverse region on earth. The areas around Puerto Maldonado and Iquitos are two of the best locales to observe this riot of life.

On the Tambopata Reserve, for example, 620 species of birds and more than 1,200 species of butterflies have been sighted within a few miles of Explorer's Inn. To put that into perspective, only about 700 species of birds and 700 species of butterflies breed in all of North America. Within the huge Manu National Park, which includes part of the eastern slope of the Andes, about 1/10 of the world's bird species can be sighted. A single tree can harbor the same number of ant species as found in the entire British Isles. A single hectare (2.4 acres) of forest might hold nearly 300 species of trees.

This huge diversity owes itself to ideal temperatures and constant moisture for growth of plants and animals and to a mixture of stability and change over the past several million years. The complex structure of the forest leads to many microhabitats for plants and animals. The diversity of plants and animals is overwhelming and the opportunity for new observations is limitless.

STARS OF THE AMAZON

Pink River Dolphin: The long-snouted pink river dolphin enters shallow waters, flooded forest, and even large lakes. Unlike the gray dolphin of river channels, this species rarely jumps out of the water.

Eats: Fish. **Weighs:** 350 lbs. **Myth:** Often blamed for pregnancies when father is unknown.

Red-and-Green Macaw: The loud, raucous shrieks first call attention to red-and-green macaws, the largest members of the parrot family in the Amazon. Clay licks near a number of jungle lodges in Madre de Dios are great places to observe these spectacular birds.

Eats: Seeds of trees and vines. **Weighs:** 3 lbs.
Length: 3 ft. **Odd habit:** Consumes clay from steep banks.

Hoatzin: The clumsy-flying, chicken-sized Hoatzin sports a long frizzled crest and bare blue skin around the eye, suggesting something out of the Jurassic. Its digestive system features a fermentation chamber and is more bovine than avian.

Eats: Leaves, especially arum. **Weighs:** 1.8 lbs.
Unusual feature: Nestlings can climb with claws on their wings. **Favorite Hangout:** Trees and shrubs in swampy vegetation near lakes.

Squirrel Monkey: The small, active squirrel monkeys live in groups of 20 to 100 or more. These common monkeys can be distinguished by a black muzzle and white mask.

Eats: Large insects and fruit. **Weighs:** 2 lbs.
Favorite Hangout: Lower and mid-levels of vine-tangled forest especially near rivers and lakes. **Associates:** Brown capuchin monkeys often hang out with the troop.

Red Howler Monkey: A loud, long, deep, roaring chorus from these large, sedentary, red-haired monkeys announces the coming of dawn, an airplane, or a rainstorm. The swollen throat houses an incredible vocal apparatus.

Eats: Leaves and fruits. **Weighs:** 8 to 23 lbs.
Favorite Hangout: Tree tops and mid-levels of forest.
Unfortunate trait: They will urinate and defecate on you if you walk beneath them.

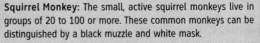

Three-toed Sloth: This slow-moving, upside down ball of fur is easiest to spot in tree crowns with open growth like cecropias. The dark mask and three large claws on the hands distinguish it from the larger two-toed sloth.

Eats: Leaves. **Weighs:** 5 to 11 lbs. **Favorite Hangout:** Tree tops and mid-levels of forest. **Unusual habit:** Sloths climb to the ground once a week to move their bowels.

Cecropia Tree: The huge, multi-lobed leaves, open growth form, and thin light-colored trunks make cecropias among the most distinctive Amazonian trees. Cecropias are the first trees to shoot up when a forest is cut or a new river island is formed. Their long finger-like fruits are irresistible to birds.

Height: Up to 50 ft. or more. **Bark:** Has bamboo-like rings. **Attracts:** Toucans, tanagers, bats, monkeys, sloths. **Relationships:** The hollow stems house stinging ants that protect the tree—beware.

Horned Screamer: A bare, white quill arches from the crown of this ungainly, dark, turkey-sized bird. Its long toes enable it to walk on floating vegetation. Occasionally it soars among vultures.

Eats: Water plants. **Weighs:** up to 7 lbs. **Favorite Hangout:** Shores of lagoons and lakes. **Relatives:** Screamers are related to ducks and geese—who would have guessed?

Russet-backed Oropendola: What the yellow tailed, crow-sized, oropendola lacks in beauty, it makes up for in its liquid voice. The remarkable three-foot long woven nests dangle in groups from an isolated tree—protection from monkeys.

Eats: Insects and fruit. **Favorite Hangout:** Forest near clearings and rivers. **Look for:** Flocks of hundreds going to and from roosting islands in the river at dusk and dawn.

Giant Amazon Water Lily: This water lily has leaves up to 7 ft. across and 6–12 inch white or pink flowers that bloom at night. The edges of the leaves bend upward. Leaf stems grow with the rising flood.

Length: Stems up to 20 ft. **Eaten by:** Fish eat the seeds. **Favorite Hangout:** River backwaters, oxbow lakes. **Sex changes:** Female parts flower the first night, then the flower turns pink and the male parts open.

TIPS:

Don't expect all those species to come out and say hello! The Amazon's great biodiversity is made possible by the jungle's sheltering, almost secretive nature. Here are tips to help train your eye to see through nature's camouflage.

1. Listen for movement. Crashing branches are the first clue of monkeys, and rustling leaves betray secretive lizards and snakes.

2. Going upstream on the river means your boat will stay steady close to shore—where all the wildlife is.

3. Look for birds in large mixed-species flocks; stay with the flock while the many birds slowly reveal themselves.

4. Concentrate your observation in the early morning and late afternoon, and take a mid-day siesta to save energy for night-time exploration.

5. Wear cloths that blend in with the environment. Exception: hummingbird lovers should wear shirts with bright red floral prints.

6. Train your eye to pick out anomalies—what might, at first, seem like an out-of place ball of debris in the tree could be a sloth.

7. At night, use a bright headlamp or hold a flashlight next to your head to spot eye-shine from mammals, nocturnal birds, frogs, boas, moths, and spiders.

8. Crush leaves and use your nose when getting to know tropical plants.

Hanging bridge over the Tambopata rainforest.

TAMBOPATA NATIONAL RESERVE & BAHUAJA-SONENE NATIONAL PARK

5 km (3 mi) south of Puerto Maldonado.

Up the Tambopata River from Puerto Maldonado is the Tambopata National Reserve, a 3.8-million-acre primary-humid-tropical-forest reserved zone about the size of Connecticut, and overlapping Madre de Dios and Puno departments. Officially separate from the reserve, but usually grouped for convenience under the "Tambopata" heading, is the Bahuaja-Sonene National Park, created in 1996 and taking its moniker from the names in the local indigenous Ese'eja language for the Tambopata and Heath rivers, respectively. (The Río Heath forms Peru's southeastern boundary with neighboring Bolivia.) The former Pampas de Río Heath Reserve along the border itself is now incorporated into Bahuaja-Sonene, and encompasses a looks-out-of-place secondary forest more resembling the African savannah than the lush tropical Amazon.

Peru works closely on joint conservation projects with Bolivia, whose adjoining Madidi National Park forms a grand cross-border 7.2-million-acre reserve area. Only environmentally friendly activities are permitted in Tambopata. The area functions partially as a managed tropical-forest reserve. The reserve's shiringa trees are an extraction source for latex. And cultivation here of *castañas*, or Brazil nuts, keeps thousands employed.

Elevations here range from 500 meters (1,640 feet) to a lofty 3,000 meters (9,840 feet), providing fertile homes for an astounding number of animals and plants. The area holds a world record in the number of butterfly species (1,234) recorded by scientists. Within the reserve, the Explorer's Inn holds the world-record bird-species sighting for a single lodge: 600 have been recorded on its grounds, 331 of those sighted within a single day, also a score no other lodging can top. ■ TIP➔ **Tambopata is the site of the most famous and largest of Madre de Dios's ccollpas; this clay lick is visited daily by 15 species of parrots and macaws, who congregate at dawn to collect a beakful of mineral-rich clay, an important but mysterious part of their diet.**

The Tambopata jungle lodges are much easier to reach—and much less expensive—than those in the Manu Biosphere Reserve, Madre de Dios's more famous ecotourism area. And Tambopata is no poor man's Manu either—its sheer numbers of wildlife are very impressive. A half-hour, early-morning flight from Cusco at S/350 round-trip takes you to Puerto Maldonado, the Tambopata jumping-off point. And in a few hours or less you can arrive by boat at most lodges here and start bird-watching that afternoon. (You'd still be on your way to Manu at that point.) Some of the lodges offer two-day/one-night packages that amount to little more than 24 hours. You need to depart very early to make it back to Puerto Maldonado for your morning flight out. Opt for at least three days here.

Jungle Days

Tufted capuchin in the Manu Biosphere Reserve..

The knock at the door comes early. "¡Buenos días! Good morning!" It's 5 AM and your guide is rousing you for the dawn excursion to the nearby ccollpa de guacamayos. He doesn't want you to miss the riotous, colorful spectacle of hundreds of macaws and parrots descending to the vertical clay lick to ingest a beakful of mineral-rich earth. Roll over and go back to sleep? Blasphemy! You're in the Amazon.

A stay at any of the remote Iquitos or Madre de Dios lodges is not for the faint of heart. You'll need to gear up for a different type of vacation experience. Relaxing and luxuriating it will not be, although some facilities are quite comfortable. Your days will be packed with activities: bird- and wildlife-watching, boat trips, rain-forest hikes, visits to indigenous communities, mountain biking, white-water rafting, and on. You'll be with guides from the minute you're picked up in Iquitos, Puerto Maldonado, or Cusco. Most lodges hire top-notch guides who know their areas well, and you'll be forever amazed at their ability to spot that camouflaged howler monkey from a hundred paces.

The lodge should provide mosquito netting and sheets or blankets, and some type of lantern for your room. (Don't expect electricity.) But check with your tour operator for a list of what to bring and what the lodge provides. Your required inventory will vary proportionally by just how much you have to rough it. Pack sunscreen, sunglasses, insect repellent, a hat, hiking boots, sandals, light shoes, a waterproof bag, and a flashlight. Also, a light, loose-fitting, long-sleeve shirt and equally loose-fitting long trousers and socks are musts for the evening when the mosquitoes come out. Carry your yellow-fever vaccination certificate and prescription for malaria prevention and an extra supply of any medicine you might be taking. Bring along antidiarrheal medication, too. You'll need a small daypack for the numerous guided hikes, and bring plastic bags to protect your belongings from the rain and humidity. Also bring binoculars, and your camera.

Everything is usually included in the package price, though you might be caught off guard by the extra price you're charged for beverages. Soft drinks and beer carry a hefty markup, and are rarely included in the quoted price.

Few things are more enjoyable at a jungle lodge than dinner at the end of the day. You'll dine family style around a common table, discussing the day's sightings, comparing notes well into the evening, knowing full well there will be another 5 AM knock in morning.

—By Jeffrey Van Fleet

WHERE TO STAY

The listings below are for lodges consisting of wooden huts raised on stilts. All provide rustic but more than adequate accommodations. Rates include river transportation from Puerto Maldonado, guides, and meals.

$$$$ **Explorer's Inn.** No place in the world tops this one for the number of bird species (600) sighted at a single lodge, though you'll need to stay more than a couple days to reach that number. Explorer's is managed by Peruvian Safaris, and accommodates tourists and visiting scientists in its thatched-roof bungalows. All can be seen navigating the lodge's 30 km (18½ mi) of trails. The lodge, the forerunner of ecolodges in the area, has a reference library and guides on-hand. There's no electricity in the rooms. The minimum stay is three days/two nights. **Pros:** Knowledgeable guides, deep in the Tambopata Reserve. **Cons:** The jungle is humid. *Reservations:* ⊠*Alcanfores 459, Miraflores, Lima* ☎*01/447–8888* 🖷*01/241–8427* ⊕*www.explorersinn.com* 📞*30 rooms* 🛇*In-room: no a/c, no phone, no TV* ⑩*AI.*

$$$$ **Fodor's Choice** ★   **Posada Amazonas.** This comfortable lodge is owned jointly by Rainforest Expeditions and the Ese'eja Native Community of Tambopata, and some of your guides are locals. The property defines "jungle chic," with mosquito nets over the beds, and wide, screenless windows to welcome cooling breezes. A canopy tower provides a great view of the rain forest. ■**TIP**➜ Transportation to the lodge is usually by a combination of a thatched-roof truck and a large wooden boat with drop-down rain curtains. A visit to a local village is made en route. Packages include all transport, lodging, meals, and guides. The minimum stay is three days/two nights. **Pros:** Good range of guided excursions. **Cons:** No electricity, but that's no surprise. ⊠*30-min drive, 1-hr boat ride, and 15-min walk from Puerto Maldonado* *Reservations:* 🖱*Av. Aramburu 166, Miraflores, Lima* ☎*01/421–8347, 877/905–3782 in U.S.* 🖷*01/421–8183* ⊠*Sunturwasi 350 (Triunfo), Cusco* 🖷☎*084/232–772* ⊠*Arequipa 401, Puerto Maldonado* 🖷☎*082/571–056* ⊕*www.perunature.com* 📞*30 rooms* 🛇*In-room: no a/c, no phone, no TV* ⊟*MC, V* ⑩*AI.*

$$$$ **Tambopata Lodge.** Peru's Libertador chain operates this lodge four hours south of Puerto Maldonado on the Tambopata River. Spacious cabins (without electricity, though with solar-powered hot water) have two bedrooms each, with porches and comfy hammocks in which to curl up at the end of a day of sightseeing on the lodge's 25 km (15½ mi) of trails. The minimum stay is three days/two nights, with meals and guides included. **Pros:** Nice rooms, good programs, trails. **Cons:** Somewhat pricey. ⊠*Nueva Baja 432, Cusco* 🖷☎*084/245–645* ⊕*www.tambopatalodge.com* 📞*28 rooms* 🛇*In-room: no a/c, no phone, no TV. In-hotel: bar, library* ⊟*AE, MC, V* ⑩*AI.*

$$$$ **Tambopata Research Center.** A six-hour upriver boat journey from the Posada Amazonas lodge brings you to this Amazon base. Here you'll see several kinds of monkeys and other rain-forest wildlife, including hundreds of macaws and parrots at the nearby clay lick. The twin rooms at the lodge don't have private baths but instead share a separate

Afternoon hammock nap at the Sandoval Lake Lodge.

Taking in high view at the Posada Amazonas Lodge.

room with four showers and another with four toilets. One research project allows you to interact with macaws. The minimum stay is five days/four nights. **Pros:** You're way out there, lots of macaws, wildlife. **Cons:** You're way out there, shared bath. ⊠*6 hrs upriver from Posasa Amazonas via boat* Reservations: ⬚*Av. Aramburu 166, Miraflores, Lima* ☎*01/421–8347, 877/905–3782 in U.S.* ☎*01/421–8183* ⊠*Sunturwasi 350 (Triunfo), Cusco* ☎☎*084/232–772* ⊠*Arequipa 401, Puerto Maldonado* ☎☎*082/571–056* ⬚*www.perunature.com* ⬚*18 rooms with shared bath* ⬚*In-room: no a/c, no phone, no TV. In-hotel: bar* ⬚*MC, V* ⬚*AI.*

MANU BIOSPHERE RESERVE

Fodor'sChoice
★

90 km (55 mi) north of Cusco.

Readers of the British children's series *A Bear Called Paddington* know that the title character "came from darkest Peru." The stereotype is quite outdated, of course, but the Manu Biosphere Reserve, often called "the most biodiverse park on earth," will conjure up the jungliest Tarzan-movie images you can imagine. And the reserve really does count the Andean spectacled bear, South America's only ursid, and the animal on which Paddington was based, among its 200 mammals.

This reserve is Peru's largest protected area and straddles the boundary of the Madre de Dios and Cusco departments. Manu encompasses more than 4½ million acres of pristine primary tropical-forest wilderness, ranging in altitude from 3,450 meters (12,000 feet) down through cloud forests and into seemingly endless lowland tropical rain forests at 300 meters (less than 1,000 feet). This geographical variety shelters a stunning biodiversity. A near total absence of humans and hunting has made the animal life less skittish and more open to observation. ■TIP➔ The reserve's 13 monkey species scrutinize visitors with the same curiosity they elicit. White caimans sun themselves lazily on sandy riverbanks, whereas the larger black ones lurk in the oxbow lakes. And expect to see tapirs at the world's largest tapir ccollpa. Giant Orotongo river otters and elusive big cats such as jaguars and ocelots sometimes make fleeting appearances. But it's the avian life that has made Manu world famous. The area counts more than 1,000 bird species, fully a ninth of those known. Some 500 species have been spotted at the Pantiacolla Lodge alone. Birds include macaws, toucans, roseate spoonbills, and 1½-meter- (5-foot-) tall wood storks.

Manu, a UNESCO World Heritage Site, is divided into three distinct zones. The smallest is the so-called "cultural zone" (Zone C), with several indigenous groups and the majority of the jungle lodges. Access is permitted to all, even to independent travelers in theory, though vast distances make this unrealistic for all but the most intrepid. About three times the size of the cultural zone, Manu's "reserve zone" (Zone B) is uninhabited but contains one of the lodges—Manu Lodge. Access is by permit only, and you must be accompanied by a guide from one of the 10 agencies authorized to take people into the area. The western 80% of Manu is designated a national park (Zone A). Authorized

7

researchers and indigenous peoples who reside there are permitted in this zone; visitors may not enter.

A Manu excursion is no quick trip. Overland travel from Cusco, the usual embarkation point, takes up to two days, in a thrilling trip over the mountains and down into the lowland plains. A charter flight in a twin-engine plane to the small airstrip at Boca Manu shaves that time down to 45 minutes and adds a few hundred dollars onto your package price. From Boca Manu you'll still have several hours of boat travel to reach your lodge. The logistics of travel to this remote part of the Amazon mean you should allow at least five days for your excursion. A week is more manageable.

WHERE TO STAY

$$$$ ☷ **Cock of the Rock Lodge.** Higher elevation means fewer mosquitoes, and this lodge perches along the Kosñipata River in the cloud forest of Manu's cultural zone. This venture of the respected InkaNatura Travel takes its name from Peru's red-and-black national bird that frequents the grounds. Bungalows have balconies, private bathrooms, and are furnished with two beds, tables, and mosquito nets, and there's an ample supply of hot water. The minimum stay is three days/two nights, with transportation and guided excursions included. **Pros:** Lots of wildlife, less mosquitoes. **Cons:** Not cheap. ⊠ *177 km (110 mi or an 8-hr drive) north of Cusco* *Reservations:* ☝ *Calle Ricardo Palma 11, Cusco* ☎ *084/255–255, 877/827–8350 in U.S.* 🖷 *084/245–973* ⊕ *www.inkanatura.com* ☏ *12 cabins* ⌕ *In-room: no a/c, no phone, no TV. In-hotel: bar* ⊟ *AE, MC, V* ⦿ *AI.*

$$$$ ☷ **Manu Cloud Forest Lodge.** High in the cloud forest of Manu's cultural zone, this lodge sits on grounds blooming with orchids and overlooking the rushing Río Unión. Rooms are rustic and spartan, with beds and tables, but all have a private bath and plenty of hot water (but no electricity). The LODGE also has a sauna. The highly respected Manu Nature Tours operates the lodge. The minimum stay is three days/two nights. Bilingual guides and ground transportation are included. **Pros:** Birds, tours, only 12 rooms. **Cons:** Fairly basic rooms. ⊠ *About 145 km (90 mi or a 6½-hr drive) north of Cusco* *Reservations:* ☝ *Av. Pardo 1046, Cusco* ☎ *084/252–721* 🖷 *084/234–793* ✉ *Conquistadores 396, San Isidro, Lima* ☎ *01/442–8980* ⊕ *www.manuperu.com* ☏ *8 rooms, 4 cabins* ⌕ *In-room: no a/c, no phone, no TV. In-hotel: bar, bicycles* ⊟ *AE, MC, V* ⦿ *AI.*

$$$$ ☷ **Manu Lodge.** Built by Manu Nature Tours from mahogany salvaged from the banks of the Manu River, the lodge is set deep in the reserve zone, the only such accommodation, overlooking the 2-km- (1-mi-) long oxbow lake called Cocha Juárez. ■**TIP→** **Frequently seen in the lake are giant river otters and black and white caimans.** The comfortable, screened-in lodge has a two-story dining area, and you have access to three habitats: the lakes, the river, and a trail network spanning 10 square km (4 square mi) of rain forest. The lodge has tree-climbing equipment to lift visitors onto canopy platforms for viewing denizens of the treetops. The minimum stay is five days/four nights (with a stay

en route at Manu Cloud Forest Lodge), and includes bilingual guides, ground transportation, and meals. There's no electricity. **Pros:** Knowledgeable guides, incredible location. **Cons:** Not for the urban minded. *Reservations:* ✉*Av. Pardo 1046, Cusco* ☎*084/252–721* 🖷*084/234–793* ✉*Conquistadores 396, San Isidro, Lima* ☎*01/442–8980* ⊕*www. manuperu.com* ⬫*12 rooms* 🛏*In-room: no a/c, no phone, no TV. In-hotel: restaurant, bar* ▭*AE, MC, V* ¶⃝*AI.*

$$$$ ⊡**Manu Wildlife Center.** As the name suggests, this is a great place for wildlife viewing, as it sits close to Manu's macaw and tapir ccollpas and encompasses 48 km (30 mi) of trails. The MWC, as it's known, is jointly owned by Cusco's InkaNatura Travel and Manu Expeditions, and services are top-notch. Raised thatched-roof bungalows have screens and wooden latticework walls as well as tiled hot-water baths. **Pros:** Wildlife central. **Cons:** Not cheap. ✉*30 min by air and 90 min by boat from Cusco. Reservations:* ⅍*Calle Ricardo Palma 11, Santa Monica, Cusco* ☎*084/255–255, 877/827–8350 in U.S.* 🖷*084/245–973* ⊕*www.inkanatura.com* ⬫*22 cabins* 🛏*In-room: no a/c, no phone, no TV. In-hotel: bar* ▭*AE, MC, V* ¶⃝*AI.*

$$ ⊡**Pantiacolla Lodge.** Named for the mountain range that forms this portion of the Andes, the Pantiacolla sits in Manu's cultural zone near the border of the national park. Cooler than many lodges, it also has fewer mosquitoes. Rooms are basic, with beds, mosquito netting, tables, and wooden floors. The company specializes in excursions to nearby indigenous Yine communities. All-inclusive package tours are available. **Pros:** Less expensive and less bugs, child-friendly. **Cons:** Basic rooms. *Reservations:* ✉*Plateros 360, Cusco* ☎*084/238–323* 🖷*084/252–696* ⊕*www.pantiacolla.com* ⬫*14 rooms with shared bath* 🛏*In-room: no a/c, no phone, no TV* ▭*AE, MC, V* ¶⃝*FAP.*

IQUITOS & ENVIRONS

Founded by Jesuit priests in the 1500s, Iquitos was once called the "Pearl of the Amazon." It isn't quite that lustrous today, but it's still a pleasant, friendly town on the banks of the Amazon River, in Peru's northeastern jungle. The jungle port, which sits near the confluence of the Río Nanay and the Río Amazonas, is only accessible by water and by air. Motor scooters outnumber cars, and the typical family transportation is a three-wheeler with a canvas top.

Iquitos, which had seen unprecedented growth and opulence during the rubber boom, became an Amazonian backwater overnight when the boom went bust. The economy slouched along, barely sustaining itself with logging, exotic-animal exports, and tobacco, banana, and Brazil-nut farming. In the early 1970s, petroleum was discovered. The black gold, along with ecotourism and logging, have since become the backbone of the region's economy. Although the main reason to drop into town is to explore the surrounding rain forest, Iquitos can grow on you as you become accustomed to the humid climate and relaxed, easy ways of its citizens. A revamped riverwalk is the popular place for an evening stroll, followed by entertainment in the riverside plaza.

GETTING AROUND

The best way to travel around the Iquitos area is by boat. There are many boats offering day and overnight cruises throughout the area. There are huge seagoing boats that will transport you all the way through Brazil to the Atlantic Ocean, tiny dugout canoes to take you deep into the jungle, and swift launches with outboard engines and canvas tops to keep you dry. It takes several days by boat to get to any large communities near Iquitos.

A number of national and international ferry lines operate from Iquitos, taking you to the town of Pucallpa, in the Ucayali department, and as far as the Atlantic Ocean in Brazil. These boats are often quite run-down, and few have staterooms. You'll need to bring a hammock and lots of bug spray. Passage to Pucallpa takes four to eight days and costs around US$40. Most boats leave from Puerto Masusa, about 3 km (2 mi) north of the Iquitos city center on Avenida La Marina.

BORDER CROSSINGS It's a three-day boat ride to the Brazilian border, unless you take the "mas rapido," which costs only $60 and takes 8–10 rough hours. As of this writing American citizens do need a special visa to enter Brazil, though these policies change quite often; check with the **Brazilian Consulate** (⊠*Sgto. Lores 363, Iquitos*) before heading there. For the most part, Peruvian boats operate only in Peruvian waters. You'll need to change boats in Brazil.

IQUITOS

1,150 km (713 mi) northeast of Lima.

A sultry port town on the Río Amazonas, Iquitos is quite probably the world's largest city that cannot be reached by road. The city has some 400,000 inhabitants and is the capital of the vast Loreto department. The area around Iquitos was first inhabited by small, independent Amazonian tribes. In the 1500s Jesuit missionaries began adventuring in the area, trying to Christianize the local population, but the city wasn't officially founded until 1757.

GETTING AROUND

The most common mode of transportation in the Iquitos area is the motocarro, a three-wheeled motorcycle with a canvas top. Service in town costs around S/1.50, whereas a trip to the outskirts costs around S/10 an hour. Always negotiate the price beforehand. There aren't many places to go by road, but exploring the outskirts and tiny hamlets around Iquitos—during the day—can be fun. Motos y Autos JB rents four-by-fours and motorcycles by the day and by the hour.

SAFETY & PRECAUTIONS Though violent crime is not common in Iquitos, pickpockets are. And remember your mosquito repellent!

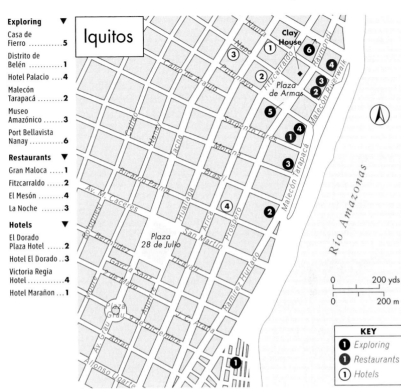

Exploring ▼

Casa de Fierro **5**

Distrito de Belén **1**

Hotel Palacio **4**

Malecón Tarapacá **2**

Museo Amazónico **3**

Port Bellavista Nanay **6**

Restaurants ▼

Gran Maloca **1**

Fitzcarraldo **2**

El Mesón **4**

La Noche **3**

Hotels ▼

El Dorado Plaza Hotel **2**

Hotel El Dorado ..**3**

Victoria Regia Hotel **4**

Hotel Marañon ...**1**

KEY

❶ Exploring
❶ Restaurants
① Hotels

ESSENTIALS

CURRENCY **Banco Continental** (✉ *Sgto. Lores 171* ☎ *065/235–421*). **Banco de Crédito** (✉ *Av. Putumayo 202* ☎ *065/233–838*). **Banco Wiese** (✉ *Av. Próspero 278* ☎ *065/232–350*).

MAIL **Serpost Iquitos** (✉ *Av. Arica 402* ☎ *065/223–812*).

MEDICAL **Clinica Adventista Ana Stahl** (✉ *Av. de la Marina 285* ☎ *065/252–528*). **Hospital Regional de Iquitos** (✉ *Av. 28 de Julio, Cuadra 15* ☎ *065/252–004*).

TAXI **Motos y Autos JB** (✉ *Yavari 702* ☎ *065/242–965*).

VISITOR INFO **iPerú** (✉ *Airport* ☎ *065/260–251*). **Tourist Information Office** (✉ *Napo 226* ☎ *065/236–144*).

WHAT TO SEE

❶ One of Iquitos's most fascinating sights is the **Distrito de Belén** *(Belén*
Fodor'sChoice *District)* along the Itaya River (an Amazon tributary). The market sells
★ goods from the area's jungle villages; you'll find sundry items from
love potions to fresh *suri* (palm-tree worms). It's not the cleanest or
sweetest-smelling market but it's worth the visit. From the center of
the market you come to the port, where you can head out on a canoe
trip through the floating Belén District. ■**TIP**➔ **This slummy area is
often called the Venice of the Amazon (a diplomatic euphemism), but pad-**

dling by canoe through the floating "neighborhoods" is really a kick. The houses are built on balsa rafts. Most of the year they float placidly on the Amazon, though during the low-water season (June–November) they sit in the mud and can attract disease-carrying mosquitoes. During high-water season (December–May), guides hire out their services for one- to two-hour trips, which normally cost around S/7. Negotiate the price beforehand. Be street smart in Belén—evening muggings have been reported so it avoid at night. Also be wary of pickpockets at all times. Stay alert, access your cash discreetly when you need it, and keep your valuables close.

2 You can take an afternoon stroll along the **Malecón Tarapacá,** the pleasant riverfront walk. Several good restaurants are here, as well as some well-maintained rubber-boom-era architecture.

3 The **Museo Amazónico** gives a unique look into the rich indigenous culture of the region, with bronzed statues of local tribespeople. The moldings were made from plastering real people. ⌧ *Malecón Tarapacá 386* ☎ *065/242–353* ⌧ *Free* ⊙ *Daily 9–6.*

4 Iquitos enjoyed its heyday as a port during the rubber boom a century ago. Some of the wealth of that time can still be detected in the *azulejos* (imported tiles) that face many buildings along the riverbank, notably the former **Hotel Palacio,** now converted into an army barracks and looking a little worn around the edges. The hotel was built in 1908. ⌧ *Putumayo and Malecón Tarapacá* ☎ *No phone* ⌧ *Free* ⊙ *Daily.*

5 An example of the interesting architecture on the Plaza de Armas is the **Casa de Fierro** *(iron house),* designed by Gustave Eiffel (of Eiffel Tower fame) and forged in Belgium. A wealthy rubber baron bought the house at the Parisian International Exposition of 1889 and had it shipped to Iquitos, where it was reassembled. Over the years the building has housed numerous businesses, including a pharmacy and, most recently, several shops and a restaurant. The building is best appreciated from the outside where the metal framework can be seen; a walk into one of the shops allows a close-up view of the interior. On the second floor is the Amazon Café. ⌧ *Putumayo 180, on Plaza de Armas* ☎ *No phone* ⌧ *Free* ⊙ *Daily 8* AM*–noon.*

6 From the small **Port Bellavista Nanay,** slightly more than 1 km (½ mi) north of downtown Iquitos on Avenida La Marina, you can hire boats to take you to the Boras and Yaguas villages. Bringing a donation of school supplies (pencils, crayons, and notebooks) is a kind gesture that will be appreciated by the Boras and Yaguas, who live in small communities near the pueblo San Andrés. A 20-minute boat ride from the port will bring you to **Pilpintuwasi Butterfly Farm,** which hosts some 42 butterfly species and also has macaws, a jaguar, and a tapir. During the dry season you'll need to walk along a forest path for 15 minutes to get to the farm. It's best to go with a guide. ⌧ *Near village of Padre Cocha on Nanay River, 5 km (3 mi) from downtown Iquitos* ☎ *065/232–665 or 065/993–2999* ⊕ *www.amazonanimalorphanage.org* ⌧ *S/26 without transportation* ⊙ *Tues.–Sun. 9–4.*

DID YOU KNOW

Walking above the Madre de Dios Preserve, you are walking above one of the world's most diverse bird habitats. More species live here than in all of North America.

WHERE TO EAT

¢–$ ✕ **Fitzcarraldo.** On the boulevard with patio and indoor dining, this restaurant overlooking the river cooks up essentials like pizza and pasta, but the Amazon fish specialties are the draw. Try the spinach salad with the friend or the venison stew. Top off the meal with a

> **CLAY HOUSE**
>
> The real Fitzcarraldo (not Klaus Kinski of the film) plied his rubber baron ways on the corner of Napo and Raymondi streets in this clay warehouse.

frothy *caipirinha* (a Brazilian drink with lime, sugar, and the sugarcane liquor *cachaça*). ⊠ *Napo 100, at El Blvd.* ☎ *065/236–536* ⊟ *AE, DC, MC, V.*

$–$$ ✕ **Gran Maloca.** The city's most elegant restaurant is in a lovely building encrusted with colorful *azulejos* (glazed tiles). They serve both local specialties and international fare; the lobster and shrimp in pepper sauce is especially good. Try the *suri al ajo* (palm-tree grubs cooked in wine and garlic sauce) for an appetizer. Gran Maloca has an extensive wine and spirits list, with locally made fruit liqueurs. ⊠ *Sargento Lores 170* ☎ *065/233–126* ⊟ *AE, DC, MC, V.*

¢ ✕ **El Mesón.** This restaurant on the riverwalk serves ample potions of regional specialties. ■ **TIP→ Try the delicious paiche, a giant fish found in jungle lakes.** Also the *pescado de loretana* (fried-fish fillet with yuca, fried bananas, and hearts-of-palm salad) is a good bet. Tapestries and paintings depicting scenes from traditional Amazonian life adorn the walls. With good views of the Amazon, this is an excellent sunset joint, though a more peaceful meal is had inside. ⊠ *Av. Malecón Maldonado 153* ☎ *065/231–857* ⊟ *AE, DC, MC, V.*

$ ✕ **La Noche.** Big windows smile onto the Amazon River from the azulejos-covered facade of this bistro. The menu has de rigueur international standards and local alternatives like fried-caiman nuggets. The *venado a la Loretana* (Loretan-style venison) is tender and yummy. This is a good night spot, with music and tasty pisco sours and the restaurant sits right on the Malecón Maldonado riverwalk. ⊠ *Malecón Maldonado 177* ☎ *065/222–373* ⊟ *No credit cards.*

WHERE TO STAY

$$$ 🛏 **El Dorado Plaza Hotel.** This five-star contemporary hotel deserves the
★ praise it wins from guests. The grand entryway has a large fountain and a glass elevator. The rooms have all the modern conveniences and are equipped with soundproof glass to protect you from the incessant cacophony of central Iquitos. Behind the hotel is a pool with a swim-up bar; a bridge arches over the pool, leading to the Jacuzzi. The hotel is in the heart of the city on the Plaza de Armas. **Pros:** Best in town, good staff. **Cons:** You could be spending your time on the river. ⊠ *Napo 252* ☎ *065/222–555* ⊕ *www.eldoradoplazahotel.com* ⇆ *56 rooms, 9 suites* ⌂ *In-room: safe. In-hotel: restaurant, room service, bars, pool, gym, laundry service, airport shuttle, parking (no fee)* ⊟ *AE, DC, MC, V* ⊚ *CP.*

$$ **Hotel El Dorado.** A small, grotto-like pool and a pleasant patio are a few of the charming amenities of this hotel a few blocks off the main square. The rooms have seen better days—the bedspreads are slightly dank from nonstop air-conditioning, and the cheap wood furniture is nicked in places. A heavy tropical odor pervades most rooms: the sweet smell of the tropics, a strange mix of sweat, overripe fruit, earth, and ozone is at first repellent and overwhelming, but you will quickly adapt and may even find the aroma

RAFT RACE

The self-proclaimed "longest raft race in the world," the Great River Amazon Raft Race is not for nervous. The race lasts three days down 132 miles of the Amazon to Iquitos and starts the 3rd week of September every year. Teams of 4 build their rafts out of balsawood (provided) and then get to paddling. Anyone can enter, but not everyone should enter.

alluring and exotic after a day or two. The hotel's restaurant, Las Rocas, is quite good. Pros: Good restaurant, pool. **Cons:** Rooms are a little dingy. ⊠*Napo 362* ☎*065/231–742* ⊕*www.masitravel.com* ⊘*dorado@TUS.com.pe* ⟲*57 rooms, 3 suites* ⌂*In-hotel: restaurant, room service, bar, pool, laundry service, airport shuttle* ▭*AE, DC, MC, V* ◯*CP.*

$–$$ **Victoria Regia Hotel.** This modern lodging has rooms dressed in cool colors that surround a courtyard with a small swimming pool. Rooms in the back are less noisy but darker. Most rooms have impressionist on the walls, blond-wood furniture, and large, comfy beds. **Pros:** Pool, good beds. **Cons:** Rooms can be dark. ⊠*Ricardo Palma 252* ☎☎*065/231–983* ⊕*www.victoriaregiahotel.com* ⟲*34 rooms, 8 suites* ⌂*In-room: safe. In-hotel: restaurant, room service, bar, pool, laundry service, airport shuttle* ▭*AE, DC, MC, V* ◯*CP.*

¢–$ **Hotel Marañon.** There's a slightly institutional feel to this ultraclean, relatively inexpensive hotel, thanks mostly to the tile floors, high ceilings, and unadorned walls. The front of the hotel faces a busy street; rooms in the back are quieter. The pool and small terrace in the back are a nice addition. **Pros:** Good value. **Cons:** Not the character choice. ⊠*Nauta 289* ☎*065/242–673* ☎*065/231–737* ⊘*hotel.maranon@ terra.com.pe* ⟲*38 rooms* ⌂*In-hotel: restaurant, room service, pool, laundry service, airport shuttle* ▭*MC, V* ◯*CP.*

NIGHTLIFE & THE ARTS

Maybe it's the proximity to the jungle and its innate, inexplicable sensuality. Whatever the reason, Iquitos heats up after dark, and the dancing and bar scene is spectacular. You should begin your night at one of the many bars along the Malecón Maldonado. **Arandú Bar** (⊠*Malecón Maldonado 113* ☎*065/243–434*) is one of the riverwalk's best bars, mainly because you get to choose the music; ask the waiter for the CD case and pick from a wide selection of modern pop and Latino disks. **La Noche** (⊠*Malecón Maldonado 177* ☎*065/222–373*) is another popular spot on the river. The ultrafunky **Café Teatro Amauta** (⊠*Amauta 250* ☎*065/233–109*) has live music and performances every night. The music is mostly regional, but you'll likely hear some international

Crocodile Nuggets, Anyone?

Amazonian cuisine, with its jungle game meats and off-color local dishes, is truly far-out. Try *chicharron de lagarto* (crocodile nuggets), *venado a la Loretana* (Loretan-style venison), *paiche* (a giant lake fish), or *suri* (palm-tree grubs). *Sarapatera* is a turtle plantain stew cooked in the turtle's shell. *Ensalada de chonta* (hearts-of-palm salad) is also quite popular.

Fruit and fish preparations evoke neighboring Brazil more than the high-mountain cuisine found elsewhere in Peru. Try *pataraschca* (steamed fish wrapped in banana leaves). *Timbuche* is a tasty catch-all fish soup made from the catch of the day. Try *tacacho*, bananas baked over coals and spiced up with a bit of pork and onion, and top it off with the ubiquitous *juanes* (rice cakes). Brazil nuts, locally called *castañas*, make a

tasty snack, and by purchasing them you'll be helping to support a sustainable ecofriendly use of the southern Amazon rain forest.

Sadly, some city restaurants incorporate endangered turtle species into their offerings. You'll see *sopa de motelo* (turtle soup served in the shell) and *muchangue* (turtle eggs) on the menu. Don't support further elimination of an already vanishing species by ordering them.

Chapo, a sweet banana-milk-and-sugar drink, is popular, as is *masato*, a beverage prepared by chewing yuca and then fermenting the saliva. For a thirst quencher that also packs a punch, look no further than *cashasa*, a liquor concocted from sugarcane. Other local drinks include *siete raizes* (seven roots), said to be a potent aphrodisiac.

tunes as well. The stage faces the road and sidewalk café. This bohemian gathering spot serves local cocktails such as *siete raizes* and *chuchuwasa*. **Discoteque Papa Piraña** (⊠*Loreto 220* ☎*No phone*) caters to a twenty-and-under crowd and has loud Latino music. **Discotec Noa** (⊠*Fitzcarraldo 298* ☎*065/222–993*) charges a cover and is the biggest, liveliest dance club in town.

SHOPPING

Stores and souvenir stands are along Malecón Tarapacá and the streets leading off the Plaza de Armas. Look for pottery, hand-painted cloth from Pucallpa, and jungle items such as preserved piranhas, seed necklaces, fish and animal teeth, blowguns, spears, and balsa-wood parrots. The **Mercado Belén** is a riot of colors and smells. You can buy everything from souvenirs to love potions to fresh-made *masato* (mashed, fermented yucca) in the market. Beware, as there are many pickpockets in the close-quartered market. Many people will offer to sell souvenirs made from snake and caiman skins and toucan beaks, but buying these items encourages the further decimation of these at-risk animals. For T-shirts emblazoned with FEDERACIÓN DE BORRACHOS DE IQUITOS (Federation of Drunks of Iquitos) or "FBI" logos, among others, try **Mad Mike's Trading Post** (⊠*Putumayo 184–B* ☎*065/222–372*). Mike's also rents camping gear and more for jungle excursions. The money goes to benefit children living on the street and to provide medical supplies for local hospitals.

INTO THE JUNGLE

The Amazon basin is the world's most diverse ecosystem. The numbers of cataloged plant and animal species are astronomical, and scientists are discovering new species all the time. More than 25,000 classified species of plants are in the Peruvian Amazon (and 80,000 in the entire Amazon basin), including the 2-meter-wide (6-foot-wide) Victoria Regia water lilies. Scientists have cataloged more than 4,000 species of butterfly and more than 2,000 species of fish—a more diverse aquatic life than that of the Atlantic Ocean. Scientists estimate that the world's tropical forests, while comprising only 6% of the Earth's landmass, may hold up to 75% of the planet's plant and animal species. This land is also the largest natural pharmacy in the world: one-fourth of all modern medicines have botanical origins in tropical forests.

Most mammals are nocturnal and difficult to spot, and hunting has made them wary of humans. ■TIP➔ You're likely to see birds, monkeys, pink freshwater bufeos (dolphins), and caimans along the Amazon River and its tributaries. You're sure to spot large blue morpho butterflies.

It's interesting and worthwhile to visit the small villages of indigenous people. When the boat stops at these settlements, you'll usually find half the village waiting to trade handicrafts for whatever you have with you; items perpetually in demand include umbrellas, hammers, fishing hooks, flashlights, sewing supplies, lipstick, clothing, and school supplies.

The best way to visit the jungle is with a prearranged tour with one of the many jungle lodges, or cruise boats. All the lodges and some cruise boats have highly trained naturalist guides. Among the activities offered are nature walks, birding tours, nighttime canoe outings, fishing, and trips to indigenous villages. Some lodges have canopy walkways that take you into the seldom-explored rain-forest canopy.

Around Iquitos there are large tracts of virgin rain forest and several reserves worth visiting. The hard-to-reach **Reserva Nacional Pacaya Samiria** sits at the confluence of the Marañón and Ucayali rivers. The reserve is Peru's second largest and encompasses more than 20,000 square km (7,722 square mi) of land, about the size of El Salvador. As with many reserves in South America, there are a number of people living in Pacaya Samiria, around 30,000 according to recent estimates. Park rangers try to balance the needs of these local communities with efforts to protect the environment, and occasionally request a minimal S/120 for seven days entrance fee. It takes about several hours by boat to reach the park and at least five days to visit it. ⌧ *Confluence of Marañón and Ucayali rivers* ☎ *No phone* ⊙ *Daily.*

★ Several smaller private rain-forest reserves are northeast of Iquitos near the confluence of the Napo and Amazon rivers. CONAPAC (Peruvian Amazon Conservation Organization) has a large 1,000-square-km (386-square-mi) multiuse reserve known as the **CONAPAC (or Sucusuri) Biological Reserve.** The Orejones tribe, whose name refers to the tribe's ritual practice of ear piercing and lobe enlargement, also has a reserve of about 50 square km (19 square mi). ⌧ *Near confluence of Napo and Amazon riv-*

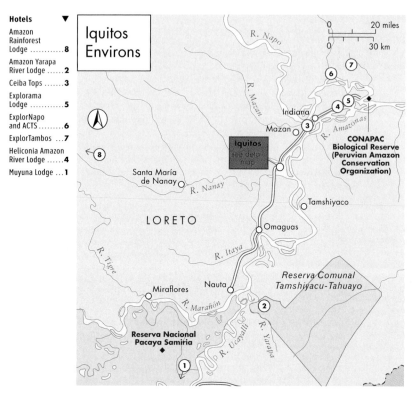

ers, 70 km (43 mi) downriver from Iquitos ☎065/252–530 *Explorama Tours, 800/707–5275 in U.S.* ⊕*www.explorama.com* ✉*Free* ⊙*Daily.*

WHERE TO STAY

Rates for the rain-forest lodges near Iquitos include transportation, meals, and guided walks. Transportation to the lodges is either by *palmcaris* (large wooden boats with thatched roofs) or speedboats. Four lodges—Ceiba Tops, Explorama Lodge, ExplorNapo, and Explor-Tambos—are owned and operated by Explorama Tours.

$$ 📷**Amazon Rainforest Lodge.** An hour by speedboat from Iquitos, this network of thatched-roof bungalows sits on the Momon River. The attractive structures, upgraded in 2007, have twin beds and private baths, and are lighted by gas lanterns. Activities include guided walks, piranha fishing, night canoeing, ayahuasca ceremonies, and visits to Yagua villages. They cater to a much younger crowd than most of the jungle lodges in the area. **Pros:** Only an hour trip from Iquitos, visits to local tribes, as well as wildlife tours. **Cons:** People splashing in the pool may not be what you came for. *Reservations:* ✉*Putumayo 159, Iquitos* ☎065/233–100 *or* 01/445–5620 🖷065/242–231 *or* 01/447–2651 ⊕*www.amazon-lodge.com* 🛏22 *bungalows* ⚒*In-room: no a/c, no*

phone, no TV. In-hotel: restaurant, bar, pool, Jacuzzi, laundry service, airport shuttle, no-smoking rooms ☐MC, V ❙◯❙FAP.

$$$$ 🛏**Amazon Yarapa River Lodge.** This lodge is at the forefront of the mar-
Fodor'sChoice   riage of ecological conservation and tourist getaway. There's all sorts
★   of solar power, composting, native wood structures built by native
peoples, even a biology lab used by Cornell University. ■**TIP→ Jungle
cruises and rainforest hikes are led by some of the best informed guides of
all the lodges.** Meanwhile the lodge has some great communal spaces,
and the rooms, some with private bath (cold water only), others are
shared, are all comfortable and well maintained. It's a 3–4 hour boat
journey from Iquitos. **Pros:** Great guides, good food. **Cons:** Rooms
with private bath are better all around. *Reservations:* ✉*La Marina
124, Iquitos* ☎*065/993–1172, 315/952–6771 in U.S.* ⊕*www.yarapa.
com* ⇆*16 rooms with shared bath, 8 rooms with private bath* ⚒*In-
room: no a/c, no phone, no TV. In-hotel: restaurant, bar, airport shuttle
☐AE, MC, V* ❙◯❙*FAP.*

$$$$ 🛏**Ceiba Tops.** Explorama's newest luxury lodge, with large picture
windows overlooking the Amazon, is 45 minutes downriver from Iquitos. After a jungle trek, you can plunge into the pool, take a nap in
your air-conditioned room, or relax with a book in a hammock. You
can even take a hot shower before dinner. The restaurant serves international cuisine and Peruvian wines. The hotel is on a several-acre
private rain-forest reserve. All meals are included in the rate. **Pros:**
Amenities on the Amazon, excursions. **Cons:** May be a little too Flor-
ida-resort-like for the Amazon. ✉*40 km (25 mi) downriver from Iquitos. Reservations:* ⌂*Av. de la Marina 340, Iquitos* ☎*065/252–530,
800/707–5275 in U.S.* 🖨*065/252–533* ⊕*www.explorama.com/ceiba-
tops.htm* ⇆*72 rooms, 3 suites* ⚒*In-room: no a/c (some), no phone,
no TV. In-hotel: restaurant, bar, pool, airport shuttle, no-smoking
rooms ☐AE, MC, V* ❙◯❙*FAP.*

$$$$ 🛏**Explorama Lodge.** Explorama's first lodge, built in 1964, comprises
several palm-thatched houses with a total of 63 rooms. Kerosene lamps
light up the covered walkways between them. Many walks are offered,
including one to the Seven Bridges Trail. The rooms are extremely
simple, as they are in most jungle lodges, and the requisite mosquito
nets ensure a night's sleep relatively free from bites. There are cold-
water shower facilities. It's 50 mi from Iquitos and the minimum stay
is two nights. **Pros:** You're definitely in the jungle here. **Cons:** Shared
bath. ✉*80 km (50 mi) downriver from Iquitos. Reservations:* ⌂*Av.
de la Marina 340, Iquitos* ☎*065/252–530, 800/707–5275 in U.S.*
🖨*065/252–533* ⊕*www.explorama.com* ⇆*63 rooms with shared
bath* ⚒*In-room: no a/c, no phone, no TV. In-hotel: restaurant, bar,
airport shuttle, no-smoking rooms ☐AE, MC, V* ❙◯❙*FAP.*

$$$$ 🛏**ExplorNapo and ACTS.** The remote ExplorNapo camp is deep in the
Fodor'sChoice   middle of the Sucusari Nature Reserve, up the Napo River, 160 km
★   (100 mi) from Iquitos and 1½ hours by boat from Explorama Lodge.
There's a 1,500-foot-long, 120-foot-high canopy walkway at the nearby
ACTS (Amazon Conservatory of Tropical Studies) for exploring the

7

seldom-seen upper-reaches of the Amazon, as well as an informative ethnological garden. Facilities at ExplorNapo are rustic, with kerosene lighting and separate cold-water shower facilities. There's a screened dining room, with occasional music performed by locals. ■**TIP→** **This is a prime place for spotting wildlife, so guided walks and canoe trips are daily activities.** The minimum stay is four nights, and you can substitute a night or two at the ExplorNapo with an overnight stay at the ACTS lodge. Though it puts you much closer to the canopy walkway, ACTS is even more rustic and has fewer facilities. Because of the remoteness of these lodges, many people spend a night at the Explorama Lodge en route to ExplorNapo and ACTS. **Pros:** Great wildlife, deep in the jungle experience. **Cons:** Far from Kansas, rustic. ⊠*160 km (100 mi) from Iquitos along Napo River. Reservations:* ⌂*Av. de la Marina 340, Iquitos* ☎*065/252–530, 800/707–5275 in U.S.* 🖷*065/252–533* ⊕*www.explorama.com* ⟿*30 rooms with shared bath* ⌂*In-room: no a/c, no phone, no TV. In-hotel: restaurant, bar, airport shuttle, no-smoking rooms* ⊟*AE, MC, V* ⦿*FAP.*

$$$$ 🏠**ExplorTambos.** This very primitive lodge is a three-hour hike from ExplorNapo. There are no rooms here—you sleep on mattresses on platforms under mosquito netting. Visits here are usually an extension of trips to Explorama Lodge or ExplorNapo. As this is the most remote lodge in the region, the chances of your seeing wildlife are quite good. But this is definitely a place for serious explorers who don't mind a little discomfort. The minimum stay is four nights. **Pros:** Total immersion in the jungle life. **Cons:** Very basic, some would say primitive. ⊠*3 hrs from ExplorNapo on foot. Reservations:* ⌂*Av. de la Marina 340, Iquitos* ☎*065/252–530, 800/707–5275 in U.S.* 🖷*065/252–533* ⊕*www.explorama.com* ⟿*Space for 16 people* ⌂*In-room: no a/c, no phone, no TV. In-hotel: restaurant, airport shuttle* ⊟*AE, MC, V* ⦿*FAP.*

$$$$ 🏠**Heliconia Amazon River Lodge.** An hour downriver from Iquitos you'll find the Heliconia, which sits on the large Yanamono reserve. The lodge has a big thatched-roof dining area. Rooms have twin beds, private bathrooms, and hot-water showers. Guides are available for fishing, night canoeing, and bird-watching. **Pros:** Great birds, fishing tours. **Cons:** Thank god for screens. ⊠*80 km (50 mi) downriver from Iquitos, Yanamono. Reservations:* ⌂*Av. Ricardo Palma 242, Iquitos* ☎*065/231–959 or 01/421–9195* 🖷*01/442–4338* ⊕*www.amazonriverexpeditions.com* ⟿*21 rooms* ⌂*In-room: no a/c, no phone, no TV. In-hotel: restaurant, bar, airport shuttle, no-smoking rooms* ⊟*AE, MC, V* ⦿*FAP.*

$$$ 🏠**Muyuna Lodge.** You go 140 km (84 mi) on the Amazon and on the Rio Yanayacu to reach this ecolodge. Guests are guaranteed to see wildlife, and the guides are very good. Seventeen thatch-roof cabins are on stilts to keep from drowning when the water rises. Private baths have cold-water showers and kerosene lanterns are for light. **Pros:** Great activities and guides, not overcrowded. **Cons:** Accommodations are fairly basic. *Reservations:* ⊠*Putumayo 163, ground fl., Iquitos* ☎*065/242–858* ⊕*www.muyuna.com* ⟿*17 cabins* ⌂*In-room: no a/c, no phone, no TV. In-hotel: restaurant, airport shuttle* ⊟*MC, V* ⦿*FAP.*

The Central Highlands

WORD OF MOUTH

"In Huancayo I taught the children in Peru Luz de Esperanza's after school program. Each day of the week I would attend a different village and teach geography Other volunteers help construct classrooms, some did house visits and provided basic knowledge on nutrition and health, and yet others help the mothers in the area build scarves or bake bread for self-income."

—SmileyKrn

WELCOME TO
THE CENTRAL HIGHLANDS

TOP REASONS
TO GO

★ **Handicrafts:** Ayacucho has *retablos*—three-dimensional scenes of religious and historical events. Quinua has ceramic workshops. The Mantaro Valley has Mates Burilados, silver filigree, and alpaca textiles.

★ **Warm Mugs:** Impromptu street vendors sell body warming drinks such as *calientitos,* a pisco-piked herbal tea, and ponche, a sweet, frothy blend of milk, sesame, cloves, cinnamon, and walnuts.

★ **Market Day:** Villagers trek in from miles around with their goods ready to hawk and trade whatever they can. Head to the Mantaro Valley and there's a market every day.

★ **Ethnotourism:** Design silver jewelry, carve gourds, play the pan flute, learn to weave, cook *papas a la hunacaina,* or help orphaned children. Huancayo has excellent interactive tourism opportunities.

★ **World's Highest Train:** Chug your way from Lima to 4,782 meters (15,685 feet) before dropping down to the valleys surrounding Huancayo.

1 **Huánuco.** Increased mining activity has increased attention to this small Andean hamlet only a few hours from the Amazon. Don't miss the Temple of the Crossed Hands of Kotosh a few kilometers from the main plaza, one of the earliest settlements in the Americas.

2 **Huánuco South to Tarma.** The road ascends to more than 5,000 meters (16,400 feet) over a barren, windswept landscape and past herds of wild alpacas and llamas. Spelunk in the deepest cave in South America, soak in a hot spring, or spot flamingos on Peru's largest lake after Titicaca.

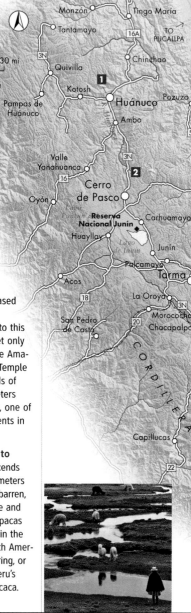

3 Tarma South to Ayacucho. Some of the country's worst roads have kept outside influences away and maintained the traditional Andean values in places such as Huancavelica. Small villages lost on high altitude, barren plains are among preferred hangouts of *soroche*, or altitude sickness, so taking it slow and drinking coca tea is the way of life here.

4 Huancayo. Among the most tourist-friendly towns in Peru, craft capital Huancayo is within a few minutes of vibrant Andean festivals and markets occurring every day. Many come for a weekend on the world's highest train, but then stay to study Spanish or take a cultural course from area craftspeople.

5 Ayacucho. Terrorism once cut Ayacucho off from the rest of the country but with stability, improved roads, and new flights to Cusco, the church-filled town is firmly on the tourist trail. This is particularly true during the weeklong celebration of Semana Santa, when a passionate and deeply religious fervor blankets the town.

GETTING ORIENTED

A mere hour east of Lima puts you in the foothills of the Andes, a windy, barren landscape where llamas and alpacas wander upon vast, puddle-filled fields. Roads and rails twist around the peaks and pass by ramshackle mountain towns before gradually sliding down from the highlands into muggy, jungle en route to Tingo María and Pucallpa. Southeast from Tarma on the way to Ayacucho is more mountain terrain, where over the centuries jagged stubs of forested stone have protected great archaeological finds.

8

Huánuco market.

Parque
Nacional
Yanachaga-
Chemillén

Oxapampa

Perené

San Ramón

20A

5S

Runatullo

Jauja
Mantaro
Valley

Concepción

Huancayo

4

3S

3

Yauncocha

Izcuchaca

Huancavelica

3A

24B

Huanta

3

Quinua

Santa Inés

Lircay

5

Ayacucho

24A

3

Rumichaca

CORDILLERA

ORIENTAL

OCCIDENTAL

THE CENTRAL HIGHLANDS PLANNER

Weather Wise

The best weather for this region is May through October, in winter and spring, when the skies are clear and daytime temperatures are moderate (nights can be frigid). The rainy season is November through April when many roads are inaccessible.

Health & Safety

Altitude Sickness. Altitude sickness, or *soroche*, is a common risk in the Andes. Drink plenty of water and coca tea, move slowly, and avoid alcohol.

Safety. The Central Highlands is not the lawless region controlled by the Shining Path that it was in the 1980s and '90s. Terrorism has been eradicated and a military presence is strong. The only major concern is conflicts between the police and illegal coca growing and narco trafficking, particularly in the area from Huánuco to Pucallpa. This has little effect on tourism; however, the occasional road block does occur.

Petty crime in cities happens less than the coast. If you take the usual traveling precautions in your hotel and when walking or driving you shouldn't have any trouble. Carry your passport and other important identification at all times. Call (☎105) for an ambulance, the fire department, or the police.

Getting Around

By Air: On Tuesday, Thursday, and Sunday, AeroCóndor (⊕ *www.aerocondor.com.pe*) flies between Ayacucho, Andahuaylas, and Lima, from where you can catch flights to Pucallpa, Trujillo, Chiclayo, and other northern towns. You can also check LC Busre (⊕ *www.lcbusre.com.pe*) for flights from Lima to Ayacucho, Huancayo, Huanuco, and other major cities outside of the Central Highlands. Flights between Ayacucho and Cusco have resumed in small planes from Andes Servicios Aereos (⊕ *www.andessac.com*). Flights are often canceled in the rainy season. Always confirm your flight in good weather, too.

By Bus: Buses from Ayacucho run to Lima, including overnight services on Los Libertadores, Ormeño, Cruz del Sur, and Expresa Molina. You can also reach Huancayo from Ayacucho (10 hours) by overnight service on Turismo Central and Expresa Molina—but prepare for a very rough road. From Huancayo, ETUCSA, Ormeño, Cruz del Sur, and Expresa Molina—have many daily buses to Lima. Expresa Molina and Empresa Hidalgo have buses to Huancavelica.

By Car: The Central Highlands have some of the country's most scenic driving routes, and roads are paved from the capital north to Huánuco and south to Huancayo. It's five hours to La Oroya, from which a gorgeous Andes panorama stretches in three directions: north toward Huánuco, east toward Tarma, and south to Huancayo. Most sights around Huancayo in the Valle del Mantaro are accessible by car. The rugged road from Huancayo to Ayacucho, which takes around 10 hours, should be traveled only by four-wheel-drive vehicles equipped for emergencies. Except for the highway, there are mostly dirt roads in this region, so be prepared.

By Train: The train journey from the capital is the most memorable travel option. The 335-km (207-mi) railway cuts through the Andes, through mountain slopes and above deep crevasses where thin waterfalls plunge down into icy streams far below. The most logical route is from Lima to Tarma and Huancayo, then south to Huancavelica and Ayacucho.

Restaurants & Hotels

On the Menu

Dining out in the Central Highlands is a very casual experience. Restaurants are mostly small, family run eateries serving regional fare. Breakfast is usually bread with jam or butter and juice. The midday lunch, the day's largest meal, combines soup, salad, and a rice and meat dish. You'll find snacks everywhere, from nuts and fruit to ice cream and sweet breads. Dinner is after 7 PM and extremely light. Don't worry about dressing up or making reservations. Tipping isn't customary, but waiters appreciate the extra change. All parts of the animal and almost every animal is considered. Guinea pig farming is among the more profitable occupations, so grilled *cuy* is a menu staple. Heartier fare comes in stews, which are spiced with ají to stave off the mountain chill.

Accommodations in the Central Highlands lean toward the very basic. Only the largest properties have air-conditioning, hot water, TVs, phones, and private baths. If you don't need pampering, and you don't expect top-quality service, you'll travel easily—and cheaply. The majority of hotels have clean, modest rooms with simple Andean motifs. Bathrooms usually have showers only, and if hot water is available it's only in the morning or evening. Most hotels have a restaurant, or at least a dining room with some type of food service. If you want a homestay experience, ask your hotel or a local travel company, who can often hook you up with hosts in the area.

Rooms are almost always available. But if you'll be traveling during the region's popular Semana Santa (Holy Week) or anniversary festivities book tours and hotels early. Also book early around the anniversary of the Battle of Ayacucho in mid-December.

While outside influences have shaped other Andean villages, the isolation in the Central highlands have kept recipes focused on local ingredients and traditions. Huancayo's local specialty is *papa a la huancaína* (boiled potato covered in yellow chili-cheese sauce), served cold with a sliced egg and an olive. *Pachamanca* (marinated meat, vegetables, potatoes, and spices) is wrapped in leaves, then slow-cooked on hot stones in an underground oven. Huánuco favorites include *picante de cuy* (guinea pig in hot-pepper sauce), pachamanca, fried trout, *humitas* (a tamalelike food made of ground corn and stuffed with various fillings), and sheep's-head broth. Ayacucho is famous for its filling, flavorful *puca picante* (a nutty pork-and-potato stew), served with rice and topped with a parsley sprig. The city's favorite drink is the warm *ponche* (flavored with milk, cinnamon, cloves, sesame, peanuts, walnuts, and sugar).

8

WHAT IT COSTS IN NUEVO SOLES

RESTAURANTS				
¢	$	$$	$$$	$$$$
under S/20	S/20–S/35	S/35–S/50	S/50–S/65	over S/65
HOTELS				
¢	$	$$	$$$	$$$$
under S/125	S/125–S/250	S/250–S/375	S/375–S/500	over S/500

Restaurant prices are per person for a main course. Hotel prices are for a standard double room, excluding tax.

Updated by Nicholas Gill

The Central Highlands are where the massive Andes crash into the impenetrable South American rain forests and winding, cloud-covered mountain roads dip down into stark desert terrain. The way of life has changed little in hundreds of years.

Most people still depend on the crops they grow and the animals they breed—including guinea pigs and rabbits. Local festivals, traditional recipes, and craft workshops date back to before Inca ever was uttered in the region. Natural beauty abounds, with thundering rivers, winding trails, and hidden waterfalls tucked into the mountainous terrain. Lago de Junín, the country's second-largest lake, is in the north.

Despite how little daily life seems to have changed, the area has been the setting for some of the most explosive events in Peruvian history: fierce wars between the Incas and the Wankas, the most important battles for independence, and the birth of Peru's devastating terrorist movement. The region was home to the Sendero Luminoso (Shining Path) terrorists and the Tupac Amaru Revolutionary Movement for almost two decades. The Sendero Luminoso, which arose in the 1960s around Ayacucho, was finally dismantled in 1992 with the arrest of its leader, Abimaél Guzman Reynoso. In 1999 then-president of Peru Alberto Fujimori led a successful manhunt for the leader of the Sendero Rojo terrorist faction, Oscar Alberto Ramírez Durand, shutting down the region's revolutionary stronghold for good. Now, apart from narco trafficking and the occasional protest from coca growers the region is relatively calm.

This beautiful region is quickly gaining prominence—particularly due to tight military checkpoints that have put drug trafficking on the decline. It's one of the few truly remote regions left in the world, although improvements in road, rail, and air services have made traveling less challenging than it was even in the late 1990s.

No one knows when the first cultures settled on the *puna* (highland plains), or how long they stayed. ■TIP→**Archaeologists found what they believe to be the oldest village in Peru at Lauricocha, near Huánuco,** and one of the oldest temples in the Americas, at Kotosh. Other nearby archaeological sites at Tantamayo and Garu also show that indigenous cultures thrived here long before the Inca or Spanish conquistadors ever reached the area.

When the Inca arrived in the late 1400s, they incorporated the already stable northern settlement of Huánuco into their empire. It eventually became an important stop along their route between the capital at Cusco and the northern hub of Cajamarca, and today Inca ruins are scattered along the pampas. Huánuco was officially founded by the Spanish in 1539 and the area quickly gained the attention of Spanish explorers, who turned Cerro de Pasco's buried gold, silver, copper, and coal into the center of the mining industry north of the Amazon basin. They ruled the region—and the country—until 1824, when Simón Bolívar's troops claimed Peru's autonomy by defeating the Spanish on the Quinua pampas near Huánuco.

HUÁNUCO SOUTH TO TARMA

Heading east, the road from modern, sprawling Lima climbs through the Andes, then splits north–south through the highlands. Working its way through the narrow crevasses and up the rugged hillsides of the Valle Mantaro, the northern road speeds endlessly forward at an elevation of 4,250 meters (13,940 feet) atop the Earth's largest high-altitude plains. This route north connects the mountain towns of La Oroya, Junín, Cerro de Pasco, Huánuco, and Tingo María, where local customs have been preserved even amid battles for independence and intrusions of modern technology. At an elevation of 3,755 meters (12,316 feet) by the confluence of the Río Mantaro and Río Yauli, La Oroya is a town of 36,000 and a main smelting center for the region's mining industry. From here you can head due east to Tarma or continue north by road or rail to the village of Junín. Still farther northwest along the eastern shores of Lago de Junín are Tambo del Sol and Cerro de Pasco.

At an elevation of 4,333 meters (14,212 feet), with more than 30,000 residents, Cerro de Pasco is the world's highest town of its size. It's also the main center for copper, gold, lead, silver, and zinc mining north of the Amazon basin. Coal is excavated from the Goyllarisquisga canyon 42 km (26 mi) north of town, the highest coal mine in the world. From here the road leads over pale, soggy Pampas de Quinua, where Simón Bolívar's troops outfought Spain in 1824.

About 80 km (50 mi) east of town, the Valle de Huachón provides gorgeous mountains for hiking and camping, while the trail north toward Huánuco runs along a spectacular road that plunges nearly 2,500 meters (8,200 feet) in the first 30 km (19 mi). Overlooking the land from an elevation of 1,849 meters (6,065 feet), Huánuco is a pleasant stopover between Lima and thick jungles around Pucullpa, or before heading south toward Huancayo and into the highlands. Farther north, spread between the Andean slopes and cloud forests, Tingo María is a jumping-off point for land adventures.

8

HUÁNUCO

365 km (226 mi) northeast of Lima; 105 km (65 mi) north of Cerro de Pasco.

At first glance Huánuco is just a picturesque collection of colonial buildings and churches along the Río Huallaga amid rocky, forested mountains: an archetypal Spanish settlement, but history runs far deeper here. Evidence of some of Peru's earliest human settlements, and some of the oldest ruins in the country, were found nearby at Lauricocha and Kotosh. Pre-Inca ruins have turned up throughout these mountains, notably at Tantamayo and Garu. Huánuco was an Inca stronghold and a convenient stopover on their route from Cusco north to Cajamarca. Thousands of Inca relics litter the surrounding pampas.

Huánuco's cool, 1,894-meter (6,212-foot) elevation makes for pleasant winter days and crisp nights, but in the rainy summer the town is just low enough to become immersed in the thick mountain fog. The Spanish-style architecture reflects the town's 1539 founding, and later buildings tell the story of Huánuco's importance as a cultural hub. Still, the original Peruvian traditions run deep, particularly during the annual Huánuco anniversary celebrations. Mountain hikes, swims in natural pools, and dips in nearby hot springs add to the area's natural appeal.

GETTING AROUND

Most of Huánuco can be seen on foot or via short, cheap cab rides. A guide is recommended for exploring beyond the city. The area is a major coca-growing region and farmers are leery about strange characters hanging about. Tours from several agencies on the Plaza de Armas will bring you to the major sites within a few hours of the city for under S/50. David Figueroa Fernandini Airport is 8 km (5 mi) away from Huánuco.

ESSENTIALS

AIRPORT **David Figueroa Fernandini Airport** (✉ *Airport Hwy., Km 6* ☎ *062/513–066*).

BUS **Expreso Huallaga** (✉ *Puente Calicanto*). **León de Huánuco** (✉ *Robles 821*). **Transportes Rey** (✉ *28 de Julio 1201*). **Turismo Central** (✉ *Capac 499*).

CURRENCY **Banco de Crédito** (✉ *2 de Mayo 1005, Huánuco* ✉ *Huánuco 699* ⊕ *www. viabcp.com*).

MAIL **Serpost** (✉ *2 de Mayo 1157* ☎ *062/512–503*).

VISITOR INFO **Oficina de Turismo** (✉ *On main plaza, Prado 714* ☎ *064/512–980*). **Incas del Peru** (✉ *Av. Giraldez 652* ☎ *064/223–303*).

WHAT TO SEE

❸ A block from the Plaza de Armas, the small **Museo de Ciencias** is a natural-history museum with multilingual displays of local crafts and weaving, shells, fossils, Inca tools, and what might be the world's largest collection of bad taxidermy. ✉ *Gen. Prado 495* ☎ *No phone* 💲 *S/2* ☷ *Mon.–Sat. 8–noon and 3–7.*

Quecha of the Andes

The Quechua are the original mountain highlands dwellers. Their traditions and beliefs have survived Inca domination, Spanish conquests, and the beginning influences of modern technology. Throughout the region, Quechua is the first language spoken and traditional costumes are still woven on backstrap looms and worn at the markets. Many Quechua make their living by farming maize and coca in the valleys or potatoes and quinoa in the higher altitudes, while other families herd llamas and alpacas on the cold, windy *puna*.

Walk through the narrow, cobbled streets of any village and you'll spot Quechua men by the large, patterned, fringed ponchos draped over their shoulders, their heads topped by matching tasseled cloths beneath big, cone-shape, felt hats. Knee-length pants are held up with a wide, woven belt that often has a local motif—such as the famous mountain train. Despite the cold, men usually wear rubber sandals, often fashioned from old tires.

Quechua women's attire is equally bright, with modern knit sweaters and a flouncing, patterned skirt over several petticoats (added for both warmth and puff). Instead of a poncho, women wear an *aguayo*, a length of saronglike fabric that can be tied into a sling for carrying a baby or market goods, or wrapped around their shoulders for warmth. Hats for the women differ from village to village; some wear black-felt caps with neon fringe and elaborate patterns of sequins and beads, whereas others wear a plain brown-felt derby. Women also wear rubber sandals for walking and working in the fields, but often go barefoot at home.

The Morochuco are a unique group of formerly nomadic Quechua who live near Ayacucho on the Pampas de Cangallo. They have light skin and blue eyes, and, unlike other Quechua, many Morochuco men wear beards. Cattle breeding and horse training are the main occupations. Renowned for their fearlessness and strength, the Morochuco fought for Peru's independence on horseback with Simón Bolívar, and local lore has it that they are the descendents of the army of Diego de Almagro, a Spanish hero killed by Pizzaro.

The Morochuco are first-rate horseback riders—women and children included—who use their swiftness and agility to round up bulls on the highland pampas. Women ride in long skirts and petticoats, whereas men don thick wool tights and dark ponchos. Both men and women wear *chullos*, a wool hat with ear flaps, beneath a felt hat tied under the chin with a red sash.

Look for gatherings of stone or adobe-brick homes with thatched roofs as you travel through the mountains. These typical Quechua homes are basic inside and out. Food is cooked either in an adobe oven next to the dwelling or over an open fire inside. Mud platforms with llama wool or sheepskin blankets make do for beds; occasionally a family will have the luxury of a wooden bed frame and grass mattress. All members of the family work in the fields as soon as they are able. Members of the *ayllu* (extended family) are expected to contribute to major projects like harvesting the fields or building a new home.

—By Holly S. Smith

8

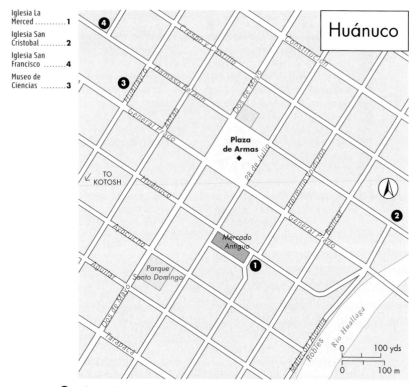

Huánuco

Plaza
de Armas

TO
KOTOSH

Mercado
Antiguo

Parque
Santo Domingo

Rio Huallaga

0   100 yds

0   100 m

❹ The 16th-century **Iglesia San Francisco** has Cusco School paintings and a few colonial-era antiques. Peek inside to see the spectacularly gilt wall and arches behind the altar. ✉*2 de Mayo y Beruan* ☏*No phone* 💲*Free* ☉*Mon.–Sun. 6–10 and 5–8.*

❶ The Romanesque **Iglesia La Merced** was built in 1600 by Royal Ensign Don Pedro Rodriguez. Colonial treasures include a silver tabernacle, paintings of the Cusco school, and the images of the Virgen Purisima and the Corazon de Jesus that were gifts from King Phillip II. ✉*Valdizan Cuadra 4* ☏*No phone* 💲*Free* ☉*Mon.–Sun. 6–10 and 5–8.*

❷ Fronting a landscape of steep, grassy mountain slopes, the **Iglesia San Cristobal**, with its three-tiered bell tower, was the first local church built by the Spanish settlers in 1542. Inside is a valuable collection of colonial-era paintings and baroque wood sculptures of San Agustín, the Virgen de la Asuncion, and the Virgen Dolorosa. ✉*San Cristobal y Beruan* ☏*No phone* 💲*Free* ☉*Mass time.*

★ In the Andean foothills at 1,812 meters (5,943 feet), **Kotosh,** a 4,000-year-old archaeological site, is famous for the Templo de las Manos Cruzadas (Temple of the Crossed Hands). Some of the oldest Peruvian pottery relics were discovered below one of the niches surrounding the main room of the temple, and the partially restored ruins are thought to have been constructed by one of the country's earliest cultures. Inside the temple you'll see re-created images of the crossed hands. The original mud set is dated 3000–2000 BC and is on display in Lima's Museo Nacional de Antropología, Arqueología, e Historia del Perú. ■TIP→The site was named Kotosh (pile) in reference to the piles of rocks found strewn across the fields. Taxi fare is S/15 for the round-trip journey from Huánuco, including a half hour to sightsee. ⊠*5 km (3 mi) west of Huánuco* ☎*No phone* ☒*S/3.50* ⊙*Daily sunrise–sunset.*

The **Pampas de Huánuco,** also called Huánuco Viejo, is a major site of Inca ruins. These fields are along the highland pampas near the town of La Unión. ⊠*10 km (6 mi) northwest of Huánuco* ☎*No phone* ☒*Free* ⊙*Daily 24 hrs.*

OFF THE BEATEN PATH

Tomayquichua. This small village was the birthplace of Micaela Villegas, a famous mestiza entertainer in the 18th century and the mistress of Viceroy Manuel de Amat y Juniet, a Spanish military hero and prominent colonial official. Also known as La Perricholi, her story was the basis of Prosper Mérimée's comic novella *Le Carrosse du Saint-Sacrement* and she was a important character along with the Viceroy in Thornton Wilder's *The Bridge of San Luis Rey.* A festival in July with parades, music, and dancing celebrates her vitality. Beautiful mountain views are the main attraction of the 2,000-meter- (6,500-foot-) high area. Sixteenth-century San Miguel Arcangel, one of the first churches built in the Huánuco area, is nearby in the village of Huacar. ⊠*18 km (11 mi) south of Huánuco* ☎*No phone* ☒*Free* ⊙*Daily 8–6.*

WHERE TO STAY & EAT

Restaurants in Huánuco are simple and small, mostly offering local cuisine with a smattering of Chinese and continental selections. Little eateries are around the plaza and its neighborhoods, and around the markets. ■TIP→Most hotels have a small restaurant, but if yours does not, your host will usually fix a meal on request. Hotels are basic, with shared cold-water baths at most budget places. Spend a little more and you'll get lots more comfort, including a private bath, hot water, and a better mattress. But don't expect the Ritz.

¢ ╳⊞ **Casa Hacienda Shismay.** About 17 km away from the city this fortresslike colonial hacienda sits on 8,650 acres amid the stunning scenery of the Esperanza Valley. Rooms are rustic and cozy, but have brick fireplaces and an endless wood supply. Hierba Buena restaurant serves regional specialties and some basic international fare. Musicians from the nearby village of San Sebastian often come during dinner to play. The hotel will arrange horseback riding, trekking, bird-watching, and homestays in the area. **Pros:** Incredible value, romantic, lots of land. **Cons:** Far from town, no public transportation, rustic. ⊠*Amarilis* ☎*062/510–040* ⊕*www.shismay.com* ➥*4 rooms* ♨*In-hotel: restaurant, laundry service, parking (no fee).*

Fodor's Choice ★

¢ ╳⊞ **Gran Hotel Cusco.** Its age shows in chipped paint, squeaky pipes, and ceiling cracks, but overall this local favorite has held up well over the decades. Rooms have the modern essentials: TV, phone, and hot shower. It's popular with visiting businesspeople, so book early for

8

weekdays. The cafeteria serves tasty Peruvian grilled meats and stews, as well as salads, and *tallarines* (noodles). **Pros:** Decent price, modern amenities. **Cons:** Showing its age, lacks frills. ⊠*Huánuco 614–616* ☎*062/513–578* ⌨*50 rooms* ⌂*In-hotel: laundry service, parking (no fee), no elevator* ☰*No credit cards.*

¢ ⊡ **Hostal Residencial Huánuco.** It's the town's favorite backpacker hang-out, where you can kick off your hiking boots and chat with new friends over a cup of *maté* (tea) in the garden. Shop the food market, then whip up your meal in the kitchen—the owners will even give cooking lessons. Hot water and laundry facilities set this hostel above other budget options. **Pros:** Friendly owners and staff, easy to meet other travelers, kitchen use. **Cons:** Pretty basic, can get crowded. ⊠*Huánuco 775* ☎*062/512–050* ⌨*23 rooms* ⌂*In-room: no phone, kitchen, no TV. In-hotel: laundry facilities, parking (no fee), no elevator* ☰*AE, MC, V.*

$ ✕⊡ **Inka Comfort.** The colonial-style building is chic, swanky, and completely out of place in simple Huánuco, which explains the bargain rate for a room. Rooms, with private baths and hot water, are modern and eclectic. Some rooms overlook the plaza, but beware of noise on mornings and weekends. Public areas are opulent yet intimate, with corners to relax in and have a quiet conversation. ∎**TIP➔The pool, sauna, and gym provide respite for those returning from long day tours of the surrounding pampas.** The Majestic restaurant is by far the best in town and serves everything from regional to international dishes. **Pros:** On the plaza, first-class service, good restaurant. **Cons:** Some rooms are noisy. ⊠*Beraun 775* ☎*062/514–222* ⎙*064/512–410* ⊕*www.grandhotel-huanuco.com* ⌨*34 rooms* ⌂*In-hotel: restaurant, pool, gym, parking (no fee), public Internet, no elevator* ☰*AE, DC, MC, V.*

Fodor's Choice
★

TANTAMAYO

158 km (98 mi) northwest of Huánuco.

The fields around Tantamayo are rich with pre-Inca ruins, some from the oldest cultures to settle in Peru. Most notable are the thick, seven-story stone skyscrapers of the Yarowilca, who flourished from AD 1200 to 1450. ∎**TIP➔Finds at Susupio, Hapayán, Piruro, and Selmín Granero are the best-preserved.** The ruins are within easy walking distance of Tantamayo village, which has a hostel and basic restaurants; or catch a bus to Tantamayo and visit the ruins without a guide.

TINGO MARÍA

129 km (80 mi) north of Huánuco.

The warmth and humidity in the Andean foothills hit you as you descend from the Huánuco highlands. Not many travelers visit this settlement at the border between mountains and jungle, as it has gotten a bad rap for being in the midst of the country's coca-growing core. It's a shame, though, to miss Tingo María's vibrance and beauty, seen in its colorful, bustling markets and frenzied festivals. A strong military presence keeps out drug smugglers from the Río Huallaga valley to the north.

With a backdrop of mountains shaped like La Belle Durmiente (Sleeping Beauty), Tingo María is a safe haven of 21,000 residents who make their living tending the surrounding coffee, rubber, and sugarcane farms. Banana and tea plantations also wind their way up the slopes, and less than 15 km (9 mi) farther out there are hidden lakes, waterfalls, and caves to explore. Most travelers come here to visit **Parque Nacional Tingo María,** in the midst of the Pumaringri mountains. Many highland and rain-forest species live here, including parrots, primates, and bats. ■ **TIP➔This is also the home of the rare, nocturnal guacharo (oilbird), a black-and-brown, owl-like bird with a hooked beak and a 1-meter (3-foot) wingspan.** You can also explore the famed **Cueva de las Lechuzas** (Las Lechuzas Cave), on the skirts of the Bella Durmiente, an enormous limestone cave that shelters an important colony of guacharos (also known as *santanas*).

GETTING AROUND

Tingo María is about three hours north of Huánuco on a paved road. You'll pass through several military checkpoints along the way, which are precautions to prevent drug trafficking and intermittent guerrilla activity. ■ **TIP➔Summer and autumn rains often cause landslides, and the road is frequently under repair.** Tingo Maria Airport is about 1½ km (1 mi) west of town. Taxis run from most airports into town, and many hotels have transport service.

WHERE TO STAY & EAT

There are plenty of small restaurants and inexpensive hotels—most with cold water, but some with private baths and cable TV.

¢ 🏨 **Villa Jennifer Farm and Lodge.** Most international travelers stay at the excellent Danish-Peruvian run lodge, a nine-room bird-watching haven on 25 acres not far from the national park. (⊠*Km 3.4, Castillo Grande* ☎*62/960–3509* ⊕*www.villajennifer.net* ⌂*In-room: no phone, no TV, fan. In-hotel: laundry facilities, parking (no fee), pool).*

VALLE YANAHUANCA

35 km (22 mi) south of Tingo María; 73 km (45 mi) north of Huancayo.

One of the longest surviving stretches of Inca road, the Qhapaq Nan, passes through the massive rocky outcrops and deep meadows of the Valle Yanahuanca. Forested hills threaded by shallow, pebbled rivers lead 4 km (2½ mi) farther to the village of Huarautambo, where pre-Inca ruins are treasures to search for in the rugged terrain. Continue along the 150-km (93-mi) Inca track and you'll pass La Union, San Marcos, Huari, Llamellin, and San Luis.

RESERVA NACIONAL JUNÍN

238 km (148 mi) south of Yanahuanca; 165 km (102 mi) north of Huancayo.

This reserve is at the center of the Peruvian puna, the high-altitude cross section of the Andes, which, at 3,900 to 4,500 meters (12,792 to 14,760 feet), is one of the highest regions in which humans live. Its boundaries begin about 10 km (6 mi) north of town along the shores of Lago de Junín, which, at 14 km (9 mi) wide and 30 km (19 mi) long, is Peru's second-largest lake after Titicaca.

Flat, rolling fields cut by clear, shallow streams characterize this cold, wet region between the highest Andes peaks and the eastern rain forest. Only heavy grasses, hearty alpine flowers, and tough, tangled berry bushes survive in this harsh climate, although farmers have cultivated the warmer, lower valleys into an agricultural stretch of orchards and plantations. The mountains are threaded with cave networks long used as natural shelters by humans, who hunted the llamas, alpacas, and vincuñas that graze on the plains. The dry season is June through September, with the rains pouring in between December and March.

The reserve is also the site of the **Santuario Histórico Chacamarca**, an important battle site where local residents triumphed over the Spanish conquistadors in August of 1824. A monument marks the victory spot. The Chacamarca Historical Sanctuary is within walking distance of Junín, and several trails lead around the lake and across the pampas. Bird fans stop here to spot birds such as Andean geese and flamingos and other wildlife on day trips from Tarma.

TARMA

350 km (217 mi) east of Lima; 25 km (16 mi) southeast of Junín.

The hidden mountain town known as "The Pearl of the Andes" has grown into a city of 155,000 whose Peruvian roots are held close in its traditions and sights. Long before the Spanish arrived, local tribes built homes and temples in the hills that frame the town, the ruins of which are still being turned up by local farmers who have plowed much of the terrain into flower and potato fields, coffee plantations, and orchards. The town's look is all Spanish, though, with a small Plaza de Armas and several colonial-style churches and mansions.

At an elevation of 3,050 meters (10,004 feet), Tarma has a cool and breezy climate, with crisp nights all year. ■TIP➔**Get out in these nights, too, as candlelight processions are a major part of the town's many festivals—notably the Fiesta San Sebastián in January, Semana Santa in April, Semana de Tarma in July, and Fiesta El Señor de Los Milagros in October.** Tarma is definitely not a tourist town, but a place to visit for true Peruvian traditions.

Sights to visit include the village of Acobamba, a 10-km (6-mi) drive from town, where you can tour the **El Señor de Muruhuay** sanctuary, where an image of the crucified Christ was said to have appeared. About

Laguna de Paca lakeside resort, near Jauja.

15 km (9 mi) northwest is the town of **San Pedro de Cajas**, well-known for its exquisite weaving and as an excellent place to buy good-quality, locally made wall hangings and rugs. You can also head northwest 28 km (17 mi) to Palcamayo, then continue 4 km (2½ mi) west to explore the **Gruta de Guagapo** limestone cave system, a National Speleological Area. Guides live in the village near the entrance and can give you a basic short tour, but you'll need full spelunking equipment for deep cavern trips.

Tarma's **Oficina de Turismo,** on the Plaza de Armas, can help you find qualified local guides for sights in the region.

ESSENTIALS

BUS **Transportes Chanchmayo** (✉ *Callao 1002* ☎ *064/321–882*). **Transportes DASA** (✉ *Callao 1012* ☎ *064/321–843*). **Transportes Junin** (✉ *Amazonas 669* ☎ *064/321–324*).

INTERNET **Colegio Santa Rosa** (✉ *Amazonas 892* ☎ *064/321–457*).

MAIL **Serpost** (✉ *Callao 356* ☎ *064/321–241*).

VISITOR INFO **Oficina de Turismo** (✉ *2 de Mayo y Lima* ☎ *064/321–010*).

WHERE TO EAT

¢ ✕**Le Break Pizzeria Cafe.** Hidden away a few blocks from the plaza, tiny Le Break is one of the town's better dining options. There's nothing Peruvian about this place, only wood-fired pizzas and pastas. It's popular with visiting Limeños. ⊠*Callao 220* ☎*064/323–334* ▭*No credit cards.*

¢ ✕**Restaurant Chavin.** This popular travelers' hangout is on the plaza. There's kitschy Andean decor—pictures of snow-covered mountains, patterned wall hangings—and lively lunchtime crowds. Hearty stews and rice dishes are the midday specials; at dinner you'll find grilled meat and even fish. ⊠*Lima 262* ☎*064/321–449* ▭*MC, V.*

¢ ✕**Restaurant Señorial.** Tarma's most upscale restaurant is still casual and chic, the place where the top of the townsfolk dine with fresh-pressed attire and just-shined shoes. The chefs show off their Andean flavors in *pachamanca* (marinated, slow-cooked meat, vegetables, potatoes, and spices) and *picante de cuy* (guinea pig in hot pepper sauce). You can also order pastas and sauces, grilled meats, and seafood. ⊠*Huánuco 138* ☎*064/323–334* ▭*No credit cards.*

WHERE TO STAY

¢ **La Florida.** Experience life at a Spanish hacienda at this charming
Fodor'sChoice bed-and-breakfast that's a 10-minute drive from Tarma. Rooms, which
★ sleep up to four guests, are furnished with period pieces, local art, and handmade textiles that evoke the 18th-century esthetic. There's even a camping section with a bathroom (S/10), and hiking trails that lead to ruins and highland villages. **Pros:** Breakfast included, hiking trails lead from property. **Cons:** Simple, car ride from town. ⊠*6 km (4 mi) north of Tarma* ☎*064/341–041, 01/344–1358 in Lima* ⊕*www.haciendalaflorida.com* ⟳*5 rooms, 6 campsites* ⚓*In-hotel: laundry service, parking (no fee), no elevator* ▭*AE, MC, V* ⧄*BP.*

¢ **Hostal Durand.** A number of budget hotels are on Jr. Lima leading from the plaza and the Durand is the best value. The rooms are clean, new, and even have private baths, hot water, and TVs. The rooms near the street are the largest and have nice views of the plaza. **Pros:** Clean, modern, cheap. **Cons:** Lacks character, above a busy street and shop. ⊠*Lima 583* ☎*064/317–434* ⟳*10 rooms* ▭*V.*

$ **Los Portales.** Considered by locals to be the best hotel in town, this colonial-style mansion surrounded by gardens offers more warmth than grandeur. Rooms, which have modern amenities and private baths with hot water, are decorated with a mix of real and reproduction antiques that complement the elegant architecture. The staff is very helpful with advice for regional sightseeing. **Pros:** Historic charm, Lima-like amenities for half the price, friendly staff. **Cons:** Out of town, often filled. ⊠*Castilla 512* ☎*064/321–411* ☎*064/322–533* ⊕*www.hoteleslosportales.com* ⟳*45 rooms* ⚓*In-hotel: restaurant, bar, laundry service, parking (no fee), no elevator* ▭*AE, DC, MC, V* ⧄*BP.*

SAN PEDRO DE CASTA

120 km (74 mi) northeast of Lima.

This compact Andean village is a collection of mud-brick and clapboard homes and shops where you can watch craftspeople and farmers at

QUECHA LESSON

Here's a small sampling of Quecha words. It won't make you fluent, but people appreciate the effort when you learn a few of words of their language.

WORDS:
House–Wasi
Mother–Mama
Father–Papa, tayta
Son–Wawa
Daughter–Wawa
Yes–Arí
No–Mana
Please–Allichu
Hello–Rimaykullayki, napaykullayki

PHRASES:
What is your name?–Imataq sutiyki?

My name is...–Nuqap...sutiymi
Good-bye–Rikunakusun
Good morning–Windía
How are you?–Ima hinalla?
Thank you–Añay

NUMBERS:
Zero–Ch'usaq
One–Huq, huk
Two–Iskay
Three–Kinsa, kimsa
Four–Tawa
Five–Pishqa, pisqa, pichqa
Six–Soqta, suqta
Seven–Qanchis
Eight–Pusaq, pusac
Nine–Isqun
Ten–Chunka

work on the highland plains. For many visitors, the town is a starting point for the three-hour, uphill hike to the unusual rock formations at **Marcahuasi**, 3 km (2 mi) from San Pedro, where winds have worn the earth into a menagerie of animal shapes. Other hiking trails weave through the grasslands around San Pedro, but you'll need to spend at least one night to get used to the high altitude. Carry a water filtration kit to drink from the lakes. San Pedro is about 40 km (25 mi) north of Chosica, on the main highway between Lima and La Oroya. Most visit on a day trip from Tarma, about 1½ hours by car or the hourly buses.

TARMA SOUTH TO AYACUCHO

The road from Tarma continues beside the spine of the mountains, alternately cutting through high-altitude plains and winding in coils alongside steep crevasses. The thin air can be biting in the shade and scorching in the mid-afternoon sun beating down on a dry, barren landscape pounded into rough grasslands between the peaks. ■TIP➔Look for spots of black, brown, and white—wild llamas and alpacas that roam this cold, rocky range. Near Pucapampa, the road rises to 4,500 meters (14,760 feet), often causing *soroche* (altitude sickness) in travelers while the resident (and rare) gray alpaca remains quite comfortable.

Still the road rises, passing tiny Santa Inés and Abra de Apacheta, the latter at 4,750 meters (15,580 feet). Somehow the scenery continues to be even more spectacular, for oxides in the earth have painted the rocks and creeks in a wash of vibrant colors. One of the highest roads in the world is 14 km (9 mi) farther, the 5,059-meter (16,594-foot) pass 3 km (2 mi) north of Huachocolpa. From here the journey is downhill into the wide, windy Valle Huanta, a landscape of lakes and hot springs, caverns, and ruins.

JAUJA

280 km (174 mi) southeast of San Pedro de Casta; 60 km (37 mi) south of Tarma.

Jauja has the distinction of having been Peru's original capital, as declared by Francisco Pizarro when he swept through the region; he changed his mind in 1535 and transferred the title to Lima. ■**TIP→Jauja still has many of the ornate 16th-century homes and churches that mark its place in the country's history.** The Wednesday and Sunday markets display Andean traditions at their most colorful, showing the other side of life in this mountain town. Although there are several moderately priced hotels, many travelers come here on a day trip from Huancayo. Those who stay usually head to the lakeside **Laguna de Paca** resort area 4 km (2½ mi) from town.

CONCEPCÍON

Fodor'sChoice *15 km (9 mi) southeast of Jauja; 25 km (16 mi) northwest of*
★ *Huancayo.*

The village of Concepcíon is the site of the 1725 **Convento de Santa Rosa de Ocopa.** Originally a Franciscan foundation whose role was to bring Christianity to the Amazon tribes, now the building has a reconstructed 1905 church and a massive library with more than 25,000 books— some from the 15th century. ■**TIP→The natural-history museum displays a selection of regional archaeological finds including traditional costumes and local crafts picked up by the priests during their travels.** A restaurant serves excellent, if simple, Andean food, and several spare but comfortable accommodations are in the former monks' quarters. Admission includes a guided tour. ☎*No phone* 💲*S/5* ⊙ *Wed.–Mon. 9–1 and 3–6.*

HUANCAYO

25 km (16 mi) southeast of Concepcíon; 40 km (25 mi) southeast of Jauja.

It's not hard to see how the modern city of Huancayo, which has close to 260,000 residents, was once the capital of pre-Inca Huanca (Wanka) culture. In the midst of the Andes and straddling the verdant Río Mantaro valley, the city has been a source of artistic inspiration from the days of the earliest settlers, and has thrived as the region's center for culture and wheat farming. A major agricultural hub, Huancayo was linked by rail with the capital in 1908, making it an endpoint on the world's highest train line. Although it's a large town, its little shops,

small restaurants, blossoming plazas, and broad colonial buildings
give it a comfortable, compact feel.

Huancayo has also been a stronghold for the toughest Peruvian
tribes, including the Huanca, who
out-fought both the Inca and the
Spanish. Little wonder that Peru
finally gained independence in
this region, near Quinua, in 1824.

> **GOOD TO KNOW**
>
> It's best to bring U.S. cash to the
> smaller towns of this region, as
> traveler's checks and credit cards
> usually aren't accepted. Travel
> agencies or larger hotels might
> change money if you're in a pinch.

■TIP➜Still, the Spanish left their mark with the town's collection of hacienda-style homes and businesses, most with arching windows and fronted
by brick courtyards with carefully groomed gardens. For an overview of
the city, head northeast 4 km (2½ mi) on Giráldez, 2 km (1 mi) past
Cerro de la Libertad park, to the eroded sandstone towers in the hillsides at Torre-Torre.

The drive from Lima to Huancayo is breathtaking, with the road rising to more than 4,700 meters (15,416 feet) before sliding down to
the valley's 3,272-meter (10,731-foot) elevation. As you enter the city,
four-lane Calle Real is jammed with traffic and crammed with store-
fronts—but look more closely and you'll see the elegant churches and
colorful markets tucked into its side streets, hallmarks of local life that
make the city so charming. Women with long black braids beneath
black-felt hats still dress in multitiered skirts and blouses with *mantas*
(bright, square, striped cloths) draped over their shoulders. Note the
intricate weavings—particularly the belts with the famous train worked
into the pattern.

8

GETTING AROUND
Although Huancayo is big, most of the areas of interest to travelers are
within walking distance of the plaza. The exceptions are the craft villages in the Mantaro Valley. Combi vans circle the city streets looking
for passengers for the 20–40-minute rides to each town or you can take
a comprehensive valley tour from any of the travel agencies in Huancayo S/50. Taxis are another option as they're quite economical.

ESSENTIALS
BUS **Cruz del Sur** (✉*Ayacucho 281* ☎*064/235–650*). **ETUCSA** (✉*Puno 220*
☎*064/232–638*). **Expresa Molina** (✉*Angaraes 334, Huancayo* ☎*064/224–501*).
Ormen[ac]o (✉*Castilla 1379* ☎*064/251–199*). **Turismo Central** (✉*Ayacucho*
274 ☎*066/223–128*).

CURRENCY **Banco de Crédito** (✉*Real 1039* ⊕*www.viabcp.com*).

INTERNET **Huancayo Internet** (✉*Loreto 337* ☎*064/233–856*).

MAIL **Serpost** (✉*Huamanmarca 350* ☎*064/231–271*).

VISITOR INFO **Oficina de Turismo** (✉*Casa de Artesana, Real 481* ☎*064/233–251*).

Huancayo

WHAT TO SEE

❷ In front of the Río Shulcas, the **Capilla de la Merced** is a national monument marking where Peru's Constitutional Congress met in 1830 and the Constitution was signed in 1839. In addition to information about this historic gathering, the Chapel of Mercy also exhibits Cusqueño paintings. ⊠*Real y Ayacucho* ☎*No phone* ⌨*Free* ⊙*Weekdays 9–noon and 3–6:30.*

❸ The **Museo Salesiano** has more than 5,000 objects. Look for the well-preserved rain-forest creatures and butterflies from the northern jungles. Local fossils and archaeological relics are also displayed at the Salesian Museum. ⊠*2 blocks west of Real, across Río Shulcas* ☎*064/247–763* ⌨*S/5* ⊙*Weekdays 8–noon and 2–6.*

❺ The **Parque del Cerro de la Libertad** is an all-in-one amusement site 1 km
⌚ (½ mi) east of the city. You can picnic in the grass, watch the kids at the playground, swim in the public pool, dine at the restaurant, or stroll through the zoo. ■**TIP➜**Folkloric dancers and musicians perform at the Liberty Hill Park amphitheater on weekends. A 15-minute walk from the park brings you to the site of Torre Torre, a cluster of 10–30-meter rock towers formed by wind and rain erosion. ⊠*Giraldez* ☎*No phone* ⌨*Free* ⊙*Daily 24 hrs.*

Tour & Travel Agencies

Ayacucho is surrounded by archaeological ruins and natural wonders, all of which can be viewed on a package tour. Morochucos Travel Services has city excursions and routes to Huari, Quinua, Valle Huanta and Vilcashuamán. Quinua Tours specializes in Ayacucho's outer ruins but also runs city tours. Wari Tours Ayacucho and A&R Tours offers explorations of the famous ruins, as well as tours of town.

Around Huancayo you can hike, bike, and explore local villages with the amazing Incas del Perú, which also has a Spanish-language school, book exchange, and folk-art collection. They will also arrange volunteering and hiking throughout the Manataro Valley and high jungle, as well as music, cooking, weaving, and gourd carving workshops. Murikami Tours and Wanka Tours are among the better options from the numerous package-tour offices in town. Turismo Huancayo organizes trips to local ruins and natural wonders.

Max Adventures in Tarma has several tour packages, local maps, and information.

Contacts: **A&R Tours** (✉ *9 de Diciembre 130, Ayacucho* ☎ *066/311-300*). **Incas del Perú** (✉ *Giráldez 652, Huancayo* ☎ *064/223-303* 📠 *064/222-395* ⊕ *www.incasdelperu. com*). **Max Adventures** (✉ *2 de Mayo 682, Tarma* ☎ *064/323-908*). **Morochucos Travel Services** (✉ *Constitución 14, Ayacucho* ☎ *066/912-261*). **Murikami Tours** (✉ *Jr. Lima 354, Huancayo* ☎ *064/234-745*). **Quinua Tours** (✉ *Asemblea 195, Ayacucho* ☎ *066/912-191*). **Turismo Huancayo** (✉ *Real 517, Huancayo* ☎ *064/233-351*). **Wanka Tours** (✉ *Real 565, Huancayo* ☎ *064/231-778*). **Wari Tours** (✉ *Independencia 70, Ayacucho* ☎ *066/913-115*).

8

❹ The focus of the beautiful **Parque de la Identidad Wanka** *(Wanka Identity Park)* is on the pre-Inca Huanca culture, which occupied the area but left few clues to its lifestyle. Pebbled paths and small bridges meander through blossoming gardens and past a rock castle just right for children to tackle. The enormous sculpture honors the local artists who produce the city's *mates burilados* (carved gourds). ✉ *San Antonio* ☎ *No phone* 🎟 *Free* ⊙ *Daily 24 hrs.*

❶ When the Spanish founded Huancayo in 1572, the **Plaza Huamanmarca** was the city center and the site of the weekly *Feria Dominical* (Sunday market). Today Huamanmarca Square is fronted by the post office, the telephone agency, and the Municipal Hall. ✉ *Calle Real between Loreto and Piura* ☎ *No phone* 🎟 *Free* ⊙ *Daily 24 hrs.*

OFF THE BEATEN PATH

Warvilca. This ruined temple was built by the pre-Inca Huanca culture. The closest village is Huari, which has a little museum on the main square with ceramic figures, pottery, and a few bones and skulls. ✉ *9 km (6 mi) from Huancayo* ☎ *No phone* 🎟 *S/15* ⊙ *Ruins: daily 10–noon and 3–5; museum: daily 10–noon.*

WHERE TO EAT

The local specialty is *papa a la huancaína* (boiled potato covered in a ají-cheese sauce), served cold with an olive. Budget restaurants with set lunch menus are on Arequipa south of Antojitos, as well as along Giráldez. You can pick up a quick morning meal at the Mercado Modelo after 7 AM and juice stands, with fresh fruit brought in daily from the high jungle, are on every street.

¢ ✗ **Antojitos.** The tasty grilled meats, wood-smoked pizzas, and hearty sandwiches at this renowned backpacker restaurant draw more than just the budget crowd. The highland sophisticates meet here for a glass of local wine, businesspeople snack on the filling lunch specials, and the live bands on weekends always draw a crowd. ⊠ *Puno 599* ☎ *064/237–950* ▭ *DC, MC, V.*

¢ ✗ **La Cabaña.** A romantic air pervades this cozy, charming restaurant
Fodor'sChoice that has long been a travelers' favorite. The cuisine combines Peruvian
★ specialties like *anticuchos* (grilled marinated beef hearts) and *calientitos* ("little hotties," a hot punch made of tea, rum, and spices) with basic continental fare like pasta, pizza, and grills. Dine in the garden on balmy days, or around the fireplace on chilly evenings. There's live music Thursday through Saturday. ■ TIP➔The owners can arrange cooking classes, Spanish lessons, music instruction, and long-term local homestays. Two hostel rooms, a book exchange, and numerous maps are available. ⊠ *Giráldez 652* ☎ *064/223–303* ▭ *MC, V.*

¢ ✗ **Detrás de la Catedral.** With the Cathedral only steps away, romantic is an understatement. Stone walls and candlighted tables calm the air that's scented with the aroma of roasted lamb, grilled trout, and pastas. Call ahead for reservations or prepare to wait. ⊠ *Ancash 335* ☎ *064/212–969* ▭ *DC, MC, V.*

¢ ✗ **Panadería Coqui.** Petite tables swathed in rippling cloths are arranged in tea-party style in the airy dining room. It's a perfectly elegant way to sample the pretty cakes and pastries while sipping espresso. Hungrier patrons can get pizza and sandwiches. Afterward, wander into the liquor shop to check out the local specialties. ⊠ *Puno 356* ☎ *064/234–707* ▭ *No credit cards.*

¢ ✗ **Restaurant Olímpico.** This upmarket restaurant, open for more than 60
★ years, still serves a downtown lunch crowd with cheap, hearty Andean specials. It's popular and always crowded, but good food is guaranteed. For a basic selection of soup, salad, meat, rice, and dessert, try the daily special. Otherwise, you can order a mix of Peruvian delicacies, including cuy, from the à la carte menu. ⊠ *Giráldez 199* ☎ *064/234181* ▭ *AE, DC, MC, V.*

¢ ✗ **Restaurant Vegetariano Nuevo Horizante.** Health food has arrived in the Andes at this vegetarian spot. Pastas, soups, and rice dishes with vegetable bases are all on the menu. The kitchen whips up yogurt, soy milk, and fruit drinks as well. You can also stock up on organic products and vitamins. ⊠ *Cajamarca 379* ☎ *No phone* ▭ *No credit cards.*

WHERE TO STAY

¢ ⌂ **La Casa de la Abuela.** Hot showers, hearty Peruvian home cooking, and a sunny garden gathering spot attract budget travelers and volunteers to this old colonial mansion. Rooms have a mix of contem-

CLOSE UP

High Train

The world's highest train rides again!

The Central Highlands are one of the country's most scenic areas, and tracks cut through the mountains and plains all the way from Lima to Huancavelica.

Unfortunately, parts of the line often aren't running, so check first at the station. These are old cars, so don't expect plush seats, clean windows, or first-class service. The most reliable section is from Huancayo to Huancavelica, a spectacular journey that's worth the discomfort.

Huancayo has two train stations, one in the town center serving Lima and one in the Chilca suburb serving Huancavelica. With the help of tour operators such as Incas del Peru that have designed weekend train packages from Lima, the train is now running regularly again. One of the most spectacular journeys in South America is the 335-km (207-mi) train route that twists through the Andes at an elevation of 4,782 meters (15,685 feet). The engine chugs its way up a slim thread of rails that hugs the slopes, speeding over 59 bridges, around endless hairpin curves, and through 66 tunnels—including the 1,175-meter- (3,854-foot-) long Galera Tunnel, which, at an altitude of 4,758 meters (15,606 feet) is the world's highest railway. A second uniquely amazing journey is from Tarma to Chanchamayo, on which the road descends almost 2,500 meters (8,200 feet) from mountains into the jungle in less than 70 km (43 mi).

The trips are about two weekends a month and depart on Thursday or Friday at 7 AM and return Sunday at 6 PM. Snacks and lunch are included in the price (S/240 round-trip). You can request oxygen if you get short of breath over the high passes.

The Huancavelica Tren Expreso departs from Huancayo Monday through Saturday at 6:30 AM and Sunday at 2 PM (S/12, 4 ½ hours). Purchase advance tickets at the station. Return trains depart from Estación Huancavelica on Avenida Leguía (067/752–898) at 6:30 AM Monday through Saturday and Sunday at 2 PM.

8

porary, colonial, and comfortably worn pieces; some are dorms, and some have private bathrooms. The shared laundry and kitchen are often busy. Pros: Extremely friendly and helpful staff, great breakfasts. Cons: Often full, not many rooms. ⊠ *Giráldez 691* ☎*064/234–383* 🖷*064/222–395* ⊕*www.incasdelperu.com* 🛏*4 rooms, 3 dormitories* 🕭*In-room: no phone, kitchen, no TV. In-hotel: laundry facilities, parking (no fee), no elevator* ⊟*No credit cards* ⫶⊘⫶*CP.*

$ 🛏 **Hostal El Marquez.** It lacks the character of Hotel Turismo, but the fairly new El Marquez is the only comparable hotel in town. The rooms have been recently renovated but remain bland. There's supposed to be 24-hour hot water so if you just want a cozy place to sleep look no further. Pros: Centrally located, recently renovated, modern comforts. Cons: Bland, the hot water isn't always hot. ⊠*Puno 294* ☎*064/219–026* 🖷*064/200–777* ⊕*www.elmarquezhuancayo.com* 🕭*In room: telephones, cable. In-hotel: laundry service, parking (no fee), publicInternet* ⊟*AE, DC, MC, V* ⫶⊘⫶*BP.*

¢   🛏 **Hotel Olímpico.** This central hotel has more charm than its larger competitors, and it's close to the center of town. Cozy rooms with modern furniture have all the amenities, including TVs, phones, and bathrooms with hot water. Pros: Right on the plaza, good price. Cons: Getting run down, not all rooms created equal. ⊠*Ancash 408* ☎*064/214–555* 🖷*064/215–700* 🛏*32 rooms* 🕭*In-hotel: restaurant, room service, laundry service, parking (no fee)* ⊟*AE, DC, MC, V.*

$ 🛏 **Hotel Presidente.** The most popular lodging with visiting Limeños has the comforts of a modern hotel, and a bland 20th-century exterior to match. Rooms, with contemporary furnishings and Andean fabrics and accents, have TVs, phones, private baths with hot water—and thin walls. There's a wheelchair-accessible elevator. Pros: Great amenities, train packages. Cons: Mostly business oriented. ⊠*Real 1138* ☎*064/231–275* 🖷*064/231–736* ⊕*www.hoteles-del-centro.com* 🛏*88 rooms* 🕭*In-hotel: laundry service, parking (no fee)* ⊟*AE, DC, MC, V* ⫶⊘⫶*BP.*

$ 🛏 **Hotel Turismo Huancayo.** The hacienda-style exterior of this elegant hotel gives it a worldly charm that sets it above the younger options. Public areas are ornate, with Peruvian paintings and local crafts and textiles. Rooms are sparkling clean, and many have TVs, phones, and private baths with hot water. ■**TIP➔Ask to see several different options before you agree to stay, as rooms vary in size, decor, view, and amenities.** Although the neighborhood is quieter than those around the plaza, the hotel is conveniently in the middle of town. Pros: Excellent service. Cons: Street and plaza in front often see protests, quality of rooms vary. ⊠*Ancash 729* ☎*064/231–072* 🖷*064/231–072* ⊕*www.hoteles-del-centro.com* 🛏*64 rooms* 🕭*In-room: no phone (some), no TV (some). In-hotel: restaurant, room service, laundry service, parking (no fee), no elevator* ⊟*AE, DC, MC, V.*

NIGHTLIFE

Huancayo's nightlife is surprisingly spunky. Many restaurants turn into *peñas* with dancing, live music, and folkloric performances from Friday to Sunday between 7 PM and midnight (though some may start and end earlier). If you arrive around or after the time the show begins, expect to pay a cover of about S/7. Dance clubs are usually open from about 10 PM to 2 AM and have a cover charge of S/10–S/14.

La Cabaña (✉ *Giráldez 652* ☎ *064/223–303*) has rollicking live *folklórico* and pop bands Thursday through Saturday. Video karaoke is the main attraction at the **Taj Mahal** (✉ *Huancavelica 1052*) when you're not dancing. A trendy crowd of young locals and the occasional backpacker heads to **Café Bizarro** (✉ *Puno 656* ☎ *No phone*) where the occasional live rock band plays bad '80s covers.

SHOPPING
Huancayo and the towns of the surrounding Valle del Mantaro are major craft centers. The region is famous for its mate burilado (large, intricately carved and painted gourds depicting scenes of local life and historic events), many of which are made 11 km (7 mi) outside of town in the villages of Cochas Grande and Cochas Chico. Silver filigree and utensils are the specialties of San Jerónimo de Tunán, and exquisite knitwear, woolen sweaters, scarves, wall hangings, and hats are produced in San Agustín de Cajas and Hualhaus.

Elegant, high-quality textiles are woven and sold at **Artesanía Sumaq Ruray** (✉ *Brasilia 132* ☎ *064/237–018*). You'll find top-quality, locally made goods near the Plaza Constitución at **Casa del Artesano** (✉ *Real 495* ☎ *No phone*), where artists sit shop-by-shop working on their various crafts. Artists' shops and stalls line the **Centro Commerical Artesanal El Manatial** (✉ *Ancash 475* ☎ *No phone*), where you can browse for clothing, textiles, ceramics, wood carvings, and many other crafts.

The city's main shopping venue is the weekend **Mercado** (✉ *Av. Huancavelica* ☎ *No phone*), which is spread down one of the city's main thoroughfares and its side streets. In particular, look for mate burilado, mantas, straw baskets, and *retablos* (miniature scenes framed in painted wooden boxes). **Mercado Mayorista** (✉ *Prolongación Ica* ☎ *No phone*), stretching around the blocks near the train station, is the daily produce market. You'll need several hours to wander through the stalls of local crafts and foodstuffs, where you'll find traditional medicines and spices among such local delicacies as gourds, guinea pigs, fish, and frogs. The **Sunday crafts market** (✉ *Calle Huancavelica* ☎ *No phone*) has textiles, sweaters, embroidery, wood carvings, and ceramics. This is a good place to shop for the carved gourds.

EN ROUTE **Valle de Mantaro.** The wide Mantaro Valley stretches northwest of Huancayo, embracing not only the Río Mantaro but also a vast area of highlands lakes and plains. Trails run along the jagged mountainsides to archaeological sites and crafts villages. By road, you'll reach Cochas Chicas and Cochas Grandes, gourd-carving centers 11 km (7 mi) north of Huancayo, with some of the most talented mate burilado artists in the country. The road west leads 10 km (6 mi) to Hualhaus, a weaving village where you can watch blankets and sweaters being crafted from alpaca and lamb's wool dyed with local plants. About 5 km (3 mi) north is San Jerónimo de Tunan, where the Wednesday market specializes in gold and silver filigree. Cross the Río Mantaro and head 10 km (6 km) west to Aco, a village of potters and ceramics

8

artists. Group tours from Huancayo cover the valley, but the roads are good enough that you can drive on your own—although you won't have a guide or a translator. Minibuses from the Avenida Giraldez also reach these villages.

HUANCAVELICA

147 km (91 mi) south of Huancayo.

Spread out high in the Andes, Huancavelica was founded in the 16th century by Spanish conquistadors, who discovered the rich veins of silver and mercury threaded through the rocky hillsides. The abundant mercury was vital in the extraction of silver from mines in Peru and Bolivia, including Potosí. Although mining was difficult at 3,680 meters (12,979 feet), the Spanish succeeded in making the city an important profit center that today has grown to a population of around 40,000.

This scenic town is sliced by the Río Huancavelica, which divides the commercial district on the south and the residential area in the north. The road is rough, but the surroundings are beautiful, a mix of quiet, clapboard-style villages fronting vast sheep pastures and snowcapped mountains. ■TIP➔If you have a good map and your own equipment excellent hiking opportunities are in the surrounding mountains.

A lack of good roads leading to the town has kept the Andean city away from the winds of change. You'll still see traditional costumes worn by women in the markets and shops and the narrow, cobbled streets are still lined with elegant, colonial-style mansions and 16th-century churches. Only the raggedy and jam-packed train to Huancayo keeps Huancavelica connected to other mountain towns. Residents from all over the region crowd the sprawling Sunday market, as well as the daily food market at the corner of Muñoz and Barranca.

Most crafts and clothing are made in the villages on the outskirts of Huancavelica, and you're welcome to visit the artisans' shops. Other neighboring explorations include the viewpoints from Potaqchiz, a short stroll up the hill from San Cristóbal. Thermal baths are on the hillside across from town.

GETTING AROUND

The town is quite compact and nearly everything of interest is confined to a few short streets in the center. Few roads lead to Huancavelica; many mountain villages can only be reached by foot. A good, albeit steep, path starts from behind the rail station and has pleasant views of the city and surrounding mountains. The altitude is a common problem to visitors here, so take it slow and drink plenty of bottled water.

The best place for contacts on local culture in Huancavelica is **Instituto Nacional de Cultura** (⊠*Plaza San Juan de Dios*), which offers language, music, and dance lessons, cultural talks, and details on historic sights and regional history. It's open Monday through Saturday 10–1 and 3–7.

ESSENTIALS

CURRENCY **Banco de Crédito** (✉ *Toledo 300* ⊕ *www.viabcp.com*).

MAIL **Serpost** (✉ *Pasaje Ferrúa* ☎ *067/752–750*).

VISITOR INFO **Ministerio de Industria y Comercio, Turismo, y Artesanías** (✉ *Nicolás de Piérola 180*).

WHAT TO SEE

Huancavelica's **Plaza de Armas** is the main gathering place. Across from the plaza is the restored 17th-century cathedral. ✉ *Toledo y Segura* ☎ *No phone* 🎫 *Free* ⊙ *Daily 24 hrs.*

The **Iglesia de San Francisco** was begun in 1673 and took six more decades to complete. The dual white towers and red stone doorway—carved with regional motifs—make the San Francisco Church one of the most attractive buildings in town. ✉ *Goodos y Tagle* ☎ *No phone* 🎫 *Free* ⊙ *Mon.–Sat. 4–6.*

The Sunday **Feria Dominical** market attracts artists and shoppers from all the mountain towns. It's a good place to browse for local crafts—although you'll get better quality (and sometimes better prices) in the villages. ✉ *Garma y Barranca* ☎ *No phone* 🎫 *Free* ⊙ *Sun. 8–3.*

OFF THE BEATEN PATH

San Cristóbal. Locals believe that these hot-spring mineral baths, found in the tree-covered slopes north of town, have healing powers. Hundreds of pilgrims come from the surrounding villages during holy days. ✉ *5 de Agosto* ☎ *No phone* 🎫 *S/0.50 private room, S/0.35 public area* ⊙ *Daily 6 AM–3 PM.*

WHERE TO STAY & EAT

Restaurants line Barranca, Toledo, and the streets around the Plaza de Armas. All are casual and have a mix of Andean and continental cuisine. Most restaurants have an à la carte menu useful for sampling several dishes. Hotels usually have restaurants, or at least a small café or dining room.

$ 🏨 **Hotel Presidente Huancavelica.** The town's top hotel is in an attractive, Spanish-colonial building on the plaza. Rooms have bland modern furnishings, but they're sizable and comfortable, with phones and hot showers. Rooms with shared baths are cheaper. The restaurant is open for lunch and dinner when the hotel is busy; otherwise, it's open for breakfast only. **Pros:** Historic building, prime plaza setting. **Cons:** Mixed amenities, pretty basic for the best hotel in town. ✉ *Carabaya y Muñoz* ☎ *067/752–760* 🖨 *064/752–760* ⊕ *www.hoteles-del-centro.com* 🛏 *45 rooms, 40 with bath* 🔑 *In-room: no phone (some), no TV (some). In-hotel: restaurant, laundry service, parking (no fee), no elevator* ▤ *AE, DC, MC, V* ⏹*BP.*

¢ ✗🏨 **Mercurio.** The modestly furnished rooms at this colonial-style hotel on the plaza are spic-and-span, with private bathrooms—some with tubs—and hot water. The restaurant serves hearty portions of Peruvian cuisine, as well as pasta. **Pros:** Great location, can't beat the price. **Cons:** Bathrooms are hot or miss, very basic. ✉ *Torre Tagle 455* ☎ *067/755–773* 🛏 *45 rooms* 🔑 *In-hotel: restaurant, laundry service, parking (no fee), no elevator* ▤ *No credit cards.*

8

QUINUA

37 km (23 mi) northeast of the Ayachuco.

Fodor'sChoice   The Battle of Ayacucho, the decisive battle against Spain in the Peru-
★   vian War of Independence, took place on the **Pampas de Quinua** grasslands 37 km (23 mi) northeast of the city, near the village of Quinua,
on December 9, 1824. Today a white obelisk rises 44 meters (144 feet)
above the pampas to commemorate how the locals firmly cemented
Peru's independence here when they defeated the Spanish. You can follow the surrounding events through exhibits in the compact Quinua
museum ⌧*Plaza de Armas* 🖃*S/5* ⊘*Mon.–Sat. 10–1 and 3–5.* Come
the first week in December to celebrate the town's role in Peru's democracy, when you'll see extravagant local performances, parties, parades,
and crafts fairs. There's a little local market on Sunday. ■**TIP**➔Quinua
is one of the craft centers of Peru. It's best known for its ceramics, and
you'll find various examples on the windowsills and rooftops of the adobe
houses. Miniature churches, delicately painted with ears of corn or
flowers, are frequently seen symbols of good luck. The ubiquitous bulls
are figures once used in festivities associated with cattle-branding ceremonies. Tours of Huari, Vilcashuaman, and Vischongo often include
Quinua, but you can also get here by bus.

AYACUCHO

*114 km (71 mi) south of Huancavelica; 364 km (226 mi) northeast
of Pisco.*

Tucked into the folds of the Andes, 2,740 meters (8,987 feet) up on the
slopes, Ayacucho is a colorful, colonial-style town. Though its looks are
Spanish—all glowing white-alabaster mansions with elegant columns
and arches—it's primarily an Indian town inhabited by people who still
speak Quechua as a first language and don traditional costume for their
daily routine. Visitors are greeted with some amazement (and lots of
warmth) in this city of 120,000 where artists are revered and celebrations like Carnaval and Semana Santa take place in a frenzy of activity
and energy. Religion is a serious pursuit, too, in this city of churches,
where more than 50 sanctuaries beckon worshippers at all hours.

Civilization in Peru began in the valleys around Ayacucho about
20,000 years ago. Dating back this far are the oldest human remains
in the country—and perhaps in the Americas—found in a cave network
at Piquimachay, 24 km (15 mi) west of the city. Over the centuries, the
region was home to many pre-Hispanic cultures, including the Huari
(Wari), who set up their capital of Huari 22 km (14 mi) from Ayacucho
some 13,000 years ago. When the Inca arrived in the 15th century, they
ruled the lands from their provincial capital at Vilcashuamán.

The Spanish came and conquered the reigning Inca tribes, and Francisco Pizarro founded Ayacucho in 1540. First named Huamanga for
the local *huamanga* (alabaster) used in handicrafts, Ayacucho grew
from a small village into a broad city known for its many colonial-style
churches. Nearly 300 years later it was the center of Peru's rebellion

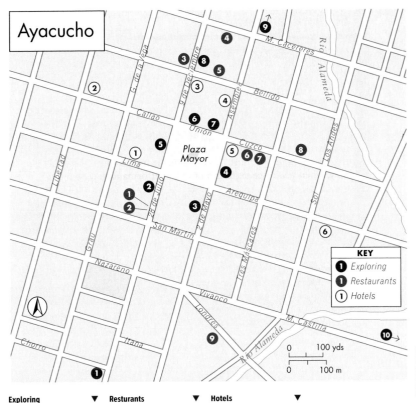

Ayacucho

CLOSE UP

Sendero Luminoso

Searching for the "Shining Path" to Peru's future, from 1980 to the mid-'90s, the revolutionary group Sendero Luminoso held Peru in the grip of a conflict that crippled governments and the economy and saw human rights abuses committed by all sides.

Fighting what they considered a Marxist revolutionary war, Sendero Luminoso first formed in the 1960s under the guidance of philosophy professor Abimael Guzman. Yet it was not until 1980, when democracy returned to Peru after 12 years of military rule, that the Sendero officially launched their "revolutionary war." Refusing to take part in the 1980 elections, the first revolutionary act of Sendero Luminoso was to burn ballot boxes in Ayacucho. By late 1981 the country was in a State of Emergency.

Sendero's philosophy was a form of extreme Marxism. Based in the countryside, with their stronghold in the highlands around Ayacucho, they aimed to replace the country's political structure with a peasant revolutionary regime. They carried out assassinations of political figures, planted bombs in cities such as Lima, and spread fear throughout the country through macabre techniques such as hanging dead dogs from lampposts, with signs around their necks spreading the Sendero message.

Claiming to fight for Peru's peasant communities, Sendero Luminoso instead committed more atrocities against those they claimed to represent than they did against the "enemy." Villages in the Peruvian highlands under Sendero control were purged, after "popular trials" of anyone connected with capitalist economy such as trade unionists, civic leaders, and managers of farming collectives. Brutality soon became associated with the Sendero's "shining" path.

As the Sendero gained more territory, the government response to the violence was no better. The military were given arbitrary powers and human rights violations and massacres committed by the military against the peasant population are well documented. The government also armed various groups, called "rondas," within peasant communities in an effort to get them to fight the Sendero themselves, all of which contributed to the escalation of brutal violence.

In the report released by the Truth and Reconcilliation commission in 2003, nearly 70,000 people were found to have been murdered or "disappeared" during the conflict. Approximately half the victims were attributed to Shining Path, and one third to government security forces.

The Dancer Upstairs, a film directed by John Malkovich, is a fascinating look at the search for, and capture of, Sendero Luminoso leader Abizmael Guzman. Guzman was captured in 1992, and with his capture the Sendero's struggle largely ended, although there have been random actions carried out as recently as 2005.

Perhaps soon to be joining Guzman in jail is former President Alberto Fujimori, who spearheaded the fight against the Sendero. After many years of seeking his extradition from Chile, in 2007 the Peruvian government was finally able to bring Fuijimori back to Peru to stand trial on corruption and human rights charges.

–By Katy Morrison

for independence from the Spanish, when the Peruvian army led by Antonio José de Sucre defeated the last Spanish at nearby Quinua on December 9, 1824. The first bells of Peru's independence were sounded at the Iglesia Santo Domingo in Ayacucho.

It took a century more before the city built its first road links west to the coast, and the road to Lima went unpaved through the 1960s. Ayacucho might have opened to tourism then, but for the influence of Abimael Guzmán, a philosophy teacher at the University of Huamanga who set up the Sendero Luminoso (Shining Path) here. From March 1982, when bombs and gunfire first sounded through the cobbled streets, thousands of Ayacuchanos fled or were killed during fighting between the Shining Path and the government. The city was nearly cut off from the rest of Peru during the early 1990s. Guzmán was finally arrested in 1992 and the Sendero Luminoso dismantled, but even with stability tourism has been slow to establish itself outside of semana Santa and the city receives only about a thousand visitors a month.

Ayacucho's resulting isolation from the modern world means that to visit is to step back into colonial days. Elegant white huamanga buildings glow in the sunlight, bright flowers spilling out of boxes lining high, narrow, wooden balconies. ■ **TIP→Beyond the slim, straight roads and terra-cotta roofs, cultivated fields climb the Andes foothills up to the snow.** Electricity, running water, and phones are unreliable, if even available. Banks and businesses are hidden in 16th-century *casonas* (colonial mansions). Women in traditional Quechua shawls draped over white blouses, their black hair braided neatly, stroll through markets packed with small fruit, vegetable, and craft stalls.

8

GETTING AROUND
Most of the city can be explored on foot as most tourist amenities, hotels, restaurants, and the bulk of the churches and colonial buildings are within a few blocks of the Plaza de Armas. Getting to out-of-the-way workshops in Santa Ana and La Libertad requires a quick cab ride. Basic city tours (S/0.20) offered at every agency depart daily and will save you much of the hassle.

Ayacucho's Alfredo Mendivil Duarte Airport is 4 km (2½ mi) from the city. You can take a taxi (about S/4), or catch a bus or colectivo from the Plaza de Armas, which will deliver you about a half block from the airport.

ESSENTIALS
AIRPORT **Alfredo Mendivil Duarte Airport** (✉ *Ejercito 950* ☎ *066/812–088*).

BUS **Ayacucho Tours** (✉ *Cáceres 880* ☎ *066/813–532*). **Cruz del Sur** (✉ *Av. Mariscal Caceres 1264* ☎ *066/812–813*). **Expresa Molina** (✉ *Cápac 273* ☎ *066/311–348 or 066/312–984*). **Los Libertadores** (✉ *Máscaras* ☎ *066/813–614*). **Ormen[ac]o** (✉ *Libertad 257* ☎ *066/312–495*).

CURRENCY **Banco de Crédito** (✉ *28 de Julio y San Martín* ⊕ *www.viabcp.com*).

INTERNET **Instituto Pacifico** (✉ *Callao 106* ☎ *066/814–299*).

MAIL   Serpost (⊠Asamblea 295 ☎066/312–224).

VISITOR INFO   La Dirección General de Industria y Turismo (⊠Asamblea 481 ☎066/812–548). Ministerio de Turismo Ayacucho (⊠Asamblea 400 ☎066/912–548). iPerú (⊠Portal Municipal 48, Plaza Mayor ☎066/318–305).

WHAT TO SEE

❶ In Casona Vivanco on the Plaza Mayor, the 17th-century **Museo Cáceres** honors Andrés Cáceres, an Ayacucho resident and former Peruvian president best known for his successful guerrilla leadership during the 1879–83 War of the Pacific against Chile. His Cáceres Museum is one of the city's best-preserved historic mansions, which today protects a mix of military memorabilia and ancient local artifacts, including stone carvings and ceramics. Note the gallery of colonial-style paintings. ⊠28 de Julio 508 ☎066/326–166 🖼S/4 ⊙Mon.–Sat. 8–noon and 2–6.

❸ Across from the Iglesia Merced on the Plaza Mayor, you'll see the colonial-style **Casa Jaúregui.** The Jaúregui House is an art gallery with paintings, sculptures, and local crafts by Peruvian artists. ⊠Plaza Mayor ☎No phone 🖼S/4 ⊙Weekdays 9–noon and 3–5, Sat. 9–1.

❷ You can't miss the ocher-color, baroque-style exterior of **La Compañía de Jesús.** The towers were added a century after the main building, which has religious art and a gilt altar. ⊠Jr. 28 de Julio y Lima ☎No phone 🖼Free ⊙Mass time.

❺ The **Prefectura,** or Boza and Solis House, is tucked into a 1748, two-story casona historica (historic mansion). Local independence-era heroine María Prado de Bellido was held prisoner in the Prefecture's patio room until her execution by firing squad in 1822. ⊠28 de Julio ☎No phone 🖼S/2 ⊙Daily 8–6.

❻ The **Museo de Arte Popular Joaquín López Antay,** in the Casona Chacón on the Plaza Mayor, has some of the region's best art. The exquisite and valuable collections include clay sculptures, silver filigree, retables, and paintings. Trace the town's history, as well as the craftsmanship behind many pieces, through photo exhibits. ■TIP→Note the gathering of looms used to weave lamb and alpaca wool into textiles and clothing. The Museum of Popular Art shares the Casona with the Banco de Credito in one of the city's best-preserved colonial-style mansions. ⊠Unión 28 ☎066/812–467 🖼Free ⊙Mon.–Sat. 9–12:30 and 2–5.

❽ The 1548 **Iglesia Santo Domingo** is now a national monument. The first bells ringing out Peru's independence from the Spanish after the Battle of Ayacucho were sounded from here. Byzantine towers and Roman arches mark the church's facade. ⊠Jr. 9 de Diciembre y Bellido ☎No phone 🖼Free ⊙Mass time.

OFF THE BEATEN PATH   **Huari.** The wide plains that make up the 300-hectare (740-acre) Santuario Histórico Pampas de Ayacucho are scattered with relics of the Huari culture, which evolved 500 years before that of the Inca. Huari was its capital, thought to have once been home to 60,000 or more residents, and its surrounding fields contain a maze of tumbled stone temples, homes, and 12-meter (39-foot) walls. This is believed to have been the first urban walled settlement in the Andes, created by a civilization whose livelihood was based on such metalworking feats as bronze weapons and gold and silver jewelry. A small museum displays skeleton bits and samples of ceramics and textiles; opening times are at the whim of the workers. You can get here cheaply from Barrio Magdalena in Ayacucho via irregular buses, which continue to Quinua and Huanta for S/3. Most travel agents in town offer guided tours to the site for around S/60. ⊠*22 km (14 mi) southeast of Ayacucho* 🕾*No phone* ⌨*Site: free; museum: S/3* 🕙*Ruins: daily 8–6; museum: hrs vary.*

➒ On display at the **Museo de Arqeología y Antropología Hipólito Unánue**, at the Centro Cultural Simón Bolívar, are regional finds from the Moche, Nazca, Ica, Inca, Canka, Chavín, and Chimu cultures. Highlights of the Hipólito Unánue Archaeology and Anthropology Museum include ceremonial costumes, textiles, everyday implements, and even artwork from some of the area's oldest inhabitants. The museum is locally referred to as Museo INC. ⊠*Av. Independencia* 🕾*066/812–360* ⌨*S/4* 🕙*Mon.–Sat. 8:30–11 and 2–5.*

➐ Built in 1550 and now the home of the Escuela de Bellas Artes (School of Fine Arts), the **Palacio de Marqués de Mozobamba** is one of the city's oldest structures. The colonial-era, baroque-style architecture includes *portales* (stone arches) in front and a monkey shaped stone fountain in the courtyard. ■**TIP→**Notice the Andean carvings of snakes, cougars, and lizards etched into the stone. Two Inca stone walls were discovered in 2003 during restorations. ⊠*Unión 47* 🕾*No phone* ⌨*Free* 🕙*Weekdays 10–4.*

➍ Walk through the plaza gardens and you'll immediately spot the twin brick bell towers of the 1612 Ayacucho **Catedral**, built by Bishop Don Cristóbal de Castilla y Zamora. Step inside to view the cathedral's carved altars with gold-leaf designs, a silver tabernacle, and an ornate wooden pulpit. Look for the plaque inside the entrance that quotes from Pope John Paul II's speech during his visit in 1985. The **Museo de Arte Religioso** exhibits antique objects from the sanctuary's early days, carvings of saints, and religious paintings; ask for visiting privileges if the doors are locked. During Semana Santa, the church hosts an extremely popular Palm Sunday candlelight procession with a statue of Christ transported on the back of a white donkey. ⊠*Asemblea* 🕾*No phone* ⌨*Free* 🕙*Church: Mass time; museum: Mon., Tues., and Sat. 9–noon and 3–5, Fri. 9–noon and 4–7.*

➓ At the end of the airport runway, the enormous **Cementerio Municipal** looks like a huge condo with multiple walls of crypts. Many of the sites date from the 1970s and 1980s, when the Sendero Luminoso held the region hostage. ⊠*End of airport runway* 🕾*No phone* ⌨*Free* 🕙*Daily 8–6.*

OFF THE BEATEN PATH

Vilcashuamán and Intihuatana. Four long hours south of Ayacucho on winding, unpaved roads is the former Inca provincial capital of Vilcashuamán, set where the north–south Inca highway crossed the east–west trade road from Cusco to the Pacific. You can still see the double-seated

8

throne and a five-tiered platform surrounded by stepped fields once farmed by Inca. An hour's walk from Vilcashuamán (or a half-hour's walk south past the main road from Ayacucho) is Inhuatana, where Inca ruins include a palace and tower beside a lagoon. Former Inca baths, a sun temple, and a sacrificial altar are also on the grounds. Check out the unusual 17-angled boulder, one of the odd building rocks that are an Inca hallmark. Ayacucho travel agencies can organize tours of both sites (S/65), or you can catch a bus or *colectivo* (small van) from Avenida Castilla on Tuesday, Thursday, and Saturday. If you take public transport, you'll have to stay overnight, as vehicles return on alternate days.

WHERE TO EAT

Outside of a few international restaurants catering to visiting tourists Ayacucho stands by its Andean specialties. The city is famous for its filling, flavorful *puca picante* (a peanutty pork-and-potato stew), served with rice and topped with a parsley sprig. ■TIP→The city's favorite **drink is the hot, creamy, pisco-spiked ponche (flavored with milk, cinnamon, cloves, sesame, peanuts, walnuts, and sugar).** The best time to sample this popular concoction is during Semana Santa. In the first week of November, Ayacuchanos are busy baking sweet breads shaped like horses, *caballos,* and babies, *guaguas,* to place in baskets for the spirits at the family gravesites. You'll find inexpensive restaurants where you can grab a cheap *almuerzo* (lunch) along Jirón San Martin. Many restaurants are closed on Sunday.

¢   33 ✗**Antonino's.** The glow of the brick oven on the rows of Chilean reds bathe the small Italian restaurant with a cozy, romantic feel. Pizzas and pastas are a safe bet, especially if you've been stuck eating regional dishes for awhile. ⊠*Cusco 144* 🕾*No phone* ▤*No credit cards.*

¢   ✗**La Brasa Roja.** Pollos a la brasa, or Peruvian rotisserie chicken, is the specialty at the tiny La Brasa Roja that's lost among the cheap hotel cafes on Jr. Cusco. Choose between a quarter, half, or whole chicken with fries and salad. ⊠*Cusco 180* 🕾*No phone* ▤*No credit cards.*

¢-$ ✗**La Casona.** Dining in this Spanish-style home is like attending an intimate, upscale party in a fine hacienda. Soft music wafts between high walls lined with paintings and woven textiles, while conversations ebb and flow at a low hum. The scent of fresh flowers decorating the glass-topped tables mixes with the delicious aromas of Peruvian specialties like *puca picante* (pork and potatoes in red sauce) and *tortas* (sweet cakes). ⊠*Bellindo 463* 🕾*No phone* ▤*MC, V.*
★

¢   ✗**Lalo's café.** Lalo's is a modern patio café with coffees, teas, pastries, and light meals. It's much more Parisian and much less Ayacucho, which attracts the city's well-to-do and NGO workers in the mornings and evenings. ⊠*Jr. 28 de Julio 178* 🕾*066/311–331* ▤*V.*

¢   ✗**Mia Pizza.** You'll make friends at this dinner-only spot where patrons sit side by side at wooden tables to snack on Italian fare. You can't miss with the pizza, cooked in an authentic wood-burning oven. The cheesy cannelloni and hearty spaghetti are also good bets. ⊠*Jr. Asembla 138* 🕾*066/311–283* ⊗*No lunch* ▤*No credit cards.*

DID YOU KNOW?

Native cultures from the Ayacucho region have been perfecting their textile skills for some 3,000 years.

¢ ✕**El Monasterio.** You can sit under the stars in the pleasant colonial courtyard at the Centro Turistico San Cristobal de Huamanga, home to several excellent restaurants and cafés, shops, and galleries. The best is El Monasterio in the near corner, which cooks up regional specialties like *puca picante* (pork-and-potato stew) and roasted cuy. ⊠*Jr. 28 de Julio 178 int 116* ☏*No phone* ⊟*V.*

¢–$ ✕**Niños.** The building is old Spanish style, but the food is modern, ranging in flavors from the meaty Andes *parrillada* (grill) to pasta and sandwiches. Come on weekends to catch bands that rock the crowd. The restaurant is across the street from the Iglesia Santo Domingo. ⊠*9 de Diciembre 205* ☏*066/814–537* ⊟*V.*

¢ ✕**Restaurant Los Alamos.** This popular backpacker hangout begins the day with serious breakfasts: hearty egg and meat dishes, pancakes, sweet breads, and the like. After dark, huge dinners, such as *pollo a la brasa* (roasted chicken) and *tallarin verdes* (noodles with pesto) are often accompanied by local bands crooning crowd favorites. ⊠*Cusco 215* ☏*066/312–782* ⊟*No credit cards.*

¢ ✕**Restaurant Urpicha.** Eating here feels like you're having dinner at
Fodor's Choice grandma's. Meals are lovingly (and slowly) prepared, but worth the
★ wait. The kitchen turns out such traditional Andean specialties as grilled cuy (guinea pig) and *puca picante,* potatoes in a spicy sauce with peanuts, rice, and pork. Drop by on a weekend to hear the best local folk groups. ⊠*Londres 272* ☏*066/313–905* ⊟*No credit cards.*

WHERE TO STAY

¢ ⌨**La Colmena Hotel.** Though the rooms are small, the quiet and pleasant courtyard make this one of the city's most popular budget options. Rooms, with plain furniture and local art, come with or without baths; hot water runs only in the morning. Rooms in the back tend to be dingy and lack light, so try for the ones facing the street. **Pros:** Great regional restaurant, close to plaza. **Con:** Dingy bathrooms. ⊠*Cusco 140* ☏*066/311–318* ⇆*18 rooms, 12 with private bath* ⌕*In-room: no TV. In-hotel: parking (no fee), no elevator* ⊟*No credit cards.*

¢ ⌨**Hotel Condeduque.** This modern hotel on a pedestrian only street lacks character, but the good price, modern amenities like clean rooms, tiled floors, TVs, Wi-Fi, and phones make up for it. The sleek upstairs mirador has nice views of the city. **Pros:** Clean, new. **Cons:** On a noisy street, better hotels for the price. ⊠*Jr. Asamblea 159* ☏*066/316–231* ⊕*www.hotelelcondeduque.com* ⊠*066/315–952* ⇆*12 rooms* ⌕*In-hotel: restaurant, laundry service, public Internet* ⊟*V* ❍*BP.*

$ ⌨**Hotel Plaza Ayacucho.** The city's most expensive hotel is in a gracious colonial building partly overlooking the Plaza Mayor. Spacious gardens and opulent sitting areas belie the modest rooms with worn carpet and nicked modern furnishings. The best (and quietest) accommodations are on the second floor, where there's a view of the terra-cotta roofs and the courtyard. You can request a balcony over the plaza, but beware the ever-present commotion outside—especially on Sunday and during festivals. **Pros:** Some rooms overlook plaza, the place to stay for Semana Santa. **Cons:** Room quality varies, stuffy atmosphere. ⊠*Jr. 9 de Diciembre 184* ☏*066/312–202* ⊠*066/312–314* ⇆*84 rooms* ⌕*In-hotel: restaurant, room service, no elevator* ⊟*AE, MC, V* ❍*BP.*

¢ ⊞**Hotel San Francisco de Paula.** At this Spanish mansion, local charm is threaded throughout the winding rooms and public areas, decorated with folk-art pieces, textiles, and crafts. Antique furnishings bring the colonial era to life, but modern room amenities like TVs and refrigerators pour on 21st-century comfort. Book a room with a balcony to enjoy the local street scene below, or dine at the rooftop restaurant for views of the city and mountains. **Pros:** Nice views of city and hills, regional art everywhere. **Cons:** Plain rooms, tacky bedspreads. ⊠*Callao 290* ⊞*066/312–353 or 066/960–3086* ⊕*www.hotelsanfranciscodepaula.com* ↩*40 rooms* ♿*In-room: refrigerator. In-hotel: restaurant, bar, laundry service, parking (no fee), no elevator* ⊟*AE, DC, MC, V* ⌾*BP.*

¢ ⊞**Hotel Santa Maria.** The only bad news in this charming new hotel is that it's three blocks from the plaza. Otherwise the blend of colonial style with modern features and bold colors make it one of the best options in Ayacucho. Wood floors and Andean décor flush out the guest rooms, while a contemporary theme runs throughout the hotel. **Pros:** Cosmopolitan vibe, great price. **Cons:** Steep walk to the plaza, doesn't feel like Ayacucho. ⊠*Jr. Arequipa 320* ⊞*066/314–988* ⊕*www.hotelesjian.com.pe* ↩*22 rooms* ♿*In-hotel: restaurant, bar, room service, pool table, laundry service, public Internet* ⊟*AE, MC, V* ⌾*BP.*

¢ ⊞**Hotel Santa Rosa.** Near the plaza, this pleasant little hotel has a pretty courtyard with gardens and a brick walkway. Rooms have a mix of antiques, handmade fabrics, and contemporary furnishings, plus unexpected modern amenities like TVs and phones. Private bathrooms have hot water only morning and evening. **Pros:** Beautiful courtyard, good restaurant, local charm with a modern feel. **Cons:** Hot water isn't all day, room sizes vary. ⊠*Lima 166* ⊞*066/314–614* ⊕*www.hotelsantarosa.com* ↩*26 rooms* ♿*In-hotel: restaurant, bar, laundry service, parking (no fee)* ⊟*V* ⌾*BP.*

NIGHTLIFE

Peña Macha (⊠*Grau 158* ⊞*No phone*) is a disco during the week but has folkloric shows and live music on weekends. At **Taberna El Buho** (⊠*Jr. 9 de Diciembre 284* ⊞*No phone*), kick back with a pisco sour and listen to '80s rock, before getting the nerve to run upstairs to sing karaoke. Admire the local art on the walls and dozens of upside-down black umbrellas on the ceiling while grabbing a drink or pizza at the **Taberna Magía Negra** (⊠*Cáceres y Vega* ⊞*No phone*).

SHOPPING

Ayacucho is the home of many of Peru's best artists, whom you can often visit at work in their neighborhood shops or galleries. Look for retablos, the multitiered, three-dimensional displays of plaster characters in scenes of the city's famed religious processions and historic battles. Good markets are in the city's outskirts, such as the busy Mercado Domingo (Sunday Market) in Huanta, an hour north.

Ayacucho's produce and meat market is the **Mercado Andrés Vivanco** (⊠*Jr. 28 de Julio* ⊞*No phone*), found behind the Arco del Triunfo in a one-story building. Shops continue for several streets behind the main building.

The Santa Ana neighborhood is a famous **weaving area,** where you can visit local artists and their galleries. In particular, look for the complex *tejidos* (textiles), which have elaborate—and often pre-Hispanic—motifs that can take more than a half-year to design and weave. These creations, made of natural fibers and dyes, can cost US$200 or more for high-quality work. **Familia Sulca** (⊠ *Cáceres 302* ☎ *No phone*) is known for its beautiful carpets. **Galería Latina** (⊠ *Plazuela Santa Ana 105* ☎ *066/528–315*) is the workshop of world-renowned weaver Alejandro Gallardo. Internationally famous weaver Edwin Sulca Lagos works out of **Las Voces del Tapiz** (⊠ *Plazuela Santa Ana 82* ☎ *066/914–242*).

Elsewhere in Santa Ana, intricate alabaster, or Huamanga stone, carvings are the specialty of **Jose Gálvez** (⊠ *Jeruslaén 12* ☎ *066/814–278*).

Many famous retablo artists live in Ayacucho, particularly around the neighborhood known as Barrio La Libertad. **Artesanías Helme** (⊠ *Bellido 463* ☎ *No phone*) has a selection of retablos and other art with delicate depictions of Andean life and religious scenes. **Artesanías Huamanguina Pascualito** (⊠ *Cusco 136* ☎ *066/811–013*) has an extensive collection of carvings. **Ohalateria Artesanías** (⊠ *Plaza de Armas* ☎ *No phone*), in the center of town, is a good place to begin studying the delicate collections. Workshops owned by the artist family **Urbano** (⊠ *Peru 308 and 330* ☎ *No phone*) are among the best places to find finely crafted retablos. In Barrio Belén, members of the **Familia Pizarro** (⊠ *San Cristóbal 215* ☎ *No phone*) carve *piedra huamanga* (alabaster sculptures) and weave fine textiles. The widest selection of handicrafts in Ayacucho, from retablos to sweaters, can be found at **Mercado Artesanal Shosaku Nagase** (⊠ *Plazoleta El Arco* ☎ *No phone*) about a kilometer north of the center.

The North Coast & Northern Highlands

WORD OF MOUTH

Magnificent places to visit are Kuelap in the city of Chachapoyas (take a plane from Lima or a bus from Chiclayo) and Chavin, in Huaraz.

—llello

WELCOME TO THE NORTH COAST & NORTHERN HIGHLANDS

TOP REASONS TO GO

★ **The Ancient World:** Along the coast, Chavín, Moche, and Chimú ruins date as far back as 3,000 BC. In the highlands are Wari sites, and Kuélap, a stunning complex built by the Chachapoyans a thousand years before Machu Picchu.

★ **Real Peru:** People are friendly, excited to talk to foreigners, and want to share their culture. The coast's warmer temperatures don't hurt either.

★ **Outdoor Adventure:** The highlands provide of trekking, climbing, and rafting, especially around Huaraz, where mountains soar above 6,000 meters (19,500 feet).

★ **Colonial Architecture:** The coastal city of Trujillo is one of the best places for colonial architecture. It's like walking into a time-warp, and you may feel inspired to wear a hoop skirt or starch your collar.

★ **Beaches:** The northern-most coast offers year-round sun, white-sand beaches, and a relaxed, tropical atmosphere, especially in Máncora and Punta Sal.

1 The North Coast. Explore almost unlimited archaeological sites, well-preserved colonial architecture, and relaxed beach towns with year-round sun and surf. Fresh seafood is abundant, the climate is warmer, and life is more relaxed.

The National Museum of the Royal Tombs of Sipan in Lambayeque.

Huaraz.

2 Huaraz & the Cordillera Blanca. Stunning snow-capped peaks, natural hot springs and incredible international food make this one of the north's most popular areas. With more than 40 peaks above 6,000 meters (19,500 feet) and the second highest peak in all the Americas, this provides spectacular views and outdoor activities.

3 The Northern Highlands. See a landscape almost untouched by the modern world, with farm pastures, mountains, and herds of cows, goats, and sheep in Cajamarca. Head to Chacapoyas, near the border of the Amazon, for extraordinary greenery and the astonishing ruins at Kuélap, often compared with Machu Picchu, but built more than a thousand years before.

GETTING ORIENTED

Travel from one geographic region to another is quite challenging and only recommended for those without time constraints. Instead, choose a region and explore accordingly: for the north coast: travel from archeological ruins to beach in a south–north direction; for Huaraz & the Cordillera Blanca, use the town of Huaraz as your focal point—from there discover glaciers, snow capped peaks, and natural hot springs; for the northern highlands, fly to Cajamarca to begin discovering the gateway to the Amazon.

9

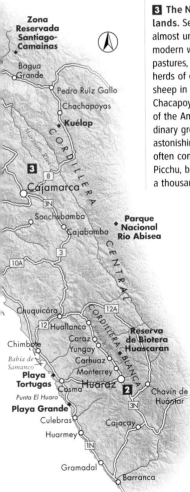

Zona Reservada Santiago-Camainas
Bagua Grande
Pedro Ruíz Gallo
Chachapoyas
Kuélap
CORDILLERA
Northern Rio
3
8
Cajamarca
3N
Sonchubamba
Cajabamba
CENTRAL
3
10A
Parque Nacional Río Abisea
Chuquicara
12A
12 Huallanca
CORDILLERA
Caraz
Chimbote
Yungay
Reserva de Biotera Huascaran
Bahía de Samanco
Carhuaz
Monterrey
BLANCA
Playa Tortugas
Casma
Huaraz
2
Punta El Huaro
3N
Chavin de Huántar
Playa Grande
Culebras
Cajacay
Huarmey
1N
Gramadal
Barranca

Cordillera Blanca.

THE NORTH COAST & NORTHERN HIGHLANDS PLANNER

Weather Wise

The weather along the north coast is always pleasant, although it's sunnier from November to May. The northern highlands weather is more capricious—rainy season is November to early May, while it's drier from mid-May to mid-September. September and October have fairly good weather, but occasional storms frighten off most mountaineers.

Health & Safety

Health. Use purified water for drinking and brushing your teeth. If you're out trekking, bring an extra bottle with you. Also, eat foods that have been thoroughly cooked or boiled. If vegetables or fruit are raw, be sure they're peeled.

Safety. In the big cities on the coast, be on your guard and take simple precautions, such as asking the concierge at the hotel to get you a taxi and carrying only the cash you need. In small coastal towns or in the highlands things are more secure, but be aware of your belongings at all times.

Altitude Sickness. In the highlands, especially Huaraz, relax for a few days and drink lots of water to avoid dehydration and altitude sickness.

Getting Around

By Air: The easiest way to get around is by plane. You'll definitely want to fly to destinations like Piura and Cajamarca. Lan (⊕ www.lan.com), Star Peru (⊕ www.starperu.com), and Aero Cóndor (⊕ www.aerocondor.com.pe) fly to most cities in the region.

By Bus: Bus service throughout the region is generally quite good. Emtrafesa (⊕ www.deperu.com/emtrafesa) runs all the way up the coast. Other reputable companies for the coastal communities include Cruz del Sur (⊕ www.cruzdelsur.com.pe) and Expreso Chiclayo (☎ 074/233–071 in Chiclayo). For the highlands, Movil (⊕ www.deperu.com/emtrafesa) is a good choice. Whenever possible, pay for a bus-cama or semi-cama, which gets you an enormous seat that fully reclines, and waitress service that includes at least one meal and a movie.

By Car: Driving can be a challenge—locals rarely obey road rules—but a car is one of the best ways to explore the region. The Pan-American Highway serves the coast. From there take Highway 109 to Huaraz and Highway 8 to Cajamarca. Small reputable rental-car agencies are in Trujillo, Chiclayo, Piura, and Huaraz. Think twice before driving to archaeological sites; some are hard to find, and it's easy to get lost on the unmarked roads. Consider hiring a driver or taking a tour. Roads in the northern highlands are always in some disrepair.

By Taxi: Taxi rides in town centers should cost around S/3; rates go up at night. A longer ride to the suburbs or town environs costs from S/5 to S/10. Negotiate the price before you head off. Taxis hire out their services for specific places, ranging from $5 and up depending on the distance, or around US$100 for the entire day.

Restaurants & Hotels

The north coast has excellent seafood, while simpler, but equally delicious, meat-and-rice dishes are more common in highlands. Some of Trujillo's fancier restaurants expect you to dress up for dinner, but most spots along the coast are quite casual. Depending on the restaurant, the bill may include a 10% service charge. If not, a 10% tip is appropriate. Throughout the region, *almuerzo* (lunch) is the most important meal of the day. It's eaten around 2 PM. *Cena* (dinner) is normally a lighter meal.

Cities along the north coast, especially Trujillo and Chiclayo, have a wide range of lodgings, including large business hotels and converted colonial mansions. The latter, usually called *casonas,* offer personalized service not found in the larger hotels. In smaller towns, such as Barranca and Casma, luxury lodgings do not exist, but you'll have no problem finding a clean and comfortable room. The highlands have excellent lodges with horse stables and hot springs; you can also find family-run inns with simple, basic rooms. Assume hotels do not have air-conditioning unless otherwise indicated.

Finding a hotel room throughout the coastal and highlands areas ought to be painless throughout the year, although coastal resorts like Máncora and Punta Sal are often jammed in summer and holiday weeks. Sports enthusiasts head to Huaraz and Cajamarca in summer so make reservations early. Plan at least two months in advance if you want to travel during Easter and Christmas, when Peruvians take their holidays.

WHAT IT COSTS IN NUEVO SOLES

RESTAURANTS				
¢	$	$$	$$$	$$$$
under S/20	S/20–S/35	S/35–S/50	S/50–S/65	over S/65

HOTELS				
¢	$	$$	$$$	$$$$
under S/125	S/125–S/250	S/250–S/375	S/375–S/500	over S/500

Restaurant prices are per person for a main course. Hotel prices are for a standard double room, excluding tax.

North Coast Menu

The coast serves mostly fresh seafood, often cold—a refreshing meal on a hot day. The highlander diet consists of root vegetables, like yucca and potato, and a variety of meats, where all parts of an animal are eaten. Both regions have spicy and nonspicy meals, so ask first.

Cabrito con tacu-tacu: This dish of kid with grilled rice, usually served with beans, tastes like Peruvian comfort food. It's rich in flavor, but has no spice.

Cangrejo reventado: This stew consists of boiled crab, eggs, and onions. Often served with yucca, this is a fresh, spicy dish.

Ceviche de mococho: Ceviche made of algae for adventurous eaters. You really get a taste of the sea and, so they say, lots of protein.

Cuy: Eating guinea pig is one of the more popular dishes in Peru. It's a good but chewy meat usually served whole so you need to decide if this is something you want to see before eating.

Shámbar: Particular to Trujillo, this bean stew is a nice, semi-spicy meat alternative.

Parrilladas: At restaurants serving parrilladas (barbecues) you can choose from every imaginable cut of beef, including *anticucho* (beef heart) and *ubre* (cow udder).

9

DID YOU KNOW?

Peru's Cordillera Blanca has more that 50 peaks that soar above 18,000 ft. The highest peak in the contiguous United States reaches only 14,505 ft.

Updated by
Aviva Baff

The North Coast and Northern Highlands are the least traveled but most diverse areas of Peru. There are beaches, mountains, green fertile valleys, dry desert, and tremendous archaeological sites and museums. The region also has the least developed tourism industry and travel often requires time and patience.

Like the rest of Peru, there's incredible history behind the cities and towns you see today. First inhabited more than 13,000 years ago, the Chavín and Moche people later built colossal cities near the coast, to be replaced over time by civilizations like the Chimú and Chachapoyas. Eventually, all these were overtaken by the Incas, followed by the Spanish. Luckily, the extensive ruins and elaborate colonial-era mansions and churches are being preserved in many areas of the north.

A place of extraordinary natural beauty, the northernmost reaches of Peru have magnificent mountains, steep sea cliffs, and vast deserts. The steep, forested hills emerge from the highlands, and trekkers and climbers from around the world converge to hike the green valleys and ascend the rocky, snow-capped peaks towering more than 6,000 meters (19,500 feet) above the sea. The coast offers spectacular white-sand beaches, year-round sun, and an abundance of fresh seafood.

As Peru becomes a more popular international destination, tourism in the north is slowly awakening, but is still light years behind Machu Picchu and Lake Titicaca. Come now and explore the relatively virgin territory that provides a rich peek into the cultural, historical, and physical landscape of Peru.

THE NORTH COAST

From pyramids to sun-drenched beaches, the north coast offers great diversity in landscape, weather, and activities. The north coast was, until recently, largely ignored by foreign tourists, but all the way up this sun-drenched stretch of coastal desert you'll find plenty of places to explore and relax, including well-preserved colonial architecture, numerous ancient ruins, excellent restaurants, reasonable beach resorts, and a friendly and relaxed people.

Rich in history and filled with an astonishing number of archaeological sites, especially from Barranca to Piura, the northern coast redefines what is "old." Visit tombs, huge adobe cities, and unbelievable mummies. Explore museums filled with artifacts that date back to 3500 BC. In the far north, especially Mancora and Punta Sal, take off your watch and sink into the sand, soak up the sun, and eat up the luscious seafood.

GETTING AROUND

Once in a city, it's extremely easy to get around via taxis or tours; however, getting from city to city requires more planning. There are flights to Tumbes, Piura, or Trujillo from Lima, but not from city to city; the best option is to start by flying into a city and either rent a car or take one of the many frequent, but long bus rides to other towns.

BARRANCA

200 km (124 mi) northwest of Lima on Pan-American Hwy.

A nondescript town with little to visit except a large Chimú temple nearby, this is a stop for those who are either determined to see every archaeological site in Peru or do not have the time to go to Trujillo or Chiclayo, but would like to see some northern ruins. To get here, head north from Lima on the Pan-American Highway through the bleak, empty coastal desert, passing several dusty villages, and arriving in Barranca.

With its seven defensive walls, the gigantic temple at **Paramonga** is worth a look. A small museum has interesting displays on Chimú culture. The archaeological site sits just off the Pan-American Highway, about 3 km (2 mi) north of the turnoff for Huaraz. For a few dollars you can take a taxi to the ruins from the nearby town of Barranca. ⊠ *Pan-American Hwy.* ☎ *No phone* 💲 *S/5* ⊗ *Daily 8–6.*

WHERE TO STAY & EAT

¢–$ ✕**Don Goyo.** Here's the best restaurant option in Barranca, offering a large selection of pizza, pasta, and grilled meat dishes. On the menu is the requisite *pollo a la brasa* (rotisserie chicken), all pizzas are served with garlic bread, and regardless of what you order, it will come with a friendly smile. Fresh, homemade yogurts and cheeses are sold on the premises. ⊠ *Jr. Gálvez 506* ☎ *01/235–2378* ▭ *No credit cards.*

¢ 🖳**Hotel Chavin.** A full-service hotel at bargain prices, this is the best deal ⟳ in Barranca. The plain concrete six-story hotel provides wood-floored rooms (ask for one in the rear if noise is a concern) and a decent restaurant serving criollo food. The staff is well-trained and detail-oriented. To relax, dip into the pool and swim up to the poolside bar, the hotel's best feature. One of the few safe places to go out at night is the **Karaoke Hotel Chavin**, in back of the first floor. **Pros:** Extensive facilities for a low

9

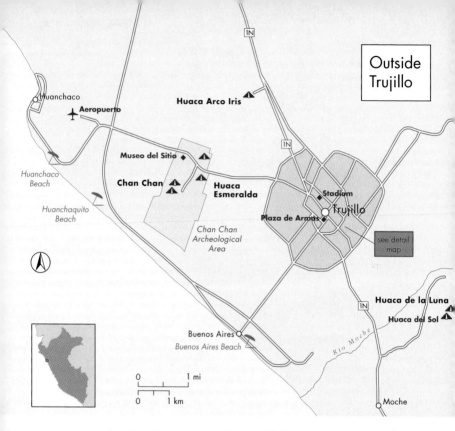

Outside
Trujillo

Huanchaco

Aeropuerto

Huaca Arco Iris

Huanchaco
Beach

Museo del Sitio

Chan Chan

Huaca
Esmeralda

Huanchaquito
Beach

Chan Chan
Archeological
Area

Stadium

Trujillo

Plaza de Armas

see detail
map

Huaca de la Luna

Huaca del Sol

Buenos Aires
Buenos Aires Beach

Rio Moche

0   1 mi

0   1 km

Moche

price. **Cons:** Location is on highly-trafficked main road. ✉ *Jr. Gálvez 222* ☎ *01/235–2358 or 01/235–2253* 🖷 *044/235–2480* ⊕ *www.hotelchavin. com.pe* 🛏 *73 rooms* ♿ *In-room: Wi-Fi. In-hotel: restaurant, Wi-Fi, pool, playground, parking (no fee)* ⊟ *DC, MC, V.*

CASMA

170 km (105 mi) north of Paramonga.

Once known as the "City of Eternal Sun," Casma, like Lima, is now subject to cloudy winters and sunny summers. However, with its leafy Plaza de Armas and a number of pleasant parks, it makes the best base for visiting the nearby ruins. If you're not into the archaeology thing, you might not want to include Casma in your itinerary.

The origins of **Sechín**, one of the country's oldest archaeological sites dating from around 1600 BC, remain a mystery. It's not clear what culture built this coastal temple, but the bas-relief carvings ringing the main temple, some up to 4 meters (13 feet) high, graphically depict triumphant warriors and their conquered, often beheaded enemies. The site was first excavated in 1937 by the archaeologist J. C. Tello. It has since suffered from looters and natural disasters. Archaeologists are still

CLOSE UP

Northern Journeys

EXPLORING THE ANCIENTS

If seeing the important archaeological sites, ruins and museums are your main priority, start your journey in Trujillo and the important Moche pyramids of the Huaca de la Luna and Huaca del Sol, as well as Chán Chán, built by the Chimú people (but be sure to take at least a day to walk around and enjoy the spectacular colonial architecture). From here, head north to Chiclayo and peer into the Tomb of Sipán and explore world-class historical museums. If you can extend your trip past a week, probably for another four to five days, take the bus from Chiclayo to Chachapoyas and visit Kuélap, a precursor to Mach Picchu built over one thousand years before.

EXPLORING THE OUTDOORS

If you want to see the spectacular mountains of the highlands, head up (and up and up) to the mountain town of Huaraz. Drink water and take a day or so to acclimatize to the altitude,

taking in the local sights and hot springs. Take a three-day trek around the Cordillera Blanca. Discuss the numerous options with your guide. If you can extend your trip past a week, head to Trujillo to enjoy the architecture and ruins (see Exploring the Ancients). Note: you can fly to Huaraz, but there's only one flight per week so it takes careful advance planning.

REST & RELAXATION

If you want to take a week to relax, fly from Lima to Piura, walk around the city, eat in one of the excellent restaurants, and sleep in one of the first-rate hotels. After a relaxing breakfast at your hotel (almost always included in the price of your room), head to Máncora or Punta Sal for the next few days. Regardless of where you stay, you'll be able to relax on the beach or poolside, and—if you're inspired to get out of your beach chair—to go on a fishing trip, learn to surf or try the even more adventurous kite-surfing.

9

excavating here, so access to the central plaza is not permitted. ■**TIP→** A trail leading up a neighboring hill provides good views of the temple complex, and the surrounding valley. A small museum has a good collection of Chavín ceramics and a mummy that was found near Trujillo. To get to the ruins, head southeast from Casma along the Pan-American Highway for about 3 km (2 mi), turning east onto a paved road leading to Huaraz. The ruins sit about 2 km (1¼ mi) past the turnoff. ☎*No phone* ✉*S/6, includes admission to Pañamarca* ☉*Daily 8–6.*

Several other ruins are near the town of Casma, but the heavily weathered Mochica city of **Pañamarca** is what to see after Sechín. Located 10 km (6 mi) from the Pan-American Highway on the road leading to Nepeña, Pañamarca has some interesting murals. If they're not visible right away, ask a guard to show you as they are often closed off. A taxi will take you to the ruins for about S/20 an hour. Negotiate the price before you leave. ☎*No phone* ✉*S/6, includes admission to Sechín* ☉*Daily 8–6.*

WHERE TO STAY & EAT

¢ ✗**El Tío Sam.** The best restaurant in Casma, this local favorite serves just about every type of seafood imaginable. The *arroz chaufa con mariscos* (shellfish with Chinese-style fried rice) is especially good, but if you're not in the mood for seafood, try the *cebiche de pato*. This isn't traditional ceviche, but cooked duck, served with rice, yucca, and beans. Don't be put off by the cement floor—the restaurant lacks polish, but it serves good food. ⊠*Av. Huarmei 138* ☎*043/411–447* 🖃*No credit cards.*

¢ 🏨**El Farol.** A respite from the dusty streets, gardens surround this pleasant hotel. Although the rooms have unsightly fluorescent lights, they're comfortable and affordable. The bamboo-walled restaurant specializes in seafood and looks onto the center gardens. **Pros:** Calm and natural beauty transports you away from the city. **Cons:** Service is a little too calm and requires patience. ⊠*Av. Túpac Amaru 450* ☎☎*043/411–064* ✍*hostalelfarol@hotmail.com* ⮐*24 rooms, 4 suites, 1 bungalow* 🛏*In-room: no phone. In-hotel: restaurant, pool, gym, laundry service, parking (no fee)* 🖃*V.*

PLAYA TORTUGAS

20 km (12 mi) north of Casma.

An easy drive from the Sechín area, this small beach is a more low-key base to explore the nearby ruins. ■**TIP➔** A ghost town in winter, it's much more pleasant, in terms of both weather and people, in summertime. The stony beach, in a perfectly round cove, surrounded by brown hills, looks drab and offers limited hotel and restaurant options, but with its fleet of fishing boats and pleasant lapping waves, it's a relaxing destination.

WHERE TO STAY

¢ 🏨**Hospedaje Las Terrazas.** A pleasant stone walkway leads from the lobby to the bamboo-ceilinged rooms. They have basic, clean rooms, each with a terrace and view of the bay. Make sure you're around for the exhilarating sunset viewing, but also take a look at the back of the hotel, where the black hills turn an eerie orange. **Pros:** Excellent views and relaxed atmosphere. **Cons:** Bland furnishing and service. ⊠*Caleta Norte, Playa Tortuga* ☎*043/961–9042* ⊕*www.lasterrazas.com* ⮐*8 rooms* 🛏*In-room: no phone, no TV. In-hotel: restaurant, parking (no fee)* 🖃*V* 🍽*CP.*

TRUJILLO

561 km (350 mi) northwest of Lima on Pan-American Hwy.

The well-preserved colonial architecture, pleasant climate, and archeological sites have made Trujillo a popular tourist destination. The Plaza de Armas and beautifully maintained colonial buildings make central Trujillo a delightful place to while away an afternoon. Occupied for centuries before the arrival of the Spaniards, ruins from the Moche and

Tours

Condor Travel and Guía Tours both organize tours to the ruins around Trujillo. Clara Bravo and Michael White are great guides for Trujillo, and also lead trips farther afield. Sipán Tours is one of Chiclayo's best tour companies for trips to the Tomb of Señor Sipán.

There are many tour companies in Huaraz; Monttrek is among the best, arranging rafting, trekking, and mountain-climbing expeditions. Clarin Tours is said to be one of Cajamarca's best. In Piura, call Piura Tours.

In Chachapoyas, contact Vilaya Tours. The company arranges tours to Kuélap, as well as the remote ruins of Gran Vilaya, which requires a 31-km (19-mi) hike, and to the Pueblo de Los Muertos, which requires a 23-km (14-mi) hike.

Contacts: **Clara Bravo and Michael White** (⊠ *Cahuide 495, Trujillo* ☎ *044/243–347* ⊕ *www.xanga. com/trujilloperu*). **Condor Travel** (⊠ *Jr. Independencia 553, Trujillo* ☎ *044/254–763* ⊕ *www.condortravel. com*). **Clarin Tours** (⊠ *Del Batán 161, Cajamarca* ☎ *076/366–829* ⊕ *www.clarintours.com*). **Guía Tours** (⊠ *Jr. Independencia 580, Trujillo* ☎ *044/245–170* ⊕ *www.guiatours. com.pe*). **Monttrek** (⊠ *Av. Luzuriaga 646, Huaraz* ☎ *043/42–1121* ⊕ *www. monttrekperu.com*). **Piura Tours** (⊠ *Jr. Ayacucho 585, Piura* ☎ *073/326–778* ✉ *piuratours@speedy.com.pe*). **Sipán Tours** (⊠ *7 de Enero 772, Chiclayo* ☎ *074/229–053* ⊕ *www.sipantours. com*). **Vilaya Tours** (⊠ *Jr. Grau 624, Chachapoyas* ☎ *041/777–506* ⊕ *www.vilayatours.com*).

Chimú people are nearby, as is a decent museum. Combine this with a selection of excellent hotels, restaurants, and cafés, and you'll see why Trujillo, officially founded in 1534, competes with Arequipa for the title of Peru's "Second City." The only serious problem for tourists is trying to fit in the time to visit all the sights—literally, since many places close from 1 to 4 for lunch.

GETTING AROUND

Almost everything is within walking distance in the center of the city and for everything else there are reasonably priced taxis. If you don't have a car, ask your hotel to arrange for a taxi for the day or to tour a specific place. For the archaeological sights, another option is to join a day tour from a travel agency.

ESSENTIALS

CURRENCY **Scotia Bank** (⊠ *Pizarro 314* ☎ *044/256–600* ⊕ *www.scotiabank.com.pe*).

MAIL **Post Office** (⊠ *Av. Independencia 286* ☎ *044/245–941*). **DHL** (⊠ *Av. Pizarro 318* ☎ *044/233–630* ⊕ *www.dhl.com.pe*).

MEDICAL **Belén Hospital** (⊠ *Bolívar 350* ☎ *044/245–281*).

PHARMACY **Boticas Fasa** (⊠ *Jr. Pizarro 512* ☎ *044/899–028*).

RENTAL CAR **Trujillo Rent-a-Car** (⊠ *Prolongación Bolivia 293* ☎ *044/420–059*).

VISITOR INFO **iPerú** (⊠ *Jr. Pizarro 402* ☎ *044/294–561* ⊕ *www.peru.info*).

ARCHEOLOGICAL SITES

Begin your archaeological exploration at the **Museo del Sitio.** The entrance fee includes admission to the museum, plus Chán Chán, Huaca Arco Iris, and Huaca Esmeralda, so hold onto your ticket (you may also go directly to the ruins and purchase the same ticket there, for the same price). ■TIP➜ This small but thorough museum has displays of ceramics and textiles from the Chimú empire. From Trujillo, take a taxi or join a tour from an agency. Each location is a significant distance from each other. Guides are available at the entrance of each site for S/10 more (S/20 Chán Chán) and are strongly recommended. At the museum, and all sites listed below, there are clean restrooms and a cluster souvenir stalls and snack shops, but no place to buy a full meal. ⊠ *Carretera Huanchaco, 5 km (3 mi) northwest of Trujillo* 🕾 *044/206–304* 🏷 *S/11, includes admissionChán Chán, Huaca Arco Iris, and Huaca Esmeralda* 🕙 *Daily 9–4:30.*

Fodor'sChoice
★

Chán Chán. The sprawling adobe-brick capital city, whose ruins lie 5 km (3 mi) west of Trujillo, has been called the largest mud city in the world. It once held boulevards, aqueducts, gardens, palaces, and some 10,000 dwellings. Within the city were nine royal compounds, one of which, the royal palace of Tschudi, has been partially restored and opened to the public. Although the city began with the Moche civilization, 300 years later, the Chimú people took control of the region and expanded the city to its current size. Although less known than the Incas, who conquered them in 1470, the Chimú were the second-largest pre-Columbian society in South America. Their empire stretched along 1,000 km (620 mi) of the Pacific, from Lima to Tumbes.

Before entering this UNESCO World Heritage Site, see the extensive photographic display of the ruins at the time of discovery and postrestoration. Then, begin at the Tschudi complex, the Plaza Principal, a monstrous square where ceremonies and festivals were held. The throne of the king is thought to have been in front where the ramp is found. The reconstructed walls have depictions of sea otters at their base. From here, head deep into the ruins toward the royal palace and tomb of Señor Chimú. The main corridor is marked by fishnet representations, marking the importance of the sea to these ancient people. ■TIP➜ You will also find renderings of pelicans, which served as ancient road signs, their beaks pointing to important sections of the city. Just before you arrive at the Recinto Funerario, where the tomb of Señor Chimú is, you pass a small natural reservoir called a *huachaque,* 44 secondary chambers surround the *recinto funerario,* where the king Señor Chimú was buried. In his day it was understood that when you pass to the netherworld you can bring all your worldly necessities with you, and the king was buried with several live concubines and officials, and a slew of personal effects, most of which have been looted. Although wind and rain have damaged the city, its size—20 square km (8 square mi)—impresses.

Huaca Arco Iris. Filled with intriguing and unusual symbolic carvings, and with an urban backdrop, is the restored Huaca Arco Iris or Rainbow Pyramid. Named for the unusual rainbow carving (the area rarely

CLOSE UP

Which Culture Was That again?

The massive walls of Chan Chan, near Trujillo, once home to 10,000 dwellings.

It's a common question after a few days of exploring the extensive archaeological sites in the north. So many different civilizations were emerging, overlapping, and converging, that it can be difficult to keep track of them all.

Chavín: One of the earliest major cultures in northern Peru is the cat-worshipping Chavín. The Chavín empire stretched through much of Peru's northern highlands and along the northern and central coasts. Artifacts dating back to 850 BC tell us that the Chavín people were excellent artisans, and their pottery, with its florid, compact style, can be seen in the museums of Trujillo and Lima.

Moche: About 500 years later, a highly advanced civilization called the Moche emerged. It was their carefully planned irrigation systems, still in use today, which turned the desert into productive agricultural land. Their fine ceramics and large Moche pyramids, still standing near present-day Trujillo and Chiclayo, give us insight about their architectural advances and daily lives. Such oddities as dragon motifs are perhaps a testament to commerce and intercultural exchange between South America and Asia. Despite voracious *huaqueros*, or looters, the tomb of the Lord of Sipán, discovered in 1987, was intact and untouched, revealing more abut their complex culture.

Chimú to Inca: The Chimú came on the scene about AD 850. That civilization continued to conquer and expand until around 1470, when it, like most others in the area, was assimilated by the huge Inca empire. The awe-inspiring city of Chán Chán, built by the Chimú, sits near present-day Trujillo. Although the Inca center of power lay farther south in the Cusco–Machu Picchu area, its cultural influence stretched far beyond the northern borders of Peru and it was near present-day Tumbes that Pizarro, the Spanish pig farmer-turned-conquistador, first caught site of the glory of the Inca empire.

9

sees rain), it's also known as the Huaca El Dragón, or Pyramid of the Dragon, because of the central role dragons play in the friezes. ■TIP→ **This structure, built by the early Chimú, also has a repeating figure of a mythical creature that looks like a giant serpent.** On the walls, mostly reconstructions, you will see what many archaeologists believe are priests wielding the knives used in human sacrifices. Half-moon shapes the bottom of most of the friezes indicate that the Chimú probably worshipped the moon at this temple. ⊠ *Pan-American Hwy., 5 km (3 mi) north of Trujillo* ☎ *No phone* 🖅 *S/11, includes admission to Chán Chán, Huaca Esmeralda, and Museo del Sitio* ☉ *Daily 9–4:30.*

Huaca Esmeralda. Much like the other Chimú pyramids, the ruins' most interesting aspects are the carved friezes, unrestored and in their original state. The images include fish, seabirds, waves, and fishing nets, all central to the life of the Chimú. Like other Chimú pyramids on the northern coast, the ancient temple mound of Huaca Esmeralda, or the Emerald Pyramid, is believed to have served as a religious ceremonial center. The pyramid is in a dangerous area so go with a guide. ⊠ *Huanchaco Hwy., 2 km (1 mi) west of Trujillo* ☎ *No phone* 🖅 *S/11, includes admission to Chán Chán, Huaca Arco Iris, and Museo del Sitio* ☉ *Daily 9–4:30.*

Fodor'sChoice ★ **Huaca de la Luna & Huaca del Sol.** When you consider that these temples were built more than 3,000 years ago, the mud and adobe pyramids near the Pan-American Highway and Río Moche are quite impressive. The Moche people were the first to spread its influence over much of the north coast and all subsequent civilizations, including the Chimú and Incas, built upon what this group began.

The smaller of the two pyramids—the only one you can actually tour—is the **Huaca de la Luna,** the Pyramid of the Moon. The adobe structure is painted with anthropomorphic and zoomorphic reliefs. ■TIP→ **Many of the figures picture the Moche god Ai-Apaec, whereas others depict fanciful creatures, notably dragons; the use of dragon images may point to cultural and commercial exchange between the cultures of South America and Asia.** The Moche expanded the pyramid several times during their reign, covering up the exterior's original reliefs. Since 1990 archaeologists have slowly uncovered the ancient layers of the pyramid. Walk through to its very heart to glimpse some of its first facades. ■TIP→ **On most days you're able to watch archaeologists as they uncover multicolor murals.** Facilities include a visitor center at the entrance, with a small craft market, cafeteria, restrooms, and parking area (free).

Although the nearby **Huaca del Sol,** or the Pyramid of the Sun, sits along the same entry road, it's not yet ready for the public. Standing more than 40 meters (130 feet) high—slightly shorter than it originally stood—with more than 140 million bricks, this is the largest adobe-brick structure in the New World. Scattered around its base are what some archaeologists believe are "signature bricks," with distinctive hand, finger, and foot marks that identify the community whose labor produced the bricks for their lords. ■TIP→ **Researchers believe that the pyramid served as an imperial palace for the Moche people.** Once a storehouse of untold treasures, it has been stripped clean over the centuries by huaqueros. So great were its riches that in 1610 the Spanish diverted the Río Moche to wash away the pyramid's base and lay bare the bounty within. Although many tourists wander around the base, this is not recommended as the structure may not be solid and it's possible to destory part of this important temple with a single step. ⊠ *10 km (6 mi) southeast of Trujillo* ☎ *044/834–901* ⊕ *www.huacadelaluna.org.pe* 💰 *S/11* ⊙ *Daily 9–4.*

> ### FARMACIA VS BOTICA
>
> Pharmacies are abundant in Trujillo and Huaraz. If the sign says farmacia, it means that there's a licensed pharmacist; if the sign says botica, it means that the products will be the same, but no actual pharmacist is there (despite the professional white coats and willingness to answer questions). Either is sufficient if you just need to buy band-aids, but go to a farmacia if you have questions.

WHAT TO SEE IN EL CENTRO

More than any other city in Peru, Trujillo maintains much of its colonial charm, especially inside Avenida España, which encircles the heart of the city. This thoroughfare replaced a 9-meter- (30-foot) high wall erected in 1687 to deter pirates. Two pieces of the wall stand at the corner of Estete and España.

❹ **Casa de la Emancipación.** This branch of Banco Continental is unlike any bank you've ever been in. Go through the central courtyard and up to the small art gallery on the right. Enjoy the current exhibition, anything from modern to traditional artwork, and see a scale model of Trujillo when it was a walled city. ■**TIP**➔ Continue to the back, taking in the chandeliers, the large gold mirrors and the small fountain, and imagine the day that, in this house, the city declared its independence from Spain on December 29, 1820. It later became the country's first capitol building and meeting place for its first legislature. ⊠ *Pizarro 610* ☎ *044/246–061* 💰 *Free* ⊙ *Mon.–Sat. 9–12:30 and 4–6:30 (frequent special events may affect these hrs).*

❶ **Casa del Mayorazgo de Facala.** The open courtyard, from 1709, is surrounded by beautiful cedar columns, greenery, and... bankers. As with many colonial mansions, this one is now owned by a bank. However, Scotia Bank welcomes tourists and clients into the house to see its wonderfully preserved beauty. Notice the classic brown stucco-covered thick adobe walls and Moorish-style carved-wood ceiling. The security guards are happy to answer questions about the house. ⊠ *Pizarro 314, entrance on corner of Bolognesí and Pizarro* ☎ *044/249–994* 💰 *Free* ⊙ *Weekdays 9:15–12:30, 3:30–6, Sat. 9:15–12:30.*

❸ **Casa Urquiaga.** The enormous, elaborately carved wooden door is a stunning entrance to this beautifully restored neoclassical mansion from the early 19th century. ■**TIP**➔ Owned by another friendly bank, go inside and look around as long as you wish—you'll clearly look like a tourist, not a client. Don't miss the lovely rococo furniture and the fine

9

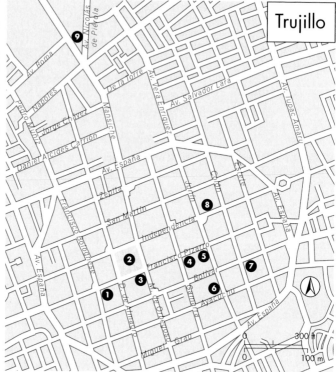

collection of pre-Columbian ceramics. ✉*Pizarro 446* ☎*044/245–382* ✉*Free* ⊙ *Weekdays 9:30–3, weekends 10–1:30.*

❼ Monasterio El Carmen. Still used as a nunnery, this handsome monastery, built in 1725, is regarded as the city's finest example of colonial art. It has five elaborate altars and some fine floral frescos. Next door is a museum, the Pinacoteca Carmelita, with religious works from the 17th and 18th centuries and an interesting exhibition on restoration techniques. ✉*Av. Colón at Av. Bolívar* ☎*No phone* ✉*S/2.5* ⊙ *Mon.–Sat. 9–1.*

❾ Museo Cassinelli. This private museum in the basement of a gas station has a 2,800-piece collection, mostly concerning indigenous cultures. Of note are some spectacular portrait vases from the Moche civilization and whistling pots, which produce distinct notes that mimic the calls of various birds. ✉*Av. Nicolás de Piérola 607* ☎*044/203–433* ✉*S/5* ⊙ *Daily 9–1 and 2–6.*

❻ Museo de Arqueología. Originally built in the 17th century, this museum displays pottery and other artifacts recovered from the archaeological sites surrounding Trujillo. There are excellent reproductions of the colorful murals found at the Huaca de la Luna, the pyramids southeast of the city. ⊠*Jr. Junín 682, at Jr. Ayacucho* ☎*No phone* 🖅*S/5* ⊗*Mon. 9–2:45, Tues.–Fri. 9–1 and 3–7, weekends 9–4.*

❽ **Museo del Juguete.** Puppets, puzzles, toys, games... what could be more fun than a toy museum? This private museum houses a large collection of toys from all over the world and shows the transformation of toys through the centuries. ■**TIP→** The toys from pre-Colombian Peru are especially interesting, giving a seldom-seen view into the daily lives of ancient people. You can't play with the toys so it may not be appropriate for very young children. ⊠*Jiron Independencia 705* ☎*044/208–181* 🖅*S/3* ⊗*Mon.–Sat. 10–6, Sun. 10–2.*

NEED A BREAK? Feel like you're part of the colonial history while enjoying delicious coffee at the Museo Café Bar. With a black-and-white-checkered marble floor, a dark-wood bar, floor-to-ceiling glass cabinents, and cushioned leather seats, it's a relaxed café in the afternoon and a hopping bar in the early evening. Advice: come to soak up the atmosphere, not to satiate your appetite. (⊠*Corner of Junin and Jiron Independencia* ☎*044/297–200* ▭*AE, DC, MC, V*).

❺ **Palacio Iturregui.** One look at the elaborate courtyard with its two levels of white columns, enormous tiles, and three-tiered chandeliers and you'll know why this is called a palace rather than a house. From the intricate white-painted metalwork to the gorgeous Italian marble furnishings, every detail has been carefully restored and maintained. Originally built in 1842, it's now the home of the private Club Central de Trujillo. Unfortunately, the club only allows visitors limited access. You may only enter, for a small fee, weekdays 8–10:30 AM and visit only the front courtyard 11–6. If you find these colonial-era mansions as fascinating as we do, get there early to visit the inside. The grand salon alone is worth it. ⊠*Pizarro 688* ☎*044/234–212* 🖅*S/5, or free to visit courtyard only* ⊗*Inside club: weekdays 8–10:30; courtyard only: Mon.–Sat. 11–6.*

NEED A BREAK? Homemade gelato is at De Marco (⊠*Pizarro 725* ☎*044/234–251* ▭*AE, DC, MC, V*), a small bistro that also serves excellent value criollo food at lunch and sponsors occasional peñas at night.

❷ **Plaza de Armas.** Brightly colored, well-maintained buildings and green grass with walkways and benches, make this one of the most charming central plazas. Fronted by a 17th-century cathedral and surrounded by the colonial-era mansions that are Trujillo's archi-

FESTIVALS

Considered the cultural capital of Peru, Trujillo is known for its festivities, including an international ballet festival, a contemporary art biennial, and a horse show. Consider coming to town for the Festival Internacional de la Primavera (International Spring Festival), held every year in late September or early October (check www. festivaldeprimavera.org.pe for the exact date). Trujillo is also busy during the last week of January, when it holds a dance competition called the National Fiesta de La Marinera. These events provide glimpses of traditional *criollo* culture.

9

tectural glory, this is not, despite claims by locals, Peru's largest main plaza, but it's one of the nicest.

WHERE TO EAT

Trujillo serves up delicious fresh seafood and a variety of excellent meat dishes. Try the ceviche made with fish or shellfish, *causa*, a northern cold casserole made of mashed potatoes and stuffed fish, tasty *cabrito al horno* (roast kid) or *seco de cabrito* (stewed kid), or *shámbar*, a bean stew tinged with mint.

$–$$ ✕ **Las Bóvedas.** This elegant restaurant in the Hotel Libertador offers
★   diners a beautiful space and delicious food. An impressive *bóveda*, or vaulted brick ceiling, line the walls of the dining room and plants fill the niches. The house specialty is the local delicacy, shámbar, garnished with *canchita* (fried bits of corn). It's served only on Monday. ⊠*Independencia 485* ☎*044/232–741* ▭*AE, DC, MC, V.*

¢–$ ✕ **De Marco.** Come to this noisy but cheerful eatery for good Peruvian
★   and Italian dishes, excellent coffee, an enormous selection of desserts, and free filtered water. Try the *seco de cabrito*, a local delicacy made of stewed goat. If you eat the freshly baked bread on the table, there's a small fee (S/0.25 each), but the special herbed butter is no extra charge. ⊠*Pizarro 725* ☎*044/234–251* ▭*AE, DC, MC, V.*

¢–$ ✕ **El Mochica.** It's crowded and busy, but a fun place to eat. Start with an industrial-size portion of spicy *cebiche de lenguado* (sole marinated in citrus), followed by rice smothered with *camarones* (shrimp) or *mariscos* (shellfish). Join the many other enthusiastic diners at this local spot. ⊠*Bolívar 462* ☎*044/224–247* ▭*AE, DC, MC, V.*

¢–$ ✕ **Romano.** Although this Trujillo establishment looks like it's seen better days in its 54 years, Romano still offers diners good food and friendly service. For dinner, enjoy seafood and pasta dishes, followed by excellent homemade desserts. Skip the dimly lighted front and, via a long, fluorescent-lighted hallway, enter the small, cozy back room with natural light and a more congenial feeling. ⊠*Pizarro 747* ☎*044/252–251* ▭*DC, V.*

$–$$ ✕ **San Remo.** People come here for the best pizza in town. Select from a large list of pizzas, with every topping imaginable, or choose one of the many other dishes, mostly pasta, but also meat and poultry options. The deer head in the entryway, the stained-glass windows, and the small wooden bar add to an old-school atmosphere. There's an excellent selection of South American and European wines. ⊠*Av. Húsares de Junín 450* ☎*044/293–333* ▭*AE, DC, MC, V* ⊘*No lunch.*

WHERE TO STAY

$$ ⊞ **Los Conquistadores.** Near the Plaza de Armas, this business hotel has large rooms with separate sitting areas. The staff is well-trained and offers a professional, no-frills hotel with quiet common areas away from the noisy street and spacious, clean rooms. The rate includes a buffet breakfast. **Pros:** Excellent location, large rooms. **Cons:** Bland furnishings, little natural light. ⊠*Diego de Almagro 586* ☎*044/244–505* ⊕*www.losconquistadoreshotel.com* ⬐*40 rooms, 13 suites* ⬧*In-*

hotel: restaurant, room service, bar, laundry service, public Internet, public Wi-Fi, parking (no fee), no-smoking rooms ⊟*AE, DC, MC, V* †◎|*BP.*

TRUJILLO TIME

Many of the museums and restaurants are closed for lunchtime from about 1 to 4 or 4:30. It can be quite hot around midday, so it's best to plan on indoor activities. It's easy to hail a taxi in Trujillo, and the in-town fare of about S/3 is quite reasonable. As always when traveling, be on your guard if you visit the market area—access your cash discreetly and keep your valuables close.

$ **⚅|Gran Bolívar.** A modern hotel hides behind the historic facade of this centrally located lodging. The spacious rooms overlook a courtyard filled with streaming sunlight. Inside the hotel is a full-service tourist agency, which offers a decent selection of local tours. Ask to see a few rooms beforehand, as some are nicer than others. **Pros:** Colonial architecture, beautiful central courtyard, central location, good staff. **Cons:** Some rooms have lots of light, others have very little. ⊠*Jr. Bolívar 957* ☎*044/222–090 or 044/223–521* ⊕*www.perunorte.com/granbolivar* ⇘*21 rooms, 7 suites* ♿*In-room: no a/c (some). In-hotel: restaurant, room service, bar, gym, spa, laundry service, billiards, airport shuttle, parking (no fee)* ⊟*AE, DC, MC, V* †◎|*CP.*

$ **⚅|Gran Hotel El Golf.** If you want to stay outside the city, this modern hotel is the best place to stay. The rooms face a large pool, surrounded by beautifully landscaped gardens and palm trees. It's a good choice for families since it has open areas for kids to play. There's a nearby golf course. **Pros:** Quiet, attractive setting. **Cons:** Can be isolating without a car. ⊠*Los Cocoteros 500, El Golf* ☎*044/282–515* 🖶*044/282–231* ⊕*www.granhotelgolftrujillo.com* ⇘*112 rooms, 8 suites* ♿*In-room: safe, Wi-Fi (some). In-hotel: restaurant, public Internet, room service, bar, pools, gym, laundry service, airport shuttle, parking (no fee), no-smoking rooms* ⊟*AE, DC, MC, V* †◎|*CP.*

$$ **⚅|El Gran Marques.** This upscale, full-service business hotel is minutes from the city center. Most of the rooms look down on a pool surrounded by lush gardens. On the roof are a small spa and sauna, and a small pool. Rooms have maroon carpets, wood furnishings, and paisley spreads. **Pros:** Very efficient service. **Cons:** Caters to business travelers and can be impersonal. ⊠*Díaz de Cienfuegos 145, Urb. La Merced* ☎*044/249–366* 🖶*044/249–161* ⇘*45 rooms, 5 suites* ♿*In-room: Ethernet, Wi-Fi. In-hotel: restaurant, room service, bar, pools, gym, spa, laundry service, parking (no fee)* ⊟*AE, DC, MC, V* †◎|*BP.*

$$–$$$ **⚅|Hotel Libertador.** On the Plaza de Armas, this elegant, upscale hotel is
★   the best choice in Trujillo. With beautiful colonial architecture, room details like pre-Colombian designs, locally tooled leather and wood furniture, and wrought-iron wall lamps, along with all the modern amenities. ∎**TIP➔** Look at your room in advance as some are smaller and don't have much natural light. If you fancy people-watching, ask for a location and beautiful architecture. **Cons:** Some rooms are better than

9

Colonial architecture abounds around Trujillo's Plaza de Armas.

others. ⊠*Independencia 485* ☎*044/232–741* ⊕*www.libertador.com.*
pe ⟿*73 rooms, 5 suites* ⌂*In-room: safe, Wi-Fi. In-hotel: restaurant,*
room service, bar, pool, gym, sauna, Wi-Fi, laundry service, parking
(no fee), no-smoking rooms ⊟*AE, DC, MC, V* ⧂*BP.*

NIGHTLIFE

A venerable men's club, **Chelsea** (⊠*Estete 675* ☎*044/257–032*) is a
good place for a drink on the weekends. **Luna Rota** (⊠*Av. América*
Sur 2119 ☎*044/228–877*) has live local music most evenings. The
dance club and casino downstairs mainly attracts a 40 and over crowd.
In a converted mansion with a friendly vibe, **Tributo** (⊠*Almagro and*
Pizarro) has live music, mainly cover or tribute (hence, the name) bands
on weekends.

SHOPPING

Along Avenida España, especially where it intersects with Junín, stalls
display locally made leather goods, particularly shoes, bags, and coats.
Be wary of pickpockets during the day, and avoid it altogether after
the sunset. For made-to-order boots or belts, check out **Creaciones**
Cerna (⊠*Bolognesi 567* ☎*044/205–679*). **Lujan** (⊠*Obregoso 242*
☎*044/205–092*) sells stylized Peruvian jewelry. **Los Tallanes** (⊠*Jr. San*
Martín 455 ☎*044/220–274*) has a wide selection of handicrafts.

HUANCHACO

12 km (7½ mi) northwest of Trujillo.

Less than half an hour away from the city, Huanchaco is a little beach community where surfers, tourists, affluent *Trujillianos*, families, and couples easily mix. With excellent restaurants, comfortable hotels and never-ending sunshine, this is a nice place to unwind for a couple of days or to live it up at one of the many annual *fiestas*. The Festival del Mar is held every other year during May, the Fiesta de San Pedro held every June 29, and multiple surfing and dance competitions happen throughout the year.

■ **TIP→** Head to the beach in the late afternoon to watch fishermen return for the day, gliding along in their caballitos de totora, traditional fishing boats that have been used for more than 1,000 years. These small, unstable boats, made from totora reeds, can be seen in Moche ceramics and other pre-Columbian handiwork. The boat's name, *caballitos*, means "little horse" and comes from how fishermen kneel on them.

Although people come to Huanchaco for the beach, one of Peru's oldest churches, **El Santuario de Huanchaco,** on a hill overlooking the village, is a nice sidetrip. The Sanctuary of Huanchaco was built on a Chimú ruin around 1540. In the second half of the 16th century a small box containing the image of *Nuestra Señora del Socorro* (Our Lady of Mercy) floated in on the tide and was discovered by locals. The image, which is kept in the sanctuary, has been an object of local veneration ever since. ✉ *At Andrés Rázuri and Unión* ☎ *No phone* 💲 *Free* ⊙ *Daily 8–6.*

THE BEACHES
The beaches around Huanchaco are popular, though the water can be rather cold.

9

Playa Malecón, north of the pier, is the town's most popular beach and is filled with restaurant afer restaurant. Local craftspeople sell their goods along the waterfront walk. Rocky **Playa Huankarote,** south of the pier, is less popular for swimming, but there's good surfing.

WHERE TO EAT

¢–$ ✗**Big Ben.** Skip the first floor and head upstairs to the terrace for great views of the beach. Enjoy Huanchaquero specialties, including *cangrejo reventado* (baked crab stuffed with eggs) and *ceviche de mococho* (algae ceviche). Only open 11–6, this open-air restaurant serves lunch and sunset drinks from a special wine list or cocktail menu. Huanchaquero specialties include *cangrejo reventado* (baked crab stuffed with eggs) and *ceviche de mococho* (algae ceviche). ✉ *Av. Victor Larco 836* ☎ *044/461–378* ⊕ *www.bigbenhuanchaco.com* ▭ *AE, DC, MC, V* ⊙ *No dinner.*

¢–$ ✗**Club Colonial.** An excellent menu, beautifully decorated, and the absolute best place to watch the sunset, this is one of the finest places to **FodorsChoice** dine in northern Peru. Club Colonial combines recipes from the Old ★ World with ingredients from the New World, coming up with wonderful combinations of fresh seafood, pasta, greens, meats, and more.

■TIP➜ There's everything from Basque-style sea bass to crepes covered with tropical fruit. The restaurant is filled with colorful colonial artifacts and has a cozy bar and an outdoor terrace. The food and atmosphere haven't changed much over the years, but this is a new location on a newly created street, so asking for directions can be tricky. It's closer to the surfers' section of the beach than the fishermen's area. ⊠Av. La Rivera 171 ☎044/461–015 ⊟AE, MC, V.

¢–$ ✗Estrella Marina. This lively restaurant on Playa Huanchaco can be noisy, but the view of the ocean is superb. Dishes are typical of the region, with plenty of fresh seafood concoctions, such as ceviche marinated in citrus juice. Whatever you order, sit upstairs for the better ocean view. ⊠Av. Victor Larco 594 ☎044/461–850 ⊟MC, V, DC.

WHERE TO STAY

¢ ☷Hostal Bracamonte. This pleasant hotel, across the boulevard from
☾ Playa Huanchac, is popular with Peruvian families, especially in summer, and has a pool set in beautifully landscaped grounds, a small restaurant, a small playground, lots of grassy areas to play in, and a good "neighborhood" feel. There's even a camping area, but it's bring-your-own-tent. **Pros:** If you have kids, this is the place to be. **Cons:** If you don't have kids, this is not the place for you. ⊠Jr. Los Olivos 503 ☎044/461–162 ⊟044/461–266 ⊕www.hostalbracamonte.com ⤒24 rooms, 8 bungalows ⚴In-room: Wi-Fi (some). In-hotel: restaurant, bar, pool, parking (no fee), Internet, Wi-Fi, game room ⊟AE, DC, MC, V.

$ ☷Las Palmeras. Across from the tranquil Playa Los Tumbos, a beach on
★ the northern end of the waterfront, Las Palmeras is a welcoming hotel once you get past the gated entrance. Its spotless rooms have terraces; most have great views of the ocean. A narrow garden with a small pool makes your stay very relaxing. Since the hotel is gated in, there's a feeling of privacy. At this writing, the hotel is in the process of building a new restaurant in front of the hotel. **Pros:** Pristine and comfortable rooms, very quiet and relaxing. **Cons:** Difficult to find behind a closed gate, prices vary based on location of the room. ⊠Av. Victor Larco 1150 ☎044/461–199 ⊕www.laspalmerasdehuanchaco.com ⤒20 rooms, 1 suite ⚴In-room: no phone, no TV. In-hotel: restaurant, pool, laundry service, room service, no elevator ⊟V.

NIGHTLIFE

Worth checking out, especially on the weekend, is **Sabes?** (⊠Larco 920 ☎044/461–555). It's a laid-back place at the northern end of the main drag with good music and drinks. A local hotspot, mainly filled with foreign travelers, is **El Kero** (⊠Av. La Rivera 115 ☎044/461–184), a restaurant and pub with an extensive menu, including Peruvian and foreign food, and loud music for the after-dinner crowd.

SIPÁN

35 km (21 mi) east of Chiclayo.

This tiny village of about 1,700 doesn't offer much, but nearby is one of the country's major archaeological sites. Arrange for a taxi or tour to take you to the tomb of the Lord of Sipán.

The **Tumba del Señor de Sipán** *(Tomb of the Lord of Sipán)* was discovered by renowned archaeologist Walter Alva in 1987. The road to the archaeological site, not far from the town of Sipán, winds past sugar plantations and through a fertile valley. You'll soon reach a fissured hill—all that remains of a temple called the Huaca Rajada. ■TIP→ **The three major tombs found here date from about ad 290 and earlier, and together they form one of the most complete archaeological finds in the Western Hemisphere.** The tombs have been attributed to the Moche culture, known for its ornamental pottery and fine metalwork. The most extravagant funerary objects were found in the tomb, now filled with replicas placed exactly where the original objects were discovered. The originals are now on permanent display in the Museo Tumbas Reales de Sipán in Lambayeque. The Lord of Sipán did not make the journey to the next world alone—he was buried with at least eight people: a warrior (whose feet were amputated to ensure that he didn't run away), three young women, two assistants, a servant, and a child. The tomb also contained a dog and two llamas. Hundreds of ceramic pots contained snacks for the long trip. Archaeological work here is ongoing, as other tombs are still being excavated. *No phone* S/8, S/20 for a guide (strongly recommended) Daily 8–5:30.

CHICLAYO

219 km (131 mi) north of Trujillo.

A lively commercial center, Chiclayo is prosperous and easygoing. Although it doesn't have any colonial architecture or special outward beauty, it's surrounded by numerous pre-Columbian sites. ■TIP→ **The Moche and Chimú people had major cities in the area, as did the Lambayeque, who flourished here from about 700 to 1370.** Archaeology buffs flocked to the area after the 1987 discovery of the nearby unlooted tomb of the Lord of Sipán. Chiclayo is a comfortable base from which to visit that tomb as well as other archaeological sites.

GETTING AROUND

For the most part, you'll need to take a taxi around Chiclayo. Within the city limits, each ride should cost about S/3 and ask for help at your hotel to negotiate anything beyond the city. Look at the map before hailing a taxi, though, because some things are within walking distance.

ESSENTIALS

CURRENCY **Banco de Crédito** (⊕ *www.viabcp.com*). **Banco de Crédito** (⊕ *www.viabcp. com*).

INTERNET   **Africa Café Web** (⊠*San José 473* ☎*074/229–431*).

MAIL   **Post Office** (⊠*Elías Aguirre 140* ☎*074/237–031*).

MEDICAL   **Clinica del Pacífico** (⊠*Av. José Leonardo Ortiz 420* ☎*074/232–141*).

PHARMACY   **Max Salud** (⊠*Av. 7 de Enero 185* ☎*076/226–201*).

VISITOR INFO   **iPerú** (⊠*Av. Sáenz Peña 838* ☎*074/205–703* ⊕*www.peru.info*).

WHAT TO SEE

The enormous **Cathedral**, dating back to 1869, is worth a look for its neoclassical facade on the Plaza de Armas, and its well-maintained central altar. ⊠*Plaza de Armas* 🎫*Free* ☉*Weekdays 6:30* AM—*1, 3–9:30, weekends closed 1–3.*

For fresh air and a great spot for people-watching, head to the **Paseo Las Musas**. The pedestrian walk borders a stream and has classical statues depicting scenes from mythology. To enjoy this the most, look up at the statues and people walking by and ignore the excessive litter along this beautiful promenade. ⊠*La Florida and Falques.*

The closest beach to Chiclayo is in the port town of **Pimentel**, 14 km (8½ mi) west of Chiclayo. Access via taxi should cost about S/15 each way. Although the beach is not so attractive, there's an interesting curved pier dating back more than a century, and many other enjoyable sights along the beach. Walk along and observe the old colonial beach houses, navy officers in white outside the maritime station, and an excessive number of young Peruvian couples walking hand in hand.

WHERE TO EAT

Much like Trujillo, Chiclayo and Lambayequ offer *cabrito, causa* and *pescado seco* (salted fish). The area is more famous for *kinkón* (pronounced much like "King Kong"), a large, crispy pastry. It's filled with *manjar blanco*, a sweet filling made of sugar, condensed milk, and cinnamon boiled down until it's thick and chewy.

$–$$$ ✕**Típico Fiesta.** Well-known for its excellent food, the Chiclayo location of this Peruvian-owned restaurant group lives up to its reputation. Start with the "Fiesta Hot Round," an appetizer sampler and order *comida norteña* (typical food of northern Peru), including sumptuous *cabrito* (kid), or other carefully prepared dishes such as imported salmon with capers. Try the special breakfast on weekends 8–11 and sit upstairs for the best ambience. ⊠*Salaverry 1820* ☎*074/201–970* ▭*AE, DC, MC, V.*

$ ✕**Marakos Grill.** Come here for the best barbecue in Chiclayo. The ★   grilled-to-perfection *parrillas* (barbecue) combinations are the best options, serving groups ranging from two to seven, and including steak, ribs, chorizo sausages and more—plus your choice of side dishes. For the more adventurous eaters, try the tender *anticucho* (beef heart) or *avestruz* (ostrich). There are two locations on the same block, both owned by the same family, one by the parents, the other by their son. Although the menus are the same, the restaurant at 696 has a more family-friendly atmosphere while the one at 490 is smaller and more intimate. ⊠*Av. Elvira Garcia y Garcia 490 and Av. Garcia y Garcia 696* ☎*074/232–840* ⊕*www.marakosgrill.com* ▭*AE, DC, MC, V.*

¢–$ ✕**Hebrón.** A friendly staff serves a wide range of national and international specialties from 7 AM to midnight daily at this centrally located eatery. There's an excellent breakfast menu, free Wi-Fi, big corner windows for good people-watching, and a playground, "Hebrónlandia," in the back. Families could easily spend half a day here. There are "children's options" on the menu, but these are dishes that kids usually like and the size/price is no different. ⊠*Av. Balta 605* ☎*074/222–709* ▭*AE, DC, MC, V.*

¢–$ ✕**Nueva Venecia.** Fantastic pizza, served on a wooden block fresh from the oven, is why this hugely popular Italian restaurant is busy every night. The list of toppings is extensive and there are some pasta choices. You might have to wait on the street to get in, and once inside you'll feel almost-stifling heat from the pizza ovens, but you're guaranteed good food and old-country charm. ⊠*Av. Balta 365* ☎*074/233–384* ▭*AE, DC, MC, V.*

¢–$ ✕**La Parra.** Despite the bland decorations, this restaurant serves delicious grilled meats. La Parra specializes in *parrilladas* (barbecues), with an extensive menu including every imaginable part of the cow. The *anticuchos* (beef heart) and *ubre* (cow udder) are well-prepared house specials. If this sounds unappetizing, you can always get grilled steak or head to the *chifa* (Chinese) restaurant next door, run by the same people. ⊠*Manuel María Izaga 752* ☎*074/227–471* ▭*AE, DC, MC, V.*

WHERE TO STAY

$$ ☖**Gran Hotel Chiclayo.** Come for a high standard of everything from the
★ well-trained staff, spacious rooms, and extra hotel amenities, including a pool, casino, restaurant, gym, and spa. An in-house travel agency can help you do everything from arrange a tour to rent a car. For this reason, the hotel is as popular with executives in town for a meeting as travelers here to see the ancient ruins. Rooms have large windows that let in a lot of light and some rooms have balconies. A buffet breakfast is included in the rate. **Pros:** Central location, first-rate accommodation and amenities. **Cons:** Occasionally large business groups overtake the hotel. ⊠*Av. Federico Villareal 115* ☎*074/234–911* 🖷*074/223–961* ⊕*www.granhotelchiclayo.com.pe* ⤶*129 rooms, 16 suites* ⚭*In-hotel: 2 restaurants, room service, bar, pool, laundry service, public Internet, Wi-Fi, gym, spa, parking (no fee)* ▭*AE, DC, MC, V* ⧀*BP.*

$$ ☖**Garza Hotel.** Don't be fooled by the bland exterior, inside there's a poolside bar and outdoor fireplace for cool nights, an admirable restaurant serving regional cuisine, efficient staff, and excellent accommodation. Enjoy the traditional artwork throughout the hotel, as well as your welcome cocktail, free breakfast, cable TV, and air-conditioning. **Pros:** First-rate service and accommodation, central location. **Cons:** Nothing makes it Peruvian, you could be anywhere in the world. ⊠*Bolognesi 756* ☎*074/228–172* 🖷*074/228–171* ⊕*www.garzahotel.com* ⤶*91 rooms, 3 suites* ⚭*In-hotel: 2 restaurants, room service, bar,*

9

pool, gym, spa, laundry service, public Internet, public Wi-Fi, parking (no fee) ☱*AE, DC, MC, V* ⓧⓄⓧ*CP.*

$ ☷ **Inti Hotel.** With newly refurbished rooms and noise-proof glass for street-side rooms, this hotel offers you one of the best deals in Chiclayo. Rooms are clean, the staff is professional, and the hotel feels busy, but not hurried. Inti Hotel is a new name. The original name was Inca Hotel, but after losing a legal battle with Cusco, a city that believes they have exclusive right to all things Inca, the hotel was forced to change its name. **Pros:** Quality rooms at a low price. **Cons:** Dimly lighted hallways and mediocre hotel restaurant. ☒*Av. Luis Gonzales 622* ☎*074/235–931* ☐*074/227–651* ⊕*www.intihotel.com.pe* ☜*62 rooms, 2 suites* ♿*In-room: no a/c (some). In-hotel: restaurant, room service, bar, laundry service, public Internet, Wi-Fi, parking (no fee)* ☱*AE, DC, MC, V* ⓧⓄⓧ*CP.*

$ ☷ **Las Musas.** People stay here for the view of the Paseo Las Musas. The hotel has standard accommodation and services, but each room overlooks the promendade. Other nice features include a waterfall and tiny koi pond at the entrance, a sixth-floor restaurant with great views of the entire city, and one suite with an enormous heart-shape Jacuzzi. **Pros:** Location and views. **Cons:** Rooms are very average. ☒*Los Faiques 101, Urb. Santa Victoria* ☎*074/239–884* ☐*074/273–450* ☜*41 rooms, 5 suites* ♿*In-hotel: restaurant, room service, bar, laundry service, public Internet, Wi-Fi, parking (no fee)* ☱*AE, DC, MC, V* ⓧⓄⓧ*CP.*

NIGHTLIFE & THE ARTS

A favorite pastime of Chiclayans is karaoke. One of the hottest places to show your vocal skills is the Gran Hotel Chiclayo's discoteque and bar **Solid Gold** (☒*Av. Federico Villarreal 115* ☎*074/234–911*).

If singing in front of strangers doesn't sound like fun, try **Bali Lounge** (☒*Av. José L. Ortiz 490* ☎*074/235–932*) for an extensive menu of high-level, expensive Peruvian and Japanese-Peruvian fusion options, top shelf liquors, imported beers, and an exuberant crowd. Starting around 11, the line for **Ozone Disco** (☒*Av. José L. Ortiz 490* ☎*074/235–932*), just next door, begins. At this discoteque, people in their early twenties to early fifties revel in the (excessively) loud music and good cocktails. The first-floor bar and dance floor costs S/10 to enter.

SHOPPING

Chiclayo's indoor **Central Market** on Avenida Balta is no longer the city's main market. Once famed for its ceramics, weavings, and charms made by local *curanderos* (folk healers), now there's mainly fresh food for sale, and a nice little "foodcourt" in the back. Head over to the larger, more popular **Outdoor Market** beginning at the intersection of Avenida Balta and Avenida Arica. This vast market has fresh meat, vegetables, and fruit from local farms, as well as clothing, pirated DVDs and CDs, handbags, and more. You can also ask at any of the stalls to point you to a shaman for immediate help or to make an evening appointment. Wander around and enjoy, but don't lose each other in the crowd. For the best handicrafts in the area, go to **Mercado Artesanal de Monsefú**, about 14 km (9 mi) south of Chiclayo. You can buy straw hats, baskets, cotton weavings, embroidery, clay pots, wall hangings, all kinds of delicious snacks, and more. It's well worth the trip (round-trip taxi from Chiclayo, including waiting for you to shop, costs about S/35).

LAMBAYEQUE

12 km (7 mi) north of Chiclayo.

This small town has some well-preserved colonial-era buildings but the reason to come is for the outstanding museums. The museums exhibit details about the Moche civilization, and the original artifacts from the tomb in Sicán.

GETTING AROUND

The town is small enough to walk around from place to place or you can take an inexpensive taxi (S/3 within town) to the different museums. To get here from Chiclayo, you can easily hire a taxi or rent a car.

WHAT TO SEE

Fodor's Choice ★ Go to the **Museo Arqueológico Nacional Brüning** to see how the different pre-Incan civilizations lived on a daily basis. Covering the Moche, Lambayeque, and other pre-Inca cultures such as the Cupisnique, Chavín, Chimú, and Sicán, there are excellent interpretive displays, showing how people fished, harvested, kept their homes. There's also a wonderful photography exhibit of the archaelogist Hans Heinrich Bruning and his experiences in Peru beginning in the late 1800s. Descriptions are in Spanish, so an English-speaking guide is recommended. ✉ *Huamachuco and Atahualpa* ☎ *074/282–110* ⊕ *www.museobruning.com* 🖃 *S/8, S/20 for a guide* ☉ *Daily 9–5.*

Fodor's Choice ★ The impressive **Museo Nacional Tumbas Reales de Sipán**, which ranks among the country's best museums, displays the real artifacts from the tomb of the Señor de Sipán, one of the greatest archaeological finds of recent years. (Why the real artifacts are not actually in Sipán is a question no one was able to answer.) The stunning exhibits detail where every piece of jewelry, item of clothing, or ceramic vase was found. ■TIP→ **English-speaking guides are available to help with the Spanish-only descriptions and confusing order of exhibits.** All bags, cameras, and cell phones must be checked before you can enter the museum. ✉ *Av. Juan Pablo Vizcardo and Guzmán* ☎ *074/283–977* ⊕ *www.tumbasreales.org* 🖃 *S/10, S/20 for a guide,* ☉ *Tues.–Sun. 9–5.*

FERREÑAFE

18 km (11 mi) northeast of Chiclayo.

Although it's produced more winners of the Miss Peru contest than any other town, Ferreñafe has other charms. The Iglesia Santa Lucia, begun in 1552, is a good example of baroque architecture. However, most visitors come to visit its excellent new museum.

Adobe Pyramids

In Túcume, 35 km (21 mi) north of Chiclayo, you can see an immense pyramid complex, including Huaca Larga, one of the largest adobe pyramids in South America, as well as dozens of smaller ones spread across a dry desert. Go first to the small museum, **Museo de Sitio**, and take a tour with an English-speaking guide to learn about the history of the nearby ruins. Then, follow your guide and climb 10 minutes to see the 26 giant pyramids, surrounded by the smaller ones, and the areas in between, which have yet to be excavated.

The rugged desert landscape, sprinkled with hardy little *algarrobo* (mesquite) trees, is probably very similar to what it looked like when—so the legend goes—a lord called Naymlap arrived in the Lambayeque Valley, and with his dozen sons founded the Lambayeque dynasty and built the pyramids we see today. ☎ 074/800–052 or 076/422–027 ☒ S/8 ☉ Daily 8–5.

Although the **Museo Nacional Sicán** offers insight into the culture of the Sicán people, there are also unique exhibits such as the *El Niño* effect and where the pre-Incan civilizations fit into world history. Visual timelines hammer home just how far back Peruvian history goes. See the exhibits introducing the Sicán (also known as the Lambayeque), including everything from common eating utensils to ceremonial burial urns, models of what their homes might have looked like, and a central room full of treasures from this coastal culture renowned for its amazing headdresses and masks. ☒ *Av. Batá Grande* ☎ 074/286–469 ⊕ *http://sican.perucultural.org.pe* ☒ S/8 ☉ *Tues.–Sun. 9–5.*

PIURA

269 km (167 mi) north of Chiclayo.

The sunny climate, friendly people, and good food make Piura a delightful stop on your way north. Since most of the major flight and bus routes to the north-coast beaches travel through Piura, stopping here is not just easy, it's often required.

As a central commercial hub and the country's fifth-largest city (population 400,000), it's hard to believe how relaxed and friendly the city is to tourists. Historically, however, it's a community used to transitions. Founded in 1532 by Francisco Pizarro before he headed inland to conquer the Incas, the community changed locations three times before setting down on the modern-day location along the banks of the Río Piura.

GETTING AROUND

The best way to get around Piura is to walk. However, inexpensive and safe taxis are available from the street if you have heavy bags or are ready for a siesta.

ESSENTIALS

CURRENCY   **Banco de Crédito** (⊕ *www.viabcp.com* ☒ *Av. Grau 133* ☎ *073/336–822*).

MEDICAL   **Hospital Cayetano Heredia** (⊠ *Av. Independencia s/n, Urb. Miraflores* ☎ *073/303–208*).

VISITOR INFO   **iPerú** (⊠ *Av. Ayacucho 377* ☎ *073/320–249* ⊕ *www.peru.info*).

WHAT TO SEE

On the city's main square, the **Catedral de Piura** is worth a visit. Built in 1588, it's one of the country's oldest churches. Inside you'll find an altarpiece dedicated to the Virgen de Fátima dating back more than 350 years. ⊠ *Plaza de Armas* ☑ *Free*.

WHERE TO EAT

¢–$ ✗ **El Arrecife.** If you couldn't tell by the name—which means the Reef— the rope chairs and tanks filled with tropical fish should inform you that this is a seafood restaurant. Choose from 14 different ceviches at this local lunch-only establishment and if you still have room, there are countless other fresh fish dishes to sample. ⊠ *Jirón Ica 610* ☎ *074/313–161* ☰ *No credit cards.*

¢–$$ ✗ **Capuccino.** This modern Peruvian restaurant has an extensive menu.
★   Traditional rice and meat dishes, as well European-inspired salads, sandwiches, and entrées mix local and imported ingredients. Whether you choose the Thai salad or *lomo saltado*, expect to savor your meal. Relax in the serene dining room and don't forget to order dessert along with the delicious cappuccino. ⊠ *Calle Tacna 786* ☎ *074/301–111* ☰ *AE, MC, V* ⊙ *Closed Sun.*

¢–$$ ✗ **La Santitos.** This *picantería* transports you to provincial Spain of long ago with cracked walls, slow service, and waitresses dressed in peasant blouses and wide-flowing skirts. The menu of mainly grilled meats and criollo-style fish dishes has a variety of tapas and main dishes, including *arroz con mariscos*, Peruvian-style paella, and a variety of lobster dishes. Still recuperating from a recent fire, the restaurant has lost some of its former charm, but the food still makes it worth a visit. ⊠ *Calle Libertad 1014* ☎ *074/309–475* ☰ *AE, MC, V* ⊙ *No dinner.*

WHERE TO STAY

$ ▦ **Hotel Costa Del Sol.** This business hotel offers modern rooms and facilities, along with excellent service. In addition to the small kidney-shape pool in the central terrace, local artwork is displayed in the common areas and every room looks out onto a simple atrium. The completion of new rooms and an upgraded hotel bar will only improve this already excellent hotel. **Pros:** Catering to business travelers means better all-around service. **Cons:** The modern architecture lacks charm; some rooms have little natural light. ⊠ *Av. Loreto 649* ☎ *074/302–864* ⊞ *074/302–546* ⊕ *www.costadelsolperu.com* ⟳ *37 rooms, 3 suites* ⌂ *In-hotel: restaurant, room service, bar, pool, gym, laundry service, parking (no fee), no-smoking rooms, Wi-Fi* ☰ *AE, DC, MC, V* ⦿ *CP.*

$$ ▦ **Los Portales.** A venerable hotel on the tree-shaded Plaza de Armas, Los
★   Portales has charming colonial architecture. In the center of its small courtyard, you'll find a fountain and umbrella-shade tables. Nearby, the pool has its own waterfall and palm-dotted island, along with a

9

decent in-hotel café and restaurant. Rooms are spacious, though the bathrooms are small and dimly lighted. **Pros:** Beautiful colonial architecture. all the modern amenities one could want. **Cons:** Some rooms are better than others. ⊠*Libertad 875* ☎*074/321–161* ⊟*074/321–161* ⊕*www.hotelportalespiura.com* ⟿*33 rooms, 2 suites* �*In-hotel: restaurant, room service, bar, pool, laundry service, airport shuttle, parking (no fee), no elevator (2 floors only), Wi-Fi* ▭*AE, DC, MC, V* ⏍*BP.*

SHOPPING

The tiny pueblo of **Catacaos**, 12 km (7 mi) southwest of Piura, is famous for its textiles, gold and silver figurines, and excellent pottery. The small market, filled with street stalls and shops, is open daily until 6 PM. Look around as much as you like, but to get the best price, only closely examine what you really want to buy. To get to Catacaos, take the Pan-American Highway. A taxi should cost around S/30 round-trip.

In Piura, **Artisanias Lucas** (⊠*Jr. Comercio 629*) does not offer the selection and prices that Catacaos has, but there is a respectable assortment of artisanal goods.

> ### HOLD ON!
>
> As a general rule, taxis are abundant, cheap, and safe throughout Peru. Enter the mototaxi, a three-wheeled motorcycle, attached to a double-seat, covered by an awning. No metal, no glass, nothing between you, the road and the other cars. The good news? Mototaxis often are slower and go only short distances. Whenever possible, take a regular taxi in a car. However, for those places—especially Máncora and Punta Sal—in which mototaxis are the main source of travel, hold on and enjoy the ride!

MÁNCORA

229 km (142 mi) north of Piura.

This laid-back beach destination, famous for its sunshine and white-sand beaches has excellent waves for surfing, fishing, and diving. Although the relaxed but dusty town has tourist offices, restaurants, and small shops, the real draw are the hotels about 2 km (1¼ mi) south along **Las Pocitas,** a lovely beach with rocky outcrops that hold tiny pools of seawater at low tide.

WHERE TO STAY

$ 🏨**Los Corales.** Directly on the beach with very reasonable rates, this
★ little lodging is one of the best deals in Máncora. The bamboo furnishing, tiled floors, colorful bedspreads, and terraces with hammocks give the rooms a tropical theme. Enjoy the tranquil seating areas, full-service restaurant, pool, and lovely stretch of beach connected to the hotel. **Pros:** Offers the same beach-side location and service at a lesser cost. **Cons:** With only 15 rooms, reservations are difficult to get. ⊠*Km 1215, Old Pan-American Hwy. N* ☎*073/258–309* ⊟*073/258–124* ⊕*www.vivamancora.com/loscorales* ⟿*15 rooms* ċ*In-room: no*

Surfers take to the waves at Mancora, the north's hotspot beach destination.

phone, no TV. In-hotel: restaurant, bar, pool, beachfront, laundry service, parking (no fee), public Wi-Fi ⊟*AE, DC, V* ⊚*CP.*

$$ ⊞**Las Pocitas.** This full-service, family-friendly hotel has a large pool, restaurant, bar, game area, and a beautiful beach. Relax in a hammock on your room's terrace or join other guests at one of the many hotel facilities. If you want to explore more than just the beach, the staff can arrange horseback riding, surfing lessons, a sailing trip, massages, and tours of nearby mangroves. **Pros:** Larger spaces than most hotels, good options for activities. **Cons:** If all you want is the beach, you can stay somewhere else for less. ⊠*Km 1162, Pan-American Hwy.* ☎*073/258–432* ⊕*www.laspocitasmancora.com* ⇲*21 rooms* ♿*In-room: Wi-Fi, no phone (some), no TV (some). In-hotel: restaurant, bar, pool, beachfront, laundry service, parking (no fee), Wi-Fi* ⊟*V* ⊚*CP.*

PUNTA SAL

25 km (15 mi) north of Máncora, 70 km (43 mi) south of Tumbes.

Sit on the beach, go for a swim, and relax in the afternoon sun—just what you want from a beach resort. That's probably why Punta Sal has become a popular vacation spot in recent years. A few kilometers north of the Pan-American Highway, hotels and resorts abound in this area, tourists and vacationing Limeños flock here for the blond-sand beach, comfortable ocean breezes, and a sunny climate.

WHERE TO STAY & EAT

$$ ✕⊞ **Hotel Caballito de Mar.** This top-notch beach resort has tropical bun-
Fodor'sChoice galows with private terraces, an excellent fresh seafood restaurant and
★ beach access. Arrange for a surfing-, diving-, or other excusion, play in
the ocean waves, or just relax in one of the comfortable lounge chairs
around the small seahorse-shape pool. All meals are included in the
standard room price, or you can opt for the cheaper breakfast-only
plan. **Pros:** First-rate service, larger family bungalows available, rea-
sonable rates. **Cons:** Only the suites have air-conditioning and minibar;
prices nearly double during peak holidays. ⊠*Punta Sal, Km 1187,
Pan-American Hwy. N* ☎*072/540–058 telefax* ⊕*www.hotelcaballi-
todemar.com* ⏎*23 rooms* ⌂*In-room: no phone, no TV (some). In-
hotel: restaurant, bar, pool, beachfront, laundry service, parking (no
fee), public Wi-Fi* ▤*AE, DC, V* �†☉|*BP, FAP.*

$–$$ ⊞ **Punta Sal Club Hotel.** Offering a variety of bungalows, rooms, and
beach areas, this upscale, all-inclusive resort is the place to go for lux-
ury and relaxation. You'll enjoy the sparkling beach, excellent service,
delicious food, and extensive activity choices, which are guaranteed
to make you forget that stress was ever a part of your life. Bungalows
are significantly better than the regular rooms so shell out the extra
soles. **Pros:** Top-quality hotel. **Cons:** Regular rooms are nothing special, rates vary by season. ⊠*Punta Sal, Km 173, Sullana-Tumbes Hwy.*
☎*072/540–088* ⊕*www.puntasal.com.pe* ⏎*12 rooms, 15 bungalow*
⌂*In-hotel: restaurant, bar, pool, beachfront, gym, spa, laundry service,
public Internet, parking (no fee)* ▤*AE, DC, V* †☉|*CP.*

THE PERU-ECUADOR BORDER

About an hour's drive north of the beach resorts of Máncora and Punta
Sal is Tumbes, the last city on the Peruvian side of the Peru-Ecuador
border. Tumbes played a major role in Peruvian history: it was here
that Pizarro first saw the riches of the vast Inca empire. In the past,
tensions were high—it wasn't until 1941 that Tumbes became part of
Peru following a military skirmish. Tensions are now minimal. Other
than its geographical and historical importance, Tumbes doesn't offer
much to tourists. While good hotels are in the city, there is little charm
and few sights. Include Tumbes in your itinerary only if you plan to
enter Ecuador via the land-border crossing here. If you go, be extra
aware of your personal belongings. Tumbes, like many border towns,
has its fair share of counterfeit money, illegal goods, and scams to get
money from foreigners.

HUARAZ & THE CORDILLERA BLANCA

The Cordillera Blanca is one of the world's greatest mountain ranges.
The soaring, glaciated peaks strut more than 6,000 meters (19,500 feet)
above sea level—only Asia's mountain ranges are higher. Glaciers carve
their lonely way into the green of the Río Santa valley, forming streams,
giant gorges, and glorious gray-green alpine lagoons. On the western

Discover Nature

Some of the most incredible flora and fauna live in protected areas near Máncora and Punta Sal. Luckily, we can visit these important ecological areas, but only do so through a reputable hotel and experienced guide. Do not believe it if someone tells you they can bring you there and back in an hour. Most trips involve extensive driving, as well as hiking and camping. Including these areas in your itinerary isn't always possible, but the experience will leave you inspired and amazed.

Santuario Nacional Los Manglares de Tumbes: Crocodiles and a diverse collection of birds live in this mangrove reserve. Accessible only by unmotorized boat, this swamp forest is where the ocean water and river water meet, providing some of the most productive ecosystems on the planet.

Parque Nacional Cerros de Amotape: This area was created to protect the equatorial dry forest and its inhabitants. Living in this area are the condor, puma, boa constrictor, and approximately 100 other species of mammals, reptiles, and birds.

Zona Reservada de Tumbes: The dry forest and humid forest exist together in this protected zone, making it one of the more interesting areas to explore. As much of the flora and fauna in this area are in danger of extinction, this also an extremely important area.

---

side of the valley is the Cordillera Negra. Less impressive than the Cordillera Blanca, its steep mountains have no permanent glaciers and are verdant and brooding. Driving along the paved stretch of road through the valley offers spectacular views of both mountain ranges. You'll find an abundance of flora and fauna in the valley and in the narrow gorges that come snaking their way down from the high mountains. Deer, *vizcacha* (rodents resembling rabbits without the long ears), vicuñas, puma, bear, and condors are among the area's inhabitants. You'll also find the 10-meter-tall (32-foot-tall) *puya raimondii* (the world's largest bromeliad), whose giant spiked flower recalls that of a century plant.

The valley between the Cordillera Blanca and the Cordillera Negra is often called the Callejón de Huaylas. It's named after the town of Huaylas in the northern part of the valley. ■ TIP➜ **The town is possibly the most important climbing and trekking destination in South America.** From here, arrange to go white-water rafting; head out on a 10-day trek through the vast wilderness; or stay closer to home, taking one-day excursions to the 3,000-year-old ruins at Chavín de Huántar, local hot springs, a nearby glacier, and an alpine lagoon. Climbers come during the dry season to test their iron on the more than 40 peaks in the area exceeding 6,000 meters (19,500 feet). The 6,768-meter (21,996-foot) summit of Huascarán is the highest in Peru and is clearly visible from Huaraz on sunny days. To the south of Huaraz, the remote and beautiful Cordillera Huayhuash offers numerous trekking and climbing excursions as well. The outdoor options are limitless.

The area has been inhabited since pre-Inca times, and Quechua-speaking farmers still toil on the land, planting and harvesting crops much as they did thousands of years ago. The land in the valley is fertile, and corn and oranges are abundant. Up above, potatoes and other hearty crops grow on the steep terrain. The goddess *Pachamama* has always provided, but she can be iron-willed and even angry at times; every now and then she will shake her mighty tendrils and a section of one of the glaciers will crumble. The resulting rock and ice fall, called an *aluvión*, destroys everything in its path. In 1970 one such aluvión resulted from a giant earthquake, destroying the town of Yungay and almost all its 18,000 inhabitants. Most of the towns throughout the area have suffered some damage from the numerous earthquakes, so not much colonial architecture survives. What remains are friendly, somewhat rugged-looking towns that serve as excellent jumping-off points for exploration of the area's vast wilderness and mountain ranges, hot springs, and 3,000-year-old ruins.

HUARAZ

400 km (248 mi) north of Lima.

Peru's number-one trekking and adventure-sports destination, Huaraz is an easy starting point for those wishing to explore the vast wilderness of the Cordillera Blanca. Unfortunately, the town has been repeatedly leveled by natural disasters. In the later part of the 20th century three large earthquakes destroyed much of Huaraz, claiming more than 20,000 lives.

Despite the setbacks and death toll, Huaraz rallied, and today it's a pleasant town filled with good-natured people. Being the most popular tourist destination in northern Peru, Huaraz also has a great international scene; while the town has few sights, the restaurants and hotels are some of the best in the region. ■TIP→ **Many businesses close between September and May, when the town practically shuts down without its hoards of climbers and trekkers**. It can be hard to find an outfitter at this time; call ahead if you plan a rainy-season visit.

GETTING AROUND

Huaraz is a small town and you can walk almost everywhere. Or, if you've just arrived and are feeling a little breathless from the altitude, take a taxi for 3 to 5 soles. To enjoy any of the nearby treks and sights, hire a guide as it's not safe to go alone.

ESSENTIALS

CURRENCY **Banco de Crédito** (⊠ *Av. Luzuriaga 691* ☎ *043/421–170* ⊕ *www.viabcp.com*). **Scotia Bank** (⊠ *José de Sucre 760* ☎ *043/721–500* ⊕ *www.scotiabank.com.pe*).

MAIL **Post Office** (⊠ *Av. Luzuriaga 702* ☎ *043/421–030*).

MEDICAL **Hospital Victor Ramos Guardia** (⊠ *Av. Luzuriaga, Cuadra 8* ☎ *043/421–861*).

RENTAL CAR **Monte Rosa** (⊠ *Jr. José de la Mar 691* ☎ *043/421–447*).

VISITOR INFO **iPerú** (⊠ *Pasaje Atusparia* ☎ *043/428–812* ⊕ *www.peru.info*).

Continued on page 399

BIG MOUNTAINS
of the Cordillera Blanca

by Oliver Wigmore

The lofty ice-clad peaks of Cordillera Blanca soar above 6,000 meters (20,000 feet) and stretch for over 100 kilometers (62 miles) north to south across the Andes. These mountains, worshipped by Andean peoples for thousands of years, are now the idols of global adventure tourism.

Explore ancient ruins, ascend icy summits at the crack of dawn, hike isolated alpine valleys, be absorbed by the endless azure blue of glacial lakes, or put your feet up at a mountain lodge.

The formation of the present Andean mountain chain began as the Nazca plate collided with and was forced beneath the South American plate, driving the ocean floor up to produce the world's longest exposed mountain range. This resulted in the formation of the Pacific coastal desert, the highland puna, and the verdant Amazon basin. Since then the Andes have been the bridging point

between these diverse environmental and ecological zones. The Cordilleras Blanca, Negra and Huayhuash, and the Callejon de Huaylas Valley were formed 4 to 8 million years ago, producing spectacular peaks and many distinct ecological niches.

The May to September dry season brings the most stable weather—and the big crowds. Increasingly people are battling the rain and snow for the isolation that comes with the off-season.

Peruvians cross a log bridge in the Jancapampa Valley, as the Cordillera Blanca looms before them.

CORDILLERA BLANCA

Taulliraju Mount, Cordillera Blanca, Huascaran National Park, Peru.

The Cordillera Blanca encompasses the mighty Huascarán, Peru's highest peak at 6,767m (22,204ft), and Alpamayo 5,947m (19,511ft), once proclaimed the most beautiful mountain in the world by UNESCO. Most of the Cordillera Blanca is within the Huascarán National Park, for which an entry ticket is required. Valid for one day or one month, these can be purchased at the entry gates or from the park headquarters in Huaraz.

Thanks to the newly paved road, the glacial lakes are now a popular day trip from Huaraz. Their beauty is still worth the trip.

HIGH POINTS

1. **The Santa Cruz Trek:** You ascend the Santa Cruz valley, crossing the Punta Union pass at 4,760m (15,617ft) beneath the breathtaking peaks, then descend to the spectacular azure blue of the Llanganuco Lakes. One of Peru's most popular alpine treks, it's often overcrowded, with litter and waste becoming a serious problem. For pristine isolation, look elsewhere.

2. **Pastoruri Glacier:** You can walk on a tropical glacier, ice-climb, ski, and witness the impacts of climate change. Popular day tours from Huaraz often combine the trip here with a visit to see the impressive Puya raimondii trees.

3. **Chavin de Huantar:** On the eastern side of the cordillera is Chavin de Huantar, where in around 900 BC the first pan-Andean culture developed. The Chavin culture eventually held sway over much of central Peru. The site can be visited on a long day trip from Huaraz.

4. **Olleros to Chavin Trek:** A short three-day trek across the Cordillera terminates at Chavin de Huantar. Guiding companies in Huaraz offer this trek with llama hauling your gear.

5. **Quilcayhuanca and Cojup Valley Loop:** This trek is becoming popular due to its relative isolation and pristine condition. It explores two spectacular high alpine valleys, crosses the 5,000m (16,404ft) Pico Choco Pass, passing beautiful glacial lakes, one of which caused the 1941 destruction of Huaraz city in a flood of mud, rocks, and ice.

6. **Laguna 69:** Spectacular glaciers encircle the lake and give it deep turquoise color. It can be seen on a long day hike from Huaraz. However, spending the night allows you to explore, and you will likely have the lake to yourself once the day trippers leave. This is an ideal acclimation trek.

7. **Alpamayo Basecamp:** An arduous week-long trek takes you on a northern route through the Cordillera, passing the spectacular north face of Nevado Alpamayo (5947m/19,511ft).

8. **Huascarán:** Peru's highest peak is one of the Cordillera's more challenging summits.

Climbing: Relatively easy three to five day guided summit climbs of Ishinka (5,550m/18,208ft), Pisco (5,752m/18,871ft) and Vallunaraju (5,684m/18,648ft) are arranged at any of the guiding outfitters in Huaraz. Prices and equipment vary—get a list of what's included. Many smaller companies operate purely as booking agencies for the larger companies.

1 The Santa Cruz Trek

Huaicayan

Cashapampa

Huaripampa

7 Alpamayo
5,947m
(19,511ft)

Pirámide

Artesonraju

Caraz

Pisco
5,752m
(18,871ft)

Caraz

6 Laguna 69

Huandoy

Chacraraju

Yanama

C O R D I L L E R A (H U A S C A R Á N)

Chopicalqui

Contrahierbas

Pueblo Libre

Yungay

8 Huascarán
6,768m
(22,204ft)

Chacas

Utla

Musho

Huaypan

Pompey

Mancos

Hualcan

C O R D I L L E R A   B L A N C A   N A T I O N A L   P A R K

Shilla

Huaicán

Copa

Copa

Bayoraju

Paqcharaju

Carhuaz

Copa Chico

Vicos

Akilpo

Ranrahirca

Marcará

Kekepatipa

Vicos

Pashpa

Toellaraju

C O R D I L L E R A

N E G R A

Anta

Joncopampa

Palcaraju

Taricá

Collón

Ishinka
5,550m
(18,208ft)

Pucaranra

Jangas

Vallunaraju
5,684m
(18,648ft)

Ranrapalca

Pico Choco

Monterrey

COJUP
VALLEY

Churup

Wilkawain

5 Quilcayhuanca and
Cojup Valley Loop

Huaraz

Pitec

QUILCAYHUANCA
VALLEY

Huchac

Macashca

A llama—member of the camelid
family and provider of wool for
Andean weavers—Chavin, Cordillera Blanca.

Río Santa

2 Pastoruri
Glacier

Chavin de
Huantar **3**

4 Olleros

Agocancha

0   3 mi
0   3 km

GOOD TO KNOW

CLIMBING HISTORY

The first climbers in the region were probably pre-Colombian priests, attempting difficult summits to perform sacred rituals atop icy summits. This climbing tradition was continued by the Spanish Conquistadors who wanted to exploit the rich sulphur deposits atop many of Peru's volcanic cones, and to show their dominance over Mother Nature. Modern climbing in the region took off in 1932 when a German-Austrian expedition completed many of the highest summits, including Huascarán Sur. Since then the peaks of the Cordillera Blanca and Peru have attracted climbers from around the world for rapid-summit sport climbs and solo summits. Extended duration expeditions and large support crews are less common here than in the Himalayas.

(above) Cullicocha; (below) Sheperds hut, Huaraz.

SAFETY TIPS

This area is a high alpine environment and weather patterns are unpredictable. Be prepared for all weather possibilities. It's not uncommon to experience snow storms and baking sun over the course of a single day, and at night temperatures plummet. Sunburn, dehydration, exhaustion, and frostbite are all potential problems, but by far the major issue is *soroche* (altitude sickness). It's extremely important to pace yourself and allow enough time for acclimatisation before attempting any long-distance high-altitude treks or climbs.

ENVIRONMENTAL CHANGE

The warming climate is producing alarming rates of retreat in glacial water reserves of the Cordillera Blanca. The heavily populated Pacific coast relies almost exclusively on seasonal run-off from the eastern Andes for water supplies and hydroelectricity. The feasibility of transporting water across the Andes from the saturated Amazon basin is now being debated.

MAPS

For serious navigation, get the Alpenvereinskarte (German Alpine Club) topographic map sheets, which cover the Cordillera Blanca over two maps (north and south). They are sold by Casa de Guias and the gift store below Café Andino. Many local expedition outfitters sell an "officially illegal" copy with a little persuasion.

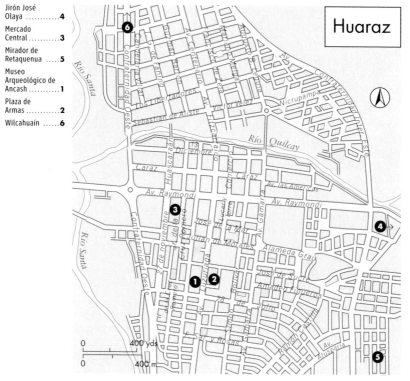

Huaraz

WHAT TO SEE

❷ Every few years, as a new mayor is elected, the town gets an updated
Plaza de Armas, which is on the corner of Luzuriaga, the town's main
drag, and José Sucre. Thanks to the current mayor, who removed a
gigantic, towering statue of Christ, the plaza provides nice views of the
surrounding mountains. There are several *ferias artesenales* (artisanal
kiosks) bordering the plaza.

❶ The small **Museo Arqueológico de Ancash** displays some very unique items,
including a mummified baby and teenager, created by covering the dead
with salt, *muña* (wild mint), *quinua* (a cornlike plant), and *izura* (pink
earth). ■**TIP→** Upstairs numerous skulls bear the scars (or rather holes)
from trepanation, the removal of bone from the skull. Additionally, the
museum has Chavín textiles and ceramics, and a delightful little park
accessible through the bottom floor. Here you'll find original carved
stones, benches, and a little café. ⊠*Av. Luzuriaga 762* ☏*043/721-551*
⊕*www.huaraz.com/museo* ⊡*S/5.60, includes a guide* ☉*Mon.–Sat.
8:15–6:30, Sun. and holidays until 5.*

❸ For a pungent look at Andean culture, head to the **Mercado Central.** At
this market you'll see fruits and vegetables grown only in the highlands
as well as *cuy* (guinea pig), chickens, ducks, and rabbits, which you

can purchase alive or freshly slaughtered. ⊠*Entrance at Jr. de la Cruz Romero and Av. Cayetano Requena.*

❹ To see Huaraz's colonial remnants, head to **Jirón José Olaya,** a pedestrian-only street where several houses with handsome facades still stand. It's best to visit on Sunday when there's a weekly *Feri[t]a de Comida Tipicos,* a regional street festival with typical food and craft stalls. ⊠*East of town center on right-hand side of Raimondi and a block behind Confraternidad Inter Este.*

❺ The **Mirador de Retaquenua,** lookout point has an excellent view of Huaraz, the Río Santa, and the surrounding mountains. It's a 45-minute walk up, but the directions are complicated so it's best to hire a guide or just take a taxi. ⊠*Av. Confraternidad Inter Sur and Av. Confraternidad Inter Este.*

❻ North of the city is a small archaeological site called **Wilcahuaín.** The Wari temple, dating back to AD 1100, resembles the larger temple at Chavín de Huántar. Each story of the crumbling three-tiered temple has seven rooms. There's a small museum and recently built basic bathroom facilities and a limited restaurant. Trained and knowledgable local students will be your guide for a small tip (suggested minimum tip: S/15). ⊠*8 km (5 mi) north of Huaraz* 🕾*No phone* 💵*S/5* 🕙*Daily 6–6.*

OFF THE BEATEN PATH

Glaciar Pastoruri. A popular day trip from Huaraz is a visit to the Glaciar Pastoruri, where you can hike around the glacier and visit a glowing blue-ice cave. ■**TIP→** **On this trip you'll ascend to well above 4,000 meters (13,000 feet), so make sure you're used to the high altitude.** Wear warm clothing, sunscreen, and sunglasses, as the sun is intense. Drink lots of water to avoid altitude sickness. The easiest and safest way to get here is with a tour company from Huaraz. The tour costs about S/20 to S/30 and takes eight hours. Admission to the glacier is S/5. You can also hire diminutive horses to take you up to the glacier from the parking lot for about S/15. It's not the most spectacular glacier in the world, but if you've never seen one up close, it's worth the trip. The glacier is south of Huaraz, off the main highway at the town of Recuay.

WHERE TO EAT

¢–$ **✕ Creperie Patrick.** With a breezy terrace upstairs and a cozy bistro
Fodor's Choice downstairs, this French eatery is an excellent choice. There's couscous
★ and fondue, as well as hard-to-find local dishes such as grilled alpaca. Don't miss the sumptuous dessert crepes and good wine selection. After almost 20 years in Peru, chef and owner Patrick has begun to make homemade delicacies including his own liquors, jams, mustards, granola, and more. ⊠*Av. Luzuriaga 422* 🕾*044/426–037* ▭*No credit cards* 🕙*No lunch Oct.–Apr.*

¢–$ **✕ El Horno.** With a terrace area for sunny afternoons and a recently
★ expanded dining room for the evenings, El Horno is a good stop any time. ■**TIP→** **Here you'll find some of the finest pizzas in Huaraz—baked by a Frenchman, no less.** The doughy crusts are superb and the service faultless. Excellent salads, sandwiches, pastas, and barbecued meats are also on the menu. If you are, by some chance, looking for French

books, there is a French-only book exchange here as well. ⊠ *Parque del Periodista 37* ☎ *043/424—617* ⊕ *www.elhornopizzeria.com* ▭ *No credit cards* ⊘ *Closed on Sundays; No lunch during the low season.*

¢–$ ✕ **Piccolo Ristorante.** Walk straight to the outdoor patio in the back to enjoy your meal in the peaceful Parque del Periodista. The Italian eatery specializes in pastas and pizza, but the international specialties like *filete de trucha a la piamontesa* (trout in herb sauce) and filet mignon round out the menu nicely. The breakfasts are especially good, as is the freshly brewed coffee. ⊠ *Jr. Julián de Morales 632* ☎ *043/427–306* ▭ *AE, DC, V.*

$–$$ ✕ **Siam de Los Andes.** Thai food high in the Peruvian Andes—who would
★ have thought? Siam de Los Andes is a true anomaly in the land of tacu-tacu and pollo a la brasa. The light, delicate, and at times extremely spicy food is the real deal; from the chicken satay to the shredded pork, it's very good. The Thailand-born owner's secret? He takes regular trips to the homeland, importing those hard-to-find ingredients. Closed during the low season. ⊠ *Augustin Gamarra 560* ☎ *043/428–006* ▭ *No credit cards* ⊘ *No lunch.*

WHERE TO STAY

$–$$ ⊡ **Hotel Andino.** A Swiss-style chalet set high on the hill above Huaraz, Hotel Andino is one of the town's best lodging. There are several types of clean, modern rooms, each with carefully planned details. Some have terraces with excellent views of the mountains, others look out on the wonderfully green interior garden; some suites have fireplaces, DVD players, and separate kitchens. Each floor has a computer with Internet access and the main floor has different seating areas, including one with a fireplace, to enjoy this tranquil hotel. **Pros:** The best views in Huaraz. **Cons:** It's just outside the heart of central Huaraz. ⊠ *Pedro Cochachín 357* ☎ *043/421–662* 🖷 *043/422–830* ⊕ *www.hotelandino.com* ⚓ *57 rooms* ♿ *In-room: safe. In-hotel: restaurant, laundry service, public Internet, parking (no fee)* ▭ *AE, DC, MC, V.*

$ ⊡ **Hotel Colomba.** The best hotel to come if you—or your kids—are
☉ high-energy and want activities. In addition to a beautiful garden setting around this hacienda-turned-hotel, there's a rock-climbing wall, soccer field, basketball court, gameroom, gym, and playground. The staff is well-trained and friendly. **Pros:** Family friendly, lots of activities. **Cons:** Some rooms are better than others, but all cost the same (ask for a room in the back with parquet floors). ⊠ *Jr. Francisco de Zela 210, Independencia* ☎ *043/421–501 or 043/422–273* ⊕ *www.huarazhotel. com* ⚓ *20 rooms* ♿ *In-hotel: room service, laundry service, public Internet, public Wi-Fi, parking (no fee)* ▭ *AE, DC, MC, V* ⅋ *BP.*

$ ⊡ **Hotel San Sebastián.** Perched on the side of a mountain, this hotel has
★ great views of the Cordillera Blanca. Many rooms have small balconies and shady terraces are scattered about the hotel. Built in the Spanish-colonial style, the hotel exudes rustic charm with plenty of pine furniture and natural sunlight. The owner is Selio Villón, a mountain guide with more than 20 years of experience. **Pros:** Reasonable rates with first-rate accommodation. **Cons:** Hotel keeps expanding, doubling

9

its capacity in two years, losing some of its "family" charm. ⊠*Jr. Italia 1124* ☎*043/426–960 or 043/426–386* 🖷*043/422–306* ⊕*www. sansebastianhuaraz.com* ⟿*30 rooms, 1 junior suite* ⌂*In-hotel: room service, laundry service, public Internet, Wi-Fi, parking (no fee), no elevator* ⊟*V.*

NIGHTLIFE

Café Andino is a funky café offering light snacks, hot and cold beverages, and a seemingly endless supply of newspapers and books in English. (⊠*Jr. Lucar y Torre 530, 3rd floor* ☎*043/421–203*). To warm yourself up at night, enjoy one of the many cool bars and dance clubs. The ever-popular **Tambo** (⊠*José de la Mar 776* ☎*043/423–416*) has low ceilings and curvy walls. There's a large dance floor where you can get down to salsa music. Just down the street from Tambos is **Makondos** (⊠*José de la Mar and Simon Bolívar* ☎*043/623–629*). The music here tends to be pop. To relax with the backpacker circuit, head to **Vagamundo** (⊠*Julián de Morales 753* ☎*043/614–374*). Join other vagabonds for a game of foosball, a movie, or dancing. For strong cocktails and loud rock music head to **Xtreme Bar** (⊠*Gabino Uribe and Luzurriaga* ☎*043/723–150*).

OUTDOOR ACTIVITIES

BIKING If you're an experienced mountain biker, you'll be thrilled at what the area offers along horse trails or gravel roads, passing through the Cordilleras Blanca and Negra. One reputable operator is **Mountain Bike Adventures** (⊠*Jr. Lucar and Torre 530* ☎*043/724–259* ⊕*www.chaki-naniperu.com*) rents bikes and has experienced guides to take you to the good single-track spots.

CLIMBING & If dreams of bagging a 6,000-meter (19,500-foot) peak or trekking TREKKING through the wilderness haunt your nights, Huaraz is the place for you. Huaraz sits at a lofty 3,090 meters (10,042 feet), and the surrounding mountains are even higher. Allowing time to acclimatize is a life-saving necessity. Drinking lots of water and pacing yourself help avoid high-altitude pulmonary edema (commonly known as altitude sickness). ■TIP➔ The climbing and trekking season runs from May through September—the driest months. You can trek during the off-season, but drudging every day through thick rain isn't fun. Climbing during the off-season can be downright dangerous, as crevasses get covered up by the new snow. Even if you're an experienced hiker, you shouldn't venture into the backcountry without a guide.

The guided treks in the region vary by the number of days and the service. You can opt for smaller one-, two-, and three-day hikes, or an expedition of 10 to 20 days. Most guided treks provide donkeys to carry your equipment, plus an emergency horse. So many outfitters are in the area that looking for a qualified company can become overwhelming. Visit a few places, talk with the guides, and make sure you're getting what you really want. **Casa de Guís** (⊠*Parque Ginebra 28/G* ☎*043/427–545* ⊕*www.casadeguias.com.pe*) is an association of certified freelance guides who offer excellent advice and personalized trips, including mountaineering and trekking as well as rock- and ice-climbing courses.

WHITE-WATER
RAFTING

There's good rafting on the Río Santa with Class 3 and 4 rapids. The freezing cold glacial river water brings heart-pumping rapids. The most-often-run stretch of river runs between Jangas and Caraz. The river can be run year-round, but is at its best during the wettest months of the rainy season, between December and April. Be prepared with the right equipment; the river is cold enough to cause serious hyperthermia. **Monttrek** (⊠ *Av. Luzuriaga 646, upstairs* ☎ *043/421–124* ⊕ *www. monttrekperu.com*) is one of the best rafting outfitters in Huaraz. The company also has friendly and experienced guides for trekking and mountaineering.

SHOPPING

Craft booths on either side of the Plaza de Armas have tables piled high with locally woven textiles. If you arrive and find that you need some gear, **Tatoo Adventure Gear** (⊠ *Jr. Simón Bolivar 26* ☎ *043/422– 066* ⊕ *www.tatoo.ws*) has a large selection of quality gear, mainly imported.

CHAVÍN DE HUÁNTAR

★ *110 km (68 mi) southeast of Huaraz.*

Although the ruins appear unimpressive at first—most of the area was covered by a huge landslide in 1945—underground you'll discover a labyrinth of well-ventilated corridors and chambers. ■**TIP**➔ **They're illumined by electric lights that sometimes flicker or fail altogether—it's wise to bring your own flashlight.** Deep inside the corridors you'll come upon the **Lanzón de Chavín.** This 4-meter-high (13-foot-high) dagger-like rock carving represents an anthropomorphic deity (complete with fangs, claws, and serpentine hair); it sits elegantly at the intersection of four corridors. Built by the Chavín, one of the first civilizations in Peru, little is known about this ancient culture, although archaeologists believe they had a complex religious sysem. The main deity is always characterized as a puma or jaguar. Lesser deities, represented by condors, snakes, and other animals, were also revered.

This is a fascinating archaeological site that you can day-trip to from Huaraz. Chavín de Huántar sits on the southern edge of Chavín, a tiny village southeast of Huaraz. On the drive from Huaraz you get good views of two Andean peaks, Pucaraju (5,322 meters/17,296 feet) and Yanamarey (5,237 meters/17,020 feet). Construction on the road may delay your journey—check on conditions before setting out. Tours from Huaraz visit the ruins, a small on-site museum, and the alpine Laguna de Querococha during the 8-hour tour. The tour costs about S/30 per person, not including the entrance fee to the ruins. If you'd prefer to get here on your own, regular buses run between Huaraz and Chavín, you can hire a guide at the entrance to the ruins. ☎ *No phone* ▱ *S/11* ☉ *Daily 8–4.*

9

GETTING AROUND

If you have a car—and an excellent map and good sense of direction—you can head out and explore the windy, confusing roads. For all others, simply hiring an inexpensive taxi when needed will ensure you arrive where you need to safely. Major trips and treks should be arranged with experienced, certified guides.

MONTERREY

5 km (3 mi) north of Huaraz.

This area provides a quiet and attractive alternative to Huaraz. For some, it can feel isolating: there isn't a town center, just hotels and restaurants spread about. There are local hot springs and a nice hiking trail just behind Hotel Monterrey that leads across a stream and up into the hills, eventually taking you to the Wilcahuaín Ruins. And you're just a 15-minute drive from Huraz.

To get to the Monterrey area, head north from Huaraz on what is popularly called the Callejón de Huaylas, passing attractive little villages and taking in spectacular scenery from the comfort of your car.

Popular with locals, **Los Baños Termales de Monterrey** is a large public bathing area where you can soak your troubles away. Although the facilities could use some refreshing, a dip in the sulfur-rich waters is quite relaxing. For a more tranquil bath, as it can get very crowded on the weekends, you can rent a private tub. Didn't bring your bathing suit on your hiking trip? Don't worry, you can buy (or rent!) one here. ⊠ *Av. Monterrey s/n, at Hotel Monterrey* ☎ *043/427–690* 💲 *S/3.50* ⊘ *Daily 6–5.*

WHERE TO STAY & EAT

$–$$ ✕ **El Cortijo.** This outdoor restaurant has the absolute best barbecue ★ around, from steaks to ribs. The plastic patio furniture, placed around the grass and centered on the large barbecue pit, add to the "down-home" feeling. Or maybe it's the swingset in the front. Either way, El Cortijo is a great place to spend part of a sunny afternoon—or perhaps the entire afternoon, as the food is plenty and the service can be slow. ⊠ *Carretera Huaraz–Caraz* ☎ *043/423–813* ⊘ *Daily 8–7* ⊟ *AE, DC, MC, V.*

$ 🏨 **El Patio de Monterrey.** A lovely hacienda built in the colonial style, El
Fodor's Choice Patio is a great lodging option for those wishing to stay in the country.
★ It's only 6 km (4 mi) from Huaraz, making it a feasible alternative for those wishing to stay near the city. Whitewashed walls, wooden beams, hand-painted tiles, greenery and flowers everywhere, and a delightful stone patio make this one of the area's loveliest lodgings. The antiques-filled rooms have a clean, provincial look. There's a small chapel here, as priests originally built the hacienda. A taxi from here to Huaraz is only S/8 so a car is not a necessity. **Pros:** Close to the city, luxurious country-estate. **Cons:** You may not see much else while you're here. ⊠ *Carretera Huaraz–Caraz, Km 206* ☎ *043/424–965* 🖷 *043/426–967* ⊕ *www.elpatio.com.pe* 🛏 *28 rooms, 4 cabañas* ⚲ *In-hotel: restaurant,*

CLOSE UP | Life in the Andes

This region of the Andes has sustained some 12,000 years of cultural development. From Guitarrero Cave through the Chavin, Huari, and Inka cultures to the present day.

The highland puna has been the breadbasket for countless generations of Andean communities. Fertile glacial plains and mineral-rich rivers provide the nutrients for the rigorous growing cycles of traditional highland crops such as potato, while lower elevations allow the production of grains including quinoa, oats, barley, wheat, and corn. The region also provides pasture for wild and domestic herds of llamas, alpacas, and vicunas. Various species of bird and waterfowl also inhabit the area and sightings of the enormous condor are possible.

To this day traditional life remains a struggle. Indigenous populations continue to eke a meagre existence from the land, while attempting to keep up with the rapidly changing face of a modernizing Peru. Increasingly young people are moving away from traditional life to find employment in the cities, mines, or Peru's booming tourism industry.

—Oliver Wigmore

laundry service, public Internet, parking (no fee) ▭AE, DC, MC, V ¶◎|CP.

CARHUAZ

35 km (22 mi) north of Huaraz.

A small, laid-back village, less touched by recent earthquakes, Carhuaz is a popular stop along the Callejón de Huaylas. A bright spot is the ice-cream shop, which scoops up excellent homemade *helado.* The town comes alive with bullfights, fireworks, dancing, and plenty of drinking during its festival honoring the Virgen de la Merced, held every year September 14–24. This is one of the best festivals in the region.

WHERE TO EAT

¢ ✗**Heladeria El Abuelo.** You won't want to miss this ice-cream shop, mostly for the fantastic flavors such as pisco sour and beer. The owner is a good source for information about the region; he also rents nice rooms in a lodge near town. ✉*Merced 727* ☎*043/494–149* ▭No *credit cards.*

YUNGAY

59 km (37 mi) north of Huaraz.

On May 31, 1970, an earthquake measuring 7.7 on the Richter scale shook loose some 15 million cubic meters of rock and ice that cascaded down the west wall of Huascarán Norte. In the quiet village of Yungay, some 14 km (8½ mi) away, people were going about their normal activities. Some were waiting for a soccer game to be broadcast on the radio, others were watching the Verolina Circus set up in the stadium.

Then the debris slammed into town at a speed of more than 200 mi per hour. Almost all of Yungay's 18,000 inhabitants were buried alive. The quake ultimately claimed nearly 70,000 lives throughout Peru.

The government never rebuilt in Yungay, but left it as a memorial to those who had died. They now call the area **Campo Santo,** and people visit the site daily. ■**TIP→** Walking through the ruined town, you'll see upturned buses, the few remaining walls of the cathedral, and, oddly, a couple of palm trees that managed to survive the disaster. There's a large white cross at the old cemetery on the hill south of town. It was here that 92 people who were tending the graves of friends and relatives were on high-enough ground to survive. You pay a nominal S/2 to enter the site.

New Yungay was built just beyond the aluvión path—behind a protective knoll. It serves as a starting point for those visiting the spectacular Laguna Llanganuco.

LAGUNAS DE LLANGANUCO

Fodor's Choice
★

Make sure your memory card is empty when you go to see these spectacular glaciers, gorges, lakes, and mountains. Driving through a giant gorge formed millions of years ago by a retreating glacier, you arrive at **Lagunas de Llanganuco.** The crystalline waters shine a luminescent turquoise in the sunlight; in the shade they're a forbidding inky black. ■**TIP→** Waterfalls of glacial melt snake their way down the gorge's flanks, falling lightly into the lake. There are many *quenual* trees (also known as the paper-bark tree) surrounding the lakes. Up above, you'll see treeless alpine meadows and the hanging glaciers of the surrounding mountains. At the lower lake, called Lago Chinancocha, you can hire a rowboat (S/3 per person) to take you to the center of the lake. A few trailside signs teach you about local flora and fauna. The easiest way to get here is with an arranged tour from Huaraz (about S/25 plus S/5 entrance fee). The tours stop here and at many other spots on the Callejón de Huaylas, finishing in Caraz.

Laguna Llanganuco is one of the gateways to the **Parque Nacional Huascarán,** a 340,000-hectare park created in 1975 to protect and preserve flora and fauna in the Cordillera Blanca. ■**TIP→** This incredible mountain range has a total of 663 glaciers and includes some of the highest peaks in the Peruvian Andes. Huascarán, which soars to 6,768 meters (21,996 feet), is the highest in Peru. The smaller Alpamayo, 5,947 meters (19,327 feet), is said by many to be the most beautiful mountain in the world. Its majestic flanks inspire awe and wonder in those lucky enough to get a glimpse. The monstrous Chopicalqui and Chacraraju rise above 6,000 meters (19,500 feet).

Within the park's boundaries you'll find more than 750 plant types. There's a tragic scarcity of wildlife in the park—most have been decimated by hunting and the loss of natural habitats. Among the 12 species of birds and 10 species of mammals in the park, you're most likely

Cordillera Huayhuash

While much smaller than the Cordillera Blanca, the main chain of the Cordillera Huayhuash is known for its isolation and pristine environment. For years the area remained essentially off limits to foreign tourism as it was a major stronghold for the Shining Path movement that wracked much of Peru's central highlands with terrorism throughout the 1980s. Today this isolation is what makes the region so special. Treks in this region are measured in weeks not days with road access and tourist infrastructure almost nonexistent. The opportunities to spot rare Andean wildlife are much greater here and the chances of meeting tour groups next to nothing. **Cordillera Huayhuash Circuit:** The major draw here is the Cordillera Huayhuash circuit. This taxing trek can take up to two weeks passing some of the region's most spectacular mountain scenery. Access to this trail was traditionally via Chiquian but the road has now been extended to Llamac. Tours and supplies are best organized in Huaraz although Chiquian does provide some limited facilities and arrieros and mules can be arranged here.

Wildlife: The isolation and pristine nature of the Cordillera Huayhuash make it an ideal place to see many of the region's rare species. **Siula Grande (6,344 meters, 20, 813 feet):** See the mountain made famous by Joe Simpson in his gripping tale of survival in Touching the Void.

Yerupaja (6,617 m, 21,709 ft): The second highest mountain in Peru.

—Oliver Wigmore

to see wild ducks and condors. With a great deal of time and an equal amount of luck you may also see foxes, deer, pumas, and viscachas.

The giant national park attracts campers, hikers, and mountain climbers. Myriad treks weave through the region, varying from fairly easy 1-day hikes to 20-day marathons. Within the park, you can head out on the popular **Llanganuco–Santa Cruz Loop,** a three- to five-day trek through mountain valleys, past crystalline lakes, and over a 4,750-meter-high (15,437-foot-high) pass. Other popular hikes include the one-day Lake Churup Trek, the two-day Quilcayhuanca–Cayesh trek, and the two-day Ishinca Trek. Check with guide agencies in Huaraz for maps, trail information, and insider advice before heading out.

Although experienced hikers who know how to survive in harsh mountain conditions may want to head out on their own, it's much safer to arrange for a guide in Huaraz. You can opt to have donkeys or llamas carry the heavy stuff, leaving you with just a daypack. The most common ailments on these treks are sore feet and altitude sickness. Wear comfortable hiking shoes that have already been broken in, and take the proper precautions to avoid altitude sickness (drink lots of water, avoid prolonged exposure to the sun, and allow yourself time to acclimatize before you head out). The best time to go trekking is during the dry season, which runs May through September. July and August are the driest months, though dry season doesn't mean a lack of rain or even snow, so dress appropriately.

Recently many hikers have decided to enter the park at night to avoid paying the hefty S/65 for a multiday pass (from 2 to 30 days). The money from these fees goes to protect the wonders of the Andes; consider this before you slip in in the dead of night. You can purchase a pass at the Huaraz office of Parque Nacional Huascarán, at the corner of Rosas and Federico Sal. ⊠ *Federico Sal y Rosas 555* ☎ *043/422–086* 💷 *S/5 day pass, S/65 multiday pass* ☉ *Daily 6–6.*

CARAZ

67 km (42 mi) north of Huaraz.

One of the few towns in the area with a cluster of colonial-era architecture, Caraz is at the northern tip of the valley—only a partly paved road continues north. North of Caraz on the dramatic road to Chimbote is the Cañon del Pato, the true northern terminus of the Callejón de Huaylas. Caraz is an increasingly popular alternative base for trekkers and climbers. While in town be sure to try the ultrasweet *manjar blanco* frosting.

WHERE TO STAY & EAT

¢ ✕🏨 **Chamanna.** This cluster of cabañas among beautifully landscaped
Fodor'sChoice gardens is the town's best lodging. Benches let you admire mountain
★ streams and towering peaks. Although not all the cabañas have private bathrooms, they are nonetheless stylish, with interesting murals and hand-hewn furniture. The restaurant serves excellent French and international cuisine. The German owner is affable and helpful. **Pros:** The distance provides peacefulness and calm. **Cons:** Hiring taxis and traveling means less time to enjoy the great outdoors. ⊠ *Av. Nueva Victoria 185* ☎ *044/689–257* ⊕ *www.chamanna.com* 🛏 *10 cabañas, 5 with bath* 🛁 *In-room: no phone, no TV. In-hotel: restaurant, laundry service, public Internet* ▤ *AE, DC, MC, V* ⫿⫿ *CP.*

THE NORTHERN HIGHLANDS

The green valleys and high mountaintops that comprise the northern highlands are certainly one of the area's biggest draws, as is the area's rich history. But few travelers venture here; it's hard to reach and far from the more popular destinations of Cusco, Puno, and Machu Picchu.

Several major archaeological sites are in the northern highlands. ■ **TIP→** **The pre-Inca fortress of Kuélap, near Chachapoyas, is one of the region's best-preserved ruins.** The region's largest town, Cajamarca, is the center for exploration and was the site of one of history's quickest and wiliest military victories. It was here in 1532 that Pizarro and his meager force of 160 Spaniards were able to defeat more than 6,000 Inca warriors and capture Atahualpa, the new king of the Inca empire. Without a king, the vast empire quickly crumbled. In and around Cajamarca you'll find a handful of Inca and pre-Inca sites. There are also chances for horseback riding and hiking in the green valleys and hills.

CAJAMARCA

865 km (536 mi) northeast of Lima; 304 km (188 mi) northeast of Trujillo.

Cajamarca is the best place to stay if you want to explore the lovely landscape and rich history of the northern highlands; from here there are a number of daylong excursions to nearby ruins and hot springs.

The largest city in the northern highlands, it's a tranquil town of more than 150,000 people. It sits in a large green valley surrounded by low hills. The name Cajamarca means "village of lightning" in the Aymara language. It's fitting, for the ancient Cajamarcans worshiped the god Catequil, whose power was symbolized by a bolt of lightning. ■**TIP→ The area around town was first populated by the Cajamarcan people 3,000 years ago, whose major cultural influence came from the cat-worshiping Chavín.** The Incas conquered the region in about 1460, assimilating the Chavín culture. Cajamarca soon became an important town along the *Capac Ñan* or Royal Inca Road.

The arrival of the Spanish conquistador Pizarro and his quick-witted defeat of the Incas soon brought the city and much of the region into Spanish hands. Few Inca ruins remain in modern-day Cajamarca; the settlers dismantled many of the existing structures to build the churches that can be seen today. The town's colonial center is so well preserved that it was declared a Historic and Cultural Patrimony Site by the Organization of American States in 1986.

GETTING AROUND

Most places are within walking distance, but taxis are abundant if you feel a little breathless from the altitude or want to go somewhere a little outside of the city center. If you like your taxi driver, arrange a pickup another day. For major exploration outside of the city, the best option is to join a tour for the day. Cajamarca is 2,650 meters (8,612 feet) above sea level. Although not very high by Andes standards, it's still quite high. Take your time, wear sunscreen, and drink plenty of water to avoid altitude sickness.

9

ESSENTIALS

CURRENCY **Banco de Crédito** (⊠ *Jr. Apurimac 717* ☎ *076/362–742* ⊕ *www.viabcp.com*). **Scotia Bank** (⊠ *Jr. Amazonas 750* ☎ *076/827–101* ⊕ *www.scotiabank.com.pe*).

MAIL **Post Offices** (⊠ *Jr. Amazonas 443* ☎ *076/82406–52045*).

MEDICAL **Hospital de Cajamarca** (⊠ *Av. Mario Urtega 500* ☎ *076/822–557*).

VISITOR INFO **iPerú** (⊠ *Av. 13 de Julio s/n* ☎ *076/823–042* ⊕ *www.peru.info*).

WHAT TO SEE

❸ **Baños del Inca.** About 6 km (4 mi) east of Cajamarca are these pleasant hot springs offering several public pools and private baths. The central bath, Poza del Inca, is an intact Incan pool with a system of aqueducts built by the Incas and still in use today. Despite the large size of the complex, it's quite relaxing and popular with the locals. ⊠ *Av. Manco Cápac* ☎ *076/348–563* 💲 *S/6* ⊙ *Daily 5–8.*

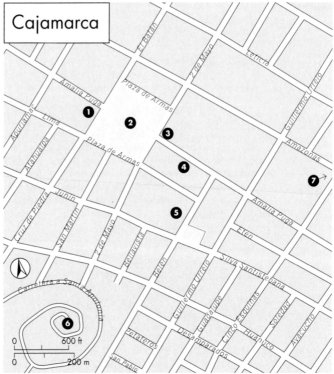

❶ **Catedral de Cajamarca.** Originally known as the Iglesia de Españoles (because only Spanish colonialists were allowed to attend services), this cathedral on the Plaza de Armas was built in the 17th and 18th centuries. It has an ornate baroque facade that was sculpted from volcanic rock. Like many of the town's churches, the cathedral has no belfry; the Spanish crown levied taxes on completed churches, so the settlers left the churches unfinished, freeing them from the tight grip of the tax collector. ⌧ *Jr. Del Batan and Amalia Puga* ☎ *No phone* 💲 *Free* ⊙ *Daily 3–6.*

❻ **Cerro Santa Apolonia.** At the end of Calle 2 de Mayo are steps leading to this hilltop *mirador,* or scenic lookout to see a bird's-eye view of the city. At the top are many carved bricks dating to pre-Columbian times. ■**TIP→** One of the rocks has the shape of a throne and has been dubbed the Seat of the Inca. According to local legend, it was here that Inca kings would sit to review their troops. You'll find pretty gardens and great views of the town. You can either walk or go by taxi (round-trip S/5). ⌧ *End of 2 de Mayo* ☎ *No phone* 💲 *S/2* ⊙ *Daily 8–6.*

OFF THE BEATEN PATH

Ventanillas de Otuzco. One of the oldest cemeteries in Peru, the Ventanillas de Otuzco (Otuzco Windows) dates back more than 3,500 years. The ancient necropolis, 8 km (5 mi) northeast of Cajamarca, is comprised of several large burial niches carved into a cliff. From afar the niches look like windows, hence the area's name. On closer inspection you see that many of the burial niches have carved decorations. Sadly, the site is slowly being eroded by wind and rain. If you're incredibly inspired by this cemetery, you can go about 30 km (18 mi) from Combayo, in the same direction, and you can visit the better-preserved Ventanillas de Combayo. A three-hour guided tour to Ventanillas de Otuzco costs around S/25.

❺ ★ El Complejo de Belén. Built in the 17th century, this large complex, originally a hospital, now houses the city's most interesting museums and a colonial church. At the **Museo Arqueológico de Cajamarca,** the town's archaeological museum, are exhibits of Cajamarcan ceramics and weavings. The pre-Inca Cajamarcans were especially famous for their excellent patterned textiles that were often dyed vivid shades of blue. The **Museo Etnográfico** has a few displays of everyday bric-a-brac—there's even an old saddle and a dilapidated coffee grinder—dating back to pre-colonial times. The **Iglesia de Belén** is a charming church with a polychrome pulpit and cupola. ⊠*Jr. Belén and Jr. Junín* ☎*076/362–903 or 076/362–997* 🎫*S/5, includes admission to entire Complejo de Belén and El Cuarto del Rescate* ⊗*Mon.–Sat. 9–1 and 3–6, Sun. 9–1.*

❹ El Cuarto del Rescate. The Ransom Chamber is the only Inca building still standing in Cajamarca and, although the big stone room itself isn't much to look at, the history is enough to make this worth a visit. Legend has it that after Pizarro and his men captured Atahualpa, the Inca king offered to fill the chamber once with gold and twice with silver. The ransom was met, but the war-hardened Spaniards killed Atahualpa anyway. ⊠*Jr. Amalia Puga 750* ☎*044/922–601* 🎫*S/5, includes El Complejo de Belén* ⊗*Mon.–Sat. 9–1 and 3–6, Sun. 9–1.*

9

❸ Iglesia de San Francisco. Built in the 17th and 18th centuries, the Church of San Francisco sits proudly on the Plaza de Armas in front of the main cathedral. The church's two bell towers were begun in republican times and finished in 1951. The church was called the Iglesia de Indios (Church of the Indians) as indigenous peoples were not allowed to attend services at the main cathedral. ■**TIP→ Inside you'll find catacombs and a small religious-art museum.** To the right of the church, the Capilla de la Virgen de Dolores is one of Cajamarca's most beautiful chapels. A large statue of Cajamarca's patron saint, La Virgen de Dolores, makes this a popular pilgrimage destination for local penitents. ⊠*Northeast corner of Plaza de Armas* ☎*No phone* 🎫*S/3 for museum* ⊗*Daily 3–6.*

❷ Plaza de Armas. Like all main colonial cities, this is the main square and includes a fountain, benches, and street vendors, making it a nice place to hang out. Built on roughly the same spot as the great plaza where the Atahualpa was captured and later killed, Cajamarca's Plaza de Armas no longer shows any sign of Inca influence, but it's good to remember. ⊠*Av. Lima and Arequipa.*

OFF THE BEATEN PATH

Cumbe Mayo. This pre-Inca site, 23 km (14 mi) southwest of Cajamarca, is surrounded by a large rock outcropping, where you'll find various petroglyphs left by the ancient Cajamarcans. There are also petroglyph-adorned caves so a guided tour is highly recommended. This site, discovered in 1937 by the famous Peruvian archaeologist J. C. Tello, also includes some of the most notable aqueducts in the Andes. Constructed around 1000 BC, the aqueduct was designed to direct the ample water from the Andes into the drier area of Cajamarca, where there was a large reservoir. Amazingly, more than 8 km (5 mi) of the ancient aqueduct are intact today. Guided tours cost around S/25 and take about four hours.

OUTDOOR ACTIVITIES

A number of hikes are in the area around Cajamarca, from the rivers of the region, to past Inca and pre-Inca ruins. Most follow the *Capac Ñan* or Royal Inca Road, that ran from Cusco all the way north to Quito. One of the most popular walks is to the pre-Inca necropolis of **Combayo.** To get to the trailhead, drive 20 km (12 mi) north of the Baños del Inca. The hike takes around four or five hours. The **Ruta del Tambo Inca** takes you to an old Inca *tambo,* or resting point. It's difficult to find this trailhead and roads sometimes get washed out during the rainy season, so ask in town to confirm the following: Drive 46 km (28 mi) from Cajamarca on the road to Hualgayoc. Near Las Lagunas turn onto a dirt road and follow the road to the milk depository at Ingatambo. The trail begins from here. The 16-km (10-mi) trip takes about eight hours. The best time to go trekking is during the dry season, May through September.

The **Association for the Rescue of the Cajamarcan Ecosystem** (⊠*Av. Manco Cápac 1098* ☎*076/894–600 Ext. 360* ⊕*www.aprec.org*) publishes an excellent guide with maps and route descriptions of many other hikes in the region. The goal is to create sustainable ecotourism in a place where the mining companies control the local economy. Their office is in the Hotel Laguna Seca. **Clarin Tours** (⊠*Jr. Del Batán 161* ☎*076/366–829* ✍*clarintours@yahoo.com*) offers trips, with English-speaking guides, to many of the ruins in and around Cajamarca.

WHERE TO EAT

¢–$$
★

✕**El Batán.** Although the food is excellent, the real feast is the visual one: the restaurant building is a beautifully restored 18th-century mansion. The patio dining area, including a stained-glass roof, has iron chairs and a stone floor. In addition to picturesque surroundings, this criollo restaurant has specialty meat dishes, a menu in Spanish and English, a small art gallery upstairs, and live music on the weekends. ⊠*Jr. Del Batán 369* ☎*076/366–025* ▭*AE, DC, MC, V* ☺*Closes at 6 on Sun.*

¢–$

✕**Cascanuez.** This is the place in Cajamarca for decadent desserts and delicious coffee. Casanuez translates to "Nutcracker," and Sugar Plum Fairies would approve of the extensive homemade pastries, tortes, and other tempting treats. There's also a small dinner and lunch menu with highland staples such as potato soup and grilled meats, but the desserts are their mainstay and important not to miss. ⊠*Av. Puga 554* ☎*076/366–089* ⊟*AE, DC, MC, V.*

¢–$ ★ ✗**El Querubino.** Here gourmet food is paired with slow service. Ask for the chef's daily specials or enjoy a large selection of dishes, such as fettucini with pesto sauce, gnocchi with herbed-sauce, roasted duck or *causa de langostinos,* mashed potatoes with shrimp. To compliment your meal, choose from the most extensive wine list in Cajamarca and enjoy the nice details, such as the monogrammed plates in pastel hues and walls painted a soft Tuscan yellow. ⊠*Av. Puga 589* ☎*076/340–900* ⊟*AE, DC, MC, V.*

> ## DRINKING THE AGUARDIENTES
>
> Homemade *aguardientes* (homemade liqueurs) are common throughout the region. They're made in sundry flavors, including *mora* (blackberry), *maracuyá* (passion fruit), *café* (coffee), and *leche* (milk). Unfortunately, there's no place that offers tourists a sample, so if you want to try one of these strong, home-brewed liqueurs, you'll have to convince a Peruvian to take you home and share his private collection.

¢–$ ✗**Salas.** Across from the Plaza de Armas, this is where to get typical food from the area. Open 7–10 daily, the menu includes authentic regional specialties such as *cuy* (guinea pig), *perico* (a lake fish), and Spanish-style tortillas. There's also an extensive selection of piscos, top-shelf liquors, and wines. Although the furnishings and staff look like they have been there since the restaurant opened in 1947, the food is fresh and delicious. ⊠*Av. Puga 637* ☎*076/362–867* ⊟*AE, DC, MC, V.*

WHERE TO STAY

$ 🖼**Hotel El Ingenio.** The best bargain in Cajamarca. Like all the other hotels, this is in a renovated hacienda with extensive grounds. There's a lovely central courtyard with a giant orange tree, well-kept gardens, and a charming wooden bar. Each room is simply decorated with antique-looking hardwood furniture and large, comfy beds. **Pros:** The same quality service at a very reasonable price. **Cons:** Some rooms are better than others. ⊠*Av. Via de Evitamiento 1611–1709* ☎*076/367–121 or 076/368–733* ⊕*www.elingenio.com* ↵*33 rooms, 6 suites* ♿*In-room: safe. In-hotel: restaurant, room service, bar, laundry service, public Internet, Wi-Fi, parking (no fee)* ⊟*AE, DC, MC, V* ⦿*CP.*

$$–$$$$ Fodor'sChoice ★ 🖼**Hotel Laguna Seca.** Come here to pamper yourself. This refurbished hacienda, which has well-manicured garden areas throughout its extensive grounds, offers private and public baths from the nearby natural thermal hot springs—in fact, each room has a large tub and direct access to this water. ■**TIP➡** Try a massage or other spa treatment, relax in the Jacuzzi, or tour the grounds on horseback. Decorated with antique-looking hardwood furniture and large, comfy beds, every detail of this hotel was chosen to help guests do one thing: relax. **Pros:** In-room natural hot spring water. **Cons:** Outside of the city limits. ⊠*Av. Manco*

9

Cápac 1098, Baños del Inca ☎*076/584–300* ☐*076/584–311* ⊕*www. lagunaseca.com.pe* ⮐*37 rooms, 5 suites* ⬧*In-room: Wi-Fi. In-hotel: restaurant, room service, bars, pools, spa, bicycles, laundry service, Wi-Fi, airport shuttle* ▭*AE, DC, MC, V.*

$ 📷**El Portal del Marques.** If you want to stay in Cajamarca's historic district, this lovely casona is an excellent choice. Surrounding two sunny courtyards, the rooms have a modern style while the common areas have hand-woven rugs and antique colonial furniture. The beds are narrow and soft. **Pros:** In the heart of Cajamarca city. **Cons:** The city can be noisy. ⊠*Jr. de Comercio 644* ☎*076/343–339* ⊕*www. portaldelmarques.com* ⮐*31 rooms, 2 suites* ⬧*In-room: safe. In-hotel: restaurant, bar, laundry service, public Internet, Wi-Fi, parking (no fee)* ▭*AE, DC, MC, V* ⦿|*CP.*

$ 📷**La Posada del Puruay.** In the countryside, this hacienda is far from
☾   the noise of Cajamarca and has extensive gardens, a trout hatchery,
★   and green hills for horseback riding and hiking. The hacienda was constructed in 1914, so the rooms have authentic touches like vaulted wood-beam ceilings. Large rosaries adorn the walls. It feels like you're visiting well-to-do relatives for a summer holiday. **Pros:** Transported to another time and place, reasonable price. **Cons:** Few rooms can be a drawback if you don't like the other guests. ⊠*Carretera Porcón, Km 4.5* ☎*076/367–028* ☎☐*076/367–928* ⮐*7 rooms, 6 suites* ⬧*In-room: VCR, Wi-Fi (some). In-hotel: restaurant, room service, bar, bicycles, playground, laundry service, airport shuttle, parking (no fee)* ▭*AE, DC, MC, V* ⦿|*BP.*

NIGHTLIFE

Los Frailones (⊠*Av. Perú 701* ☎*076/344–272* ⊕*www.losfrailones. com*) has an air of sophistication not often found in these parts. This beautifully renovated casona has antiques throughout. The waiters dress in monks' robes. The house has several levels, where you'll find a grill, a dance floor, and a cozy pub. There are peñas on weekends and sometimes during the week. **Up & Down** (⊠*Tarapacá 782* ☎*No phone*) has a dance floor in the basement with overwhelmingly loud salsa and pop music. **Cowboy Pub** (⊠*Amalia Puga 212* ☎*076/365–529*) is a local watering hole, popular with the town's miners.

SHOPPING

The town of **Llacanora,** 13 km (8 mi) from the city on the road to the Baños del Inca, is a typical Andean farming community, now a cooperative farm, famous for agriculture and making reed bugles. People come to see the traditional village, but there are also several shops around town to buy locally produced goods.

CHACHAPOYAS

460 km (285 mi) east of Chiclayo.

At the *ceja de la selva* (jungle's eyebrow), Chachapoyas is the capital of Peru's Amazonas department. ■**TIP→ The town is a good jumping-off point for exploring some of Peru's most fascinating and least-visited pre-**

Inca ruins. The giant fortress at Kuélap, and the ruins of Purunllacta and Gran Vilaya are nearby. Despite the Amazonas moniker, there's nothing junglelike about the area around Chachapoyas. The surrounding green highlands constitute what most people would call a highland cloud forest. Farther east, in the region of Loreto (won by Peru in the 1942 border dispute with Ecuador), you'll find true jungle.

Chachapoyas is a sleepy little town of 20,000. It has a well-preserved colonial center and one small archaeological museum. Chachapoyas—difficult to reach because of the poor roads through the mountains—is most easily accessed from Chiclayo. Infrequent flights arrive here from Lima as well.

GETTING AROUND
In town, everything is close and within walking distance. There are plenty of taxis, but you'll have little chance of needing one. To get to the archaeological sites, you must go with a guide. The most enjoyable and cost-effective way of doing this is with a tour. There's no public transportation and you cannot hire a guide once at the sites.

ESSENTIALS
CURRENCY **Banco de Crédito** (⊠ *Jr. Ortiz Arrieta 576* ☎ *041/777–430* ⊕ *www.viabcp.com*).

MEDICAL **Hospital Chachapoyas** (⊠ *Jr. Triunfo, Cuadra 3* ☎ *044/777–354*).

VISITOR INFO **iPerú** (⊠ *Jr. Ortiz Arrieta 588* ☎ *041/477–292* ⊕ *www.peru.info*).

WHAT TO SEE
The **Iglesia Santa Ana** is the town's oldest church. It was one of Peru's first "Indian churches," where indigenous people were forced to attend services. The church was built in the 17th century and is on a small square of the same name. ⊠ *Av. Santa Ana.*

Showing artifacts from the area's ancient civilizations, a small display of Chachapoyan ceramics is at the **Museo Arqueologico.** You'll also find a ghoulish display of mummies lying in the fetal position. ⊠ *Jr. Ayacucho 504* ☎ *041/477–045* 🎫 *Free* ⏰ *Wekdays 8–1 and 2–4:45.*

This small, rocky natural hot spring, a few blocks west of the Plaza de Armas at the **Pozo de Yanayacu** isn't much, but is nice to look at. It's said the spring magically appeared during a visit from Saint Toribio de Mogrovejo. ⊠ *Jr. Salamanca, 2 blocks west of Jr. Puno.*

OFF THE BEATEN PATH

Purunllacta. About 35 km (22 mi) southeast of Chachapoyas are the ruins of Purunllacta, a good place for hiking. With pre-Inca agricultural terraces, dwellings, ceremonial platforms, and roads extending for more than 420 hectares, but few tourists, this can be peaceful and also boring as you have no explanation of what you're seeing. To get here, drive to the town of Cheto. From the town it's a one-hour walk uphill to the site. Few people know about this or go, so ask in Cheto for directions to the trailhead, and don't be alarmed if you have to ask more than one person. There's no entrance fee.

9

The circular structures at the pre-Inca city of Kuélep.

WHERE TO EAT

¢ ✗ **El Tejado.** With windows overlooking the town's Plaza de Armas, this is one of the most elegant eateries in Chachapoyas. The criollo food is serviceable, and the staff is most attentive when the *dueña* (owner) is around. ✉ *Jr. Santo Domingo 424* ☎ *041/477–592* ▤ *No credit cards.*

CERAMIC STOP

About 10 km (6 mi) north of Chachapoyas is the tiny pueblo of **Huancas,** whose citizens are well-known for their pottery; this is a good place to buy artisanal goods and locally made ceramics.

¢ ✗ **La Tushpa.** Probably the best eatery in town, La Tushpa has good grilled steaks served with homemade *chimichuri* (a green sauce made with herbs, garlic, and tomatoes). There are also pizzas and other items from the on-site bakery. Though the place feels institutional, the restaurant is more welcoming than most in the region, thanks to an extremely friendly waitstaff. Make sure to look at the Andean textiles hanging on the walls. Ask to see the owner's orchard garden, which he keeps above the restaurant. ✉ *Jr. Ortiz Arrieta 769* ☎ *041/477–478* ▤ *V.*

WHERE TO STAY

¢ ▨ **Gran Hotel Vilaya.** A pleasant, if slightly antiseptic, hotel in the center of Chachapoyas, the Gran Hotel Vilaya has rooms with simple wooden furnishings. The service is quite friendly, and there's a good in-house travel agency. **Pros:** Good service. **Cons:** Unattractive concrete building. ✉ *Jr. Ayacucho 755* ☎ *041/477–664* ▤ *041/478–154* ⊕ *www.hotel-*

vilaya.com ⏎*19 rooms, 1 suite* &*In-room: no phone, safe. In-hotel: bar, laundry service, airport shuttle* 🖃 V 🔟CP.

¢ 🏨**Hostal Casa Vieja.** This colorful old house, with its bougainvillea-
★ filled courtyard and pleasant terraces is the finest in Chachapoya. There's a charming salon with a fireplace and upright piano. The rooms vary greatly; ask to see a handful before you decide. No. 3, with its large sitting area and chimney, is the nicest. **Pros:** Amazing old house with modern touches. **Cons:** Some rooms are better than others. ✉*Jr. Chincha Alta 569* ☎041/477–353 ⊕*www.casaviejaperu.com* ⏎*11 rooms, 3 suites* &*In-hotel: restaurant, room service, laundry service, Wi-Fi, airport shuttle* 🖃V.

¢ 🏨**Puma Urco.** Simple, clean rooms and friendly staff make this a good budget alternative. Most rooms have large beds with flowers painted over the headboards. However, the walls are paper-thin. This is a good choice if all other options are full. **Pros:** Good location. **Cons:** Very basic rooms. ✉*Jr. Amazonas 833* ☎041/477–871 ⏎*20 rooms* &*In-room: no phone. In-hotel: laundry service* 🖃*No credit cards.*

NIGHTLIFE & THE ARTS

La Reina (✉*Jr. Ayacucho 727* ☎041/477–618) has a large selection of local *aguardientes* (locally distilled liquors) in flavors that range from *leche* (milk) to *mora* (blackberry). **La Estancia** (✉*Jr. Amazonas 861* ☎041/478–432) is a friendly pub. The owner loves to chat with the customers about the region's history and natural beauty.

KUÉLAP

★ *72 km (45 mi) south of Chachapoyas.*

The most impressive archaeological site in the area is the immense pre-Inca city of Kuélap. Most visitors to this region come solely to see the grand city. Little is known about the people who built it; archaeologists have named them the Chachapoyans or Sachupoyans. They were most likely a warlike people, as the city of Kuélap is surrounded by a massive defensive wall ranging from 6 to 12 meters (20 to 40 feet) high. The Chachapoyans left many cities and fortresses around the area. In 1472 they were conquered by the Inca Huayna Capac. ■**TIP➜ If you've been to Machu Picchu, or just seen photographs, you'll recognize many similarities in this complex, built almost a thousand years before.**

A visit to Kuélap is an all-day affair. The city sits at a dizzying 3,100 meters (10,075 feet) above sea level, high above the Río Utcubamba. The oval-shape city has more than 400 small, rounded buildings. The city's stonework, though rougher than that of the Inca, has geometric patterns and designs, adding a flight of fancy to a town seemingly designed for the art of war. The most interesting of the rounded buildings has been dubbed El Tintero (the Inkpot). Here you'll find a large underground chamber with a huge pit. ■**TIP➜ Archaeologists hypothesize that the Chachapoyans kept pumas in this pit, dumping human sacrifices into its depths.**

9

It's best to visit Kuélap with a tour group from Chachapoyas. The trip costs around S/60 per person. Vilaya Tours, in the Grand Hotel Vilaya, is highly recommended. Remember to bring a hat for protection from the sun. Take frequent rests and drink lots of water to avoid altitude sickness. ✉ *72 km (45 mi) south of Chachapoyas* ☎ *No phone* 🎫 *S/11.20* ⊙ *Daily 6–6.*

UNDERSTANDING PERU

English-Spanish
Vocabulary

SPANISH VOCABULARY

	ENGLISH	SPANISH	PRONUNCIATION
BASICS			
	Yes/no	Sí/no	see/no
	Please	Por favor	pore fah-**vore**
	May I?	¿Me permite?	may pair-**mee**-tay
	Thank you (very much)	(Muchas) gracias	(**moo**-chas) **grah**-see-as
	You're welcome	De nada	day **nah**-dah
	Excuse me	Con permiso	con pair-**mee**-so
	Pardon me	¿Perdón?	pair-**dohn**
	Could you tell me?	¿Podría decirme?	po-dree-ah deh-**seer**-meh
	I'm sorry	Lo siento	lo see-**en**-toh
	Good morning!	¡Buenos días!	**bway**-nohs **dee**-ahs
	Good afternoon!	¡Buenas tardes!	**bway**-nahs **tar**-dess
	Good evening!	¡Buenas noches!	**bway**-nahs **no**-chess
	Goodbye!	¡Adiós!/¡Hasta luego!	ah-dee-**ohss/ah**-stah **lwe**-go
	Mr./Mrs.	Señor/Señora	sen-**yor**/sen-**yohr**-ah
	Miss	Señorita	sen-yo-**ree**-tah
	Pleased to meet you	Mucho gusto	**moo**-cho **goose**-toh
	How are you?	¿Cómo está usted?	**ko**-mo es-**tah** oo-**sted**
	Very well, thank you.	Muy bien, gracias.	**moo**-ee bee-**en**, **grah**-see-as
	And you?	¿Y usted?	ee oos-**ted**
	Hello (on the telephone)	Diga	**dee**-gah
NUMBERS			
	1	un, uno	oon, **oo**-no
	2	dos	dos
	3	tres	tress
	4	cuatro	**kwah**-tro
	5	cinco	**sink**-oh

6	seis	saice
7	siete	see-**et**-eh
8	ocho	**o**-cho
9	nueve	new-**eh**-vey
10	diez	dee-**es**
11	once	**ohn**-seh
12	doce	**doh**-seh
13	trece	**treh**-seh
14	catorce	ka-**tohr**-seh
15	quince	**keen**-seh
16	dieciséis	dee-**es**-ee-**saice**
17	diecisiete	dee-**es**-ee-see-**et**-eh
18	dieciocho	dee-**es**-ee-**o**-cho
19	diecinueve	**dee-es**-ee-new-**ev**-eh
20	veinte	**vain**-teh
21	veinte y uno/veintiuno	**vain**-te-**oo**-noh
30	treinta	**train**-tah
32	treinta y dos	train-tay-**dohs**
40	cuarenta	kwah-**ren**-tah
43	cuarenta y tres	kwah-**ren**-tay-**tress**
50	cincuenta	seen-**kwen**-tah
54	cincuenta y cuatro	seen-**kwen**-tay **kwah**-tro
60	sesenta	sess-**en**-tah
65	sesenta y cinco	sess-**en**-tay **seen**-ko
70	setenta	set-**en**-tah
76	setenta y seis	set-**en**-tay **saice**
80	ochenta	oh-**chen**-tah
87	ochenta y siete	oh-**chen**-tay see-**yet**-eh
90	noventa	no-**ven**-tah
98	noventa y ocho	no-**ven**-tah-**o**-choh
100	cien	see-**en**

101	ciento uno	see-**en**-toh **oo**-noh
200	doscientos	doh-see-**en**-tohss
500	quinientos	keen-**yen**-tohss
700	setecientos	set-eh-see-**en**-tohss
900	novecientos	no-veh-see-**en**-tohss
1,000	mil	meel
2,000	dos mil	dohs meel
1,000,000	un millón	oon meel-**yohn**

COLORS

black	negro	**neh**-groh
blue	azul	ah-**sool**
brown	café	kah-**feh**
green	verde	**ver**-deh
pink	rosa	**ro**-sah
purple	morado	mo-**rah**-doh
orange	naranja	na-**rahn**-hah
red	rojo	**roh**-hoh
white	blanco	**blahn**-koh
yellow	amarillo	ah-mah-**ree**-yoh

DAYS OF THE WEEK

Sunday	domingo	doe-**meen**-goh
Monday	lunes	**loo**-ness
Tuesday	martes	**mahr**-tess
Wednesday	miércoles	me-**air**-koh-less
Thursday	jueves	hoo-**ev**-ess
Friday	viernes	vee-**air**-ness
Saturday	sábado	**sah**-bah-doh

MONTHS

January	enero	eh-**neh**-roh
February	febrero	feh-**breh**-roh
March	marzo	**mahr**-soh
April	abril	ah-**breel**

May	mayo	**my**-oh
June	junio	**hoo**-nee-oh
July	julio	**hoo**-lee-yoh
August	agosto	ah-**ghost**-toh
September	septiembre	sep-tee-**em**-breh
October	octubre	oak-**too**-breh
November	noviembre	no-vee-**em**-breh
December	diciembre	dee-see-**em**-breh

USEFUL PHRASES

Do you speak English?	¿Habla usted inglés?	**ah**-blah oos-**ted** in-**glehs**
I don't speak Spanish	No hablo español	no **ah**-bloh es-pahn-**yol**
I don't understand (you)	No entiendo	no en-tee-**en**-doh
I understand (you)	Entiendo	en-tee-**en**-doh
I don't know	No sé	no seh
I am American/British	Soy americano (americana)/ inglés(a)	soy ah-meh-ree-**kah**-no (ah-meh-ree-**kah**-nah)/in-**glehs**(ah)
What's your name?	¿Cómo se llama usted?	koh-mo seh **yah**-mah oos-**ted**
My name is . . .	Me llamo . . .	may **yah**-moh
What time is it?	¿Qué hora es?	keh **o**-rah es
It is one, two, three . . . o'clock.	Es la una./Son las dos, tres . . .	es la **oo**-nah/sohn lahs dohs, tress
Yes, please/No, thank you	Sí, por favor/No, gracias	**see** pohr fah-**vor**/no **grah**-see-us
How?	¿Cómo?	**koh**-mo
When?	¿Cuándo?	**kwahn**-doh
This/Next week	Esta semana/ la semana que entra	**es**-teh seh-**mah**-nah/ lah seh-**mah**-nah keh **en**-trah
This/Next month	Este mes/el próximo mes	**es**-teh mehs/el **proke**-see-mo mehs
This/Next year	Este año/el año que viene	**es**-teh **ahn**-yo/el **ahn**-yo keh vee-**yen**-ay

Yesterday/today/ tomorrow	Ayer/hoy/mañana	ah-**yehr**/oy/ mahn-**yah**-nah
This morning/ afternoon	Esta mañana/ tarde	es-tah mahn-**yah**-nah/ **tar**-deh
Tonight	Esta noche	es-tah **no**-cheh
What?	¿Qué?	keh
What is it?	¿Qué es esto?	keh es **es**-toh
Why?	¿Por qué?	pore **keh**
Who?	¿Quién?	kee-**yen**
Where is . . . ?	¿Dónde está . . . ?	**dohn**-deh es-**tah**
the train station?	la estación del tren?	la es-tah-see-on del trehn
the subway station?	la estación del tren subterráneo?	la es-ta-see-**on** del trehn soob-teh-**rrahn**-eh-oh
the bus stop?	la parada del autobus?	la pah-**rah**-dah del ow-toh-**boos**
the post office?	la oficina de correos?	la oh-fee-**see**-nah deh koh-**rreh**-os
the bank?	el banco?	el **bahn**-koh
the hotel?	el hotel?	el oh-**tel**
the store?	la tienda?	la tee-**en**-dah
the cashier?	la caja?	la **kah**-hah
the museum?	el museo?	el moo-**seh**-oh
the hospital?	el hospital?	el ohss-pee-**tal**
the elevator?	el ascensor?	el ah-**sen**-sohr
the bathroom?	el baño?	el **bahn**-yoh
Here/there	Aquí/allá	ah-**key**/ah-**yah**
Open/closed	Abierto/cerrado	ah-bee-**er**-toh/ ser-**ah**-doh
Left/right	Izquierda/derecha	iss-key-**er**-dah/ dare-**eh**-chah
Straight ahead	Derecho	dare-**eh**-choh
Is it near/far?	¿Está cerca/lejos?	es-**tah sehr**-kah/ **leh**-hoss
I'd like . . .	Quisiera . . .	kee-see-ehr-ah
a room	un cuarto/una habitación	oon **kwahr**-toh/ **oo**-nah ah-bee-tah-see-**on**
the key	la llave	lah **yah**-veh
a newspaper	un periódico	oon pehr-ee-**oh**-dee-koh
a stamp	un sello de correo	oon **seh**-yo deh koh-**reh**-oh

I'd like to buy . . .	Quisiera comprar . . .	kee-see-**ehr**-ah kohm-**prahr**
cigarettes	cigarrillos	ce-ga-**ree**-yohs
matches	cerillos	ser-**ee**-ohs
a dictionary	un diccionario	oon deek-see-oh-**nah**-ree-oh
soap	jabón	hah-**bohn**
sunglasses	gafas de sol	**ga**-fahs deh sohl
suntan lotion	loción bronceadora	loh-see-**ohn** brohn-seh-ah-**do**-rah
a map	un mapa	oon **mah**-pah
a magazine	una revista	**oon**-ah reh-**veess**-tah
paper	papel	pah-**pel**
envelopes	sobres	so-brehs
a postcard	una tarjeta postal	**oon**-ah tar-**het**-ah post-**ahl**
How much is it?	¿Cuánto cuesta?	**kwahn**-toh **kwes**-tah
It's expensive/ cheap	Está caro/barato	es-**tah kah**-roh/ bah-**rah**-toh
A little/a lot	Un poquito/ mucho	oon poh-**kee**-toh/ **moo**-choh
More/less	Más/menos	mahss/**men**-ohss
Enough/too much/too little	Suficiente/ demasiado/ muy poco	soo-fee-see-**en**-teh/ deh-mah-see-**ah**-doh/**moo**-ee poh-koh
Telephone	Teléfono	tel-**ef**-oh-no
Telegram	Telegrama	teh-leh-**grah**-mah
I am ill	Estoy enfermo(a)	es-**toy** en-**fehr**-moh(mah)
Please call a doctor	Por favor llame a un medico	pohr fah-**vor ya**-meh ah oon **med**-ee-koh

ON THE ROAD

Avenue	Avenida	ah-ven-**ee**-dah
Broad, tree-lined boulevard	Bulevar	boo-leh-**var**
Fertile plain	Vega	**veh**-gah
Highway	Carretera	car-reh-**ter**-ah
Mountain pass	Puerto	poo-**ehr**-toh
Street	Calle	**cah**-yeh
Waterfront promenade	Rambla	**rahm**-blah

Wharf	Embarcadero	em-bar-cah-**deh**-ro

IN TOWN

Cathedral	Catedral	cah-teh-**dral**
Church	Templo/Iglesia	**tem**-plo/ee-**glehs**-see-ah
City hall	Casa de gobierno	kah-sah deh go-bee-**ehr**-no
Door, gate	Puerta portón	poo-**ehr**-tah por-**ton**
Entrance/exit	Entrada/salida	en-**trah**-dah/sah-lee-dah
Inn, rustic bar, or restaurant	Taverna	tah-**vehr**-nah
Main square	Plaza principal	plah-thah prin-see-**pahl**
Market	Mercado	mer-**kah**-doh
Neighborhood	Barrio	**bahr**-ree-o
Traffic circle	Glorieta	glor-ee-**eh**-tah
Wine cellar, wine bar, or wine shop	Bodega	boh-**deh**-gah

DINING OUT

Can you recommend a good restaurant?	¿Puede recomendarme un buen restaurante?	**pweh**-deh rreh-koh-mehn-**dahr**-me oon bwehn rrehs-tow-**rahn**-teh?
Where is it located?	¿Dónde está situado?	**dohn**-deh ehs-**tah** see-**twah**-doh?
Do I need reservations?	¿Se necesita una reservación?	seh neh-seh-**see**-tah **oo**-nah rreh-sehr-bah-**syohn**?/
I'd like to reserve a table . . .	Quisiera reservar una mesa . . .	kee-**syeh**-rah rreh-sehr-**bahr** oo-nah **meh**-sah . . .
for two people.	para dos personas.	**pah**-rah dohs pehr-**soh**-nahs
for this evening.	para esta noche.	**pah**-rah **ehs**-tah **noh**-cheh
for 8:00 p.m.	para las ocho de la noche.	**pah**-rah lahs **oh**-choh deh lah **noh**-cheh

A bottle of . . .	Una botella de . . .	**oo**-nah bo-**teh**-yah deh
A cup of . . .	Una taza de . . .	**oo**-nah **tah**-thah deh
A glass of . . .	Un vaso de . . .	oon **vah**-so deh
Ashtray	Un cenicero	oon sen-ee-**seh**-roh
Bill/check	La cuenta	lah **kwen**-tah
Bread	El pan	el pahn
Breakfast	El desayuno	el deh-sah-**yoon**-oh
Butter	La mantequilla	lah man-teh-**key**-yah
Cheers!	¡Salud!	sah-**lood**
Cocktail	Un aperitivo	oon ah-pehr-ee-**tee**-voh
Dinner	La cena	lah **seh**-nah
Dish	Un plato	oon **plah**-toh
Menu of the day	Menú del día	meh-**noo** del **dee**-ah
Enjoy!	¡Buen provecho!	bwehn pro-**veh**-cho
Fixed-price menu	Menú fijo o turistico	meh-**noo fee**-hoh oh too-**ree**-stee-coh
Fork	El tenedor	el ten-eh-**dor**
Is the tip	¿Está incluida la	es-**tah** in-cloo-**ee**-dah
included?	propina?	lah pro-**pee**-nah
Knife	El cuchillo	el koo-**chee**-yo
Large portion of savory snacks	Raciónes	rah-see-**oh**-nehs
Lunch	La comida	lah koh-**mee**-dah
Menu	La carta, el menú	lah **cart**-ah, el meh-**noo**
Napkin	La servilleta	lah sehr-vee-**yet**-ah
Pepper	La pimienta	lah pee-me-**en**-tah
Please give me	Por favor déme	pore fah-**vor deh**-meh
Salt	La sal	lah sahl
Savory snacks	Tapas	**tah**-pahs
Spoon	Una cuchara	**oo**-nah koo-**chah**-rah
Sugar	El azúcar	el ah-**thu**-kar
Waiter!/Waitress!	¡Por favor Señor/Señorita!	pohr fah-**vor** sen-**yor**/sen-yor-**ee**-tah

EMERGENCIES

Look!	¡Mire!	**mee**-reh!
Listen!	¡Escuche!	ehs-**koo**-cheh!
Help!	¡Auxilio! ¡Ayuda! ¡Socorro!	owk-**see**-lee-oh/ ah-**yoo**-dah/ soh-**kohr**-roh
Fire!	¡Incendio!	en-**sen**-dee-oo
Caution!/Look out!	¡Cuidado!	kwee-**dah**-doh
Hurry!	¡Dése prisa!	**deh**-seh **pree**-sah!
Stop!	¡Alto!	**ahl**-toh!
I need help quick!	¡Necesito ayuda, pronto!	neh-seh-**see**-toh ah-**yoo**-dah, **prohn**-toh!
Can you help me?	¿Puede ayudarme?	**pweh**-deh ah-yoo-**dahr**-meh?
Police!	¡Policía!	poh-lee-**see**-ah!
I need a policeman!	¡Necesito un policía!	neh-seh-**see**-toh oon poh-lee-**see**-ah!
It's an emergency!	¡Es una emergencia!	ehs **oo**-nah eh-mehr-**hehn**-syah!
Leave me alone!	¡Déjeme en paz!	**deh**-heh-meh ehn pahs!
That man's a thief!	¡Ese hombre es un ladrón!	**eh**-seh **ohm**-breh ehs oon-lah-**drohn**!
Stop him!	¡Deténganlo!	deh-**tehn**-gahn-loh!
He's stolen my . . . pocketbook. wallet. passport. watch.	Me ha robado . . . la cartera. la billetera. el pasaporte. el reloj.	meh ah rroh-**bah**-doh . . . lah kahr-**teh**-rah lah bee-yeh-**teh**-rah ehl pah-sah-**pohr**-teh ehl rreh-**loh**
I've lost my suitcase. money. glasses. car keys.	He perdido mi maleta. mi dinero. los anteojos. las llaves de mi automóvil.	eh pehr-**dee**-doh mee mah-**leh**-tah mee dee-**neh**-roh lohs ahn-teh-**oh**-hohs lahs **yah**-behs deh mee ow-toh-**moh**-beel

TELLING TIME AND EXPRESSIONS OF TIME

What time is it?	¿Qué hora es?	keh **oh**-rah ehs?
At what time?	¿A qué hora?	ah keh **oh**-rah?
It's . . .	Es . . .	ehs . . .
one o'clock.	la una.	lah **oo**-nah
1:15.	la una y cuarto.	lah **oo**-nah ee **kwahr**-toh
1:30.	la una y media.	lah **oo**-nah ee **meh**-dyah
It's . . .	Son las . . .	sohn lahs . . .
1:45.	dos menos cuarto.	dohs **meh**-nos **kwahr**-toh
two o'clock.	dos.	dohs
morning.	la mañana.	Lah mah-**nyah**-nah
afternoon	la tarde.	lah **tahr**-deh
It's midnight	Es media noche	ehs **meh**-dyah **noh**-cheh
It's noon	Es mediodía	ehs meh-dyoh-**dee** ah
In a half hour	En media hora	ehn **meh**-dyah **oh**-rah
When does it begin?	¿Cuándo empieza?	**kwahn**-doh ehm-**pyeh**-sah?

PAYING THE BILL

How much does it cost?	¿Cuánto cuesta?	**kwahn**-toh **kwehs**-tah?
The bill, please.	La cuenta, por favor.	lah-**kwen**-tah pohr fah-**bohr**
How much do I owe you?	¿Cuánto le debo?	**kwan**-toh leh **deh**-boh?
Is service included?	¿La propina está incluida?	lah proh-**pee**-nah ehs-**tah** een-kloo-ee-dah?
This is for you.	Esto es para usted.	**ehs**-toh ehs pah-rah oos-**tehd**

GETTING AROUND

English	Spanish	Pronunciation
Do you have a map of the city?	¿Tiene usted un mapa de la ciudad?	**tyeh**-neh oos-**tehd** oon **mah**-pah deh lah syoo-**dahd**?
Could you show me on the map?	¿Puede usted indicármelo en el mapa?	**pweh**-deh oo-**stehd** een-dee-**kahr**-meh-loh ehn ehl **mah**-pah?
Can I get there on foot?	¿Puedo llegar allí a pie?	**pweh**-doh yeh-**gahr** ah-**yee** ah pyeh?
How far is it?	¿A qué distancia es?	ah keh dees-**tahn**-syah ehs?
I'm lost.	Estoy perdido(-a).	ehs-**toy** pehr-**dee**-doh(-dah)
Where is . . .	¿Dónde está . . .	**dohn**-deh ehs-**tah** . . .
the Hotel Rex?	el hotel Rex?	ehl oh-**tehl** rreks?
. . . Street?	la calle . . . ?	lah **kah**-yeh . . . ?
. . . Avenue?	la avenida . . . ?	lah ah-beh-**nee**-dah . . . ?
How can I get to . . .	¿Cómo puedo ir a . . .	**koh**-moh **pweh**-doh eer ah . . .
the train station?	la estación de ferrocarril?	lah ehs-tah-**syon** deh feh-rroh-cah-**rreel**?
the bus stop?	la parada de autobuses?	lah pah-**rah**-dah deh ow-toh-**boo**-ses?
the ticket office?	la taquilla?	lah tah-**kee**-yah?
the airport?	el aeropuerto?	ehl ah-eh-roh-**pwehr**-toh?
straight ahead	derecho	deh-**reh**-choh
to the right	a la derecha	ah lah deh-**reh**-chah
to the left	a la izquierda	ah lah ees-**kyehr**-dah
a block away	a una cuadra	ah **oo**-nah **kwah**-drah
on the corner	en la esquina	ehn lah ehs-**kee**-nah
on the square	en la plaza	ehn lah **plah**-sah
facing, opposite	enfrente	ehn-**frehn**-teh
across	al frente	ahl **frehn**-teh
next to	al lado	ahl **lah**-doh
near	cerca	**sehr**-kah
far	lejos	**leh**-hohs

ON THE BUS

I'm looking for the bus stop.	Estoy buscando la parada de autobuses.	ehs-**toy** boos-**kahn**-doh lah pah-**rah**-dah deh ow-toh-**boo**-sehs
What bus line goes . . . north? south? east? west?	¿Qué línea va . . . al norte? al sur? al este? al oeste?	keh **lee**-neh-ah bah . . . ahl **nohr**-teh? ahl soor? ahl **ehs**-teh? ahl oh-**ehs**-teh?
What bus do I take to go to . . .	¿Qué autobús tomo para ir a . . .	keh ow-toh-**boos** **toh**-moh **pah**-rah eer ah . . .
Can you tell me when to get off?	¿Podría decirme cuándo debo bajarme?	poh-**dree**-ah deh-**seer**-meh **kwan**-doh **deh**-boh bah-**hahr**-meh?
How much is the fare?	¿Cuánto es el billete?	**kwahn**-toh ehs ehl bee-**yeh**-teh?
Should I pay when I get on?	¿Debo pagar al subir?	**deh**-boh pah-**gahr** ahl soo-**beer**?
Where do I take the bus to return?	¿Dónde se toma el autobús para regresar?	**dohn**-deh seh **toh**-mah ehl ow-toh-**boos** **pah**-rah rreh-greh-**sahr**?
How often do the return buses run?	¿Cada cuánto hay autobuses de regreso?	**kah**-dah **kwahn**-toh ahy ow-toh-**boo**-sehs deh rreh-**greh**-soh?
I would like . . . a ticket. a receipt. a reserved seat. first class. second class. a direct bus. an express bus. ticketed luggage.	Quisiera . . . un billete un recibo un asiento numerado. primera clase. segunda clase. un autobús directo. un autobús directo. equipaje facturado.	kee-**syeh**-rah . . . oon bee-**yeh**-teh oon reh-**see**-boh oon ah-**syehn**-toh noo-meh-**rah**-doh pree-**meh**-rah-**klah**-seh seh-**goon**-dah **klah**-seh oon ow-toh-**boos** dee-**rehk**-toh oon ow-toh-**boos** ehks-**preh**-soh eh-kee-**pah**-heh fahk-too-**rah**-doh

ACCOMMODATIONS

I have a reservation.	Tengo una reservación/ una reserva.	**tehn**-goh **oo**-nah rreh-sehr-vah-**syohn**/ . . . **oo**-nah rre-**sehr**-vah
I would like a room for . . .	Quisiera una habitación por . . .	kee-**syeh**-rah **oo**-nah ah-bee-tah-**syohn** pohr . . .
one night.	una noche.	**oo**-nah **noh**-cheh
two nights.	dos noches.	dohs **noh**-chehs
a week.	una semana.	**oo**-nah seh-**mah**-nah
two weeks.	dos semanas.	dohs seh-**mah**-nahs
How much is it . . .	¿Cuánto es . . .	**kwahn**-toh ehs . . .
for a day?	por día?	pohr **dee**-ah?
for a week?	por una semana?	pohr **oo**-nah-seh-**mah**-nah?
Does that include tax?	¿Incluye impuestos?	een-**kloo**-yeh eem-**pwehs**-tohs?
Do you have a room with . . .	¿Tiene una habitación con . . .	**tyeh**-neh **oo**-nah ah-bee-tah-**syohn** kohn . . .
a private bath?	baño privado?	**bah**-nyoh pree-**bah**-doh?
a shower?	una ducha?	**oo**-nah **doo**-chah?
air-conditioning?	aire acondicionado?	**ay**-reh ah-kohn-dee-syoh-**nah**-doh?
heat?	calefacción?	kah-leh-fak-**syohn**?
television?	televisor?	teh-leh-bee-**sohr**?
hot water?	agua caliente?	**ah**-gwah kah-**lyehn**-teh?
a balcony?	balcón?	bahl-**kohn**?
a view facing the street?	vista a la calle?	**bees**-tah ah lah **kah**-yeh?
a view facing the ocean?	vista al mar?	**bees**-tah ahl mahr?
Does the hotel have . . .	¿Tiene el hotel . . . ?	**tyeh**-neh ehl oh-**tehl** . . . ?
a restaurant?	un restaurante?	oon rrehs-tow-**rahn**-teh?
a bar?	un bar?	oon bahr?
a swimming pool?	una piscina/ alberca (Mexico)?	**oo**-nah pee-**see**-nah/ ahl-**behr**-kah?
room service?	servicio de habitación?	sehr-**bee**-syoh deh ah-bee-tah-**syohn**?
a safe-deposit box?	una caja de valores/ seguridad?	**oo**-nah **kah**-hah deh bah-**loh**-rehs/ seh-goo-ree-**dahd**?

laundry service?	servicio de lavandería?	sehr-**bee**-syoh deh lah-vahn-deh-**ree**-ah?

I would like . . .	Quisiera . . .	kee-**sye**-rah . . .
meals included.	con las comidas incluidas.	kohn lahs koh-**mee**-dahs een-**kluee**-dahs
breakfast only.	solamente con desayuno.	soh-lah-**men**-teh kohn deh-sah-**yoo**-noh
no meals included.	sin comidas.	seen koh-**mee**-dahs
an extra bed.	una cama más.	**oo**-nah **kah**-mah mahs
a baby crib.	una cuna	**oo**-nah **koo**-nah
another towel.	otra toalla.	**oh**-trah **twah**-yah
soap.	jabón.	hah-**bohn**
clothes hangers.	ganchos de ropa.	**gahn**-chohs deh **rroh**-pah
another blanket.	otra manta.	**oh**-trah **mahn**-tah
drinking water.	agua para beber.	**ah**-gwah **pah**-rah beh-**behr**
toilet paper.	papel higiénico.	pah-**pehl** ee-**hye**-nee-koh

This room is very . . .	Esta habitación es muy . . .	**ehs**-tah ah-bee-tah-**syohn** ehs muee . . .
small.	pequeña.	peh-**keh**-nyah
cold.	fría.	**free**-ah
hot.	caliente.	kah-**lyehn**-teh
dark.	oscura.	ohs-**koo**-rah
noisy.	ruidosa.	rruee-**doh**-sah

The . . . does not work.	No funciona . . .	noh foon-**syoh**-nah
light	la luz.	lah loos
heat	la calefacción.	lah kah-leh-fahk-**syohn**
toilet	el baño.	ehl **bah**-nyoh
the air conditioner	el aire acondicionado.	ehl **ay**-reh ah-kohn-dee-syo-**nah**-doh
key	la llave.	lah **yah**-beh
lock	la cerradura	lah seh-rah-**doo**-rah
fan	el ventilador.	ehl **behn**-tee-lah-**dohr**

outlet	el enchufe.	ehl ehn-**choo**-feh
television	el televisor.	ehl teh-leh-bee-**sohr**

May I change to another room?	¿Podría cambiar de habitación?	poh-**dree**-ah kahm-**byar** deh ah-bee-tah-**syohn**?

Is there . . .	¿Hay . . .	ahy . . .
room service?	servicio de habitación?	sehr-**bee**-syoh deh ah-bee-tah-**syohn**?
laundry service?	servicio de lavandería?	sehr-**bee**-syoh deh lah-vahn-deh-**ree**-ah?

E-MAIL AND THE INTERNET

Where is the computer?	¿Dónde está la computadora?	**dohn**-deh eh-**stah** lah kohm-poo-tah-**doh**-rah
I need to send an e-mail.	Necesito enviar un correo electrónico.	neh-seh-**see**-toh ehn-**byahr** oon koh-**reh**-yoh eh-lehk-**troh**-nee-koh
Can I get on the Internet?	¿Puedo conectarme con el internet?	**pweh**-doh koh-nehk-**tahr**-meh ahl **een**-tehr-net?
Do you have a Web site?	¿Tiene página web?	**tyeh**-neh **pah**-hee-nah web?

BARGAINING

Excuse me.	Perdón.	pehr-**dohn**
I'm interested in this.	Me interesa esto.	meh een-teh-**reh**-sah **ehs**-toh
How much is it?	¿Cuánto cuesta?	**kwahn**-toh **kwehs**-tah?
It's very expensive!	¡Es muy caro!	ehs muee **kah**-roh!
It's overpriced. (It's not worth so much.)	No vale tanto.	noh **vah**-leh **tahn**-toh
Do you have a cheaper one?	¿Tiene uno más barato?	**tyeh**-neh **oo**-noh mahs bah-**rah**-toh?
This is damaged— do you have another one?	Está dañado, ¿hay otro?	ehs-**tah** dah-**nyah**-doh, ahy **oh**-troh?
What is the lowest price?	¿Cuál es el precio mínimo?	**kwahl** ehs ehl **preh**-syoh **mee**-nee-moh?
Is that the final price?	¿Es el último precio?	ehs ehl **ool**-tee-moh **preh**-syoh?
Can't you give me a discount?	¿No me da una rebaja?	noh meh dah **oo**-nah rreh-**bah**-hah?

I'll give you . . .	Le doy . . .	leh doy . . .
I won't pay more than . . .	No pago más de . . .	noh **pah**-goh mahs deh . . .
I'll look somewhere else.	Voy a ver en otro sitio.	voy ah behr ehn **oh**-troh **see**-tyoh
No, thank you.	No, gracias.	noh, **grah**-syahs

TOILETRIES

toiletries	objetos de baño	ohb-**jeh**-tohs deh **bah**-nyoh
a brush	un cepillo	oon seh-**pee**-yoh
cologne	colonia	koh-**loh**-nyah
a comb	un peine	oon **pay**-neh
deodorant	desodorante	deh-soh-doh-**rahn**-teh
disposable	pañales	pah-**nyah**-lehs deh-
diapers	desechables	seh-**chah**-blehs
hairspray	laca	**lah**-kah
a mirror	un espejo	oon ehs-**peh**-hoh
moisturizing lotion	loción humectante	loh-**syohn** oo-mehk-**tahn**-teh
mouthwash	enjuague bucal	ehn-**hwah**-geh boo-**kahl**
nail clippers	cortauñas	kohr-ta-**oo**-nyahs
nail polish	esmalte de uñas	ehs-**mahl**-teh deh **oo**-nyahs
nail polish remover	quitaesmalte	kee-tah-ehs-**mahl**-teh
perfume	perfume	pehr-**foo**-meh
sanitary napkins	toallas sanitarias	toh-**ah**-yahs sah-nee-**tah**-ryahs
shampoo	champú	chahm-**poo**
shaving cream	crema de afeitar	**kreh**-mah deh ah-fay-**tahr**
soap	jabón	hah-**bohn**
a sponge	una esponja	**oo**-nah ehs-**pohn**-hah
tampons	tampones	tahm-**poh**-nehs

tissues	pañuelos de papel	pah-**nyweh**-lohs deh pah-**pehl**
toilet paper	papel higiénico	pah-**pehl** ee-**hyeh**-ee-koh
a toothbrush	un cepillo de dientes	oon seh-**pee**-yoh deh **dyehn**-tehs
toothpaste	pasta de dientes	**pahs**-tah deh **dyehn**-tehs
tweezers	pinzas	**peen**-sahs

Travel Smart Peru

TRANSPORTATION

Because of the long distances involved, most travelers choose to fly between the major cities of Peru. The good news is that domestic flights are surprisingly inexpensive, often less than $100 per segment.

TRAVEL TIMES FROM LIMA		
To	By Air	By Car/Bus
Cusco	1 hour	24 hours
Puno	2 hours	19 hours
Arequipa	1¼ hours	15 hours
Trujillo	1 hour	9 hours

■TIP➔ Ask the local tourist board about hotel and local transportation packages that include tickets to major museum exhibits or other special events.

■ BY AIR

Almost all international flights into Peru touch down at Aeropuerto Internacional Jorge Chávez, on the northwestern fringe of Lima. Flying times are for nonstop flights to Lima: from Miami 5 hours 45 min; Dallas 7 hours 12 min; Houston 6 hours 45 min; Los Angeles 8 hours 35 min; and from New York 7 hours.

Departure taxes on international flights from Lima are US$30.25 and domestic flights US$6.05. These taxes, paid after you check in for your flight, must be paid in cash, either in U.S. dollars or Peruvian nuevos soles. If you're paying in dollars, try to have the exact amount ready, as you'll be given change in local currency. It's a good idea to wait to convert your nuevos soles back to dollars until after you pay the departure tax.

The least expensive airfares to Peru are priced for round-trip travel. Airlines generally allow you to change your return date for a fee; most low-fare tickets, however, are nonrefundable.

Buying an airline ticket in Peru is often cheaper than abroad. For example, a recent ticket for a one-way flight from Lima to Cusco cost $149 online in the U.S. and $86 from a Peruvian travel agent. If you have a flexible schedule, this is a great way to save money.

Airlines & Airports Airline and Airport Links.com (⊕www.airlineandairportlinks.com) has links to many of the world's airlines and airports.

Airline Security Issues Transportation Security Administration (⊕www.tsa.gov) has answers for almost every question that might come up.

AIRPORTS

Peru's main international point of entry is Aeropuerto Internacional Jorge Chávez (LIM), on the northwestern fringe of Lima. It's a completely modern facility with plenty of dining and shopping options. There are ATMs and currency exchange offices in the main terminal and the arrivals terminals. These are nowhere to be found in the departures terminal, so do your banking before heading through security.

Airport Information Aeropuerto Internacional Jorge Chávez (✉Av. Faucett s/n ☎01/517–3100 ⊕www.lap.com.pe/ingles).

GROUND TRANSPORTATION

If your hotel doesn't offer to pick you up at the airport, you'll have to take a taxi. There will be a line of sleek black cars just outside the main terminal. Agree on a price before getting in or allowing the driver to handle your luggage. A taxi to most places in the city should cost no more than US$15. It's a 20-minute drive to El Centro, and a 30-minute drive to Miraflores and San Isidro.

FLIGHTS

Dozens of international flights touch down daily at Lima's Aeropuerto Internacional Jorge Chávez, mostly from other Latin American cities. But there are also plenty from the U.S. American flies from Miami, Continental flies from Houston and Newark. Delta has daily flights from Atlanta, and Spirit has connections through Fort Lauderdale. The South American–based airline Lan flies from Los Angeles, Miami, and New York's JFK. Air Canada flies from Toronto.

If you're flying from other Latin American cities, you have a wide range of regional carriers at your disposal. Lan has flights from most major airports in the region, as does Taca. Copa, affiliated with Continental, flies from its hub in Panama City. Aeroméxico flies from Mexico City, Aerolineas Argentinas flies from Buenos Aires, Avianca from Bogota, and Lacsa from San José, Costa Rica.

With four mountain ranges running through Peru plus a large swath of the Amazon jungle, flying is the best way to travel between most cities and towns. Lan, which in the past few years has become the carrier with the most national flights, departs several times each day for Arequipa, Cusco, Juliaca, Puerto Maldonado, and Trujillo. Aero Cóndor has daily flights to Arequipa Cusco, and Iquitos. Star Perú flies to Arequipa, Cusco, Juliaca, Iquitos, and Trujillo, and Taca Peru flies to Arequipa and Cusco.

Airline Contacts Aerolineas Argentinas (☎800/333-0276 in North America, 01/513-6575 in Lima ⊕www.aerolineas.com.ar). **Aeroméxico** (☎800/237-6639 in North America, 01/421-3500 in Lima ⊕www.aerolineas.com.ar). **Air Canada** (☎888/247-2262 in North America, 01/241-1457 in Lima ⊕www.air-canada.com). **American Airlines** (☎800/433-7300, 01/211-7000 in Lima ⊕www.aa.com). **Avianca** (☎800/284-2622 in North America, 01/444-0747 in Lima ⊕www.avianca.com). **Continental Airlines** (☎800/523-3273 for U.S. and Mexico reservations, 800/231-0856 for international reservations, 01/712-9230 in Lima ⊕www.continental.com). **Copa** (☎800/359-2672 in North America, 01/610-0808 in Lima ⊕www.copaair.com). **Delta Airlines** (☎800/221-1212 for U.S. reservations, 800/241-4141 for international reservations, 01/211-9211 in Lima ⊕www.delta.com). **Lan** (☎866/435-9526 in North America, 01/213-8200 in Lima ⊕www.lan.com). **Taca** (☎800/400-8222 in North America, 01/511-8222 in Lima ⊕grupotaca.com).

Domestic Airlines Aero Cóndor (☎01/614-6014 ⊕www.aerocondor.com.pe). **Lan** (☎01/221-3764 ⊕www.lan.com). **Star Perú.** ☎01/705-9000 ⊕www.starperu.com. **Taca Peru** (☎01/446-0033 ⊕grupotaca.com).

❚ BY BUS

The intercity bus system in Peru is extensive, and fares are quite reasonable. Remember, however, that distances between cities can be daunting. It's best to use buses for shorter trips, such as between Lima and Ica or between Cusco and Puno. That way you can begin and end your trip during daylight hours. If you stick with one of the recommended companies, like Cruz del Sur or Ormeño, you can usually expect a comfortable journey.

Second-class buses (*servicio normal*) tend to be overcrowded and uncomfortable, whereas the more expensive first-class service (*primera clase*) is more comfortable and much more likely to arrive on schedule.

Bus fares are substantially cheaper in South America than they are in North America or Europe. Competing bus companies serve all major and many minor routes, so it can pay to shop around if you're on an extremely tight budget. Always speak to the counter clerk, as competition may mean fares are cheaper than the official price posted on the fare board.

For the 14-hour journey between Lima and Arequipa, Cruz del Sur's fares for its top service, called *Cruzero,* is about $32. Its less-expensive service, called *Imperial,* is $22. Oremño's top service is called *Royal Class* and the one-way fare from Lima to Arequipa is around US$26, and *Business Class* is around $13.

Tickets are sold at bus-company offices and at travel agencies. Be prepared to pay with cash, as credit cards aren't always accepted. Reservations aren't necessary except for trips to popular destinations during high season. Summer weekends and major holidays are the busiest times. You should arrive at bus stations early for travel during peak seasons.

Bus Information Cruz del Sur (⊠Av. Javier Prado 1109, San Isidro, Lima ☎01/225–6163 ⊕www.cruzdelsur.com.pe). **Ormeño** (⊠Av. Javier Prado Este 1059, San Isidro, Lima ☎01/472–1710 ⊕www.grupo-ormeno.com.pe).

▌ BY CAR

Should you rent a car in Peru? In general, it's not a great idea to have a car in Peru. Driving is a heart-stopping experience, as most Peruvians see traffic laws as suggestions rather than rules. That said, there are a few places in Peru where having a car is a benefit, such as between Lima and points south on the Pan-American Highway. The highway follows the Pacific Ocean coastline before it cuts in through the desert, and stops can be made along the way for a picnic and a swim. The highway is good, and although there isn't too much to see along the way, it's nice to have the freedom a car affords once you get to your destination.

If you rent a car, keep these tips in mind: outside cities, drive only during daylight hours, fill your gas tank whenever possible, and make sure your spare tire is in good repair. In some areas, drivers caught using a cell phone while driving receive a hefty fine, especially on the coastal highway following the cliff along the Pacific Ocean between Lima and Miraflores, and San Isidro.

If you plan to rent a car it's best to make arrangements before you leave home, and book through a travel agent who will shop around for a good deal. If you plan to rent during a holiday period, reserve early. Consider hiring a car and driver through your hotel, or making a deal with a taxi driver, for some extended sightseeing. Drivers often charge an hourly rate regardless of the distance traveled. You'll have to pay cash, but you'll often spend less than you would for a rental car.

The minimum age for renting a car in Peru is 25. All major car-rental agencies have branches in downtown Lima as well as branches at Jorge Chávez International Airport that are open 24 hours.

The cost of rental cars varies widely, but is generally between $18 and $28 for a compact, $30 to $41 for a full-size car. A $10 collision damage waiver is usually added to your bill. Always make sure to check the fine print, as some companies give you unlimited mileage whereas others give you between 200 and 240 km (124 and 150 mi) free, then charge you a hefty 25 cents for every kilometer you drive above that.

Massive road-improvement programs have improved highways. But elsewhere, including some parts of Lima, roads are littered with potholes. Outside of the cities, street signs are rare, lighting is nonexistent, and lanes are unmarked. Roads are straight along the coast, but in the mountains they snake around enough to make even the most steady driver a little queasy.

And then there are the drivers. When they get behind the wheel, Peruvians are very assertive. Expect lots of honking and last-minute lane switching when you're in a city. On the highways you'll encounter constant tailgating and passing on blind curves. Take our word for it and leave the driving to someone else.

The major highways in Peru are the Pan-American Highway, which runs down the entire coast, and the Carretera Central, which runs from Lima to Huancayo. Most highways have no names or numbers; they're referred to by destination.

Always give the rental car a once-over to make sure that the headlights, jack, and tires (including the spare) are in working condition. Note any existing damages to the car and get a signature acknowledging the damage, no matter how slight.

GASOLINE
Gas stations are almost never found in the middle of the large cities. Most are on the outskirts, and are often difficult to find. Make sure to ask your rental company where they're located. Stations along the highways are few and far between, so don't pass up on the chance to gas up. Many stations are now open 24 hours.

PARKING
If you have a rental car, make sure your hotel has its own parking lot. If not, ask about nearby lots. In the cities, guarded parking lots that charge about $1 an hour are common.

ROADSIDE EMERGENCIES
The Touring and Automobile Club of Peru will provide 24-hour emergency road service for members of the American Automobile Association (AAA) and affiliates upon presentation of their membership cards. Members of AAA can purchase good maps at low prices.

Emergency Services Touring and Automobile Club of Peru (✉ César Vallejo 699, Lince, Lima ☎ 01/221-2432 ⊕ www.touringperu.com.pe).

RULES OF THE ROAD
In Peru your own driver's license is acceptable identification, but an international driving permit is good to have. They're available from the American and Canadian automobile associations and, in the United Kingdom, from the Automobile Association and Royal Automobile Club. These international permits, valid only in conjunction with your regular driver's license, are universally recognized; having one may save you a problem with local authorities.

Speed limits are 25 kph–35 kph (15 mph–20 mph) in residential areas, 85 kph–100 kph (50 mph–60 mph) on highways. Traffic tickets range from a minimum of $4 to a maximum of $40. The police and military routinely check drivers at road blocks, so make sure your papers are easily accessible. Peruvian law makes it a crime to drive while intoxicated, although many Peruvians ignore that prohibition.

▋ BY TRAIN

PeruRail is operated by Orient-Express, the same company that runs one of the most luxurious and famous trains in the world, the Venice Simplon Orient Express between London and Venice. Since the company took over in 1999 it has been making constant improvements. First-class cars have been added to most trains, with dining services, improved washroom facilities, and observation cars for unhindered viewing of the passing landscape.

Trains run along three different routes: between Cusco and Machu Picchu, between Ollantaytambo and Machu Picchu, and between Cusco and Lake Titicaca. In addition there's a line between Puno and Arequipa that's operated for groups only. Tickets can be purchased at train stations, through travel agencies, or on the Internet. During holidays or high season it's best to get your tickets in advance.

The most popular route runs between Cusco and Machu Picchu. Several different trains make the 3½-hour trip: the Backpacker ($96 round-trip), the Vistadome ($142 round-trip), and the Hiram Bingham ($588 round-trip). The Backpacker is the most basic service, but it's more than comfortable. The Vistadome is a bit more comfortable, has rooftop windows for a better view, and snacks in both directions. There's also a fashion show and a kitschy traditional dance performance. All tour groups and most independent travelers choose this level of service. The most deluxe service, the Hiram Bingham, has four carriages, two dining cars, and a bar car with observation deck. Brunch is served en route to Machu Picchu, and on the return, dinner is offered from a five-course à la carte menu. Is it worth the expense? At four times the price of the Vistadome, we'd say no. Note that this train doesn't leave from Cusco, but from the nearby town of Poroy.

Travelers visiting the Sacred Valley take the trains that run between Ollantaytambo and Machu Picchu. There's a Backpacker ($86 round-trip) and a Vistadome ($120 round-trip). Keep in mind that some people leave on one route and return on another, making it possible to depart from Cusco, visit Machu Picchu, and then head to the Sacred Valley. You can also do this same trip in reverse, of course.

One train a day takes passengers on the 10-hour trip between Cusco and Puno on Lake Titicaca. The train is divided into two classes, the spare Backpacker ($22 one-way) and the plush Andean Explorer ($143 one-way). The same food served on the Andean Explorer is available for a small fee on the Backpacker, making it a much better deal.

Note that there are two different train stations in Cusco. Estación San Pedro serves the Machu Picchu route, and Estación Wanchaq serves the Lake Titicaca route.

Reserve and purchase your ticket as far ahead as possible, especially during holidays or high season. Reservations can be made directly with PeruRail through its Web site, or through a travel agency or tour operator.

Reservations PeruRail (☎084/238-722 ⊕ www.perurail.com).

Train Stations Estación San Pedro (Cusco–Machu Picchu route) (✉Cascaparo s/n, near Mercado Central ☎084/23-5201 or 084/22-1352). **Estación Wanchaq (Cusco–Lake Titicaca route)** (✉Av. Pachacutec 503 ☎084/23-8722 or 084/221-992).

ESSENTIALS

■ ACCOMMODATIONS

It's always good to take a look at your room before accepting it; especially if you're staying in a budget hotel. If it isn't what you expected, there might be several other rooms from which to choose. Expense is no guarantee of charm or cleanliness, and accommodations can vary dramatically within a single hotel. Many older hotels in some of the small towns in Peru have rooms with charming balconies or spacious terraces; ask if there's a room *con balcón* or *con terraza* when checking in.

If you ask for a double room, you'll get a room for two people, but you're not guaranteed a double mattress. If you'd like to avoid twin beds, you'll have to ask for a *cama matrimonial* (no wedding ring seems to be required).

The lodgings we list are the cream of the crop in each price category. We always list the available facilities, but we don't specify whether they cost extra; when pricing accommodations, always ask what's included and what costs extra. Properties are assigned price categories based on the range between their least and most expensive standard double room at high season (excluding holidays) to the most expensive. Properties marked ✕🖼 are lodging establishments whose restaurants warrant a special trip.

■ **TIP→** Assume that hotels operate on the European Plan (**EP**, no meals) unless we specify that they use the Breakfast Plan (**BP**, with full breakfast), Continental Plan (**CP**, continental breakfast), Full American Plan (**FAP**, all meals), Modified American Plan (**MAP**, breakfast and dinner) or are all-inclusive (**AI**, all meals and most activities).

APARTMENT & HOUSE RENTALS

Apartment rentals are not a viable option in most parts of Peru. However, they're becoming more popular in Lima. One company that has proven reliable is Inn Peru, which rents apartments in the neighborhood of Miraflores. You can get a roomy two- or three-bedroom apartment for less than you'd pay for a shoebox-size hotel room.

Contacts Home Away (☎512/493–0382 ⊕www.homeaway.com). **Inn Peru** (☎945/607–2173 in U.S., 01/9857–8350 ⊕www.innperu.com). **Villas International** (☎415/499–9490 or 800/221–2260 ⊕www.villasintl.com).

BED & BREAKFASTS

Bed-and-breakfasts are a popular option all over Peru, but especially in tourist areas like Cusco, Arequipa, and Puno. Many are in charming older buildings, including colonial-era homes built around flower-filled courtyards. Breakfast ranges from a roll with butter and jam to a massive buffet.

Reservation Services Bed & Breakfast.com (☎512/322–2710 or 800/462–2632 ⊕www.bedandbreakfast.com) also sends out an online newsletter. **Bed & Breakfast Inns Online** (☎615/868–1946 or 800/215–7365 ⊕www.bbonline.com). **BnB Finder.com** (☎212/432–7693 or 888/547–8226 ⊕www.bnbfinder.com).

HOME EXCHANGES

With a direct home exchange you stay in someone else's home while they stay in yours. Some outfits also deal with vacation homes, so you're not actually staying in someone's full-time residence, just their vacant weekend place.

Exchange Clubs Home Exchange.com (☎800/877–8723 ⊕www.homeexchange.com); $59.95 for a 1-year online listing. **HomeLink International** (☎800/638–3841 ⊕www.homelink.org); $90 yearly for Web-only membership; $140 includes Web access and two catalogs. **Intervac U.S.** (☎800/756–4663 ⊕www.intervacus.com); $78.88 for Web-only membership; $126 includes Web access and a catalog.

HOTELS

Peru uses a rating system of one to five stars for its accommodations. A hotel can have one to five stars, an apart-hotel (a hotel with apartmentlike rooms) three to five, and a hostel one to three. Lodgings with fewer stars are not necessarily inferior—they may only be missing an amenity or two that may not be important to you, such as a telephones or television in the rooms. The name of a hotel does not necessarily have anything to do with its luxuriousness. A *posada*, for example, can be at the high, middle, or low end.

▮ COMMUNICATIONS

INTERNET

E-mail has become a favorite way to communicate in Peru. Lima, Cusco, and other larger cities have dozens of Internet cafés. Even on the shores of Lake Titicaca you can stop in a small shop and send an e-mail message back home for about $1. And many of the country's airports, including Lima's Jorge Chávez International Airport and Cusco's Teniente Alejandro Velasco Astete International Airport, offer free wireless connections if you're traveling with your own laptops. Even hotels that don't have wireless in their rooms will probably have a strong signal in the public areas.

Computer keyboards in South America are not quite the same as ones in English-speaking countries. Your biggest frustration will probably be finding the @ symbol to type an e-mail address. You have to type Alt+Q or some other combination. If you need to ask, it's called *arroba* in Spanish.

If you're traveling with a laptop, carry a converter if your computer isn't dual voltage. (Most are these days.) Carrying a laptop could make you a target for

thieves. Conceal your laptop in a generic bag, and keep it close to you at all times.

Contacts Cybercafes (⊕www.cybercafes. com) lists more than 4,000 Internet cafés worldwide.

PHONES

The good news is that you can now make a direct-dial telephone call from virtually any point on earth. The bad news? You can't always do so cheaply. Calling from a hotel is almost always the most expensive option; hotels usually add huge surcharges to all calls, particularly international ones. In some countries you can phone from call centers or even the post office. Calling cards usually keep costs to a minimum, but only if you purchase them locally. And as expensive as international mobile phone calls can be, they are still usually a much cheaper option than calling from your hotel.

To call Peru direct, dial 011 followed by the country code of 51, then the city code, then the number of the party you're calling. (When dialing a number from abroad, drop the initial 0 from the local area code.)

CALLING WITHIN PERU

To get phone numbers for anywhere in Peru, dial 103. For an operator dial 100, and for an international operator dial 108. To place a direct call, dial 00 followed by the country and city codes. To call another region within the country, first dial 0 and then the area code.

LOCAL DO'S & TABOOS

CUSTOMS OF THE COUNTRY

Peru is one of South America's most hospitable nations. Even in the overburdened metropolis of Lima, people are happy to give directions, chat, and ask a question you'll hear a lot in Peru, *De dónde vienes?* (Where are you from?). Peruvians are quite knowledgeable and proud of the history of their country. Don't be surprised if your best source of information isn't your tour guide but your taxi driver or hotel desk clerk.

GREETINGS

In the cities, women who know each other often greet each other with a single kiss on the cheek, whereas men shake hands. Men and women often kiss on the cheek, even when being introduced for the first time. Kissing, however, is not a custom among the conservative indigenous population.

SIGHTSEEING

To feel more comfortable, take a cue from what the locals are wearing. Except in beach towns, men typically don't wear shorts and women don't wear short skirts. Bathing suits are fine on beaches, but cover up before you head back into town. Everyone dresses nicely to enter churches. Peruvian women wearing sleeveless tops often cover their shoulders before entering a place of worship.

OUT ON THE TOWN

Residents of Lima and other large cities dress up for a night on the town, but that doesn't necessarily mean a jacket and tie. Just as in Buenos Aires or Rio de Janiero, you should dress comfortably, but with a bit of style. In smaller towns, things are much more casual. You still shouldn't wear shorts, however.

LANGUAGE

Spanish is Peru's national language, but many indigenous languages also enjoy official status. Many Peruvians claim Quechua, the language of the Inca, as their first language, but most also speak Spanish. Other native languages include the Tiahuanaco language of Aymará, which is spoken around Lake Titicaca, and several languages in the rain forest. But English is now routinely taught in schools, and many older people have taken classes in English. In Lima and other places with many foreign visitors, it's rare to come across someone without a rudimentary knowledge of the language.

A word on spelling: since the Inca had no writing system, Quechua developed as an oral language. With European colonization, words and place-names were transcribed to conform to Spanish pronunciations. Eventually, the whole language was transcribed, and in many cases words lost their correct pronunciations. During the past 30 years, however, national pride and a new sensitivity to the country's indigenous roots have led Peruvians to try to recover consistent, linguistically correct transcriptions of Quechua words. As you travel you may come across different spellings and pronunciations of the same name. An example is the city known as Cusco, Cuzco, and sometimes even Qosqo.

To reach an AT&T operator, dial 171. For MCI, dial 190. For Sprint, dial 176.

CALLING OUTSIDE PERU

For international calls you should dial 00, then the country code. (For example, the country code for the U.S. and Canada is 1.) To make an operator-assisted international call, dial 108.

Access Codes AT&T Direct (☎800/225–5288). **MCI WorldPhone** (☎800/444–4444). **Sprint International Access** (☎800/793–1153).

CALLING CARDS

Public phones use phone cards that can be purchased at newsstands, pharmacies, and other shops. These come in denominations ranging from S/10 to S/100. Your charges will appear on a small monitor on the phone, so you always know how much time you have left. Instructions are usually in Spanish and English.

MOBILE PHONES

If you have a multiband phone (some countries use different frequencies than what's used in the United States) and your service provider uses the world-standard GSM network (as do T-Mobile, Cingular, and Verizon), you can probably use your phone abroad. Roaming fees can be steep: 99¢ a minute is considered reasonable. And overseas you normally pay the toll charges for incoming calls. It's almost always cheaper to text message than to make a call, since text messages have a very low set fee.

If you just want to make local calls, consider buying a new SIM card (note that your provider may have to unlock your phone for you to use a different SIM card) and a prepaid service plan in the destination. You'll then have a local number and can make local calls at local rates. If your trip is extensive, you could also simply buy a new cell phone in your destination, as the initial cost will be offset over time.

■**TIP**➜ If you travel internationally frequently, save one of your old mobile phones or buy a cheap one on the Internet; ask your cell phone company to unlock it for you, and take it with you as a travel phone, buying a new SIM card with pay-as-you-go service in each destination.

Contacts Cellular Abroad (☎800/287–5072 ⊕www.cellularabroad.com) rents and sells GMS phones and sells SIM cards that work in many countries. **Mobal** (☎888/888–9162 ⊕www.mobalrental.com) rents mobiles and sells GSM phones (starting at $49) that will operate in 140 countries. Per-call rates vary throughout the world. **Planet Fone** (☎888/988–4777 ⊕www.planetfone.com) rents cell phones, but the per-minute rates are expensive.

■ CUSTOMS & DUTIES

You're always allowed to bring goods of a certain value back home without having to pay any duty or import tax. But there's a limit on the amount of tobacco and liquor you can bring back duty-free, and some countries have separate limits for perfumes; for exact figures, check with your customs department. The values of so-called "duty-free" goods are included in these amounts. When you shop abroad, save all your receipts, as customs inspectors may ask to see them as well as the items you purchased. If the total value of your goods is more than the duty-free limit, you'll have to pay a tax (most often a flat percentage) on the value of everything beyond that limit.

When you check through immigration in Peru put the white International Embarkation/Disembarkation form you filled out in a safe place when it's returned to you. You will need it when you leave the country. If you lose it, in addition being delayed, you may have to pay a small fine. You may bring personal and work items; a total of three liters of liquor; jewelry or perfume worth less than $300; and 400 cigarettes or 50 cigars into Peru without paying import taxes. After that, goods and gifts will be taxed at 20% their value up to $1,000; everything thereafter is taxed at a flat rate of 25%.

U.S. Information U.S. Customs and Border Protection (⊕ www.cbp.gov).

▌ EATING OUT

Most smaller restaurants offer a lunch-time *menú,* a prix-fixe meal ($2–$5) that consists of an appetizer, a main dish, dessert, and a beverage. Peru is also full of cafés, many with a selection of delicious pastries. Food at bars is usually limited to snacks and sandwiches.

The restaurants we list are the cream of the crop in each price category.

For information on food-related health issues, see Health below.

MEALS & MEALTIMES

Food in Peru is hearty and wholesome. Thick soups made of vegetables and meat are excellent. Try *chupes,* soups made of shrimp and fish with potatoes, corn, peas, onions, garlic, tomato sauce, eggs, cream cheese, milk, and whatever else happens to be in the kitchen. Corvina, a sea bass caught in the Pacific ocean, is superb, as is a fish with a very large mouth, called *paiche,* that is found in jungle lakes and caught with spears. Or try piranha—delicious, but full of bones. *Anticuchos* (marinated beef hearts grilled over charcoal) are a staple. Peru's large-kernel corn is very good, and it's claimed there are more than 100 varieties of potatoes, served in about as many ways. And there is always *ceviche,* raw fish marinated in lemon juice and white wine then mixed with onions and red peppers and served with sweet potatoes, onions, and sometimes corn.

Top-notch restaurants serve lunch and dinner, but most Peruvians think of lunch as the day's main meal, and many restaurants open only at midday. Served between 1 and 3, lunch was once followed by a siesta, though the custom has largely died out. Dinner can be anything from a light snack to another full meal. Peruvians tend to dine late, between 7 and 11 PM.

Unless otherwise noted, the restaurants listed in this guide are open daily for lunch and dinner.

RESERVATIONS & DRESS

Peruvians dress informally when they dine out. At the most expensive restaurants, a jacket without a tie is sufficient for men. Shorts are frowned upon everywhere except at the beach, and T-shirts are appropriate only in very modest restaurants.

In this book we only mention reservations specifically when they are essential or when they are not accepted. For popular restaurants, book as far ahead as you can (often 30 days), and reconfirm as soon as you arrive. We mention dress only when men are required to wear a jacket or a jacket and tie.

WINES, BEER & SPIRITS

Peru's national drink is the pisco sour, made with a pale grape brandy—close to 100 proof—derived from grapes grown in vineyards around Ica, south of Lima. Added to the brandy are lemon juice, sugar, bitters, and egg white. It's a refreshing drink and one that nearly every bar in Peru claims to make best. Tacama's Blanco de Blancos from Ica is considered the country's best wine. Ica's National Vintage Festival is in March.

Peruvian beer (*cerveza*) is also very good. In Lima, try Cristal and the slightly more upscale Pilsen Callao, both produced by the same brewery. In the south it's Arequipeña from Arequipa, Cusqueña from Cusco, and big bottles of San Juan from Iquitos, where the warm climate makes it taste twice as good. In Iquitos locals make Chuchuhuasi from the reddish-brown bark of the canopy tree that grows to 100 feet high in the Amazon rain forest. The bark is soaked for days in *aguardiente* (a very strong homemade liquor) and is claimed to be a cure-all. However, in Iquitos, it has been bottled and turned into a tasty drink for tourists.

ELECTRICITY

The electrical current in Peru is 220 volts, 50 cycles alternating current (AC). A converter is needed for appliances requiring 110 voltage. U.S.-style flat prongs fit most outlets.

Consider buying a universal adapter, which has several types of plugs in one lightweight, compact unit. Most laptops and mobile phone chargers are dual voltage (i.e., they operate equally well on 110 and 220 volts), so require only an adapter. These days the same is true of small appliances such as hair dryers. Always check labels and manufacturer instructions to be sure. Don't use 110-volt outlets marked FOR SHAVERS ONLY for high-wattage appliances such as hair-dryers.

Contacts Steve Kropla's Help for World Traveler's (⊕ www.kropla.com) has information on electrical and telephone plugs around the world. **Walkabout Travel Gear** (⊕ www. walkabouttravelgear.com) has a good coverage of electricity under "adapters."

EMERGENCIES

The fastest way to connect with the police is to dial 105. For fire, dial 116. The Tourism Police, part of the National Police of Perú, exists for the security and protection of travelers. Officers are usually found in around hotels, archaeological centers, museums, and any place that is frequently visited by tourists. They almost always speak English.

Foreign Embassies Canada (⊠ Jr. Libertad 130, Miraflores ☎ 01/444–4015). **New Zealand** (⊠ Av. Natalio Sánchez 125, El Centro ☎ 01/433–4738). **United Kingdom** (⊠ Av. Larco 1301, Miraflores ☎ 01/617–3050). **United States** (⊠ Av. La Encalada, Cuadra 17, Monterrico ☎ 01/434–3000).

HEALTH

The most common illnesses are caused by contaminated food and water. Especially in developing countries, drink only bottled, boiled, or purified water and drinks; don't drink from public fountains or use ice. You should even consider using bottled water to brush your teeth. Make sure food has been thoroughly cooked and is served to you fresh and hot; avoid vegetables and fruits that you haven't washed (in bottled or purified water) or peeled yourself. If you have problems, mild cases of traveler's diarrhea may respond to Imodium (known generically as loperamide) or Pepto-Bismol. Drink plenty of fluids; if you can't keep fluids down, seek medical help immediately.

Infectious diseases can be airborne or passed via mosquitoes and ticks and through direct or indirect physical contact with animals or people. Some, including Norwalk-like viruses that affect your digestive tract, can be passed along through contaminated food. If you are traveling in an area where malaria is prevalent, use a repellent containing DEET and take malaria-prevention medication before, during, and after your trip as directed by your physician. Condoms can help prevent most sexually transmitted diseases, but they aren't absolutely reliable and their quality varies from country to country. Speak with your physician and/or check the CDC or World Health Organization Web sites for health alerts, particularly if you're pregnant, traveling with children, or have a chronic illness.

Medical Insurers **International Medical Group** (☎800/628-4664 ⊕www.imglobal. com). **International SOS** (⊕www.international-sos.com). **Wallach & Company** (☎800/237-6615 or 540/687-3166 ⊕www.wallach.com).

SHOTS & MEDICATIONS

No vaccinations are required to enter Peru, although yellow fever vaccinations are recommended if you're visiting the jungle areas in the east. It's a good idea to have up-to-date boosters for tetanus, diphtheria, and measles. A hepatitis A inoculation can prevent one of the most common intestinal infections. Those who might be around animals should consider a rabies vaccine. As rabies is a concern, most hospitals have anti-rabies injections. Children traveling to Peru should have their vaccinations for childhood diseases up-to-date.

According to the Centers for Disease Control and Prevention (CDC), there's a limited risk of cholera, typhoid, malaria, hepatitis B, dengue, and Chagas' disease. Although a few of these you could catch anywhere, most are restricted to jungle areas. If you plan to visit remote regions or stay for more than six weeks, check with the CDC's International Travelers Hot Line.

Health Warnings **National Centers for Disease Control & Prevention** (CDC ☎877/394-8747 international travelers' health line ⊕www.cdc.gov/travel). **World Health Organization** (WHO ⊕www.who.int).

SPECIFIC ISSUES IN PERU

The major health risk in Peru is traveler's diarrhea, caused by viruses, bacteria, or parasites in contaminated food or water. So watch what you eat. If you eat something from a street vendor, make sure it's cooked in front of you. Avoid uncooked food, food that has been sitting around at room temperature, and unpasteurized milk and milk products. Drink only bottled water or water that has been boiled for several minutes, even when brushing your teeth. Order drinks *sin hielo,* or "without ice." Note that water boils at a lower temperature at high altitudes and may not be hot enough to rid the bacteria, so consider using purification tablets. Local brands include Micropur.

Mild cases of traveler's diarrhea may respond to Imodium, Pepto-Bismol, or Lomotil, all of which can be purchased in Peru without a prescription. Drink plenty of purified water or tea—chamomile (*manzanilla*) is a popular folk remedy.

The number of cases of cholera, an intestinal infection caused by ingestion of contaminated water or food, has dropped dramatically in recent years, but you should still take care. Anything raw, including ceviche, should only be eaten in the better restaurants.

Altitude sickness, known locally as *soroche,* affects the majority of visitors to Cusco, Puno, and other high-altitude cities. Headache, dizziness, nausea, and shortness of breath are common. When you visit areas over 10,000 feet above sea level, take it easy for the first few days. Avoiding alcohol will keep you from getting even more dehydrated. To fight soroche, Peruvians swear by *mate de coca,* a tea made from the leaves of the coca plant.

Soroche is also a problem in the Andes. Spend a few nights at lower elevations before you head higher. If you must fly directly to higher altitudes, plan on doing next to nothing for the first day or two. Drinking plenty of water or coca tea or taking frequent naps may also help. If symptoms persist, return to lower elevations. If you have high blood pressure or a history of heart trouble, check with your doctor before traveling to high elevations.

Mosquitoes are a problem in tropical areas, especially at dusk. Take along plenty of repellent containing DEET.

You may not get through airport screening with an aerosol can, so take a spritz bottle or cream. Local brands of repellent are readily available in pharmacies. If you plan to spend time in the jungle, be sure to wear clothing that covers your arms and legs, sleep under a mosquito net, and spray bug repellent in living and sleeping areas. You should also ask your doctor about antimalarial medications. Do so early, as some vaccinations must be started weeks before heading into a malaria zone.

Chiggers are sometimes a problem in the jungle or where there are animals. Red, itchy spots suddenly appear, most often *under* your clothes. The best advice when venturing out into chigger country is to use insect repellent and wear loose-fitting clothing. A hot, soapy bath after being outdoors also prevents them from attaching to your skin.

OVER-THE-COUNTER REMEDIES

Over-the-counter analgesics may curtail soroche symptoms, but consult your doctor before you take them, as well as any other medications you may take regularly. Always carry your own medications with you, including those you would ordinarily take for a simple headache, as you will usually not find the same brands in the local *farmacia* (pharmacy). However, if you forgot, ask for *aspirina* (aspirin). Try writing down the name of your local medication, because in many cases, the druggist will have it or something similar.

▌ HOLIDAYS

New Year's Day; Easter holiday, which begins midday on Maundy Thursday and continues through Easter Monday; Labor Day (May 1); St. Peter and St. Paul Day (June 29); Independence Day (July 28); St. Rosa of Lima Day (August 30); Battle of Angamos Day, which commemorates a battle with Chile in the War of the Pacific, 1879–81 (October 8); All Saints' Day

(November 1); Immaculate Conception (December 8); Christmas.

▌ MAIL

Letters sent within the country cost S/2.50 for less than 20 grams; anything sent to the United States and Canada costs S/5.50. Bring packages to the post office unsealed, as you must show the contents to postal workers. Mail service has been improving, and a letter should reach just about anywhere in a week from any of the main cities. For timely delivery or valuable parcels, use FedEx, DHL, or UPS.

DHL, FedEx, and UPS all have offices in Peru. Because of the limited number of international flights, overnight service is usually not available.

▌ MONEY

Peru's national currency is the nuevo sol (S/). Bills are issued in denominations of 5, 10, 20, 50, and 100 soles. Coins are 1, 5, 10, 20, and 50 céntimos, and 1, 2, and 5 soles. At this writing, the exchange rate was almost exactly S/3 to the U.S. dollar.

You'll want to break larger bills as soon as possible. Souvenir stands, craft markets, taxi drivers, and other businesses often do not have change.

Currency Conversion Google (⊕www.google.com). Oanda.com (⊕www.oanda.com) XE.com (⊕www.xe.com)

■**TIP→** If you're planning to exchange funds before leaving home, don't wait till the last minute. Banks never have every foreign currency on hand, and it may take as long as a week to order.

ATMS & BANKS

Your own bank will probably charge a fee for using ATMs abroad; the foreign bank you use may also charge a fee. Nevertheless, you'll usually get a better rate of exchange at an ATM than you will at a currency-exchange office or even when changing money in a bank. And extracting funds as you need them is a safer option than carrying around a large amount of cash.

■ TIP→ **PIN numbers with more than four digits are not recognized at ATMs in many countries. If yours has five or more, remember to change it before you leave.**

ATMs (*cajeros automáticos*) are widely available, especially in Lima, and you can get cash with a Cirrus- or Plus-linked debit card or with a major credit card. Most ATMs accept both Cirrus and Plus cards, but to be on the safe side bring at least one of each. Note that if your PIN code is more than four digits it might not work in some places.

ATM Locations MasterCard Cirrus (☎800/424–7787 ⊕www.mastercard.com). **Visa Plus** (☎800/843–7587 ⊕www.visa. com/atm).

CREDIT CARDS
Throughout this guide, the following abbreviations are used: **AE**, American Express; **DC**, Diners Club; **MC**, Master-Card; and **V**, Visa.

It's a good idea to inform your credit-card company before you travel. Otherwise, the credit-card company might put a hold on your card owing to unusual activity—not a good thing halfway through your trip. Record all your credit-card numbers—as well as the phone numbers to call if your cards are lost or stolen—in a safe place, so you're prepared should something go wrong. Both MasterCard and Visa have general numbers you can call (collect if you're abroad) if your card is lost, but you're better off calling the number of your issuing bank, since MasterCard and Visa usually just transfer you to your bank; your bank's number is usually printed on your card.

Although it's usually cheaper (and safer) to use a credit card abroad for large purchases (so you can cancel payments or be reimbursed if there's a problem), note that some credit-card companies *and* the banks that issue them add substantial percentages to all foreign transactions, whether they're in a foreign currency or not. Check on these fees before leaving home, so there won't be any surprises when you get the bill.

■ TIP→ **Before you charge something, ask the merchant whether or not he or she plans to do a dynamic currency conversion (DCC). In such a transaction the credit-card** *processor* **(shop, restaurant, or hotel, not Visa or MasterCard) converts the currency and charges you in dollars. In most cases you'll pay the merchant a 3% fee for this service in addition to any credit-card company and issuing-bank foreign-transaction surcharges.**

Dynamic currency conversion programs are becoming increasingly widespread. Merchants who participate in them are supposed to ask whether you want to be charged in dollars or the local currency, but they don't always do so. And even if they do offer you a choice, they may well avoid mentioning the additional surcharges. The good news is that you *do* have a choice. And if this practice really gets your goat, you can avoid it entirely thanks to American Express; with its cards, DCC simply isn't an option.

For costly items, try to use your credit card whenever possible—you'll come out ahead, whether the exchange rate at which your purchase is calculated is the one in effect the day the vendor's bank abroad processes the charge or the one prevailing on the day the charge company's service center processes it at home.

Major credit cards, especially Master-Card and Visa, are accepted in most hotels, restaurants, and shops in tourist areas. If you're traveling outside major cities, always check to see whether your hotel accepts credit cards. You may have to bring enough cash to pay the bill.

Before leaving home make copies of the back and front of your credit cards; keep one set of copies with your luggage, the other at home.

Reporting Lost Cards American Express
(☎800/528–4800 in U.S., 336/393–1111 collect from abroad ⊕www.americanexpress. com). **Diners Club** (☎800/234–6377 in U.S., 303/799–1504 collect from abroad ⊕www.dinersclub.com). **MasterCard** (☎800/627–8372 in U.S., 636/722–7111 collect from abroad ⊕www.mastercard.com). **Visa** (☎800/847–2911 in U.S., 410/581–9994 collect from abroad ⊕www.visa.com).

CURRENCY & EXCHANGE
You can safely exchange money or cash traveler's checks in a bank, at your hotel, or at *casas de cambio* (exchange houses). The rate for traveler's checks is usually the same as for cash, but many banks have a ceiling on how much they will exchange at one time.

■ TIP➜ Even if a currency-exchange booth has a sign promising no commission, rest assured that there's some kind of huge, hidden fee. (Oh . . . that's right. The sign didn't say no *fee*.). Rates are always better at an ATM or a bank.

■ PACKING

For sightseeing, casual clothing and good walking shoes are desirable and appropriate, and most cities don't require formal clothes, even for evenings. If you're doing business in Peru, you'll need the same attire you would wear in U.S. and European cities: for men, suits and ties; for women, suits for day wear, and for evening, depending on the occasion—ask your host or hostess—a cocktail dress or just a nice suit with a dressy blouse.

Travel in rain-forest areas will require long-sleeve shirts, long pants, socks, sneakers, a hat, a light waterproof jacket, a bathing suit (if you want to swim), sunscreen, and insect repellent. You can never have too many large resealable plastic bags (bring a whole box), which are ideal for storing film, protecting offi-

cial documents from rain and damp, and quarantining stinky socks.

If you're visiting the Andes, bring a jacket and sweater, or acquire one of the hand-knit sweaters or ponchos crowding the marketplaces. Evening temperatures in Cusco are rarely above the 50s. For beach vacations, you'll need lightweight sportswear, a bathing suit, a sun hat, and lots of sunscreen. Peruvians are fairly conservative, so don't wear bathing suits or other revealing clothing away from the beach.

Other useful items include a travel flashlight and extra batteries, a pocketknife with a bottle opener (put it in your checked luggage), a medical kit, binoculars, and a calculator to help with currency conversions. A sarong or light cotton blanket can have many uses: beach towel, picnic blanket, and cushion for hard seats and, most important, always travel with tissues or a roll of toilet paper as sometimes it's difficult to find in local restrooms.

Weather Accuweather.com (⊕www.accuweather.com). **Weather.com** (⊕www.weather. com)

■ PASSPORTS & VISAS

Visitors from the United States, Canada, the United Kingdom, Australia, and New Zealand require only a valid passport and return ticket to be issued a 90-day visa at their point of entry into Peru.

Make two photocopies of the data page of your passport, one for someone at home and another for you, carried separately from your passport. While sightseeing in Peru, it's best to carry the copy of your passport and leave the original hidden in your hotel room or in your hotel's safe. If you lose your passport, call the nearest embassy or consulate and the local police. Also, never, ever, leave one city in Peru to go to another city (even for just an overnight or two) without carrying your passport with you.

GENERAL REQUIREMENTS FOR PERU

Passport	Valid passport required for U.S. residents
Visa	Not necessary for U.S. residents with a valid passport
Vaccinations	Yellow fever vaccination required for those visiting infected areas
Driving	Driver's license required
Departure Tax	US$30.25 for international flights; US$6.05 for domestic flights; payable in cash only

■ RESTROOMS

In Lima and other cities, your best bet for finding a restroom while on the go is to walk into a large hotel as if you're a guest and find the facilities. The next best thing is talking your way into a restaurant bathroom; buying a drink is a nice gesture if you do. Unless you're in a large chain hotel, don't throw toilet paper into the toilet—use the basket provided—as unsanitary as this may seem. Doing so can clog the antiquated plumbing. Always carry your own supply of tissues or toilet paper, just in case.

Public restrooms are usually designated as *servicios higiénicos*, with signs depicting the abbreviation SS.HH.

Find a Loo The Bathroom Diaries (⊕ www. thebathroomdiaries.com) is flush with unsanitized info on restrooms the world over—each one located, reviewed, and rated.

■ SAFETY

Be street-smart in Peru and trouble generally won't find you. Money belts peg you as a tourist, so if you must wear one, hide it under your clothing. If you carry a purse, choose one with a zipper and a thick strap that you can drape across your body; adjust the length so that the purse sits in front of you. Carry only enough money to cover casual spending. Keep camera bags close to your body. Note that backpacks are especially easy to grab and open secretly. Finally, avoid wearing flashy jewelry and watches.

Many streets throughout Peru are not well lighted, so avoid walking at night, and certainly avoid deserted streets, day or night. Always walk as if you know where you're going, even if you don't.

Use only "official" taxis with the company's name emblazoned on the side. Don't get into a car just because there's a taxi sign in the window, as it's probably an unlicensed driver. At night you should call a taxi from your hotel or restaurant.

Do not let anyone distract you. Beware of someone "accidentally" spilling food or liquid on you and then offering to help clean it up; the spiller might have an accomplice who will walk off with your purse or your suitcase while you are distracted.

Women, especially blondes, can expect some admiring glances and perhaps a comment or two, but outright come-ons or grabbing are rare. Usually all that is needed is to ignore the perpetrator and keep walking down the street.

■ TIP➔ Distribute your cash, credit cards, IDs, and other valuables between a deep front pocket, an inside jacket or vest pocket, and a hidden money pouch. Don't reach for the money pouch once you're in public.

Contact Transportation Security Administration (TSA; ⊕ www.tsa.gov).

■ TAXES

A 19% *impuesto general a las ventas* (general sales tax) is levied on everything except goods bought at open-air markets and street vendors. It's usually included in the advertised price and should be included with food and drink. If a business offers you a discount for paying in cash, it probably means they aren't charging sales tax (and not reporting the transaction to the government).

By law restaurants must publish their prices—including taxes and sometimes a 10% service charge—but they do not always do so. They're also prone to levy a cover charge for anything from live entertainment to serving you a roll with your meal. Hotel bills may also add taxes and a 10% service charge.

Departure taxes at Lima's Aeropuerto Internacional Jorge Chávez are US$30.25 for international flights and US$6.05 for domestic flights.

▌ TOURS

Many people visiting Peru do so as part of a tour package. Nothing wrong with that, especially for those who don't speak Spanish or are unaccustomed to foreign travel. On the other hand, do you really want to see the same sights as everyone else? There's no reason that you can't book your own tour. It's easy to arrange a custom itinerary with any travel agent.

Several Lima-based companies can arrange trips around the city as well as around the country. The most professional is Lima Tours, which offers tours of the city and surrounding area as well as the rest of the country. Lima Vision has some excellent tours, including several that include lunch at a traditional restaurant or a dinner show.

Recommended Companies Lima Tours
(✉Belén 1040, El Centro ☎01/619-6900
⊕www.limatours.com.pe). **Lima Vision** (✉Jr. Chiclayo 444, Miraflores ☎01/447-7710
⊕www.limavision.com).

▌ VISITOR INFORMATION

ONLINE TRAVEL TOOLS

Andean Travel Web, an independent Web site, has great information about regional destinations. Assisting travelers is iPerú, which has English- and Spanish-language information about the city and beyond. The Web site, in English and Spanish, is extremely helpful in planning your trip.

The most thorough information about Peru is available at South American Explorers. This nonprofit organization dispenses a wealth of information. You can also call ahead with questions, or just show up at the beautiful clubhouse in Miraflores and browse through the lending library and read trip reports filed by members. It costs US$50 to join, and you can make up for that with discounts offered to members by hotels and tour operators.

All About Peru Andean Travel Web
(⊕www.andeantravelweb.com). **iPerú**
(☎01/574-8000 in Peru ⊕www.peru.info/perueng.asp).

South American Explorers (☎01/445-3306 in Peru, 800/274-0568 in U.S. ⊕www.saexplorers.org).

INDEX

NOTES

ABOUT OUR AUTHORS

Aviva Baff (Ch. 9, North Coast & Northern Highlands) was a New York City Teaching Fellow, earning her teaching certification and Master's degree. She now lives in Lima, teaching and traveling.

Michael Collis (Ch. 7, Amazon Basin) grew up in England. At 49 he moved to Iquitos, where he founded the Great River Amazon International Raft Race in 1999. In 2002 he founded the English language newspaper the *Iquitos Times*.

Nicholas Gill (Ch. 8, Central Highlands) is a Lima-, Peru-, and NYC-based food/travel writer and photographer. He has authored, contributed to, and shot numerous guidebooks of Latin America. His work also appears in *The Columbus Dispatch, Sherman's Travel,* and other newspapers, magazines, and websites.

Michelle Hopey (Ch. 4, Southern Coast to Lake Titicaca) holds an MS in journalism from Boston University and has written for a number of US newspapers, covering everything from crime to national politics. Today, Michelle splits her time between Latin America and Boston.

Zoe Ponce Massey (contributed to Experience Chapter) lives in Lima, working freelance in photography and as the editor of a Peruvian Cuisine Web site.

Katy Morrison (Ch. 3, The South; ch. 5 Cusco & the Sacred Valley) is a freelance writer who has traveled throughout Central and South America. While updating this book, Katy enjoyed perfecting her salsa moves and learning the correct technique for eating guinea pig (with your fingers).

Diana P. Olanos (contributed to Experience chapter) graduated from Pace University in Pleasantville, New York, with a BA in Media and Communications. She now edits and writes for LivingInPeru.com.

Ruth Anne Phillips (In Focus: Nazca Lines) earned her Ph.D. in Art History with a specialization in the Pre-Columbian Andes in May 2007. She has taught at various colleges in and around New York City. She has published on the relationship between Inca structures and the sacred landscape.

Paul Steele (In Focus: Visible History) has a PhD on Inca culture history from the University of Essex in England that looked at the Inca myth-stories of origin. He is the author of the *Handbook of Inca Mythology.*

Mark Sullivan (Ch. 1, Lima; In Focus: Food in Peru, Essentials) is a former Fodor's editor who has traveled extensively in South America. He has also written and edited for Fodor's South America and Central America books.

Jeffrey Van Fleet (Ch. 5, Cusco & the Sacred Valley; Ch. 6 Machu Picchu & the Inca Trail, contributed to Experience Chapter) is a regular writer for Costa Rica's English-language newspaper *The Tico Times*. Jeff has also contributed to Fodor's guides to Costa Rica, Guatemala, Argentina, Chile, and Central and South America.

Doug Wechsler (in Focus: The Jungle Life) has studied and photographed wildlife in the Amazon and tropical forests around the world. He is Director of VIREO, the world's most comprehensive collection of bird photographs, at The Academy of Natural Sciences in Philadelphia. Wechsler (www.dougwechsler.com) has authored 22 children's books about nature.

Oliver Wigmore (In Focus: Big Mountains) After completing degrees in Archaeology, Geography and Marine Science in New Zealand, Oliver went walkabout. Between ski seasons in Canada and archaeological digs in Belize and Ecuador, Oliver has spent much time exploring South and Central America. Falling in love with the magic and diversity of Peru, he can't stay away from the place.